METATHEORY FOR THE TWENTY-FIRST CENTURY

Metatheory for the Twenty-First Century is one of the many exciting results of over four years of in-depth engagement between two communities of scholar-practitioners: critical realists and integral theorists. Building on its origins at a symposium in Luxembourg in 2010, this book examines the points of connection and divergence between critical realism and integral theory, arguably two of the most comprehensive and sophisticated contemporary metatheories. The Luxembourg symposium and the four that followed explored the possibilities for their cross-pollination, culminating in five positions on their potential for integration, and began the process of fashioning a whole new evolutionary trajectory for both integral theory and critical realism. The contributors to this book bring together critical realism and integral theory in order to explore the potential of this collaboration for the advancement of both. Highlighting the ways in which these metatheories can transform scholarship and address the most pressing global issues of the twenty-first century, this book will be of interest to students, scholars and practitioners in the areas of metatheory, philosophy, social theory, critical realism, integral theory and current affairs more generally.

Roy Bhaskar (1944–2014) was the chief architect of the philosophy of critical realism and the author of many acclaimed and influential works, including *A Realist Theory of Science*, *The Possibility of Naturalism*, *Scientific Realism and Human Emancipation*, *Reclaiming Reality*, *Philosophy and the Idea of Freedom*, *Dialectic: The Pulse of Freedom, Plato Etc.*, *Reflections on meta-reality* and *From Science to Emancipation*. Prior to his death, while this book was in preparation, he was founding chair of the International Centre for Critical Realism and World Scholar at the UCL Institute of Education, University of London.

Sean Esbjörn-Hargens is the founder of MetaIntegral, a network of organizations that apply integrative metatheories to global challenges. He is also the executive editor of the *Journal of Integral Theory and Practice* and editor of the SUNY Series in Integral Theory.

Nicholas Hedlund is executive director of the Integral Research Center (www.integralresearchcenter.org) and a PhD researcher at University College London, Institute of Education (University of London), where he is conducting emancipatory social research into the philosophical, cultural and psychological dimensions of climate change.

Mervyn Hartwig is founding editor of the *Journal of Critical Realism* and principal author and editor of the *Dictionary of Critical Realism*.

ONTOLOGICAL EXPLORATIONS

Other titles in this series:

METATHEORY FOR THE TWENTY-FIRST CENTURY

Critical realism and integral theory in dialogue

Edited by Roy Bhaskar, Sean Esbjörn-Hargens,
Nicholas Hedlund and Mervyn Hartwig

MATT —

WITH GRATITUDE FOR YOUR

FRIENDSHIP

/

Routledge
Taylor & Francis Group

LONDON AND NEW YORK

NICK

First published 2016
by Routledge
2 Park Square, Milton Park, Abingdon, Oxon OX14 4RN

and by Routledge
711 Third Avenue, New York, NY 10017

Routledge is an imprint of the Taylor & Francis Group, an informa business

British Library Cataloguing in Publication Data
A catalogue record for this book is available from the British Library

Library of Congress Cataloguing in Publication Data
   Metatheory for the twenty-first century: critical realism and integral theory in
   dialogue / edited by Roy Bhaskar, Sean Esbjörn-Hargens, Nicholas Hedlund, and
   Mervyn Hartwig.
      pages   cm. – (Ontological explorations)
   1. Metatheory.   2. Critical realism.   I. Bhaskar, Roy, editor
   B842.M48   2015
   149'.2–dc23   2015023808

ISBN: 978-0-415-82000-4 (hbk)
ISBN: 978-0-415-82047-9 (pbk)
ISBN: 978-1-315-68933-3 (ebk)

Typeset in Bembo
by Out of House Publishing
Printed in Great Britain
by Ashford Colour Press Ltd, Gosport, Hants

CONTENTS

FIGURES

TABLES

CONTRIBUTORS

Roy Bhaskar (1944–2014) was the chief architect of the philosophy of critical realism and the author of many acclaimed and influential works, including *A Realist Theory of Science*, *The Possibility of Naturalism*, *Scientific Realism and Human Emancipation*, *Reclaiming Reality*, *Philosophy and the Idea of Freedom*, *Dialectic: The Pulse of Freedom*, *Plato Etc.*, *Reflections on meta-reality* and *From Science to Emancipation*. Prior to his death, while this book was in preparation, he was founding chair of the International Centre for Critical Realism and World Scholar at the UCL Institute of Education, University of London.

Mark G. Edwards PhD is a lecturer at the Business School, University of Western Australia. He teaches in the areas of business ethics and organizational change. His research focuses on knowledge integration and global sustainability.

Sean Esbjörn-Hargens PhD is the founder of MetaIntegral, a network of organizations that apply integrative metatheories to global challenges. He is also the executive editor of the *Journal of Integral Theory and Practice* and editor of the SUNY Series in Integral Theory.

Mervyn Hartwig PhD is founding editor of *Journal of Critical Realism* and principal author and editor of the *Dictionary of Critical Realism*.

Nicholas Hedlund PhD(c) is executive director of the Integral Research Center (www.integralresearchcenter.org) and a PhD researcher at University College London, Institute of Education (University of London), where he is conducting emancipatory social research into the philosophical, cultural and psychological dimensions of climate change.

Paul Marshall PhD(c) is a doctoral candidate at UCL, Institute of Education, working on a synthesis of critical realism, integral theory and complex thought.

Markus Molz PhD is managing director of the Alliance for the Future, co-founder and coordinator of the University for the Future Initiative, founding board member of the Institute for Integral Studies and associate editor of *Integral Review*. He works on an integral redesign of higher education to catalyze the Great Transition.

Tom Murray EdD is a senior research fellow at the University of Massachusetts School of Computer Science and is chief visionary and instigator at Perspegrity Solutions. His projects include research on supporting "social deliberative skills" and deep reflective dialogue in online contexts. He is an associate editor for *Integral Review*, and he has published many articles on integral theory as it relates to education, contemplative dialogue, leadership, ethics, knowledge-building communities, epistemology and postmetaphysics.

Michael Schwartz PhD is a professor at Georgia Regents University, USA, where he teaches art history and the philosophy of art and aesthetics. He is co-founding Executive Officer of the Comparative and Continental Philosophy Circle and the Art and Aesthetics Editor at Integral Life. He has published in several disciplines, including art history, continental philosophy, comparative philosophy, social theory and metatheory.

Zachary Stein EdD received his doctorate in the philosophy of education from Harvard University. He is Core Faculty and Associate Director of Student Assessment at Meridian University, Academic Director at the Center for Integral Wisdom and a Co-Founder of Lectica, Inc.

Roger Walsh MD, PhD is professor of psychiatry, philosophy and anthropology at the University of California at Irvine.

FOREWORD

The potentials of metatheory

Roger Walsh

The knowledge explosion not only continues, but continues to accelerate. Just how much it is accelerating is shown in the calculations of Eric Schmidt (2010), the CEO of Google, who estimated that "There were 5 exabytes [of information] created between the dawn of civilization through 2002, but that much information is now created every two days and the pace is increasing." One exabyte is 10^{18} bytes, and that is a *lot* of data. No wonder we feel inundated with information and drowning in data.

There were several kinds of response to this avalanche of information. One was intellectual fragmentation as knowledge disciplines became increasingly dissociated. Another was increasing specialization as individuals focused ever more narrowly, knowing more and more about less and less. This fragmentation and specialization were obvious across multiple domains such as the sciences, the humanities, and medicine.

Yet another response was reductionism, both within and between disciplines. For example, within psychology, successive schools claimed that their unique focus offered *the* supreme explanatory principle by which the overwhelming complexity of behavior could be best understood and modified. For example, behaviorists argued that behavior was largely determined by reinforcers. In making this claim, the behaviorists aimed to replace the psychoanalysts, who focused on understanding and modifying unconscious psychodynamic forces. Yet the behaviorists were replaced in turn by cognitive therapists, who emphasized the primacy of thoughts.

Large-scale reductionism between disciplines also thrived. Scientific materialism became the largely unquestioned de facto philosophy of science, while social constructivism thrived in the humanities. Likewise, E. O. Wilson advanced sociobiology as a sweeping evolutionary explanation of individual and social behavior, while neural eliminative materialism claimed that psychology would soon disappear by reducing explanations of behavior and mind to neuroscience (Churchland, 2013).

Theories are powerful, and reductionistic programs such as these hold enormous implications for our understanding of reality and humanity. For reality, Whitehead (1967) lamented that scientific materialism reduces nature to "a dull affair, soundless, scentless, colorless; merely the hurrying of material endlessly, meaninglessly" (p. 69). However, he went on to point out that "this position on the part of the scientist was pure bluff."

The effects of reductionism on our views of human nature were even more pain-ful. Humans were downgraded to mere machines: the stimulus–response machines of behaviorists, the "wet computers of artificial intelligence," and for evolutionary biologists "a peculiarly baroque example of the lengths to which nucleic acid is prepared to go to copy itself" (Chedd, 1973, p. 606).

Francis Crick (1994, p. 3) added to these reductionisms with his own brand of neuronal reductionism which he called "the astonishing hypothesis." Its central claim is that:

> You, your joys and your sorrows, your memories and your ambitions, your sense of personal identity and free will, are in fact no more than the behav-ior of a vast assembly of nerve cells and their associated molecules. As Lewis Carroll's Alice might have phrased it: "You're nothing but a pack of neurons".

Of course many people pointed out the multiple problems with reductionism. Back in 1964, the psychologist Gordon Allport wrote that "by their own theor-ies of human nature, psychologists have the power of elevating or degrading that same nature. Debasing assumptions debase human nature, generous assumptions exalt them." Speaking more generally about the problem of reductionism, Edgar Morin argued that:

> The reductionistic approach, which consists in relying on a single series of factors to regulate the totality of problems associated with the multiform cri-sis we are currently in the middle of, is less a solution than the problem itself.
> *(Morin & Kern, 1999, p. 128)*

Several schools emerged to counter these reductionistic forces, and within psych-ology, two of these schools – humanistic and transpersonal – were forerunners of integral theory. Humanistic psychology emphasized unique human experience over abstraction, potentials rather than pathologies, and central human concerns such as meaning and purpose rather than simple behaviors and mechanisms. Transpersonal psychology went further and attempted to create an integrative psychology that included ordinary and alternate states of consciousness, psychological and spiritual dimensions, as well as Eastern and Western perspectives.

Both schools had their influence and provided doors through which profes-sionals could explore issues outside the often narrow and reductionistic confines of conventional academia. However, both made only initial inroads into academic and intellectual culture.

The unfortunate result is that today reductionism rules much of academia. Scientific materialism provides the usually unexamined and unquestioned worldview dominating science. In the humanities, the excesses of postmodernism and social constructivism dominated in many places, but are now fading. In the mental health field, neuroreductionism reigns, and the answer to almost every ill is a pill, while lifestyle factors – often remarkably powerful and important – are largely ignored (Walsh, 2011).

Reductionistic approaches tend to explain "away" uniquely human endeavors such as art and religion in terms of lower-order phenomena. A century earlier, Karl Marx had interpreted art and religion in economic terms. Now they are repeatedly interpreted, and often interpreted away, in neural and/or evolutionary terms. For example, the neuroscientist Ramachandran (2009) claims that "many of history's great religious leaders have had TLE" (temporal lobe epilepsy). Likewise, Francis Crick – who received a Nobel prize for identifying the structure of DNA, but who was obviously ignorant of the massive differences between conventional and postconventional religions – reportedly dismissed religion as the unfortunate product of a mischievous, mutant molecule he named "theotoxin."

The need for metatheory

Clearly there is a need for big-picture metatheories that can address these major intellectual issues. Such metatheories would serve what Zachary Stein in his excellent chapter calls a "discourse regulative function" for opening intellectual inquiry and individual disciplines to more fruitful and less reductionistic perspectives (Chapter 1, this volume). More specifically, effective metatheories of human nature and behavior will perform at least ten major beneficial functions:

1 They will include and integrate multiple perspectives and disciplines, thus providing a fruitful metaperspective.
2 Effective metatheories will embrace epistemological pluralism, and employ epistemologies and methodologies appropriate to each discipline and domain.
3 They will encompass the ever growing complexity of scientific, social, global, and ecological systems.
4 Fruitful metatheories of human nature will include a developmental dimension. This will allow them to incorporate the vitally important findings of developmental psychology, which recognize different levels of adult psychological maturity. For example, there are enormous differences in the cognitive capacities, processes, and worldview of someone at the concrete operational level of cognitive development, as opposed to someone at the more mature post-formal operational level. Likewise, in ethics, there are enormous differences in the values and attitudes of people at conventional and postconventional levels. For example, at the conventional "maintaining norms" schema level, whatever "God" or the law says is unreflectively assumed to be true and sacrosanct. However, for people at the postconventional schema level, values are

open to questioning and evaluation (Thoma, 2006). I emphasize this developmental dimension for five crucial reasons:

- Once adult development is recognized, then it becomes apparent that conventional "normality" is not the ceiling of developmental possibilities, and that postconventional potentials await us.
- The recognition of postconventional potentials can encourage us to foster them individually and collectively (Walsh, 2014).
- A developmental perspective enables us to make sense of many contemporary challenges – such as cultural conflicts over issues such as abortion, racism, and feminism – which reflect usually unrecognized developmental differences.
- The significance of psychological development is often underappreciated, even in sophisticated metatheories such as critical realism and complex thought.
- Metatheorizing may require postconventional and post-formal levels of cognition such as James Baldwin's *aesthetic imagination* and *theoretical intuition*, Aurobindo's *higher mind* and *intuitive mind*, Edgar Morin's *complex thought*, and Ken Wilber's *vision-logic.*

5 Full metatheories will include religion without inappropriately pathologizing it or reductionistically dismissing it (Wilber, 2006). By employing a developmental perspective they will recognize the enormous differences between, for example, *conventional religion* – which centers on believing a narrative – and *postconventional* (or better *transconventional*) religion, which centers on psychological and contemplative practices for producing healing, transformation, and maturation.

6 Corrective metatheories will counter the recurrent tendencies – which seem to be part of our psychological make-up – to fall into inappropriate oversimplification, reductionism, and mistaking the part for the whole.

7 Metatheories can also serve a eudaimonic function that helps us reflect more effectively on the nature of a good life, and ways in which it can be fostered.

8 Socially valuable metatheories will offer tools and perspectives that foster effective social and political critiques. Specifically, these theories will help social analysts unveil inefficiencies, injustices, and pathologies built into our social and political systems, and offer in their stead constructive alternatives.

9 A crucial function for contemporary metatheories is to address the great social, global, and ecological crises of our time. Our species and our planet are imperiled, and effective metatheories can help us navigate these perils to avert the very real prospect of ecological and civilizational collapse.

10 Finally, helpful metatheories will help us recognize and explore both individual and collective potentials and thereby foster them so as to support individual, social, and global flourishing. Only in this way can we mature – individually

out of our conventional limitations, and collectively out of what is probably our evolutionary adolescence – into the further reaches of human possibilities (Elgin, 2000).

Contemporary metatheories

The recognition of the need for encompassing metatheories is certainly urgent, but is also not new. As Zachary Stein points out, as far back as the nineteenth century, two great thinkers – James Mark Baldwin and Charles Sanders Peirce – saw the need and constructed sophisticated systems that were impressive in their scope. Peirce, who was not known for his intellectual humility, wrote that he hoped:

> To make a philosophy like that of Aristotle, that is to say, to outline a theory so comprehensive that, for a long time to come, the entire work of human reason, in philosophy in every school and kind, in mathematics, in psychology, in physical science, in history, in sociology, and in whatever department there may be, shall appear as the filling up of its details
>
> *(Peirce, 2000, p. 168)*

But the world was not yet ready for such metatheories and their impact was limited. Now the time is ripe, and towards the end of the twentieth century, big-picture theories and metatheories began to reappear.

One that received significant publicity was E. O. Wilson's (1998) theory of consilience, meaning the convergence of evidence from diverse sources. It focused primarily on the sciences and was still largely reductionistic in its attempt to explain human behavior.

Around the same time, three more comprehensive and less reductionistic metatheories began to emerge: Roy Bhaskar's *critical realism*, Ken Wilber's *integral theory*, and Edgar Morin's *complex thought*. In response, researchers such as Mark Edwards (2009) began to outline a new field of theoretical studies to formally examine the nature, creation, and criteria of metatheories. Now these three great systems are meeting formally for the first time. What will happen?

When different theories meet there are many possible responses including the following five major possibilities (see also Sean Esbjörn-Hargens, Chapter 3, this volume, for further ideas and the preface and introduction to this volume):

- defensive dismissal of the validity and value of alternate theories;
- mutual enrichment, which will hopefully always occur;
- the identification of common factors: what ideas, dimensions, levels and epistemologies do the theories hold in common?
- assimilative integration: In this response, elements of one theory are assimilated into another theory. This is something that metatheories do routinely, and thereby enrich and enlarge themselves;

- the formation of a novel integrative theory that effectively synthesizes and integrates the elements of the original constitutive theories.

Thanks to the editors and contributors to this volume we can already see that the first alternative of defensive dismissal will not dominate. Rather, this book is a model of mutual respect, enrichment, and the identification of common factors and differences. Beyond this, chapters such as that by Paul Marshall (Chapter 4, this volume), with his remarkably wide-ranging scholarship and formidable synthesizing abilities, point to integrative possibilities.

This book is a wonderful tribute to Roy Bhaskar, whose great mind was guided by an equally great heart. This book is also an enormously important contribution, and helps advance metatheory as a crucial intellectual contribution to the twenty-first century. On behalf of us all, I thank the creators – Ken Wilber, Roy Bhaskar, and Edgar Morin – for creating the three metatheories meeting here, and the editors and contributors to this fine book for bringing them together for our benefit.

References

Allport, G. (1964). The fruits of eclecticism: Bitter or sweet. *Acta Psychologica, 23,* 27–44.

Chedd, G. (1973). Evolution in a test tube. *New Scientist,* 58(849), 606–608.

Churchland, P. (2013). *Touching a nerve: The self as brain.* New York: W. W. Norton.

Crick, F. (1994). *The astonishing hypothesis: The scientific search for the soul.* New York: Charles Scribner's Sons.

Edwards, M. (2009). *Organizational transformation for sustainability: Integral metatheory.* New York: Routledge.

Elgin, D. (2000). *Promise ahead: A vision of hope and action for humanity's future.* New York: William Morrow.

Morin, E., & Kern, B. (1999). *Homeland Earth: A manifesto for the new millennium* (S. M. Kelly & R. Lapointe, Trans.). Cresskill, NJ: Hampton Press.

Peirce, C. (2000). *Writings of Charles S. Peirce: A chronological edition* (Vol. 6). Bloomington: Indiana University Press.

Ramachandran, V. (2009). Self awareness: The last frontier. http://edge.org/conversation/self-awareness-the-last-frontier.

Schmidt, E. (2010). Google CEO Eric Schmidt talks about three fundamental technology trends: mobile, clouds and networking. www.theguardian.com/media/video/2010/jul/02/google-eric-schmidt-activate.

Thoma, S. (2006). Research on the defining issues test. In M. Killen & J. Smetana (Eds.), *Handbook of moral development* (pp. 67–92). Newark, NJ: Lawrence Erlbaum.

Walsh, R. (2011). Lifestyle and mental health. *American Psychologist, 66*(7), 579–592.

Walsh, R. (Ed.). (2014). *The world's great wisdom: Timeless teachings from religions and philosophies.* Albany, NY: SUNY Press.

Whitehead, A. (1967). *Science and the modern world.* New York: Macmillan.

Wilber, K (2006). *Integral spirituality: A startling new role for religion in the modern and postmodern world.* Boston, MA: Shambhala.

Wilson, E. O. (1998). *Consilience: The unity of knowledge.* New York: Alfred Knopf.

PREFACE

Roy Bhaskar

Editors' note. Roy Bhaskar died, sadly, before he could write a preface to this book. However, he communicated to us that he had been developing his thoughts for the preface, which he shared in his introductory remarks to the third critical realism and integral theory symposium, 'Integrative Metatheories in the Twenty-First Century: Forging New Alliances for Planetary Flourishing in the Anthropocene', at the UCL Institute of Education, London, on 22 July 2014. Thus, we believe that the edited transcript of his remarks, and the ensuing dialogue, makes a very good substitute. It is also a splendid tribute to Roy himself, who had only a few months to live and was in considerable pain throughout the presentation. We feel this preface also captures in a lively way the spirit of dialogical engagement out of which this volume has been produced.

Roy Bhaskar. Because I'm not very well and have to leave early, I'm going to combine my welcome to you with a few words I was going to say in my response at a later stage. So I'm welcoming you, first, to this extension of the IACR conference here over the last four days – through the pre-conference workshop, six days in all – and I hope you enjoyed it. I welcome you all to a continuation of the discussions we've been having since 2010/2011.

Without going into the informal discussions we had at the time, the first meeting in the series was a four-day event organized by Sean Esbjörn-Hargens and Nicholas (Nick) Hedlund in San Francisco in September 2011 at John F. Kennedy University. We'd met the year before in Luxembourg. We established a firm friendship and an immediate sense of connection. I was very pleased to see that Sean had started reading my work. I had read a little bit of Ken Wilber a long time ago, I think in the 1990s. Of course I was impressed by it, but I haven't made any attempt to systemically use it. Sean and I decided it would be a great idea to have a symposium, a meeting between representatives of integral theory (IT), people who came from the critical realist (CR) tradition, and a few individuals who were familiar with both or represented additional valuable perspectives. So this meeting happened in September 2011 and it was an extremely wonderful occasion, I think we all agree. There were a lot of very frank exchanges. But actually the interesting thing is that most people found these exciting and energizing rather than, you know, depressing. I enjoyed it very much also because we had a hopeless summer in England, and of course San Francisco in September is absolutely gorgeous, so I used to go out for a couple of hours in the middle of the day and just sit there, in the sun.

There were various responses to the symposium, including a published exchange between Tim Rutzou and Paul Marshall, who was there on the critical realist side, but who had already been Sean's student and knew quite a bit about IT. And then these exchanges developed. In the *Journal of Integral Theory and Practice* there was, not really an exchange between me and Ken, but my attention was drawn to something Ken had said, and so I replied to it. He didn't really reply to my piece, but I was sandwiched between two bits of Ken as if it was an exchange. I think that sort of missed the point, really, of an exchange, but I am hoping to meet Ken at some point. Of course I admire and respect what he has done.

Then, in terms of physical meetings, there was the one-day pre-conference symposium at the San Francisco Integral Theory Conference last year, July 2013. But this time, coming from normally rainy, dank UK, the weather in San Francisco was hopeless.[1] Nonetheless, it was a lovely conference. I enjoyed very much the hospitality and I met some old friends, but I met lots of new people too. I was amazed at the degree to which IT-ers were seeking to apply critical realism. They were reading it and discussing it and applying it; this was a wonderful thing actually, and it was a very impressive conference.

We also got a contract with Routledge for a book, which is what we're going to be discussing today, or it's going to structure our discussions. That's more or less what we decided to do in having a third symposium here.

What I'm going to talk about now is various different ways in which I feel CR and IT can, or cannot, work together. I'm talking about CR and IT, not complex thought (CT), to make it very concrete and focused, because none of us is a particular expert on CT, though Paul is writing a thesis that includes it. But not including CT simplifies the choices I feel that we've got as individuals or even as a group; these are the same with respect to complex thought, whether you're a critical realist or an integral theorist.

I think there are four very clear alternative positions, perhaps five, that have already become a little bit *un*clear. To understand them, it would be best if you read some of the dialogues, such as the one between Paul and Tim. But I think even if you haven't read any of the dialogues or any papers exploring the relationship between CR and IT, you could still understand these four or five positions. I think there are four people here who exemplify the four positions, so I might as well put their names to them. The first I think is Sean Esbjörn-Hargens' (I'm not trying to be entirely accurate, it's more about a position than about Sean). Let's call this position *complex integral realism* (CIR). I'll describe that in a moment. The second position,

TABLE P.1 Overview of five positions

Positions abbreviated	Full name	Exemplary individuals and chapter in this volume	Description
1. CIR	Complex integral realism	Sean Esbjörn-Hargens Chapter 3	Preservative synthesis
2. P(CIR)	The possibility of complex integral realism	Paul Marshall Chapter 4	Potential synthesis
3. CRIT	Critical realist integral theory	Nick Hedlund Chapter 5	Non-preservative synthesis
4. CR/IT	Critical realism/integral theory resonance	Mervyn Hartwig Chapter 7	Resonance, but no synthesis possible
5. CR||IT	Critical realism and integral theory incommensurability	Tim Rutzou	No fruitful dialogue; incommensurable

which I think is Paul Marshall's, could be described as *the possibility of complex integral realism* P(CIR). The third position, which I think is Nick Hedlund's, could be called *critical realist integral theory* (CRIT). The fourth position is one I think Mervyn Hartwig is close to – it's somewhere between Mervyn and Tim Rutzou, who's unfortunately not here. It is that CR and IT have a resonance, there is a resonance between them, but they can't be synthesized (CR/IT). There might be times when they can be cross-fertilizing each other, but this isn't synthesis. Then a fifth position, represented by Tim Rutzou (2012, 2014), would be that no dialogue is really going to be fruitful, it would be of mere academic interest or something like that. This could be represented as CR\|\|IT. CR and IT each have their own effective and worthwhile trajectories, but contact between them is not really going to be very fruitful. They're basically incommensurable. See Table P.1 for an overview of these five positions.

So the first position is the one that some of us held after the 2011 symposium, that actually there are absences in critical realism which integral theory seeks to fill, and vice versa. Looking at it as a critical realist, IT doesn't seem to have an ontology, it doesn't really fully buy into the critique of actualism, and it also doesn't seem to be very strong in dealing with change. But then IT could say, 'Well, CR doesn't have the same kind of epistemological taxonomy that we have, and there are various other areas in which CR is defective.' So if we put the two together, it's like a jigsaw puzzle: 'Wow! We could have this great jigsaw.' What was involved in this notion was the notion of a preservative synthesis, that these two traditions could be synthesized into a new position, which incorporated preservatively the prehistory of CR and IT. So that's a very clear line. The idea of a jigsaw that many of us have, and as it is exemplified by Sean's and Paul's papers (Chapters 3 and 4 in this volume, respectively), suggests that synthesis is a strong possibility.

But a problem with it became very clear to me when I was discussing a draft of Paul's thesis and some papers he was going to publish – I hope you don't mind me saying this, Paul, I might be caricaturing you, but I hope not too much. Paul would talk about the need for understanding the critique of the epistemic fallacy within ontology, and then he would go on to talk about Ken's work as having an ontology and as being realist. Of course the question is: '*Does* it have an ontology and does it have a fully adequate ontology?' There were also problems when we went into work in IT that had been done under the partial influence of critical realism, because there is talk of enactment, and the principle of enactment seems to us to be very close to positivism. The idea is that things don't really exist until you can enact them, epistemologically or in a laboratory or something like that; whereas for critical realism there is a deep ontology, which constitutes scientific laws, generative mechanisms, structures and fields that exist outside and long before human life. So there is a clear contradiction between the demands of critical realist ontology and the theory of enactment. Then some of us became worried by the multiple object theory, say as applied to climate change (e.g. Sean's work; Esbjörn-Hargens, 2010). This is the view that there are lots of different phenomena one is talking about, but for me anyway it's clear that climate change is a unitary, but very complex phenomenon, which has many different modes of interpretation by different agents, situated with different perspectives, material interests and worldviews. So for me it's a unitary phenomenon, and I think it's necessary to understand that it is, in order to address it properly. So the multiple object theory seems suspect. And it seemed to me that if you were going to integrate critical realism with integral theory, you would have to reject bits of the prehistory of both. So it couldn't be a preservative synthesis. So I rather pressed Paul, saying, 'You can't combine these two, you simply have to make up your mind.' Then he came back at me by saying, 'Well, I'm not really at the stage of forming a theory or anything like that. What I'm doing' – and these are my words not Paul's – 'is just sketching possibilities and scenarios.' So you can regard this as a very full picture of what might happen at the retroductive stage of scientific theorizing, at the stage where you've got a lot of multiple generative mechanisms and you put them all together on the same piece of paper or in the same research profile, and you know you can't apply them all together but you're looking for the one that you can apply or, to put it in terms of what I call the DREIC model, you're looking for which to eliminate. Then it might be that the resulting one is a synthesis or a combination of bits of CR and bits of IT, for example, but there would be clearly rejected other bits. So this is a second position, which I'm attributing to Paul for the sake of the argument today, that what he is doing is the *possibility* of complex integral realism. And some theorists in the future – perhaps not so far in the future, or it may be a long, long time – will come up with an effective synthesis, but based on previous non-preservative work on the two theories. This is not really an applicable position before you do the work that it presupposes, that is of eliminating the possibilities.

So then the third position is a position from which you can work today, and I have to say I'm very sympathetic to it. This I would call critical realist integral theory (CRIT). This is the sort of position that I think Nick is aspiring to work towards, though again I don't want to prejudge what he's going to say in his thesis.[2] It basically says – well, the way I would develop it without attributing it to Nick (though I did tell him, 'Have a look at Iskra's CRAT (Nunez, 2014) [not CRAP!], and it could be that this is the way he is actually developing it) is to embed elements of IT that are strong within a robust critical realist ontology. So you don't make any pretences to be synthesizing the two, what you do is you say, Well, I've got to accept something like a critical realist ontology. Plus the second element is the critical realist critique of philosophy, which I think is very strong, and in particular the critique of 'the unholy trinity' of Western philosophy, which is the epistemic fallacy; third, what I call the primal squeeze on the Platonic/Aristotelian fault-line, or more simply, actualism; and fourth, ontological monovalence, which is the generation of a purely positive account of being. But there are other elements, I think, within the critical realist system or composite work we've already done, which I think it would be absolutely essential for any synthesis to take on. For example, the critique of individualism, and we have a very strong sense of structure, of social structure being real. You can find that in Ken Wilber, but the overwhelming emphasis is an individualist one. So I think there would have to be a correction there. So let's say the third and fourth thing that would have to be corrected is individualism and lack of a realist account of social structure, so four elements of IT are critiqued that would inform CRIT. When you are doing your CRIT work in the field of climate change, that will be based on a critical realist ontology. I think that is a strong, and a very good way of moving forward.

But then there's also the position that it would be very difficult to do this, and perhaps we just ought to accept that we've both got lovely theories, beautiful systems which we imagine are in some sort of reciprocity so that we can smile at each other and we can have lovely conferences together, in nice places, and we should meet every year if we can get the money together and resonate, bounce off each other. So this is CR/IT resonance. Then the position would be that we can cross-fertilize and mutually infuse each other. And this is how most scientific theories actually work, by importing models or building models by importing cognitive material from another field. Because the question of the sort of mirror image or the illusion of the mirror image at the September 2011 symposium is quite an impressive one, there would be lots of cross-fertilization. It is clear that IT has a very powerful epistemic taxonomy, so critical realists should use that. And then again it's clear that critical realism has a very strong ontology, and so integral theorists should use that. But there wouldn't be any attempt to say this is a super-unified theory, it would just be very useful and fruitful cross-fertilization. Now of course that's the fourth position, and I think Mervyn is somewhere between the third and the fourth. If he was *at* the fourth, that would be very convenient – but I'm not trying to push you there, Mervyn.

Mervyn Hartwig. I *am* at the fourth.

Roy. Okay, that's very good, thanks a lot!

What we have to notice of course with CRIT, the third position that I identified with Nick, is that it doesn't have to be a global theory, it's possible to have regional theories and local theories. Nick might do a very good piece with respect to climate change, but without the supposition that it could be applied across the board. Of course it might be that it *can* be applied across the board.

So those are the four positive alternatives. The fifth alternative is the no dialogue, or no *fruitful* dialogue position, which I don't think Tim Rutzou is quite at, but he is close to it. I mean he's had exchanges with Hans Despain on this, and I think he's on his final position. But it is an *arguable* one, so that's a position we have to bear in mind.

Mervyn. This would be a position where a critical realist or an integral theorist might take the view that okay, there are areas in which you could get some benefits from dialogue with IT or with CR, but it might be more important to dialogue with critical theory or some other theory. It's not necessarily an absolute rejection.

Roy. No, that's right, and of course there are lots of intermediate positions between the fourth and the fifth that would be a sort of magpie position. You know, if I've got a lacuna in my theory let me go as a magpie and pick something. I look at critical theory first, perhaps, and then poststructuralism. If it's not there, OK, let's go back to my old friend.

Otto Laske. It seems to me there's a sixth position. There are more than that, but a sixth would say that to take two ready-made theories and try to connect them is an encumbrance, an unnecessary encumbrance on spontaneous dialectical thinking, and that one should rather begin with dialectical thinking itself and spin out of it a synthesis that may well take pieces from here and there, but unencumbered by these —

Roy. The two monoliths. Yes, that's very good. Perhaps in your presentation today you could go into that a bit more. Have we got any more comments?

Michael Schwartz. Yes, I just wonder if a way of framing these two isn't just positions but process.

Roy. Absolutely. Yes.

Michael. And we approach this by a hermeneutical prejudgment from the positions we already have. I thought that's a little bit of what I was hearing from Otto, what does the dialogic process look like rather than what are the actual positions we're looking at.

Roy. Yes, well of course, but you could still say that at any moment in time with respect to any topic of enquiry, then you would have these positions.

Michael. I agree.

Roy. So yes, of course we have to bear in mind the process. Now I'm sure I've been very unfair to Sean, so I'll let him speak.

Sean Esbjörn-Hargens. Yes, just briefly because we'll get into this more when we go into my paper. I don't feel I'm promoting the strong version of synthesis in the way that I was hearing it presented by you. I think my impulse – and maybe I'm not very successful in expressing that impulse in my writings at this point – is more along the lines of Otto's dialectical process. The notion of *trialectics* that I'm trying to bring forward and discuss in my paper is more about bringing these three theories – CR, IT, and complex thought (CT) – into dynamic engagement with each other and then seeing what kinds of synthetic and non-synthetic possibilities emerge. So I'm not advocating a simplistic preservative synthesis as much as what might be called an emergent synthesis. I'm fine with being a representative of position one, but I think my real inquiry is something slightly different and more in the direction of a kind of dialectical encounter between all three integrative metatheories where a new emergent 'meta-meta' theory or simply a new metatheory informed by the best aspects of all three begins to take shape. That's why I've drawn so heavily on Mark Edwards' work on integrative pluralism to frame my paper. Because I am aware of my own strong tendency for a kind of *über*-synthesis, but I'm not wanting that impulse to colonize the emergence of what I am calling complex integral realism. I sense the value of CIR lies in the mystery of what might emerge when we place these three integrative metatheories into deep contact with each other in a dialectical and generative inquiry.

Roy. Yes, well I think integrative pluralism is a great term. I used it in *Scientific Realism and Human Emancipation*. Of course we're not just looking at it synchronically as a decision or choice that we have now, but also in terms of a developing process over time, and I think that's a fruitful way of proceeding. I'd like to couple that with Paul's position, because that's the intention: in the future there would be this engagement and what he's actually doing is just mapping out the possibilities, possible scenarios. And then you would have to make all the judgments, when it came to a particular theory, at some point in the future when you felt able to do it. But in the moment we could just enjoy the process, which is a very nice thing to be able to do, of course. And in a way this is what we have been doing for the last three years.

Mark Edwards. I'm thinking that my sort of perspective and position on the spectrum is not really represented. I'm not really interested in some level of synthesis between two or three different viewpoints, but the whole clearing, in what big-picture philosophies and scientific theories exist. And what are the conditions of that clearing, and what are the separations and distinctions between different philosophies and science within that sort of meta-level space? I think those sorts of preconditions that actually define that clearing have not really been well articulated outside the particular sort of position within that. My interest has been in what are the enabling conditions that allow a conscious, reflexive understanding of this meta-level.

Roy. So this is like a kind of meta-underlabouring. Before we can get down to synthesizing or elements of synthesis, we have to meta-underlabour. We have to clear the ground.

Mark. Particularly a scientific underlabouring. How you get a scientific grasp of this stuff as opposed to a philosophical one.

Roy. Well, I think that's a very important part of what we should be doing. So if you like you could add that to the six or seven we've got now, because that's an important aspect of it. But of course it won't rule out the need for one of the first four, because when you come to seek to apply it to the world, then of course you have to move out of it – well, you can be in the clearing, but you would have to move to a different level to make assessments about the world. The basic problem is, 'Are critical realist and integral theory perspectives about the world compatible?'; or, to make that fuller, 'To what extent are they compatible?' Clearly there is some compatibility, but equally there is some incompatibility, and I do not think it is possible to coherently apply a theory of enactment with a critical realist ontology – and if enactment is very important to integral theory, or phases of integral theory anyway, and ontology is absolutely indispensable for critical realism, there is a problem.

Gary Hampson. I just want to add to your point, Mark, about the attractor of science in relation to this debate in addition to that of philosophy. I would like to add a third, which is aesthetics or beauty or art. I think that often gets under-appreciated and I think we need to be aware of that attractor as well.

Roy. Great.

Hans Despain. I just want to say that I think what you outlined for us is really useful. There's something very organic that came out of that in the discussion. I see a commonality between what Otto, Mark and Michael said earlier. Actually, I think what Gary just said goes right into that, which is that there is going to be a process here. I think that's a very important thing. To take a step back and ask, 'What are the intentions of critical realism, how did it evolve, what are the intentions of IT, and so on?' But I think it's the process, and it might break down what you did outline, which I think has been very useful, in very curious ways.

Roy. Yes, I think there is a process. But the constraint is explaining phenomena in reality, and then we will come up against this problem. So perhaps I'm just posing a problem that will come up when we seek – you see, my initial enthusiasm for this project was geared to the idea that, well, this would be a deeper vehicle, a bigger toolkit, a more comprehensive one for explaining and dealing with the crises that we've got in the world today. And it's the sort of thing that can't be postponed to a very nice social and intellectual aesthetic process, because those problems are urgent and if you take the title of Nick's thesis, which is 'Towards a Critical Realist Integral Theory of Climate Change', I mean, that's just the sort of thing we want and need, and I think we need it in economics as well. So I do want this process to go on. I think it's a beautiful process, a lovely process and it may have very rewarding, dialectically unforeseeable offshoots in the future, and should definitely continue, so I'm not trying to stop it in any way. But it would be a better process if it was also capable of generating good explanatory theories.

Otto. It seems to me we also need to consider that what we call the global crisis is testimony to the present state of human thinking, and that that actually may be the crux of the matter, that human thinking is not at a level at which it can appreciate it's embeddedness in reality. So that's an educational problem in my view, that until we can bring up a human's thinking and development as a whole to a level where it becomes unquestionably important to consider the consequences of our actions in nature, little can be done. So it's really not about the crisis – it *is* a crisis, but it's a crisis of human thinking.

Roy. Oh yes, I totally agree with you, I think that's absolutely the case. But the problem is that we can't wait: we have to have this new thinking now. Of course it's always difficult when you have to speed up new thinking, it's better for the new thinking to take its time. But the ecological crisis is something that humanity has to act on now, and the economic crisis, or the political-economic crisis could explode at any minute. There are crises that we haven't talked about in the conference, really, relating to war and violence, that are here, with us now. We need to be able to understand them and to transform those situations. So that's what I think we need to do, we must. We need a perspective of understanding and relating to crisis now even while we wait for new thinking to catch up. And as intellectuals what we do is we try and make this new thinking happen as quickly as possible, including to ourselves.

Otto. But in acting don't we also have to consider that the individual mind develops over an entire lifespan and that we cannot impose solutions that will not be accepted, because the people's thinking is not at a level where you can even understand it?

Roy. Yes, but I also think that in particular circumstances the human mind is capable of a great leap. I'm thinking for example of the minds of the Chilean miners trapped underground. In crisis situations we act from what I call our ground-states. Everyone has a ground-state. You don't have to wait to the end of your life to feel it, to know it. In a crisis many people – most people I would say – will act from their ground-states; that will be their first response. And then, when they starting talking to other people and a lot of intellectual arguments are put to them with various emotional charges, they will move away from their ground-states. Then at the end they will be just in their egos in my sense, acting selfishly or panicking.

Paul Marshall. From what Otto is saying, it sounds like the core difference between integral theory and critical realism is that critical realism stresses that the main cause of the present crisis is external social structures and power relations —

Roy. No, I think the main cause of the ecological and economic crises has to be understood in terms of four-planar social being. The very conception of human being that we have is atomistic, egocentric; the notion of reason that we have is of abstract universality. These notions are of course held by particular people, the behaviour we have is of particular people, but they are also objectified in social structures. And we have to act on all four planes simultaneously, that's the most important. Yesterday at the post-conference workshop on metaRealism

I was talking about the importance of self-referentiality. So what you say isn't true of critical realism as fully developed – by me at any rate.[3] I don't think that you will get any social change, any really significant social change, without transformation of all four planes of social being, and you can't do anything without acting on your self, because that will be the thing that will produce the change in other things.

Editors' note. Soon after his comments above, Roy excused himself from the event as he was not feeling well. The group continued to discuss a number of the chapters in this volume. We felt this was a perfect place to end this Preface as these words from Roy are close to his last words for the printed record. We also feel that Roy discussing the primacy of self-change is a very good (if slightly abrupt) note to end on.

Notes

1   In contrast to the September 2011 symposium at John F. Kennedy University, the weather at the July 2013 conference was cool and foggy, as is often the case in the summertime in San Francisco.
2   Roy served as Nick Hedlund's PhD supervisor at the UCL Institute of Education from 2012 to the time of his death in 2014.
3   As 'fully developed' implies, it is true of original CR up to a point.

References

Esbjörn-Hargens, S. (2010). An ontology of climate change: Integral pluralism and the enactment of multiple objects. *Journal of Integral Theory and Practice*, 5(1), 143–174.

Nunez, I. (2014). *Critical realist activity theory: An engagement with critical realism and cultural-historical activity theory*. London: Routledge.

Rutzou, T. (2012). Integral theory: A poisoned chalice? *Journal of Critical Realism*, 11(2), 215–224.

Rutzou, T. (2014). Integral theory and the search for the Holy Grail: On the possibility of a metatheory. *Journal of Critical Realism*, 13(1), 77–83.

ACKNOWLEDGEMENTS

This book is the outcome of four years of dialogical engagement between critical realism and integral theory in which many people and a number of organizations and institutions played an invaluable role. The engagement might never have happened had Mark Edwards not encouraged Sean Esbjörn-Hargens to check out critical realism at the 2008 Integral Theory Conference and had Markus Molz and the Institute for Integral Studies (Germany) not organized an international symposium in Luxembourg that brought the four editors of this volume together. We are deeply grateful to Mark and Markus for this. Special thanks go to the Integral Institute for largely funding the first symposium that got the engagement seriously under way, and to John F. Kennedy University for hosting it. For hosting the second, third and fourth symposium we must thank the MetaIntegral Foundation, UCL Institute of Education, University of London, and Sonoma State University, respectively. In organizing the symposia, the lead role was taken by the Integral Research Center, and for this we are most grateful. Other important roles were played by the International Centre for Critical Realism and the International Association for Critical Realism (London) and by the organizers of the 2013 Integral Theory Conference, Mark Forman and Jordan Luftig (San Francisco); in many ways, critical realism 'arrived' in the integral community as a metatheory at this conference, and we are deeply appreciative of the warm reception the conference gave Roy Bhaskar. Special thanks must go to Roy's partner, Rebecca Long, for her care and support of Roy at this and the London symposium and for helping to organize the latter; and to Gary Hampson for recording the proceedings in London. Thanks also to the *Journal of Integral Theory and Practice* and *Journal of Critical Realism* for publishing important exchanges and articles arising from the dialogue. We are thankful to Roger Walsh and Markus Molz, who provided much support and inspiration for this project, and also offered excellent and insightful contributions, in the Foreword and Afterword, respectively. We are deeply indebted to Alan Jarvis of Routledge (the publisher of a range of book series on critical realism) for his generous encouragement and support for our project and his ready willingness to go to a second volume when this, the first one, burst its bounds. Many thanks also to Emma Chappell of Routledge for her valuable editorial assistance. Above all we thank the many participants in the symposia and our co-authors for their lively and creative input.

INTRODUCTION

On the deep need for integrative metatheory in the twenty-first century

Nicholas Hedlund, Sean Esbjörn-Hargens, Mervyn Hartwig, and Roy Bhaskar[1]

1 Introduction: toward a free-flourishing planetary society in the twenty-first century

The twenty-first century is a radically new era, unprecedented in human geo-history, marked by deep and complexly interrelated global crises: ecological, economic, political, moral, and existential, to name but some of pertinence. These complex problems or crises present extraordinary dangers and pitfalls, as well as great opportunities and potentials. Due to their profound interdependencies and feedback loops, these complex and intractable crises can best be understood as a singular socio-ecological crisis, or what we call the *metacrisis* (see below). Clearly, this meta-crisis is the most complex and urgent challenge of the twenty-first century. It is a ubiquitous, real-world phenomenon, whose unprecedented complexity profoundly transcends the boundaries of our traditional academic disciplines and specialized research methodologies. Indeed, the metacrisis is a complex, multifaceted totality or "laminated system" (Bhaskar, Frank, Høyer, Næss, & Parker, 2010) which is far more complex than can adequately be addressed by piecemeal, mono-disciplinary approaches and methodologically restricted research programs. Such approaches fail to account for all its facets and their dynamic, non-linear interrelationships and are therefore incapable of providing adequate holistic accounts of the metacrisis.

In this context, comprehensive and sophisticated *integrative* frameworks are needed for three main reasons. First, complex twenty-first-century problems and the metacrisis at large demand frameworks that go beyond the proliferating fragmentation of knowledge and 'grasp the big picture'; that is, support us to effectively account for the intricate multidimensionality and dynamism of the metacrisis, foster coordination and integration across disciplinary boundaries and knowledge domains, and ultimately help generate transformative praxis that can optimize the conditions for planetary flourishing. Second, integrative metatheory can serve a crucial emancipatory function by helping us to identify the real causes of social pathology, oppression, and alienation. Third, to resolve the metacrisis we need to expand the purview of our vision and imagination to develop ideas about what human beings are capable of and what are the conditions for their universal free flourishing; metatheory is well placed to assist with this by articulating an integrated descriptive, normative, and aesthetic vision of a concrete utopian, eudaimonic world and a coherent program for global transformation in the coming decades. Without such a vision we cannot even 'see' what kind of planetary society is possible. The world itself – what Bhaskar (1993/2008) refers to as alethic truth, the reality principle and axiological necessity – seems to be demanding transformation to new intellectual formations and structures of consciousness that can support new modes of praxis and engagement, apt for our contemporary context. Such formations can not only help to avert biocatastrophe but also to actualize the world's evolutionary potentials and profound opportunities for human development and spiritual maturation on the way to the emergence of a freely flourishing Earth community.[2]

In this way, integrative metatheory can contribute to a 'lifeworld transformation' wherein illusory or demi-real modes of thinking and acting are shed and a deeper understanding of who we are as a species, our *raison d'être*, and our place in the field of nature is cultivated. The way we understand ourselves in the world powerfully informs how we relate to and shape the world in and through the activities that reproduce or transform our social structures. That is, metatheories tend to undergird our collective modes of thought and vision around which we organize our societies. Metatheories can be viewed as the formalized intellectual expression and rationalization and/or reconstruction of larger cultural worldviews[3] that are in resonance with social structures. They begin as micro-level cultural phenomena that often function as blueprints for more diffuse meso- and macro-level worldviews and social structures. Therefore, apt metatheories – these new intellectual formations – are of paramount concern if we are likewise to help birth the new cultural and social formations demanded by the planetary moment. As Charles Taylor (2004) has argued, a careful study of history reveals that often what began as 'theories' held by a few eventually come to profoundly inform and shape the social imaginary, first amongst intellectual elites and then in the public sphere and society at large.[4] In this way, one can argue that the history of socially influential ideas – metatheories and metanarratives – has tended to be a primary and disproportionate driver in the trajectory of cultural history as a whole. Thus, if we are seeking deliberate transformation of our worldview and social formation to address our complex problems, the level of metatheory appears to be a powerful leverage point.

Yet, while there are some countervailing trends (see section 3), much of the contemporary academy remains hypnotized by either the hyper-analytic, hyper-specialized, fragmented gaze of late modernity, or the sliding scale of postmodern relativism and its antipathy to integrated knowledge and meta-level understanding. Together these two orientations offer inadequate understanding(s) of our many complex problems and their root causes, let alone the socio-ecological crisis at large. Without being able to adequately illumine such root causes, the academy remains largely impotent to address and help transform them. This point is underscored by the fact that, to date, the dominant metatheories of modernity, such as positivism, have not only failed to alter fundamental trajectories of human-induced ecological degradation (Biermann *et al.*, 2012; IPCC, 2014) but are in fact deeply implicated as underlying causal forces contributing to such trends, as has been widely argued by philosophers and social theorists alike (Bhaskar, 2002/2012, ch. 2; Wilber, 1995).

This book therefore takes a fresh look at the role of metatheory in the twenty-first century. Throughout the volume, we showcase a variety of perspectives on what metatheory is, and what it ought to become to adequately grasp and address the unique and urgent context of our planetary moment. Our aim is to help ignite the potentials of integrative metatheory as an emancipatory, visionary, and transformational force vis-à-vis our complex twenty-first-century challenges. We try to make the case that metatheory in the appropriate form provides indispensable intellectual scaffolding for the crucial psychological, cultural, and social transformations demanded by a world in metacrisis.

We do this through, first, reflection on the role and function of metatheory in geo-historical context; and, second, the development of metatheory through an exploratory-dialogical encounter between what are arguably amongst the most sophisticated contemporary metatheories, *critical realism* and *integral theory* (and to some extent *complex thought*).[5] The book brings together a number of voices that we feel collectively forge a bold new mosaic vision on the role of metatheory in supporting planetary flourishing in the twenty-first century. Indeed, it is a key intention of this book to embolden our collective movement toward such a free-flourishing planetary society in the twenty-first century.

In the remainder of this Introduction we circle back on the state of the world in more detail and review various concepts of our complex problems, and briefly highlight what an integrative metatheoretical lens can bring to their understanding. This is followed by a discussion of metatheory in which we review various definitions on the way to offering an overarching, integrative meta-definition, which we call *metatheory 2.0*. Metatheory 2.0 stands in contrast with metatheory 1.0, which is associated with the integrative monism of modernity (see section 3). We then delineate some of the key criteria for such integrative metatheory apt for deployment in a twenty-first-century global context, and situate this relative to metatheories of the past. Finally, we provide a historical overview of dialogical encounter between critical realism and integral theory in which this anthology and its companion volume (Bhaskar, Esbjörn-Hargens, Hedlund, & Hartwig, forthcoming) were forged, before summarizing each chapter in the book.

2 Hypercomplexity, wicked problems, and the metacrisis

A scientific review of the state of the world reveals a planet undergoing rapid and potentially catastrophic changes, many of which are or may become irreversible. The balance of the great biogeochemical cycles of the Earth system have been disrupted by human activities, perhaps most notably the carbon and nitrogen cycles. The former has led to changes in the global climate system and destabilized the generally favorable conditions that we have enjoyed over the past 10,000 years of the Holocene epoch. At the time of writing, we have exceeded a concentration of 400ppm CO_2 in the atmosphere and are on a warming trajectory that is more rapid and intense than some of the 'worst case' projective scenario models of years past (IPCC, 2000, 2014). Climate change means in the first instance an increasing onslaught of extreme-weather events (hurricanes and typhoons, tornadoes, floods, droughts, wildfires, etc.) (IPCC, 2014), which are already destroying lives, impacting communities, and undermining humanity's capacity to survive and thrive in the twenty-first century and beyond. Unchecked burning of fossil fuels and deforestation practices will only increase this undermining of the conditions for the possibility of human flourishing until critical thresholds are crossed and we start to experience systems collapse (whether on an economic, social, or ecological level). In addition to climate change and other biogeochemical disruptions, we have critically contaminated much of the planet's water, air, and soil. Moreover, we are undergoing a human-driven loss of species known as the Sixth Extinction, unparalleled since the time of the dinosaurs 65 million years ago. Other key (interrelated) concerns include topsoil loss, deforestation, ocean acidification and plastification, overfishing and the collapse of aquatic ecosystems, bioaccumulation of toxins (which threaten primarily mammals at the top of the food chain, namely, us humans), endocrine disruption, depletion of ground water and crucial fossil aquifers, and desertification[6] – and all this while more than 7 billion humans continue to reproduce and consume natural resources at exponentially increasing rates.

On the social plane, widespread poverty, starvation, income and wealth inequality, and social injustice – along with problems with health and obesity – persist. Corporate power has corrupted politics in many so-called advanced democracies, to the point where they are teetering on the edge of oligarchy (as appears to be the case in the United States). The media, which is supposed to be the Fourth Estate in a functional democracy, has been consolidated and corporatized. There is a widespread mood of existential alienation, disenchantment, anomie, and mental disorder. And there is widespread disagreement in the public sphere about the status of these complex issues and how best to respond to them.

The emergent global context, scale, and profound interdependency of many of the aforementioned ecological and social problems has led theorists to coin a range of neologisms to underline their novelty and urgency. According to Scharmer (2009), many of these issues can better be conceptualized as "hypercomplex problems." Such problems are characterized by the following three features: *dynamic complexity* (defined by cause and effect being distant in space and time); *social complexity* (defined by divergent and often conflicting interests, cultures, and worldviews among diverse stakeholders); and *emerging complexity* (defined by disruptive patterns of innovation and change in situations in which the future cannot be predicted and addressed by the patterns of the past).

Other theorists, such as Hulme (2009), use the term 'wicked problems' in an attempt to illuminate the novel and dynamic qualities of complexity associated with many of our twenty-first-century challenges, such as climate change. The notion of wicked problems, introduced by Rittel and Webber (1973), was used originally in social planning to describe a problem that is resistant to simple resolution due to the complex, open-systemic interdependencies of its multiple natural and social facets as they dynamically morph, reconfigure into emergent relational networks, and feedback on each other in complex, non-linear ways. The term 'wicked' is used, not in the sense of evil or any other normative judgment, but rather to refer to resistance to simple resolution. Moreover, because of such complex interdependencies, the effort to solve one aspect of a wicked problem may reveal or create other problems, much like Hercules found in trying to slay the Hydra, according to the ancient Greek myth.

Due in part to their intricate interdependencies and networked feedback loops, while many of the aforementioned distinct problems could be understood as 'wicked' or 'hyper-complex' in their own right, we believe they can be more adequately understood together as a complex multiplicity or crisis that is more than the sum of its parts. Edgar Morin (1999) refers to this multiplicity of interconnected wicked or hypercomplex problems as the "polycrisis." The polycrisis is marked by an emergent and unprecedented level of human impact on the very structure of the Earth system that some authors refer to as the *Anthropocene.*[7]

Our own preferred term for this complex multiplicity is 'metacrisis'. This is in part because for us it is not just a polycrisis in the sense that it is multifaceted or there are many interconnected objective or 'exterior' crises or wicked problems occurring (e.g., political, economic, and ecological). These interconnected crises are also situated in a(n) (inter)subjective context of 'interior' meaning making (semiosis), construal and response that includes philosophical, scientific, religious, existential, worldview, and psychospiritual dimensions that are essential to include in an adequate understanding of the complex dynamics in play in order to facilitate more effective responses. In other words, what distinguishes the metacrisis from the polycrisis is that, while the latter highlights that there are many different crises occurring simultaneously and recognizes that many of these are interconnected, the former goes a step further and uses integrative metatheoretical frameworks and distinctions to reveal the subjective as well as objective, semiotic as well as 'material', 'interior' as well as 'exterior' dynamics in play.[8] Whereas poly refers to 'many' crises and their objective interconnection, meta refers in addition to their higher-order unity as a complex totality or singularity that includes human construals and interventions and the possibility of a more adequate metaview that grasps real future possibilities. Meta implies an overarching unity or identity that holds and operates on the differences in their subjective as well as objective complexity. The notion of the metacrisis thus challenges the idea of an exclusively technological set of solutions to our global challenges. Because, in a context of generalized power$_2$ (power-over) relations both construals and responses will be contested, resolution of the metacrisis will involve among other things "*hermeneutic* hegemonic/counter-hegemonic struggles" (Bhaskar, 1993/2008, p. 62, our emphasis). Metatheory is needed *inter alia* to orient and support the coordination of these struggles globally. Its metaview offers an integrated perspective of the human subject in relation to the world. Without it, we can't even 'see' the polycrisis, let alone construe it adequately or relate to it effectively; with it, new realities and leverage points for impact are highlighted. Metatheories have co-evolved or co-emerged with the metacrisis. On the one hand the metacrisis demands and in part drives the emergence of integrative metatheory. On the other hand integrative metatheories allow one to see and engage the metacrisis in its full holistic complexity. They thus present us with unprecedented opportunities for helping to effect a transition to a new sustainable form of life. They can help empower us to make it through the collective rite of passage that the metacrisis necessitates.

As mentioned above, critical realism, integral theory, and complex thought are arguably among the most sophisticated contemporary integrative metatheories. We feel that all three can learn from each other in profound ways and so become more robust and powerful for addressing the global moment, both individually and collectively. This volume is all about advancing this strategic vision – building concrete utopian vistas and *phronesis* or situated power-aware *practical wisdom* (Bhaskar, 1993/2008; Flyvbjerg, 2001; Tyfield, 2015) and compelling, realistic theories and practices of transition and transformation that operate from and toward real future possibilities.

3 Metatheory and the emergence of integrated knowledge

There are many important approaches that have contributed to the integration of knowledge in the face of widespread disciplinary and methodological fragmentation emerging across the planet. These include inter-, multi-, cross-, trans-, and postdisciplinarity; post-normal science (Funtowicz & Ravetz, 1993); mixed methods approaches (Creswell, 1998; Creswell & Plano Clark, 2011; Johnson & Onwuegbuzie, 2004; Tashakkori & Teddlie, 1998); developmental action-inquiry (Torbert, 1991, 2000a, 2000b, 2001, 2004); action research (Chandler, 2003; Reason & Bradbury, 2001; Reason & Torbert, 2001); systemic intervention (Midgley, 2001); integrated assessment modeling (Parson, 1995); team science (Bennett, 2010; Trochim *et al.*, 2008); earth systems science (Earth, 2014); biological "integrative pluralism" (Mitchell, 2003); the "synthetic philosophy of contemporary mathematics" (Zalamea, 2013); "integrative thinking" in organizational development (Martin, 2009); "cybersemiotics" (Brier, 2013); Bryan Norton's (2005) approach to sustainability through adaptive ecosystem management; "interpersonal neurobiology" (Siegel, 2012); "transmodernism" (Dussel, 1995, 2002); "integration and implementation sciences" (Bammer, 2013); meta-analysis (Cooper, 2009); and systematic reviews (Gough, 2013).

These integrative approaches are being developed within a single discipline or knowledge domain, or between a limited selection of them. A much smaller number of approaches attempt to 'include' or encompass in some sense all the general domains of human knowledge – from the arts and humanities to the social and natural sciences. These are the 'heavyweight' integrative metatheories of our time: critical realism, founded by Roy Bhaskar (1944–2014); integral theory founded by Ken Wilber (1949–); and complex thought, founded by Edgar Morin (1921–). They represent some of the most advanced expressions of macro-level integrated knowledge that encompass, and/or articulate an orienting metatheory for all domains of human inquiry. In order to situate the particular status of these three metatheories, a deeper discussion of metatheory in general is called for.

Metatheory fell on hard times in the post-sixties cultural milieu in which postmodernism and poststructuralism flourished in the humanities and much of the social sciences. There was a widespread disdain for abstract, big-picture thinking and grand metanarratives (Lyotard, 1984). Many of the ensuing critiques, which accused metatheories of having hegemonizing, totalizing ambitions that ignored the diversity of the world and its construction within discourse, have a certain validity, but in our view apply largely to what we call 'old-school metatheory' or metatheory 1.0. Metatheory 1.0 is essentially modern positivist metatheory, rooted in discredited metaphysical assumptions, and insufficient in its methodological transparency. For example, this kind of metatheory was prominent amongst some of the *philosophes* of the European Enlightenment, such as the founder of positivism in its modern sense, Auguste Comte (1798–1857). Comte developed various big-picture theories, including speculative developmental schemes, inadequately grounded in either transcendental or empirical methods. Comte's metatheory was born largely of speculation, unchecked by the rigors of scientific peer-review, proclaiming a unilinear, triumphalist developmental progression from 'primitive' levels of social evolution towards the 'civilized' status represented by the modern West and its 'positive' knowledge.[9] Furthermore, it is an example of a monistic approach to the integration of knowledge in the form of grand and totalizing theory. According to Edwards (2010, p. 51), "one central aim of modernist social science is to search for theoretical monism" – what George Ritzer (2001) refer to as the aim "to discover general laws of human society and to put them together systematically in the form of [grand] sociological theories" (p. 116). This form of theorizing is certainly a form of big-picture theory, but is not grounded in a procedural rationality; that is, a transparent methodology available for social validation or refutation in an open, democratic style. As Edwards notes, "a key reason that overarching theory in particular has always struggled to gain scientific credibility is its lack of a solid methodological basis" (p. 46); to which critical realism would add that its metaphysical assumptions are often vulnerable to transcendental critique; and integral theory would add that it also lacks adequate epistemic reflexivity (e.g., situating its claims in relation to relevant structures of interiority). The proclamation of such grand metanarratives, popular in the eighteenth and nineteenth centuries, clearly grounded in Eurocentric biases and power dynamics much more than rigorous empirical analysis, touted under the pseudo-objective guise of 'positive social science', has been a major contributor to the cultural trauma in the

TABLE I.1 Metatheory 2.0 principles

Methodological transparency and judgemental rationalism
Epistemic reflexivity and relativity
Ontological realism and comprehensiveness
Integrative pluralism

TABLE I.2 Metatheory α and β

Metatheory α	Metatheory β
Metaphilosophy	Meta-science
Philosophy of science	Science
A priori from historically relative premises	*A posteriori*
Transcendental arguments plus immanent critique	Conceptual clarification and synthesis plus immanent critique
Abstract and formal	Concrete and substantive
Philosophical ontology	Scientific ontology
Ex ante in relation to empirically-grounded theory	*Ex post* in relation to empirically-grounded theory

West in relation to metatheory and to the barrenness of much social science. To be clear, such a power$_2$-laden and -rationalising metatheory has little to do with a metatheory for the twenty-first century, except insofar as the latter builds on a demonstration that the former is false, misleading, or inadequate. We hesitate to call it a 'metatheory' at all; its name within critical realism is 'ideology' (see especially Bhaskar, 1986/2009).

In contrast to metatheory 1.0 and in keeping with an understanding of it as ideology, we propose the notion of *metatheory 2.0*, a broad category of metatheorizing that we argue is fit for the twenty-first century.[10] Metatheory 2.0 can be defined as a form of big-picture or integrative theory grounded in the following criteria or principles: methodological transparency and judgemental rationalism, epistemic reflexivity and relativity, ontological realism and comprehensiveness, and integrative pluralism (see Table I.1). Methodological transparency refers to the reflexive disclosure of the methodology and methods (or injunctions) from which knowledge claims are derived. Thus, metatheory 2.0 adheres to a procedural rationality or methodological transparency that is open to ongoing rigorous assessment or criticism in terms of clearly defined validity criteria. Moreover, it sustains the possibility of judgemental rationalism, which will in general depend on ethical reflexivity and responsibility, in the context of the actuality of epistemic relativity and the necessity of ontological realism. In addition, metatheory 2.0 engages a robust epistemically reflexive inquiry in relation to the assumptions and salient epistemic structures of the research – a kind of researching the researcher (Hedlund,

2008) – so as to both situate one's knowledge claims therein and potentially mitigate problems of inter-individual variability and subjective bias (Hedlund, 2008, 2010). Both methodological transparency and epistemic reflexivity enrich the dialogical process connected to the final stage of the research process – that of social validation. Given our epistemic fallibility as embodied personalities engaged in epistemically relative inquiries, one function of such practices is to enhance the peer-review process surrounding the relative validity, utility, strengths, and limitations of the knowledge claims of a given researcher. In the absence of reflexive transparency, it can be rather difficult to assess aspects of the relative validity of the 'view from nowhere' that many researchers implicitly assume (Edwards, 2010; Nagel, 1986). Ontological realism is the critical realist view that the object of inquiry is existentially intransitive in relation to the investigator and relatively or absolutely intransitive causally. Ontological comprehensiveness refers to the inclusion of all key dimensions, planes, or contours of reality known to humans – including real generative mechanisms and structures in the subjective, social, and natural domains – in the purview of one's metatheorizing. This does not necessarily mean that one is integrating theory from all of these domains *per se*, but rather that all these domains are considered and one's metatheorizing is situated within this context. Finally, metatheory 2.0 is an expression of integrative pluralism, as opposed to an integrative monism (as in metatheory 1.0). Integrative pluralism has two declensions, epistemological (emphasized by integral theory) and ontological (highlighted by critical realism). In relation to the problem of theoretical pluralism (for example, in the social sciences), the monistic approach of metatheory 1.0 attempts to assert a singular, totalizing, abstract, and universal overarching theory that does not account either for competing perspectives or the real depth and diversity of the world. In contrast, integrative pluralism in its epistemological mode "retains an appreciation for the multiplicity of perspectives while also developing new knowledge that connects their definitive elements to build more expansive, 'roomier' metatheoretical frameworks" (Edwards, 2010, p. 16). For critical realism, integrative pluralism, or developing integrative pluralism, is also and most fundamentally another name for a philosophical ontology that grasps the world as asymmetrically stratified and differentiated, dynamic and interconnected (Bhaskar, 1986/2009, p. 101).

Metatheory 2.0 has two distinct modes: *metatheory* α (alpha) and *metatheory* β (beta). Distinguishing *metatheory* α from *metatheory* β along the lines of Bhaskar's distinction between *metaphysics* α and *metaphysics* β,[11] the former is concerned to articulate a general metatheory for the sciences through formal transcendental investigation of their presuppositions and those of human practical activity more generally, whereas the latter subjects the general conceptual frameworks actually deployed in scientific research and practical programs to critical scrutiny and synthesizes their findings. Both 'underlabor' for science, and both also deploy the method of immanent critique, absenting absences in other approaches and theories and in their own past phases to arrive at more adequate and complete conceptual formations. Metatheory α is the chief task critical realist philosophy sets itself, while metatheory β is the main focus of integral theory and complex thought, as well as

Edwards' (2010) approach to scientific metatheorizing. The former's transcendental method proceeds *a priori* but conditionally from historically relative premises and issues in a general philosophical ontology; the latter proceeds *a posteriori* and issues in a general scientific ontology; and each articulates a cognate epistemology and methodology. While the findings of metatheory α are *ex ante* in relation to the findings of science, they must in the long run be consistent with those findings; the findings of metatheory β build critically on the findings of science and are thus *ex post*.[12] Since science itself deploys an essentially transcendental procedure,[13] the two kinds of metatheory beautifully complement each other. Both are intended to play an orienting and facilitating rather than prescriptive role in relation to substantive scientific enquiries; deploying a metatheory in some substantive enquiry has been usefully likened to using a word processor with an operating system running in the background. Each science has an ontology, epistemology, and methodology specific to its subject matter, for which metatheory intends to underlabor in its specificity rather than provide a ready-made blueprint for all that can be mechanically applied.

Having distinguished metatheory 1.0, or ideology, from metatheory 2.0, or metatheory for the twenty-first century – as well as its two modes of α and β – we can now turn to look at the encounter between critical realism and integral theory and the various advancements and outcomes that ensued.

4 A history of the CR–IT dialogues

In this section we present the historical context of the symposium series between critical realism (CR) and integral theory (IT), which provides more details to the general outline provided by Roy Bhaskar in his opening remarks in the Preface. We have chosen to provide a detailed overview of the encounter between these two schools of thought because we feel that it provides disclosure with respect to the method of exploratory-dialogical encounter from which the contents of this book were largely derived. We also feel that a more detailed historical overview can offer value by potentially informing other similar initiatives.

This volume – and its sister volume *Metatheory for the Anthropocene: Emancipatory Praxis for Planetary Flourishing* (Bhaskar *et al.*, forthcoming) – are among the many exciting results of over four years of deep dialogical engagement between two communities of scholar-practitioners: that of critical realism, on the one hand, and integral theory, on the other. The books, in many ways, can be seen as the result of systematic exploration and inquiry into the relationship of two of the planet's most comprehensive integrative metatheories and how each might be impacted and transformed through such an encounter; we were curious to see what kind of 'mutant hybrid-offspring' might be born through their cross-pollination, and how they might mutually empower each other with respect to real-world engagement vis-à-vis the complex global challenges of the twenty-first century. Thus, this book and its sister volume can be seen as a report of the results of employing an integrative methodology of dialogical engagement and cross-pollination of two schools of metatheoretical thought in the context of four symposia over the course of five years. We will describe highlights of each of the symposia in turn.

A meeting of minds: University of Luxembourg, June 2010

In June 2010 a number of the world's leading integrative metatheorists and philosophers converged, for the first time, at the University of Luxembourg for the international symposium "Research across Boundaries," organized by Markus Molz and the German-based Institute for Integral Studies, to engage a historic meeting of minds and hearts.[14] Among those scholars were the four editors of these two volumes: Roy Bhaskar, Sean Esbjörn-Hargens, Nicholas (Nick) Hedlund, and Mervyn Hartwig.[15] At this academic gathering Roy and Sean were both in the same section devoted to "Integrative Frameworks Crossing Multiple Boundaries." During the course of the event they had the opportunity to connect both in and out of session and immediately struck up a friendship. During their conversations they discovered their mutual love for and interest in philosophical meta-approaches to reality, and with growing excitement began to explore the resonances between critical realism and integral theory and how they can learn from each other. Roy, Sean, and Nick stayed in touch afterwards and soon began to envision and organize a symposium in the San Francisco Bay Area.

Symposium 1: John F. Kennedy University, San Francisco Bay Area, September 2011

In the fall of 2011, the Integral Research Center and Integral Institute, in partnership with the International Centre for Critical Realism, hosted the inaugural Critical Realism and Integral Theory Symposium at John F. Kennedy University in the San Francisco Bay Area. This four-day event was planned by Roy, Sean, and Nick to bring together established scholars from both approaches to explore the points of similarity and divergence. The goal was to create a generative space of inquiry and dialogue, edgy in its capacity to be critical of each approach, while at the same time being constructive. In order to encourage a level of intimacy and depth among participants, only 15 people were invited from each approach. Integral theory participants included:

- Sean Esbjörn-Hargens, USA
- Clint Fuhs, USA
- Nick Hedlund, USA/the Netherlands
- Jordan Luftig, USA
- Michael Schwartz, USA
- Robb Smith, USA
- Zak Stein, USA
- Roger Walsh, USA
- Lisa Waters, USA.

Critical realist participants included:

- Eirin Annamo, Norway
- Roy Bhaskar, UK
- Hans Despain, USA
- MinGyu Seo, South Korea
- Mervyn Hartwig, UK
- Neil Hockey, Australia
- Paul Marshall, Spain/UK
- Leigh Price, UK/South Africa
- Tim Rutzou, UK/Australia
- Nick Wilson, UK.

In addition to these two major groups there was a third group of metatheorists who were not identified with either CR or IT but were familiar with both. They were invited to offer a reflective engagement outside of identification with either approach, help each approach see its blind spots, and provide an overarching view of integrative metatheory. These participants included:

- Gary Hampson, Czech Republic/UK
- Bonnie Roy, USA
- Lauren Tenney, USA.

Additionally, there were a number of participants who attended parts of the event, including:

- Annick de Witt, the Netherlands/USA
- Ray Greenleaf, USA
- Sushant Shresta, USA/Nepal
- Vernice Solimar, USA.

Over the course of our four days together, we had the opportunity to get to know each other in some depth. During our long formal sessions in dialogue, each side had the opportunity to introduce itself philosophically. It was a very exciting time in which we were learning each other's theoretical languages, and identifying many striking similarities, complementarities, and broad resonances. While we were also beginning to note some key differences and potential areas of incommensurability, this was not a strong focus, and we did not go into these in depth. The predominant note was a vital sense of optimism as we oriented ourselves to the possibilities for collaboration and integration. We were in a kind of 'honeymoon' phase in which a mood of warmth and generosity prevailed, and there was a strong sense among some, if not many, that the deficiencies of each approach synchronistically seemed to correspond with the strengths of the other, such that two metatheories might fit together in an almost yin-yang sense of complementarity, or like two pieces of a puzzle. In line with this enamoured mood, Esbjörn-Hargens (2011) wrote the following reflecting on his experience at the symposium:

> It was a very engaging four days and I think it is fair to say that both meta-approaches will never be the same. The similarities between the metaphilosophy of Bhaskar and the metatheory of Wilber are simply stunning. Furthermore, the ways they complement each other via their unique combination of strengths and limitations is remarkable. For example, integral theory excels at articulating a sophisticated and nuanced theory of epistemology whereas critical realism is unsurpassed in presenting a multilayered and complex theory of ontology. Integral theory has a primary focus on individuals and their growth and development all the way till nondual realization. Critical realism has a primary focus on society and the injustices therein which must be addressed for collective emancipation.
>
> The main area of divergence that emerged occurred around integral theory's postmetaphysical notion of enactment and critical realism's critique of neo-Kantianism and their notion of the Real. While the complexities of the exchanges around this are too multifaceted to get into here, I will just say that I felt more alive in those moments than I ever have before. It was just thrilling to be at the intersection between critical realism and integral theory and watching both approaches having to confront some deep epistemological and ontological issues; issues that likely will have a major impact on both schools of thought as they continue to unpack the implications of what the other school was pointing out to them.
>
> In short, there were a number of deep exchanges between the two groups. integral theory has a lot to learn from critical realism and vice versa. The critical realists raised some good critiques and identified areas of underdevelopment within integral theory and we did the same for them. I feel that integral theory has found a soul mate in critical realism (and Bhaskar's philosophy of metaReality). I learned as much about integral theory over these last four days as I did about critical realism. Thus, this four-day encounter served both schools of thought in helping each one to make their own approach an object of their collective awareness. Therein lies the subject to object principle, which is the driver of growth and transformation. I honestly feel that integral theory will never be the same now – it has and will continue to be transformed by its encounter with the critical realism 'other.' In fact, there are already a variety of ongoing exchanges, collaborations, and engagements between the members of the symposium from both communities of discourse. For integral theory to mature into its post-formal potential as a meta-framework for theory and practices, ongoing events such as this will be essential and I believe are now inevitable.
>
> *(p. v)*

Some of the most notable creative outcomes of this first symposium include:

- A number of academic articles in both *Journal of Critical Realism* and the *Journal of Integral Theory and Practice* were published that extended and deepened the engagement.
  - *Journal of Critical Realism* published three articles inspired by the symposium. These are Paul Marshall's "The meeting of two integrative metatheories";[16] Timothy Rutzou's "Integral theory: A poisoned chalice?";[17] and Hans Despain's "Integral theory: The salubrious chalice?"[18]
  - Marshall's article offers a fine overview of the points of connection and divergence between critical realism and integral theory and a constructive vision of how the two approaches might interact in mutually enhancing ways.
  - Rutzou's article essays a philosophical critique of integral theory from a critical realist perspective.
  - Despain's article analyses the potential theoretical benefits offered by integral theory. While endorsing some of Rutzou's points, it argues that integral theory offers much to critical realism in the form of developmental theories, cultural anthropology and transpersonal psychology.
  - The *Journal of Integral Theory and Practice* published four articles on critical realism and its relationship to integral theory: Paul Marshall's "Toward an integral realism: Part I: An overview of transcendental realist ontology"[19] and "Ken Wilber on critical realism";[20] Roy Bhaskar's "Considerations on 'Ken Wilber on critical realism'";[21] and Ken Wilber's "In defence of integral theory: A response to critical realism."[22]
  - Marshall's first article discusses how integral theory might benefit from critical realism by providing an in-depth overview of critical realism's foundational transcendental realist ontology, including a review of relevant background philosophies informing it.
  - Marshall's second article was written as a summary for Roy Bhaskar of Ken Wilber's position on critical realism. The article was based on an exchange between Marshall and Wilber as a part of the journal review process.
  - Bhaskar's article is a response to Marshall's summary, which was hoped to have initiated a more direct conversation between Bhaskar and Wilber.
  - Wilber's article was written as a long endnote for his forthcoming book, volume 2 of the Kosmos Trilogy, prior to his 'exchanges' with Marshall and Bhaskar, and originally posted on the Integral Life website: www.integrallife.com.
- A strategic partnership was established between the International Centre for Critical Realism at the UCL Institute of Education, University of London and the San Francisco-based MetaIntegral Foundation in general, as well as with the Integral Research Center in particular. This partnership became the institutional underpinning for the CR–IT symposium series, as well as for the present volume and its sister volume.

- A post-conference workshop on metaReality following the 2012 International Association of Critical Realism Conference, "Global Challenges and Critical Realism Debates," at Rhodes University in South Africa, was partly dedicated to constructively exploring the relationship between critical realism and integral theory.
- A group of American participants from New England, including Hans Despain, Zak Stein, Lauren Tenney, and Bonnie Roy, formed an ongoing dialogue group.
- Paul Marshall's PhD thesis project evolved into an exploration of the interface of critical realism, integral theory, and Edgar Morin's complex thought – a shift that was importantly inspired by the symposium. Paul continued to engage in mutually provocative dialogues in this area with Roy, whom he studied under at the UCL Institute of Education at the University of London.
- In the wake of the symposium, Nick Hedlund, who at the time was a PhD student at the California Institute of Integral Studies, began to collaborate with Roy Bhaskar. Roy eventually invited him to study under him at the UCL Institute of Education, University of London. Through the symposium and subsequent dialogue with Roy, Nick underwent an intellectual revolution, moving from a primary identification with the philosophy of enactivism to a modified critical realist position. The trajectory of this revolution is broadly expounded in Nick's chapter in this volume.
- In the summer of 2012, Roy, Sean, and Nick consolidated a vision for the present volume, wrote a proposal, and secured a contract with Routledge. They began to invite contributors to submit précis, from which the submissions were selected for publication in the book.
- Sean Esbjörn-Hargens, in collaboration with Mark Forman and Jordan Luftig, began to envision the 2013 Integral Theory Conference in San Francisco. The conference was deeply inspired by the kind of dialogical engagement of bringing these metatheories together exemplified in the symposium. The conference sought to bring into dialogue three key integral metatheories – integral theory, critical realism, and complex thought – and thus redefine the field no longer in terms of Wilberian integral theory exclusively, but rather in terms of the dynamic confluence of these three metatheories.

Symposium 2: Integral Theory Conference, San Francisco, July 2013

The second symposium was held as a pre-conference event of the Integral Theory Conference (ITC) in San Francisco in July of 2013. This day-long international symposium, "Metatheory for the Twenty-First Century: Critical Realism and Integral Theory in Dialogue," was held for invited critical realists and integral theorists to converge once again and advance the dialogue. As noted above, a major theme of the third Integral Theory Conference, "Connecting the Integral Kosmopolitan," was exploration of the relationship(s) between integral theory and critical realism, as well as that of complex thought. Roy Bhaskar delivered a keynote address, along with the French philosopher and founder of complex thought, Edgar Morin. The conference marked Roy's introduction to the integral community at large, which Roy was rather delighted by. We felt that the integral community mirrored back to Roy the deep value of his 'spiritual turn' and subsequent vision of metaReality, whereas in the critical realist community it has been much more controversial. In the integral community, Roy's work, in all three of its major phases, was received in a wider context, which was important for Roy. Roy and Edgar Morin also met and conversed with each other. This constituted a historic confluence of their respective metatheoretical streams worth noting in its own right. Moreover, several prominent critical realists attended and presented. Numerous presentations at the conference were devoted to exploring points of contact between these two metatheories, and two new award categories for conference papers, "best engagement with critical realism" and "best engagement with complex thought," were included by the conference organizers.[23] Thus, the second symposium, though it remained predominantly focused on the meeting of just two of these metatheories, was a kind of microcosm of the macrocosm of the conference – and in many ways, the whole conference was inspired by the kind of engagement demonstrated at the first symposium at JFK University, nearly two years earlier.

While we very much built on the generative dialogical encounter that we began at the first symposium, the focus of the second one was beginning to turn from a more (meta)theoretical approach to the realm of praxis and application in a contemporary planetary context. Thus the one-day San Francisco symposium focused on the ways in which these two (and other) integrative metatheories can join forces to transform scholarship and address the most pressing global challenges of the twenty-first century – from climate change to the global economic crisis to the need for new forms of education. Over the course of the event, we sought to create a space of free-flowing exchange and nurture a rich field of mutual understanding that would continue to inspire future engagement and development within and between both approaches.

This symposium also saw the beginning of collective work on the present volume (which grew into two volumes). Accepted précis, along with several chapter drafts for the book, were sent to participants prior to the symposium, providing an opportunity for reflection on the themes and theses presented therein, and were used as a starting point for our engagement. We wanted, once again, to create a generative space of inquiry and dialogue that was critical, but this time the focus was more oriented to real-world solutions. More specifically, dialogue focused on the ways both metatheories (and various interfaces and syntheses) could be employed in creative ways that illuminate reality and pathways toward holistic social-cultural transformation in the face of contemporary 'wicked problems.' This, we felt, was the optimal focal point for our dialogue, as opposed to focusing primarily on the debate around how each theory 'maps onto' – or fails to map onto – the other.

Many of the same scholars participated in this symposium, though some important critical realist voices were missing, and there were also some new faces. We again invited some metatheorists who were familiar with both (and other) approaches to provide some triangulation and contextual engagement from an 'external' vantage point. Naturally, being a part of the Integral Theory Conference, there were more integral theorists and fewer critical realists this time around. Integral theorists included:

- Bruce Alderman, USA
- Annick de Witt, the Netherlands/USA
- Sean Esbjörn-Hargens, USA
- Clint Fuhs, USA
- Nick Hedlund, USA/the Netherlands
- Gilles Herrada, USA/France
- Ed Kelly, Ireland
- Lynette Lee, USA
- Jordan Luftig, USA
- Tom Murray, USA
- Aftab Omer, USA
- Matthew Rich, the Netherlands/South Africa
- Michael Schwartz, USA
- Zak Stein, USA.

Critical realists included:

- Roy Bhaskar, UK
- Hans Despain, USA
- Paul Marshall, Spain/UK
- Leigh Price, UK/South Africa.

Other metatheorists included:

- Mark Edwards, Australia
- Gary Hampson, Czech Republic/UK
- Adam Robbert, USA
- Bonnita Roy, USA.

The San Francisco symposium not only deepened the engagement and alliance between CR and IT but also brought to light the potential for engagement with Morin's complex thought (and also other approaches, such as speculative realism or actor-network theory). There was also a sense of excitement about Roy's keynote address and critical realism being formally introduced to the integral community, as well as that of complex thought.[24] In addition to the group dialogue in the symposium, Paul Marshall gave a short presentation that offered an overview of each of the three metatheories – arguing that there is an important dialogue, complementarity, and potential integrative synthesis in bringing the three metatheories together. It seemed that nearly everyone was impressed and inspired by this vision that Paul had articulated with such clarity, sophistication, and eloquence. In this way, the horizon of our engagement seemed to widen.

Beyond this bright and buoyant sense of possibility, during this symposium (and the time in between the two), we were starting to substantively metabolize and comprehend each other's positions, having done more background reading and research, and as a result come to understand more fully some of the key differences in our respective metatheories. For example, CR's critique of the *epistemic fallacy* and *actualism* and the ways in which they arguably play out in the context of IT, as well as IT's critique, in various inflections, of what would later be named by Zak Stein (see Stein's chapter in *Metatheory for the Anthropocene*) as the *cognitive maturity fallacy*, and the case that CR succumbs to it. However, this greater appreciation for the differences was generally backgrounded, and the sense of solidarity and broad agreement foregrounded. There was likely more dissent in the community than many of us realized at this symposium, but the focus on real-world emancipation seemed to captivate our attention and – for the moment – overshadow our differences. Moreover, at that point, we had only read each other's précis and a few draft chapters – but, as we would learn, the 'devil of disagreement' often lies in the details, which were largely yet to be thoroughly expounded in the chapters.

Noteworthy outcomes that emerged between the second and third symposia include the following:

- Many individuals in the integral community began referencing critical realism in their work – so the integral community has had major uptake in citation of CR material.

  - We estimate that 30–40 percent of integral scholars who presented papers at ITC 2013 – and a disproportionate 50–60 percent of the prominent leadership in the integral community – have engaged with critical realism. Such engagement, has been highly generative, and will likely have lasting impacts on the field.

- The 2013 International Association for Critical Realism (IACR) conference in Nottingham, UK, featured another post-conference day devoted to metaReality, including its relationship to integral theory.
- In early 2014, *Journal of Critical Realism* published two additional articles furthering the CR–IT debate: Timothy Rutzou's "Integral theory and the search for the Holy Grail: On the possibility of a metatheory,"[25] and Hans Despain's "Integral theory and the search for earthly emancipation: On the possibility of emancipatory and ethical personal development."[26]
- Initially conceived as a single anthology, in the spring 2014 the burgeoning length of the book provoked us to propose that the original book be split into two stand-alone volumes: the present one, and its aforementioned companion *Metatheory for the Anthropocene: Emancipatory Praxis for Planetary Flourishing* (forthcoming). While the present book takes up a more theoretical focus, *Metatheory for the Anthropocene* is concerned, as the title implies, with questions of a more applied, practice-oriented nature.

- At the 2014 European Integral Conference in Budapest, Ken Wilber delivered a keynote address and engaged in a subsequent question-and-answer-style dialogue (over Skype). In the question-and-answer period Wilber was asked what he was working on recently, and, according to Frank Visser, "[O]ne of the topics he mentioned was to write about what he saw as 'serious problems' in the philosophy of critical realism, which could possibly result in a Wilber-6 phase of his work."[27]
- Gary Hawke, a British scholar-practitioner of integral theory and critical realism, produced an online audio and video series of interviews with Roy Bhaskar, "Introduction to Critical Realism," in an effort to make critical realism more accessible. These materials are available on YouTube. Also see Gary Hawke's website at: www.alethic-coaching.org/
- In the spring of 2014, Roy proposed that Mervyn Hartwig join the editorial team to assist with the burgeoning workload. Sean and Nick agreed and Mervyn came on board.

Symposium 3: UCL Institute of Education, University of London, July 2014

The third symposium, "Integrative Metatheories in the Twenty-First Century: Forging New Alliances for Planetary Flourishing in the Anthropocene," was held at the UCL Institute of Education, University of London, as a post-conference event following the 17th annual International Association for Critical Realism Conference, "From the Anatomy of the Global Crisis to the Ontology of Human Flourishing."[28] In some respects, the conference took up the dialogical spirit of ITC 2013, albeit to a much lesser degree, and built on it. Several integral theorists presented at the IACR conference, and some noteworthy dialogues ensued.

This one-day symposium was again intended to help forge new alliances across theoretical boundaries in which we could practically apply our joint insights to addressing pressing real-world challenges in the emergent context of the Anthropocene, such as climate change. The present volume and its companion served as a strong basis for the London symposium. As such, it was a much more structured event than either of the two prior symposia. Authors read each other's chapter drafts, engaged in deep dialogue, critique, and constructive inquiry. Chapters were sent out for all to read and served as the basis for group dialogue. Specifically, select authors were paired based on thematic resonance. Each author briefly summarized the key points of their own chapter before the paired author offered criticisms and inquiry points and opened up a group discussion on it. The feedback and insight from the symposium was woven into further chapter revisions. Each chapter was already the result of the cross-pollination forged in the prior symposia, but this second cycle of reflection, constructive critique, and dialogue constituted a kind of meta-level cross-pollination. This, we feel, led to a more refined, integrated final product – which you are now holding in your hand or reading on your screen.

Mirroring the context at ITC 2013, because the London symposium was under the umbrella of the IACR Conference, there were more critical realists than integral theorists, and there were again some new participants. Those who attended included:

- Eirin Annamo, Norway
- Roy Bhaskar, UK
- Hans Despain, USA
- Mark Edwards, Australia
- Sean Esbjörn-Hargens, USA
- Gary Hampson, Czech Republic/UK
- Mervyn Hartwig, UK
- Gary Hawke, UK
- Nick Hedlund, USA/the Netherlands
- Neil Hockey, Australia
- Otto Laske, USA
- Paul Marshall, Spain/UK
- Iskra Nunez, USA/Mexico
- Lene Nyhus, Norway
- Tim Rutzou, UK/Australia
- Michael Schwartz, USA
- Tone Skinningsrud, Norway
- Nick Wilson, UK.

Overall, in the London symposium, the mood of maturity and charged dialectic predominated. The core differences had been drawn out and the sense of critique and discord had become more pronounced. So this symposium had a stronger sense of the incommensurability and points of difference, which marked a new, more sober and mature mode of engagement. It was easy to think we all agreed when we were just talking, but when people actually completed and shared their chapters, it quickly clarified the differences. We could then really see where everyone stood and thus begin a level of substantive and nuanced debate that previously was not possible. Roy was only able to articulate the five positions (see preface) after reading the chapters. Writing the chapters made the details a lot clearer. Of course part of the reason the differences showed up more strongly at the London symposium was simply that more CR scholars showed up at the IACR conference, but they weren't so sympathetic to IT that they would fly across the world for a one-day event (i.e., ITC, 2015).

The honeymoon phase had ended, but, it seemed, there was enough passion and resonance – perhaps most prominently around our shared commitment to emancipation and flourishing in the real word – to keep us going. While the sense of difference indeed became more pronounced in this symposium, the focus on real-world service functioned as a concurrent and countervailing tendency that built solidarity as well. In many ways, it felt like a deep connection and alliance had emerged which was not only founded on a *prima facie* sense of resonance and complementarity, but also a respect for some very deep (and sometimes charged) differences and disagreements. Indeed, we were discovering, it was often precisely in this sense of dialectic and difference that the most potent and provocative transformational potentials dwelled.

However, there was a paradoxical sense in which the hermeneutics of generosity in the spirit of the engagement seemed to hold and contain such discord. It felt as though we had moved into a shared space in which there was enough intimacy, understanding, and solidarity for us to be more unabashedly real and raw with each other. The passion and love for reality, truth, and wisdom was tangible. Our hearts were fully in it and the sense of deep care for our beautiful and imperilled world was profoundly palpable. There was a potent emotional sense of shared love and concern for the planet and alignment around the project of emancipation, yet a deep sense that our differences were also present. As we dialogued, explored, critiqued, and inquired together, it felt as though we had moved from more of a pseudo-community to real community, in that we were able to incorporate conflict and difference in a full and robust way, yet do so with respect and trust in our enduring bond and shared commitment. There was something of intense beauty in holding this dialectical tension in our hearts and minds; by the end of the last session, nearly all of us of found ourselves moved to tears. There was a sense that we had moved from an emphasis on identity in the first symposium, and slowly developed the sense of difference in and through the second, and were now arriving at a sense of strong difference simultaneously with that of identity – a kind of dynamic and messy identity-in-difference.

It was a special day – and for many of us, our last with Roy, our dear friend whom many of us hold as a great, deeply loving man and philosophical genius at a level that is difficult to appreciate at this point in history. Roy presented his typology of five positions within the CR–IT dialogue (presented in the Preface and developed below), as a useful way for us to reflect on the multi-year engagement and the positions represented in the room (and the books). This felt like an apt offering for our moment, as there was a sense that we had reached a point of culmination and maturation in the process and had, in some respects, settled into various positions along a spectrum of identity and difference. However, as was reflected in Otto Laske's suggestion that there is more of a dynamic dialectic than a settled sense of positions, the atmosphere of the exchange felt far from settled. Rather, there was a potent sense of passionate, vital, and transformational-dialectical charge suffusing and impelling the collective field. Interestingly, dialectical thinking seemed to have been a key point of contention, both in terms of critiques along the lines of 'having a dialectical metatheory' as a position and 'embodying dialectical thinking' as an integrated cognitive-emotional-social mode of engaging the process.

Other than a number of postgraduate seminars at the UCL Institution of Education, this was to be Roy Bhaskar's last public performance. He died four months later, on November 19. Roy devoted his life to a struggle to win the intellectual high ground for a global society of universal free flourishing and was greatly appreciated and loved by all who knew him well for his cheerfulness, his generosity, his warmth and inclusiveness, his talent for making people feel very special and give their best and above all for his gentleness and his love. These qualities were richly in evidence at the symposium, even in illness. Without Roy's exuberant support, the CR–IT dialogue would never have happened. His absence from the process will make a huge difference, but we will draw inspiration and strength from his life and his affirmation of the creative powers and potentials of human beings as such. Among his last words as he left the symposium, underlining the primacy of self-change in the demi-real, were: "We are all TINA compromise formations." When we get rid of the compromises, human creative potentials are unleashed.

Symposium 4: Integral Theory Conference, Sonoma State University, San Francisco Bay Area, July 2015

The forth CR-IT symposium, "From Metatheory to Metapraxis: Critical Realism, Integral Theory, and Emancipatory Impact," was held as a post-conference event of the 2015 International Integral Theory Conference, hosted by Sonoma State University. Whereas the previous symposia explored a multitude of themes as expressed in the various chapters of this book and its companion volume, this one-day symposium was an opportunity to reflect on the largely finished books, the key critiques each metatheoretical school had of the other, and how these are of practical consequence for emancipatory action. This pursuit was not one of mere abstraction, but rather was grounded in a commitment to 'seriousness' or the coherence of theory and practice. The sensibility of this symposium, in highlighting the move from metatheory to meta-praxis, from right view to right action, was closely aligned with the theme of the overall conference: "Integral Impacts: Using Integrative Metatheories to Catalyse Effective Change". In this spirit, we looked at next steps in the dialogue and how we can more effectively build alliances across metatheoretical boundaries in service of real-world emancipatory impact and planetary flourishing. In contrast to the previous symposia, this one was not by invitation, but was open to all conference attendees. Participants included:

- Alina Abraham, USA
- Bruce Alderman, USA
- Byron Belitsos, USA
- Ken Burrows, USA
- Annick De Witt, the Netherlands
- Gene Dunaway, USA
- Sean Esbjörn-Hargens, USA
- Jed Fox, USA
- Nick Hedlund, USA
- Mary Janicke, USA
- Chandana Kulasuriya, India
- Lynette Lee, USA

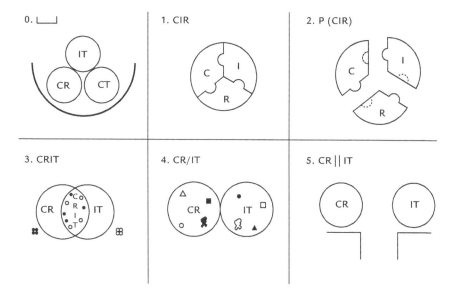

FIGURE I.1 Typology of metatheory encounters

- David MacLeod, USA
- Lisa Norton, USA
- Terri O'Fallon, USA
- David Orneallas, USA
- Michael Schwartz, USA
- Farsam Shadab, USA
- Zak Stein, USA
- Isabelle Wachsmuth, Switzerland
- William Wandall, USA
- Chris Zdenek, USA

We began the day by focusing intently on the epistemic fallacy, with sessions on the epistemic fallacy and the critique of IT, and epistemic fallacy and the 'defense' of IT. Part of this dialogue engaged Ken Wilber's keynote address at the conference, "At the Frothy Edge of Geopolitical Impact: Nation Building in Ukraine (and a Brief Look at Pluralistic Ontology)," in which critical realism was heavily referenced. The dialogue that ensued explored the fascinating and subtle space 'in between and beyond' the more polar debates of past symposia in which the orientation tended to focus on whether or not IT commits the epistemic fallacy (in the sense of an either/or). It seemed as though we were collectively beginning to forge a 'third way' beyond this more polar orientation (and exploring the contours of the possibility of a both/and).

In the later part of the symposium, we heard from integral theorist Zak Stein about his collaborative work with critical realist Hans Despain, articulating what new forms of emancipatory metatheoretical praxis can look like in mobilizing both

IT and CR for purposes of diagnosis and strategic intervention in the domain of educational reform in the United States. These conversations were so rich that we ended up developing two more chapters for the companion volume to this book – one on the epistemic fallacy and one on the applied metatheoretical collaboration of Zak Stein and Hans Despain. The Sonoma symposium will therefore be discussed further in the companion volume. We completed the day with a ritual and moment of gratitude for Roy Bhaskar.

5 A typology of metatheory encounters

In the Preface, Roy Bhaskar outlines five positions in the engagement between critical realism and integral theory.[29] As noted, the Preface is based on the transcript of Roy's opening remarks at the third symposium in London. In the dialogue following Roy's remarks, Mark Edwards introduced a sixth position that we feel is quite useful to specify. In this section we review the positions Roy outlines and develop this framework further. We do so for several reasons. First, we feel that these six positions are useful for different metatheoretical communities to consider when encountering each other. The order presents a spectrum of possible positions that can be inhabited; while many variations on them are possible, these seem to be the main types. Second, as explained below, we realized after the fact that the table of contents we had intuitively arrived at was ordered in terms of these six positions. As such, we feel that it is useful to invoke this typology as a way of understanding and contextualizing the chapters in this volume (see section 6 below).

In addition to the five positions Roy outlined in the Preface, we have included the additional position inspired by Mark Edwards' comments. In his exchange with Roy, Mark makes the point that there is also a position that is focused on the context or "clearing" of the integrative metatheory engagement, as opposed to the specific content or metatheories being engaged. Since this position signifies the conditions or context for any encounter between integrative metatheories to occur we have placed it prior to the other five positions and used a zero to designate it. Using a '0' in this way both preserves the order of Roy's typology and serves to signify the clearing that this position is highlighting. This position can also be signified with a keyboard by "|_____|" to represent the context in which metatheories, in this case CR, IT, and CT, are engaged with each other. In sum, these six positions essentially move from a general clearing of engagement (position 0) to decreasing degrees of compatibility or integration (positions 1–4) to incommensurability and non-dialogue (position 5). Moreover, it is worth noting that Roger Walsh, in his excellent Foreword, provides a resonant typology of five major possibilities that arise in response to the meeting of (meta)theories (p. xvi). These likewise are oriented along a continuum of commensurability and integration and have a rough correspondence to some of the positions we outline, yet add nuance and additional inflections.

Interestingly, as we mentioned, when we first began to order the table of contents for this volume we intuitively organized the chapters in an order that reflects the sequence of these six positions. Since this volume is about dialogue between two or three integrative metatheories we decided not to include a chapter representing position 5 – no fruitful dialogue – though interested individuals can read Tim Rutzou's articles in *Journal of Critical Realism*. We find it noteworthy that in the course of the four symposia, articles and chapters were generated that illustrate all six positions. In addition, some chapters in this volume may contain arguments associated with more than one position. So these six positions should not be reified. Rather they serve as general or ideal types of distinct orientations that can occur across a spectrum of possibilities.

6 In this volume

The first two chapters of the volume represent in various ways position 0. We open the volume with Zachary Stein's "Beyond nature and humanity: reflections on the emergence and purposes of metatheories." In this chapter, Stein takes a metaview on metatheories. Adopting an 'expressive' style rather than a 'persuasive' one, he explores the notion of 'metatheory' and provides a historical reconstruction drawing on some key figures (e.g., Peirce, Baldwin, Piaget, and Habermas) that contribute to contemporary understandings of the practice and philosophy of metatheory. He discusses the normative nature and function of metatheories, with a focus on their evolutionary and developmental framings. Stein ends by linking his reflections to the metatheory projects of Wilber and Bhaskar. This chapter serves the volume by helping to ground our current project in the historical and philosophical contexts that have set the stage for our dialogical encounter. Stein invites us to simultaneously look backward and forward as to the purpose of integrative metatheories.

Building on the theme of reflecting on and delineating the clearing of integrative metatheorizing the next chapter is Mark G. Edwards' "Healing the half-world: ideology and the emancipatory potential of meta-level social science." Edwards is well known for his ground-breaking work in articulating the architecture of integral meta-studies. In this chapter he furthers his project by exploring the healing and emancipatory potential of a meta-level social science. To do this he examines Bhaskar's triadic lens "Absolute-Relative-Demi-reality" and its meta-ontological implications for reflexive social science. To deepen this inquiry he juxtaposes Bhaskar's lens with Wilber's meta-hermeneutic engagement with the Absolute-Relative lens. Edwards leverages both Bhaskar's and Wilber's approaches to illustrate how an emancipatory social science could be developed. In doing this, Edwards not only illustrates the process of engaging multiple integrative metatheories to support emancipatory aims, but he demonstrates the value of drawing on both critical realism and integral theory for such a project. In other words, Edwards illuminates the process of creating a meta-context by engaging specific metatheories.

Next we have Sean Esbjörn-Hargens' "Developing a complex integral realism for global response: three meta-frameworks for knowledge integration and coordinated action." This is an ambitious chapter that can be viewed as a representative of position 1, though Esbjörn-Hargens' intent is more about developing a 'meta-praxis' of creating an integral metatheory. To illustrate this he places critical realism, integral theory, and complex thought into a 'trialectical' encounter that serves to address the blind spots of each approach. Drawing on the key strengths of each integral metatheory, Esbjörn-Hargens develops three meta-frameworks (one for each of the domains of epistemology, methodology, and ontology) to support this meta-praxis. This chapter provides a powerful example of what a preservative synthesis between the three integral metatheories might consist of and as such paves the way for further development of such a complex integral realism.

Complementing the previous chapter, Paul Marshall's "Towards a complex integral realism" serves to provide a detailed analysis of the key concepts and frameworks of all three integrative metatheories (critical realism, integral theory, and complex thought) and their resulting common ground. Marshall does an excellent job of discussing the areas of cross-fertilization between these three metatheories. In contrast to Esbjörn-Hargens' chapter, which uses the three integrative metatheories to go 'meta-meta,' Marshall uses them to go 'meta-micro' and provide a detailed overview of the similarities and differences between all three. He concludes his chapter by identifying some of the key features of a 'complex integral realism.' This chapter serves as an illustration of position 2 and the possibility of a synthesis between these three integrative metatheories.

In "Rethinking the intellectual resources for addressing complex twenty-first-century challenges: towards a critical realist integral theory" Nicholas Hedlund rolls up his philosophical sleeves and begins the hard work of creating a non-preservative synthesis between critical realism and integral theory. He calls the result a CRIT – a critical realist integral theory – and this represents position 3, which is characterized by a non-preservative synthesis (i.e., some elements from each theory are negated in order to create the synthesis). To do this, he examines in detail the epistemological and ontological positions of each metatheory. Then he critiques each metatheory in light of the other theory. This systematic analysis does much to lay the groundwork for considering what a CRIT might consist of. This chapter does a great job of detailing the philosophical challenges each metatheory poses to the other and how they might be reconciled into a new vision.

In a similar, but less systematic and synthetic, spirit to Hedlund, Michael Schwartz explores the complementary and divergent natures of critical realism and integral theory. In "After integral gets real: on meta-critical *chiasma* of CR and IT" he identifies a number of points of contact between both metatheories and how each can be enhanced by distinctions and perspectives from the other. Schwartz begins with the polarized domain of being and knowing. It is polarized in the sense that this is where the most obvious clashes of perspectives occur between the two traditions. Next he explores the important role that negativity and nothingness plays in both metatheories. This sets the stage for him to explore the role of schemes: CR's stratified ontology of horizontal depth and IT's stratified ontology of vertical height. He concludes with a discussion of nonduality, a view that both schools include as important and foundational to their approaches. While in some respects Schwartz's chapter appears to be oriented to process as much as position, we nonetheless feel that this chapter represents a view that falls between positions 3 and 4.

Striking a more first-person reflective tone, Mervyn Hartwig's "Why I'm a critical realist" represents position 4. Hartwig holds that there are important resonances between critical realism and integral theory and that each can benefit from an encounter with the other. However, he argues that there are fundamental incommensurable aspects that render any real synthesis (preservative or otherwise) impossible. This chapter in effect has two streams of discourse occurring simultaneously. On the one hand there is the narrative of Hartwig's philosophical journey with critical realism and an argument that the metacrisis can be resolved only by an epochal transition to a global society based on solidarity and love, as thematized by critical realism. On the other hand there are his robust endnotes, which provide a context for him to unpack some salient points about the limits of integral theory and its incommensurability with critical realism. This structure serves to highlight how the practice of philosophy is wonderfully always *inter alia* a very personal and biographical process.

The final chapter of the volume is Tom Murray's "Contributions of embodied realism to ontological questions in critical realism and integral theory." This chapter takes a different approach from previous chapters in that it is less concerned with the relationship or possible synthesis between critical realism and integral theory. Instead, Murray draws on the field of embodied philosophy (à la Lakoff and Johnson's position of embodied realism) to augment both CR and IT. He introduces a number of the core distinctions and findings of embodied realism and illustrates how these notions can ground integrative metatheories like CR and IT. He focuses on epistemological and ontological issues, which is quite useful given that it is within these contexts that most of the philosophical challenges and opportunities exist between these two approaches. In some respects this final chapter represents position 0 in that it foregrounds the process of integrative metatheorizing and helps establish the clearing of such metathinking and meta-practice. However, we felt that this was an apt chapter to complete this volume with, as it highlights how the dialogue that has occurred to date, and is in part represented by the chapters in this volume, can be further developed, expanded, and deepened by drawing on other philosophical traditions beyond the sphere of integrative metatheories as such. Besides, given the abstract nature of integrative metatheories, this chapter is useful in anchoring them in our embodied experience, making us more aware of the epistemic drives and multiple metaphors we can use to navigate, in fruitful ways, the many lines of inquiry that the encounter between integrative metatheories opens up.

Together these eight chapters serve to illustrate a wide range of potential positions of relationship between critical realism and integral theory (and in some cases complex thought as well). In addition, various other bodies of work and philosophical traditions are drawn on to support the inquiry around the possible relationships that can be supported between these integrative metatheories. Our authors argue for and against various degrees of synthesis, augmentation, and complementarity as well as making a case for incommensurability and outright disagreement. On the whole we feel they do a formidable job of documenting the range of philosophical issues that have been present in our series of symposiums while highlighting the value of bringing two different groups of scholar-practitioners together for dialogue and engagement.

We are very pleased to conclude the volume with an Afterword by Markus Molz, who, as noted above, is largely responsible for planting the seeds – at the Luxembourg symposium in 2010 – for what grew into this five-year (and counting) dialogue between leading scholar-practitioners of critical realism and integral theory (as well as other notable positions). Molz's Afterword helps situate the generative encounter documented in this volume within an even larger inquiry around the importance of creating interspaces of engagement between different streams of integrative and even non-integrative metatheories. We welcome Molz's reflections as they serve to further our own commitment to using what has transpired between the communities of critical realism and integral theory as a way of exploring and modeling the transformative and emancipatory potential of bringing different metatheories into intimate contact with each other.

7 Conclusion

As you read this volume and engage the many perspectives and positions presented herein, we hope you will be inspired to make your own contributions to the ongoing exploration of the deep need for integrative metatheories in the twenty-first century. Integrative metatheories can make a significant contribution to birthing a thriving planetary civilization. These contributions will be even more potent to the extent that different traditions of metatheory engage each other and find ways to support the emancipatory aims of each other. This process of engagement begins with people – like you – who are drawn to metatheory and its potential contributions to actualizing a eudaimonic world. So we invite you to seriously consider how you might you contribute to the ongoing project that has been initiated in these pages.

Acknowledgement

We would like to thank Annick de Witt for her valuable support and feedback on an earlier version of this Introduction.

Notes

1 Roy passed away before we completed this Introduction. We have decided to include his name in authorship since his involvement with the project and input into the contents of the introduction remained formative.
2 Bhaskar (2002/2012, xxixf., lxxif. and *passim*) deploys the theory of generalized co-presence – the enfoldedness at the most fundamental level of everything within

everything else – to argue that any movement, however small, toward universal free flourishing as we 'dive' to our ground-states, will tend to invoke a reciprocal response in all other beings, thus magnifying such actions in a dialectically resonant way. The dive to the ground-state is thus, he argues, "the mechanism of the universal silent revolution, a mechanism which is clear but whose form and effect cannot be predicted. However, given this mechanism, no one should underestimate the effect of any act they perform. Historicism, in the sense of predicting the future, is totally flawed. All we can say is that if the species, and our planet in a recognizable form, is to survive, only through such mechanisms as this will it happen. In the silence and everywhere, simultaneously the dawn breaks – this is the periodicity of the sunrise" (p. lxxx).

3 According to some generalized definitions, metatheory "involves the study of the epistemological, ontological, methodological, or axiological premises on which any theoretical statement rests" (Edwards, 2010, p. 39) and functions as an overarching interpretive lens (see section 3 for a more nuanced discussion on the definitions of metatheory). Worldviews have been defined as "overarching systems of meaning and meaning-making that to a substantial extent inform how we interpret, enact, and co-create reality; they are complex constellations of epistemic capacities, ontological presuppositions, and ethical aesthetic values that converge to dynamically organize a synthetic apprehension of the world" (De Witt & Hedlund, in press). Indeed, there is a striking resonance between these. For more on worldviews, see the work of Dutch social scientist Annick De Witt (Hedlund-de Witt, 2013a, 2013b; A. Hedlund-de Witt & Hedlund-de Witt, 2013).

4 As Randall Collins argues in *The Sociology of Philosophies* (2000), rather than ideas emerging prefabricated from the minds of a few great thinkers or being created by 'cultures', small groups are the source of most intellectual innovations. Such intellectual innovations then impact and shape the culture at large.

5 For an introductory overview of each of these metatheories see: Esbjörn-Hargens (2010) for integral theory, Bhaskar (2016, forthcoming) and N. Hedlund-de Witt (2012) for critical realism, and Montuori (2013) for complex thought.

6 Genetic engineering as well as the development of artificial intelligence are likewise potentially high-stakes experiments that come to mind as potentially major twenty-first-century threats to humanity and the biosphere. However, unlike the issues presented above, which are grounded in strong scientific consensus, these may or may not turn out to pose significant threats.

7 This concept, popularized by the Dutch Nobel prize-winning atmospheric chemist Paul Crutzen (see Crutzen & Stoermer, 2000), signifies a new geological epoch marked by the profound and far-reaching causal power of human, social life in shaping the evolutionary trajectory of Earth system processes. This new epoch contrasts with previous epochs, which have been identified by stratigraphic and fossil data, the most recent being the generally hospitable and climatically stable Holocene. See the companion book to this volume: *Metatheory for the Anthropocene: Emancipatory Praxis for Planetary Flourishing* for an extended discussion of the notion of the Anthropocene.

8 In line with this, a critical realist metatheory of crisis recently articulated by Bob Jessop (2015) stresses the semiotic and hermeneutic dimensions of crises as well as their more objective dimensions.

9 Such approaches have been deconstructed by numerous (postmodern and poststructuralist) philosophers, anthropologists, and sociologists alike, mainly because of their Eurocentric, neo-colonial, and derogatory implications, and their commitment to an oversimplified ontological parsimony that is out of step with the complexities of the empirical evidence (de Witt & Hedlund, 2015, in press; G. Marshall, 1998). The underpinning metaphysics of positivism is devastatingly critiqued by Bhaskar (e.g., 1989/2011).

10 Our notion of metatheory 2.0 is very much in alliance with the work of Mark Edwards (2010) and his development of a scientific method of metatheorizing and integral meta-studies (also see Chapter 2 in this volume). The work of George Ritzer (1991, 2001, 1990) is likewise an approach to metatheorizing that our notion of metatheory 2.0

is likewise somewhat inspired by and builds on. However, Ritzer's work tends to focus on empirically-grounded sociological metatheorizing, whereas our approach cuts across disciplines. Fiske and Schweder's (1986) work is also worth noting as a relatively contemporary set of perspectives on metatheory in the social sciences.

11 Bhaskar (1986/2009, pp. 19–20).

12 Following Ritzer (1991, 2001) and Colomy (1991), four sub-types of metatheory β may be distinguished. Metatheory β1 studies extant theory to produce a metatheory that overarches some or all of a theoretical domain, that is, some part of a discipline's theory, all of a discipline's theory, or multiple disciplines (Ritzer's Mo). Metatheory β2 studies theory in preparation for the production of new theory on unit level, rather than an overarching new metatheory (Ritzer's Mp). Metatheory β3 studies an existing theory for purposes of attaining a deeper reflective understanding of it, but does not attempt to produce new theory or metatheory (Ritzer's Mu). Metatheory β4 is used to assess the conceptual adequacy and scope of other metatheories and theories (Colomy's Ma). Given that we have scanned across the horizon of extant theoretical definitions of metatheory, we consider our definitional scheme to be a kind of meta-definition along the lines of Metatheory β1.

13 Bhaskar (1979/2015, pp. 50–51).

14 The international symposium "Research across Boundaries: Advances in Theory-Building" brought together, for the first time, "around 30 leading researchers from more than 15 countries and as many different research areas. They are representatives of an array of contemporary integrative frameworks and research practices." According to the organizers, the goal of the symposium was "to foster dialogues among them and additional participants through plenum, small-group and open space sessions, in order to discover common concerns and stimulating differences regarding advanced boundary-crossing research approaches." Please see http://dica-lab.org/rab/ for more details on the symposium and www.integral-studies.org/ for information on the Institute for Integral Studies.

15 Other scholars at the Luxembourg symposium contributing chapters to this volume include Mark Edwards and Gary Hampson.

16 P. Marshall (2012b).

17 Rutzou (2012).

18 Despain (2013).

19 P. Marshall (2012c).

20 P. Marshall (2012a).

21 Bhaskar (2012).

22 Wilber (2012).

23 Best engagement with critical realism was awarded to Nick Hedlund for an earlier version of his chapter in this volume. Best engagement with complex thought was awarded to Sean Kelly, Adam Robbert, and Sam Mickey for their paper "The varieties of integral ecologies: Kosmopolitan complexity and the new realisms."

24 In addition to Edgar Morin, a number of other notable scholars of complex thought attended and presented at the conference, including Sean M. Kelly and Alfonso Montuori of the California Institute of Integral Studies.

25 Rutzou (2014).

26 Despain (2014).

27 Visser goes on to note that: "(During the past Integral Conference in 2013, Roy Bhaskar's critical realism was contrasted with Wilber's integral philosophy, and some scholars have suggested integral theory was in need of a 'grounding in ontology', which subsequently Wilber denied. In his understanding, integral theory was complete as it is. This is quite a sophisticated debate we have to leave to the professionals to work out. Paul Marshall and Nick Hedlund-de Witt, two students of Bhaskar who I met at the conference, are involved in this meta-integral debate.)" See www.integral-world.net/visser69.html.

28 Moreover, this event built on the momentum of the increasing coordination and collaboration amongst integrative scholar-practitioners in Europe following the 1st Integral European Conference (Budapest, May 8–11, 2014), where Annick de Witt, Gary Hampson, Nick Hedlund, Paul Marshall, Matthew Rich, and others presented.

29 The positions Roy articulates are as follows: (1) complex integral realism (CIR), exemplified by Sean Esbjörn-Hargens in Chapter 3, and characterized by 'preservative synthesis'; (2) the possibility of complex integral realism (P(CIR)), exemplified by Paul Marshall in Chapter 4, and characterized by 'potential synthesis'; (3) critical realist integral theory (CRIT), exemplified by Nick Hedlund in Chapter 5, and characterized by 'non-preservative synthesis'; (4) critical realism/integral theory resonance (CR/IT), exemplified by Mervyn Hartwig in Chapter 7, and characterized by 'resonance, but no synthesis possible'; (5) critical realism and integral theory incommensurability (CR | |IT), exemplified by Tim Rutzou in his *Journal of Critical Realism* articles, and characterized by 'no fruitful dialogue; incommensurable.'

References

Bammer, G. (2013). *Disciplining interdisciplinarity: Integration and implementation sciences for researching complex real-world problems*. Canberra: ANU E Press.

Bennett, L. M., Gadlin, H., & Levine-Finley, S. (2010). Collaboration and team science: A field guide. Retrieved June 1, 2015, from https://ccrod.cancer.gov/confluence/download/attachments/47284665/TeamScience_FieldGuide.pdf?version=1&modificationDate=1271730182423.

Bhaskar, R. (1979/2015). *The possibility of naturalism: A philosophical critique of the contemporary human sciences*. London: Routledge.

Bhaskar, R. (1986/2009). *Scientific realism and human emancipation*. London: Routledge.

Bhaskar, R. (1989/2011). *Reclaiming reality: A critical introduction to contemporary philosophy*. London: Routledge.

Bhaskar, R. (1993/2008). *Dialectic: The pulse of freedom*. London: Routledge.

Bhaskar, R. (2002/2012). *The philosophy of metaReality: Creativity, love and freedom*. London: Routledge.

Bhaskar, R. (2012). Considerations on "Ken Wilber on critical realism". *Journal of Integral Theory and Practice, 7*(4), 39–42.

Bhaskar, R. (2016, forthcoming). *Critical realism in a nutshell*, edited by Mervyn Hartwig. London: Routledge.

Bhaskar, R., Esbjörn-Hargens, S., Hedlund, N., & Hartwig, M. (Eds.). (2016, in press). *Metatheory for the anthropocene: Emancipatory praxis for planetary flourishing*. London: Routledge.

Bhaskar, R., Frank, C., Georg Høyer, K., Næss, P., & Parker, J. (Eds.). (2010). *Interdisciplinarity and climate change: Transforming knowledge and practice for our global future*. London: Routledge.

Biermann, F. Abbott, K., Andresen, S., Bäckstrand, K., Bernstein, S., & Betsill, M. M. (2012). Transforming governance and institutions for global sustainability: Key insights from the Earth System Governance Project. *Current Opinion in Environmental Sustainability, 4*(1), 51–60.

Brier, S. (2013). *Cybersemiotics: Why information is not enough*. Toronto: University of Toronto Press.

Chandler, D., & Torbert, B. (2003). Transforming inquiry and action: Interweaving 27 flavors of action research. *Action Research, 1*(2), 133–152.

Collins, R. (2000). *The sociology of philosophies: A global theory of intellectual change.* Cambridge, MA: Harvard University Press.

Colomy, P. (1991). Metatheorizing in a postpositivist frame. *Sociological Perspectives,* 34(3), 269–286.

Cooper, H. (2009). *Research synthesis and meta-analysis: A step-by-step approach.* Thousand Oaks, CA: Sage.

Creswell, J. W. (1998). *Qualitative inquiry and research design: Choosing among five traditions.* Thousand Oaks, CA: Sage.

Creswell, J. W., & Plano Clark, V. L. (2011). *Designing and conducting mixed methods research.* Thousand Oaks, CA: Sage.

Crutzen, P. J., & Stoermer, E. F. (2000). *Global Change Newsletter,* 41, 17–18.

De Witt, A., & Hedlund, N. (in press). Towards an integral ecology of worldviews: Reflexive communications for climate solutions. In S. Mickey, S. M. Kelly, & A. Robbert (Eds.), *Integral ecologies: Culture, nature, knowledge, and our planetary future.* New York: SUNY Press.

Despain, H. (2013). Integral theory: The salubrious chalice? *Journal of Critical Realism,* 13(2), 507–517.

Despain, H. (2014). Integral theory and the search for earthly emancipation: On the possibility of emancipatory and ethical personal development. *Journal of Critical Realism,* 13(2), 183–188.

Dussel, E. (1995). *The invention of the Americas: Eclipse of "the other" and the myth of modernity* (M. D. Barber, Trans.). New York: Continuum.

Dussel, E. (2002). World-system and trans-modernity. *Nepantla: Views from South,* 3(2), 221–244.

Earth, Future. (2014). Retrieved November 15, 2014, from www.icsu.org/future-earth/ who on.

Edwards, M. G. (2010). *Organizational transformation for sustainability: An integral metatheory.* New York: Routledge.

Esbjörn-Hargens, S. (2010). An overview of integral theory. In S. Esbjörn-Hargens (Ed.), *Integral theory in action: Applied, theoretical and constructive perspectives on the AQAL model* (pp. 33–64). New York: SUNY Press.

Esbjörn-Hargens, S. (2011). Editorial introduction. *Journal of Integral Theory and Practice,* 6(3), v.

Fiske, D. W., & Shweder, R. A. (Eds.). (1986). *Metatheory in social science: Pluralisms and subjectivities.* Chicago: University of Chicago Press.

Flyvbjerg, B. (2001). *Making social science matter: Why social inquiry fails and how it can succeed again* (S. Samson, Trans.). Cambridge: Cambridge University Press.

Funtowicz, S. & Ravetz, J. (1993). Science for the post-normal age. *Futures,* 25(7), 739–755.

Gough, D., Oliver, S., & Thomas, J. (Eds.). (2013). *An introduction to systematic reviews.* Thousand Oaks, CA: Sage.

Hedlund, N. H. (2008). Integrally researching the integral researcher. A first-person exploration of psychosophy's holding loving space practice. *Journal of Integral Theory and Practice,* 3(2), 1–57.

Hedlund, N. H. (2010). Integrally researching integral research: Enactive perspectives on the field. *Journal of Integral Theory and Practice,* 5(2), 1–30.

Hedlund-de Witt, A. (2013a). *Worldviews and the transformation to sustainable societies: An exploration of the cultural and psychological dimensions of our global environmental challenges* (Unpublished doctoral dissertation). VU University, Amsterdam.

Hedlund-de Witt, A. (2013b). Worldviews and their significance for the global sustainable development debate. *Environmental Ethics,* 35(2), 133–162.

Hedlund-de Witt, A., & Hedlund-de Witt, N. H. (2013). *The state of our world, the state of our worldview(s): The Integrative Worldview Framework as a tool for reflexive communicative action and transformation.* Paper presented at the Transformation in a changing climate, University of Oslo.

Hedlund-de Witt, N. H. (2012). Critical realism: A synoptic overview and resource guide for integral scholars. Retrieved December 12, 2012, from https://foundation.metaintegral. org/sites/default/files/Critical%20Realism_4-12-2013.pdf.

Hulme, M. (2009). *Why we disagree about climate change: Understanding controversy, inaction and opportunity.* Cambridge: Cambridge University Press.

IPCC. (2000). *Emissions scenarios.* Cambridge: Cambridge University Press.

IPCC. (2014). *Climate change 2014: Impacts, adaptation, and vulnerability. Part A: Global and sectoral aspects. Contribution of Working Group II to the Fifth Assessment Report of the Intergovernmental Panel on Climate Change.* Ed. C. B. Field & V. R. Barros. Cambridge: Cambridge University Press.

Jessop, B. (2015). The symptomatology of crises, reading crises and learning from them: Some critical realist reflections. *Journal of Critical Realism, 14*(3), 238–271.

Johnson, R. B., & Onwuegbuzie, A. J. (2004). Mixed methods research: A research paradigm whose time has come. *Educational Researcher, 33*(7), 14–26.

Lyotard, F. (1984). *The postmodern condition: A report on knowledge.* Minneapolis: University of Minnesota Press.

Marshall, G. (1998). *The Oxford dictionary of sociology.* Oxford: Oxford University Press.

Marshall, P. (2012a). Ken Wilber on critical realism. *Journal of Integral Theory and Practice, 7*(4), 35–38.

Marshall, P. (2012b). The meeting of two integrative metatheories. *Journal of Critical Realism, 11*(2), 188–214.

Marshall, P. (2012c). Toward an integral realism. Part 1: an overview of transcendental realist ontology. *Journal of Integral Theory and Practice, 7*(4), 1–34.

Martin, R. (2009). *The opposable mind: Winning through integrative thinking.* Cambridge, MA: Harvard Business Review Press.

Midgley, G. (2001). *Systemic intervention: Philosophy, methodology, and practice.* New York: Springer.

Mitchell, S. D. (2003). *Biological complexity and integrative pluralism.* Cambridge: Cambridge University Press.

Montuori, A. (2013). Complex thought: An overview of Edgar Morin's intellectual journey. Retrieved August 14, 2013, from https://foundation.metaintegral.org/sites/default/files/ Complex_Thought_FINAL.pdf.

Morin, E., & Kern, A. B. (1999). *Homeland Earth: A manifesto for the new millennium* (S. M. Kelly & R. Lapointe, Trans.). Cresskill, NJ: Hampton Press.

Nagel, T. (1986). *The view from nowhere.* Oxford: Oxford University Press.

Norton, B. G. (2005). *Sustainability: A philosophy of adaptive ecosystem management.* Chicago: University of Chicago Press.

Parson, E. A,. & Fisher-Vande, K. (1995). Searching for integrated assessment: A preliminary investigation of methods, models, and projects in the integrated assessment of global climatic change. University Center, MI: Consortium for International Earth Science Information Network (CIESIN).

Reason, P., & Bradbury, H. (2001). *Handbook of action research.* London: Sage.

Reason, P., & Torbert, W. (2001). The action turn: Toward a transformational social science. *Concepts and Transformation, 6*(1), 1–37.

Rittel, Horst W. J., & Webber, Melvin M. (1973). Dilemmas in a general theory of planning. *Policy Sciences, 4*(2), 155–169.

Ritzer, G. (Ed.). (1990). *Frontiers of social theory: The new syntheses.* New York: Columbia University Press.

Ritzer, G. (1991). *Metatheorizing in sociology*. Lexington, MA: Lexington Books.

Ritzer, G. (2001). *Explorations in social theory: From metatheorizing to rationalization*. Thousand Oaks, CA: Sage.

Rutzou, T. (2012). Integral theory: A poisoned chalice? Rut *Journal of Critical Realism*, 11(2), 215–224.

Rutzou, T. (2014). Integral theory and the Holy Grail: On the possibility of a metatheory. *Journal of Critical Realism*, 13(1), 77–83.

Scharmer, O. (2009). *Theory u: Leading from the future as it emerges*. San Francisco, CA: Berrett-Koehler.

Siegel, D. (2012). *Pocket guide to interpersonal neurobiology: An integrative handbook of the mind*. New York: W. W. Norton.

Tashakkori, A., & Teddlie, C. (1998). *Mixed methodology. Combining qualitative and quantitative approaches* (Vol. 46). Thousand Oaks, CA: Sage.

Taylor, C. (2004). *Modern social imaginaries*. Durham, NC: Duke University Press.

Torbert, W. (1991). *The power of balance: Transforming self, society and scientific inquiry*. Newbury Park, CA: Sage.

Torbert, W. (2000a). A developmental approach to social science: A model for analyzing Charles Alexander's scientific contributions. *Journal of Adult Development*, 7(4), 255–267.

Torbert, W. (2000b). Transforming social science: Integrating quantitative, qualitative, and action research. In F. T. Sherman & W. Torbert (Eds.), *Transforming social inquiry, transforming social action* (pp. 67–92). Boston, MA: Kluwer Academic Publishers.

Torbert, W. (2001). The practice of action inquiry. In P. R. H. Bradbury (Ed.), *Handbook of action research* (pp. 250–260). London: Sage.

Torbert, W. (2004). *Action inquiry: The secret of timely and transforming leadership*. San Francisco, CA: Berrett-Koehler.

Trochim, W. M., Marcus, S. E., Masse, L. C., Moser, R. P., & Weld, P. C. (2008). The evaluation of large research initiatives: A participatory integrated mixed-methods approach. *American Journal of Evaluation*, 29(1), 8–28.

Tyfield, D. (2015). What is to be done? Insights and blind-spots from cultural political economy(s) (review essay). *Journal of Critical Realism*, 15(5).

Wilber, K. (1995). *Sex, ecology, spirituality: The spirit of evolution*. Boston, MA: Shambhala.

Wilber, K. (2012). In defense of integral theory: A response to critical realism. *Journal of Integral Theory and Practice*, 7(4), 43–52.

Zalamea, F. (2013). *Synthetic philosophy of contemporary mathematics*. New York: Sequence Press.

1

BEYOND NATURE AND HUMANITY

Reflections on the emergence and purposes of metatheories

Zachary Stein

Introduction: metatheory as humanity's vocabulary of self-transformation[1]

> [With] self-consciousness comes the possibility of *transforming* ourselves by adopting new vocabularies, redescribing, and so reconstructing our selves and discursive institutions. While all of us are in some sense *consumers* of such new vocabularies, it is the special calling of some to *produce* them. And among those producers some take the construction of unique, potentially transformative vocabularies as the project by commitment to which they understand and define themselves. Among that group, some seek to produce those new vocabularies precisely by trying to understand the phenomena of sapience, normativity, conceptuality, reason, freedom, expression, self-consciousness, self-constitution, and historical transformation by subversive, empowering vocabularies. Those are the philosophers. They are charged neither with simply understanding human nature (human history), nor with simply changing it, but with changing it *by* understanding it.
>
> *(Brandom, 2009, p. 150)*

We humans are a self-interpreting species for whom the practice of recollecting and redescribing ourselves is a crucial necessity. For us the reconstruction of identity is a continuous process wherein the *past* is selectively crafted into a *history*. It is a creative and self-constitutive exercise. We come to know each other and ourselves not by exchanging resumes (mere inventories of events), but by telling our stories. And our stories change as we do; they reflect what actually happened and what we think is worth remembering, they reflect who we were, who we are, and who we would like to become. Neglecting this retrospective task results in identity confusion, leaving us fragmented, meandering, and directionless. Some argue that the species as a whole faces an impending identity crisis as the unchecked proliferation of informational and biological technologies create abrupt discontinuities in the intergenerational fabric of the lifeworld, catapulting us out of history and into forms of life that are incongruent and incomprehensible (Habermas, 2003; Fukuyama, 2002). These concerns about possible futures appear realistic when they are seen in the context of the obvious identity confusions that already characterize large swaths of the academy, especially in the humanities and social sciences (Kagan, 2009; Menand, 2010). The disciplines traditionally responsible for the self-interpretation of the species do not have a coherent interpretation of themselves.

This chapter expresses a certain understanding of the origins and purposes of metatheories. Remembering (recollecting and redescribing) who we are as metatheorists should go a long way toward bringing order to the disorder and fragmentation of the academy. The proliferation of robust metatheories should in turn foster the emergence of more substantive and coherent voices in the public sphere, which is otherwise becoming increasingly irrational, inarticulate, and superficial. What follows is a certain type of scholarly intervention. It involves a historical reconstruction of core intellectual themes that have shaped a given field, addressing this reconstruction to participants in that field, and thus affecting how they understand their efforts. Both Brandom (2002, 2009) and Habermas (1971) have executed projects of this type – in philosophy and critical theory respectively – and both have discussed the unique methodological issues involved. The reconstruction of a cumulative trajectory or tradition is both a discovery and a creation. It is also both descriptive and prescriptive. We remember what we think is worth remembering, which depends in part on who we want to become, yet who we want to become is a reflection of who we think we have been all along. This kind of complex hermeneutic exercise is indispensable for assuring the continuity of intellectual traditions. Retrospective reconstructive work sets the necessary staging for concerted constructive efforts.

Importantly, these kinds of reconstructions are always partial. The story I tell here is but *one* story (and a regrettably brief and unelaborated one at that). There are other stories worth telling. And I encourage the reconstruction of different stories. In one sense this chapter can be read as having a merely *expressive* intent, as opposed to its being read as if it were crafted to persuade or convince. This does not mean what follows is arbitrary or irrelevant, or that it cannot be persuasive. The long tradition of expressive philosophical projects – from Schelling, Nietzsche, and Emerson through Derrida, Rorty, West, and Brandom – would suggest quite the opposite. Many have been *influential* while yet only claiming to express themselves, especially regarding issues too deep to really argue about. So while I am adopting a somewhat unconventional argumentative strategy, it is not an unreasonable one.

I have adopted this argumentative strategy mainly in response to the state of the discourse surrounding the term *metatheory*, which has been so variously characterized (e.g., Edwards, 2008; Fiske & Shweder, 1986; Overton, 2007; Ritzer, 1991; 1992). At first pass the term can simply be understood as referring to a type of super-theory built from overarching constructs that organize and subsume more local, discipline-specific theories and concepts. Roughly: whereas a theory within a discipline typically takes the world as data, metatheory typically takes other theories as data. Beyond this first pass, however, the discourse about metatheory gets very complex very fast (see Ritzer, 1992). A highly abstract, ornate, and self-referential academic niche has emerged. And as a result there has been a flowering of interesting intellectual work concerning metatheory. This is not a situation unique to the discourse about metatheory. Nor do I write this intending a criticism of the field. This is how things stand in most fields, even those with seemingly straightforward subjects, such as *human memory* (see Hacking, 1995).

But things get even more complex and contested if *philosophy* is not partitioned off from metatheory (a move I have never seen justified) and if the whole discourse about *interdisciplinarity* and *transdisciplinarity* is also thrown into the mix (e.g., Gibbons *et al.*, 1994; Klein, 2005; Stein, 2007). When the net is cast broadly what comes into view is an expansive and unprecedented proliferation of reflective activity about knowledge production processes in post-industrial socio-cultural contexts. The task of cataloging the various genera and species that populate this intellectual landscape is a daunting one. And the idea of offering some new theoretical creature that might survive seems misguided, as the diversity on the current scene suggests probable redundancy. So my strategy has been to look back to a time before the Cambrian Explosion, as it were – a time before the contemporary cacophony – to find the key progenitors in hopes that this approach might allow for clarity about the core properties that characterize metatheoretical endeavors.

What results, I think, is a compelling account wherein metatheory is understood as a unique extension of more traditional modes of philosophy. First emerging in the later half of the nineteenth century, metatheory grew up as a response to advances in psychology that would transform epistemology, and to socio-economic transformations affecting the institutionalization of knowledge production (e.g., the birth of the complex departmentalized research university). It emerged to serve a normative function as a result of cognitive, disciplinary, and discursive necessities, ultimately positioning itself as a locus of responsibility for setting the trajectory of high-level discourses and reflective cultural practices. Of course, today metatheorists claim to be doing all kinds of things, such as serving descriptive, deconstructive, or even decorative functions. I am aware of the various ways we metatheorists might understand ourselves, but I choose to offer a vision that emphasizes the distinctly normative core of metatheoretical endeavoring. Others are welcome to tell stories that construe metatheory differently, perhaps as a more recent and poly-focal form of academic activity. I personally prefer to see metatheory as the continuation by new means of classic philosophical efforts, where highly reflective individuals take responsibility for discursively constructing conceptual innovations aimed at bringing coherence to the state of knowledge for the sake of shaping human history.[2]

Below I trace the origins of metatheory to Kant and Hegel, who gave it to Emerson and a host of young Hegelians on both sides of the Atlantic. Then I profile the metatheoretical projects of Charles S. Peirce, James Mark Baldwin, Jean Piaget, and Jürgen Habermas, whom I characterize as key progenitors of contemporary metatheory. They all self-consciously appropriated and transformed the philosophical traditions they inherited in order to address the rapidly changing contexts of knowledge production they faced. The results are best understood as metatheoretical endeavors that are explicitly related to a specific philosophical tradition concerned with the function, role, and purpose of humanity in an evolving universe. A look at Ken Wilber and Roy Bhaskar brings the narrative up to date. This historical reconstruction is intended to remind contemporary metatheorists of a set of related issues and themes, which I will quickly foreshadow.

The metatheorists discussed below all address the place of humanity in an evolving universe, each seeking to articulate a way of preserving human reason and morality in a thoroughgoing evolutionary context – including both natural and cultural evolution. This relates to each theory's focus on, and the distinctly *normative* nature of, humanity; that is, they were each out to show that we are the makers and followers of rules, values, and ideals, not just passive nodes in causal systems; we reflectively strive to create what *ought* to be from what *is*. This common focus on the function of the normative in nature appears as one of the ways that metatheories have kept alive more traditional philosophical and religious themes, including such problems as free will, post-conventional morality, and the possibility of creating radically new and more humane cultural and social conditions. The tie between metatheory and religious or spiritual visions of humanity seems to be intrinsic. Not only do all the theorists discussed below display long-standing interests in religious questions and investigations, their theories were shaped by these concerns as much as others. Moreover, because these theories are so broad and because they take humanity as their focus their content will tend toward areas traditionally the subject of philosophical or religious discourse. So even while metatheories may not directly address these existential issues, many are intrinsically relevant and are often raised despite the intention of authors to keep them off the table.[3]

However, as abstract and complex as these theories are they are not "views from nowhere" (Nagel, 1986). All the metatheorists discussed below offer theories that can account for themselves – they eat their own tails – because they are tied into traditions in psychology and human development that can explain the emergence of metatheoretical capabilities, in both the individual mind-brain and in communities of inquiry and practice. Beginning with Peirce and Baldwin, metatheoretical constructs have been reflectively wielded as the most advanced ideas around, coming into use only "beyond formal operations" (in what Baldwin called the "super-logical" levels of cognitive development). Since then these kind of constructs have been called: post-formal (Piaget), post-conventional (Kohlberg; Habermas), dialectal (Basseches), 2nd-tiered vision-logic (Wilber), meta-systemic (Commons), and single principled (Dawson; Fischer). Developmental psychologists agree that these high-level constructs have particular properties and potentials, two of which strongly characterize all the theories discussed here. Metatheoretical constructs serve a discourse-regulative function – they emerge from a kind of discursive mastery, which gives way to an ability to reflect on the norms of discourses and pursue new languages for *norming the norms* – this is a basic characteristic of post-conventional discourse-interventions. Once these constructs emerge they can be re-tooled to serve a general discourse-regulative function: within a single discourse (e.g., discourse-specific metatheory, like meta-psychology); between discourses (e.g., interdisciplinary metatheory, like systems theory); or across indefinite discourses, including public and non-academic (e.g., philosophical metatheory, like critical realism or integral theory). Post-formal constructs serve as epistemic adjudicators within and between disciplines (this is the meta-critical aspect of metatheory; or simply *metacritique*), but they also mediate between the sciences and the everyday communication of the lifeworld – giving humanity new languages with which to understand itself (this is the metanarrative function of metatheory; or simply *metanarrative*).

Metatheoretical languages articulate norms beyond those set by existing social conditions, including current scientific understandings of nature and the meaning of the evolutionary emergence of humanity. Metatheorists traffic in constructs that lead beyond both nature and humanity; they provide languages designed to recreate humanity's understanding of itself. This is discussed below as *the normative function of metatheoretical endeavors*. Metatheory has inherited from philosophy the function of providing for humanity's languages of self-transformation – which is the task of leading humanity beyond itself by re-articulating a shared vision of human nature and the nature of the universe.

Humanity as the emergence of the normative from the natural

> We are symbols, and inhabit symbols.… Our expressions, or namings, [or theories,] are not art, but a second nature, grown out of the first, as a leaf out of a tree. What we call nature, is a certain self-regulated motion, or change; and nature does not leave another to baptize her, but baptizes herself; and thus through the metamorphosis again.
>
> *(Emerson, from "The Poet")*

Emerson was not the first to speculate about the function of humanity in nature; but he was one of the most articulate. Beyond merely positioning humanity in the natural world, Emerson offered a vision in which humans have a role to play, a task ordained – a function – in nature. The continuity of human history with natural evolution would become a theme in American philosophy (Schneider, 1963). Following the influential examples of Herbert Spencer and Auguste Comte, a set of speculative Americanized 'cosmic histories' were articulated by the likes of John Fiske (1874) and Francis Ellingwood Abbot (1885). Lester Frank Ward (1887), the St. Louis Hegelians (Leidecker, 2007), John Dewey (1898), and others (Mead, 1936) would all argue that cultural evolution should be understood as being in important ways continuous with cosmic evolution. These early voices, like those of Peirce and Baldwin, toiled in Emerson's shadow. Of course, Emerson toiled in the shadow of Kant, who first tentatively and cryptically suggested that the laws humanity gives itself are best read as an autonomous extension of the self-regulative processes of the natural world. According to this view, humanity's *autonomy* – literally, its self-legislating capability – represents nature's crowning innovation, wherein are found startling advances toward novelty and complexity. Importantly, a capacity for autonomy entails the acceptance of responsibility. This is the root of the notion that humanity is somehow accountable for the trajectory of evolution.

According to the tradition I am reconstructing here – from Kant through Emerson to Peirce, Baldwin, Piaget, Habermas, and Wilber – the function of humanity in nature is a *normative* one. It is a function contingent upon the autonomy of humanity in an evolving world and humanity's reflective knowledge of this situation. This tradition suggests that we are responsible for directing the trajectory of evolution, and we know it (or ought to). Emerson offered his evocative and ennobling calls for self-determination with this broad context in mind. Kant argued that humanity ought to facilitate the transformation of the *kingdom of nature* into the *kingdom of ends* by proceeding such that the norms of our actions might be fit to serve as universal laws (akin to natural laws). Peirce wrote about it in terms of our having a responsibility to lay down new cosmic habits. These views highlight the directive, regulative, trajectory-setting – that is, the *normative* – function of humanity in nature.

This philosophical tradition focusing on the normative function of humanity is where the first metatheoretical endeavors emerged. Metatheories emerge, as Peirce's work exemplifies, in order to regulate and oversee whole sets of discourses – serving a normative function vis-à-vis more local, discipline-specific theories and concepts. Metatheories set the trajectory for broad segments of culture and knowledge production. This saddles the metatheorist with unique responsibilities.

Along these lines, many of Kant's arguments were set in the context of specific views about the responsibilities of philosophers in the public sphere and beyond. In the final sections of the *Critique of Pure Reason*, Kant (1998, B867) lays out a distinction between two general types of philosophers: *scholastic-reductionist* and *cosmopolitan-comprehensivist*. The former perpetuates the fragmentation of knowledge by exercising the power of philosophy in isolated contexts and for partial purposes. The latter embodies a postmetaphysical vision of philosophy wherein the philosopher serves a normative function in the public sphere, explicating the *teleologia rationis humanae*, being a legislator of reason's future, and an immanent catalyst of the *corpus mysticum*. This was some of Kant's motivation when he (1983a, 1983b) articulated one of the earliest and most influential normative global metanarratives in a series of publications about the history of human civilization and the necessary future emergence of a global governance system.[4] In its wake Habermas and Bhaskar have both articulated normative global metatheories concerned with the trajectory of cultural evolution – both trace a lineage to Kant via Hegel and Marx as well as other nineteenth-century European thought-leaders. It seems Wilber can trace a lineage to Kant via Baldwin, Peirce, Piaget, and Emerson, all cosmopolitan agents building metatheories to fit normative functions. With this backward glance we are positioned to consider the shape of the metatheories that came before ours as well as those that are to come.

Peirce's metatheoretical *modus operandi*

> The word *normative* was invented by the school of Schleiermacher.… But we must trace its introduction into common speech, to Wundt. It is taken from the Latin verb *normo*, to square.… The majority of writers who make use of it tell us that there are three normative sciences: logic, aesthetics, and ethics. The doctrines of the true, the beautiful, and the good, a triad of ideals which has been recognized since antiquity.… Logic is the theory of *right* reasoning, of what reasoning *ought* to be, not of what it *is*. On that account, it used to be called a *directive* science, but of late years the adjective *normative* has been generally substituted.
>
> *(Peirce, 1931 p. 5)*

Peirce was a towering but controversial figure on the intellectual scene of his day. He was by any measure a prodigious polymath, with a working mastery of well over a dozen sciences, a mathematician, logician, metaphysician, and an epistemologist. He was one of the few American academics on the world stage during the middle of the nineteenth century, and was the first American to be elected as a member of an international scientific organization. But he was never able to gain the institutional support and positioning in the American academy that many thought he deserved. Both his personality and the substance of his intellectual contributions made it difficult for him to secure a position. As would be the case for Baldwin two decades later, a scandal forced Peirce to leave Johns Hopkins University.[5] And like Baldwin, Peirce was a metatheorist during a time when it was unacceptable to be one. During the last decade of his life he faded into obscurity, eventually dying in poverty in rural Pennsylvania. He was known as the greatest genius of his generation to a few (including William James and Theodore Roosevelt), but completely unknown to most.[6]

Yet Peirce toiled away at his work, even as he was starving to death in the Delaware River Valley. He ultimately built what is one of the most profound philosophical systems ever constructed. As Peirce explained it:

> [I intend] to make a philosophy like that of Aristotle, that is to say, to outline a theory so comprehensive that, for a long time to come, the entire work of human reason, in philosophy of every school and kind, in mathematics, in psychology, in physical science, in history, in sociology, and in whatever other department there may be, shall appear as the filling up of its details.
>
> *(Peirce, 2000, p. 168)*

This system has exerted a wide-ranging influence, from philosophers like Popper (1966) to linguists like Chomsky (1979), both of whom see Peirce as one of the most significant philosophers to have lived. His continued relevance for a wide range of fields outside philosophy, including semiotics (a field which he founded), cognitive science, and computer science, is evidenced by what amounts to an academic cottage industry, where scholarship is burgeoning (see Misak, 2004).

For the purposes of the story I am telling here, it is important to see that Peirce's work was a response to the unprecedented transformations affecting academic knowledge production processes in the later half of the nineteenth century (Ketner & Kloesel, 1986). On one reading, Peirce's philosophical system can be understood as general semiotics, analytically equipped for *overseeing*, *explicating*, and *evaluating* different kinds of beliefs at multiple levels – from propositions, to arguments, to discourses. Peirce executes this ambitious project by utilizing a variety of philosophical methods – methods Baldwin would claim exemplify the exercise of aesthetic imagination, or theoretical intuition (what today developmentalists would call *post-formal thought*).

Peirce surveyed a broad expanse of sciences and inductively explicated an evolutionary hierarchy akin to a biological taxonomy (Kent, 1987; Peirce, 1931). He built a system of existential graphs wherein the relations between propositions are explicated via logically uniform concept maps (Peirce, 1933; Shin, 2002). He also clarified the intersubjective conditions for the possibility of reliable knowledge production, arguing that inquiry-oriented communication communities must have an open and inclusive structure predicated on trust, honesty, and reciprocity (Apel, 1995; Peirce, 1984a). And of course, as a final example, it is well known that underlying his whole system was a set of three *primordial concepts* – in Kant's sense of being transcendentally basic – that he characterized as syncategorematic categories, and once correlated with the three basic pronouns: I, Thou, and It (Habermas, 1992; Peirce, 1982). In all of these instances Peirce was out to build metatheoretical constructs that could play a role in adjudicative processes concerning the value of our cognitive wares.

Moreover, Peirce positioned his discourse-regulative project atop a broader evolutionary vision of the universe where the strivings of humanity are continuous with the evolution of the cosmos (Peirce, 2000, 1934; Esposito, 1980; Hausman, 1993). Peirce articulated a sophisticated and empirically grounded evolutionary ontology where all events are semiotic processes that co-evolve toward increasing complexity, autonomy, self-awareness, and possible harmony. Peirce's *pansemiotic* evolutionary theory was a unique (postmetaphysical) view in so far as it was explicitly offered as a hypothesis amenable to correction in light of forthcoming empirical data. It greatly influenced Whitehead (1978) and continues to intrigue and inspire scholars in the physical and biological sciences (Prigogine & Stengers, 1984) and philosophy (Apel, 1994).

This understanding of evolution allowed Peirce to bring his overarching normative concerns about the trajectory of academic discourses in line with a venerable philosophical tradition that articulated the radical significance of humanity's cultural endeavors in terms of a cosmic evolutionary unfolding. Ultimately, Peirce, with a look in Kant's direction, envisioned humanity as capable of multitudinous self-correcting intellectual and ethical endeavors, which ought to result in an ideal communication community coterminous with the cosmos. In this postmetaphysical eschatology, the ideals of *harmonious love between all beings* and *unconditional knowledge about all things* stand as goals to be approached asymptotically. With this thought Peirce rearticulates a philosophical motif that can be traced back through Emerson, Schelling, and Kant to the obscure cipher of Böhme's mystical Protestant religiosity and its ancient Hebraic and Neoplatonic roots.

Baldwin's meta-dictionary and his views of the higher stages

> We see experience establishing, of itself, a synthetic mode of apprehension. To our mind, the course of the history of thought makes it plain that the quest for such a mode of experience presents the only hope of a lessened strife among points of view; for in such a mode of process evidence would be present to show that the entire system of experience is expressive of reality, and that only in the organization of the whole are the respective roles of this and that function to be made out. [Thus] the need of carrying out to their legitimate outcome all the hints that consciousness gives as to its unreduced and undivided epistemological calling. [This calling] does not deny the epistemological value of any of the mental functions, or the force of any of the theories which are based respectively upon one or other of the functions; on the contrary, its aim is to discover the synthetic adjustment of their claims with the larger whole.
>
> *(Baldwin, 1915, p. 226)*

James Mark Baldwin was a massive figure on the intellectual scene of his day. During the height of his influence he was mentioned in the same breath as William James, John Dewey, and Pierre Janet, on both sides of the Atlantic. He was arguably the most significant American psychologist of the nineteenth century – while James gave psychology a face, publishing the indelible *Principles of Psychology*, Baldwin gave it legs, institutionalized it, building labs and starting journals. His writings were widely cited, translated into many languages, and several of his books were considered as standards in the field.[7] And though his theories have had a lasting impact on a variety of areas – from developmental psychology (Kohlberg, 1981; Piaget, 1932) and psychoanalysis (Lacan, 1977) to evolutionary biology (Weber & Depew, 2003), evolutionary epistemology (Campbell, 1987), and integral theory (Wilber, 1999) – he is not the household name he once was.

Given his former stature and the continuing relevance of his ideas, many have speculated about the reasons for his present obscurity (Broughton & Freeman-Moir, 1982). A scandal did leave him blacklisted in American academia, and his departure did clear the way for behaviorism, as John B. Watson assumed control of Baldwin's prestigious faculty position and numerous journal editorships (see Wozniak, 2001). However, Baldwin did continue to write prolifically while exiled in France, was eventually elected a foreign correspondent to the French Academy (the highest honor that can be given to a non-citizen), and then received the Legion of Honor for his charity and relief work in France during World War I. The standard story is that institutional rearrangements and broad changes in the academic *Zeitgeist* secured his fate as a footnote in the history of psychology. There is certainly an element of truth in that account, but there is a deeper reason for Baldwin's neglect, I believe. It has to do with the fact – and the parallels here with Peirce are remarkable, as I will show below – that he was doing metatheory when it was unacceptable to do so.

His later works are nearly universally considered to be obscure, speculative, and worthless to contemporary psychology (Boring, 1929; Richards, 1987; Weber & Depew, 2003; although see Broughton & Freeman-Moir, 1982[8]). This is, I believe, because these works (Baldwin, 1911, vols. 1–3; 1913, vols. 1–2; 1915) unlike his earlier works (1895; 1897) are not offered in the spirit of experimental psychology. Baldwin's later works are offered as metatheoretical interventions, aimed at organizing the existing state of discourse in the human sciences, biology, and the humanities into a common framework, a *comprehensive developmental theory of reality*.

Baldwin's moves beyond psychology toward metatheory were undoubtedly catalyzed by his work as editor of the *Dictionary of Philosophy and Psychology* (Baldwin, 1905).[9] The *Dictionary* stands as one of the most impressive transnational scholarly efforts ever. Explicitly comprehensive in its ambitions, its four massive volumes cover the majority of academic knowledge that existed at the turn of the last century. It contains contributions from hundreds of academics on well over a thousand topics, serving as a veritable *who's who* and *what's what* for the nineteenth-century academy. The *Dictionary* remains unrivaled as a scholarly achievement in certain respects – getting a remarkable amount of knowledge under one roof, with attention to codifying common terminology and efforts at clarifying the structure of the epistemological relations between the disciplinary perspectives in play. And Baldwin oversaw the entire project, making emendations or substantial contributions to almost every entry.

Importantly, the ambitious encyclopedic effort coincided with Baldwin's appointment to Johns Hopkins University, the first modern research university in America. This was a dynamic time in the history of academic institutions (Cremin, 1988; Kerr, 1963; Menand, 2010). The sciences began to gain hegemony and the disciplines were subdividing and multiplying at a dizzying rate. No student of nineteenth-century thought can ignore the profound and pervasive impacts resulting from the professionalization and concomitant departmentalization of knowledge production in the years immediately preceding the publication of Baldwin's *Dictionary*. It was in these years that the academy began to assume the shape it has today, with a vast array of siloed, specialized disciplinary areas. It is hard to see Baldwin's *Dictionary* as anything but a response to what was becoming an increasingly fragmented and sprawling intellectual landscape, an unprecedented academic landscape he found himself in the middle of at Johns Hopkins.

But while he was in the middle of it institutionally, he was also in the middle of it theoretically, as his interests turned at this time toward articulating a metatheoretical developmental epistemology. He moved beyond the focused experimental orientations that characterized his earlier psychological works. Baldwin began to construct an overarching model that could account for the wide variety of knowledge he was compiling for the *Dictionary*, the various types of validity-claims, and the related methods of investigation. Moreover, it was a model that would ultimately account for his *ability* to organize this knowledge, providing an account of the genesis of metatheoretical constructs as high-level emergent products of cognitive developmental processes. From where I sit it is critical to see – although it is often overlooked – that the publication of the *Dictionary* immediately preceded Baldwin's work on *Thought and Things* (1911, vols. 1–3).

In *Thought and Things*, the *magnum opus*, he offers a *convergent view* of human epistemological development, putting forward a model in which the higher stages are mainly integrative and reconciliatory – functioning to transcend the dualisms and differentiations carefully and necessarily built up as the child develops in relation to culture and nature. Baldwin suggests that psychological growth is best thought of in terms of different *lines or domains of development*, which he refers to as *developmental modes*. Each mode is a relatively distinct skill or capacity, exercised in relation to different aspects of reality. Modes cluster together because they have similar external *controls*, thus forming distinct object domains. Different disciplines, methods, and their related validity-claims can be organized in terms of differential mode-recruitment profiles. And at a more abstract level this same strategy provides Baldwin with a way to build a system of epistemological categories. At its highest reaches the model contains a central division between *logical* and *practical* modes – a distinction that retrofits Kant's differentiation of *theoretical* and *practical* reason. This is the difference between science and morals, between objectivity and intersubjectivity; I–It set apart from I–Thou–We. For Baldwin (and others, e.g., Piaget, Habermas, and Wilber), the two most basic modes of development are those that cluster around objects (I–It; objectivity) and those that cluster around people (I–Thou–We; intersubjectivity/subjectivity).

In any case, late in the life course, according to Baldwin's model, these different lines reach a point of complexity and divergence such that they call for the creation of a specific type of new concept, built to transcend but include the differences between the logical and the practical – to reconcile science with the perspectives of the lifeworld. New constructs emerge and begin serving a discourse-regulative function – overseeing, organizing, and regulating whole fields of discourse. With a nod to Kant, Baldwin characterizes this emergent developmental capacity as the *aesthetic imagination*. In Baldwin's words:

> The outcome of our investigation, broadly stated, is that in the aesthetic imagination … *the processes of experience [can] come together after having fallen apart*. Each of the cognitive modes [i.e., lines] … sets up, as is its nature to, a reference in which *the real for it, its real, is found*. But in each case *its real*, not

the real, is postulated or presupposed, since the control that is discovered is the outcome of this or that special mode and stage of psychic function. The protest of the aesthetic imagination is against just this partialness of each of the modes of "real" meaning. Its own ideal, on the contrary, is one of completeness, of reunion, of *reconciliation*; it gives us the "real" which is absolute in the sense that its object is not relative to, and does not fulfill, one type of interest only to the exclusion of others.

(Baldwin, 1911, vol. 3, p. 13)

In Baldwin's model the aesthetic imagination emerges during the course of late-stage cognitive and socio-moral development. It leads to the construction of a variety of *trans-logical* and *trans-practical* constructs. These constructs function across multiple domains and disciplines to oversee, integrate, and regulate important reconciliatory syntheses. For example, Baldwin states that at this stage the individual begins to yearn for views that overcome the distinctions between mind and body, theory and practice, and the ideal and the actual.

Most relevant to this discussion is what Baldwin called *theoretical intuition*, a name he gives to what results when the aesthetic imagination is exercised in the domain of theoretical or logical pursuits, such as science. As Baldwin describes, "By theoretical intuition is meant the immediate apprehension or perception of rational principles as such, these principles being looked upon as constitutive or regulative of knowledge" (Baldwin, 1911 vol. 3, p. 234). Thus, according to Baldwin's developmental model, whole theories, methods, and discourses come to be regulated by the products of late-stage psychological growth. A capability comes online that allows for the creation of metatheoretical constructs that serve a normative function.

This way of understanding the higher reaches of human epistemological development would buoy Baldwin's continued metatheoretical endeavors, most notably his ambitious attempt at building a *comprehensive developmental theory of reality* (Baldwin, 1915). According to this vision, human experience, as elaborated through cultural evolution, is the apex of cosmic evolutionary development, giving a unique significance to our moral, epistemological, and for Baldwin most importantly, our aesthetic strivings. For Baldwin, with homage to Kant's third *Critique* and the Romantics it inspired, it is in the reconciliatory immediacy and world-disclosing power of aesthetic experience that the fullness of reality is revealed, transcending but including all the partial modes of experience built up over the course of biological, cultural, and individual evolution. Thus do the aforementioned *aesthetic imagination* and its *theoretical intuitions* function to guide the trajectory of cultural evolution. And so the function of humanity in the natural world is a normative one – to redeem, reconcile, and resuscitate the full reality and meaning of the universe. But this is getting ahead of our story.

For now it should be noted that Baldwin's theorizing ate its own tail. He offered a theoretical account of the very cognitive processes that he recruited in his metatheoretical endeavoring. He argued that metatheoretical constructs, which organize and regulate whole discourses and theories, were a necessary outgrowth of epistemological development. I pointed out that he began his forays into metatheory after executing a massive project that got him intimately acquainted with the full range of knowledge production processes then extant. So Baldwin's story teaches that the emergence of metatheory involves an *ability* to reflect on a range of knowledge production processes and recognize that they need regulating, organizing, and direction setting. This ability was inimitably exemplified by Charles S. Peirce, who faced the same unprecedented academic environment as Baldwin, and who also took the metatheoretical high road. It is also an ability exemplified in the work of Jean Piaget, who was directly influenced by Baldwin's metatheoretical endeavors.

Piaget's comprehensive structuralism: between the natural and the normative

> So we can speak of self-regulation, but only at the risk of its being confused with life itself.
>
> *(Piaget, 1971a, p. 148)*

Near the end of Chapman's (1988) *tour de force* on the development of Piaget's thought he suggests that Piaget be ranked among those who articulated perspectives that gave new meaning to human life in the context of evolutionary change. He mentions several thinkers with comparable visions, including Bergson, Teilhard de Chardin, Jantsch, Waddington, Polanyi, and Whitehead. To this list could be added Baldwin, Peirce, Aurobindo, and Wilber. The common denominator here is not a shared worldview (although their views are similar, there are important differences) but rather a shared ambition to reposition humanity in relation to our growing fund of scientific knowledge about the natural world.

Piaget first grappled with this ambition as a young man when he drafted an autobiographical novel, *Recherche*, confessing his desire to foster the integration of religious values and scientific knowledge (see Piaget, 1977, for a partial translation). He approached the problem in terms of two related sets of concerns. On the one hand, he offered a principled classification of the sciences with the intention of organizing knowledge and ensuring interdisciplinary quality control. On the other hand, he offered a provisional but comprehensive explanatory framework involving evolutionary processes thought to regulate the development of both the natural world and of human cognition and civilization. He would later chide himself for his "adolescent metaphysical speculations" (Piaget, 1952) and as he began work in psychology his concerns about the integration of science and religion faded.[10] However, the broad research program he outlined in his youth remained intact (Smith, 2002; Chapman, 1988). His principled classification of the sciences reappears repeatedly in his work, largely unchanged (e.g. Piaget, 1971b, 1970c). As does his desire to articulate a comprehensive explanatory framework involving developmental processes that cut across biological, psychological and epistemological perspectives (e.g. Piaget

1972, 1971). It was when he was in his early twenties that Piaget began reading Baldwin. He even labeled his research program after Baldwin's: *genetic epistemology* or *genetic structuralism*, although a more descriptive heading might be: *comprehensive developmental structuralism*.

Piaget's early reflections on the organization of different methods took off from Comte's famous classification of the sciences. However, where Comte saw a strict hierarchy of relationships between the sciences, with mathematics at the bottom, physics in the middle, and sociology at the top, Piaget saw a 'circle of sciences' bound together via symbiotic relations. Physics is not foundationless; to ensure quality control it must engage in epistemological reflections of a logical-mathematical type. Epistemology in turn requires psychology and sociology to remain grounded and these must be in dialogue with biology. And of course, biology shades into physics, which as already noted, is not foundationless. And so the circle of sciences closes back in on itself. This may appear like a vicious circle, but Piaget construes it as a spiral, with the different sciences progressing in concert and collaboration. This basic view would serve Piaget for the rest of his career. But as we will see below, what began as a speculative endeavor would end up as a methodologically sophisticated stance about the nature of interdisciplinarity, grounded in a synoptic view of the intellectual landscape. For now we should note the systematic place he gave to normative considerations (i.e., epistemology) and the intimate relations between those considerations and psychology, and in turn between psychology and biology.

Alongside these reflections about methods Piaget also began to sketch an ambitious explanatory framework targeting ubiquitous evolutionary processes common to both biological life and the life of the mind. With reference to Bergson and Aristotle, the young Piaget laid out a proposal for a science of 'forms' that would traffic in extremely general models of self-organization and development. Roughly, this would be a science offering explanations predicated upon the continuity of life and mind and capable of explaining the forms of intellectual development in terms analogous to the forms of biological evolution. Even at this early juncture Piaget identified equilibration as a process fit to this task. Biological life and evolution are governed by a tendency towards equilibration between organism and environment. This same tendency characterizes the life of the mind as it develops toward an equilibration between subject and object. Thus models of equilibration processes should have great explanatory power, cutting across biological, psychological, sociological, and epistemological perspectives.

It is no secret that equilibration processes maintained a central place in Piaget's explanations of cognitive development. What is less well known is just how much explanatory power he attributed to this concept. In fact, he never really relinquished the bold hypotheses of his youth. He always maintained that certain very general explanatory constructs could be used to explain the evolution of biological organisms and the development of intelligence at all levels. However, what began as a set of metaphysical beliefs about the continuity of life and mind and the directionality of evolution itself would end up as a grounded metatheoretical stance informed by a variety of interdisciplinary endeavors. As explored below, these transdisciplinary metatheoretical constructs exemplify Baldwin's highest level of *theoretical intuition*, and, like Peirce's philosophical architectonics, they serve a discourse-regulative function.

Before going on to discuss Piaget's mature views a few things should be noted about the musings of his youth, which centered on creating a new discourse capable of positioning human values and norms in the natural world. In particular, Piaget was looking to resolve a crisis of faith that left him torn between the knowledge endorsed by scientific worldviews and the strong ethical convictions that are the fruits of religious beliefs. His solution was a complex view of evolution in which human cognition and civilization could be understood as the creative and autonomous extensions of universal developmental processes. According to such a view we can in some ways identify the ideals we strive for, be they truth or justice, with the trajectory of evolution in general.

But Piaget's vision was as far from a crude teleology as it was from reductionism. As his principled classification of methods makes clear, he was careful to differentiate the natural from the normative, even while he posited their continuity. This differentiation entails, strictly speaking, that questions concerning normative issues (such as those in epistemology and in some psychology) cannot be addressed by methods devised for explaining and describing natural phenomena, and vice versa. He was indeed looking for a single comprehensive discourse (his proposed "science of forms") but he was not looking to expand biological categories beyond their proper range of application or to bring mental and normative categories to bear in explaining things best explained by the natural sciences. Thus he was looking for a kind of *tertium quid* (Smith, 2002), a kind of third discourse capable of transcending but including the differentiation of the mental and the physical and the natural and the normative. This ambition played out in his mature views in terms of a comprehensive developmental structuralism, which was a radically interdisciplinary endeavor.

In the late 1960s Piaget was involved with UNESCO's ambitious efforts to characterize the nature and status of interdisciplinary endeavors worldwide. Out of these efforts he produced a trio of slim volumes (Piaget 1970a, 1970b, 1970c). In my mind this work represents his most concerted attempt at elaborating the epistemological structure of interdisciplinary knowledge production. And in these three books we find the 'circle of sciences' he elaborated in his youth reconstructed and justified in relation to a wide variety of considerations. In effect he offers a series of complex reflections, both sociological and philosophical, on what different methods and approaches have to offer, on their points of convergence, and their contrasts.

In particular he lays out principled arguments about important and fundamental similarities between explanatory models from very different disciplines (e.g., dynamical systems modeling), while at the same time drawing clear distinctions between certain broad knowledge domains (e.g., the human sciences and the natural sciences). This is the same tension that characterized the speculations of Piaget's youth. Key differentiations between distinct domains and methods are subsumed within a broader vision of unity. This unity is conceived in terms of certain universal developmental processes, which unfold differentially across distinct domains, from the biological to the psychological and epistemological.

Unfortunately, the framework Piaget lays out in these three books is difficult to grasp. His writing is always more evocative than it is explicative. So I offer one reading and do not claim to have crafted a definitive exegesis. At a very general level, Piaget makes distinctions between three broad approaches: Biology, the Human Sciences, and Philosophy. These are rough divisions that refer to deep epistemological issues that Piaget struggles to make clear, and they reflect the basic categories outlined by Peirce and Baldwin. In establishing these metatheoretical distinctions (and their discourse-regulative function) he appeals to philosophical debates surrounding certain primordial epistemic (and methodological) differentiations: understanding vs. explanation (1970c); natural sciences vs. human sciences (1970c, p. 60); descriptions vs. prescriptions (1970a, p. 53); causality vs. entailment (1970b, p. 18). Broadly speaking he was characterizing the difference between the *natural* and the *normative*.

Both the natural and the normative are the general categories that must be subsumed by a truly comprehensive developmental structuralism. Thus, echoing his early desire for a 'science of forms' common to life and mind, Piaget suggests that there are dynamic developmental processes that cut across both categories. Where he brings his own work on the dynamic development of structures of intelligence into view alongside work concerning processes of self-organization in biology we begin to see the contours of his proposed framework. Appealing to Waddington and von Bertalanffy, Piaget notes the wide applicability of models that represent structured and self-regulating wholes. Dynamic systems models in biology offer formalized structural accounts of the regulations and interactions between organisms and environments. These models are remarkably analogous to the models Piaget produced to explain processes of intellectual development. However, and this is a crucial point that is often overlooked, these types of models are analogous, not identical.

Piaget uses a nuanced account to differentiate dynamic systems models suitable for biological science from dynamic systems models suitable of use in studying human cognition and society. The point is that when we model cognitive processes we must often appeal to explicitly followed and interpreted rules, values, and signs, whereas when we model biological processes we can make no such appeals. It is useful to see this difference in terms of the status and role of norms in behavior and cognition. Rules, values, and signs can be appealed to in the explanation of norm-laden behaviors and cognition because they are reflected upon as such by the organism being studied. When we observe a child making a judgment we have before us a normative fact. The child follows a rule that is deemed valuable and that will eventually be amenable to explicit statement, revision, and reflection. As Piaget explains:

> The term "normative facts" has been happily introduced in to the general vocabulary ... to describe that which constitutes a norm for the subject and, at the same time, an object of analysis for the observer engaged in studying both the behavior of the subject and the norms he recognizes.... [For

example] normative facts are studied in genetic psychology when the question is to discover how subjects who were originally insensitive to certain logical norms come to regard them as essential through a process depending partly on their life in the community and partly on the internal structure of the action envisaged.

(Piaget, 1970c, pp. 8–9)

This distinction between normative facts and natural facts is crucial. Biological structures and functions are not like the 'normative facts' that confront us when we study human cognition and behavior. When we study the regularities of a paramecium's reaction to its environment we have before us a natural fact. The structural, functional, and informational antecedence of the paramecium's behavior are not understood or reflected upon by the paramecium itself. Natural facts are those that can be understood irrespective of the intensions and consciousness of the thing being studied. This distinction between normative facts and natural facts relates back to the primordial epistemic (and methodological) differentiations noted above: e.g., natural sciences vs. human sciences; causality vs. entailment.

Piaget's big point is that normative facts (e.g., acts of judgment), natural facts (e.g., regularities of reaction), and everything in between are best explained in terms of dynamic self-regulating processes that maintain wholeness, facilitate emergence, and tend toward equilibration. Thus, as noted above, the comprehensive developmental structuralism Piaget has in mind would be composed of dynamic and developmental explanatory constructs that generate isomorphic theoretical models in the physical, biological, and human sciences. Equilibration is thus an explanatory construct that ties the development of human cognition and civilization to the evolution of life itself; what catalyzed it catalyzes us. And so the radical hypothesis of Piaget's youth looms large in his mature vision.

And yet Piaget emphasizes the "isomorphism" – not identity – between models of equilibration across the different domains. He tempers his unifying thrust with cautions about both reductionism, i.e., "the tendency which consists of suppressing the original characteristics of the higher order and reducing them ... to the processes of the lower orders" (Piaget, 1971a, p. 39), and projection, i.e., "the tendency which leads people to project onto the phenomena of inferior orders the characteristics of phenomena of the higher orders" (p. 38). Thus, despite instances where he offers an ontology of process and development, he never entirely neglects the reflective engagement with methodological perspectives that framed the categorical distinctions traced above.

In the end, I read his claims about the isomorphism of models across the natural and the normative as attempts to suggest the existence of certain ubiquitous evolutionary processes, ones best thought of as universal 'forms' governing the development of the entire universe. But he never exactly puts his metaphysical cards on the table. Although I think he does prophesize a single unified discourse fundamentally geared into these primordial developmental processes (Piaget, 1971d). One gets the impression that Piaget takes the variety of structuralisms he inventories in his interdisciplinary reflections as harbingers of some single structuralism that would disclose the formal structure of all things. We have seen that Piaget's vision of a comprehensive developmental structuralism remained remarkably consistent over the course of his career. As it was progressively refined its most general contours become clear.

Piaget argued that developmental processes are ubiquitous (from mind and life, to matter and energy), so that they must be categorized in terms of the different ways in which they can be understood. The *natural* and the *normative* signify a set of epistemologically deep-seated distinctions that can be used to categorize different types of methodological perspectives. Piaget suggested we might hope for the emergence of a discourse geared into the primordial developmental processes that cut across these different perspectives. Paralleling the possibility of a unified discourse explaining all developmental processes, he also suggested we pursue a certain type of interdisciplinarity. Piaget's comprehensive metatheoretical discourse-regulative constructs serve as meta-norms, which can guide us toward the construction of more adequate interdisciplinary research programs. The key to this claim is the insight that we must find some way to systematically deal with normative issues in human development (Smith & Voneche, 2006; Wilber, 1999; Habermas 1990, 1984, 1987a).

The lesson here is less about Piaget's speculative claims and more about his indefatigable desire to find a place for the normative in nature. There are a variety of metatheoretical orientations that lean heavily on dynamic systems models and emphasize the primacy of context and dynamism over mechanistic forms of reductionism (Overton, 2007; Lazlo, 1972; Mareschal *et al.*, 2007). These are great; but they don't deal with the normative.

Understanding an obligation (either epistemic or ethical) entails accounting for both its (normative) necessity and its (natural; e.g., reliable) efficacy and impact. The latter involves causal regularities of the human brain and accompanying socialization, but the former involves concerns about the validity of the obligation itself. Irrational obligations cannot be necessary despite whatever rhetorical efficacy and impact might result from their social currency, while rational obligations are necessary and binding despite social pressure to the contrary.

If the only categories we have are the objective ones offered by systems theory, how do we make distinctions between what *is* and what *ought* to be? The goal of equilibration between organism and environment must itself be justified when discussing human development in cultural and social contexts. Post-conventional moral identities are worthy of pursuit but not because they bring persons into an equilibrium with surrounding cultural expectations. As Habermas (1987a) has made clear, the major liability of dynamic systems approaches in the human sciences is their inability to deal with the full complexity of normative issues. And like Piaget, he suggests that this inability is built into the basic methodological perspectives on which they rely.

Habermas' critical and comprehensive developmental structuralism

> [Postmodern capitalistic social structures] have evidently found some func-
> tional equivalent for ideology formation. In place of the positive task of meet-
> ing certain needs for self-interpretation by ideological means, we have the
> negative task of preventing holistic self-interpretations from coming into
> existence.... *Everyday consciousness* is robbed of its power to synthesize; it
> becomes *fragmented*.... The attempts at an *Aufhebung* of philosophy and art
> were rebellions against structures that subordinated everyday consciousness to
> the standards of exclusive expert cultures developing according to their own
> logics.... Everyday consciousness sees itself thrown back on traditions whose
> claims to validity have already been suspended; where it does escape the spell
> of traditionalism, it is hopelessly splintered. In place of "false consciousness"
> we today have a "fragmented consciousness" that blocks enlightenment.
>
> *(Habermas, 1987a, p. 355)*

Growing up reading American mass-produced copies of John Dewey in post-war
Germany while learning of government-sanctioned genocide in real time over the
radio, Habermas was predisposed to being concerned about the relations between
evolutionary thought and the normative foundations of democracy. Habermas wrote
his dissertation on Schelling and the problem of free will, and through a friendship
with the great Kabbalistic scholar Gershom Scholem, he undertook extensive considerations of the Lurianic theological principles of *tsim-tsum* and *tikkun*.[11] Again the
echoes of Jakob Böhme can be heard in this normative view of cosmic evolution
that has long been the esoteric core of Marxist theories about cultural evolution
(Kołakowski, 1978). Like Piaget, mystical themes stay mostly dormant in Habermas'
social-philosophy. However, in his most recent work, Habermas has returned to
questions about free will, evolution, and the role of faith and religious practice in
private life and the public sphere (Habermas, 2008).

Habermas' project has always been metatheoretical, aiming for an interdisciplinary problem-focused approach for understanding human normativity – positioning human agency as a unique factor in natural and social systems. Beginning
with *On the Logic of the Social Sciences* (1988), Habermas engages in a philosophical
critique of existing research projects in the social sciences and looks toward a synthesis between *causal-natural* and *hermeneutic-normative* methods of understanding
human agency. Deepening this interdisciplinary metatheory of society, *Knowledge
and Human Interests* (Habermas, 1971) has the same goal of positioning humanity in
both the nature of the biosphere and the "second nature" of social systems created
and maintained by humans. A metatheoretical set of "anthropologically deep seated
human interests" are taken directly from Peirce's philosophy of science, Dilthey's
hermeneutics, and Freud's psychoanalysis. These distinct metatheoretical orientations – natural science of control and prediction (Peirce); historical understanding

of self-clarification and intergenerational transmission (Dilthey); normative discourse of diagnostic self-objectification and healing (Freud) – these basic knowledge constitutive interests are potentially complementary and mutually supportive. They are each true but partial – no one metatheoretical orientation covers all basic human interests. This means that if one is taken out of portion (as the sciences of control and prediction have been in the post-industrial West) then a distortion of culture and the intergenerational transmission of the lifeworld results. As a project in 'methodological self-clarification,' this early period is an underlaboring for the metatheoretical framework that emerges in Habermas' later writings, which provides a critical theory of our current historical moment.

Legitimation Crisis (1973) begins Habermas' use of developmental structuralist models, including Luhmann's dynamic systems models of society and Piaget's developmental epistemology. The goal in this first work of the middle period is to recast a Marxist theory of cultural evolution in terms of modern system dynamics and advances in the social sciences. The central concepts are offered as a discourse-regulative intervention, especially the distinction between *system* and *lifeworld* as metatheoretical orientations to understanding society. The lifeworld is about the 'inside' of human society, it is the culture as it is experienced, as replete with norms, values, selves, and linguistically mediated mutual understandings. The system is different, it is functional-strategic and does not require participation in shared norms and values, it requires only that a limited range of rules be followed in order to simplify relationships along technical lines. Examples of this are markets, as well as bureaucratic hierarchies in the military or corporation. The system runs on proxies of consent (money, bureaucratic power); the lifeworld runs on actual consent, from shared ideals guiding communicative action, to simple mutual agreement about the meaning of words or the basic requirements of logic that are a presupposition even of disagreement (Cooke, 1997).

The system–lifeworld distinction is at the heart of Habermas' middle period, which includes his two-volume master work, *The Theory of Communicative Action* (1984, 1987a). It is in this work that the full normative thrust of Habermas' metatheoretical project is revealed as a system of transdisciplinary investigations into the very nature of human communication – especially non-institutionalized forms of legitimate power and communicative action. The result is a comprehensive developmental structuralism focusing on a set of primordial communicative conventions and presupposition of discourse, such as the primordially perspectival parts of speech: I/We/It; and the distinction between theoretical-instrumental reason and practical-communicative reason. These are all used as broad orienting metatheoretical constructs in a discourse-regulative reconstruction of the emergence and continued evolution of modern and postmodern socio-cultural totalities.

Similar to Piaget's models, which Habermas uses throughout this middle period, metatheory becomes a dynamic structural and developmental approach that differentiates and clarifies the normative aspects of human behavior, thought, and agency. Like Peirce, Habermas also builds a principled framework of basic philosophical categories that can be used as a kind of general semiotics (or what Habermas calls a formal-pragmatics of communication).[12] This is a metatheoretical system analytically equipped for *overseeing, explicating,* and *evaluating* different kinds of beliefs at multiple levels – from propositions, to arguments, to discourses. But there is more to Habermas' metatheoretical *modus operandi* than this highly formal metatheory of human communicative action. The system of categories he uses enables a critique of existing conditions. *Between Facts and Norms* (1996) applies the metatheoretical constructs from Habermas' theory of communicative action to the state of legal theory and the state of the normative discourses that continue to work with the principles of and practices of democracy. One central mechanism by which the "system colonizes the lifeworld" is through intensive processes of legal bureaucratization that re-regulate forms of social life traditionally regulated through lifeworld consensus-based value-intensive mechanisms. From health care to education, the expansion of human service industries in post-industrial society has lead to regulatory agencies that increasingly translate the problems of the lifeworld into the vocabulary of systems. Generally, instead of pursuing the institutionalization of forms of political discourse free from domination that might legitimately guide our joint future, postmodern social systems are regulated by the imperatives of system maintenance and efficiency.

In his most recent work Habermas further defends and clarifies human normativity, using metatheoretical constructs to regulate and guide the scope of validity of different disciplines. As the human sciences expand their reach, they make claim to more and more of the lifeworld's so-called 'folk-psychology.' Habermas (2003, 2007) has suggested that in many cultural groups models from the human sciences have supplanted traditional (religious) languages of self-understanding. Unlike models in the physical sciences, which affect the lifeworld eventually mainly in the form of technological innovation, the human sciences affect the lifeworld directly by shaping the action-orienting self-understandings of individuals. Habermas argues that those who produce knowledge in these fields should consider the fact that the scientific languages they create become available to function as resources for identity construction. For example, radically counterintuitive, fragmented, and reductionist scientific accounts are *irresponsible* (not just wrong) in so far as the likelihood of their being adopted as self-descriptors is high and the appropriateness of their serving this function is low. This is not an argument against bold hypothesis generation and materialist research programs in the human sciences, nor is it an argument against increasing the scientific understanding of human beings. It is an argument against a form of scientism that aims to systematically contradict deep-seated aspects of the self-understanding of the species. Irresponsible scientific generalizations run the risk of undermining the language games enabling autonomous ethical agency and human dignity (Habermas, 2007). The concerns Habermas expresses have to do with the premature conclusions and promissory notes of a burgeoning but still immature neuroscience. This is a field that has been remarkably attractive to the popular media. It is affecting legal discourse and practice, education, and marketing, while at the same time generally shaping the way large numbers of people understand their behaviors and relationships (Kagan, 2009; Stein, della Chiesa, Hinton, & Fischer, 2011).

Habermas clarifies the role of metatheory as an adjudicator both between different sciences and between the sciences in general and the complex discourse of the lifeworld. This orientation toward crafting a reconciliation between the scientific disciplines and between these disciplines and the lifeworld is a signature of Habermas' philosophical metatheory. The idea is most clearly stated in an essay from his middle period (that happens to make extended references to Kant, Piaget, and Peirce):

> The compartmentalization [of knowledge] constituting as it does a hallmark of modernity … poses problems. First how can reason, once it has been thus sundered, go on being a unity on the level of culture. And second, how can expert cultures, which are being pushed more and more to the level of rarefied, esoteric forms, be made to stay in touch with everyday communication…. Reaching understanding in the lifeworld requires a cultural tradition that ranges across *the whole spectrum*, not just the fruits of science and technology. As far as philosophy is concerned, it might do well to refurbish its link with the totality by taking on the role of interpreter on behalf of the lifeworld. It might then be able to help set in motion the interplay between the cognitive-instrumental, moral-practical, and aesthetic-expressive dimensions that have come to a standstill today like a tangled mobile.
>
> *(Habermas, 1990, pp. 17–19)*

These integrative and reconciliatory tasks look a lot like the tasks characterizing Baldwin's highest levels of human development, which he thought were populated by integrative constructs of the aesthetic and theoretical imagination. Like Peirce and Piaget, Habermas executes this ambitious project by utilizing a variety of philosophical methods – methods Baldwin would claim exemplify the exercise of aesthetic imagination, or theoretical intuition, and which Habermas self-consciously recognizes as *post-formal thought*. Habermas (1990, p. 8) has his metatheory eat its own tail as he positions the cognitive operations necessary to produce it in terms of Piaget's theory of cognitive development. With post-formal operations comes the possibility of taking on the metatheoretical task of regulating the evolution of whole discourses and large swaths of culture – of creating a new language and framework with which to *norm the norms* of discourse-specific practices. Metatheory is both metanarrative (in translating between the sciences and the public sphere) and metacritique (in adjudicating the epistemic position of the various scientific disciplines). This tradition of normative metatheory was brought into the twenty-first century by a variety of figures, of whom Ken Wilber and Roy Bhaskar are among the most important and influential.

Wilber, Bhaskar, and the shape of contemporary metatheories[13]

> These are *orienting generalizations*: they show us, with a great deal of agreement, where the important forests are located, even if we can't agree on how many trees they contain…. If we take these types of largely-agreed-upon

orienting generalizations from the various branches of knowledge (from physics to biology to psychology to theology), and if we string these orienting generalizations together, we will arrive at some astonishing and often profound conclusions, conclusions that, as extraordinary as they might be, nonetheless embody nothing more than our already agreed upon knowledge. The beads of knowledge are already accepted: it is only necessary to provide the thread to string them together into a necklace … working with broad orienting generalizations … delivers up a broad orienting map of the place of men and women in the Universe, Life and Spirit, the details of which we can all fill in as we like.

(Wilber, 1995, p. 5)

At the outset I raised the possibility of a species-wide identity crisis that would render humanity incomprehensible to itself. This is one way of recasting the idea – handed down from Marx and Dewey, through Habermas, to Wilber – that non-synchronic patterns in socio-cultural development have resulted in a situation where our techno-scientific capabilities far outstrip our ethico-political visions and organizations. Just as unprecedented scientific advances expand the reach and efficacy of our communication and biomedical technologies, the fields tasked with expressing an understanding of what humanity is have been rendered speechless by their own confusions. The proliferation of self-descriptions provided by contemporary biologically oriented human sciences offer a fragmented and reductionistic picture, while the humanities and social sciences, underfunded and undervalued, pursue opportunistic and conservative research agendas (Kagan, 2009). In the same historical moment we find ourselves with the knowledge and power to reliably and strategically affect the central nervous system as a means for canalizing behavioral conformity, our *normative discourses* (the normative sciences, as Peirce would call them) are in disarray — these are the discourses that address how things *ought* to be with society and its discursive institutions. In the coming decades, as the global information explosion continues and networks of communicational connectivity encircle the Earth, we will be using them to debate the meaning of our humanity – striving to articulate a set of global values that might allow us to understand ourselves as the inhabitants of a globalized techno-economic and communications infrastructure. The academy – the so-called 'multiversity' – is not built to provide humanity with a coherent picture of itself. The desperate trumpeting of interdisciplinary in colleges and research labs is a testament to this (Menand, 2010).

This twenty-first-century academy demands a new kind of metatheoretical project. Here I explore Wilber (1995, 1999, 2006) and Bhaskar (1986, 1993), who offer complementary comprehensive philosophical metatheories. That they are together in many ways the focus of this volume is not surprising. I'd argue their appeal is in part because the centerpieces of their theories look like the centerpieces of the metatheoretical tradition I've just reconstructed. Across all these thinkers there is a shared set of shared philosophical commitments, constructs, and methods, including: reconstructive/transcendental arguments; social science conceived as an axiology of freedom; ontological emergence, change, and evolution; stratified selves/compound individuals; differentiated and laminated social realities; transformational bio-psycho-social models of human agency; and the immanent possibility of geo-historical evolutionary 'progress' toward a eudaimonistic society.

As has been noted elsewhere (Esbjörn-Hargens, 2010; this volume) there are two important metatheoretical constructs that Wilber and Bhaskar's systems share: a fourfold model of social reality and a transformational bio-psycho-socio-cultural model of human action. Both ideas are clearly represented by Wilber's four quadrants and Bhaskar's four-planer social cube. These models represent human social reality, and thus the structure of human action, as a 'four-planer' or 'four-quadrant' autopoietic dynamic. That is, according to these models, social reality consists of at least an individual, in a cultural and social system that is reproducing itself in relation to natural realities, both those internal to the social reality (individual psycho-biology) and those that are external (the biosphere). Put differently, both models are attempts to represent the full complexity of the social realities addressed by the human sciences, which must account for at least the interplay of: individual agency and psychology; cultural/hermeneutic reproduction and transmission; social-systems and institutional structures; and the natural realities of the body and biosphere. Some critical realists have argued that Wilber's quadrants are prone to reification (Cartesian planes, even); but this is an inaccurate exegesis of Wilber's writings. As Hans Despain (2013) argues, as well as others more familiar with Wilber's work (Esbjörn-Hargens, 2010), the quadrants are a heuristic and they point to the same dynamic 'stratified ontology' represented by Bhaskar's four-planer social being/transactional model of human agency. A fully articulated account of the confluences and contrasts between the two systems would include (among other things) levels of development (both individual and socio-cultural), psychological frameworks for transcendence, spirituality, and metaReality, as well as commitments to universally efficacious evolutionary processes, from the individual to the geo-historical and cosmic.

However, the most important difference between these two metatheories is their difference of emphasis concerning the priority of metacritique and metanarrative. Hans Despain (2013: p.9) writes (augmented slightly to fit the terms used here):

> Critical realism [CR], dialectical critical realism [DCR] and the philosophy of metareality [PMR; e.g., Bhaskar's various theories] do not constitute a "metatheory" in the sense that integral theory does. Whereas integral theory is a quintessential metatheory as a [metanarrative] synthesis (by mainly one thinker in Ken Wilber) of psychology, sociology, anthropology, religion, physics, ecology, etc., CR, DCR, and PMR are ontological orientations for science, social science and emancipatory projects. I resist strongly the idea that CR, DCR, and PMR constitute a metatheoretical [metanarrative]. Rather it is better understood as an ontological orientation with contingent potential to manifest a metatheoretical [metanarrative].… Integral theory is metatheory [as metanarrative]. Dialectical critical realism is [metatheory] as metacritique.

Indeed, Bhaskar offers an evolving framework of post-analytical work in the philosophy of science that argues against reductionist ontologies and articulates alternate non-reductive ontologies that allow for depth psychology, human agency, self-consciousness, and self-transformative praxis. This is his project, in the tradition of Kant, Peirce, and Habermas: to take the tools of mainstream academic philosophy and use them to create a philosophical ontology that explains and clarifies the normative aspects of human reason and agency (and for there to be things like emergence, non-linear causality, and evolution in the natural world). Bhaskar is thus among the meta-critics and meta-methodologists, like Edwards (2009) and Esbjörn-Hargens (2010), who argue for and clarify the methodological and ontological underpinnings of integrative metanarratives – e.g., they lay the groundwork for richly articulated meta-psychologies and meta-sociologies – the most provocative of which is Wilber's integral theory.

Wilber's metatheory evolved across several iterations as an elaborate integration of existing theories in the social, biological, and physical sciences. Beginning in psychology and transpersonal psychology, Wilber's (1977) concept of a "spectrum of consciousness" served a discourse-regulative metatheoretical function in facilitating the integration a wide variety of systems in developmental psychology, both East and West. Expanding the scope of the integrative metatheory to include sociology and anthropology (Wilber, 1981, 1983), a metanarrative began to emerge that would characterize humanity in terms of evolutionary processes, both individual human development as well as the dynamics of socio-cultural evolution. Pulling from Habermas and Piaget, as well as the dynamical and autopoietic factions of cognitive science and social theory, Wilber (1999) would eventually construct a comprehensive metatheory of developmental psychology, housing a related set of sub-theories of the self, socialization, spirituality, meditative states, personality types, and developmental lines. This system of psychology is nested in a larger "theory of everything" (Wilber, 1995, 2006) – the integral model – consisting of a family of sub-theories, including the aforementioned system of categories known as the four quadrants; a set of 20 basic principles governing the evolution of dynamical systems throughout the natural, biological, social, and psychological worlds; and a variety of other metatheoretical normative provocations, chiding humanity's ability to understand itself as the normative edge of an evolving Kosmos.

But focused as it is on building a "map of human potential" and clarifying "the farther reaches of human nature," integral theory has "lacked a sustained critique of the development of capitalism, the capital-labor nexus, finance-debtor relations, and contemporary master-slave-type-relations generally" (Despain, 2013). Which is to say that the metanarrative offered by Wilber has not been welded in the service of sustained socio-political metacritique. The materials for such a critique are in Wilber's work, they just have not been used to this end. This is perhaps the most promising avenue for the future integrations of these two metatheories. Bhaskar's metacritique provides materials and methods for considering the injustice and irrationality of existing social formations, especially capitalistic market cultures. This critique suggests that in many contemporary social worlds the "stratified self" – the person – is disfigured and de-agentified from having developed in the context of oppressive relationships. Whereas Bhaskar provides tools for identifying processes of ideology formation in the social totality, Wilber gives tools for diagnosing and treating the deformations of personality that result. The deterioration of subjectivity that results from growing up under the oligopolistic neo-liberal domination of the global order cannot be understood without a complex psycho-social framework. Metatheoretically guided transformative practice informed by an integral theory of human development and a dialectal critical realist theory of social totalities compels us toward creating forms of social life that provide for the full development of non-alienated and autonomous individuals. This suggests the extension of deliberative democratic decision-making beyond representative government and into the entire economy – the democratization of workplaces and democratization of production and investment – and this is to be done in the interest of liberating the fullness of human potential.

Conclusion: the shape of metatheories to come

> As soil is to an agricultural society, consciousness is to ours. Some groups seek to mine it like coal, and they tend to create the smog in the noosphere that now surrounds the planet Earth with bad movies and worse TV. Other groups seek to parasitize it and feed off the sex and violence as Homeric gods hovering over the odors of burnt sacrifice. And a few techno-mystic souls imagine that some quantum shift is at hand … as we evolve out of biology and into technology. We probably won't have to wait long to find out. The new electronic media have sped things up and made the old normalcy of objective reality nonviable. They have pushed us into an "up or out" scenario in which we either shift upward to a new culture of higher spirituality, turning our electronic technologies into new cathedrals of light, or slide downward into darkness and an abyss of cultural entropy, fighting it out in a final war of all against all. As H. G. Wells warned during the beginning of this period of Planetization: "The future is a race between catastrophe and education."
>
> *(Thompson, 2009, pp. 29–30)*

In a set of publications I have addressed issues of quality control at the level of interdisciplinary knowledge production and education, and suggested that metatheoretical constructs play a necessary role in epistemologically responsible approaches to interdisciplinarity (Stein, 2007; Stein, Connell, & Gardner, 2008). Specifically, I suggested that metatheoretical constructs, such as the four quadrants (Wilber, 1995), the ideal speech situation (Habermas, 1998), and the classic syncategorematic categories (Peirce, 1984), play an important function in both disciplinary and interdisciplinary discourse. This function can be characterized variously, as the setting of quality-control parameters, or the clarification of our epistemic and ethical responsibilities. Metatheoretical constructs can be built to oversee, regulate, and direct disciplinary and interdisciplinary knowledge production. Metatheory, as I see it, serves an important normative function on the contemporary academic scene.

But the contemporary relevance of transforming knowledge production processes goes beyond the academy. Problem-focused interdisciplinary think tanks are beginning to play an increasingly important role in an emerging global network of change-oriented institutions. While some – such as the Club of Rome and branches of the OECD – have been around since the 1970s, the past decade has seen a proliferation of action-oriented institutes that span traditional disciplinary boundaries for the sake of producing usable knowledge about pressing global problems. The State of the World Forum, Integral Institute, Center for Integral Wisdom, and the Future of Humanity Institute at Oxford are four examples out of literally dozens. The United States Federal Government and the United Nations continually create specific problem-focused interdisciplinary initiatives, and readily draw from those already producing usable knowledge in the public sphere. Above I have expressed what I think the role of metatheory is in this constellation of conditions, in the academy and beyond. It is to weave a coherent overarching set of normative constructs, organizing and regulating the specialized discourses in view, with an eye to comprehensiveness, and a voice resonant with the lifeworld.

As above, this view of metatheory is controversial. But the idea here is not to displace or replace the self-understanding of metatheorists who take themselves as scientists pursuing descriptive projects with objective methods. Rather, the intention is to remind big-picture thinkers that this kind of scientific self-understanding is not the only option. Putting arguments about the crypto-normativism of ostensibly descriptive projects aside (Habermas, 1987b), I claim only that we metatheorists might want to think differently about what we do. I sketched the contours of a tradition that weds the normative function of metatheory to ideas about the *autonomy* and *self-directedness – the normative nature* of human cultural evolution. I suggested that metatheorists are those concerned about the trajectory of knowledge production processes and reflective cultural practices. According to this view metatheorists build specific kinds of high-level constructs that have a normative thrust. Their interventions aim at affecting the proprieties of our discursive practices.

Hand-wringing about the liabilities accompanying these kinds of explicitly normative projects is to be expected. While performative contradictions plague arguments against normative endeavors – prescribing the wholesale rejection of prescriptions – there are legitimate worries worth attending to. Worries about the institutionalization of centralized discursive authorities are warranted, as are concerns about the nefarious political affordances of *evolutionary ideologies* (Farber, 1998). Yet these are not necessary accoutrements to the vision of metatheory outlined above.

Every key player in my account – Kant, Emerson, Baldwin, Peirce, Piaget, Habermas, Wilber, and Bhaskar – is each a stanch, articulate, and influential proponent of the free and open discursive practices that characterize the best scientific communities and democratic public spheres. Against the backdrop these thinkers provide, the criticism that normative metatheoretical endeavors would be coercive enterprises, aimed at stifling discourse, innovation, and free inquiry is misguided. The idea that metatheorists *oversee* and *regulate* various discursive practices does not entail that metatheorists are *overseers*. Rather they are just the most reflective and visionary *participants* in knowledge production processes, arguing about preferable or regrettable trajectories for sets of disciplines, suggesting syntheses, but wielding nothing other than the unforced force of the better argument. I support the institutionalization of metatheoretically guided knowledge production because the exercise of normative authority in these contexts is *not* merely a matter of power-broking. Sweeping arguments to the contrary betray a lack of nuance about what normative authority looks like and reflect the sorry state of our normative discourses more generally.

As the quotation beginning this concluding section suggests, we inhabitants of the post-industrial West share a lifeworld characterized by the devaluation of overarching and totalizing ideologies (also see Bell, 2000). And we still associate the very idea of normative authority with the dark legacy of politically operationalized all-encompassing worldviews. The story told above about the fractioning (and factioning) of the modern research university is but one sub-plot in a larger narrative about recent transformations in the self-understanding of the species. No doubt, the specter of an evolutionary ideology has loomed at least since Darwin first articulated an objective mechanism governing evolutionary processes. But the slow and persistent emergence of an evolutionary worldview has not counteracted broader tendencies toward a radically polycentric and conflict-ridden cultural environment. Even putting aside its rejection by traditionalists preferring non-scientific accounts, evolution is an ambiguous and contested concept, especially with regards to its broader ethico-political implications (Wilber, 1995; Wilson, 1975). The suggestions I offer here assume that heterogeneity and pluralism will continue to characterize cultural evolution. Exercising the normative function of metatheory does not entail the homogenization of cultural practices and discursive institutions in the name of evolutionary progress. Placing metatheory in an evolutionary context does not entail taking on the worst baggage from over a century's worth of attempts at resuscitating ideology in evolutionary garb (Farber, 1998).

Shadow boxing aside, the goal of this chapter has been to *remember* and *express* – to reconstruct a thread in the history of metatheory with the hope of affecting the shape of metatheories to come. More work remains to be done filling out the rest of this history and, more importantly, building metatheories that fit the specifications thus reconstructed. I have already begun this constructive metatheoretical work in a series of publications that address the use of *metrics* in contexts where human lives are under scrutiny, from the diagnostic categories that structure the delivery of psychopharmacological interventions to the standardized testing infrastructures that frame educational opportunity (Stein, Dawson, & Fischer, 2010; Stein, della Chiesa, Hinton, & Fischer 2011; Stein & Hiekkinen, 2009). Overseeing complex multidisciplinary areas of concern, these interventions involve the construction of metatheoretical constructs that serve as normative parameters. I argue the merits of setting a new trajectory for the various discursive practices involved with the institutionalized measurement of human functioning, suggesting directions more comprehensive, responsible, and responsive to the singularity and vulnerability of individuals. Moreover, as others have shown (Jaques, 1976; Nussbaum, 2006; Sen,

1999), the possibilities of cultural evolution and justice in the coming decades hinge on the kinds of *metrics* we choose to build and use when assessing the properties of human lives that bear on political and economic decision-making. Our systems of measurement determine who we think we are and what we do to each other. Consider how SAT scores and GDP reports affect the self-perceptions of individuals and nations respectively, how partial they are as indices, and how drastically they alter the distribution of resources. But these considerations bring us full circle, back to the idea that we are responsible for the creation of the metatheoretical languages we would use to re-describe and re-create ourselves.

Notes

1   Parts of this chapter were previously published as: Z. Stein (2010). On the normative function of metatheoretical endeavors. *Integral Review*, 6(3), 5–22; The ideas in the section on Piaget originated in: Z. Stein (2008). On the possibilities of a comprehensive developmental structuralism: The natural, the normal, and the normative. Paper presented at the Annual Meeting of the Jean Piaget Society. Quebec City, Canada.
2   It may be that I am merely reconstructing part of the lineage of a certain *type* of metatheory. Perhaps the type of metatheory I am reconstructing here is better understood as a species of *philosophical* metatheory, which can be set apart from *scientific* metatheory (Ritzer, 1991). Or perhaps it should be called, *integral* metatheory (Edwards, 2007; Esbjörn-Hargens & Zimmerman, 2009; Hamilton, 2008; Lazlo, 2004; McIntosh, 2007; Mascolo & Fischer, in press; Wilber, 1995; 1999). I have no objections to the idea that what follows is merely a reconstruction of a certain *type* of metatheory. It may be that what I have in mind is not even metatheory, but a kind of philosophy. Call it what you will in the long run, I call it metatheory here for rhetorical purposes. I return to this issue in the conclusion.
3   This is not a problem for the metatheorists discussed here. But it is for some self-declared reductive metatheoretical positions, such as eliminative materialism (Churchland); systems theory (Luhmann; Wolfram), and the various bio-centric evolutionary syntheses (Wilson). The breadth of these metatheories results in questions and visions of religious scope and significance, which the authors deal with either awkwardly or dismissively.
4   For the full scope of Kant's ideas concerning socio-cultural evolution, see Fenves, 1991. For Kant's life and the political complexities and editorial compromises surrounding his radical views, see Cassirer, 1981. And for the contemporary relevance of Kant's cosmopolitan political vision, see Habermas, 2006. Finally, for Kant's views on *normativity*, a concept central to his whole philosophy, see Brandom, 2009; Korsgaard, 1996.
5   A footnote is warranted about the fact that both Peirce and Baldwin were dismissed from the academy due to sexual scandals. (Baldwin was caught in a club that also served as a brothel; Peirce got a divorce and married a [very] young French woman.) But a full discussion of the shadows of these men, the mores of Victorian America, and the complex and personal nature of the academic politics involved would take us too far afield (see Brent, 1998; Richards, 1987).
6   For an account of Peirce's life, which had the plot line of a Greek tragedy, see Brent, 1998.
7   For an account of Baldwin's life and work, see Boring, 1929; Richards, 1987; Wozniak, 2001.
8   Yet even Broughton only really pays attention to the first volume of Baldwin's three-volume *magnum opus*.
9   For an account of how profoundly the project affected Baldwin's thought, see Wozniak, 2001.

10 Although see Chapman 1988, pp. 68–73, where Piaget's mature religious views are reconstructed out of a series of topical essays Piaget wrote in the late 1920s, revealing a system of beliefs similar to those espoused in his youth, e.g. "immanentism…. The tendency toward higher forms of organization provides humanity with higher values…. God is identified with *directionality* and our striving to realize the ideal … thus to struggle for the good and the true … is to collaborate with God." See also, pp. 432–437, where Chapman suggests that Piaget's religious views continued to serve as a real source of motivation throughout his life.

11 Consider the fluency and power of Habermas' exegesis of Scholem's exegesis of the great Hasidic Master Isaak Luria: "The question of how evil is possible at all in a world created by God can only be given coherent formulation when we … take it back into the origin of the divine life-process itself. This is what Luria's original idea of the *tsim-tsum* achieves. God, who in the beginning is everything, withdraws into himself … through this initial contraction there arises … a nature [or evolution] of God, a knot of willfulness and a sense of I-ness (egoity). The polar tension between this dark ground in God and His radiating love already determines the ideal process of creation and evolution, which occurs in God's body and thought. [The light of God] which has been poured out and disappeared must be raised up again to its legitimate place or origin. The resurrection of restitution of the original order – the *tikkun* – would finally have reached its goal with the creation of the second … creation [which] emerges from the inner depths of God in and continues in the external history of the world" (Habermas, 2002, p. 143).

12 Habermas (1998) draws the line from his formal pragmatics through Chomsky's Universal Grammar to the various universal, formal, and philosophic/logical grammars articulated by Peirce as part of his General Semiotics.

13 I would like to thank Ken Wilber for a series of e-mail exchanges in March of 2014, which prompted many of the reflections offered here.

References

Abbot, F. (1885). *Scientific theism*. Boston, MA: Little & Brown.

Apel, K. O. (1994). Transcendental semiotics and hypothetical metaphysics of evolution. In E. Mendieta (Ed.), *Karl-Otto Apel: Selected essays* (Vol. 1) (pp. 207–231). Atlantic Highlands, NJ: Humanities Press.

Apel, K. O. (1995). *Charles Sanders Peirce: From pragmatism to pragmaticism*. Atlantic Highlands, NJ: Humanities Press.

Baldwin, J. M. (1895). *Mental development in the child and the race*. New York: Macmillan.

Baldwin, J. M. (1897). *Social and ethical interpretations in mental development*. New York: Macmillan.

Baldwin, J. M. (Ed.). (1905). *Dictionary of philosophy and psychology* (Vols. 1–4). New York: Macmillan.

Baldwin, J. M. (1911). *Thought and things: A study in the development of meaning and thought or genetic logic* (Vols. 1–4). New York: Macmillan.

Baldwin, J. M. (1913). *History of psychology* (Vols. 1–2). London: Watts.

Baldwin, J. M. (1915). *Genetic theory of reality*. New York: J. P. Putnam's Sons Press.

Bell, D. (2000). *The end of ideology*. Cambridge, MA: Harvard University Press.

Bhaskar, R. (1986). *Scientific realism and human emancipation*. New York: Verso.

Bhaskar, R. (1993). *Dialectic: The pulse of freedom*. New York: Verso.

Boring, E. G. (1929). *A history of experimental psychology*. New York: Appleton-Century.

Brandom, R. (2002). *Tales of the mighty dead: Historical essays in the metaphysics of intentionality*. Cambridge, MA: Harvard University Press.

Brandom, R. (2009). *Reason in philosophy: Animating ideas.* Cambridge, MA: Harvard University Press.

Brent, J. (1998). *Charles Sanders Peirce: A life.* Bloomington: Indiana University Press.

Broughton, J. M., & Freeman-Moir, D. J. (Eds.). (1982). *The cognitive developmental psychology of James Mark Baldwin.* Norwood, NJ: ABLEX Press.

Campbell, D. T. (1987). Evolutionary epistemology. In G. Radnitzky & W. W. Bartley (Eds.), *Evolutionary epistemology, theory of rationality, and the sociology of knowledge* (pp. 47–90). La Salle, IL: Open Court.

Cassirer, E. (1981). *Kant's life and thought.* New Haven, CT: Yale University Press.

Chapman, M. (1988). *Constructive evolution: Origins and development of Piaget's thought.* New York: Cambridge University Press.

Chomsky, N. (1979). *Language and responsibility.* New York: Pantheon Books.

Cooke, M. (1997). *Language and reason .* Cambridge MA: MIT Press.

Cremin, L. (1988). *American education: The metropolitan experience, 1876–1989.* New York: Harper and Row.

Despain, H. G. (2013). Integral theory: The salubrious chalice. *Journal of Critical Realism,* 12(4), 507–517.

Dewey, J. (1898). Evolution and ethics. *The Monist,* 8(3), 322–341.

Edwards, M. (2007). "Every today was a tomorrow": An integral method for indexing the social mediation of preferred futures. *Futures,* 40(2), 173–189.

Edwards, M. (2008). Where is the method to our integral madness: An outline for an integral meta-studies. *Journal of Integral Theory and Practice,* 3(3), 165–194.

Edwards, M. (2009). *Organizational transformation for sustainability: An integral metatheory.* New York: Routledge.

Esbjörn-Hargens, S. (2010). An ontology of climate change: integral pluralism and the enactment of multiple objects. *Journal of Integral Theory and Practice,* 4(5), 143–174.

Esbjörn-Hargens, S., & Zimmerman, M. E. (2009). *Integral ecology: Uniting multiple perspectives on the natural world.* Boston, MA: Integral Books, Shambhala.

Esposito, J. (1980). *Evolutionary metaphysics: The development of Peirce's theory of categories.* Athens, OH: Ohio University Press.

Farber, P. (1998). *The temptations of evolutionary ethics.* Los Angeles: University of California Press.

Fenves, P. (1991). *A peculiar fate: Metaphysics and world-history in Kant.* Ithaca, NY: Cornell University Press.

Fiske, J. (1874). *Outlines of a cosmic philosophy.* London: Macmillan.

Fiske, D. W., & Shweder, R. A. (Eds.). (1986). *Metatheory in social science.* Chicago: University of Chicago Press.

Fukuyama, F. (2002). *Our posthuman future.* New York: Farrar, Straus, and Giroux.

Gibbons, M., Limoges, C., Nowontny, H., Schwartzman, S., Scott, P., & Trow, M. (1994). *The new production of knowledge: The dynamics of science and research in contemporary societies.* London: Sage.

Habermas, J. (1971). *Knowledge and human interests.* Boston, MA: Beacon Press.

Habermas, J. (1973). *Legitimation crisis.* Boston, MA: Beacon Press.

Habermas, J. (1984). *The theory of communicative action. Vol. 1: Reason and the rationalization of society* (T. McCarthy, Trans.). Boston, MA: Beacon Press.

Habermas, J. (1987a). *The theory of communicative action. Vol. 2: Lifeworld and system, a critique of functionalist reason* (T. McCarthy, Trans.). Boston, MA: Beacon Press.

Habermas, J. (1987b). *The philosophical discourse of modernity.* Cambridge, MA: MIT Press.

Habermas, J. (1988). *On the logic of the social sciences.* Cambridge, MA: MIT Press.

Habermas, J. (1990). *Moral consciousness and communicative action.* Cambridge, MA: MIT Press.

Habermas, J. (1992). Peirce on communication. In *Post-metaphysical thinking: Philosophical essays* (pp. 88–114). Cambridge, MA: MIT Press.

Habermas, J. (1996). *Between facts and norms: Contributions to a discourse theory of law and democracy.* Cambridge, MA: MIT Press.

Habermas, J. (1998). *On the pragmatics of communication* (M. Cooke, Ed. & Trans.). Cambridge, MA: MIT Press.

Habermas, J. (2002). A conversation about God and the world. In *Religion and Rationality: Essays on reason, God, and modernity* (pp. 147–167). Cambridge, MA: MIT Press.

Habermas, J. (2003). *The future of human nature.* Cambridge: Polity Press.

Habermas, J. (2006). *The divided West.* Cambridge: Polity Press.

Habermas, J. (2007). The language game of responsible agency and the problem of free will: How can epistemic dualism be reconciled with ontological monism? *Philosophical Explorations,* 10(1), 13–50.

Habermas, J. (2008). Religion in the public sphere: Cognitive presuppositions for the "public use of reason" by religious and secular citizens. In *Between religion and naturalism* (pp. 114–148). Malden, MA: Polity Press.

Hacking, I. (1995). *Rewriting the soul: Multiple personality disorder and the sciences of memory.* Princeton, NJ: Princeton University Press.

Hamilton, M. (2008). *Integral city: Evolutionary intelligences for the human hive.* Gabriola Island, B.C.: New Society.

Hausman, C. (1993). *Charles S. Peirce's evolutionary philosophy.* New York: Cambridge University Press.

Jaques, E. (1976). *A general theory of bureaucracy.* London: Heinemann Educational.

Kagan, J. (2009). *The three cultures: Natural sciences, social sciences, and the humanities in the 21st century.* New York: Cambridge University Press.

Kant, I. (1983a). Idea for a universal history with a cosmopolitan intent. In *Perpetual peace and other essays* (pp. 29–40) (T. Humphrey, Trans. & Ed.). Indianapolis: Hackett Publishing.

Kant, I. (1983b). To perpetual peace: a philosophical sketch. In *Perpetual peace and other essays* (pp. 107–144) (T. Humphrey, Trans. & Ed.). Indianapolis: Hackett Publishing.

Kant, I. (1998). *The critique of pure reason* (P. Guyer, Trans.). New York: Cambridge University Press.

Kent, B. (1987). *Charles S. Peirce: Logic and the classification of the sciences.* Montreal: McGill University Press.

Kentner, K., & Kloesel, C. (Eds.). (1986). *Peirce, semiotic, and pragmatism: Essays by Max H. Fisch.* Bloomington: Indiana University Press.

Kerr, C. (1963). *The uses of the university.* Cambridge, MA: Harvard University Press.

Klein, J.T. (2005). *Humanities, culture, and interdisciplinarity.* Albany, NY: SUNY Press.

Kohlberg, L. (1981). *Essays on moral development. Vol. 1: The philosophy of moral development.* New York: Harper and Row.

Kołakowski, L. (1978). *Main currents of Marxism. Vol 1: Founders.* Oxford: Oxford University Press.

Korsgaard, C. (1996). *The sources of normativity.* New York: Cambridge University Press.

Lacan, J (1977). *Écrits: A selection* (A. Sheridan, Trans.) New York: W.W. Norton.

Lazlo, E. (1972). *Introduction to systems philosophy.* New York: Harper & Row.

Lazlo, E. (2004). *Science and the Akashic field: An integral theory of everything.* Rochester, VT: Inner Traditions.

Leidecker, K. (2007). *Yankee teacher: The life of William Torrey Harris.* s.l.: McMaster Press.

McIntosh, S. (2007). *Integral consciousness and the future of evolution: How the integral worldview is transforming politics, culture, and spirituality.* St. Paul, MN: Paragon House.

Mareschal, D., Johnson, M., Sirois, S., Spratling, M., Thomas, M., & Westermann, G. (2007). *Neuroconstructivism* (Vols. 1–2). Oxford: Oxford University Press.

Mascolo, M. F., & Fischer, K. W. (in press). The dynamic development of thinking, feeling, and acting over the lifespan. In R. M. Lerner & W. F. Overton (Eds.), *Handbook of life-span development. Vol. 1: Biology, cognition, and methods across the lifespan*. Hoboken, NJ: Wiley.

Mead, G. H. (1936). *Movements of thought in the nineteenth century*. Chicago: University of Chicago Press.

Menand, L. (2010). *The market place of ideas: Reform and resistance in the American university*. New York: W. W. Norton.

Misak, C. (Ed.). (2004). *The Cambridge companion to Peirce*. New York: Cambridge University Press.

Nagel, T. (1986). *The view from nowhere*. Oxford: Oxford University Press.

Nussbaum, M. (2006). *Frontiers of justice: Disability, nationality, species membership*. Cambridge, MA: Harvard University Press.

Overton, W. F. (2007). A coherent introduction to systems philosophy – toward a new paradigm of contemporary thought. Metatheory for dynamic systems: Relational organicism-contextualism. *Human Development*, 50, 154–159.

Peirce, C. S. (1931). Book one: Elements of logic. In C. Hartshorne & P. Weiss (Eds.), *The collected papers of Charles S. Peirce* (Vol. 2) (pp. 3–129). Cambridge, MA: Harvard University Press.

Peirce, C. S. (1933). Book two: Existential graphs. In C. Hartshorne & P. Weiss (Eds.), *The collected papers of Charles S. Peirce* (Vol. 4) (pp. 293–470). Cambridge, MA: Harvard University Press.

Peirce, C. S. (1934). Book one: Ontology and cosmology. In C. Hartshorne & P. Weiss (Eds.), *The collected papers of Charles S. Peirce* (Vol. 6) (pp. 11–283). Cambridge, MA: Harvard University Press.

Peirce, C. S. (1982). I, it, and thou: A book giving instruction in some of the elements of thought. In The Pierce Edition Project (Ed.), *Writings of Charles S. Peirce: A chronological edition* (Vol. 1) (pp. 45–47). Bloomington: Indiana University Press.

Peirce, C. S. (1984). On a new list of categories. In Pierce Edition Project (Ed.), *Writings of Charles S. Peirce: A chronological edition* (Vol. 2) (pp. 49–59). Bloomington: Indiana University Press.

Peirce, C. S. (1984a). Grounds for the validity of the laws of logic: Further consequences of four incapacitates. In Peirce Edition Project (Ed.), *Writings of Charles S. Peirce: A chronological edition* (Vol. 2) (pp. 242–273). Bloomington: Indiana University Press.

Peirce, C. S. (2000). A guess at the riddle. In Peirce Edition Project (Ed.), *Writings of Charles S. Peirce: A chronological edition* (Vol. 6) (pp. 166–203). Bloomington: Indiana University Press.

Piaget, J. (1932). *The moral judgment of the child*. London: Routledge and Kegan Paul.

Piaget, J. (1952). [Autobiography]. In E. G. Boring, H. S. Langfeld, H. Werner, and R. M. Yerkes (Eds.), *A history of psychology in autobiography* (Vol. 4, pp. 237–256). New York: Russell & Russell.

Piaget, J. (1970a). *Main trends in psychology*. New York: Harper & Row.

Piaget, J. (1970b). *Main trends in interdisciplinary research*. New York: Harper & Row.

Piaget, J. (1970c). *The place of the sciences of man in the system of sciences*. New York: Harper & Row.

Piaget, J. (1970d). *Structuralism* (C. Maschler, Trans.). New York: Harper & Row.

Piaget, J. (1971a). *Biology and knowledge*. Chicago: University of Chicago Press.

Piaget, J. (1971b). *The insights and illusions of philosophy*. New York: World Publishing.

Piaget, J. (1972). *The principles of genetic epistemology* (W. Mays, Trans.). London: Routledge & Kegan Paul.

Piaget, J. (1974). *Adaptation and intelligence*. Chicago: University of Chicago Press.

Piaget, J. (1977). *The essential Piaget: An interpretive reference guide* (H. G. Gruber & J. J. Voneche, Eds.). New York: Basic Books.

Piaget, J. (1978). *Behavior and evolution*. New York: Random House.

Popper, K. (1966). *Of clocks and clouds*. St. Louis, MO: Washington University Press.

Prigogine, I., & Stengers, I. (1984). *Order out of chaos*. New York: Bantam.

Richards, R. J. (1987). *Darwin and the emergence of evolutionary theories of mind and behavior*. Chicago: University of Chicago Press.

Ritzer, G. (1991). *Meta-theorizing in sociology*. Lexington, MA: Lexington Books.

Ritzer, G. (Ed.). (1992). *Metatheorizing*. Newbury Park: Sage.

Schneider, H. (1963). *A history of American philosophy*. New York: Columbia University Press.

Sellars, W. (2006). *In the space of reasons*. Cambridge, MA: Harvard University Press.

Sen, A. (1999). *Choice, welfare, and measurement*. Cambridge, MA: Harvard University Press.

Smith, L. (2002). Piaget's model. In U. Goswami (Ed.), *The Blackwell handbook of childhood cognitive development* (pp. 515–538). Oxford: Blackwell.

Smith, L. (2006a). Norms and normative facts in human development. In L. Smith & J. J. Voneche (Eds.), *Norms in human development* (pp. 103–141). New York: Cambridge University Press.

Smith, L. (2006b). Norms in human development: Introduction. In L. Smith & J. J. Voneche (Eds.), *Norms in human development* (pp. 1–35). New York: Cambridge University Press.

Smith, L., & Voneche, J. J. (Eds.). (2006). *Norms in human development*. New York: Cambridge University Press.

Shin, S. J. (2002). *The iconic logic of Peirce's graphs*. Cambridge, MA: MIT Press.

Stein, Z. (2007). Modeling the demands of interdisciplinarity. *Integral Review, 4*, 91–107.

Stein, Z. (2008). On the possibilities of a comprehensive developmental structuralism: The natural, the normal, and the normative. Paper presented at the Annual Meeting of the Jean Piaget Society. Quebec City, Canada.

Stein, Z, Connell, M., & Gardner, H. (2008). Thoughts on exercising quality control in interdisciplinary education: Toward an epistemologically responsible approach. *Journal of Philosophy of Education, 42*(3–4), 401–414.

Stein, Z., & Hiekkinen, K (2009). Metrics, models, and measurement in developmental psychology. *Integral Review, 5*(1), 4–24.

Stein, Z., Dawson, T. L., & Fischer, K. W. (2010). Redesigning testing: Operationalizing the new science of learning. In M. S. Khine & I. M. Saleh (Eds.), *The new science of learning: Computers, cognition, and collaboration in education* (pp. 207–224). New York: Springer Press.

Stein, Z., della Chiesa, B., Hinton, C., & Fischer, K. (2011). Ethical issues in educational neuroscience: Raising children in a brave new world. In J. Illes & B. J. Sahakian (Eds.), *The Oxford handbook of neuroethics* (pp. 803–822). Oxford: Oxford University Press.

Thompson, W. I. (2009). *Transforming history*. Great Barrington, MA: Lindisfarne Books.

Ward, L. (1887). *Dynamic sociology* (Vols. 1–2). New York: Appleton.

Weber, B., & Depew, D (Eds.). (2003). *Evolution and learning: The Baldwin effect reconsidered*. Cambridge, MA: MIT Press.

Whitehead, A. N. (1978). *Process and reality*. New York: Macmillan.

Wilber, K. (1977). *The spectrum of consciousness*. Wheaton, IL: Quest Books.

Wilber, K. (1981). *Up from Eden*. Wheaton, IL: Quest Books.

Wilber, K. (1983). *A sociable God*. New York: McGraw-Hill.

Wilber, K. (1995). *Sex, ecology, spirituality*. Boston, MA: Shambhala.

Wilber, K. (1999). *Integral psychology*. Boston, MA: Shambhala.

Wilber, K. (2006). *Integral spirituality*. Boston, MA: Shambhala.

Wilson, E. O. (1975). *Sociobiology: The new synthesis*. Cambridge, MA: Harvard University Press.

Wozniak, R. (2001). Development and synthesis: An introduction to the life and work of James Mark Baldwin. In R. Wozniak (Ed.), *Selected works of James Mark Baldwin* (Vol. 1) (pp. v–xxxi). Bristol: Thoemmes Press.

2

HEALING THE HALF-WORLD

Ideology and the emancipatory potential of meta-level social science

Mark G. Edwards

1 Introduction

> We do live in a half-world. It is a world in which we have potentials that we cannot fulfil.... We are living very fractured forms of a life that we could live, and the world could, even now, be a world of plenty – poverty could be abolished – but we live in the midst of poverty.
>
> *(Bhaskar & Hartwig, 2010, p. 161)*

We live in an unhealthy demi-reality or half-world of extraordinary potential infused with unremitting harm and constraint. We live in a world that wastes more than one third of its total food production (FAO, 2011), where 1.5 billion people are obese or overweight (Keats & Wiggins, 2014), while more than 840 million people suffer from daily hunger and undernourishment (FAO, 2013). We enjoy and utilise, as never before, the products of science and technology while the scientific facts of impending catastrophic global warming are ignored and deliberately misrepresented to attain political power and secure corporate interests (Oreskes & Conway, 2010). The world provides unprecedented opportunities for personal growth while unfettered economic growth strips future generations of their environmental inheritance and burdens them with unimaginable levels of financial debt (Gosseries & Meyer, 2009; Roemer & Suzumora, 2007). We live in a world where the wealth of some is built on the poverty of others (Collins, 2012).

Many of these predicaments are self-induced in that we believe in and utilise inadequate political, cultural, religious, scientific and commercial ideologies and their associated identities and practices to deal with these ills and, consequently, end up reproducing them in new and sometimes even more vicious forms. All this is taking a massive toll on the viability of the planet's systems (Whiteman, Walker & Perego, 2013). It is becoming daily more evident that better planetary management of our activities is required but also that our ideologies are too narrow, too half-formed and too reductionist to meet the contemporary social and planetary challenges that we all face. If sustainable and sustaining forms of society are to be established then an active science of ideology, of its dangers and potentials, is a priority. This scientific task is no different from the long history of emancipatory endeavours that have gone before. Whether it is in the realm of politics, health, education, spirituality or commerce, the intentional pursuit of greater freedom, happiness and collective well-being has been a constant preoccupation in personal and socio-cultural domains of life and we have developed elaborate ideologies to pursue these quests for freedom.[1] These emancipatory ideologies derive, in significant part, from how we have viewed the relationship between truth and falsity, right and wrong, salvation and damnation, wealth and poverty, the whole and the part, the one and the many and perhaps most crucially the absolute and the relative. Consequently, how we approach emancipatory interests today will be heavily influenced by how we assemble and utilise the Absolute-Relative lens. While it may appear to be a rather archaic philosophical distinction, this fundamental lens has implications and repercussions that ripple down through the centuries and into our current times whether we acknowledge them or not.

In this chapter I draw connections between how Bhaskar and Wilber treat the Absolute-Relative (nondual-duality) lens and how these treatments result in differing views of the emancipatory role of the social sciences. The concept of ideology and how it can be studied is central to these distinctions. Ideologies are key factors in how humans interact with each other and with the planet. A social science of ideology is vital if we are to deal in balanced ways with the global imperatives we currently face. Hence, I explore some aspects of Bhaskar's philosophy of metaReality within this context of ideology. More specifically, I discuss Bhaskar's tripartite model of demi-reality, dualistic reality and nonduality and argue that his philosophical system sets out the logical grounds for establishing a meta-level social science of ideology.

In what follows, I first very briefly outline the philosophical study of ideology, which has been referred to as systematic ideology (Walford, 1990, 1977) or meta-ideology[2] (Rehn, 2008). Next, I define meta-ideology with reference to the topic of meta-studies in general and briefly point out some important distinctions between philosophical and scientific meta-level studies. After these preliminaries, I discuss Bhaskar's tripartite model of reality and Wilber's preservation of the bipartite model focusing on the respective implications these models have for recognising the emancipatory role of the social sciences. The chapter ends with a reflection on the implication of meta-ideology for dealing with contemporary global challenges.

2 Ideology in brief

Ideology is the system of conscious and unconscious concepts, theories, worldviews and assumptions that underpin a person's or group's goals, expectations and actions.

An ideology is a system in that it is a comprehensive vision, a meta-perspective that connects and coordinates diverse ideas, plans, policies, attitudes into some, at least partially, coherent guiding overview. Every emancipatory quest, every political, educational, commercial or cultural goal inherently involves ideology. Ideologies are not only private or personal systems of abstract thought but are expressed and enacted in the world to shape physical and social environments and bring about change.

Interestingly, ideology was first proposed in the post-revolutionary turmoil of eighteenth-century France as the formal scientific study of big ideas and big theories. The political revolution created a cultural space in which revolutionary new domains of scientific study could be pursued. At the vanguard of this new scholarly movement was the soldier, politician and philosopher Antoine Destutt de Tracy. Tracy proposed that politics and economics needed to be based on the science of ideas and on the critical analysis of social and political judgements and he coined the term ideology to refer to this science. Tracy intended this new science "to establish a sound 'theory of the moral and political sciences'" (Tracy, cited in Kennedy, 1979, p. 355). Tracy and those who gathered around him wanted this science of ideology to have real practical importance in changing people's living conditions. He believed that:

> A scientific study of ideas could foster a better understanding of the human condition such that social relations could be arranged to materially reflect real human aspirations, desires and needs. In this way, 'ideology', as a science of ideas, is grounded in the real, where the 'real' is intuitively theorized as the human condition itself, or as a form of human nature that is perfectible and amenable to systematic analysis.
>
> *(Porter, 2006, p. 3)*

The circle of scholars that Tracy attracted shared an interest in how the big picture or integrated overviews could contribute to a better understanding of the practical. One of Tracy's colleagues, Joseph Marie de Gérando,[3] who authored a famous series entitled "Comparative History of Philosophical Systems, Considered in Relation to the Principles of Human Knowledge",[4] commented that (Gérando, 1822):

> All science is truly an 'ideology' or a reasoning on our ideas, and if this expression has any defect it is its universality which renders it too vague. Far from being subject to the criticism that it is unreal, it can perhaps only be accused of having too broad a meaning.

Very soon after Tracy, Gérando, Cabaniš and others proposed the scientific study of ideology Napoleon Bonaparte condemned them as 'ideologues' reportedly saying something to the effect that Tracy and his supporters "abstracted themselves from the practical realities of political life and insisted on developing fanciful theories that were impractical and doctrinaire in equal measure" (cited in Porter, 2006, p. 3). Not for the first time we see here the political opportunist (and we might include here the scientific positivist) misunderstanding the enactive capacity of abstract ideas to change practical realities and the central importance of the study of thought and theory as an applied scientific enterprise. Like Napoleon, contemporary critics of big-picture research also miss the connection between ideology as a science of ideas and the emancipatory and pragmatic purposes of that science.

Yet, from the very beginning, the study of ideology has been driven by emancipatory motivations. Cabaniš, one of Tracy's colleagues and a leading 'ideologue', described the work of his colleagues as "a true science of liberty" and the ideologues' programme of scientific education played a central role in establishing the National Institute of Sciences and Arts, today's French Academy of Sciences, in the years immediately following the French Revolution. Tracy's ideology was intended from the beginning to be a meta-level discipline that held primary place among the other schools in that it was "finally the greatest of arts, for whose success all the others must cooperate, that of regulating society" (Tracy, cited in Kennedy, 1979, p. 355).

Marx also dealt with ideology in the context of liberty but from a very different angle from the French ideologues. He and Engels took the concept and shifted its referent considerably from a science of ideas to the critical notion of an overarching system by which dominant social institutions legitimise their power through their capacity to instil "false consciousness" in the populace (Eyerman, 1981). He defined ideology as all those values, cultural practices, conceptions of the world and symbolic systems that support one way of ordering society over another (Kennedy, 1979). He proposed that those with control of the economic world had the resources to promote ideologies that maintained their privileges. With Marx's critique of ideology as false consciousness, the term took on a pejorative connotation where ideology was a hegemonic process of privileged ideas imposed on socialised into others through (re)education. This reformulation of the concept also focused on the personal reproduction of ideology in individual thoughts and actions.

The post-Marxist philosopher Louis Althusser extended this idea to reframe ideology as the means by which selves are informed on their subjective identity. Ideologies are internalised as personal identities. As such ideologies can promote and/or hinder human development. Althusser has it that we cannot know ourselves outside of ideology and that all our behavioural engagements are encounters with the overarching structure of ideological practices and institutions and that these mediate the emergence of self-identity. We literally acquire our identities by seeing ourselves mirrored in the material manifestation of ideologies. Ideologies not only inform the macro-levels (and mundo-levels) of social systems and societal structures but the meso- and micro-levels of human subjects and interpersonal relations (Žižek, 1989). Later philosophers, particularly those of the Frankfurt school of critical theory, contributed further with a more fine-grained analysis of the means by which ideologies are institutionalised and communicated (Althusser, 1971; Žižek, 2012).

Bhaskar's contribution to the study of ideology has been significant. One of the reasons for this is critical realism's respect for ontological categories that are not just the outcomes of epistemological processes but are inherent in social conditions.

Ideological programmes create categories that take on their own causal power and objectivity. Furthermore, the ways in which reality is ideologically constituted can possess greater and lesser levels of cultural, moral, artistic and scientific fit or concurrency with the aspirations of individuals and groups impacted on by those ideologies. In other words, as Bhaskar says, ideologies can be false but real. They can have very little relevance to the cultural aspirations of a people and yet have immense real impact when those ideologies are hammered onto community life through systems of political, commercial and military power. The categories and lenses that an ideology employs are "constitutive of reality itself" (Bhaskar, 2002a, p. 54). They are causally efficacious in shaping societies, personal lives and natural systems. Bhaskar says that:

> [R]eality is pre-categorised, but in the social world the way in which reality may be categorised may be false. Social reality is conceptually dependent; the categories in terms of which we understand social reality may be systematically false, illusory, or misleading, and that is the clue to the concept of ideology. Ideology is a categorically confused reality. It is real but it is false. This is a possibility and an actualised possibility in social reality. The true nature of social reality is there 'beneath' the falsity.
>
> *(Bhaskar, 2002a, p. 54)*

I would add to this the idea that ideologies, their categories, lenses and practices, are always partly true and partly false and, while not unremittingly one or the other, they can be judged as more or less partial, balanced, developed, integrative, reflexive, just, aesthetic and so on. Some tasks of emancipatory forms of social sciences are to develop meta-evaluative criteria, and apply those criteria to perform evaluative assessments on the degree and kinds of partialities ideologies might possess.

Ideologies operate to provide intellectual, political and moral legitimacy to the whole experience and understanding of personal and social realities and to our behavioural reproduction of those realities in physical space and social relations. In a positive vein, ideologies ensure the cohesion of social worlds by regulating relationships, tasks and activities and the biological and physical spaces in which they are pursued. Ideologies can, however, also serve to maintain maladaptive and ultimately harmful practices, mindsets and cultures. Ideologies are crucial for enacting socio-cultural realities and global futures. Consequently, it is important that social science develop a capacity to rigorously study ideologies. However, while philosophers have developed very sophisticated knowledge of ideologies, the same cannot be said of sciences. The reason for this is essentially that the social sciences have not, to this point, fully institutionalised or articulated a meta-level science that can systematically investigate ideology. So, before looking at Bhaskar's call for a truly emancipatory social science, I will describe what one form of meta-level science looks like and discuss why it is different to the philosophical investigation of ideology.

Meta-level social science recognises at least three layers of scientific activity – the empirical, the middle range and the meta-level. Acknowledging these three layers of activity enables a critical engagement with the interdependencies between the very process of inquiry and its outcomes. When science is regarded from a conventional realist perspective, these interdependencies can be all too easily ignored and/ or hidden. Ideologies can be concealed under the veil of modernist assumptions and objectivist methods. Ideologies are aspects not only of collective and personal life but of the global system. They are partly constitutive not only of what we think but of what we do and not only of what we do in the present, but of how we enact the future. Ideologies can have positive and negative impacts on every level of existence from the micro of the private, from the meso and macro of the public to the mundo of the global. Consequently in the twenty-first century, in the age of climate change and global crises that result from human ideologies and activities, we desperately need a science that actively studies ideology. Because science, as with all knowledge systems, is itself ideological, this means that an ideology of ideologies, a science of meta-ideology is called for.[5] Obviously this necessarily includes a meta-reflexivity (Latour, 1988; Pels, 2000) that acknowledges the important limitations as well as possibilities of that move. But to reject meta-level scientific knowledge as either methodologically impossible or epistemologically unattainable is to neglect perhaps the most important topic of twenty-first-century life. How can we promote the healthy and restrain the harmful aspects and impacts of our big ideological pictures? What kinds of metatheory building and testing methods and analytical and interpretive systems might enable a meta-level science? How might a meta-science of ideology combine a deconstructive-critical and a constructive-appreciative perspective in engaging with the transformative power of big ideas and ideologies?

3 What is meta-level science?

Since its inception in the eighteenth century, ideology has been conceived of as a metadiscipline, that is, as a philosophy/science that takes other conceptual systems as its subject matter. The study of ideology involves the analysis of the practices and systems of thought that maintain and reproduce a certain social system. Knowledge production systems, political, scientific and moral practices, cultural worldviews and all manner of big (systemic) pictures are the 'data', the units of analysis of ideological studies. As such the study of ideology constitutes a variety of meta-level social science. Meta-level science is like any other form of scientific inquiry and it includes all the complexities and ambiguities that go along with being a form of science. It needs to build and test its conceptual products. It needs to transparently describe its methods and goals. It needs to state its truth claims and gather observational and experiential evidence to support those claims.

The key qualities that differentiate meta-level science from other scientific practices are not that it is more philosophical (although it is commonly more appreciative of philosophical perspectives) or less methodological (although it often lacks good methodological transparency and rigour) or that it deals with abstract, unreal, intangible, subjectivities (in fact meta-level studies deal with, among other things, the most real and most tangible of all realities – the big pictures, worldviews and enacted practices that constrain and shape the worlds we live in). The key differentiator between meta-science and other sciences is the categorically different kind of data that meta-level science works with (Edwards, 2014b).

In very simple terms, science can be arbitrarily categorised according to whether it is interested in making sense of empirical data, conceptual data or theoretical data (see the discussion of the 'scientific continuum' in Alexander, 1987). Empirical data is collected via the measurement and recording of direct observations and experiences. In the social sciences we have demographics, population studies, epidemiology, census surveys, observational studies, descriptive case studies, sensory-motor experiments and all those streams of disciplinary-based research that focus on counting, observing, describing, measuring and recording of sensory-motor experience and behaviour whether at the individual or collective level. Conceptual data is collected by recording and collating concepts, attitudes, feelings, thoughts, meanings, explanations, reasons, accounts and all those ideational aspects of life. Conceptual data of this kind emerges through inquiry into the conceptual world of thoughts and ideas. Finally, theoretical or second-order conceptual data is collected through recording and collating theories, models, systemic explanations, paradigms and all systems of understanding and explanation. Theoretical data of this kind emerges through inquiry into the conceptual world of ideas and their systemisation in models, theories, research paradigms and all organised big-picture constructions. In short, empirical research simply records, describes and measures observations and experiences to produce systematic representations of empirical data. Middle-range or first-order conceptual research operates on those records, descriptions and measurements to produce systematic explanations or theories of empirical and conceptual data. Second-order research or metatheoretical research operates on the middle range of theories and models to produce meta-level research, also called metatheoretical evaluation (Edwards & Kirkham, 2013), metatheorising (Ritzer, 2007), multiparadigm inquiry (Lewis & Kelemen, 2002) or grand theory (Turner & Boynes, 2006), amongst other terms.

In many ways the distinction between empirical, middle-range, and meta-level science reflects the ontological strata that Bhaskar (1975) described in his first book *A Realist Theory of Science*. Empirical science can be associated with the empirical stratum of sensory experience and perception, middle-range science can be associated with the stratum of 'the actual', of events and situations and meta-level science can be associated with the stratum of 'the Real' and of the generative causes of the conditions of human events and experiences. These associations will be further explored in a later section where we map out the kinds of social science suitable for exploring these various territories.

There are several qualities that mark out meta-level social science from such things as transdisciplinary, interdisciplinary, multidisciplinary research. First, contemporary meta-level research accommodates both pluralism and integration. It recognises the need for appreciating the diversity of perspectives as well as the need for their integration in some form. Hence, meta-level science is based on the methodological assumption of integral pluralism (Dallmayr, 2010). Second, because meta-level science intentionally adopts a reflexive position and operates on the conceptual products of other activities, e.g. scientific, political, commercial, educational, it necessarily entails a conscious reflexivity. As such it is accompanied by a reflexive awareness around the epistemological, axiological, ontological, teleological and methodological assumptions on which it is grounded. Third, because meta-level research is scale-independent and not bound by disciplinary boundaries, it can cut across, between, within and over traditional research boundaries, including those that define traditional academic and community-based centres of knowledge production. Finally, what might be called an integral meta-studies (Edwards, 2008, 2010) combines all these elements with a global-scale focus to address multilevel challenges over intergenerational time spans and across intercultural standpoints.

4 Scientific and philosophical meta-studies

The essential difference between philosophy and science is that philosophical systems are built and evaluated with reference to internal logics, transcendental arguments and first principles while scientific systems are built and evaluated through empirical and conceptual data. For a philosophical theory to be taken seriously, its propositions need to be internally consistent within its own self-referential axioms and core assumptions. For scientific theory to be taken seriously it must provide evidence based on the collection and analysis of data. Philosophy looks up to the reasoned arguments of systems of logic, while science looks down to the systematic collection of evidence to build and/or evaluate its products. It is no accident that, in the famous painting *The School of Athens* by Raphael, Plato, the philosopher, is pointing up to the heavens to justify his idealistic philosophising while Aristotle, the empiricist, points down to the Earth as his source of knowledge. But as I have noted previously, the data from which science constructs and tests its products does not need to be only empirical or first-order conceptual but can also take conceptual and theoretical form.

Bhaskar's notion of the 'underlabouring' function of critical realism is a form of meta-level philosophising. Hostettler (2010, p.9) says that:

> Critical realist underlabouring is critique whose negative moments provide effective criticism of existing philosophies and whose positive moment is not always fully appreciated: it discloses and reconstructs the very structures of meaning. That is, it successfully applies its own conceptions of depth-structure and social transformation to philosophy and science. Critical realist philosophy deals with the internal relations of scientific discourse; with the deep, categorial, structures of language and meaning.

There are several meta-functions of philosophical research mentioned here. Bhaskar's work provides "criticism of existing philosophies", of disclosing and reconstructing "the very structures of meaning", of applying "conceptions of depth-structure and social transformation to philosophy and science" of dealing with the "internal relations of scientific discourse" and the "deep, categorial, structures of language and meaning". All of these underlabouring functions are intentionally and unashamedly meta-level activities. All these capacities are employed when the full toolkit of critical realist lenses are used to analyse and evaluate ideology.

Similarly, Wilber's integral theory can be regarded as metatheoretical in that it is the product of analyses of other theories and scientific and cultural models. In his book *Integral Psychology*, for example, Wilber (1999) compares, contrasts and calibrates over 100 different developmental models from more than 70 separate researchers and cultural traditions to propose a general metatheoretical lens for structural development. Using lenses derived from his metatheoretical work, Wilber has also proposed a meta-method which he calls Integral Methodological Pluralism (IMP). IMP is a meta-level framework for locating and explicating multiple social science methods within eight perspectival zones (Wilber, 2006). While Wilber does not offer a systematic study of ideology, many of his critical analyses of the limitations of particular theories call out the "hidden interests, hidden power claims" that are definitive of ideologies (Wilber, 2001, p. 457).

Many of the major schools of philosophy of the twentieth century, including Marxist, neo-Marxist, Frankfurt school, poststructuralist and critical realist philosophies, have contributed to our understanding of the function and impact of ideologies. It is no coincidence that all of these schools are, at least in part, meta-philosophies in that they provide powerful criticisms of other systems of thought. The scientific study of ideology, however, still lags well behind. There are many reasons for this. First, scientific meta-level research is still very much in its infancy as a recognisable scientific activity. Second, there has been little work on developing rigorous methods for studying ideology more systematically. Third, the postmodern concern with whether any truly scientific study of big pictures can be performed without imposing further ideological layers (the Mannheim paradox) has stymied the development of scientific approaches. On this question it is important to recognise that the social sciences are also inherently ideological. They are systems of beliefs and practices and cultural identities that reproduce themselves to maintain a particular social order. But unlike ideologies from political, educational, commercial domains, the social sciences are equipped with an inbuilt critical capacity to construct and test their products through evidential analysis, critical peer engagement and social validation. This does not mean that problems of bias, relativism, false objectivism, ethnocentrism, the 'God Trick' of unconscious standpoint do not rear up in social science, but possibilities for countervailing critical assessments always exist. The solution to the inherent ideology problem is not to withdraw from the field (as most social sciences have done over the last 50–60 years) but to be more reflexively aware and conscious in adopting the basic scientific stance of transparency, rigour, deference to the data, critical engagement and peer validation. As Apter remarks (1964, p. 30): "With respect to ideology, social science differs from all others in one respect. The only antidote for it is more of it, addressed to solidarity and identity problems." Again, here in Apter's words we see reference to the pursuit of the study of ideology in a context of liberation. The social sciences should study ideology through social "solidarity" and addressing "identity problems".

One example where the study of ideology is of immediate and increasing import- ance is the challenge of global climate change. As the realities of human-induced climate change (HICC) impacts hit home, the real battle ground will become less over whether HICC is a fact or not, and more over what the policy response should be. The battle will move from one defined by the analysis of atmospheres and oceans by empirical science to one defined by the analysis of ideologies by social science. For example, as the urgency of the climate crisis escalates, the ideological debate over government regulation versus market-based solutions will take centre stage and scientific arguments will play an important role in providing evidence for and against these different ideologies. In his recent review of the role of psychology in limiting the impact of climate change, Stern made the point that "values, attitudes, beliefs, worldviews, and emotional reactions" (Stern, 2011, p. 309) are crucial players in policy and that "public support for policies to limit climate change is associated with environmental worldviews and fundamental values" (Stern 2011, p. 309). He also remarks that "Opposition to such policies is also linked to values and political ideology" (Stern 2011, p. 309). I would go further and say that values, worldviews and ideologies are associated with all policy responses to HICC. Unlike the debate between the climate scientists and the deniers, the debate over policy response to global climate change will be between people who all accept the empirical science but who differ in their political and cultural ideologies. The debate will be based not on the acceptance or rejection of science but on the more difficult territory of what kind of ideology a person adheres to.

To summarise, as with the movement from rejecting and avoiding climate pol- icy responses to more sustaining and balanced responses, the movement from the half-world of demi-reality to a healed world of balanced duality will be assisted through the scientific investigation of ideologies and big pictures. This move requires a new role for the social sciences through the development of such metadisciplines as critical meta-studies (Edwards, 2014a). Bhaskar's reformulation of the traditional Absolute-Relative lens to include 'demi-reality' provides a context for a meta-level social science that can contribute to planetary stewardship and the development of a critical science of ideology. Exploring the differentiation of demi-reality and dual- ity highlights the need for a meta-level form of science that supports a deepening reflexivity and evaluative capacity that does not currently exist within conventional understandings of social science research.

5 Bhaskar's tripartite lens and emancipatory science

Many of the major ideologies that are globally dominant in these early decades of the twenty-first century, for example, globalism (Petras & Veltmeyer, 2001), neo-liberalism (Mudge, 2008), global terrorism (Payne, 2009), consumerism (Clarke, 2010), managerialism (Cunliffe, 2009; Deem & Brehony, 2005), religious fundamentalism (Emerson & Hartman, 2006) and market fundamentalism (Block & Somers, 2014), are harmfully reductive in that they limit our human potential, they degrade and devalue natural systems that have taken many millions of years to accrue, and they reproduce false, partial and dehumanising visions in our individual and collective identities on a global scale.[6] It is important to acknowledge that they have become global ideologies because they tap into important truths about humanity and its capacity for creating socio-cultural and technological innovation. But they also reproduce socio-cultural systems and mindsets that result in harmful power relations, impoverished worldviews and distorted forms of communication. Bhaskar (2002a) has talked of the damaging domination of such ideologies and the imbedded social ills that result from them. He also stresses the capacity for social science, and particularly of metatheoretical science, to adjudicate on the half-truths and false forms of knowing and acting that emerge from this 'demi-reality' of entrenched ideologies. Bhaskar says that:

> The task of social science is to penetrate that demi-reality through to the underlying reality and situate the conditions of possibility of the removal of illusion, of systematically false being.
>
> *(Bhaskar, 2002a, p. 55, emphasis in the original)*

One means for the removal of systematically false being and doing is through critical reflection upon our underlying big pictures. This task of developing critical metatheories and overarching systems of ideas that can comment on the partialities of predominating views will be a central task for twenty-first-century social science. This is true not only for those radical ideologies that are clearly reductive and damaging but also for any ideological alternative, any systems of ideas and practices that are proposed to benefit human potentials and planetary systems. All ideologies are reductively partial in some way and this makes their scientific study even more important. The critique that all meta-perspectives have limits is entirely valid, but this should act to encourage metatheoretical pluralism in meta-level research rather than avoid it. A movement from ongoing battle between partial ideologies to a reflexive evaluation of their relative contributions and limitations is precisely what Bhaskar's vision of an emancipatory social science enables. It does this because the Relative world of ideologies is not monological. There are better and worse ideologies. There are ideologies that disable and constrain and there are ideologies that enable and facilitate. So how does it do this?

Bhaskar's tripartite model of dualism (the demi-real), duality (relative reality) and the nondual (absolute reality) provides a useful map for emancipatory philosophies, sciences and practices of all kinds. It opens transformative possibilities and energies that are not directed towards the Absolute realm of the nondual but toward the Relative domain of a more balanced and a more reflexively aware duality.

> [T]he world of duality, and its dominance by categorial untruth and illusion in what I have called 'demi-reality' remains real and in need of transformation even when we understand how it is sustained by the world of nonduality.
>
> *(Bhaskar, 2012, p. 42)*

One of the central motivations for seeking meta-level integration lies in dealing with the foundational existential paradox of emancipation. Issues of good and bad, identity and change, knowledge and ignorance and life and death can all be usefully set within the context of the quest for liberation. Bhaskar's tripartite model of dualism, duality and nonduality opens up a clearing where the social sciences and critical philosophies can contribute to emancipatory dynamics across all three layers of reality. It enables: (i) a deconstructive critique of metatheories involved in creating and maintaining the dualistic nature of the demi-real; (ii) a constructive evaluation of more balanced and integrative metatheories in a flourishing duality of the Relative; and (iii) an integrative critique of all knowledge systems in support of 'pointing out'[7] capacity for signalling pathways to the nondual.

This tripartite distinction provides a source for many other elements of Bhaskar's work and, in many ways, describes the movement of his own philosophical journey. The movement from concerns with ideology (dualism) to transformation (duality) to transcendental dialectics (nonduality) are reflected in the shift from the underlabouring work of his early books to the emancipatory, explanatory and ideology critique of his middle period to the dialectical focus on transformative practice and agency and now his contemporary focus on metaReality and spiritual identity. We also see in his reference to the current dominance of untruth and illusion the seed of his emphasis on social science as a source of emancipatory knowledge. We see in his reference to the world of transformational duality the idea of a social science that can inform transformative social relations and institutions. Demi-reality emphasises the need for scientific, cultural and political critique and we see in Bhaskar's appreciation for transformation the germ of his focus on consciousness and transcendence as starting points for a more comprehensive philosophy of growth and development. The tripartite description of the Absolute-Relative lens also runs through the basic elements of (i) realist ontology in the intransitive dimension of science (critical acknowledgement of real harm and concrete constraints on freedom in the demi-real); (ii) epistemological relativism in the transitive or social dimension of science (critical deconstruction of the demi-real and reconstruction of a balanced duality); and (iii) judgmental rationalism in the intrinsic aspect of science (the capacity of metaReality to assess qualitative distinction in various scientific domains, i.e. one is better at 'pointing out' than the other).

According to Bhaskar we are "dual beings embodying both duality and dualism" (Bhaskar, 2002, p. 21). In addition to having a Nondual basis to our essential nature

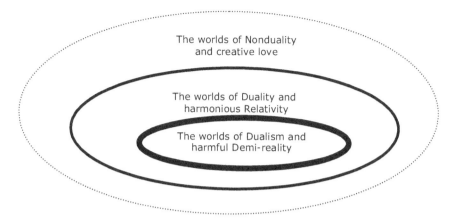

The worlds of Nonduality
and creative love

The worlds of Duality and
harmonious Relativity

The worlds of Dualism and
harmful Demi-reality

FIGURE 2.1 Bhaskar's tripartite lens

and ground qualities we also have lots of dualistic qualities which "block, constrain, drain our ground-states". The world of demi-reality is the domain of ideological illusion in that it limits basic human freedoms, capacities, potentials and opportunities. It both imposes and engenders differentiated confusion and all kinds of active and passive harm. The world of duality is one that is still bound by contradictions and oppositions but these are held within a context of deep humanism and authentic intersubjective and interobjective communications and mutualities. Eudaimonia and flourishing diversities are the outcomes of a world of balanced duality. Duality is the domain of reflexive rationality, healthy relationality and open potentiality. The relatively healthy worlds of duality descend into the half-world of demi-reality via the corruptive force of 'power over' rather than 'power to', of domination through fear and 'master-slave relationships'. Within and beyond all that, and providing the base for any kind of relationship, identity or experience is the cosmic envelop of nonduality where everything and every experience has its ground-state there and its true nature. Nonduality is the realm of profound and immediate openness to differentiated unity.

The task of the social sciences is to make the ideology of the demi-real into the praxeology of a balanced duality of relative reality; to heal the wounds inflicted by the causal efficacy of demi-reality by critically reforming its partialities, reductionisms and rationalisations as well as their enactment onto the world. As Gunnarsson puts it:

> In our world, the unavoidable duality of relative reality has turned into dualism, antagonism and split. This is what Bhaskar calls demi-reality, characterized by master–slave relations and instrumentalist modes of being. Bhaskar argues that, really, demi-reality is an illusion, but since illusions are casually efficacious it is nevertheless in that sense real.
>
> *(Gunnarsson, 2011, p. 424)*

Relativity, partiality and duality are features of all embodied existence but these do not necessarily involve harm to others, intentional or otherwise. On the contrary, the world of duality has emerged not only on the basis of sensory, psychological and social distinctions but also to enable ethical judgements of good and bad, better and worse. Duality comes into being partly as a response to the human need for improving our personal and collective well-being. Not only does Bhaskar's tripartite lens recognise the stratification and relative value of Duality over Dualism, it clarifies how Non duality penetrates the Relative. For example, that Nonduality expands and infuses through the realm of Duality through loving, unconditional modes of being which transcend dualities and differences. But the demi-real can also be clarified through the reflexive rationality of an integrative and pluralistic science whose explicit purpose it is to secure human and ecological dignities and freedoms. Emancipatory sciences of ideology are one of the primary means for enabling this process of critically engaging with false consciousness and practices of the demi-real to facilitate the emergence of an affirming realm of balanced Duality.

Bhaskar understands ordinary reality as limiting the possibilities of being. Hence it is a form of 'demi-reality'. Some of the elements of demi-reality are exploitation, oppression, conflict, commodification, egoism, environmental degradation, alienation, aggression, apathy and cynicism (Bhaskar, 2002a). These elements entail our isolation and lack of connection and include aspects of dualism. Consequently, false knowledge – which from the view of metaReality includes limiting oneself to demi-reality – refers to ideas that seem real but do not correspond in an adequate way to an object of reference (Bhaskar, 2002a). For Bhaskar, then, metaReality is dialectical: while the 'parasitic' nature of demi-reality is acknowledged, a distinct potential of metaReality emerges as that which liberates and produces a new emergent mode of existence (Bhaskar, 2002b). This liberation, however, is not a matter of moving someone beyond demi-reality; on the contrary, it is an act of transformation by embodied beings that enable the agent to qualitatively change societies through praxis.

6 Implications of the tripartite model

One implication of Bhaskar's philosophy of metaReality is that the role of social science in supporting emancipatory purposes is greatly expanded and, consequently, social science research can be thought of and performed in new ways. With the reformulation of the traditional Absolute-Relative lens to include 'demi-reality' the arena for critical reasoning and scientific inquiry is hugely expanded. As it becomes more obvious that humanity, whether it wants to or not, must take on the mantle of planetary stewardship, so it becomes more incumbent upon us that we inquire into the meta-ideologies that drive the behavioural patterns of planetary social systems. The meta-level opens up and requires of researchers a kind of reflexivity that lies outside conventional understandings of scientific research. Meta-level social science recognises at least three layers of scientific activity – the empirical, the middle range and the meta-level. Acknowledging these three layers of activity enables a critical engagement with the interdependencies between the very process of inquiry and its outcomes. When science is regarded from a conventional realist perspective, these interdependencies can be all too easily ignored and/or hidden. Ideologies can be concealed under the veil of modernist theories and objectivist methods. Bhaskar's addition of the notion of the 'demi-real' to the Absolute-Relative distinction creates an important underlying dynamic that opens the way for a truly emancipatory and reflexive social science.

The various interpretive, processual and reflexive turns of postmodernism have forced conventional science to face the issues of grounding assumptions, foundational premises, core beliefs and the ideologies that accompany these fundamentals. But this deconstructive (postmodern) phase in meta-level analysis needs to be complemented by a reconstructive phase. The basic philosophical and scientific issues of ontology, epistemology, praxeology, methodology and axiology require not only analytical critique but also synthetical, critical engagement in performing meta-level research.

Bhaskar's use of the additional layer of the demi-real is extremely useful for clarifying the role of science as an emancipation endeavour. For example, in the field of science education, Zymbelas argues that "Roy Bhaskar's philosophy of metaReality creates the middle way to theorize emancipation in critical science education" (2006, p. 665). Zembylas proposes that:

> The idea that science education has a 'critical' purpose – i.e. its function is, among other things, to challenge social institutions, public policies and practices so as to bring progressive change – is a possibility that deserves attention.
>
> *(Zembylas, 2006, p. 665)*

The purpose of a critical social science is then to "constantly and explicitly problematize the relationship between beliefs and their social functioning" (Zembylas, 2006, p. 666). To provide even more detail on the emancipatory potentials of the social sciences we can cross Bhaskar's tripartite model of levels of reality with his ontological strata of empirical experience, actual events and the real (causal factors) (Bhaskar, 2008). This stratified and inclusive ontology recognises the role of human agency in the constitution of the real and the actual. Tsoukas explains how human agency constructs "the domains of closure" for aligning these strata.

> *Causal powers* are located in the real domain and their activation may give rise to patterns of *events* in the actual domain, which in turn, when identified, become *experiences* in the empirical domain. The distinction between causal powers and patterns of events implies that the former may be out of phase with the latter. It is up to human agency (typically manifested in experiments) to construct the conditions of closure so that the domains of *real* and *actual* can be fitted together, and thus for the causal powers to give rise to patterns of events.
>
> *(Tsoukas, 1994, p. 291)*

TABLE 2.1 Ontological strata and their relations to levels of reality

		LEVEL OF REALITY		
		Dualism	Duality	Nonduality
ONTOLOGICAL STRATA	Empirical experience	*Felt harm* The world of physical, emotional, psychological and social pain and anguish.	*Felt well-being* The world of balanced ecological, physical, emotional, psychological and social well-being.	*Felt nonduality* The perceptual substrate for identity with any realm of felt experience or perception.
	Actual events	*Harmful events* The world of personal and collective alienation, and corrupted relationships.	*Healthy events* The world of personal and social freedoms, consensual power relations.	*Nondual events* The connectedness of events across ecological, social, temporal spheres.
	Causal factors	*Causes of harm* The causes of unmet potentials, master–slave relations, reductionist harmful ideologies.	*Causes of balance and growth* The world of enacted balance, healthy growth, realised potential, ideologies based on integrative reason and action.	*Absolute causes* The world of underlying causal dynamics and structures, e.g. beauty, truth, love, power, relationality, identity.

Each of these ontological strata can be considered within the context of the functions of Demi-reality, Duality and Nonduality. Table 2.1 outlines some categories of reality that emerge from combining these metatheoretical lenses. Empirical experience is what we encounter on the strata of sensory-motor perception. We can empirically, corporeally experience bodily harm, physical well-being and embodied unity and love. The stratum of actual events includes all occasions and situations that exist beyond immediate sensory perception. Actual events can be harmful and alienating, or conducive to personal and collective well-being, or expressive of radical connectedness and interpenetration. Finally, the stratum of the real and its causal processes can prevent and hinder the realisation of potentials on every ontological level. This combination of lenses creates a map for plotting the emancipatory potential open to science.

The non-exclusionary nature of these distinctions operates so that the Demi-reality is included in Duality which is itself included within Nonduality. Similarly, the empirical ontological stratum is included within the actual which is included within the real. This crucial quality of inclusiveness has the implication that emancipation is not a rejection of any particular strata or realm but a process of greater embrace and involvement at all levels.

As discussed in preceding sections, the 'Level of reality' dimension in Figure 2.1 outlines the general direction of emancipation. The social sciences can assist in moving from the harms of Demi-reality to the actualised potentials of balanced Duality. The spiritual sciences, e.g. contemplative science, selfless service and spiritual occupation, operate to transform the realities of Duality into the Nondual. The dimension of 'Ontological strata' can be used to delineate the holarchy of scientific orders. Empirical science studies empirical experience, middle-level science studies actual

TABLE 2.2 Emancipatory movements, ontological strata and levels of reality

Ontological Domains		LEVEL OF REALITY		
		Demi-reality	Duality	Nonduality
The perceptual e.g. analysing human biology	Empirical science	*Felt harm* — [A] →	*Felt well-being*	*Felt nonduality*
The conceptual e.g. analysing human psychology	Middle-range science	*Harmful events* — [B] →	*Healthy events* — [D] →	*Nondual events*
The inceptual e.g. human ideology	Meta-level science	*Causes of harm* — [C] →	*Causes of balance, Growth and well-being*	*Absolute causes of Nondual fulfilment*

events and meta-level science studies causal factors and, of most interest in this discussion, the real ideologies that create Demi-reality or which help us move to a more balanced world of relative well-being. Table 2.2 plots the various movements that open up when an emancipatory social science explores different levels of reality as a function of their ontological level.

Movement A: Emancipatory forms of empirical social and medical science aim for the movement from Demi-reality to Duality at the ontological strata of felt experience and embodied encounter through such things as describing and recording the prevalence of biological diseases and the environmental conditions that stunt healthy physical growth. In particular, the medical and therapeutics sciences, for example, epidemiology, disease control and public health interventions, are focused on alleviating this kind of felt harm.

Movement B: Emancipatory forms of middle-range social science aim for movement from Demi-reality to Duality at the ontological strata of conceptual reality. This is attempted through the development of environmental and psycho-social research paradigms that support economic wealth, organisational growth, community development, general personal health and well-being, psychotherapies and all kinds of interventions to promote efficiencies and effectiveness in human communities and ecological systems that sustain them.

Movement C: Emancipatory forms of meta-level science aim to transform the Demi-reality of unmet potentials, socially imposed constraints and inequities into a more balanced world of relative peace and well-being where human potentials are supported by natural, political and educational systems. Emancipatory meta-level science does this through the analysis of all kinds of conceptual systems including ideologies, scientific and everyday subjective theories, formal and informal models of practice and sense-making frameworks. It should be noted that emancipatory meta-level science not only investigates the macro- and mundo-structures of political and economic existence but also the micro- and meso-world of personal, interpersonal and group-level ideology and its impact within, for example implicit theorising, mindsets, personal and group worldviews.

Movement D: Emancipatory forms of spiritual science aim to transform all forms of dualism, duality and relativity into an inclusive experience of Nondual being and doing. These forms and traditions of spiritual science have previously existed outside of mainstream scientific discourse and activity. In recent times, however, there have been moves to introduce transformative practices and methods of scientific exploration within formal academic institutions. This process is in its very formative stages of development.

It needs to be pointed out that there are pathological and poorly developed forms of each of these different kinds of emancipatory science. A full description of the kinds of shortcomings that emancipatory sciences can possess is an important topic but space does not permit me to enter into that discussion here. For the moment, I point out that the tendency of scientific disciplines towards specialisation and fragmentation also leads to a lack of integration that can actually intensify human suffering and the degradation of natural systems. For example, the unbridled pursuit by mainstream economic science of achieving high standards of living through economic growth in isolation from other sciences, e.g. ecology, environmental health and health promotion, is irreparably degrading the global planetary system. Integration and boundary-crossing capacities are needed to address these kinds of issues and they can only really be achieved through movement C, through meta-level transdisciplinary research. At the same time, however, it is in movements A and B that the focus of most energy has been invested and this is compounding the unintended consequences of narrow views of well-being and how it can be achieved.

A final observation is that movement C, the process of moving from Demi-reality to balanced Duality through meta-level science, is also an important precursor for movement D and the involvement of spiritual sciences of contemplative and service-based practice. Without a thorough basis of meta-level science it is not likely or even desirable that spiritual sciences gain an established foothold in academic life. Spiritual practices and religious traditions are among the most ideological of human endeavours and their capacity to support human eudaimonic life and planetary flourishing from a scientific perspective will depend on their critical engagement with meta-level science.

7 Wilber's use of the bipartite lens

In contrast to Bhaskar's tripartite lens, Wilber retains the traditional Absolute-Relative bipartite form but focuses instead on its multiple interpretations. Wilber has discussed the bilateral Absolute-Relative lens in varying contexts including Buddhist (Theravada, Mahayana and Vajrayana), Hindu (Advaitic Vedanta) and Western philosophic (Hegel, Fichte) and mystical traditions (Eckhardt). Rather than develop the facets and expression of the lens itself, Wilber explores the reinterpretation of this lens over time. Or more accurately, Wilber investigates the relational aspects of the lens in sophisticated and nuanced ways. Metatheoretical lenses can be viewed using two basic distinctions, the lens facets that define its key structural components and the lens relationships that define the interactions between those components. For example, Wilber has described a metatheoretical lens that distinguishes between interior and exterior realities. The lens has two facets: the interior world of subjective thoughts, feelings and values and the exterior world of behaviours and systems. The relationship between these two facets is one of complementarity in that they arise together but in diametrically contrasting poles of opposition–collaboration. The point here is that metatheoretical lenses can be developed or interpreted (or misinterpreted) by focusing on their lens facets (interior or exterior facets in our example) or on their lens relationships (bilateral opposition in our example). For lens facets it is typically their number and description that is developed and articulated with greater precision over time. Wilber has done this, for example, with his detailed descriptions of the developmental holarchy lens of structures of growth. For lens relationships it is the type of relationship and the sophistication in how it is interpreted that demonstrates progress. Wilber has done this, for example, with his exposition of the relationship between pre-conventional, conventional and post-conventional stages in the developmental holarchy lens.

Rather than proposing any further facets to the Absolute-Relative lens, Wilber has tracked the different interpretive frames that have been used to draw out its internal lens relationships. His emphasis has been on the evolution of interpretations of the Absolute-Relative meta-lens. His contributions have been in the comparative task of showing how particular interpretations of this lens can initiate important cultural insights that stimulate the emergence of new perspectives and practices. Despite its fundamental importance for meta-level research, the change in how a particular form or morphology of an explanatory lens has been interpreted over time has not been acknowledged in the literature.[8] Although he does not specifically point this out, Wilber's analysis of the impact of changing interpretations of the Two Truths doctrine is an example of this metatheoretical phenomenon. Wilber has acknowledged the crucial importance of the Absolute-Relative lens not only in the Two Truths doctrine in Buddhism but also for how Western formal philosophy has discussed ontological issues such as the existence and relationship between mind and body and ethical issues regarding free will. How we manage and apply this lens has systematic and long-lasting impact on a great range of difficult philosophical topics that ripple through into the ontologies, epistemologies, axiologies and methodologies of all the sciences. In Wilber's words:

> This intractable dualism [of 'the Absolute versus the relative'], I maintain, is the central dualism in the Western tradition, and it would appear and reappear in numerous disguises: it would show up as the dualism between noumenon and phenomena, between mind and body, between free will and determinism, morals and nature, transcendent and immanent, subject and object, ascending and descending … these are essentially the same dualism.
>
> *(Wilber, 1997, pp. 83–84)*

Such dualities often shape the basic structures of ideologies and how they are enacted. For example, Wilber has discussed in detail the evolution of thought on the mind–body problem (Wilber, 2000) and how this has impacted on Western views of the body, the relationship between humanity and the natural world and on the emergence of various forms of environmentalism (Wilber, 2001). All this demonstrates the enactive power of ideologies to shape socio-cultural systems and environments of all kinds.

While Wilber has analysed the impact of the Absolute-Relative lens at the macro level, his approach to emancipation is largely concerned with personal freedom and with the liberation of the individual through contemplative practices. This has focused his interest in emancipatory topics on Eastern attempts to connect the Two Truths doctrine with meditative practices. For example, he points out that:

> When it comes to the nature of enlightenment or realization, this means that a complete, full, or nondual realization has two components, absolute (emptiness) and relative (form). The 'nonconceptual mind' gives us the former, and the 'conceptual mind' gives us the latter. Put it this way: when you come out of nonconceptual meditation, what conceptual forms will you embrace? If you are going to enter the manifest realm – if you are going to embrace not just nonconceptual nirvana but also conceptual samsara – then what conceptual forms will you use? By definition, a nondual realization demands both 'no views' in emptiness and 'views' in the world of form.
>
> *(Wilber, 2006, p. 108)*

This passage points out the immediate relevance for how absolute emptiness and relative form are conceived and expressed to enable right views and right practice to be enacted and followed. So again, we find in Wilber's work this powerful hermeneutic connection between how we conceptualise reality and the analysis of ideological and emancipatory questions. In a very lengthy footnote in his book *Sex, Ecology, Spirituality*, Wilber (2001) tracks the history of how the Two Truths doctrine has been reinterpreted in Buddhism to give a historical mapping of different views on first-person emancipation. This work shows how the emergence of new schools is associated with new interpretations and applications of the doctrine. Each school is characterised by different logics, different explanatory frames and enacted practices for understanding and manifesting emancipatory goals. Wilber discusses the changes that occur through the centuries in the way the Absolute-Relative lens is thought about and behaviourally applied. He shows how, even though the lens itself does not change in form, that is, it retains its basic meta-morphology of opposing definitional poles/limits, it undergoes significant epistemological reinterpretation resulting in new methods, new ontologies and new enacted realities, in other words, in new spiritual ideologies. For example, the early Theravada Abhidharma provided a reading of the relationship between the Relative truth of the self and the Absolute truth of Nonduality that required a movement from the illusion of Relative truth to the reality of Absolute truth. Centuries later the early Mahayana built on the

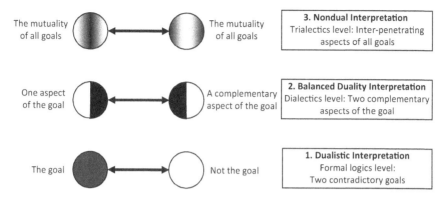

The mutuality of all goals ←→ The mutuality of all goals

3. Nondual Interpretation
Trialectics level: Inter-penetrating aspects of all goals

One aspect of the goal ←→ A complementary aspect of the goal

2. Balanced Duality Interpretation
Dialectics level: Two complementary aspects of the goal

The goal ←→ Not the goal

1. Dualistic Interpretation
Formal logics level:
Two contradictory goals

FIGURE 2.2 Levels of interpretation of metatheoretical lenses

logics of this Theravada Abhidharma interpretation to emphasise the dialectical relationship between the poles of the Absolute-Relative lens. Wilber points out that Nargarjuna, the great Mahayana philosopher-sage, applied a "dialectical analysis" to the lens (Wilber, 2001, p. 719). His dialectical analysis is designed to show that the opposing facets of the lens are not to be seen through either/or formal logics but through dialectical both/and logics. The dualistic interpretation of the Absolute and Relative poles as separate and irreconcilable is replaced by an interpretation of lens relationships as intimately co-dependent.

According to Wilber, in later interpretations from the Yogachara, Advaitic Vedanta and Vajrayana schools, the relationship between the Absolute/Nondual and the Relative/phenomenal world/self undergoes a further interpretive shift. The Absolute and the Relative are not in direct dualistic opposition, they are not simply in co-dependent relationship, but now the Relative is regarded, *in itself*, as a bridge to the Nondual. The Relative and the Absolute are now in an embodied relationship. Perhaps the most famous expression of this is in the poem 'Song of Zazen' by Zen master Hakuin Zenji: "This very body, the Buddha". The relative world of body, physical incarnation, emotion, sensory experience, is the very manifestation of the Nondual and is the means, the bridge through which this already and always present reality is realised. From this final interpretation of the lens, the Relative is the actual domain of Nondual emancipation.

Figure 2.2 shows how this transformation in interpretive complexity is aligned with associated forms of logic. This principle of different levels of logical interpretation of a lens is discussed in detail in a seminal article on the logics of contradiction and paradox in organisational change by Ford and Ford (1994, 758). The authors used the word 'logics' in a holistic sense:

> As used here, logics, or points of view, refer to "the underlying assumptions, deeply held, often unexamined, which form a framework within which reasoning takes place" (Horn, 1983: 1). Logics, which are similar to paradigms (Kuhn, 1970), frames (Bartunek, 1989), interpretive schemes (Ranson,

Hinings, & Greenwood, 1980), worldviews (Lincoln, 1985; Schwartz & Ogilvy, 1979), and deep structures (Gersick, 1991), are something more than what a person thinks or feels. They also are more than metaphors (Morgan, 1986; Ortony, 1979); they are fundamental and coherent sets of organizing principles that are unquestioned and unexamined assumptions about the nature of reality. They provide the lenses through which we view everything, telling us "what is real, what is true, what is beautiful, and what is the nature of things" (Lincoln, 1985: 29).

Adopting this language, one could speak of the logics of the bilateral Absolute-Relative lens as a sense-making process which interprets, organises and enacts what we regard as the real nature of things. Consequently, any bilateral lenses can be interpreted and applied: (i) at the formal logic level of analysis as oppositions; (ii) at the dialectical level as interdependent complementarities; and (iii) at the trialectical level as interpenetrating mutualities (Ford & Ford, 1994). Wilber's review of the literature on the various interpretations of the Two Truths doctrine in Buddhism might be seen as recapitulating this formal–dialectical–trialectical pattern. However, the interpretive progression from formal dualism to dialectical duality to trialectical nondualism is one thing, whether it actually gets updated in form is another. As the name suggests, *tri*-alectical logics are best depicted in terms of at least three points of distinction. The paradox of a bilateral lens needing to have at least three elements in its depiction immediately raises the transformation aspect of trialectical logics. For example, rather than the bilateral form for the trialectical depiction of Nonduality in Figure 2.2, a more suitable representation would be a three-point relationship (see Figure 2.3). Again all this relates to the 'bridging' and 'pointing out' exercises and representations, in that, although all representations of the relationship between Absolute and the Relative are inadequate, some are more inadequate than others. There are weaknesses and limitations obviously in all depictions but, nonetheless some are better than others for 'pointing out' purposes, for particular kinds of instructional injunctions.

The relevance of this point is seen when understanding why Bhaskar redraws the Absolute-Relative polarity to now include three elements. The inclusion of a third form or facet of reality introduces a form of logics not present in other interpretations of the lens and, consequently, opens forms of analysis that are otherwise missed. Figure 2.1 and Tables 2.1 and 2.2 represent Bhaskar's tripartite version of the Absolute-Relative lens as a holarchy rather than as a linear three-facet lens. This

The goal as no goal   The mutuality of all goals   No goal as the goal

FIGURE 2.3 Trialectical interpretation as a bilateral metatheoretical lens

is because his description of the relationship between Demi-reality, Duality and Nonduality involves a nested holarchical relationship (Bhaskar, 2002b).[9] By the way, this is also why Bhaskar describes the realisation experience in terms of "shedding" those elements of consciousness and behaviour that inhibit the awareness of the Nonduality. Because of the holarchical relationship all that is needed is the letting go of inhibiting layers of self rather than the radical removal of one self for another.

As I have proposed, Wilber's explication of the Two Truths lens is a meta-hermeneutic analysis of a spiritual-religious ideology. His analysis shows the power that these immensely important lenses have in shaping culture and social and personal practices. In reviewing Wilber's work on this topic it is noteworthy that the progression from one interpretation to another is inclusive in that the latter includes the former. Dialectical analysis includes formal logic and trialectical analysis includes the dialectic. Nothing is lost but much is opened up. Wilber is not the first to have pointed out this need for hermeneutical development in sense-making and sense-giving tools like metatheoretical lenses. I would like to briefly mention here three examples of this kind of meta-hermeneutics, one from Buddhist, one from Hindu and one from Christian traditions. The first is the exposition of the Two Truths doctrine by Dongshan Liangjie, a remarkable ninth-century Chán teacher. Dongshan composed a poetic series of koans, the Five Ranks, that reveal the complex relationship between the Contingent (Relative) and the Essential (Absolute). The Five Ranks consist of two cycles of five poetic verses. For the first time, an in-depth commentary in English on Dongshan's Five Ranks is now available (Bolleter, 2014). In the introduction to this important work, the author, Ross Bolleter, connects Dongshan's cycles and verses with earlier expositions of the Two Truths doctrine. Bolleter points out that:

> Each cycle focuses in a different way on the relationship between the timeless, inexpressible realm of our essential nature and the contingent realm of life and death, where myriad beings, things, and events appear as separate and unique.
>
> *(Bolleter, 2014, p. 10)*

Dongshan's first cycle, 'The Cycle of the Essential and the Contingent' (Bolleter, 2014), recapitulates previous renderings of the Two Truths doctrine but also adds his own unique insights to present five perspectives on the relationship between conventional and ultimate truth. The first and second verses of the first cycle 'The Contingent within the Essential' and the 'The Essential within the Contingent' present a formal perspective. The third and fourth verses 'Arriving within the Essential' and 'Approaching from the Contingent' present a dialectical perspective, and the fifth verse 'Arriving at Concurrence' presents a trialectical perspective.

The second example of a trialectical expression of the Two Truths is from the Great Sayings or Mahavakyas of Advaitic Vedantism. These again recapitulate formal, dialectical and trialectical expressions. They can roughly be represented by the statements that (Thatamanil, 2009; Williams, 2010): (1) The [Relative] world and the egoic self are completely illusory and unreal. (2) Brahman [the Absolute], the creator of the [Relative] world, alone is real. (3) The [Relative] world is *ananya* – 'not different' – from its cause, Brahman [the Absolute]. The first two statements juxtapose formal dualities that together set up a dialectical tension. The third statement imposes a trialectical paradox that cannot be resolved via any dialectical or formal working out. It is this tension that is the starting point for practice.

The same tension can be seen in the third example of a trialectical interpretation of the Absolute-Relative lens in the Catholic doctrine of the Holy Trinity. Here we have the Absolute creator, the Father (Transcendent Absolute), together with the Son (the Immanent Relative) and the Holy Spirit (the mediating Intercessor). Again we have the similar dynamic of dialectical tension in the Absolute transcendence and Relative Immanence being reinterpreted in the trialectical logics of a ubiquitously available experience of the Holy Spirit.

> Our first thought of the Holy Spirit, of course, is the realization that there is a Holy Spirit, and that the Holy Spirit is God-in-us or God-upon-us or God-among-us everywhere and anywhere. Our second thought of the Holy Spirit flows from the first: that the Spirit is ubiquitous – everywhere, always, in all creation…. That leads to a third thought, logical and hard to dispute, but too-seldom acknowledged: the Holy Spirit pre-exists all religions, cannot be contained by any single religion, and therefore can't be claimed as private property by any one religion.
>
> *(McLaren, 2012, p. 58)*

This trialectic formulation once again makes the profane sacred, the mundane a pathway to transcendence and the phenomenal-historical a universal story of real actual mystery.

In the trialectical interpretation of the Absolute-Relative, science plays a crucial role in the emancipatory movement towards the Nondual. By healing the half-world of Demi-reality and building eudaimonic habitats, meta-level social science enables the conditions for the conscious intimation of the Absolute. Perhaps more importantly, meta-level social science requires a level of meta-reflexivity that itself enacts Nonduality. This is the kind of emancipatory social science of which Bill Torbert writes in his collaborative developmental action inquiry (Torbert, 2013). Torbert wishes to contribute to "the vast field of first-person research/practice and adult development leading toward empirically rare action-logics that are theoretically associated with increasingly timely and transforming action and inquiry" (2013, p. 266). This kind of social science puts its "primary focus on presencing inquiry for timely action amidst real-time interactions with others" (2013, p. 294). Special emphasis is placed on the emancipatory role of the social sciences not only for the movement from the Demi-real to balanced Duality but from balanced Duality to Nonduality (this emancipatory dynamic is what movement D in Table 2.2 is indicating).

This role for science is not emphasised in Wilber's analysis of scientific inquiry into relative knowledge and one reason for this is his lack of a more differentiated description of the facets of a metatheoretical lens for exploring the relationship between the Absolute and the Relative. Wilber has discussed with great insight how the "eye of mind" can peer into the Absolute but from his perspective it always reports back with confounding paradox rather than emancipatory potential (Wilber, 1990). There is no place for social science, meta-level or otherwise, in Wilber's vision for realising the Nondual. His position is that, "Of course science can find no evidence for the Absolute; nor can it find evidence disproving an Absolute. When science is honest, it is thoroughly agnostic and thoroughly quiet on those ultimate questions" (Wilber, 2006, p. 188). This is in some ways true and in some ways false. A meta-level social science can indeed ask ultimate questions – What is freedom? What is truth? What is real? Innovative science builds up and answers these questions with evidence from the domain of the Relative. In so doing, emancipatory social science explores evidence from the half-world of ideological harms to support a reflexive dynamic for ongoing development towards greater freedom and fullness in life. A simple two-facet representation of the Absolute-Relative lens inhibits seeing this emancipatory potential because it always relegates any relative knowledge to the realm of complete illusion where it can only be "thoroughly agnostic and thoroughly quiet on those ultimate questions". This impoverished view of science, meta-level or otherwise, and which flows out of the simple dualistic rendering of the Absolute-Relative lens, is one reason why a science of emancipation has been neglected in Western knowledge traditions. Bhaskar's development of a more nuanced lens is one reason why his philosophy explores the potential of science to contribute to a true social science of freedom.

8 Conclusion

I have explored here two different meta-level presentations of the Absolute-Relative lens and their implications for emancipatory social science that can help to heal the half-world of partial ideologies. Both Bhaskar's tripartite model of the Demi-real, Duality and Nonduality and Wilber's meta-hermeneutic analysis point to potential avenues for the development of emancipatory meta-level science. In applying these ideas, I have proposed that meta-level social science opens up and requires of researchers a kind of reflexivity that lies outside conventional understandings of scientific research, one that fundamentally involves a critical engagement with the ideologies and worldviews that shape our local and global existence and visions of the future. The contention here is that Bhaskar's addition of the notion of the 'Demi-real' to the Absolute-Relative distinction creates an important scientific domain that opens the way for an emancipatory and reflexive social science that has only previously existed in proto-form.

The ideological implications of different readings of the Absolute-Relative lens are many and each of them is important. Slavoj Žižek, the cultural critic and critical philosopher, has written about one particularly relevant ideological problem that exemplifies this issue. When the Absolute-Relative lens is used in a formal, dualistic form, the quest for subjective emancipation, which is typically taken up in Buddhist and other Eastern first-person enlightenment practices, may lead to a type of quiescence that reinforces some problematic aspects of contemporary consumerist culture. An unhappy alliance between first-person meditational practices and passive consumerist identities results in a kind of uncritical other-worldliness that does not challenge the ideological structures that imprison and degrade social and ecological communities (cf. Bhaskar's transcendent realism). He proposes (Žižek, 2005) that:

> Such Eastern wisdom, from 'Western Buddhism' to Taoism, is establishing itself as the hegemonic ideology of global capitalism. But while Western Buddhism presents itself as the remedy against the stress of capitalism's dynamics – by allowing us to uncouple and retain some inner peace – it actually functions as the perfect ideological supplement.

His observation that hybrid versions of dualistic Buddhist and capitalist ideologies are trapping us within a 'virtual capitalism' of harmful mindsets and practices is an important one. When quiescent Buddhism reinforces a passive consumerism we enter a non-critical ideological identity that seeks emancipation in an other-worldly Absolute. We pursue a science that is the handmaiden of a corporate world interested in building technological gadgets that entertain rather than in inner and outer technologies that enable community potentials.

> Thus we need not fully engage ourselves in the capitalist game, but play it with an inner distance. Virtual capitalism could thus act as a first step toward 'liberation.' It confronts us with the fact that the cause of our suffering is not objective reality – there is no such thing – but rather our Desire, our craving for material things. All one has to do then, after ridding oneself of the false notion of a substantial reality, is simply renounce desire itself and adopt an attitude of inner peace and distance. No wonder Buddhism can function as the perfect ideological supplement to virtual capitalism: It allows us to participate in it with an inner distance, keeping our fingers crossed, and our hands clean, as it were.
>
> *(Žižek, 2005)*

Žižek's point here is exactly concerned with ideologies that arise and co-create each other when meta-level disciplines are undeveloped and unable to offer new understandings for healing the world of dualistic ideologies. Both Wilber and Bhaskar, in different ways, provide some very preliminary bases for exploring meta-level territory. Wilber's contributions to understanding the Absolute-Relative lens, as I have outlined above, lie in his meta-analysis of lens relationships. Bhaskar's contributions lie in his meta-analysis of lens facets. Clearly a meta-level social science of any ideological system, whether based on the Absolute-relative lens or not, needs to include both of these meta-level research activities. In terms of my own mapping of meta-studies, Wilber's focus has been on the meta-hermeneutics, while Bhaskar's has been on the meta-methodological and metatheoretical as regards this particular lens. It seems that the hermeneutic emphasis of Wilber has orientated him towards interior aspects of emancipation and on the Eastern strength of first-person liberation. In contrast, Bhaskar's methodological and theoretical focus has opened up the exterior aspects of emancipation and of the Western strength of second- and third-person liberation (e.g. psychotherapeutic and democratic freedoms respectively). Acknowledging and describing the changing nature in how the Absolute-Relative lens has been interpreted and tracking these shifts with the associated changes in thinking and practices, structures and cultures is of immense importance for understanding the role of ideology in psycho-social change. To some degree Wilber has done this for the developmental holarchy lens of stages of growth and for the ecological holarchy lens of multilevel nestedness but much of this has been done without specific recognition of the need for concomitant elaboration in the description of the lens itself. While Wilber has done this for the developmental holarchy lens of human altitudinal growth the same cannot be said for his treatment of the Absolute-Relative lens.

When meta-level science is honest it expresses its emancipatory ideals that include bodies and minds, personal consciousness but also collective structures, cultural mindsets and ideologies. Science is not only about finding evidence to disprove existing theories, it is also about building new theories that explain the new evidence more fully. The long-term potential of meta-level social science is that it can work towards the critical evaluation of any ideology and in this way be a 'pointing-out' knowledge system that enacts Nondual potentials.

Notes

1 I am using the notion of ideology here in its very broadest sense of an ideational or philosophical system that is embedded in a corresponding set of practices. Different terms might well be nominated for scientific, political and mystical ideologies but I am bracketing them all under this very general usage to emphasise that the purpose of ideologies is closely linked with the striving for freedom, liberation and emancipation.

2 The term meta-ideology is also used by Abrutyn and Turner (2011) to denote aggregates of ideological systems; for example, a political ideology might combine with a biased media and with educational and scientific ideologies to form an extended kind of meta-ideology. I suggest that a better descriptor here would be hyper-ideology as the prefix meta- implies a reflexive layer of intentional inquiry and integration that is not present in a simple aggregation of diverse ideologies.

3 Gérando had a significant influence on the American Transcendentalists and particularly on Emerson. Gérando offered an integrative philosophy that traced how different theories and schools of philosophy, Eastern and Western, dealt with the primary questions that had engaged serious thinkers for millennia. Gérando drew on evidence from sources such as the Indian *Mahabharata* and the Chinese *The Invariable Milieu*. Under Gérando's influence, Emerson and others in the Transcendental movement recognised that that Hindu, Chinese and Persian schools of thought were at least as valuable as their Hebrew, Greek and Christian counterparts.

4 *Histoire comparée des systèmes de philosophie, considérés relativement aux principes des connaissances humaines.*

5 Recognising that science is itself ideological immediately brings us into the notion of infinite regression of ideologies and the possible compounding of ideological falsities, but that danger is itself not resolved by ignoring the study of ideology. The problem of multiple layers of reflexivity is not dealt with by rejecting reflexive imperatives. In fact the opening up of the meta-level study of ideology actually enables reflexive capacities to emerge and it is through those capacities that the scientific qualities of evidential, methodological and dialogical solutions to the problem of infinite regress and compounding error are situated.

6 This view is itself reflective of my own ideological commitments, but the issue is how accurate, balanced and reflective of, as Bhaskar would put it, healthy dualities are they? Do my ideological commitments rely on ideological lenses that are more or less dualistic, partial, reductive and therefore false than other kinds of ideologies? This is the key point in arguing for a science of ideology to answer these kinds of questions and to adjudicate on the veracity and alethic truth of these kinds of propositions that I am making.

7 'Pointing out' here refers to the notion that scientific knowledge systems, particularly meta-level studies, can provide useful methods, data, interpretive frames and validation processes for checking, validating and informing understandings and practices concerning spiritual knowledge/experience domains.

8 For more discussion of the form, or metamorphology, of metatheoretical lenses, see Edwards, 2010, ch. 2.

9 Of course, Wilber also employs the holarchical lens variety for several other purposes, but does not specifically use it in this case.

References

Abrutyn, S., & Turner, J. H. (2011). The old institutionalism meets the new institutionalism. *Sociological Perspectives,* 54(3), 283–306. doi: 10.1525/sop.2011.54.3.283

Alexander, J. (1987). *Twenty lectures: Sociological theory since World War II.* New York: Columbia University Press.

Althusser, L. (1971). *On ideology.* London: Verso.

Apter, D. (Ed.). (1964). *Ideology and discontent.* New York: Free Press of Glencoe.

Bhaskar, R. (1975). *A realist theory of science.* Leeds: Leeds Books.

Bhaskar, R. (2002a). *From science to emancipation: Alienation and the actuality of enlightenment.* Boston, MA: Sage.

Bhaskar, R. (2002b). *MetaReality: The philosophy of metaReality.* Boston, MA: Sage.

Bhaskar, R. (2008). *A realist theory of science.* London: Routledge.

Bhaskar, R. (2012). Considerations on 'Ken Wilber on critical realism'. *Journal of Integral Theory and Practice,* 7(4), 39–42.

Bhaskar, R., & Hartwig, M. (2010). *The formation of critical realism: A personal perspective.* New York: Taylor & Francis.

Block, F., & Somers, M. R. (2014). *The power of market fundamentalism: Karl Polanyi's critique.* Boston, MA: Harvard University Press.

Bolleter, R. (2014). *Dongshan's five ranks: Keys to enlightenment.* Boston, MA: Wisdom.

Clarke, M. (2010). *Challenging choices: Ideology, consumerism and policy.* Bristol: Policy Press.

Collins, C. (2012). *99 to 1: How wealth inequality is wrecking the world and what we can do about it.* San Francisco, CA: Berrett-Koehler.

Cunliffe, A. L. (2009). *A very short, fairly interesting and reasonably cheap book about management.* London: Sage.

Dallmayr, F. R. (2010). *Integral pluralism: Beyond culture wars.* Lexington: University Press of Kentucky.

Deem, R., & Brehony, K. J. (2005). Management as ideology: The case of 'new managerialism' in higher education. *Oxford Review of Education,* 31(2), 217–235. doi: 10.2307/4618615

Edwards, M. G. (2008). Where's the method to our integral madness? An outline of an integral meta-studies. *Journal of Integral Theory and Practice,* 3(2), 165–194.

Edwards, M. G. (2010). *Organizational transformation for sustainability: An integral metatheory.* New York: Routledge.

Edwards, M. (2014a). Meta-studies. In A. Michalos (Ed.), *Encyclopedia of quality of life and well-being research* (pp. 4012–4015). Dordrecht: Springer.

Edwards, M. G. (2014b). A metatheoretical evaluation of chaordic systems thinking. *Systems Research and Behavioral Science,* 31, 160–180. doi: 10.1002/sres.2193

Edwards, M. G., & Kirkham, N. (2013). Situating 'Giving Voice to Values': A metatheoretical evaluation of a new approach to business ethics. *Journal of Business Ethics.* doi: 10.1007/s10551-013-1738-7

Emerson, M. O., & Hartman, D. (2006). The rise of religious fundamentalism. *Annual Review of Sociology,* 32, 127–144. doi: 10.1146/annurev.soc.32.061604.123141

Eyerman, R. (1981). False consciousness and ideology in Marxist theory. *Acta Sociologica,* 24(1–2), 43–56. doi: 10.1177/000169938102400104

FAO. (2011). *Global food losses and food waste.* Rome: Food and Agriculture Organization of the United Nations.

FAO. (2013). *The state of food insecurity in the world: The multiple dimensions of food security.* Rome: Food and Agriculture Organization of the United Nations.

Ford, J. D., & Ford, L. W. (1994). Logics of identity, contradiction, and attraction in change. *Academy of Management Review,* 19(4), 756–785.

Gérando, J. M. de (2013). *Histoire comparée des systèmes de philosophie, considérés relativement aux principes des connaissances humaines (Comparative history of philosophical systems considered in relation to the principles of human knowledge).* Paris: National Library of France.

Gosseries, A., & Meyer, L. H. (2009). *Intergenerational justice.* Oxford: Oxford University Press.

Gunnarsson, L. (2011). Love – exploitable resource of 'no-lose situation'? *Journal of Critical Realism,* 10(4), 419–441.

Hostettler, N. (2010). On the implications of critical realist underlabouring: A response to Heikki Patomäki's 'After critical realism?'. *Journal of Critical Realism,* 9(1), 89–103.

Keats, S., & Wiggins, S. (2014). *Future diets: Implications for agriculture and food prices.* London: Overseas Development Institute.

Kennedy, E. (1979). 'Ideology' from Destutt de Tracy to Marx. *Journal of the History of Ideas,* 40(3), 353–368. doi: 10.2307/2709242

Latour, B. (1988). The politics of explanation: An alternative. In S. Woolgar (Ed.), *Knowledge and reflexivity: New frontiers in the sociology of knowledge* (pp. 155–176). London: Sage.

Lewis, M. W., & Kelemen, M. L. (2002). Multiparadigm inquiry: Exploring organizational pluralism and paradox. *Human Relations,* 55(2), 251–275.

McLaren, B. (2012). Rethinking the doctrines of the Trinity and the Holy Spirit. *Tikkun,* 27(3), 13–59.

Mudge, S. L. (2008). What is neo-liberalism? *Socio-Economic Review,* 6(4), 703–731. doi: 10.1093/ser/mwn016

Oreskes, N., & Conway, E. M. (2010). *Merchants of doubt: How a handful of scientists obscured the truth on issues from tobacco smoke to global warming.* New York: Bloomsbury Press.

Payne, K. (2009). Winning the battle of ideas: Propaganda, ideology, and terror. *Studies in Conflict & Terrorism,* 32(2), 109–128. doi: 10.1080/10576100802627738

Pels, D. (2000). Reflexivity: One step up. *Theory, Culture & Society*, 17(3), 1–25. doi: 10.1177/02632760022051194

Petras, J. F., & Veltmeyer, H. (2001). *Globalization unmasked: Imperialism in the 21st century*. London: Zed Books.

Porter, R. (2006). *Ideology: Contemporary social political and cultural theory*. Cardiff: University of Wales Press.

Rehn, A. (2008). Speaking out: On meta-ideology and moralization. A prolegomena to a critique of management studies. *Organization*, 15(4), 598–609. doi: 10.1177/1350508408091009

Ritzer, G. (2007). Metatheory. In G. Ritzer (Ed.), *The Blackwell encyclopedia of sociology*. London: Blackwell.

Roemer, J. E., and Suzumora, K. (Eds.). (2007). *Intergenerational equity and sustainability*. Basingstoke: Palgrave Macmillan/International Economic Association.

Stern, P. (2011). Contributions of psychology to limiting climate change. *American Psychologist*, 66(4), 303–314.

Thatamanil, J. J. (2009). Ecstasy and nonduality: On comparing varieties of immanence. *Journal of Hindu–Christian Studies*, 22(8), 19–24.

Torbert, W. R. (2013). Listening into the dark: An essay testing the validity and efficacy of collaborative developmental action inquiry for describing and encouraging transformations of self, society, and scientific inquiry. *Integral Review: A Transdisciplinary & Transcultural Journal for New Thought, Research, & Praxis*, 9(2), 264–299.

Tsoukas, H. (1994). What is management? An outline of a metatheory. *British Journal of Management*, 5(4), 289–301.

Turner, J. H., & Boynes, D. (2006). The return of grand theory. In J. H. Turner (Ed.), *Handbook of sociological theory* (pp. 353–378). New York: Kluwer/Plenum.

Walford, G. W. (1977). *An outline sketch of systematic ideology*. London: Walsby Society.

Walford, G. [W.] (1990). *Beyond politics: An outline of systematic ideology*. London: Calabria Press.

Whiteman, G., Walker, B., & Perego, P. (2013). Planetary boundaries: Ecological foundations for corporate sustainability. *Journal of Management Studies*, 50(2), 307–336. doi: 10.1111/j .1467-6486.2012.01073.x

Wilber, K. (1990). *Eye to eye: The quest for the new paradigm* (3rd ed.). Boston, MA: Shambhala.

Wilber, K. (1997). *The eye of spirit: An integral vision for a world gone slightly mad*. Boston, MA: Shambhala.

Wilber, K. (1999). *Integral psychology: Consciousness, spirit, psychology, therapy*. Boston, MA: Shambhala.

Wilber, K. (2000). *Sex, ecology, spirituality: The spirit of evolution*. Boston, MA: Shambhala.

Wilber, K. (2001). *Sex, ecology, spirituality: The spirit of evolution* (2nd ed.). Boston, MA: Shambhala.

Wilber, K. (2006). *Integral spirituality*. Boston, MA: Shambhala.

Williams, M. (2010). Knowledge, cosmic generation and the world in Madhva's interpretation of Chāndogyopaniṣad 6. *Rivista di Studi Sudasiatici*, 4, 63–74.

Zembylas, M. (2006). Science education as emancipatory: The case of Roy Bhaskar's philosophy of meta-Reality. *Educational Philosophy & Theory*, 38(5), 665–676.

Žižek, S. (1989). *The sublime object of ideology*. New York: Verso.

Žižek, S. (2005). Revenge of global finance. Institure for Public Affairs, Chicago. Retrieved May 1, 2014. Available from: http://inthesetimes.com/article/2122.

Žižek, S. (2012). *Mapping ideology*. London: Verso.

3
DEVELOPING A COMPLEX INTEGRAL REALISM FOR GLOBAL RESPONSE

Three meta-frameworks for knowledge integration and coordinated action

Sean Esbjörn-Hargens

Introduction

As the twenty-first century gets underway we are witnessing an increase in disciplinary differentiation and fragmentation and an increase in integrative approaches within and across disciplines and knowledge domains (Bammer, 2013). This trend is likely to continue throughout this century, involving a paradoxical increase in both fragmentation and integration. It is unlikely that there is some integral omega point in the near or distant future wherein the hazards of fragmentation will someday finally be overcome. Rather, I see this as one of the primary polarities of the twenty-first century (and beyond), wherein both fragmentation and integration increase together as interdependent opposites. Similar to how insects and flowers have propelled each other's evolution, integration and fragmentation need each other and cannot really exist without one another. So the issue is not about getting rid of or overcoming fragmentation, rather it is about developing forms of integration for navigating it. As a result of the increasing complexity of our world and the ensuing fragmentation humanity is developing more sophisticated and wide-ranging integrative maps, models, methodologies, and metrics.

Since the beginning of the twenty-first century we have seen an increasing number of what I call "pioneers of integration." These are individuals who are developing integrative approaches within or across disciplines as a way of dealing with the explosion of information and theories that one must take into account to have a complete and relevant response to contemporary challenges. Some notable pioneers of integration include: Fernando Zalamea's (2013) "synthetic philosophy" for contemporary mathematics; Sandra Mitchell's (2003) "integrative pluralism," which she has developed in response to dealing with biological complexity; and Roger Martin's (2009) "integrative thinking" in business and organizational development.

In addition to the pioneers of integration like those noted above, who are developing integral approaches within or across a handful of knowledge domains, there is a smaller group of pioneers of "meta-integration." These are individuals proposing big visions of reality that aim to include the pearls of wisdom from all of humanity's knowledge domains in an integrated way. Among these pioneers of meta-integration three individuals stand out: Ken Wilber (b. 1949), Roy Bhaskar (1944–2014), and Edgar Morin (b. 1921).[1] Over the last 30 years all three have created an integral metatheory: integral theory, critical realism, and complex thought, respectively.[2] An integral metatheory is a big-picture theory of reality that emerges out of the coordinated integration of the key insights from dozens of theories from disciplines and knowledge domains spanning the arts and humanities, social sciences, and natural sciences.

Thus, at the same time that the wicked problems of the twenty-first century are coming into focus we see the emergence of integral metatheories. I believe these two developments are deeply interconnected. Wicked problems are wicked in that they are global and they defy national, cultural, organizational, and disciplinary boundaries.[3] Basically they are bigger than the modernist and postmodernist frameworks we have to make sense of them and a sufficient response to them requires a high level of coordination across many perspectives, scales of analysis, and types of organizations. The emerging integral metatheories are uniquely positioned to help address the wicked problems of the twenty-first century and it might even be said that anything short of an integral metatheory might not be sufficient in addressing such larger-than-life issues. In any event, integral metatheories can make a unique contribution to how we understand and respond to the challenges of the twenty-first century.

Given the unique role integral metatheory can play in helping humanity to hold and respond to the complexity of the twenty-first century, I feel that each of the three integral metatheories noted above have an important contribution to make in developing more adequate responses to the challenges we face currently as a planetary civilization and will serve us well as we confront additional challenges in the decades ahead. For this reason I have been an advocate of scholar-practitioners associated with each of these integral metatheories to be engaged with each other's work.[4] Each metatheory has unique strengths to offer a more complete view of reality and our responses to it.[5]

My goal in this chapter is to sketch out a meta-praxis of developing an integral metatheory that results from the collaborated efforts of scholar-practitioners from different integrative traditions working together using multiple integrative frameworks and approaches to combine the strengths and insights of integral theory, critical realism, and complex thought.[6] Thus, this "meta-praxis" is meta in that it goes beyond the practices and frameworks of a single scholar-practitioner community. This is important because to address the global crises and knowledge fragmentation of the twenty-first century, I believe we benefit immensely from a coordinated effort that draws on multiple integral metatheories and their application. Echoing Paul Marshall's lead I refer to this integral *meta*-metatheory as *complex integral realism*. This name nicely uses one of the words from the name of each of the three metatheories being synthesized (i.e., *complex* thought + *integral* theory + critical *realism*).[7]

These three integral metatheories are singled out as primary contributors to the ongoing development of a complex integral realism for the following reasons:

1 The founders of each integral metatheory are all contemporaries and began developing their respective approaches in the 1970s, so their work has emerged in part as a response to our global moment. Bhaskar's first book, *A Realist Theory of Science*, was published in 1975. Wilber's first book, *The Spectrum of Consciousness*, was published in 1977. Morin wrote the first volume of his six-volume magnum opus *La méthode* in 1977.[8] Each of these publications was to become foundational to each of their respective corpora.
2 They have produced large bodies of work, having written between 15 and 50 books each, which have been a catalyst for the production of a sizeable secondary literature around their writings.
3 They each have written chapters and books in or about fields associated with the arts and humanities, social sciences, and natural sciences – so they all cross disciplinary boundaries in their writings.
4 Their respective integral metatheories are currently being applied in 35–50 disciplines – this is as much or more application than any other integral metatheories can claim.
5 Each of the founders and the metatheories they have developed can be viewed as having a particular strength in one of the three major value spheres as associated with first-, second-, and third-person perspectives. Futhermore, they have complementary secondary and tertiary strengths, which makes them uniquely suited to contribute to complex integral realism.
6 Each of the founders and their metatheories include horizontal (e.g., subjectivity, intersubjectivity, and (inter)objectivity) and vertical (e.g., the stratification of reality) complexity.
7 Each of the founders and their metatheories emphasize the irreducible nature of reality and provide a metaview of reality that is highly inclusive of a wide range of humanity's insights.
8 All three metatheories provide convincing critiques of both modernism and postmodernism and position themselves as that which comes after postmodernism while striving to include the best of the premodern, modern, and postmodern periods.
9 All three of these integral metatheories emphasize planetcentric awareness and action and thus are quite global in scope and scale.
10 They each emphasize the role of their metatheories in supporting individual and social emancipation.

For these ten reasons the three integral metatheories developed by Wilber, Bhaskar, and Morin are viewed as uniquely situated to be synthesized into a complex integral realism. This chapter focuses on introducing some of the essential features of complex integral realism. It does this by presenting three new meta-frameworks I have created to support the development of complex integral realism. The first is the Metadisciplinary Framework, which is inspired in large part by complex thought's commitment to transdisciplinarity. The second is the Integral Pluralism Matrix, which is inspired in large part by integral theory's commitment to epistemological and methodological pluralism. The third is a model of nine distinct ontological domains that emerge from combining two integral lenses, which is inspired in large part by critical realism's commitment to ontology. So as you can see each of the three meta-frameworks being introduced in this chapter draws its inspiration from at least one of the above integral metatheories. These three meta-frameworks support knowledge integration in a powerful way. Knowledge integration of this sort, I argue, will be increasingly valuable for developing large-scale sophisticated responses to the global challenges of the twenty-first century and beyond.

Before presenting each of these frameworks I first want to set the stage by discussing the theoretical reflexivity that is gained by placing the three integral metatheories into engagement with each other. I will then illustrate this value through a comparative example of how all three metatheories include four irreducible dimensions in their approach. Then I will introduce Mark Edwards' (2010) approach to integral meta-studies, which provides an important context for the project of developing complex integral realism. In short this chapter has a double purpose: developing the rationale for a complex integral realism and articulating a meta-praxis of developing integral metatheory. The former is more substantive, while the latter is more methodological. These two purposes are integrated in this chapter via a recursive enactment: I am using the three proposed meta-frameworks of complex integral realism presented in this chapter to enact complex integral realism: a "metaintegral" ouroboros.

Even integral metatheories can do shadow work

The seed inspiration for this chapter comes from a quotation from Ken Wilber (2001) where he explains:

> But I should say that I hold [integral theory] very lightly. Part of the difficulty is that, at this early stage, all of our attempts at a more integral theory are very preliminary and sketchy. It will take decades of work among hundreds of scholars to truly flesh out an integral theory with any sort of compelling veracity. Until that time, what I try to offer are suggestions for making our existing theories and practices just a little more integral than they are now.

Reflecting on this quotation from time to time I arrived at the provocative idea that integral theory might not be as integral as it thinks it is or aspires to be. I came to feel that there is a real danger in assuming integral theory has included most of the enduring truths from many domains simply because it arguably has a framework and set of distinctions that could do so. In other words, there is an important difference between its integrative capacity and its current competency in integration. Having such a robust integral capacity is one thing, fully realizing it is another. As Wilber points out in the above quotation it will take decades and the work of hundreds of scholars to support integral theory in realizing its full mature potential. So I began to realize that within integral theory: there might be some important pieces of reality not yet integrated, maybe we as integral theorists were putting some square theoretical pegs in round application holes, and some things just do not always fit neatly into the four quadrants. I was left wondering, what are the blind spots, what are the square pegs, where are things messier than integral theory is able to fully acknowledge in its eloquent symmetry and parsimonious mapping? This led me to ask: how can integral theory or any integral metatheory for that matter do "shadow work?" Shadow work is a psychological phrase referring to the process of an individual becoming aware of those (often unsavory) aspects of oneself that you are not aware of or that you do not want to acknowledge. As a result these dimensions of self remain in the shadows out of the light of self-acknowledgement and self-awareness. Since shadow work is an important part of integral theory, especially in the context of what it calls integral life practice (see Wilber, Patten, Leonard, & Morelli, 2008), it felt appropriate that shadow work should not be confined to human transformation and maturity but also to theory building. This is in alignment with complex thought's notion of "auto-critique" and critical realism's notion of theory-practice congruence.

Extending this insight to the other two metatheories being considered here: complex thought and critical realism likely fall short of their own idealized versions of themselves. For example, complex thought might not be as self-reflective as it could be and critical realism might not be as critical or realist as it imagines itself to be. Thus, my vision of complex integral realism is that it becomes more aptly complex, more integral, and more realist through the engagement of other integral metatheories and their proponents and thoughtful critics.

For a number of reasons theoretical reflexivity is important for the health and growth of integral theory, critical realism, and complex thought as distinct bodies of work as well as for the synthetic version being proposed here: complex integral realism. First, each integral metatheory is not as integral, complex, or realist as it could be – there will always be things each approach leaves out, marginalizes, overemphasizes, and distorts. Second, while there is no Integral Meta-Omega point – where everything is finally integrated in a big kosmic embrace (unless we are talking about the Pristine Moment of Now) – each integral metatheory like any approach can evolve and become more mature, comprehensive, and nuanced over time. Third, one way for each integral metatheory to become more reflective as an approach is to have its proponents engage practitioners of other integral metatheories, whereby it will – through critical engagement and exploratory dialogue – come to see what it currently cannot see. I like to think of this as "theoretical shadow work," where a dynamic relationship with other integral meta-approaches serves as a meta-praxis for theoretical 'self-reflection' and development.

In short, I envision an integral/complex/critical approach to the ongoing development of each of these respective metatheories. This approach recognizes that each metatheory is not as mature or comprehensive as it could be, and so we continually strive to further develop each one through respectful inquiry and debate with other streams of integrative thought and practice. By placing each integral metatheory in direct dialogue with the others we can come to appreciate the strengths and limits of all three metatheories. By doing this we can then engage in creating a complex integral realism that integrates the strengths of each metatheory into a more robust metatheory that is more capable of tending to the wicked problems of the twenty-first century. These problems are so big and so complex, that no single theory, not even a single integral metatheory, can fully deal with and respond to it. But if we combine the best of all three metatheories, then we will be much better equipped to face the challenges of the twenty-first century.

Now, I want to turn our attention to an illustrative example of the value of placing these three integral metatheories into dialogue with each other and how that enables us to combine the best of all of these integral metatheories.

Tetradynamics: a comparative illustration

By way of illustrating the similarities and differences of these three metatheories I want to present how each one of them includes what I call a tetradynamic.[9] A tetradynamic is a graphical way to show the relationship between four primary dimensions of reality: experience, behavior, culture, and systems. For Wilber these four dimensions are the basis of his AQAL model, specifically the four quadrants. For Bhaskar these four dimensions are the basis for his Four-Planar Social Being. For both Wilber and Bhaskar these four dimensions and the integrative frameworks they have created to represent them occupy central places in their respective metatheories. For Morin, these dimensions are not formulated into a central framework within his metatheory but they show up in several places in his writings as he presents the complexity of reality. Below are quotations and diagrams from each theorist to illustrate how they each uniquely include these important irreducible dimensions.

Wilber's four quadrants

The four quadrants are the central integral framework within integral theory. All the other elements (e.g., levels of complexity) are situated within the four quadrants. Wilber first introduced these quadrants in 1995 in his *magnum opus Sex, Ecology, Spirituality* (SES). Prior to that the focus of his theory-building was around the integration of levels of psychological and cultural development with states of consciousness. Wilber's groundbreaking work in these areas positioned him as one of about three leading figures in the field of transpersonal psychology. With the publication of SES Wilber's integral theory was born and he began to move away from an exclusive identity with transpersonal psychology.

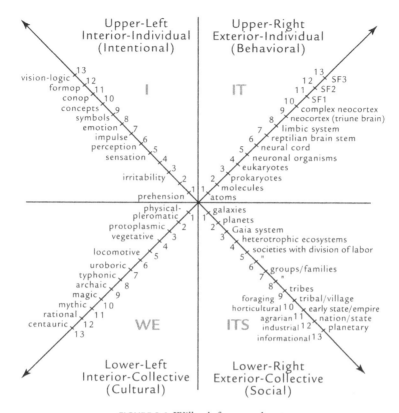

FIGURE 3.1 Wilber's four quadrants

As Wilber (1995) explains: "My position is that every holon has these four aspects or four dimensions (or four 'quadrants') of its existence, and thus it can (and must) be studied in its intentional, behavioral, cultural, and social settings. No holon simply exists *in* one of the four quadrants: each holon *has* four quadrants" (p. 129). Figure 3.1 below provides a classic chart of Wilber's four quadrants.

In addition to the iconic figure and its variations found throughout Wilber's writings, Wilber often uses pronouns to refer to the four quadrants. For example:

> Did you ever notice that major languages have what are called 1st-person, 2nd-person, and 3rd-person pronouns? The **1st-person** perspective refers to "the person who is speaking," which includes pronouns like *I, me, mine* (in the singular) and *we, us, ours* (in the plural). The **2nd-person** perspective refers to "the person who is spoken to," which includes pronouns like *you* and *yours*. The **3rd-person** perspective refers to "the person or thing being spoken about," such as *he, him, she, her, they, them, it,* and *its.*
>
> *(Wilber, 2007, p. 66, emphasis in original)*

Thus, in integral theory first-person, second-person, and third-person perspectives are represented by the pronouns I, we, and it respectively. These "primordial perspectives" are also linked with the value spheres of the Beautiful, the Good, and the True:

> The Beautiful, the Good, and the True are simply variations on 1st-, 2nd-, and 3rd-person pronouns found in all major languages, and they are found in all major languages because Beauty, Truth, and Goodness are very real dimensions of reality to which language has adapted. The 3rd person (or "it") refers to objective Truth, which is best investigated by science. The 2nd person (or "you/we") refers to Goodness, or the ways that we – that you and I – treat each other, and whether we do so with decency, honesty, and respect. In other words, basic morality. And 1st person deals with the "I," with self and self-expression, art and aesthetics, and the Beauty that is in the eye (or the "I") of the beholder.
>
> *(Wilber, 2007, p. 67)*

Wilber often refers to the Beautiful, the Good, and the True as "the Big Three" and uses art, morals, and science; self, culture, and nature; and subjectivity, intersubjectivity, and objectivity to refer to them. In the context of the quadrants the True is divided into both its singular ("it") and plural ("its") expressions (i.e., objectivity and interobjectivity).

Bhaskar's four-planar social being

Bhaskar first introduced the *four-planar social being* in 1993 in *Dialectic*, which marked the beginning of the third phase of Bhaskar's work – dialectical critical realism. Bhaskar also refers to the Four-Planar Social Being as the "social cube." Bhaskar (1993) sees the four planes of the social cube as being "dialectically interdependent" dimensions which constitute social life. As Bhaskar, Frank, Høyer, Næss, and Parker (2010) explain: "[The four-planar social being] revolves around the idea that every social happening or event occurs on at least four planes: 1. The plane of material transactions with nature; 2. The plane of social interactions between people; 3. The plane of social structure *sui generis*; and 4. The plane of the stratification of the embodied personality" (p. 11). Figure 3.2 shows the classic visual representation of the four-planar social being from *Dialectic*.

Bhaskar's four planes align with Wilber's four quadrants in a striking way where one is left with the sense that in some important ways they are talking more or less about the same dimensions albeit with a slightly different emphasis or focus (see Table 3.1). Note: this table is not to be viewed as presenting a 1:1 correlation between integral theory's four quadrants and critical realism's four planes but rather to highlight the fact that there appears to be some striking referential overlap.

A deeper exploration of the similarities and differences between Bhaskar's four planes and Wilber's four quadrants would benefit both approaches.[10] For example, how might integral theory enrich its understanding of the social expressions of the four quadrants

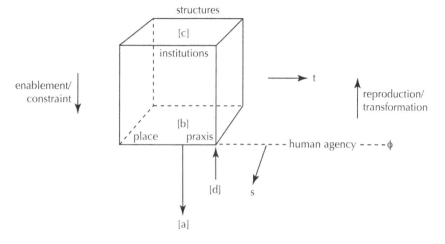

[a] = plane of material transaction with nature
[b] = plane of inter-/intra-subjective (personal) relations
[c] = plane of social relations
[d] = plane of subjectivity of the agent

FIGURE 3.2 Bhaskar's four-planar social being (Bhaskar, 1993)

and how might critical realism expand its understanding of the way these four planes occur within individuals? What might be gained for integral theory to have a less symmetrical presentation of the four quadrants – what additional relationships between each quadrant might come into focus? What might become available for critical realism to have a more symmetrical presentation of the four planes – what new relationships between the planes would be revealed? With these kinds of questions in mind let us now turn to Morin's own inclusion of these four essential dimensions of reality.

Morin's recursive approach to complexity

One of the hallmarks of Morin's writings is his use of the principle of recursivity, which he often represents visually through arrows or lines between words to show

TABLE 3.1 Bhaskar's planes and Wilber's quadrants

Bhaskar's Four Planes	Wilber's Four Quadrants
"The plane of material transactions with nature"	Upper Right quadrant of objectivity
"The plane of social interactions between people"	Lower Left quadrant of intersubjectivity
"The plane of social structure *sui generis*"	Lower Right quadrant of interobjectivity
"The plane of the stratification of the embodied personality"	Upper Left quadrant of subjectivity

how dimensions are in complex co-constitutive relationship with each other. Below are three examples of Morin describing the recursive relationship between the same four dimensions that Bhaskar and Wilber are working with above in the context of (1) a complex understanding of an individual; (2) the "uniduality" of the relationships between humans and nature; and (3) how individuals and society participate in the "*computo–cogito* loop".

Example 1: the complex subject

In the passage below we find a striking similarity with Wilber's own use of pronouns. Like Wilber, Morin claims that these pronouns and the dimensions they represent arrive together. You cannot have one without the other.

> This means that when "I" speak, it is also a "we" that speaks, the we of that warm collectivity of which we are a part. But there is not only the "we": "They" also speak when "I" speak, a "they" which is the voice of a more cold and anonymous collectivity. In every human "I" there is a "we" and a "they." The I, therefore, is not something pure, nor is it alone. The I could not speak were it not for "they."
> And there is obviously the "it" which speaks too. "Das Es." What is the it? The biological machine, something organizational that is even more anonymous than the "they." Thus, every time I speak, "they" speak, and "it" speaks, which has led some to think that the "I" does not exist. Unidimensional thinking only sees the "they" and so is blind to the "I." Conversely, those who only see the "I" dissolve the "they" and the "it," whereas *a complex understanding of the subject allows us to join together, in an indissoluble manner, the "I" with the "we", and both of these with the "they" and the "it."*
> *(Morin, 2008, p. 80, emphasis in original)*

Given that Wilber and Morin have both arrived at their integral/complex use of pronouns independently it would seem that these pronouns and the quadrants (Wilber) and planes (Bhaskar) they represent might in fact be irreducible and co-constitutive. Such similarities (and differences) raise a number of interesting meta-questions, which are beyond the scope of this chapter.

Example 2: the uniduality of human reality

Here is Morin (2001) discussing the "uniduality" of human reality in the context of our relationship with the natural world:

> Both of these paradigms [of simplification] preclude conception of the *uniduality* (natural ↔ cultural, cerebral ↔ psychic) of human reality and also preclude conception of both implication and separation in the relation between man and nature. Only a complex paradigm of implication/distinction/conjunction would allow such a conception.
> *(p. 22)*

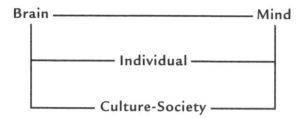

FIGURE 3.3 Morin's *computo–cogito* loop

Here we see Morin use four words (i.e., natural, cultural, cerebral, psychic) that map closely onto Wilber's quadrants and Bhaskar's planes. Similar to Wilber's notion of tetra-meshing wherein all four quadrants co-arise, Morin is proposing a recursive relationship between these dimensions where they are simultaneously distinct from each other and part of an integrated whole (i.e., a uniduality).

Example 3: the computo–cogito *loop*

Here is Myron Kofman (1996) depicting Morin's "unidual" approach. Morin is describing here the complex relationship between brain (*computo*) and mind (*cogito*) and culture-society where "individuals and societies co-operate in the [recursive] loop which connects them to brain-mind" (p. 85).

In Figure 3.3 you can see the recursive relationship between the brain and mind in an individual and how that is recursively related to culture-society. It is interesting that "culture" and "society" are two ways Wilber uses to distinguish between inter-subjectivity and interobjectivity and label the lower-left quadrant and lower-right quadrant respectively. So here Morin seems to be highlighting that the subjective mind, objective brain, intersubjective culture, and interobjective society recursively create each other in an ongoing loop.

What is striking about all the tetradynamic examples above is they each in their own way find a type of integral wholeness through the inclusion of these four dimensions. Each theorist includes these four dimensions in a signature way. For instance, Wilber uses his quadrants to highlight the four major dimensions and perspectives of individual holons (e.g., cells, plants, animals, humans); social holons only have the collective quadrants and artifacts or heaps of things can only be looked at from the four quadrants, they do not themselves possess four quadrants. Thus, the four quadrants are primarily an integral framework for understanding individuals in a comprehensive way.

In contrast, Bhaskar's four-planar social being is primarily about understanding social events in a comprehensive way. Unlike Wilber's starting point of the individual and their consciousness Bhaskar's starting point is the social event. Also, Bhaskar's "social cube" is much more visually complex and arguably abstract than Wilber's four quadrants. Wilber's quadrants have a simplicity and elegance to them and can be grasped more intuitively. Also, the relationship between the four dimensions is logically more obvious in Wilber's figure than Bhaskar's.

Morin's inclusion of these four dimensions is true to his style of being less symmetrical and more organic. Morin's focus is more on thinking complexly and creating a method of inclusion rather than a standard framework or system. Thus, unlike Wilber and Bhaskar, whose four quadrants and social cube are important frameworks in their metatheories, Morin avoids such visual representations and chooses instead to use his principle of recursion to include all four dimensions in different ways in different moments.

Over the years I have come across dozens of authors singling out these four dimensions as irreducible.[11] In looking at the five tetradynamic examples above one can see how each integral metatheory uniquely and similarly includes these four primary dimensions of reality. Something important is revealed by each of their presentations. This underscores the point that any integral metatheory would need to include these dimensions – ideally not just in one way, but in multiple ways. By comparing and contrasting how each of these metatheorists includes these irreducible dimensions of reality we can gain much insight into what each approach emphasizes and misses and we can come to each tetradynamic with fresh eyes having engaged the others. Also, the above examples give us a sense of the value of placing these integral metatheories in dialogue with each other to combine their strengths in the formation of a complex integral realism. We can also begin to see the role comparative analysis can play in creating a meta-praxis for developing an integral metatheory.

Now that I have pointed out that each integral metatheory can benefit from doing its own theoretical shadow work and have provided a comparative example of a key element of each of their theories I want to turn to the enactment of complex integral realism.

An integral meta-studies framework and methodology

In his groundbreaking work Mark Edwards (2010) has sketched out a scientific approach to the development of integral metatheories and has introduced a systematic approach to the creation of an integral meta-studies framework. His work has been very influential on me and my thinking about how to expand integral theory and now how to create a meta-praxis that would develop a complex integral realism. A complete application of Edwards' work to my vision of complex integral realism is beyond the scope of this chapter. Thus, my aim here is to situate the development of complex integral realism within the context of Edwards' vision. In doing so I hope to inspire others to take up Edwards' (2010) eight-phase methodology for building metatheory and his four-branch integral meta-studies framework to join me and others like Paul Marshall in enacting a more complex, more integral, and more realist metatheory grounded in the pioneering work of Wilber, Bhaskar, and Morin.[12] In fact, one of the primary tasks I envision for complex integral realism is to draw on all three integral metatheories in developing an explicit form for each of the four branches of integral meta-studies: metatheory, meta-methodology, meta-data-analysis, and meta-hermeneutics.[13] Each of the three integral metatheories

TABLE 3.2 Some responses to the issue of theoretical pluralism

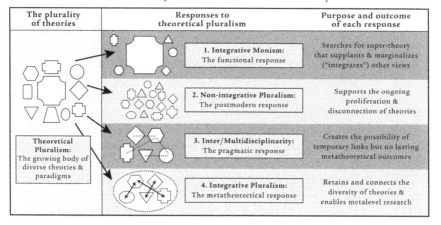

The plurality of theories	Responses to theoretical pluralism	Purpose and outcome of each response
	1. Integrative Monism: The functional response	Searches for super-theory that supplants & marginalizes ("integrates") other views
	2. Non-integrative Pluralism: The postmodern response	Supports the ongoing proliferation & disconnection of theories
Theoretical Pluralism: The growing body of diverse theories & paradigms	**3. Inter/Multidisciplinarity:** The pragmatic response	Creates the possibility of temporary links but no lasting metatheoretical outcomes
	4. Integrative Pluralism: The metatheorectical response	Retains and connects the diversity of theories & enables metalevel research

under consideration here has something to offer each of these branches and together they can create a dynamic multidimensional approach to each.

Within the context of Edwards' (2010) work one of the most important distinctions I want to introduce right away is between *integrative monism* and *integrative pluralism* (see Table 3.2). Integral theory has at times been viewed by scholars as a form of integrative monism, largely as a result of Wilber's rhetorical style and his emphasis on integral theory being a "theory of everything." In contradistinction to this I have often said that integral theory is best thought of as a "theory of anything," meaning it can be used in any context with any content, but does not necessarily include or account for all of reality in spite of its desire to do so and to be a robust framework that can support that intention.[14] It feels important to make it clear that what I am advocating here in creating complex integral realism is an integrative pluralism, not an integrative monism.

This distinction between integrative monism and integrative pluralism is important to emphasize since the very project of wanting to integrate three big integral metatheories is at risk of evoking images of forging "the one ring to rule them all." Edwards' (2010) framing of his own work eloquently explains and captures my own intention in this chapter:

> The intention here is not to bring theories together in order to create the biggest and the brightest super-theory that subsumes other explanations and understandings. Every theoretical position that has some valid research basis or authentic tradition of cultural knowledge behind it has something to offer and we need to find ways of integrating those insights while also respecting their characteristic and often conflicting differences. What I am suggesting here is not just another call for eclecticism or more interdisciplinary research. These responses to theoretical pluralism do not possess the necessary capacities for systematically linking multiple perspectives into an integrative

framework. What is required is a balance between an integrative synthesis and a respect for the pluralism of perspectives.

(pp. 1–2)

The proposed project here of developing complex integral realism is in no way envisioned as diminishing the value and importance of each integral metatheory on its own terms. In other words, I see each integral metatheory as retaining its autonomy and continuing to develop as a distinct integral metatheory. In fact, it is crucial to the health of complex integral realism that these three traditions of integral metatheory continue to grow and develop as unique lineages of integrative thought and action. So in no way does complex integral realism serve as some integrative replacement of these three other integral metatheories. In fact, I imagine a scenario where the development of complex integral realism serves to contribute to the future development of each unique metatheory and in turn that further development contributes to a more robust complex integral realism. I envision this as an integrative pluralism matrix of confluence and contrast, where synthesis is only one – albeit an exciting one – of the many important relationships needed for a dynamic and healthy encounter between these three metatheories.[15] In fact, we can draw on the three distinct logics (i.e., developmental, dialectical, and dialogical) that each integral metatheory advocates. (See the Appendix to this chapter for a table of 22 categories expressed in all three integral metatheories.) This would enable a multifold of relationships (e.g., antagonist, complementary, absence, negativity, competitive, and differentiation) between these three approaches. In addition, the relationship between the three metatheories and complex integral realism can be both *holonic* (where the parts – the three metatheories – are also each a whole and the whole – complex integral realism – is also a part of something larger, wider, deeper) and *holographic* (where the whole – complex integral realism – is also found in the parts – the three metatheories). Furthermore, how we go about bringing these three integral metatheories together can be informed by each of their primary activities: mapping (integral theory) their similarities and differences; critiquing (critical realism) each metatheory and thereby exposing their blind spots, contradictions, and inconsistencies; and reflecting (complex thought) on the epistemic distortions and complex relationships involved within and between the metatheories and the scholar-practitioners involved in creating complex integral realism.

In this way, by drawing on the different logics, whole/part relationships, and primary activities, to just name a few of the more obvious frames that can be evoked, of each integral metatheory we avoid subjugating the project of defining and developing complex integral realism to the preferences or philosophy of any one of them. That said I am a dyed-in-the-wool integral theorist who loves integration, synthesis, symmetry, and mapping. As a result my approach in this chapter to the project of complex integral realism is likely for better or worse to lean in this direction in spite of my desire otherwise. Thus, it will be important for other scholar-practitioners to complement and critique what I am doing here and contribute to the defining and development of complex integral realism by privileging other starting points or approaches to the cross-pollination I am advocating for here. What I am most excited about in the creation of complex integral realism is to have its enactment actually embody the unique wisdom contained within each integral metatheory. As a result there is a recursivity between my twofold aim of developing CIR and a meta-praxis for developing integral metatheory. In summary, how might we develop complex integral realism in a way that is attentive to the methodological concerns of Edwards and honors the unique logos of how each metatheory itself was created over thirty years?[16]

Framework 1: complex integral realism's metadisciplinary framework

Having set the stage for why the project of complex integral realism is worthwhile and having sketched out how we might go about it let me propose an initial definition, which builds on much of the discussion up to this point:

> Complex integral realism is an *amalgamated post-formal integral metatheory* committed to *integral pluralism*. It is *amalgamated* in the sense that it is largely the result of combining the strengths and unique contributions of three distinct integral metatheories: complex thought, integral theory, and critical realism. It is *post-formal* in the sense that it embraces paradox, ambiguity, messiness, dialectics, and self-reflectivity within a meta-systemic (i.e., systems of systems of systems) synthetic context that embodies integrative pluralism (opposed to integrative monism). It is *integral* in the sense that it integrates subjective (1st-person), intersubjective (2nd-person), and (inter)objective (3rd-person) aspects of reality (horizontal dimension) with stratified aspects of reality (vertical dimension). It is *metatheoretical* in the sense that it draws on and coordinates valid knowledge from theories associated with formal and informal disciplines found in the arts, humanities, social sciences, and natural sciences (i.e., it is metadisciplinary). Its commitment to *integral pluralism* is expressed through its honoring and incorporating eight major forms of integral pluralism (e.g., epistemological, methodological, and ontological pluralism).

This definition is meant as a starting point for further elaboration and engagement. There are two important aspects of this definition that have not been discussed yet in this chapter: complex integral realism's metadisciplinary orientation and its commitment to integral pluralism. It is to these two features that the rest of this chapter now turns.

Each of the three integral metatheories has a distinct relationship and approach to going beyond disciplinarity. Complex thought is strongly associated with transdisciplinarity. In fact, Morin is viewed as one of the founders of this movement (see Nicolescu and Montuori, 2008). Critical realism is strongly associated with interdisciplinarity, as can be evidenced by the following volumes devoted to topics of applied critical realism: *Interdisciplinarity and Climate Change*, *Interdisciplinarity and Well-Being*, and *Integrating Knowledge through Interdisciplinarity Research*. Elsewhere I define integral theory as postdisciplinary, by which I mean an integral approach can be applied equally successfully in disciplinary, multidisciplinary, interdisciplinary, and transdisciplinary approaches.[17]

In solidarity with these boundary-crossing approaches to disciplines, complex integral realism takes a *metadisciplinary* approach. Metadisciplinary is defined here as a meta-systemic approach to disciplines that includes four orders of disciplinary integration: disciplinary theories, integral and integrative theories, integral metatheories, and complex integral realism. Hence the metadisciplinary framework that is offered here is to support knowledge integration across multiple scales and disciplines. The first three orders correspond with Edwards' (2010) holarchy of sense-making: theoretical level, paradigm level, and metatheoretical level. The fourth order is less a higher level and more a robust version of the integral metatheoretical level. Here are all four orders:

- **Order 1:** *Disciplinary theories* associated with specific fields (e.g., evolutionary theory, semiotics, and consciousness studies).
- **Order 2:** *Integral and integrative theories* (e.g., Aurobindo's integral yoga, Latour's action-network theory, and Habermas' communicative action).
- **Order 3:** *Integral metatheories* (i.e., Wilber's integral theory, Bhaskar's critical realism and Morin's complex thought).
- **Order 4:** *Complex integral realism.*

In addition to an integrative vertical dimension as represented by these orders of disciplinary organization, the metadisciplinary framework I present below also has an integrative horizontal dimension. For this I use the triadic structure of 1st-person (1p), 2nd-person (2p), and 3rd-person (3p) perspectives (e.g., as found in Bill Torbert's (2004) action inquiry as well as in integral theory (Wilber 1995, 1999)). These three domains also correspond, as noted above, to the value spheres of the Beautiful, the Good, and the True and to the pronouns I, We and It. In summary, the metadisciplinary framework advanced here has a vertical dimension of four orders of increasing holonic integration and the horizontal dimension has three primary distinct but related domains of knowledge acquisition. In what follows I provide a brief tour of this framework and describe how it contributes to the development of complex integral realism.

To begin with, Order 1 contains at least 45 disciplines with 15 associated with each of the major knowledge domains (see Figure 3.4). The idea here is that multiple disciplines and their associated key theories contribute to an integral understanding of 1st-person (1p), 2nd-person (2p), and 3rd-person (3p) dimensions. Note that many of the disciplines listed could and do contribute to more than one of the knowledge domains. For example philosophy is listed as contributing to the 1p knowledge domain but it has theories that can also contribute to 2p and 3p

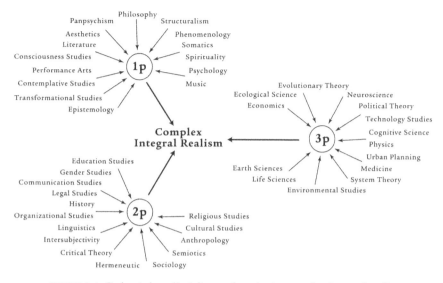

FIGURE 3.4 Order 1: key disciplinary theories in complex integral realism

domains. So the point is not to assign any discipline exclusively to a particular domain but rather provide illustrative examples of how various disciplines can contribute to a more complex, integral, and realist understanding of humans and the world around us. This important point applies to all the examples provided below and Figures 3.2–3.8. The value of the arrangement in Figure 3.4 is that it provides a systematic way to draw on dozens of relevant theories to develop the most comprehensive understanding of each of these distinct and interrelated domains of reality. It is also a way to practice theoretical reflexivity to see if you are including theories from one knowledge domain more so than others. Thus, the metadisciplinary framework is to be viewed in a dynamic and contributory way, not a rigid and reductive way. It is meant to help us see more theories and include them in an integrative way.

At Order 2 we find the same structure of knowledge integration as above. The difference here is that the contributing theories are integral or integrative theories. Order 2 contains at least 24 examples of these theories with eight associated with each of the major knowledge domains (see Figure 3.5). *Integral theories* are typically anchored or strongly connected to a single discipline but bring an integral view to bear on their object(s) of study (e.g., Sorokin's integral sociology is an integral theory of sociology working to bring together the various theories in sociology in an integral embrace; see Jeffries 2005). *Integrative theories* are not necessarily situated within a discipline and often are the result of several disciplines or theories being integrated into a new field (e.g., Science and Technology Studies, which integrates theories from psychology, philosophy, sociology, history, and political science among others). Order 2 is where a lot of the interdisciplinary theories are to be found since most integral and integrative theories draw on or incorporate insights

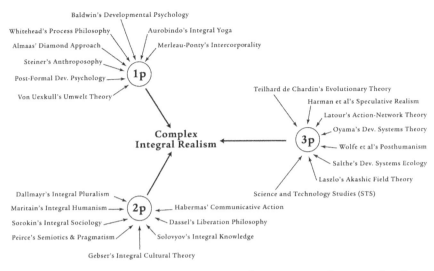

FIGURE 3.5 Order 2: key integral and integrative theories in complex integral realism

from other disciplines, often from their primary knowledge domain (e.g., Almaas' (2000) Diamond Approach draws on a variety of 1p theories from psychology and spirituality).

At Order 3 we have at least three integral metatheories, with one associated with each of the primary knowledge domains (see Figure 3.6). Unlike the integral or integrative theories found at Order 2, which are doing inclusive work primarily within one or two of the three knowledge domains, integral metatheories work with disciplines and theories from all three major knowledge domains from both Order 1 and Order 2 in an effort to provide a metaview of reality, not just a metaview on some part of reality.[18] Thus, all three integral metatheories presented here have an integral approach that explicitly includes 1p, 2p, and 3p realities in a non-reductive way. However, my observation in studying these three metatheories closely for years is that each one actually has a primary strength in one of the three primary knowledge domains. Upon reflection this is not so surprising, since each of the chief architects has built their integral metatheories by standing primarily in one of the primary knowledge domains and then increasingly drawing on theories from the other domains to create a more inclusive and comprehensive view of reality. For example, as noted above Wilber was viewed as one of the leading figures in the field of transpersonal psychology for over 20 years. This was in large part due to his integrative work at the intersection of psychology and spirituality. Thus, consciousness studies was and remains his primary strength even though he has an integral metatheory that provides a comprehensive view of reality and he has written extensively on 2p and 3p realities and the importance of including all three knowledge domains in any integral effort. Another indication of integral theory's 1p strength is Wilber's signature descriptions of psychological development and its relationship

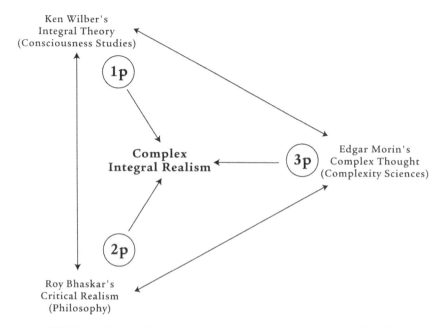

FIGURE 3.6 Order 3: key integral metatheories in complex integral realism

with expanded states of awakened consciousness where an individual experiences ultimate freedom from contraction and suffering. This focus on individual liberation is a cornerstone of integral theory. In addition to integral theory's strength in the first-person knowledge domain it also contributes key aspects of its integral architecture to the development of complex integral realism. For example, it has a robust articulation of the co-constitutive nature of the three knowledge domains (or, in its parlance, the four quadrants).

By associating each integral metatheorist with a specific knowledge domain I am in no way wanting to minimize their inclusion and engagement with the other two knowledge domains. In fact, they all have a lot to say about all three domains. After all, that is what makes an integral metatheory. However, I am wanting to emphasize their domain strengths in the service of identifying what their greatest contribution to complex integral realism might be. When I realized that each integral metatheory and its associated chief architect could be viewed as having a primary strength with one of the three primary knowledge domains I had a eureka moment. It might even be fair to say that complex integral realism was born in that moment, as I had a full-blown "vision-logic" experience and could see the implications of bringing the best of each metatheory to bear on a more complex, more integral, and more realist metatheory of reality.

I noted above that integral theory's strength is arguably consciousness studies and thus can be associated with the 1p knowledge domain. Let me now say a little bit about the strength of the other two integral metatheories. Critical realism's strength is identified as philosophy and is associated with the 2p knowledge domain. Bhaskar has developed his metatheory at the intersection of philosophy of science and philosophy of social science. He is an Oxford-trained philosopher and has been a professional philosopher since 1975. One of the hallmarks of Bhaskar's emphasis on the 2p knowledge domain is how he employs critical philosophy on behalf of social emancipation and the development of a eudaimonic (i.e., a flourishing) society. This 2p focus on social emancipation nicely complements integral theory's 1p focus on individual liberation. Part of its 2p strength includes a number of philosophical practices such as immanent critique, explanatory critique, retroduction, and transcendental argumentation.[19] In addition to these philosophical practices it contributes a very substantial set of philosophical distinctions (e.g., a 500-page dictionary with over 500 entries has been published to support individuals in engaging with critical realisms discourse; see Hartwig 2007). Together these philosophical practices and distinctions are essential to the development of complex integral realism. For example, immanent critique (i.e., using a theory's own terms to reveal its internal contradictions) can be applied to all three integral metatheories as a way of doing theoretical shadow work and leveraging the unique aspects of each metatheory as checks and balances against the shortcomings of the other two.

Adding to the other two strengths is complex thought's strength in the complexity sciences such as cybernetics, information theory, and systems theory. As a result it is associated with the 3p knowledge domain. Ever since his one-year sojourn in California at the Salk Institute in 1969, the complexity sciences have been an organizing dimension of Morin's approach. These complexity sciences figure prominently in most of his writings including his six-volume *magnum opus La méthode*. You can see their influence in many of his signature contributions such as the principle of recursivity, his critiques of both atomism and holism, transdiciplinary research, his use of the concept chaosmos, which is connected to his tetragram of order/disorder/interactions/organization, and the many different whole-part relationships he identifies and describes, to name a few. This strength in the complexity sciences is important to developing complex integral realism because, as Morin is fond of pointing out, they remind us that reality is full of disorder, incompleteness, uncertainty, and asymmetry. This serves as an important corrective to integral theory's symmetric elegance and critical realism's philosophical precision. As one of the leading American scholars of Morin's work, Alfonso Montuori (2013, p. 17), explains:

> Morin reminds us that every form of knowledge, every theory, and particularly any effort to develop an integrative perspective such as integral theory [or critical realism] is a construction, which draws on specific sources (and not others) as a result of choices, but also because of historical contingencies and the personal preferences of the theorists. This process of construction gives us an indication of the limitations of any view, no matter how capacious and integrative it is, but also points to the openness of the creative process that is involved in any such construction – the ongoing dance of constraints and possibilities that marks all paths of inquiry (Ceruti, 1994).

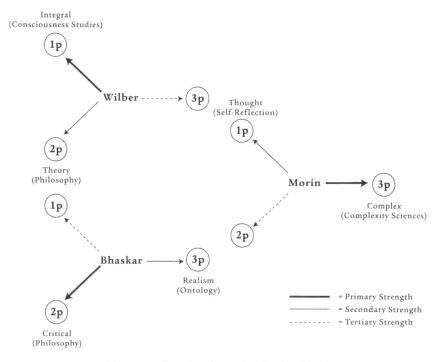

FIGURE 3.7 Complex integral realism's trialectics

In fact, these three integral metatheories and their chief architects have several lay-ers of triadic complementarity between their primary, secondary, and even tertiary strengths. This results in "integral trialectics" where each metatheory is contributing to and being augmented by the other two metatheories in important ways at their distinct levels (see Figure 3.7). As noted above, in the Appendix to this chapter there are 22 areas of complementarity listed between these three metatheories. Some of these areas have been touched on in the course of this chapter. While a full descrip-tion of all the areas listed in the Appendix is beyond the scope of this chapter, I have chosen to include this Appendix to inspire other scholar-practitioners to dive into the process of defining and developing a complex integral realism. This Appendix is meant to be suggestive of potential areas of similarity and difference and is not offered in any definitive way. See Marshall (this volume) for an exploration of many of these noted areas between the three metatheories as well as additional ones.

One of the fascinating discoveries I had in mapping out these three degrees of complementary strength is that the two-word name of each integral metatheory is expressive of their primary and secondary strength, with the first word of their name arguably connected to the primary strength and the second word connected to the secondary strength. For example, critical realism's primary strength is a "crit-ical" philosophy (2p) and its secondary strength is a "realist" ontology (3p). A similar pattern occurs for all three metatheories (see Figure 3.7). After I diagramed this out

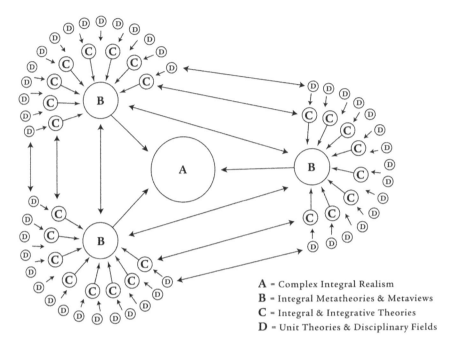

A = Complex Integral Realism
B = Integral Metatheories & Metaviews
C = Integral & Integrative Theories
D = Unit Theories & Disciplinary Fields

FIGURE 3.8 Complex integral realism's metadisciplinary framework of knowledge integration

I felt it underscored the following important point: reality is too multidimensional and mysterious for any single person – even an integral metatheorist – to have a primary strength in more than one major knowledge domain. In this context, it is not surprising that each metatheorist can be seen as having a primary and secondary strength associated with two of the three primary knowledge domains and furthermore that the name of their integral metatheory would actually indicate those strengths. Thus, we benefit from all three sets of complementary strength (i.e., primary, secondary, and tertiary) in developing a more complex, more integral, and more realist metatheory.

In summary, the three orders of theoretical contribution (i.e., disciplinary theories, integral and integrative theories, and integral metatheories) discussed above are combined through an integrative pluralism to create complex integral realism's metadisciplinary framework of knowledge integration (see Figure 3.8). Within this framework, theories from all three orders interact in multiple ways (vertically and horizontally) to continually produce as synthetic a view of reality as possible while still honoring the mystery and multiplicity of that reality which is always receding from conceptual, visual, and linguistic description.[20]

One of the results of the complex integral realism's metadisciplinary framework is not only the theoretical pluralism it generates within and across the various holarchical orders of complexity but it also generates a pluralism of approaches

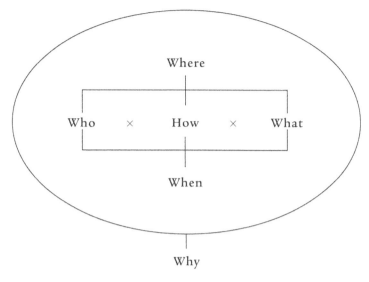

FIGURE 3.9 The 6Ws model of enactment

to important domains such as epistemology, methodology, and ontology. What is needed is a coordinating system for doing integrative work within and across these various forms of pluralism. To accomplish this I have created the Integral Pluralism Matrix, which consists of eight distinct forms of interrelated pluralism. It is to this matrix I now turn.

Framework 2: complex integral realism's Integral Pluralism Matrix

The foundation of the Integral Pluralism Matrix is an expanded version of the Who × How × What framework I developed in the context of my work in integral ecology. This framework was initially created to better understand the multidimensional aspects of environmental phenomena. I wanted a simple framework that could allow me to discuss the epistemological (the Who), methodological (the How), and ontological (the What) contributions to any ecological unit of analysis (e.g., an event or organism). In an endnote in *Integral Ecology* I noted, inspired by Brian Eddy, that one could also include spatial "Where" and temporal "When" dimensions in this framework (see Esbjörn-Hargens & Zimmerman, 2009, p. 599, n.10). Then in writing an article on the ontology of climate change, Mark Edwards suggested "Why" (i.e., a theoretical dimension) be added to this framework as well (see Esbjörn-Hargens, 2010a, p. 170, n.31). Thus, the Who × How × What framework was expanding into the Who × How × What × When × Where × Why framework. But listing them in order did not seem that useful in spite of its comprehensiveness. So I began working on a way to arrange these visually that not only included all six variables but did so in a way that highlighted the same core relationships between these essential variables. The result of my efforts is the 6Ws model of enactment: (i.e., **W**ho, Ho**w**, **W**hat, **W**hen **W**here, and **W**hy) (see Figure 3.9).[21]

The 6Ws model of enactment presents the six essential variables involved with the enactment of phenomena understood in a complex integral realist sense.[22] These six variables can be approached in three layers of analysis: *contents, contexts, concepts.* The first layer, and at the core of the enactment dynamic, is the relationship between the Who (the subject), the How (the method), and the What (the object). These three variables co-constitute each other as indicated by the recursive lines and multiplication symbol (i.e., ×) between them. They represent the *contents of analysis.*

The second layer of analysis is to understand that these variables always occur within a background of Where (space) and When (time). This background space is represented in the diagram as the space between the inner recursive loop and the outer circle. These two variables are connected to the inner recursive loop by the lines above and below the How, which enable the When and Where to influence the Who, How, and What as well as the other way around. These two variables represent the *contexts of analysis.*

The third layer of analysis is to understand that the prior two layers and the relationships between their five variables are always viewed through a frame of Why (a formal or folk theory or theories). In other words, the way the relationships between these five variables are accounted for constitutes the Why (the theory of interpretation about how the subjects, methods, and objects are related to each other within time and space). Thus, the influence of this variable is represented by an encompassing circle that shapes how we understand the relationship between the five variables and is in turn shaped by those relationships. This last variable represents the *concepts of analysis.* The 6Ws model of enactment includes the key variables that should be accounted for when describing enacted phenomena.

Each of the variables within the 6Ws model occupies a place that is home to a specific form of integral pluralism, with the Why variable being associated with three distinct forms of integral pluralism. This is because all three of these forms of pluralism are able to answer the question of "Why?" although they do it from very different perspectives. Below is a short description of each form of pluralism associated with the variables of the 6Ws model:

- **Who:** Integral Epistemological Pluralism (e.g., multiple perspectives and worldviews)
- **How:** Integral Methodological Pluralism (e.g., multiple methods of research and knowledge acquisition)
- **What:** Integral Ontological Pluralism (e.g., multiple objects and ontologies)
- **When:** Integral Temporal Pluralism (e.g., multiple time scales and horizons)
- **Where:** Integral Spatial Pluralism (e.g., multiple spatial dimensions)
- **Why$_1$:** Integral Soteriological Pluralism (e.g., multiple emancipatory aims)
- **Why$_2$:** Integral Theoretical Pluralism (e.g., multiple theories and paradigms)
- **Why$_3$:** Integral Axiological Pluralism (e.g., multiple ethical and aesthetic values).

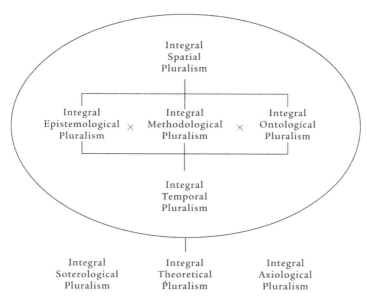

FIGURE 3.10 The integral pluralism matrix

Complex integral realism's approach to the pluralism in each of these domains is a metatheoretical one where there is a commitment to retain and connect the diversity of positions and perspectives to enable meta-level research (i.e., Edwards' (2010) "integrative pluralism"). When we replace the 6W variables with their integral pluralism equivalencies we get the Integral Pluralism Matrix (see Figure 3.10)

The Integral Pluralism Matrix includes the major forms of pluralism that are important to have a more complex, more integral, more realist understanding of reality. Typically, including two or three forms of integral pluralism is sufficient to include for most initiatives. Nevertheless, the Integral Pluralism Matrix supports us in being aware of additional forms of pluralism that we might include or consider at various points in a project. Thus, it is not necessary to include all eight forms of pluralism; rather this matrix serves to provide an overview of the total integral pluralistic landscape that is available to us.

Also, scholar-practitioners can "plug in" preferred pluralistic frameworks and distinctions within the matrix (see Figure 3.11). For example, for Integral Spatial Pluralism you could use integral theory's gross-subtle-causal-nondual framework, which might be a good choice in that Bhaskar's metaReality also includes the nondual. For Integral Epistemological Pluralism you could use integral theory's stage-state lattice (aka the Wilber–Combs Lattice). For Integral Methodological Pluralism you could use complex thought's transdisciplinary principles. For Integral Ontological Pluralism you could use critical realism's depth ontology and in particular the strata of generative mechanisms. For Integral Temporal Pluralism you could use the simple past-present-future framework.[23] For Integral Theoretical Pluralism you could use all three of the integral metatheories discussed in this chapter. So even

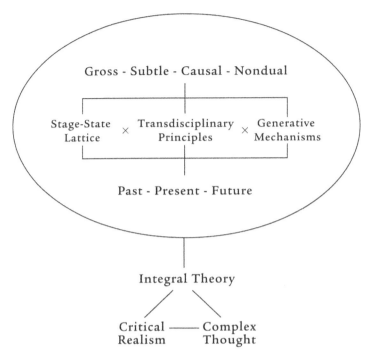

FIGURE 3.11 The integral pluralism matrix with CIR "plug-ins"

though you are using specific integrative frameworks (from each of the integral metatheories) for specific forms of integral pluralism within the matrix, you can still draw on all three metatheories for understanding the complex, integral, and realist relationships between all the variables.

Now let me provide a brief illustration of how the Integral Pluralism Matrix can be used to support specific applications to global issues. Imagine you are a marine ecologist charged with leading a study on the population decline of the Pacific Bluefin Tuna (the What) in the Northern Pacific Ocean (the Where). Because of the complexity of the issue you have decided to use a number of different methodologies (the How) such as in-depth interviews, ethnographical research, and statistical analysis. You know that you need to include as many stakeholder worldviews (the Who) as possible for sustainable solutions to emerge. Your report is supposed to cover the data from the last six years – since 2008 – and make recommendations for the next fourteen, till 2028 (the When). Given the global scale of the issue and the many dimensions you are trying to bring together in exploring possible responses, you have decided to draw on complex integral realism (the Why) as your integral metatheory. By mapping these variables onto the matrix you create a simple meta-map that helps you see all the key variables involved in your project and better understand the relationships between them. A meta-map like this can actually serve to communicate a lot of information and provide you with a metaview to see the whole system and discover new interconnections (see Figure 3.12).

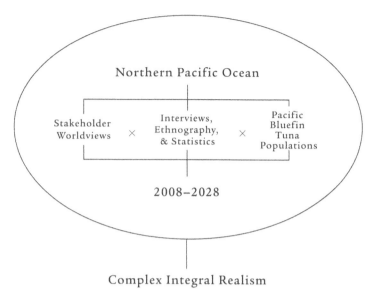

FIGURE 3.12 The integral pluralism matrix in action

Given the complexity that can accompany an approach like complex integral realism that is informed by integral pluralism I want to focus on what I consider to be the most important forms of pluralism to include in most projects. The essential variables I believe are the theories (Why) we use to describe how subjects (Who) use methods (How) to understand objects/reality (What). This I propose is the basic unit of enactment (see Figure 3.13).

In Figure 3.13, we see how enactment involves subject-method-object or Who-How-What co-arising and co-implicated in important ways in the context of theory or the Why.[24] Note the line between them is a double arrow, indicating that causality moves in both directions and is not just a linear process of subject →

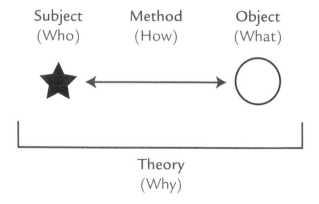

FIGURE 3.13 Enactment

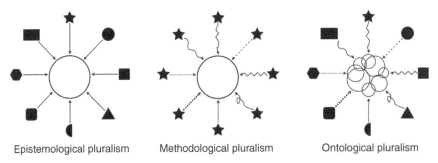

Epistemological pluralism   Methodological pluralism   Ontological pluralism

FIGURE 3.14 The three major forms of integral pluralism

method → object. This represents an enactive relationship between knowing and being, subject and object. Furthermore, the relationship between these elements is explained by a particular theory, or "the Why": the explanatory narrative that accounts for and enacts particular relations and interpretations between subjects, the methods they use, and the objects they enact. There might, however, be some aspects of objects that are withdrawn and evade enactment. As Mark Edwards (2010) points out – drawing on Anthony Giddens' (1987) notion of a *double hermeneutic* – "Theory not only creates meaning, it also concretely informs and shapes its subject matter" (p. 42). In other words, theory is not merely interpretive but to some extent, and in certain conditions is actually constitutive. Integral Theoretical Pluralism is important in part because it highlights the enactive nature of theories and metatheories. This double hermeneutic must be addressed, I believe, if we are to have a fully reflective, recursive, realist, and postmetaphysical view of enactment. Thus, complex integral realism draws on its three integral metatheories (Integral Theoretical Pluralism) to support myriad forms of enacting these three variables: Integral Epistemological Pluralism, Integral Methodological Pluralism, and Integral Ontological Pluralism. As Figure 3.14 illustrates, Epistemological Pluralism is characterized by multiple perspectives looking at an object, Methodological Pluralism is characterized by subjects using multiple methods to look at an object, and Ontological Pluralism is characterized by subjects using methods to look at a multiple, overlapping, net-worked object.

When we combine these three forms of pluralism together, our simple version of enactment (Figure 3.13) becomes a complex integral realist version of enactment (see Figure 3.15). It draws on all three integral metatheories to produce a sophisti-cated understanding of enactment.

Above I have highlighted the particular importance of three forms of Integral Pluralism for complex integral realism. Now I want to point out how each of the three integral metatheories contributes in different degrees to each of these three important forms of pluralism. This helps illustrate how Integral Theoretical Pluralism supports all the other forms of pluralism in the matrix. In what fol-lows I will identify a few of the ways each integral metatheory contributes to a pluralistic understanding of epistemology, methodology, and ontology. Starting

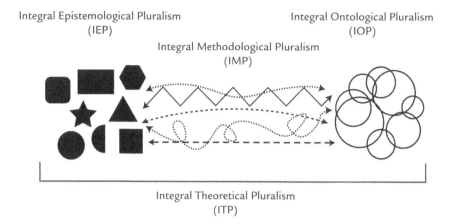

Integral Epistemological Pluralism
(IEP)

Integral Ontological Pluralism
(IOP)

Integral Methodological Pluralism
(IMP)

Integral Theoretical Pluralism
(ITP)

FIGURE 3.15 A complex integral realist version of enactment

with Integral Epistemological Pluralism, complex thought contributes epistemic reflexivity, integral theory contributes a rich taxonomy of horizontal and vertical epistemic structures, and critical realism contributes a view of a stratified embodied personality. With Integral Methodological Pluralism, complex thought contributes a well-developed transdisciplinary approach to research, integral theory contributes a powerful map of eight methodological families or zones, and critical realism contributes a robust background in doing interdisciplinary research. With Integral Ontological Pluralism, complex thought contributes a sophisticated view of the complexity sciences and how the researcher is implicated in the analyzed, integral theory contributes an understanding of the enactment of objects in relationship to the methods used and the subjects using those methods, and critical realism contributes a very valuable depth ontology and a very sophisticated philosophy of science. These various contributions are indicated in Table 3.3.

As Table 3.3 illustrates, while each integral metatheory has various degrees of contribution to the three forms of Integral Pluralism, they all have something to

TABLE 3.3 Various contributions to integral pluralism

Integral Theoretical Pluralism	Integral Epistemological Pluralism	Integral Methodological Pluralism	Integral Ontological Pluralism
Complex Thought	⬤	●	●
Integral Theory	⬤	⬤	●
Critical Realism	·	⬤	⬤

Size of circle indicates level of contribution: ● = small ⬤ = medium ⬤ = large offer each one and even the small or medium contributions become valuable in the context of complex integral realism's commitment to integrative pluralism. Also Table 3.3 highlights how each form of pluralism greatly benefits from the contributions from each integral metatheory. By way of going deeper into the last column of Table 3.3 and further illustrating the value of synergizing these three integral metatheories I want to propose how we might begin to enact a complex integral realist ontology. In short, I want to take a closer look at what an integral ontological pluralism might consist of in the context of complex integral realism.

Framework 3: complex integral realism's Ontological Domains Lattice

Ontology is the study of what is real. A complex integral realist ontology is the study of what is real in at least three main ontological dimensions (physical and systems ontologies, social and cultural ontologies, and psychological ontologies), which each contain three different ontological strata (The Real, the Actual, and the Empirical). This results in a lattice of nine different ontological domains that can be considered in an integral metatheory. This lattice is the result of combining Bhaskar's Depth Ontology lens with Wilber's often-used tripartite lens of 1st-, 2nd- and 3rd-person dimensions.[25] Note here I am foregrounding 1st-, 2nd-, and 3rd-person *ontological dimensions* (i.e., worldspaces) in contrast to 1st-, 2nd-, and 3rd-person *epistemological perspectives* (i.e., worldviews).[26] It is important to note, however, that within integral theory perspectives and dimensions are viewed as different sides of the same postmetaphysical coin – they tetra-arise within the four quadrants. Within each of the three ontological dimensions identified above there are distinct 1st-, 2nd-, and 3rd-person "objects." The development of a comprehensive and useful typology of integral objects, while beyond the scope of this chapter, is a worthwhile project that could further shed light on the kind of realism being advocated here.[27]

As Table 3.4 highlights, the Real and its generative mechanisms occur within each of the three major ontological dimensions and these underlying structures create the 1st, 2nd-, and 3rd-person phenomena associated with each dimension. For example, a psychological mechanism (e.g., a low level of emotional development) produces psychological events (e.g., an inability to take critical feedback from others), which results in the experience of psychological objects (e.g., the person in question feeling ashamed in front of their coworkers when their supervisor comments on their performance). Similarly, a social and cultural mechanism (e.g., a democratic cultural episteme) produces a social and cultural event (e.g., a grassroots revolution in the face of oppressive conditions), which results in the experience of specific social and cultural objects (e.g., anti-government flyers). These two examples – a low level of emotional development and a democratic cultural episteme – are both dealing with "interior" ontologies. The next example illustrates an "exterior" ontology, which is more typical of what people have in mind when they are discussing ontology. A physical mechanism (e.g., a person's DNA) produces

TABLE 3.4 The Ontological Domains Lattice

Ontological Dimensions

	Physical & Systems Ontologies (3rd-person dimensions)	Social & Cultural Ontologies (2nd-person dimensions)	Psychological Ontologies (1st-person dimensions)
The Real (i.e., underlying generative/ causal mechanisms or structures that create phenomena)	Physical & System Mechanisms (e.g., 4 laws of thermodynamics, morphic fields, genetic programs)	Social & Cultural Mechanisms (e.g., cultural epistemes and intersubjective structures)	Psychological Mechanisms (e.g., psychological structures – vertical and horizontal)
The Actual (i.e., events – observed or not)	Physical & Systems Events & Things (e.g., the extinction of dinosaurs, urban pollution)	Social & Cultural Events & Things (e.g., object-relations, The American Revolution)	Psychological Events & Things (e.g., personality traits, mental disorders)
The Empirical (i.e., experiences and broad empirical observations)	Experiences of Physical & Systems Objects (e.g., tornados, brain states)	Experiences of Social & Cultural Objects (e.g., food prices, poverty)	Experiences of Psychological Objects (e.g., emotions, thoughts)

Ontological Strata (left vertical label)

a physical thing (e.g., a slightly misshapen heart), which results in the experience of specific physical objects (e.g., an inability to run very fast or very long). Each of these three strata (the Real, the Actual, and the Empirical) is real – i.e., has ontological status. So "realness" is not just confined to the "top" strata of the Real, though the Real has the unique property according to critical realism of being able to be out of phase with the strata of the Actual and the Empirical. In short, within complex integral realism all nine ontological domains and their associated mechanisms, events and things, and experienced objects are equally real. The contents of one domain are not more real than the other but they are real in different ways. One of the tasks of complex integral realism is to draw on the three integral metatheories under consideration here to develop a more sophisticated view of the contents of and relationships between these nine ontological domains.

By expanding Bhaskar's depth ontology through adding a horizontal dimension we bring to critical realism an expanded view of ontology that can include more explicitly ontological dimensions associated with the interiors of individuals and collectives. Similarly by adding to integral theory's 1st-, 2nd-, and 3rd-person dimensions a stratified view of ontology we can better understand which ontological aspects within each dimension are independent, withdrawn, and enacted. Critical realism tends to emphasize the mind-independent nature of ontological realities (i.e., they are not dependent on human perception to exist). Object-oriented ontology and speculative realism tend to emphasize the withdrawn nature of ontological realities (i.e., the object is not exhausted by its being encountered by another object – important aspects of the object always remain hidden or withdrawn from the moment).[28] Integral theory in contrast tends to emphasize the enacted nature of ontological realities (i.e., the structures of consciousness and the methodologies used to disclose phenomenon do not simply discover something "out there" but bring them into existence in a participatory fashion).[29] Complex integral realism explores the contributions all three positions make to articulating a more synthetic understanding of realism.

The result of combining Bhaskar's and Wilber's triadic lenses is a multidimensional depth ontology or an "integral depth ontology" for short. There are a number of additional ontological lenses within integral theory that can be included in the development of this integral depth ontology such as the three strands of valid knowledge; the notion of broad empiricism; the eight zones of Integral Methodological Pluralism; the three eyes of knowing (Eye of Flesh, Eye of Mind, and the Eye of Spirit); the three realms of gross, subtle, and causal; and so on. For example, it will be important to explore which of the three strata (and the resulting nine domains) the various eight zones of integral theory are best suited to investigate. Can Zone 2 methods reveal psychological structures of the Real?[30] And are Zone 1 methods confined to the strata of the Empirical through their focus on our experiences of psychological objects? Likewise there are going to be additional important ontology lenses within critical realism and complex thought (e.g., Morin's theory of organization and the scientific ontology he lays out in the first two volumes of *Method*, where he provides a detailed analysis of the intricacies of physical and biological evolution) as well as from contemporary schools of thought such as speculative realism that can be included in the development of a complex integral realism.

Furthermore Table 3.4 helps us see more clearly the ways in which integral theory and critical realism complement each other. Each one of them has something to offer the development of an integral depth ontology. For instance critical realism has spent more time focused on making the case for the strata of the Real and has spent less time exploring the details of the Actual and the Empirical. In contrast, integral theory has a lot to say about the scientific ontologies associated with the Actual and the Empirical. Then within the strata of the Real, critical realism has a lot to say about physical and (social) systems ontologies. Whereas, integral theory has a lot to say about (natural) systems ontologies as well as social/cultural and psychological ontologies. Of course critical realism has things to say about social/cultural ontologies, and metaReality (Bhaskar 2002a, 2002b) has much to say about psychological ontologies but there appear to be complementary ontological strengths between these two integral metatheories. A quick example can further illustrate this complementarity: critical realism tends to point to external social systems (3rd-person dimension) for understanding how individuals are oppressed; integral theory highlights the role internal social and cultural worldview structures (2nd-person dimension) within individuals play in perpetuating their own oppressive conditions. So emancipating people requires shifts in both external social systems and internal social/cultural worldviews. Bringing in complex thought can serve to further shore up the various areas of complementarity identified above.[31]

Metadisciplinary Framework × Integral Pluralism Matrix × Ontological Domains Lattice

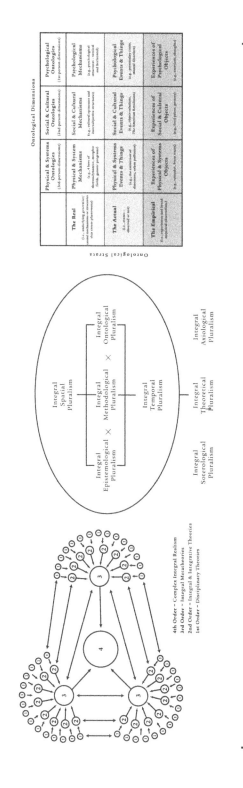

Complex   Integral   Realism

FIGURE 3.16 The enactment of complex integral realism

This section has aimed to begin an exploration about how might we develop an integral depth ontology that avoids a one-size-fits-all ontology by taking into account key distinctions from the three metatheories being discussed in this chapter. As an initial starting point I have focused on Bhaskar's depth ontology and Wilber's use of 1st-, 2nd-, and 3rd-person dimensions. Much work remains to more fully develop an integrative theory of ontology, which is all the more reason we need a meta-praxis to support an optimal level of cross-pollination and metadisciplinary engagement between the three integral metatheories explored in this chapter.

Conclusion

In this chapter I opened by pointing out the global trend toward more fragmentation and integration. I highlighted that there are an increasing number of "pioneers of integration" and that among these there are a few "pioneers of meta-integration". I identified three integral metatheories and made the case for combining their strengths into an integral *meta*-metatheory that I am calling complex integral realism. I highlighted the value of placing these metatheories into relationship with one another and how it can serve as a form of theoretical shadow work exposing blind spots and weak areas. I then illustrated how all three metatheories include four primary dimensions in unique and similar ways. This served to underscore my point that combining these integral metatheories provides a lot of value. I then introduced Mark Edwards' work around integral meta-studies as a context for the project of developing complex integral realism. At this point I introduced a metadisciplinary framework that could further develop complex integral realism. Then I presented the Integral Pluralism Matrix and its eight forms of pluralism as a way of working with the wide range of insights generated by the metadisciplinary framework. Finally, to go deeper into one form of pluralism I introduced nine distinct ontological realms and began to sketch an integral typology of objects.

Together these three meta-frameworks are combined to visually represent complex integral realism (see Figure 3.16). Each framework represents one of the variables of enactment (Who × How × What) in the context of Why (as presented in Figures 3.13 and 3.15). Thus, here I am recursively applying the meta-frameworks of complex integral realism to enact complex integral realism. So these frameworks *are both produced by and producers of* complex integral realism. This is the enactment of an integral metatheory, where its own frameworks are folded back onto itself to foster theoretical congruence and embodiment. First, the Metadisciplinary Framework represents the Who in terms of the many theories (i.e., disciplinary, integral and integrative, and meta-) that serve as stakeholders in a more complex, integral, realist metaview of reality. So each theory represents key perspectives complex integral realism wants to engage and include. Second, the Integral Pluralism Matrix represents the How in terms of the many pluralisms that are involved in the enactment of phenomena in a more complex, integral, realist metaview of reality. So each form of pluralism represents key enactment variables complex integral realism wants to embrace and incorporate. Note how at the center of the Integral Pluralism Matrix is Integral Methodological Pluralism. Thus, at the heart of this matrix is methodological pluralism, which is enacted in the context of the entire matrix of pluralisms surrounding it. Third, the Ontological Domains Lattice represents the What in terms of the many ontological domains and their associated objects that are part of the world in a more complex, integral, realist metaview of reality. So each ontological domain represents key types of objects that complex integral realism wants to acknowledge and understand. Together these frameworks create a theoretical meta-who, meta-how, and meta-what and enact a meta-why: complex integral realism.

Each of these frameworks, as this chapter has argued, supports knowledge integration and coordinated action. Both are increasingly necessary for the kinds of global response needed to address our planetary metacrisis (see the Introduction in this volume for an extended discussion of metacrisis). My aim in this chapter has been to show how the development of complex integral realism can serve to create the kind of integral metatheory needed to respond to the global challenges of the twenty-first century. The kinds of global issues we face are compounded by the disciplinary and organizational fragmentation prevalent in our postmodern moment. Thus, our global response requires an unprecedented level of knowledge integration and coordinated action. I believe integral metatheories in general and complex integral realism in particular have a lot to contribute to both. As Edwards (2010) eloquently states:

> Global problems of the scale that we currently face require a response that can navigate through theoretical pluralism and not be swallowed up by it. In saying that, twenty-first-century metatheories will need to be different from the monistic, grand theories of the past. They will have to be integrative rather than totalising, pluralistic rather than monistic, based on science and not only on philosophy, methodical rather than idiosyncratic, find inspiration in theories from the edge more than from the centre and provide means for inventing new ways of understanding as much as new technologies.
>
> *(p. 223)*

I believe complex integral realism is exactly this kind of metatheory that Edwards is describing. At the beginning of the twenty-first century we are witness to the maturation of several distinct metatheories and now these metatheories are beginning to interact and transform each other. There is much value in the scholar-practitioners of one metatheory becoming familiar with the distinctions of the others. In addition, it is important for these scholar-practitioners to engage each other so we can understand their distinctions from the inside out, not just through our own preferred lenses. This will allow us and our metatheories to be transformed by them shining a light on our own blind spots and let us be supported by their strengths and expertise. There is much richness to be gained by drawing on their work in our own writings and applications so we can cross-pollinate and create a meta-knowledge ecology. Even better would be doing joint projects together – with metatheoretical teams of research and practice comprised of individuals with fluency in one or more integral metatheory (e.g., see the chapter in Volume 2 on climate change).

The future of integral metatheory has never looked brighter than it does standing here at the birth of the twenty-first century. May we seriously consider the valuable role integral metatheories can play in creating a thriving planet and flourishing humanity for the next 1,000 years and beyond. Then hearing the clarion call of our own unique contribution to that eudaimonic vision let us roll up our collective sleeves and place our integral metaviews into emancipatory action.

Acknowledgements

I would like to thank Nick Hedlund, Paul Marshall, and Bruce Alderman for their extensive comments on an earlier draft of this chapter, which proved invaluable, and Roy Bhaskar for comments on Table 3.4.

Notes

1   For an introductory overview of each integral metatheory, see Esbjörn-Hargens (2010b) for integral theory, Hedlund-de Witt (2012) for critical realism, and Montuori (2013) for complex thought.
2   In this chapter I am using "integral metatheory" to be synonymous with "integrative metatheory".
3   The notion of "wicked problems" was introduced by Rittel and Webber in 1973. There are many different descriptions of what constitutes a wicked problem but no generally agreed upon criteria. However, features such as there not being a definitive solution, the involvement of multiple stakeholders with various mental models and worldviews, and the changing nature of the problem and how it is understood are often characteristics of "wicked problems".
4   For example, the series of symposisa between integral theory and critical realism held since 2010 (see Introduction, this volume).
5   Inspired by a vision of what might be possible if these three integral metatheories were in deeper engagement with each other, Mark Forman and I decided to invite both Roy Bhaskar from London and Edgar Morin from Paris to serve as keynote speakers at the third international Integral Theory Conference. This conference took place in 2013 in San Francisco. The theme of the conference was "Connecting the Integral Kosmopolitian" and was aimed at expanding the field of integral theory by exposing participants to the complementarity of all three integral metatheories. This event enabled an unprecedented level of contact and exchange between scholar-practitioners associated with these integral metatheories. This chapter is a further development of the opening keynote I gave at this conference.
6   By way of providing some epistemic reflexivity it is important to note that I am not equally familiar with each metatheory under consideration. I have the most familiarity with integral theory, and while I have studied Morin's complex thought for years there is very little of his work translated into English. I discovered critical realism in 2008 and have increasingly become familiar with its metaview. Thus, this chapter is not about presenting a definitive meta-comparison between these approaches (see Marshall 2012a, 2012b, 2012c, this volume, and in press).
7   In a similar vein, Hedlund (this volume) and others are referring to the synthetic combination of critical realism and integral theory as a critical realist integral theory (CRIT).

8 In 1969 Morin spent a year in California at the Salk Institute for Biological Studies. This was a pivotal period in his life as it was during this year he discovered the complexity sciences, which are a hallmark of complex thought. This year is detailed in Morin's book *California Journal* (1970). So while Morin had already written a number of books prior to Vol. 1 of *La méthode* (1977) it was *La méthode* that really marks the formal beginning of complex thought.

9 See Esbjörn-Hargens (2014) for an overview of tetradynamics.

10 Another area to explore is how critical realism's notions of transcendental self, transcendental agency, transcendental identity, and transcendental holism overlap with integral theory's four quadrants. Integral theory has a lot to offer critical realism's notion of transcendental self and how to work with the ego and embodied personality to bring it into alignment with what critical realism calls the ground-state.

11 See Esbjörn-Hargens (2014, Appendix 1) for a dozen additional examples of authors presenting their own versions of the four quadrants.

12 "More of" is not being used here to imply that more of each of these aspects is necessarily better but rather to highlight more of the best aspects of each of the three metatheories. In addition to considering all three together there is value in placing each one in dyadic encounter with each of the others for a more in-depth hermeneutic encounter.

13 And it could go the other way too: using meta-methodology to generate meta-data analyses, which are interpreted and contextualized in a meta-hermeneutics, and culminating in a metatheory (or meta-metatheory).

14 I believe integral theory can be viewed as both a theory of everything and a theory of anything, with the former not necessarily being a form of integrative monism. However, I am sympathetic to individuals who read Wilber's "theory of everything" as an integrative monism, as I believe Wilber needs to do more to distance his rhetoric from integrative monist interpretations.

15 There are different possible methods or meta-praxes for bringing together these metatheories, so you will get different "meta-data" which can be interpreted differently. For example, look at the controversy in homing in on the question of transcendental realism and the epistemic fallacy in Wilber-5. In some ways, the murky social scientific waters we are swimming in are further clouded when dealing with metatheories.

16 See Appendix G, "Logoi of Teachings," in Almaas (2004) for a discussion of different logos in the context of the wisdom traditions.

17 See Esbjörn-Hargens & Zimmerman (2009, p. 47).

18 The theories and disciplines currently listed in Figure 3.5 for Order 2 are likely more commonly associated with integral theory. Thus, for example, a critical realist might populate Order 2 with different theories around each knowledge domain than I have here. This is fine and welcomed as these charts are meant to be illustrative, not definitive.

19 See Hedlund-de Witt (2012, pp. 9–10), for a brief description of each of these.

20 Note that Figure 3.8 is limited in its ability to represent the wide range of recursive and influential relationships I have in mind for this framework. One would have to imagine a three-dimensional rendering with hundreds of arrows connecting various circles.

21 These six "W's" form a common framework used in journalism for capturing the essential elements of good reporting. It is not surprising to me that these same elements would be essential for good kosmic storytelling.

22 In the context of this chapter the notion of enactment is understood to be postmetaphysical à la Wilber in important respects but also realist in important respects à la Bhaskar, with some essential elements of epistemic reflectivity à la Morin. A full treatment of this version of enactment will be left for another time. However, I do discuss this more below in the final section on ontology.

23 A more complex temporal model can be found in Starr and Torbert (2005), who discuss a pluralist approach based on their single-, double-, triple- loop learning model: zero-dimensional time, one-dimensional time, two-dimensional time, three-dimensional time…

24 One of the key issues to consider is how aspects of the What do not necessarily co-arise with the Who, How, and Why, as the What can have its own ontological autonomy and being. This raises the issue of in what ways aspects of the What are withdrawn.

25 I am choosing to use this triadic structure over Wilber's quadratic structure for a couple of reasons. First, since I am using this triadic structure in the first part of this chapter I feel it useful to retain this structure for this section. Second, I am wanting to use the triadic structure since in my view it represents the most minimal structure one can use in this context and still be integral. So I want to promote a philosophical baseline for the development of an integral depth ontology. Third, I see philosophical value and metatheory value in using the triadic structure in this context since it nicely aligns with many other philosophical uses of this "Big Three" triad (e.g., Plato's Good, True, and Beautiful; Kant's three critiques; and Habermas' validity claims). Fourth, it is easy enough to expand this triadic structure into a quadratic one. Expanding Table 3.4 in this fashion would result in 12 (not 9) ontological domains.

26 For the purposes of this chapter "social and cultural ontologies" is being used to refer to the content of the lower-left whereas "physical and systems ontologies" is being used to refer to the UR (physical) and LR (systems) ontologies, the latter of which includes the social and natural systems.

27 For critical realism the notion of objects tends to be most often associated with the strata of the Real, though it is worth noting that there is no entry in the *Dictionary of Critical Realism* (Hartwig, 2007) for "object". However, according to Paul Marshall (personal communication), "In critical realism, the criterion for ascribing reality to something is that it be causally efficacious in the world. So all interior objects or structures or mechanisms are already real for critical realism – even illusions are real for critical realism since they affect the mind and intentional agency. For critical realism, 'object' is a global term for something that is real, a real entity, something that is existentially intransitive, a detached referent. Critical realism also talks of transitive and intransitive objects of knowledge with cognitive objects in the transitive dimension and real structures and mechanisms in the intransitive dimension." In contrast, integral theory tends to view objects as those things that are disclosed through methodologies be they an interior object (e.g., enacted through 1st-person phenomenology techniques) or an exterior object (e.g., enacted through 3rd-person empirical tools). These different uses of "object" have obscured the dialogue between critical realists and integral theorists. Thus much value will be garnered by clarifying how each integral metatheory uses key terms and concepts like "objects." Also a full elucidation of the nine ontological domains and their objects would benefit from engaging Bruno Latour's (2005) notion of actors, Graham Harman's (2011) typology of two objects (real and sensual) with two qualities (also real and sensual), Levi Bryant's (2011) typology of four objects (bright, dim, dark, and rogue), and Timothy Morton's (2013) hyperobjects and their five characteristics (viscous, molten, nonlocal, phased, and interobjective). The inclusion of these second-order theories of objects would be an important part of the integral ontological pluralism advocated here.

28 Levi Bryant (2011) is a Bhaskar-influenced speculative realist who uses "object" in a critical realist sense and argues that objects can be withdrawn because they exist in the Real and this allows them to be withdrawn. In contrast, if objects existed exclusively in the strata of the Empirical then they could be fully disclosed and not have a withdrawn nature. Integral theory's notion of enactment can be presented in a way that makes room for withdraw (see Esbjörn-Hargens & Zimmerman's (2009) discussion of "there is no single tree": pp. 174–181).

29 In the context of this chapter I am adopting a weak form of enactment (i.e., epistemology and/or method is sometimes or in some respects constitutive of being) as opposed to a strong form (epistemology and/or method is entirely constitutive of being). The latter I believe is incommensurable with critical realism and so serves as a non-starter for the synthetic engagement I am advocating here. Thus, in the context of complex integral realism I am taking a position of weak constructivism/sophisticated realism. At the same

time I encourage integral theory as a distinct lineage of metatheoretical thought/practice to continue to develop and defend a strong version of enactment.

30 Within many of the eight zone methods there is an implicit and in some cases an explicit form of retroduction. Especially in the case of the more rigorous forms of developmental structuralism (Zone 2). The whole method of rational reconstruction is a form of retroduction, which is arguably a more empirically grounded form of transcendental argumentation. Foucault's focus on cultural epistemes is an example of left-hand quadrant analysis that is trying to arrive at a speculative theory of the Real and explains various events we see. Piaget does this also when he starts with the empirical observations and looks for what the patterns of the events are here, what are the skills that people are manifesting, and then how do we deduce what are the conditions for the possibility of those skills coming forth; then he deduces the psychological structures.

31 See Marshall (2012a, p. 207) and this volume.

References

Almaas, A. H. (2000). *The pearl beyond price*. Boston, MA: Shambhala.

Almaas, A. H. (2004). *The inner journey home*. Boston, MA: Shambhala.

Bammer, G. (2013). *Disciplining interdisciplinarity: Integration and implementation sciences for researching complex real-world problems.* Canberra, Australia: Australian National University Press.

Bhaskar, R. (1975). *A realist theory of science* (1st ed.). Leeds: Leeds Books.

Bhaskar, R. (1993). *Dialectic: The pulse of freedom*. New York: Routledge.

Bhaskar, R. (2002a). *Reflections on metaReality: Transcendence, emancipation and everyday life.* London: Sage.

Bhaskar, R. (2002b). *MetaReality: Creativity, love and freedom*. London: Sage.

Bhaskar, R. (2012). Considerations on "Ken Wilber on critical realism." *Journal of Integral Theory and Practice, 7*(4), 39–42.

Bhaskar, R., Frank, C., Høyer, K. G., Næss, P., & Parker, J. (2010). *Interdisciplinarity and climate change: Transforming knowledge and practice for our global future.* London: Routledge.

Bhaskar, R., Høyer, K.G., & Næss, P. (2011). *Ecophilosophy in a world of crisis*. New York: Routledge.

Bhaskar, R., Danermark, B., & Leigh, P. (2014). *Interdisciplinarity and well-being: an essay in applied critical realism.* New York: Routledge.

Bryant, L. (2011). *The democracy of objects*. Ann Arbor, MI: Open Humanities Press.

Edwards, M. (2010). *Organisational transformation for sustainability: An integral metatheory.* New York: Routledge.

Esbjörn-Hargens, S. (2010a). An ontology of climate change: Integral pluralism and the enactment of multiple objects. *Journal of Integral theory and Practice, 5*(1), 143–174.

Esbjörn-Hargens, S. (2010b). Overview of integral theory. In S. Esbjörn-Hargens (Ed.), *Integral theory in action: Applied, theoretical and constructive perspectives on the AQAL model* (pp. 33–64). New York: SUNY Press.

Esbjörn-Hargens, S. (2014). *TetraDynamics: Quadrants in action*. San Francisco, CA: MetaIntegral Foundation Press.

Esbjörn-Hargens, S., & Zimmerman, M. (2009). *Integral ecology: Uniting multiple perspectives on the natural world.* Boston, MA: Integral Books.

Giddens, A. (1987). *Social theory and modern sociology*. Cambridge: Polity Press.

Harman, G. (2011). *The quadruple object*. Alresford: Zero Books.

Hartwig, M. (Ed.). (2007). *Dictionary of critical realism*. London: Routledge.

Hedlund-de Witt, N. (2012). Critical realism: A synoptic overview and resource guide for integral scholars. Resource paper. MetaIntegral Foundation. Retrieved August 15, 2014: https://foundation.metaintegral.org/sites/default/files/Critical%20Realism_4-12-2013.pdf.

Holland, D. (2015). *Integrating knowledge through interdisciplinarity research*. London: Routledge.

Jeffries, V. (2005). Pitirim A. Sorokin's integralism and public soliology. *American Sociologist*, Fall/Winter, 66–87.

Kofman, M. (1996). *Edgar Morin: From big brother to fraternity*. Chicago: Pluto Press.

Latour, B. (2005). *Reassembling the social: An introduction to actor-network-theory*. Oxford: Oxford University Press.

Marshall, P. (2012a). The meeting of two integrative metatheories. *Journal of Critical Realism*, 11(2), 188–214.

Marshall, P. (2012b). Toward an integral realism. Part 1: An overview of transcendental realist ontology. *Journal of Integral Theory and Practice*, 7(4), 1–34.

Marshall, P. (2012c). Ken Wilber on critical realism. *Journal of Integral Theory and Practice*, 7(4), 35–38.

Marshall, P. (in press). *Towards a complex integral realism*. London: Routledge.

Martin, R. (2009). *The opposable mind: Winning through integrative thinking*. Cambridge, MA: Harvard Business Review Press.

Mitchell, S. (2003). *Biological complexity and integrative pluralism*. Cambridge: Cambridge University Press.

Montuori, A. (2013). Complex thought: An overview of Edgar Morin's intellectual journey. Resource Paper. MetaIntegral Foundation, retrieved August, 2014: https://foundation.metaintegral.org/sites/default/files/Complex_Thought_FINAL.pdf.

Morin, E. (1970/2008). *California journal*. Brighton: Sussex Academic.

Morin, E. (1977/2009). *El método 1: La naturaleza de la naturaleza* (The method 1: Nature of nature). Madrid: Ediciones Cátedra.

Morin, E. (2001). *Seven complex lessons in education for the future*. Paris: UNESCO Publishing.

Morin, E. (2008). *On complexity*. Cresskill, NJ: Hampton Press.

Morton, T. (2013). *Hyperobjects: Philosophy and ecology after the end of the world*. Minneapolis: University of Minnesota Press.

Nicolescu, B., and Montuori, A. (2008). *Transdisciplinarity: Theory and practice*. Cresskill, NJ: Hampton Press.

Starr, A., & Torbert, W. (2005). Timely and transforming leadership inquiry and practice: Toward triple-loop awareness. *Integral Review*, 1, 85–97.

Torbert, B (2004). *Action inquiry: The secret of timely and transforming leadership*. San Francisco, CA: Berrett-Koehler.

Wilber, K. (1977). *The spectrum of consciousness*. Boston, MA: Quest Books.

Wilber, K. (1995). *Sex, ecology, spirituality: The spirit of evolution*. Boston, MA: Shambhala.

Wilber, K. (1999). *Integral psychology*. Shambhala, MA: London.

Wilber, K. (2001). On the nature of a post-metaphysical spirituality. Retrieved August 20, 2014: www.kenwilber.com/Writings/PDF/ResponsetoHabermasandWeis_CRITICS_2003.pdf.

Wilber, K. (2007). *Integral spirituality: A startling new role for religion in the modern and postmodern world*. Boston, MA: Shambhala.

Wilber, K., Patten, T., Leonard, A., and Morelli, M. (2008). *Integral life practice*. Boston: Integral Books.

Zalamea, F. (2013). *Synthetic philosophy of contemporary mathematics*. New York: Sequence Press.

APPENDIX

	INTEGRAL THEORY	CRITICAL REALISM	COMPLEX THOUGHT
Meta-Approach	Meta-Theory	Meta-Critique	Meta-Method
Disciplinarity	Postdisciplinarity	Interdisciplinarity	Transdisciplinarity
Type of Thinking	Integral	Critical	Complex
Causality	Tetra-mesh	Generative mechanisms	Retroactive and Recursive
"Homebase" Fields	Psychology and Religion	Philosophy and Social Theory	Sociology and Complexity Sciences
Spirituality	Contemplative (phenomenology)	Secular/Everyday (transcendental argument)	Natural (creativity)
Whole/Part Relationships	Holonic (Whole is a Part)		Holographic (Whole is in Part)
Primary Sciences	Human	Social and Experimental	Natural
Philosophical Emphasis	Epistemology	Ontology	Methodology
Epistemology–Ontology	Integrates	Disambiguates	Complexifies
Knowledge	Enactive	Transcendental and Critique	Complex
Famous Fallacy	Pre/Trans	Epistemic	
Logics	Developmental: *Differentiation Transcendence Integration*	Dialectical: *Thesis Antithesis Synthesis Negativity Absence*	Dialogical: *Antagonist Complementary Competitive* [no expectation of synthesis]
Emancipation	Individual	Social	Social
Philosophical Context	American Postmodernism	British Empiricism	French Deconstructivism
Liberating Activity	Shadow work/ Integral Life Practice	Social critique	Self-critique
Primary Activity	Mapping (Third-person emphasis)	Critiquing (Second-person emphasis)	Reflecting (First-person emphasis)
Subject/Agent	Kosmic Address	Agency in Structure	Researcher in the analyzed object
Critique of Atomism & Holism	Gross and Subtle Reductionism		Part/Whole
Critique of Culture	Postmodernism	Modernism	Simple Thinking
Global Influence	Canada, USA, Australia, Germany, Brazil, Japan, Holland	England, Scandinavia, South Africa	French-speaking Africa, Latin America, Italy, Spain, France
Ethical Focus	Basic Moral Imperative (First-person emphasis)	Eudemonistic Society (Second-person emphasis)	Homeland Earth (Third-person emphasis)

FIGURE 3.A1 Complex integral realism trialectics

4

TOWARDS A COMPLEX INTEGRAL REALISM

Paul Marshall

Introduction

The focus of this chapter is three contemporary integrative metatheories: critical realism, integral theory and complex thought. All three began to be constructed, and were essentially finalised, around the same time – from the mid-1970s to the early–mid 2000s – and each has their founding father and chief architect: Roy Bhaskar, Ken Wilber and Edgar Morin, respectively. They have also all undergone a series of developmental phases, with each subsequent phase building on and deepening – in a more or less preservative sublation – the anterior phases. Critical realism has gone through three major phases – basic or original critical realism (1975–late 1980s), dialectical critical realism (early 1990s) and the philosophy of metaReality (early 2000s); integral theory has moved through five phases, with phase four (1995) representing its first fully mature expression with the AQAL framework; and complex thought emerged as a result of a third 'genetic or paradigmatic reorganisation' of Morin's thinking (starting in the mid-1970s)[1]. Furthermore, their main foci are distributed between psychology, spirituality and individual emancipation (integral theory); philosophy, the social sciences and social emancipation (critical realism); and the physical and biological sciences, a generalised anthropology and human emancipation (complex thought), thus providing a rich and broad knowledge base for understanding the reality of the world, society and ourselves. They offer a host of insights, analyses, frameworks, cognitive resources and conceptual tools that, together, form a *complex, integral realist metatheory* that can help us deal more effectively with the difficult and urgent problems of today's world.

In this chapter, I offer a preliminary examination of what such a complex, integral realist metatheory might look like.[2] I begin with a brief sketch of the three metatheories' core strengths and signature innovations, and then outline some of the ways in which the three metatheories resonate and converge, the general common ground they share, at the same time pinpointing some of the different strengths and approaches within that common ground. I then consider how the combination of this common ground, varying strengths and different emphases facilitates rich possibilities for cross-fertilisation and synergy, focusing on a number of key areas: post-formal perspective; ontology and epistemology; inter/transdisciplinarity; ethics and emancipation; and spirituality. Finally, I distill all the above, suggesting a number of key features or essential ingredients that a *complex integral realism* might possess.

Core strengths

The introduction has mentioned some areas in which each metatheory has focused on. These areas naturally coincide with their strengths, which will now be briefly considered.

Starting with critical realism, there is no doubt that its signature innovation and core strength is its depth ontology. This was outlined in its first sub-phase of transcendental realism and then gradually extended and deepened in subsequent phases to include mind, intentional agency, social structures and the vast realms of non-being (absence) and nonduality. Unlike the other two metatheories, this core strength emerged at the very beginnings of critical realism, acting as a solid foundation on which the rest of the philosophical edifice was constructed. It serves as the basis for its epistemology, its ethics and emancipation, its approach to interdisciplinarity, its dialectics and spirituality, with the latter two in turn deepening and strengthening its ontology and all the areas based on it. It was established through the use of transcendental argument (from experimental activity) and immanent critique (of empiricism), two philosophical resources it has made extensive use of. While critical realism started from within the philosophy of science and a focus on the natural sciences, its main concern, from its critical naturalism sub-phase on, has been the social sciences and their emancipatory role – and freedom, transformative ethical praxis and social emancipation as a whole. We could therefore say that its core strengths include: its depth ontology, philosophy and philosophical tools, ethics and social emancipation, dialectics and a secular spirituality based on philosophical reflection.

Integral theory's signature innovation and core strength is clearly its AQAL framework, established in its main work, *Sex, Ecology, Spirituality* (1995), and developed in subsequent works to include an integral methodological pluralism. The AQAL framework includes its powerful taxonomy of levels, lines and quadrants. Another core strength is its focus on spirituality, psychology and individual emancipation. Whereas critical realism started with science and ended, in metaReality, with (a secular) spirituality, and while complex thought rejects any form of transcendent spirituality, integral theory began straight off with a powerful embrace of Eastern (and also Western) spirituality, combining it with Western psychology until they eventually coalesced into one of its four key dimensions of reality (the upper-left quadrant). This quadrant possesses a rich mixture of developmental lines taken from constructivist developmental psychology; a structuring of psychopathologies and corresponding therapies; considerations of therapeutic practices and of psycho-dynamic and shadow work taken from Western depth psychology; a deep analysis of states of consciousness and contemplative phenomenology – drawn from the great wisdom traditions – and their relation to structures of consciousness; an examination of different personality typologies and a theory of the self – making it integral theory's strongest quadrant and another of its core strengths. It points to individual emancipation and is backed by a well-developed integral transformative (or life) practice, which is an additional strength of integral theory.

The signature innovation and core strength of complex thought is its (closely connected) complex epistemology and theory of organisation, which is based on an examination of the physical and biological sciences. The former involves a deep critique of the 'paradigm of simplicity' and an outline of a 'paradigm of complexity' that makes use of the systems and complexity sciences, critiques of classical science and logic, and the Western dialectical tradition to develop a number of tools and principles with which to capture and honour the complexity of phenomena. It also leads naturally into a transdisciplinarity via a *unitas multiplex* in which the various relatively autonomous disciplines unite to capture this complexity. The latter entails a conception of nature as *physis*, which Morin likens to Spinoza's notion of nature as the "very source of creation and organisation".[3] He generalises *physis* as 'active organisation' that runs through the physio-, bio- and noospheres (or *physis*, *bios* and *anthropos*) and links them together. And it is this organisation, not matter, which evolves – into the more complex organisational forms of life and mind. The core strengths of complex thought are thus its focus on the physical and biological sciences, its theory of organisation, its epistemology and transdisciplinarity. Other strengths include its biological theory of self and its intense focus on a 'generalised anthropology' (on *homo complexus*), from which stems a complex ethics.

This quick sketch already reveals a number of clear differences in focus and strengths – the natural, social and (interior) human sciences; (a generalised) anthropology, philosophy and spirituality/psychology; human (non-transcendent) emancipation, social emancipation and individual emancipation; epistemology, ontology and enactment (epistemology and methodology).[4] The next section will outline some of the common ground within which these different strengths and emphases operate.

Common ground

One of the first points of convergence to stand out is the *integrative, maximally inclusive and non-reductionist* nature of the three metatheories, their attempt to respect and capture reality in its full complexity and multidimensionality. Integral theory aims to include and integrate as much of reality and human knowledge as possible into a coherent whole (via its signature innovation, the AQAL framework or matrix, backed by its integral methodological pluralism). Critical realism provides an original depth ontology (its signature innovation) that is maximally inclusive, embracing as real everything that is causally efficacious in the world, ranging all the way from illusions to the nondual. And complex thought argues for the use of an open rationality to dialogue with reality on its own terms, not subjected to some rigid epistemological or rationalised straitjacket, and so respecting phenomena in their full complexity. All three are consequently staunchly anti-reductionist, rejecting the 'paradigm of simplicity's' *exclusive* use of analytical thought, reductionism, rigid formal logic and specialisation. They include the above, once purged of their less wholesome or even pathological aspects,[5] in a more expansive "union of simplicity and complexity" (complex thought[6]), with analytical thought "dialectically over-reached as a precious gem"[7] (critical realism), and in a 'vision-logic' that 'transcends and includes' formal operational rationality (integral theory).

By moving into complexity, dialectical thinking and vision-logic, each metatheory displays a '*post-formal' cognition*[8] that goes beyond both the atomism of analytical thinking (reduction of wholes to parts) and the holism of systems thinking (reduction of parts to wholes). Such post-formal cognition aims to capture the full complexity of phenomena, respecting their multidimensionality, their multiple ontological strata, their full context and their holistic interrelationships and non-linear causality. It sees phenomena as open systems that undergo transformation and as forming part of larger systems and metasystems, and it is often associated with dialectical thinking. Each metatheory has its particular strengths in this area – dialectical complexity (critical realism and complex thought), AQAL metasystematic taxonomy (integral theory), critique of systems theory (integral theory and complex thought) – that, as we shall see, might supplement and enrich the others.

Another example of their integrative, maximally inclusive and post-formal approach is their openness to sources of knowledge beyond empirical science (and philosophical reflection), which, between them, include all established first-, second- and third-person methodologies used in the various sciences, as well as art, poetry and literature, self-introspection, mystical experience and contemplative phenomenology. Such an open epistemological embrace is also reflected in their approach to premodernity, with all three, in their own different ways, recognising and including its insights and contributions to knowledge as well as pointing to elements (e.g. magic and myth) that still form fundamental aspects of modern humanity. All three extract the enduring truths not only of premodernity but also of modernity and postmodernity, while at the same time rejecting their false-hoods or less wholesome aspects. They attempt to move beyond both modernity and the postmodern reaction to modernity, beyond the 'flatland' (integral theory), paradigm of simplicity (complex thought) and irrealist, actualist and ontologically monovalent (critical realism) metaphysic that has dominated science and philosophy for so long. And again, as we shall see, their different emphases here make for mutual enrichment.

Another area of resonance, this time rather broad and perhaps with as many differences as similarities, is their *realism and approach to ontology*. Critical realism is clearly the most explicit and unashamedly realist, with its innovative depth ontology forming the cornerstone of its whole edifice. It is a solid, robust ontology that, I will argue, has a great deal to offer integral theory and complex thought, which also clearly presuppose the existence of a mind-independent reality.[9] But because of the general taboo against ontology and its conflation with epistemology (critical realism's epistemic fallacy), both complex thought and integral theory have tended to avoid ontology. Nevertheless, this has also facilitated an emphasis on epistemology in both, leading to a number of insights into the knower/subject's epistemic structures (integral theory) and vulnerability to epistemological distortions (complex thought) that can strengthen critical realism's epistemology and construal of the transitive dimension. The possibilities of cross-fertilisation between the ontology and epistemology of all three metatheories are especially suggestive.

Furthermore, all three have a *stratified vision of reality*, with integral theory forging an ingenious updating and reworking of the Great Chain (Holarchy) of Being through its AQAL framework; critical realism in a three-pronged stratified approach (into the intransitive and transitive dimension; the real, actual and empirical domains; and the multiple strata of reality); and complex thought and integral theory both adopting Teilhard de Chardin's division of reality into the physiosphere, biosphere and noosphere (or complex thought's *physis, bios, anthropos*). Again, as we shall see, their different approaches here can bolster each other.

A natural consequence of their non-reductionist, dialectically complex and post-formal approach is an *inter- or transdisciplinarity*. Most open-system phenomena contain a number of dimensions, internal and external causality, multiple ontological strata and complex interrelationships that inevitably require an inter- or transdisciplinarity. An exclusively specialised, disciplinary and reductionist approach to such phenomena (e.g climate change, well-being or human nature) is clearly inappropriate and violates this complexity. All three metatheories take such an interdisciplinary approach, with complex thought stressing epistemology, critical realism ontology and integral theory enactment (epistemology and methodology). Again, these different emphases within an overall common approach suggest rich possibilities for cross-fertilisation.

In contrast to much of modern philosophy and science, all three metatheories are *strong defenders of interiority, the subject and agency – and of both universals and particulars (singularity)*. This is absolutely crucial to any 'post-postmodern' philosophy, with fundamental ethical and emancipatory implications. Modern science tends to reduce interiors to exteriors (integral theory's 'flatland'), while the abstract universality of modernity ignores singularity; and postmodern philosophy tends to reduce the individual subject (and thus agency) to intersubjective networks, while its championing of diversity and pluralism often ignores the universal commonalities that all humans share. Against this, all three metatheories defend interiority (integral theory most elegantly and consistently), a dialectical universality or *unitas multiplex* that embraces universal commonalities and singularity (with different philosophical, anthropological and developmental approaches[10]) and the 'relative' autonomy of the subject with its own emergent powers and transformative agency (critical realism with a strong philosophical defence and complex thought with a strong scientific one). Pooling together their different strengths and approaches could provide a formidable defence.

Interiority is related to *spirituality* and the subject and agency to *ethics and emancipation*. These are two final, and fundamental, areas in which the three metatheories' different emphases, within an overall common ground and similar emancipatory concern, promise fruitful possibilities of cross-fertilisation. They differ, for example, in their emancipatory focus (individual, social and human emancipation), their praxis (integral; transformative ethical praxis; constant self-examination), their ethical grounding (developmental/Spirit; ontology/dialectics/ground-state; 'ethics without foundation'/faith in certain values) and their spiritual orientation ('reverent' spirituality based on contemplative phenomenology; secular spirituality based on philosophical reflection; immanent spirituality and secular terrestrial religion[11]) – all of which lends itself to a creative tension and synergetic potential.

One further area of potential cross-fertilisation which needs to be mentioned, and which is linked to these two areas of spirituality and ethics and emancipation, is that of human nature. Complex thought, especially, has focused on this question and its rich notion of *homo complexus* can combine with critical realism and metaReality's model of human nature, based on its notions of concrete universal ↔ singular and four-planar social being, and integral theory's powerful upper-left quadrant and developmental approach to provide a robust *complex integral realist philosophical anthropology* that can serve as a basis for a similar complex integral realist ethics and integrated eudaimonics.

Suggestions for cross-fertilisation

I will now consider how the different strengths and emphases of each metatheory, within this shared common ground, might contribute to, enrich and bolster the others. I will structure this around a number of key domains already identified: post-formal perspective, ontology and epistemology, inter- and transdisciplinarity, ethics and emancipation, and spirituality. Given the space available, only a preliminary sketch highlighting the essential features will be possible.

Post-formal perspective

The various strengths in this area have already been pinpointed: dialectical complexity; AQAL metasystematic taxonomy; critique of systems theory; and an attempt to move beyond both modernity and postmodernity. I will argue that the first two can nourish each other and that the different critiques of systems theory and approaches to premodernity, modernity and postmodernity can complement, enrich and deepen one another.

Dialectical complexity ↔ AQAL taxonomy/upper-left quadrant

Critical realism has elaborated a sophisticated general theory of dialectic that reviews the Western dialectical tradition as a whole and elucidates a "non-preservative sublation of Hegelian dialectic".[12] In so doing, it provides a whole host of philosophical and conceptual tools that enable us to better grasp the dialectical complexity of phenomena, including holistic interrelationships, non-linear causality and real change and transformation.[13] Complex thought also provides a reworking of (especially Hegel's) dialectic (which it calls dialogic), offering further conceptual tools, especially its dialogic principle, its principle of organisational recursion and its notion of polycentric circuit, to capture complexity.[14] Integral theory contains an implicit, but unelaborated dialectical complexity, and the explicit emphasis on dialectical connections, complex interrelationships and holistic causality by both metatheories can help bring it to the fore, giving its quadrants a more nuanced, dialectical intricacy and its levels and directionality a more messy, non-linear, less 'ladder-like' feel (which it has sometimes been accused of).

With regard to the quadrants, complex thought applies its notion of recursive circuits to its twin trinities of individual-species-society and brain-mind-culture (which loosely map onto the four quadrants),[15] while critical realism uses the same principle of recursion in its 3L totality and transformational model of social activity (TMSA), which it later "generalize[s], dialectize[s] and substantialize[s]" into four-planar social being (which coincides with the four quadrants even more closely).[16] Applying this recursive complexity, and the general emphasis on dialectical relationships, to integral theory's quadrants would make more explicit the implicit dialectical connection *between* them that is manifested through its emphasis on both the irreducible nature of each quadrant and their simultaneous 'tetra-meshing' and co-arising. And applying such dialectical complexity *within* the quadrants, especially the powerful upper-left quadrant, might prove particularly fruitful, since it would help safeguard against any tendencies to reduce individuals to particular aspects of consciousness that have been abstracted out in isolation. This can occasionally occur in the *use of* (not necessarily as a natural consequence of) integral theory's developmental levels, for example, which has been rightly criticised.[17] Infusing integral theory with the explicit dialectical complexity of critical realism and complex thought can help protect against such misuse, emphasising that consciousness is a transformational system in which the various components[18] are inseparable and yet distinct (which is the very definition of a dialectical relationship or connection), all causally co-determining and affecting each other – and causally affecting and being affected by the other quadrants or planes.[19] In return, integral theory can deepen both critical realism and complex thought with one of its core strengths: the psychological sophistication of its upper-left quadrant, with its levels, lines, types, states and psychodynamics.[20]. Combining these strengths would enable us to capture a fuller, more complex picture of each individual, and ensure that we honour their unique singularity.

As to integral theory's levels and directionality, the reworked dialectics and complexity of critical realism and complex thought can help highlight how such directionality operates through a dialectical process that is open, realist, grounded in the material world, non-linear, messy and susceptible to regressions and detotalisation (and even collapse).[21] In return, integral theory can enrich both critical realism and complex thought with its AQAL metasystemic taxonomy, which can provide them with a much more complete and coherent picture of the overall thrust and synchrony of development through the four quadrants and the three spheres (physio-, bio- and noospheres). They can together map a long-term, complex directionality in the process of evolution as a whole and, more specifically, of human development, that is moving towards greater complexity and consciousness (all three), a post-'planetary iron age' (complex thought),[22] a more eudaimonistic society (critical realism), the evolution of Spirit-in-action (integral theory) and of the ground-state (metaReality).[23] Such a direction is undetermined, uncertain, unpredictable, mysterious and messy but one that is urged forward by absence (critical realism), Spirit/Eros (integral theory), the ground-state and the cosmic envelope (metaReality) and creative, active organisation in a 'tetragram' together with order, disorder and random interactions (complex thought)[24] – while at the same time being dependent on the ethical agency and transformative praxis of human beings who are conditioned (and, of course, enabled) by biological, psychological, socio-cultural constraints and hampered by heteronomous orders of determination. Combining the various perspectives can reveal a complex, messy directionality driven by some form of creative force that is open to a number of coherent interpretations, from secular (complex thought, critical realism) to secular spiritual (metaReality) to contemplative spiritual (integral theory).

Critiques of systems theory

Systems theory is a manifestation of systems thinking, and both are reactions against the atomism (reduction of wholes to parts) of classical science, and yet they tend to go to the other pole and adopt a holism that reduces parts to wholes and so remain within the same 'fundamental Enlightenment paradigm' (integral theory) or 'paradigm of simplicity' (complex thought) as atomism.[25] Both integral theory and complex thought adopt its enduring truths[26] but reject its inadequacies, basing their critiques on their core strengths: the integral quadrant framework and the 'paradigm of complexity' and theory of organisation. Integral theory rejects its 'subtle reductionism' or 'flatland holism', which reduces all interiors (left-hand quadrants) to exteriors (right-hand quadrants), and its failure to distinguish between individual and social hierarchies (which is what its upper- and lower-right quadrants do). This is a nice example of how the AQAL framework can be used in a simple yet powerful way to critique partial positions that are insufficiently integrative and all-inclusive. Together with its notions of holons (part/whole) and holarchies (nested, natural hierarchies of holons) – adopted from Koestler – they illustrate how integral theory 'transcends and includes' systems theory and the complexity sciences, situating them in the lower-right quadrant and, more specifically, zone 8 of its integral methodological pluralism. The AQAL framework is a powerful tool that could supplement and prove useful to both critical realism and complex thought.

Complex thought also 'transcends and includes' systems theory, emerging as it did out of "a linking together, confrontation, problematization, transformation and complexification" not only of the systems and complexity sciences but also of philosophy of science (Bachelard, Popper, Kuhn, Lakatos, Holton, Feyerabend), critiques of formalism (Ladrière), reflections on the nature of science (Husserl and Heidegger) and the Western dialectical tradition (Heraclitus, Nicholas de Cusa, Pascal, Hegel, Marx, Adorno, Jung, Bohr, Gödel, Lupasco).[27] Complex thought critiques the holism of systems theory for its "blindness to the parts as parts ... its myopia with respect to organisation as organisation and its ignorance of the complexity at the heart of any complex unity".[28] Both the whole and the parts, together with their interrelationships and organisation, need to be integrated in an explanatory complex whole – in a polyrelational circuit.[29] Its whole theory of organisation – which stresses organisation over system and places it in a dialogical, recursive 'tetragram' with order, disorder and interactions that operate throughout the three spheres of the universe, "enabl[ing] *physis* to emerge, unfold, constitute and organize itself"[30] – and general focus on the physical and biological sciences can supplement and bolster both integral theory and critical realism in a number of ways.

First, it coincides with critical realism's stress on the partial, fissured, incomplete nature and insufficiency of totality (adopting Adorno's "Totality is the non-truth"[31]), and like integral theory it emphasises the always uncertain nature of a whole given its embeddedness within other wholes *ad infinitum* (Koestler and Wilber's holon and holarchy). As a result, preference should not be given to wholes over parts since the collapse of a whole might give rise to a richer emergent that had been repressed by 'organisational constraints'. In this sense the whole is not just more but also *less* than the sum of its parts, thus stressing the stifled potential (linking to critical realism's real domain and notion of absence, and integral theory's as yet unfolded potential) of phenomena.[32]

Second, its critique of systems theory and holism can combine with integral theory's AQAL critique to form a richer vision, while its general analysis of totality, parts and wholes can combine with dialectical critical realism's 3L totality (with notions like sub-totalities, holistic causality, mediation, constellationality, duality and hiatus-in-duality) to form a fuller conception.[33] Furthermore, complex thought's theory of organisation can provide a more detailed analysis of the intricacies of the generative, self-organising nature of the universe, supplementing integral theory's broad evolutionary taxonomy with theoretical sophistication based on the physical and biological sciences. And complex thought's biological theory of the subject – emergent out of *physis* with relative autonomy – could also serve as a useful supplementary tool for integral theory and critical realism's notion of the subject and agent (and vice versa) (see section on ethics and emancipation). Finally, by creatively integrating the scientific research and insights of Terrence Deacon's recent 'theory of emergent dynamics'[34] – which shows a strong resonance not only with (a) complex thought's emphasis on organisation and constraints and his biological theory of the subject, but also (b) dialectical critical realism's notion of absence as causally efficacious;[35] (c) metaReality's ontologically differentiated 'panpsychism' or panentheism; and (d) the general, evolutionary vision of all three metatheories that emphasises the creative and in some sense enchanted nature of the cosmos, its unity (seamless connection of the three spheres), our at-homeness within it and the reintegration of meaning, value, purpose – it should be possible to establish an even more robust *complex integral realist metatheory* and vision.

Premodernity, modernity and postmodernity

The approaches of each metatheory to premodernity, modernity and postmodernity both overlap and differ. With regard to premodernity, all three embrace its axial rationality,[36] which they see as a more balanced form of rationality than modernity's,[37] while integral theory and metaReality take on board premodernity's enchanted cosmos with its spiritual infrastructure, defending an absolute nondual realm that sustains the relative realm of duality.[38] Complex thought stresses the existence of rationality, myth and magic in all periods (due to their being constituent parts of humanity), against the modern notion (in fact 'myth') that rationality began, and myth and magic ended, with modernity.[39] This last point is reached from a different perspective but coincides with integral theory's and Gebser's insistence that the various structures of consciousness that human ontogenetic and phylogenetic development passes through, remain active (included) even though they have been essentially transcended. Morin bases this on an analysis of the psychic world, on the power of the imaginary and myth in humans,[40] while integral theory's perspective is based on a thorough analysis and synthesis of cognitive and constructivist developmental psychology (and Gebser's cultural philosophy).[41] These last two perspectives could be combined to form a deeper vision of reason, myth and magic, while the philosophical arguments for nonduality of metaReality could be combined with the phenomenological ones of integral theory to form a powerful case for nonduality and the essential spiritual nature of reality (see section on spirituality for further discussion on such cross-fertilisation).

Regarding modernity, critical realism and complex thought are especially critical,[42] while integral theory, seeing modernity as the latest expression of the rational ('orange') structure of consciousness, has a more appreciative take overall. Integral theory actually coincides with many of critical realism's and complex thought's critiques of modernity and adds some more of its own,[43] while complex thought and critical realism embrace many of the enduring truths highlighted by integral theory.[44] But their different underlying approaches – one predominantly developmental and interior, the other primarily socially emancipatory and exterior, and stemming from a (critical) Marxist legacy – make for a fruitful exchange. Integral theory could benefit from the socio-politically more critical and sensitive analysis of modernity, as well as from the more nuanced analysis of its historical and philosophical development,[45] while critical realism and complex thought could benefit from an analysis that takes into account a deeper underlying process of unfolding structures of consciousness. In this way, both the pathologies of modernity and its developmental advance over what preceded it could be laid bare in a more balanced, thorough and richer analysis that includes both an interior and exterior perspective. The internal liberating force, together with its potential for oppression, contained in this rational and individualistic structure of consciousness might, for example, be seen as having begun with the axial age, East and West, in a more balanced form,[46] later manifesting in Roman civilisation with a heightened individualism,[47] to then re-emerge with modernity – slowly establishing itself over 200 years through first the Renaissance,[48] then the Reformation[49] and finally the Enlightenment/Scientific Revolution. This process left a positive, emancipatory legacy – its emphasis on reason and evidence over myth and established authority; its promotion of democracy and the dignity, rights and flourishing of the individual; its gear shift from an ethnocentric to a more worldcentric stance;[50] the 'fraternal face of humanism', critical and self-critical thinking and classical political liberalism of thinkers like Spinoza, Locke, Rousseau, Voltaire, Montaigne, Montesquieu and Wilhelm von Humboldt[51] – but its accentuated individualism ended up manifesting itself in an atomistic ego isolated from, and in conflict with, others and the world, which it objectified and approached with an instrumental rationality and abstract analytical thought. Whatever the causes for such deviation – e.g. its coinciding with capitalism and industrialisation, socio-political, cultural and psychological causes, the perhaps difficult-to-avoid consequence (given the emergent nature of humanity out of *physis* and *bios*) of human individuation, all of which could be analysed using the combined tools of the three metatheories – it would seem clear that what is required to regain balance is to maintain the positive elements of humanism, the Enlightenment and the emancipatory potential of science, and also to turn inwards to offset its exclusive focus on the objectified exterior, and in doing so begin to confront and integrate our shadow/*demens* elements and reconnect with a deeper spiritual fount and closer contact with the human essence. Further, the abstract, analytical, instrumental reasoning of *Verstand* needs to be balanced by a reaching out to the dialectical, intersubjective reason of *Vernunft*, as all three metatheories insist upon.[52] Some of the later phases of the philosophical and political discourse of modernity (from Romanticism to German idealism to Marxism to utopian socialism and anarchism to postmodernism, each with its own imbalances and blind spots) can be seen as attempts to redress these imbalances – while others (like neo-liberalism) can be seen as further unhealthy deviations. And the three metatheories can be seen as all attempting to redress the imbalances further, reworking Hegel's closed, deterministic and irrealist dialectic (critical realism and complex thought), replacing abstract universality with dialectical universality (all three), embracing the interiors (all three) and our deeper spiritual source (integral theory and metaReality) and attempting to step out of the modern/postmodern groove to a new, healthier space of greater freedom and solidarity (all three).

Moving on to postmodernity, this can be seen as essentially a reaction against modernity, with many of the three metatheories' critiques coinciding with those of postmodernism: modernity's philosophical conception of man as an atomistic, autonomous, rational ego/subject, its instrumental rationality and abstract universality – a toxic trio that contributed to the exploitation and oppression manifested in capitalism, the repression of non-European, non-modern, marginalised and minority voices, and the domination of humans over nature, mind over body and emotions, the noosphere over the biosphere. And the postmodernists additionally denounced modernity's naïve epistemology and objectivism. In response, they fiercely championed singularity, diversity, difference and pluralism; insisted on the constructed nature of reality and the fact that reality is always interpreted; stressed the contextual dependence of meaning; and highlighted the intersubjective (linguistic and cultural) networks in which the individual is embedded and which mould the subject's perceptions and consciousness. All three metatheories embrace these postmodern insights,[53] but they also all reject the extreme variants that more often than not characterise postmodernism and post-structuralism: (a) their rejection of universality *in toto*; (b) their strong social constructionism that denies any mind-independent reality; (c) their claim that there is only interpretation and thus no objective truth; (d) their deconstructive assertion that no meaning exists or can be conveyed; (e) their judgmental relativism which claims that no belief is more adequate than another; (f) their Nietzschean perspectivism which converts life into a pastiche rather than a (partial) totality; (g) their reduction of the human subject to intersubjective networks.

The different approaches of the three metatheories, from within a common ground, to postmodernism's critiques, insights and extreme variants again make for a fruitful dialogue. Integral theory pays a great deal of attention to postmodernity,[54] offering clear accounts and adopting a weak social constructionist position in phase four, but then moving to a stronger social constructionism in its postmetaphysical phase five with a distant and even dismissive stance towards ontology. There is currently a debate within integral theory on the wisdom of this move, with recent writings of Wilber being more accepting of ontology.[55] This will be discussed more in the next section on ontology and epistemology. Complex thought does not discuss postmodernism directly very much, but it clearly adopts a weak social constructionism, an implicit belief in the mind-independence of reality and in accounts of reality being more or less correct, a strong notion of *unitas multiplex* that embraces both universality and singularity/diversity, a powerful assertion of the relative autonomy of the subject, and thus of the possibility of agency, and a notion of a structured whole. Of the three, critical realism is the metatheory that provides the strongest defence against the extreme variants of postmodernism, thanks to its sophisticated depth ontology, which can arguably strengthen the other two metatheories quite considerably and can underpin the *realist* base of a potential *complex integral realist* metatheory. And by combining this depth ontology with (a) critical realism's own additional stress on judgmental rationality, dialectical universality, totality and agency; (b) integral theory's stress on universal levels and principle of unfoldment, its positioning of postmodernism within its lower-left quadrant together with its rejection of quadrant absolutism and powerful defence of the individual subject and its structured AQAL totality; and (c) the aforementioned aspects of complex thought, we have the basis of an extremely robust position that is immune to postmodernism's excesses and marks a move beyond the general modern/

postmodern 'flatland', 'simplicity', 'irrealist/actualist/monovalent' paradigm that has dominated philosophy and science, knowledge and society for so long.

Ontology and epistemology

According to critical realism,[56] there has been a general irrealist tendency within Western philosophy as a whole that has privileged epistemology over ontology, starting with the Greeks, moving through what Bhaskar calls the "Cartesian-Lockean-Humean-Kantian paradigm",[57] and reinforced in the twentieth century by the dual linguistic turn in both analytical philosophy (logical positivism, linguistic analysis and Rortian neo-pragmatism) and continental philosophy (Nietzsche, Saussure and French poststructuralism). But there appears to be a shift in recent years, in both analytical and continental philosophy, a shift that was predated especially by critical realism's depth ontology (but also by Rom Harré, E. H. Madden and George Molnar[58]). In analytical philosophy, recounts Groff, there has recently emerged, starting in the 1990s, a "'second wave' of dispositional [powers-based] realism", that has brought "causal powers … back on centre stage, philosophically – for the first time in centuries".[59] And in continental philosophy, the even more recent movement of speculative realism involves a number of thinkers who no longer follow "the repetitive continental focus on texts, discourse, social practice and human finitude", but are rather "speculating once more about the nature of reality independently of thought and of humanity more generally". They generally endorse Quentin Meillassoux's notion of correlationism, which critiques the anti-realism of continental philosophy, where "reality appears in philosophy only as a correlate of human thought"[60] – which resonates strongly with critical realism's epistemic fallacy (the conflation of epistemology and ontology), which Bhaskar traces back to the Greeks and argues affects all Western philosophy. These are encouraging developments which, arguably, might reflect a general move beyond a 'mental structure of consciousness' (à la Gebser) that has tended to conflate reality with mind – exemplified by Parmenides' "Thinking and being are one and the same"[61] and critiqued in the epistemic fallacy and correlationism – and that adopts a non-anthropocentric position and open rationality that dialogues respectfully with reality, allowing it to speak for itself without being strained through rigid epistemological, ideological or rationalised constructions. A position, however, which of course also recognises the always already interpreted and translated, socially produced nature of knowledge (postmodernism, weak social constructionism, philosophy of science), as well as the epistemic structures (stressed by integral theory) and epistemological distortions (stressed by complex thought) that the knowing subject is inevitably conditioned by (see below).

Both complex thought and integral theory before phase five are essentially realist in that they accept the mind-independent nature of reality, though in a much less explicit and elaborated form than critical realism. In its postmetaphysical phase five, integral theory becomes somewhat ambivalent, inconsistent and contradictory on this point, with Wilber seemingly torn between his previous phase-four commitment to "intrinsic features of the world that are registered by the senses" so that "in that general sense they have objective reality",[62] and a desire to make spirituality acceptable to modernity and postmodernity via a theory of enactment that prioritises epistemology and methodology over ontology, displaying a number of passages that present clear examples of critical realism's epistemic fallacy.[63] However, recent writings have shown a slight backtracking and a more accepting and less dismissive stance towards ontology,[64] and his latest writing on this topic actually invites integral theorists to ground integral theory in critical realist ontology if they so wish, arguing that doing so "doesn't change the fundamental items of the Integral Framework in the least", only its "meta-understanding".[65] Such a grounding would strengthen integral theory considerably, I shall argue, as well as aligning it with the important new general shift in philosophy towards ontology and realism and beyond a subordination of ontology to epistemology, a shift that finally escapes the Western philosophical and mental structure's conflation of mind and reality. Wilber is probably right in arguing that it would leave the fundamentals of integral theory intact, although it *would* entail a reconsideration of a number of notions – like enactment and kosmic address – of integral theory's postmetaphysical phase five, which, in their current form, would not be able to rest coherently alongside a critical realist ontology. Nevertheless, if we combine these insightful notions, in weaker versions, with the critical realist ontology and complex thought's epistemology, then we should be able to come up with a viable and cogent synthesis that includes (a) the kosmic address of both the perceiving subject and perceived object – an extremely fruitful notion; and (b) how, generally, the consciousness of the knowing subject (with all its conditioning structures and distorting components – see below), together with the injunctions and methods it uses, gain access to, and knowledge of, a mind-independent reality.[66]

Wilber's invitation to ground integral theory in critical realist ontology implicitly recognises its benefits, and here I will briefly sketch what some of these might be – for both integral theory and complex thought – as well as how critical realism can benefit from their epistemological insights. Critical realism offers an approach to ontology that goes beyond both naïve realism (of pre-Kantian critical philosophy) and Kant (and all the metatheories that have stemmed from Kant). It rehabilitates ontology in a sophisticated way that enables us to embrace both a weak social constructionism (as both complex thought and integral theory up to phase four do) and a strong realism that disambiguates ontology from epistemology and clearly asserts the mind-independent nature of reality. And in so doing it offers a powerful critique of Kant and the empirical realism and ontological actualism[67] that Kant inherited from Hume and that implicitly underlies all current mainstream metatheories in both the natural and social sciences: from positivism to hermeneutics to neo-Kantianism to social constructionism and postmodernism. It provides a new underlying metaphysics that, unlike both Hume's and Kant's, endorses a powers-based causality, where necessity is grounded in the phenomenal world, one based on a stratified ontology that adds a 'real' domain with generative, transfactual structures, mechanisms and powers that lie beyond, and produce, 'actual' events. It therefore provides, unlike Hume's and Kant's metaphysics, a solid grounding for causal agency and, together with the subsequent deepening of its ontology to include mind, social structures, absence and nonduality, offers a powerful philosophical basis for transformative ethical praxis, real change and social emancipation, geo-historical directionality and the actualisation and realisation of ever-deeper potentialities and needs. On the critical realist metacritical account of Western philosophy, it constitutes a radical break not just with Hume and Kant – and therefore all current mainstream metatheories – but also the whole tradition, all the way back to Parmenides, which has displayed a predominantly irrealist, actualist and ontologically monovalent bias. The recent emergence of similar realist positions in both analytical and continental philosophy suggests that the time for such a break is ripe. And this break, with this depth ontology, is, given the extensive shared common ground, fully compatible with,[68] and advantageous to, both integral theory and complex thought – not only grounding agency, ethics and emancipation but also providing protection against judgmental relativism and ontological support for inter/disciplinarity and spirituality (see sections below, and note 66).

In return, the core strengths of complex thought (epistemology) and integral theory (its upper-left quadrant) can infuse critical realism and its transitive dimension/epistemology with greater sophistication, especially with respect to the knowing subject. Both integral theory and complex thought go more deeply into the human psychic world than critical realism, with the former stressing especially developmental structures of consciousness[69] that condition an individual's worldview and perception of reality, and the latter emphasising a host of internal factors that distort the subject's perception and conception of reality.[70] Both therefore underline the need for greater self-reflexivity, with integral theory urging that researchers undergo a first-person self-assessment guided by the components of the upper-left quadrant,[71] and complex thought insisting that we subject knowledge to a meta-point of view that involves objectifying ourselves, recognising our subjectivity and becoming self-reflexive and self-critical. The incorporation of such insights and emphases – of such epistemic structures and epistemological distortions – into critical realism's transitive dimension would strengthen it considerably, given that critical realism tends to emphasise only the fact that knowledge is socially produced. By adding this psychological/interior dimension to epistemology, we supplement the modern/Marxist stress on the social structural/economic base conditioning of consciousness, the philosophy of science's emphasis on the cultural and paradigmatic conditioning of knowledge (Kuhn, Feyerabend) and the postmodern highlighting of the intersubjective cultural and linguistic network conditioning of knowledge and consciousness. And by also insisting on the genetic/species/biological/neurophysiological, etc.[72] conditionings of consciousness (and therefore knowledge) – both complex thought and integral theory focus on this – we end up with a four-quadrant (integral theory), four-planar (critical realism), trio of trinities[73] (complex thought) appreciation of conditioning influences on the epistemic subject. Such a psychologically, socially, culturally and biologically aware epistemology (and transitive dimension), combined with a sophisticated, philosophically grounded ontology (intransitive dimension), makes for a powerful base upon which to build a *complex integral realism*.

A few other points of cross-fertilisation also need mentioning: two specific points in relation to the developmental structures and lines of integral theory's upper-left quadrant, and one regarding the three metatheories' general overall epistemological stance. Integral theory's developmental structures and lines can be seen as critical realist generative mechanisms of the real domain of the mind, thus providing critical realism with an extra level of explanatory power. Critical realism describes mind as an emergent power with causal efficacy in the world via human intentional agency, with reasons (understood as a combination of cognitive beliefs and conative desires) acting as causes. These developmental structures, which have been brought forth and rigorously studied by constructivist developmental psychology, exert a powerful influence on people's desires, beliefs and reasons, and from there behaviour and action, and can be incorporated into critical realism's (and complex thought's) explanatory toolkit as a deeper layer of causal structures in the real domain of the mind. The same applies, of course, to any additional psychological mechanisms, like the other components of the upper-left quadrant and complex thought's sources of epistemological distortions. The levels and lines of constructivist developmental psychology, however, are particularly powerful and empirically well established.

The other point related to these developmental structures is that they act not only as structures of liberation and developmental unfolding, not only as paths to eudaimonia and emancipation. They are also, potentially, *internal individual* structures of oppression, which can be brought to the fore, and so complement the emphasis made by critical realism (and complex thought) on *external, social* 'power$_2$' structures of oppression and subjugation. This dual emancipatory/oppressive nature of structures of consciousness, together with the internal focus of integral theory and the external focus of critical realism and complex thought, was remarked upon in the discussion on modernity. And it can be applied in general to analyses of both collective and individual instances of oppression. Individual and collective development, in integral theory's (and constructivist developmental psychology's) rendering, unfold in a broad sequence of ever-increasing awareness, sense of identity and moral embrace – from ego- to socio- to ethno- to world- to planet- to cosmocentric. Consequently, adults at earlier stages of development – especially in particular lines like those of self-identity, social-emotional and moral development – where one's circle of embrace is closed in on a small group or even just oneself, naturally tend to more oppressive power$_2$ relations than those at later stages. Other factors are, of course, involved – like psychological health, socio-economic situation, cultural and political climate, etc. – and heavily influence the expression of such developmental structures, with each structure possessing both healthy and unhealthy manifestations. Nevertheless, these structures are highly generative, and need to be taken into account in any analysis of oppression and subjugation – and also emancipation and liberation. Again, they arguably constitute a powerful additional explanatory and analytical tool for both critical realism and complex thought.

With respect to the general epistemological stance of the three metatheories, there are a number of ways in which they could nourish each other. Critical realism's epistemology is a logical outcome of its transcendental realist ontology, with a 'logic of scientific discovery' that involves a reiterative movement from manifest phenomena (invariants/regularities) to the underlying causal structures and mechanisms producing them.[74] It describes each science as revealing ever-deeper strata that explain, without explaining away, previous higher-order strata; and with the sciences themselves ordered into successive strata of ever more complex, or less basic, subject matter (from physics, to chemistry to biology …), thus reflecting the broad holarchy of developmental stages described by integral theory. It also extends this logic from the natural to the social sciences, providing an 'essential unity of scientific method' appropriate to both and taking into account the ontological and epistemological limits of naturalism in the social sphere.[75] From there it develops methodological schema for both applied and theoretical explanations in social scientific research, as well as an interdisciplinary approach based on its emphasis on generative mechanisms, open system phenomena with multiple ontological strata and laminated systems[76] (see section of inter/transdisciplinary). Such an epistemology and methodology, with its robust ontological base, can fruitfully inform both complex thought and integral theory, which lack this ontological grounding. In turn, integral theory's epistemological pluralism (based on its taxonomy of epistemic structures,[77] as we have seen), integral methodological pluralism (which highlights the need to include all methodologies, not just those favoured by the natural and systems sciences) and stress on enactment and 'kosmic address' (which combines the perspective/quadrant and methodology used to access the object plus the developmental level of the subject) can enrich critical realism and complex thought. A dialogue between such different epistemological, methodological and theoretical positions and emphases could lead to a richer, more balanced integral realist approach that reflects the complex relationship between ontological object/world and epistemic subject/knower. And by inviting complex thought into the conversation, with its epistemological complexity, its emphasis on a *unitas multiplex* of knowledge systems in a broad transdisciplinarity aided by a number of conceptual tools to help capture the complexity of reality (see next section), we can move towards an even more comprehensive *complex integral realist* approach to ontology, epistemology and methodology.

Inter/transdisciplinarity

As we have seen, all three metatheories, given their post-formal, non-reductionist and integrative nature, tend naturally towards some form of interdisciplinarity. Inter- and transdisciplinarity have both been defined in a number of different ways and rest alongside other related approaches like multidisciplinarity, crossdisciplinarity, metadisciplinarity and postdisciplinarity. Critical realism emphasises an interdisciplinarity based on its depth ontology, complex thought highlights a transdisciplinarity based on its epistemological complexity and integral theory stresses a metadisciplinarity based on its integral methodological pluralism, although they all incorporate the other related approaches to provide a more nuanced position.[78] Their common objective, however, is to honour and capture the complexity and multidimensionality of phenomena, something they all do through a synthetic, integrative approach – and so the broad umbrella term of 'integrative inter- (or trans-) disciplinarity' might be appropriately applied to all three. To achieve this common goal, each metatheory, through their respective ontological, epistemological or methodological prisms, offers different conceptual tools that could inform and benefit the others.

Critical realism highlights the open systemic nature of phenomena which, combined with its depth ontology, entails that all phenomena are subject to a number of causal structures and generative mechanisms, very often from a number of distinct ontological levels (thus forming 'laminated systems'[79]). Its version of interdisciplinarity therefore involves the synthesis and integration of the knowledge of these different generative mechanisms, leading to an emergent integrative outcome. It also stresses the need for transdisciplinarity, by which it means the creative deployment of cognitive resources from a variety of different fields and disciplines. Its transdisciplinarity is therefore epistemological in essence, in contrast to the ontological base of its interdisciplinarity.[80] This less-developed transdisciplinary focus of critical realism can benefit from the transdisciplinarity that stems from complex thought's core strength of epistemological complexity, while the latter can gain from the strong, ontologically-based interdisciplinarity of critical realism. Together, they provide an impressive array of conceptual and explanatory tools to capture and understand the nature of complex phenomena. These include, from critical realism, the notions of open system phenomena, laminated system, four-planar social being, seven-scalar social being, concrete universal ↔ singular with its multiple quadruplicity, holistic complexity, real determinate absence and the philosophy of metaReality principles of universal solidarity and axial rationality to facilitate the crossdisciplinarity required to integrate the different perspectives from each discipline.[81] And from complex thought, they include the notions of polycentric circuit, *physis* as active organisation, the dialogic principle, the holographic principle, the principle of organisational recursion, a *unitas multiplex* of relatively autonomous disciplines that open up and loosen the boundaries that separate them, a stress on conjunction and synthesis rather than just disjunction and analysis, and a thorough critique of the 'paradigm of simplicity' that promotes reductionism, decontextualisation and hyperspecialisation. Many of these tools from each metatheory overlap, having emerged naturally out of a similar post-formal position, but some do not and so offer the other fresh perspectives. The key gift that critical realism can present to complex thought in this area is its depth ontological perspective on interdisciplinarity together with the tools specific to that perspective, since this is a perspective that complex thought lacks. In turn, complex thought can offer critical realism its more epistemological focus, which attempts to provide common tools or 'linking operators' – a common epistemological language that can complement critical realism's common ontological language – that help the different disciplines communicate, open them up to interdisciplinary dialogue and bridge the gap between C.P. Snow's 'two cultures'. In this way they can join forces to prevent the violation of the intrinsic complexity of reality. Furthermore, complex thought's epistemological focus places more emphasis on integrating the knowing subject into the research process, highlighting the numerous epistemological distortions to which it is vulnerable (as we saw in the previous section) and the resulting need for constant self-vigilance.

And this last point connects us to integral theory, which also places significant emphasis on knowing the knower. As we saw, its developmental approach brings together a complex array of developmental lines that develop through broad structures of consciousness that determine how a subject/knower perceives and conceives reality. This 'taxonomy of epistemic structures' constitutes an epistemological pluralism of multiple perspectives through which the subject (the who), together with specific injunctions or methods (the how), enact or bring forth the object being investigated (the what).[82] In conjunction with the notion of kosmic address, this enactive position highlights the crucial importance of the position within the AQAL matrix from which the knowing subject is situated while observing the object of study (which has its own kosmic address). And as such, it has a great deal to offer both critical realism and complex thought: providing a sophisticated 'depth epistemology' and consequent stress on integrating the knower into knowledge, as well as insisting on a methodological pluralism and how the method one uses determines what partial 'side' of the object one captures. But its focus is tilted too far towards the 'who' and 'how', leaving the 'what' with very little intrinsic essence.[83] This is where critical realism's depth ontology, which underpins its approach to interdisciplinarity, can help balance integral theory's 'integrative interdisciplinarity' or metadisciplinarity organised around its integral methodological pluralism.

So together, the three metatheories could constitute a *complex integral realist* 'integrative inter/transdisciplinarity' that offers a host of conceptual tools to capture the complexity and multidimensionality of phenomena, a common epistemological and (depth) ontological language to foster communication between disciplines, the integration of the knowing subject into knowledge via a (depth) epistemology and constant epistemological self-vigilance, and an equal pluralistic respect for, and understanding of, the complex essential nature of the phenomena under study, of the knowing subject and of the array of methods and perspectives available.

Ethics and emancipation

In the 'Common ground' section, we saw how all three metatheories provide a strong defence of the subject and agency, which is intimately connected to both ethics and emancipation. And we saw how integral theory emphasises individual emancipation and grounds its ethics in its core strengths of developmental levels and spirituality (Spirit); how critical realism stresses social emancipation and a transformative ethical praxis based on *its* core strengths of ontology, dialectics and secular spirituality; and how complex thought embraces a (non-transcendent) human emancipation based on its stress on complexity, a constant self-examination and faith in certain values.

Given the depth of the topic and the limited space available, I will make just a few suggestions for cross-fertilisation based on the three metatheories' respective strengths in this area. The critical realist emphasis on social emancipation and transformative ethical praxis is based on a robust philosophical defence of the subject and agency (seen as "embodied intentional causality or process"[84]) via its synchronic emergent powers materialism (SEPM) and its transformational model of social activity (TMSA), later fortified by its four-planar social being and its 2E negativity and 4D transformative praxis whereby 'agents absent absences/ills' in a dialectic of freedom. This defence of agency is incorporated into a social emancipatory ethics that includes additional tools like explanatory critique – which critiques cognitive ills (false beliefs and their causal factors) and non-cognitive ills (unsatisfied human needs and potentials and factors that prevent their realisation); an emancipatory axiology that propels humans from 'primal scream to eudaimonia' and underlies a rational directionality of geo-history; and an ethical naturalism (that grounds ethics in facts and science) combined with a moral realism (which distinguishes between the real and actual domains of moral reality) that enables us to know moral truths, to derive an ought from an is, values from facts.[85] While the other two metatheories also possess powerful defences of the subject and agency – and can consequently reinforce each other in this terrain – critical realism offers some powerful sociological and philosophical tools to critique actual society and morality that the other two lack. Furthermore, it grounds its ethics and social emancipation in science, realism and, above all, its original depth ontology, something that both integral theory and complex thought, given their implicit realism and the compatibility of critical realism's sophisticated ontology, could greatly benefit from.

The philosophy of metaReality goes beyond dialectical critical realist ethics by grounding it in an expanded ontology that includes a spiritual infrastructure to reality and an absolute realm of nonduality that sustains and underpins the relative world of duality. This nondual realm, argues Bhaskar, is the deep interior of being, an essential constituent of social life and also the ontological foundation of the cosmos – the foundational level of being that is immanent in all subsequent emergent levels of reality/being. By extending ontology to include spirituality and nonduality, metaReality becomes a philosophy based on identity and unity, rather than critical realism's base of non-identity, thus considerably strengthening its emancipatory intent. It enables it to go beyond the critical realist critique of 'demi-reality' (the world of duality sharpened into dualism, split, fear, hate and alienation) and its attempt to reveal the deeper structures and potential transformation of relative reality in order to show that a non-oppressive duality is possible. By bringing the nondual ground to the surface through transcendental argument from everyday social activity, it helps tip the scales in the emancipatory "struggle, in our present epoch, of nonduality and demi-reality for the realm of relative (dual) reality" in favour of the former.[86] And integral theory can add its weight to the scales, complementing the philosophy of metaReality with its own powerful embrace of spirituality and nonduality, based not on philosophical reflection and transcendental argument but on the contemplative phenomenology of the great wisdom traditions and mystical experience. Together, these two different ways of revealing the nondual, spiritual ground of reality can promote both social emancipation and an ethics that recognises the ultimate spiritual essence of all being (see section on spirituality).

Integral theory's main focus, however, as we have seen, is on individual emancipation based on an 'integral transformative (or life) practice' that facilitates both 'horizontal translation' (healing at specific structure-stages: 'cleaning up'), 'vertical transformation' (from one structure-stage to the next: 'growing up') and also horizontal state-stage development (stabilisation at ever-deeper states: 'waking up'). Its ethics are largely dependent on this process of individual self-transformation, which enables development to levels that embrace an ever-wider circle of awareness, care and compassion and depth of ethical regard for others – a development towards ultimate identity of self and other. This focus on individual transformation and emancipation (via especially its strong upper-left quadrant) is one of its strengths and can partake in a fruitful exchange with critical realism's focus on social transformation and emancipation.[87] The latter, especially in the philosophy of metaReality, also stresses the need for a 'practical, this-worldly mysticism' in which personal and social transformation are inextricably linked, but lacks the elaborated personal praxis that integral theory can provide – which in turn lacks the social scientific tools and socially emancipatory depth-praxis of critical realism. Integral theory has a number of other useful notions and distinctions,[88] and argues for an integral ethics that includes all four quadrants, including social and political activism, but its key strength and focus is on personal healing, transformation and emancipation. Combining this with critical realism's social transformative praxis, each one boosting the other's secondary focus, and with the additional help of complex thought's approach (see below), can make for a comprehensive complex integral realist emancipatory praxis and ethics.

The ethics and emancipation of complex thought differs in a number of ways from integral theory and critical realism's. While, like the other two metatheories, it defends an emergent subject with relative autonomy and causally efficacious powers, it rejects any grounding for its ethics either in spirituality or ontology, and embraces a human emancipation that involves moving beyond the 'planetary iron age', continuing hominisation and civilising earth.[89] It argues for an ethics without foundations – as part of the general epistemological crisis in foundational certainty – but one nevertheless dependent on a re-vitalisation and relinking of its individual-society-species trinity.[90] This dialogically interrelated trinity gives rise to an 'auto- (or self)-ethics', a 'socio-ethics' and an 'anthropo-ethics', respectively, which are also inextricably connected, with special emphasis on the first given its mediating role in the latter two. Complex thought's self-ethics involves a hard process of constant self-examination and self-observation, of developing a 'metapoint of view' in order to objectivise, decentre and relativise oneself. It involves patiently building up a self-reflexivity and "rehabilitat[ing] introspection, disdained by both objectivist psychologies and depth psychologies for whom only the psychotherapist is qualified to plumb the mental depths".[91] Morin, of course, recognises the importance of psychotherapy and the help of a third-person perspective for self-knowledge, but insists on the need for both "extraspection" and introspection, combining them in an "auto-hetero-examination".[92] He recognises and highlights the difficulties and traps of introspection,[93] but insists that it – together with self-criticism, 'psychic gym', a recursive ethics ("evaluating our evaluations, judging our judgments, criticizing our criticisms"[94]), resistance to moral self-righteousness and a personal responsibility linked to solidarity – is vital for an ethics designed to "resist our own inner barbarism".[95] A turn inwards is required to offset the modern emphasis on the exterior, and complex thought's insistence on constant self-examination and introspection can complement integral theory's equal insistence on 'extraspection', shadow work and psychotherapy – together with metaReality's insistence on a 'practical mysticism' – to form a complex integral realist base for a powerful individual ethics, individual integrity and transformation.

Another strength of complex thought is its complex anthropology, which guides its complex ethics and especially its 'anthropo-ethics'. It attempts to understand human nature and the human condition in its full complexity, highlighting humanity's deep connection to the cosmos and nature; recursively linking reason, affectivity and impulse; brain, mind and culture; the individual, society and species; insisting on the continuing presence of myth and magic in modern humankind and especially on the dialogic of *homo sapiens* and *homo demens* in a *homo complexus* that also includes counterparts to the modern emphasis on the rational, utilitarian and technological nature of humanity.[96] It also connects human diversity with human commonality in a *unitas multiplex* of the universal and singular, entailing a universal ethics that goes beyond the abstract universality of modern lay ethics like Kant's and distorted (in their exoteric versions) universal ethics of religions like Christianity, Buddhism and Islam – in other words a dialectical universality (like critical realism and integral theory, as we have seen) and a 'planetary humanism' facilitated by the planetary era that now unites humanity concretely. An anthropo-ethics aims to integrate this complexity and common human destiny in our individual consciousness, taking full responsibility for the future of humanity and our 'Homeland Earth'. It thus involves, using integral theory's developmental sequence, a world- and planetcentric consciousness that "transcends and includes" the egocentrism (where each individual-subject is the "centre of reference and preference") that we need to live, the ethno- or 'genocentrism' (where our family and clan are the centre of reference and preference) we inherit via our genes/species, and the 'sociocentrism' in which "our society imposes itself as the centre of reference and preference".[97]

The complex anthropology of complex thought, which Morin has forged over a period of 50 years in numerous works from *L'homme et la mort* (1951) to *L'humanité de l'humanité* (2001b), could be combined with the critical realist notion of human nature (based especially on its notion of concrete universal ↔ singular and four-planar social being), integral theory's four quadrants (especially its powerful upper-left quadrant and developmental taxonomy) and both metaReality's and integral theory's grounding of the human essence in spirit and nonduality to form a robust complex integral realist model of human nature – which could then in turn serve as a solid basis for a complex integral realist ethics.

Spirituality

If we were to place the three metatheories in a spectrum of spiritual focus, integral theory would be at one end, critical realism/philosophy of metaReality in the middle and complex thought at the other. As we saw, integral theory started off with a fully spiritual approach, a position it has maintained throughout and one that has made spirituality one of its core strengths. Critical realism, on the hand, began with science and only embraced an explicit spirituality in its last metaReality phase – although in retrospect we can see a natural progression from basic critical realism's real domain to dialectical critical realism's real determinate absence to metaReality's emptiness and the ground-state, each notion plumbing ever-greater depths. As to complex thought's approach to spirituality, we have seen how it categorically rejects any form of transcendent spirit/god/cosmic envelope, but does provide a vision of *physis* that could be broadly interpreted as a kind of 'immanent spirituality' à la Spinoza – though one thoroughly grounded in science. Its theory of organisation sees nature as *physis*, which pervades all reality as active organisation, and Morin himself likens this conception to Spinoza's notion of nature as the "very source of creation and organisation".[98] It depicts nature/*physis* as generative, self-creating and self-organising, with organisation acting together with order, disorder and interactions to form a 'tetralogical loop' that underlies the "great game of cosmogenesis" and is the "immanent principle of transformations and organization" that enables *physis* to "emerge, unfold, constitute and organize itself".[99] As was mentioned in the section on the critique of systems theory, Morin's theory of organisation – and biological theory of the subject – could enter into dialogue with Deacon's strongly resonant theory of emergent dynamics to provide a solid scientific account of creative evolution from the Big Bang on through the three spheres (physio-, bio-, noosphere).

   This scientific account of evolution might then be examined for potential synthesis with integral theory's and the philosophy of metaReality's 'panpsychic' or panentheist visions, both positing a spiritual infrastructure to the universe and consciousness as enfolded in all being. MetaReality's defence of a universe endowed with a spiritual infrastructure and pervasive (latent or manifest) consciousness is primarily philosophical, using a transcendental argument from everyday social activity, while integral theory's is primarily phenomenological, based on mystical experience and the contemplative phenomenology of the great wisdom traditions. Integral theory also embraces a 'reverent' spirituality, while metaReality talks of a secular spirituality, with the ground-state replacing the immanent divine and the cosmic envelope transcendent God/Spirit.[100] Such a potential synthesis would thus combine a scientific account of creative evolution, a philosophical/secular deduction of pervasive consciousness and nonduality and a phenomenological/reverent assertion of a fully immanent and transcendent Spirit. It would have to filter out the strengths and weaknesses of each position, and a dialogue between Bhaskar and Wilber on their different 'panpsychic' positions, and also between Deacon's vision and both critical realism/metaReality and integral theory, has already begun.[101] At first glance, it would seem that all three metatheories and Deacon share a common ground that emphasises the creative, and in thus some sense enchanted, nature of the cosmos, the unity and open totality of the universe with its three spheres intimately connected (via active organisation, emergent dynamics, Spirit/Eros, 3L totality and emergent strata, nondual ground-states/cosmic envelope), and embraces interiority and an emergent subject and subjectivity. It would also seem that such a synthesis would be wise not to use the term panpsychism, due to its anthropocentric baggage and myriad versions that can lead to misunderstanding. Wilber seems fairly comfortable with the term,[102] although he prefers 'paninteriorism', Bhaskar uses the term in scare quotes,[103] Morin would never use the term and Deacon is 'strongly allergic to panpsychic views'.[104] What is required is a position that respects the evidence of contemplative science (rigorous contemplative phenomenology backed by rational and philosophical reflection and ancient, respected lineages that conduct peer-group appraisal via confirmation or falsification/refutation), includes the rigour of philosophical/transcendental argument and incorporates the findings of empirical science. (Depth) phenomenology, philosophy and science are each able to access different aspects of reality and the knowledge they each disclose, when done well, needs to be respected and integrated.[105]

There is other potential for cross-fertilisation in this area, some of which has already been discussed in earlier sections: the directionality of evolution, ethics and emancipation and an individual transformative praxis. The different positions on spirituality strongly affect each metatheory's approach to these questions, which needs to be spelled out a little more, especially their position on the essential nature of human (and all) being. But first, I would like to add one more element to the account of complex thought's overall position on spirituality/religion. We saw how Morin categorically rejects any form of transcendent god and yet adopts a Spinozan-like vision of a creative nature/*physis* that could loosely be interpreted as an immanent spirituality. His rejection of a transcendent god, and consequently of "other-worldly salvation", places him squarely in this world and his focus on human and earthly emancipation. He also rejects any form of ideological "this-worldly salvation" emerging from the disguised terrestrial religions of European modernity based on reason (à la Robespierre) or science (à la Comte or Marx). But he does accept a 'third type' of secular, earthly religion that embraces an "omnipresent mystery" (revealed by the absence of God), love (like Christianity) and compassion (like Buddhism), and urges use of the power of religion (etym.: 'relink') to promote the fellowship, "communication and communion" that "we need in order to continue hominization and to civilize the Earth".[106] Such a religion would connect with the ideal of fellowship that the other types also possess, but without revelation, God or ideology. While clearly different from integral theory's and metaReality's immanent/transcendent approach (see below), it shows how all three metatheories embrace some element of religion or spirituality as a basis for emancipation.

MetaReality went through religion (in its transcendental dialectical critical realist sub-phase) to reach spirituality, which Bhaskar eventually saw as a presupposition not only of religious practices but also for all emancipatory projects (which he realised at the beginning of his 'spiritual turn') and even of everyday life (which he saw with the philosophy of metaReality). Integral theory likewise, this time right from the start, moved directly to the deep spiritual core that lies beneath all the great religions and made it the basis of its emancipatory focus. And complex thought uses the universal fellowship inherent in religion to promote civilisational advance.

There exists, however, a gulf between complex thought's limited spirituality and integral theory and metaReality's approach. Unlike complex thought, the latter two embrace: (a) a transcendent Spirit/cosmic envelope; (b) a spiritual infrastructure to the universe; (c) an absolute realm of nonduality that underpins and sustains the relative world of duality; (d) consciousness as enfolded in all being; and (e) this spiritual ground being our, and all sentient beings', essential nature. This strongly affects their approach especially to ethics, emancipation and individual transformation/praxis. I would argue that integral theory and metaReality's spiritual position is the stronger one – spirituality being one of their strengths – especially when their phenomenological and philosophical approaches are combined. As such, it could considerably bolster complex thought, especially via its assertion of the spiritual deep essence of human being, which reaches an interior depth with ground-state qualities[107] that lies beyond the mind, and the nondual ontological foundation of the cosmos that sustains relative reality. Such a position would strengthen complex thought's generalised anthropology, supplement its theory of organisation, offer a foundation to its ethics and enhance its transformative praxis/self-ethics. And, as we have seen, complex thought has much to offer integral theory and critical realism/metaReality in these areas. There is thus a great deal of room for cross-fertilisation in a number of areas, with the solid spiritual base laid down by integral theory and metaReality playing a significant role.

There are of course differences between integral theory and metaReality's approaches to spirituality, for example in their position on 'panpsychism',[108] but the common ground outlined above is more significant. Within this common ground integral theory's strength is in its analysis and integration of the spiritual insights and contemplative phenomenology of the great wisdom traditions, including their deep exploration of states of consciousness and the 'subtle and causal' realms and bodies, their meditative cartographies and meditative state-training (through the state-stages). It also examines the complex relation between states and structures of consciousness, between state-stages and structure-stages, with models like the 'Wilber–Combs Lattice',[109] and introduces powerful notions like the 'three faces of God' based on its four quadrants. MetaReality's strength is in its philosophical defence of nonduality via transcendental argument, arguing that an absolute realm of unity/identity or nonduality acts as an ontological foundation for the relative world of difference or duality and is the 'deep interior or fine structure' of being. It also emphasises an 'esoteric sociology of everyday life' where transcendence is a ubiquitous and vital constituent of social life. And it offers a number of key notions like co-presence, the theory of transcendental identification in consciousness and reciprocity.[110] Together they provide two different approaches to a common spiritual ground that can be fruitfully combined. Their combined, common spiritual vision is obviously an advance on traditional, exoteric/ethnocentric religions, but also on the spiritual, esoteric core of the great wisdom traditions in a number of ways. First, it incorporates the findings of science, the modern notion of evolution and the insights of postmodernity. Second, it contextualises consciousness within the other dimensions of reality (via the four quadrants/four-planar social being). Third, it offers, as well as a phenomenological justification, a purely philosophical defence of spiritual reality and nonduality and places them within a philosophical ontology grounded in science. And, finally, it breaks through beyond the impersonal 'True Self' highlighted by the great wisdom traditions to the expression of a personal 'unique self' (integral theory) or singularised ground-state or dharma (metaReality), reflecting the post-formal notions of dialectical universality, concrete universal ↔ singular and *unitas multiplex* that all three metatheories highlight.[111] It is, in short, with elements of complex thought's take added on, a vision that integrates the spiritual insight and depth phenomenology of premodernity; the science, universal 'fraternal humanism', evolutionary paradigm and stress on the dignity and flourishing of the individual of modernity; and the concrete pluralism and singularity emphasised by postmodernity – transcending and including all three in a post-formal, complex integral realist world spirituality that is open to both a reverent and secular interpretation.

   A final point to make in this area is on the relation of spirituality to philosophy. All three metatheories provide critiques of Western philosophy: complex thought via its critique of the paradigm of simplicity (especially the rigid use of Aristotelian formal logic and the Cartesian method); critical realism through its sophisticated metacritique that highlights its ontologically monovalent, analytical, actualist and irrealist bias; and integral theory offering a critique and overview through a radically spiritual prism.[112] These three critiques could fruitfully gain from each other since they all tap into a number of crucial truths and point to different flaws and absences: for example, the analytic problematic (all three); the privilege of epistemology over ontology/epistemic fallacy and the denial of real determinate absence and non-being (critical realism); and the general lack of interiority and especially deep interiority/spirituality (especially integral theory but also critical realism/metaReality). The critical realist and integral theory analyses of the Greeks (Parmenides, Plato and Aristotle) and German Idealists, for example, are very different and might lead to some interesting additional insights for both. The critical realist metacritique is especially strong, philosophy being one of its core strengths, but the integral theory spiritual critique offers many insights (e.g. its discussion of the 'Ascenders and Descenders', the latter's split into the 'ego and eco camps', its outline of a 'Western Vedanta', its appraisal of the German Idealists) that could supplement it – as well as being richly informed itself by the critical realist critique. The insights and critical analyses of all three could, together, form a powerful critique of Western philosophy, providing a philosophical/historical basis for a complex integral realist critique and vision for the twenty-first century.[113]

Some key features of a complex integral realism

Having outlined the common ground shared by the three metatheories, together with their particular strengths and emphases and a number of ways in which, in some specific areas, these different approaches within this common ground might result in some constructive cross-fertilisation, we can now attempt to distill it all in a brief preliminary sketch of what some of the key features or essential ingredients of a *complex integral realism* might be.

First, it would integrate the signature innovations of each metatheory – the AQAL framework, a depth ontology and an open embrace of the complexity of reality – as well as their combined knowledge of both the natural, social and human sciences, and of phenomenology, philosophy, anthropology and spirituality. Second, it would present a post-formal vision that is dialectically sensitive, developmentally sophisticated, taxonomically elegant and that embraces the best of premodernity, modernity and postmodernity. Third, it would present a sophisticated philosophical ontology that moves beyond both Hume and Kant (and all the metatheories that derive from them), that is all-inclusive and that is clearly disambiguated (and yet also inseparable) from epistemology. This epistemology would be psychologically, socially, culturally and biologically aware, highlighting the numerous filters, prisms, distortions and conditioning that affect the consciousness of the knowing subject, yet also affirming the possibility of access to, and knowledge of, a mind-independent reality. Fourth, it would adopt an integrative inter/transdisciplinarity that provides a common ontological, epistemological and methodological language that fosters communication between disciplines, common conceptual tools to capture the complexity and multidimensionality of phenomena, the integration of the knowing subject into knowledge and an equal respect for the Who, the What and the How of knowledge. Fifth, It would provide a robust defence of both the subject and agency, insisting on the subject's relative autonomy and causally efficacious powers, which serves as the starting point of an ethics and individual and social emancipatory/transformative praxis ultimately grounded in a nondual, spiritual ontology and a complex integral realist model of human nature. This human nature would be seen as possessing a complex mix of recursively linked psychological components, embedded in social, cultural and geo-historical conditions, emergent from and thus intimately connected to nature and the cosmos and whose essence, like all beings, is spiritual in nature. Sixth, it would depict the universe as a unified, holistic and open totality, possessing a spiritual infrastructure and a tendential directionality that is moving creatively and non-linearly towards ever-greater external complexity and internal consciousness, with humanity striving through its transformative praxis towards ever-greater freedom, universal flourishing and self-realisation. Finally, it would include a deeper interiority that reaches down to the nondual absolute reality that underpins and sustains the relative world of duality and is our essential nature, allowing for both a 'reverent' spirituality based on contemplative phenomenology and a 'secular' one based on philosophical reflection.

This rapid outline of some of the key features of a possible complex integral realism will obviously need fleshing out, refining and expanding. It will also need to be supplemented or complemented by a more critical approach that focuses more on the differences. My particular approach has aimed to be above all a constructive and appreciative one, focusing on the points of convergence and exploring the huge potential for synergy and cross-pollination that exists between these three, in many ways complementary, metatheories. And I have taken this approach not only due to my own natural inclinations and particular skill sets but also because I feel it is important to firmly emphasise the many commonalties that exist between the three metatheories before (or while) embarking on a more incisive, critical approach. Given what is at stake – the gradual construction of a metatheory that combines the varying strengths of three already powerful metatheories in order to better confront the pressing problems we now face – it would seem wise to first establish a robust common foundation and explore the potential for mutual enrichment and integration. That could then accompany the necessary critical element, potentially helping make the dialogue more open and perhaps palliating a little the inevitable tendency to protect and defend one's own preferred metatheory.

In his Foreword to this book, Roger Walsh outlines five major scenarios that can occur when different theories or metatheories meet. My position embraces the middle three – mutual enrichment, the identification of common factors and to some extent assimilative integration – and actively avoids the first depreciative approach: defensive dismissal of the validity and virtue of the others. I have made no attempt in this chapter at Walsh's final possible scenario – the construction of a new and full integrative synthesis (one that would undoubtedly include additional integrally formed approaches and philosophies) – but believe such an attempt to be an exciting future project. And it remains in the future since the dialogue between critical realism and integral theory is still in its early stages, and with complex thought even more so. Moreover, the construction of a cogent, viable synthesis would require a more critical approach, which, as I mentioned, might benefit from being accompanied by approaches that emphasise and appreciate the extensive common ground. Finally, on this question of synthesis, I'd like to endorse Sean Esbjörn-Hargens' position in his chapter in this volume, which calls for an 'integral pluralism' (as opposed to an integral monism). This position highlights the need to balance an integrative synthesis with a respect for the unique development and lineage of each metatheory, leading to a recursive, spiralling exchange between developments of a complex integral realism and each integrative metatheory.

Conclusion

This chapter has discussed some of the ways in which critical realism/meta-Reality, integral theory and complex thought might enter into a constructive, mutually beneficial dialogue in order to start building a complex integral realist integrative synthesis. There has been a lively dialogue between integral theory and critical realism over the last couple of years, clearly illustrated by this book, a dialogue in which complex thought has recently joined.[114] The common ground shared by all three metatheories greatly facilitates such a dialogue, synthesis and cross-fertilisation, making it an exciting endeavour with promising potential. Their open, post-formal, integrative framework, one which aims to respect and capture the full complexity of reality and move beyond the flaws of modernity and postmodernity, provides a refreshing and necessary base upon which to confront the complex problems of the twenty-first century. The first step would seem to be the construction of a complex integral realist position that combines the strengths of each metatheory in a coherent fashion – a position that can gradually be worked into a fuller integrative synthesis – and this chapter is a preliminary attempt towards that end. A logical next step would be to apply that position to specific areas. One could, for example, attempt to construct a complex integral realist model of human nature, given that so much depends on how we see ourselves and our place in the scheme of things. All three metatheories have invaluable insights here, as was commented on in this chapter. From there, we could then build a number of complex integral realist positions: for example, a complex integral realist ethics; a complex integral realist transformative praxis; a complex integral realist eudaimonics; and a complex integral realist exercise in concrete utopianism. The three metatheories have all been over 30 years in the making and have only come to full fruition and maturity in the last decade, and this has occurred at a time when we desperately need a deeper, fuller, more integrative understanding of society, ourselves and the world. We would be unwise not to make full use of their combined insights and knowledge.

Acknowledgements

I would like to give special thanks to Roy Bhaskar, not only for his valuable feedback and encouragement on this book chapter but also for his careful guidance and supervision of my thesis until his sad passing away. I would also like to thank Sean Esbjörn-Hargens and Mervyn Hartwig for pointing me to, respectively, the work of Edgar Morin and Terrence Deacon. Finally, I would like to thank my fellow participants in the various symposia held on critical realism and integral theory over the last four years.

Notes

1 Morin (1994/2005). All quotations from Morin in this chapter from works that have not been translated into English – those with Spanish titles in the bibliography – are my translations from the Spanish translations.
2 See Marshall (2012b) for a discussion on the possibilities of an 'integral realism' – and also a detailed overview of critical realist depth ontology, especially the first foundational sub-phase of transcendental realism. See also Marshall (2012a) for a previous discussion of the mutual enrichment between integral theory and critical realism.

3 Morin with Tager (2008/2010, p. 168). Nature is no longer the mechanical, inert sub-stance of classical science but once again generative, self-creating and self-organising, and in that sense re-enchanted (while Morin firmly rejects any transcendent Spirit or notion of God, his view of *physis* could be argued as being a kind of 'immanent spirituality' à la Spinoza, though thoroughly grounded in science).

4 These strengths correspond to complex thought, critical realism and integral theory, respectively. See Esbjörn-Hargens' ITC 2013 keynote presentation for a more exten-sive list of comparative emphases between the three metatheories. https://foundation.metaintegral.org/ITC/Papers. See also the appendix to his chapter (this volume).

5 For example, their rejection of contradiction, ambiguity and uncertainty; their inability to see the limits of formal logic (and determinism), rather than accepting a looser logic that includes a reworked dialectic (critical realism and complex thought); analytical thought's inappropriate use of atomism and decontextualisation with respect to com-plex phenomena; a hyperspecialisation in which there is no communication between disciplines and a complete split between the natural and human sciences. Morin (2008, p. 6) points to a variety of its 'pathologies': of the mind ("hyper-simplification that makes us blind to the complexity of reality"); of ideas (in the "form of idealism, where the idea obscures the reality it is supposed to translate, and takes itself alone as real"); of theory (which manifests as "doctrinarism and dogmatism, which turn the theory in on itself and petrify it"); and of reason (in the form of "rationalisation, which encloses reality in a system of ideas that are coherent but partial and unilateral, and do not know that a part of reality is unrationalisable, and that rationality's mission is to dialogue with the unrationalisable").

6 Morin with Tager (2008/2010, p. 147).

7 Bhaskar (1993, p. 191).

8 A term used in cognitive developmental psychology to refer to the stage of cognitive development beyond Piaget's formal operational thinking. This involves placing things and events within larger systems and metasystems and so seeing multiple, non-linear causality; is often equated with dialectical or complex thinking and is an integrative both/and rather than an either/or mode of thought; and sees phenomena as open sys-tems that undergo transformation and can deal with their relationships over time. See e.g. Commons & Bresette (2006), and Basseches (2005). It is generally considered to begin with systems thinking and then go beyond that, as all three philosophies here do – they all critique the holism/'subtle reductionism' of systems theory, for example, either explicitly (complex thought and integral theory) or implicitly (critical realism). Integral theory makes extensive use of cognitive and constructivist developmental psychology models and the term post-formal.

9 This is true especially of complex thought, as well as integral theory through phase four. Integral theory's phase five, however, is more ambivalent here, which I consider in a num-ber of places below. See e.g. notes 62 and 66. See also Hedlund's chapter in this volume.

10 Referring, respectively, to critical realism, complex thought and integral theory.

11 The different emphases in brackets follow, respectively, integral theory, critical realism and complex thought. The 'immanent spirituality' of complex thought is a broad inter-pretation, not anything explicitly mentioned by Morin, and is discussed in the relevant section below.

12 Bhaskar (1993, p. xxxi). See also Bhaskar (1994) and Norrie (2010). Marshall (2012b) gives a short overview of Bhaskar's reworking of Hegelian dialectic.

13 These are developed in its MELD schema of 1M non-identity, 2E negativity, 3L totality and 4D transformative praxis. Especially important is the 2E notion of absence, under-stood as "real determinate absence that exists in things, as part of … their natural neces-sity" (Norrie, 2010, p. 13). It is real absence that is present in things and which, through real negation, is inextricably linked to change. Also the 3L notion of holistic causality. See Bhaskar (1993, 1994) and Norrie (2010).

14 Morin is indebted not only to Hegel but also to a number of other Western dialecti-cians, including Heraclitus (his favourite), Nicholas de Cusa, Pascal, Marx, Adorno, Jung,

Bohr, Gödel and Lupasco (see Morin (1994/2005, 1991/2009, pp. 184–188). The dialogic principle involves relationships that are simultaneously complementary and antagonistic. Organisational recursion is where "the products and effects are at the same time causes and producers of what produces them" (Morin, 2008, p. 49). This breaks free from "the linear idea of cause and effect, of product/producer, or structure/superstructure, because everything that is product comes back on what produces it in a cycle that is itself self-constitutive, self-organising and self-producing" (Morin, 2008, pp. 49–50). A polyrelational circuit involves *parts* (or elements), *interrelations, organisation* and *whole*, where each is defined in relation to all the others, with organisation as 'nuclear'. Thus the parts, for example, are defined by their unique characteristics or properties (including those that are inhibited, unactualised or invisible within the whole), their interrelationships, "the perspective of the organisation in which they operate, and the perspective of the whole in which they are integrated" (Morin, 2008, p. 102).

15 See e.g. Morin with Tager (2008/2010, p. 156) and Morin (2001b/2009, pp. 58–59), on how these processes affect the trinity individual-species-society.

16 Bhaskar (1993, p. 160). See Marshall (2012a) for a comparison between the four quadrants and four-planar social being. It should be noted that critical realism's four-planar social being was first formulated, in the guise of the 'social cube', in 1978/79, and first published in *Scientific Realism and Human Emancipation* (1986) (personal communication from Roy Bhaskar, 17 January 2014). Integral theory's four quadrants was first formulated shortly before it was published in *Sex, Ecology, Spirituality* (1995).

17 See e.g. Otto Laske (2012), who laments the tendency by some who use Wilber's work on developmental levels to reduce a person to his/her developmental level.

18 These components are stressed especially by integral theory, but also by complex thought: the developmental levels and lines; the different personality typologies; constructive and destructive emotional states; states of consciousness as a whole; the whole psychic world of needs, desires and fantasies; projections and identifications; the dialogic of *homo sapiens/demens*; neuroses, shadow elements and repressed or yet to unfold potentials; possession by ideas.

19 Laske's (2008) 'constructive developmental framework (CDF)' offers one such example of a more dialectical approach to developmental levels and consciousness. Unlike integral theory, it (a) researches the dialectical, complex, causally recursive interrelationships between different developmental lines (especially those between the social-emotional, epistemic and cognitive lines of development); (b) incorporates dialectical thinking within the cognitive domain (using Basseches' empirical studies of dialectical thinking, which sees dialectical thinking as emerging after the development of formal logical thinking); (c) combines Basseches' empirical approach and Bhaskar's philosophical reworking of Hegel and the MELD schema of dialectical critical realism to organise a manual of dialectical thought forms; and (d) links the behavioural/psychological dimension to developmental levels.In a little more detail, Laske's CDF integrates social-emotional development (Kegan's Orders of Consciousness, cognitive development (logical, epistemic and dialectical thinking: Piaget, Jacques, Kitchener and King, Basseches/Bhaskar) and a behavioural/psychological dimension. He considers behaviour as dependent on the way a person's combined cognitive and social-emotional development (her 'evolving self') manages the relationship between her ego's needs and internal and external pressures (i.e. the relationship between Freud's id, ego, superego and real world). The two key cognitive and social-emotional strands of development are considered a dialectical, transformational system that are "both separate and inseparably linked" (2008, p. 137), with Kitchener and King's stages of reflective judgement (called *epistemic positions* by Laske) acting as a bridge between the two. "Cognitive processes … enhance epistemic position in a feedback loop, and this enhancement is directly transferred to the social-emotional line of development." Moreover, "epistemic position is also a filter for social-emotional influences on cognitive development" (2008, p. 138). The combination of social-emotional stage and epistemic position (which Laske calls *stance* – the stance one takes when confronted with the social

and physical world) – determines whether a person's cognitive *tools* are restricted to logical thought or can include those of dialectical thinking. In order to close in on an individual's unique singularity (Laske uses this framework for both developmental research and coaching), Laske deploys a social-emotional interview, a cognitive interview and a behavioural/psychodynamic questionnaire, with the first providing a very generic picture, the second a more specific picture of the individual and the third "address[ing] the individual's uniqueness and unique capabilities and challenges, including those that delay or make impossible either social-emotional or cognitive development, or both" (2012, p. 16).

20 See Marshall (2012a) for a discussion on this point with relation to critical realism. The points raised would apply equally to complex thought, although complex thought places a greater emphasis on the psychological dimension than critical realism (e.g. volumes 3 and 4 of *Le Méthode*) and has much to offer integral theory here (see sections on epistemology and ethics).

21 That is, as opposed to Hegel's more rigid, closed, idealist, linear, mechanistic dialectic and his deterministic historicism. Morin and Bhaskar also stress, contra Hegel, that preservative sublation in the real world is the exception rather than the rule, and Morin emphasises the vital role played by random events and chance – based on his study of the physical and biological sciences – while Bhaskar highlights the driving force of absence. Morin also stresses that Hegel's dialectic involves a way of thinking, not a logic, and consequently "has no internal corrective, no logical defense system.… All dialectic that is freed from the constraints of Aristotelian logic can turn into a shameless game and sleight of hand that escapes the constraints of reality" (1991/2009, p. 199). But despite these shortcomings, Morin embraces dialectical thought as an example of complex thought that "can work with contradictions, but not dissolve them" and that a 'looser' logic can accept. It exposes the shortcomings of formal logic and its inability to deal with the complexity of reality. It is clear here that Morin, like Bhaskar (1993), criticises the limitations and exclusive use of formal logic but embraces it in a more encompassing whole that includes dialectical thinking (and a reworked Hegelian dialectic).

22 In Morin's less explicitly spiritual outlook, humanity is embarked on an 'unknown adventure' in which it must attempt to move beyond the 'Planetary Iron Age', and, with the help of a more complex form of thought (post-formal or integral or open, non-linear dialogical thinking), "save the planet, civilize the Earth [and] unify humankind while safeguarding its diversity", in order to make Homeland Earth a "heaven haven" (Morin, 1993/1999, pp. 141–142).

23 In metaReality, the relative world of duality is sustained and underpinned by a nondual ground that is the ontological foundation of the cosmos. This foundational level is immanent in all subsequent emergent levels of reality/being and is an ingredient in all beings as their *ground-state*, "which both embodies the qualities necessary to bind the universe together as a whole and at the same time is always specifically differentiated in the species or being concerned" (Bhaskar, 2002a, p. xiii). So the ground-state is unique in every species and every being, and all ground-states are bound together in what Bhaskar calls the *cosmic envelope*. The ground-state qualities of humanity "include energy and intelligence (albeit enfolded as a potential to be elicited and manifested in the appropriate circumstances) and consciousness, creativity, love, the capacity for right-action and therefore for the fulfilment of the beings intentionality, in this case the intentionality of its dharma or its ground-state" (Bhaskar, 2002c, p. 55). Our ground-state is our 'transcendentally real self', or the 'alethic truth of human beings'.

24 For Morin, organisation, together with order, disorder and interactions, form a 'tetralogical loop' that underlies the "great game of cosmogenesis" and is the "*immanent principle of transformations and organization*" that enables *physis* to "emerge, unfold, constitute and organize itself" (Morin, 1977/2009, pp. 74–75).

25 For integral theory, the fundamental Enlightenment paradigm contained "two warring camps: atomism (or gross reductionism) and holism (or subtle reductionism)" (Wilber, 1995/2000, p. 586).

26 For complex thought: its central notion of system as a complex unity rather than an elementary one, a whole that cannot be reduced to the sum of its parts; its notion of system as ambiguous; and its natural affinity with transdisciplinarity, allowing for both "the unity of science and the differentiation of the sciences" (Morin, 2008, p. 10). The 20 tenets of integral theory (see Wilber, 1995) are based largely on the systems and complexity sciences.

27 Morin (1994/2005, pp. 211–212, 274–275). "Western dialectical tradition" in the sense that they all dealt with contradiction, the last three through science.

28 Morin (2008, p. 101).

29 See note 14.

30 Morin (1977/2009, pp. 74–75). See also note 24.

31 Morin (1994/2005, p. 207). By this Adorno meant, comments Morin, "that the impossibility of grasping the totality made any pretention towards totality a non-truth".

32 See e.g. Morin (2008) on these points.

33 There is no systematic critique of systems theory in critical realism, but its dialectical critical realism, especially its 3L totality, is an implicit critique of the insufficiencies of systems theory and holism. There is also a recent publication by a critical realist, John Mingers, on *Systems Thinking, Critical Realism and Philosophy* (2014). For 3L totality, see Bhaskar (1993) and Norrie (2010).

34 Deacon (2013). Also Deacon and Cashman (2012).

35 See Hartwig (2013) for an excellent review, and also critical realist critique of, Deacon's work, especially his 'Incomplete Nature'. In this review Hartwig focuses on the (b) and (c) resonances, and on also some of those of (d) in relation to dialectical critical realism and metaReality.

36 And also elements of indigenous societies, which did not form part of the axial revolution, like their close relationship with nature and the land and certain faculties or qualities that were subsequently lost. Critical realism, especially, stresses this. Integral theory, via Gebser and its notion of developmental lines, points to the positive elements or 'efficient' expression of each structure of consciousness, while at the same time pointing to their 'deficient' mode and how each later structure transcends and includes earlier ones. It points, for example, to lines of development like polyphasic maturity, which are much more developed in indigenous cultures than in modern ones. Polyphasic "refers to a culture's general access to different states of consciousness … [and] many indigenous cultures embrace access to and cultivation of states of awareness, while rational Western societies tend to emphasize rational waking consciousness at the exclusion of other modes of experiencing reality" (Esbjörn-Hargens, 2010b, p. 10). However, drawing on cognitive anthropology and, among others, Habermas, integral theory also points to the 'global syncretism' or 'indissociation' that underlies the magical-animistic structure of consciousness, which, according to Wilber, Romantics mistake for integration. (Here, of course, Wilber is talking about the original, pre-historic human of the magic-foraging era, not indigenous peoples who are living today and who have undergone their own development.) The biosphere and noosphere, argues Wilber, had still not been differentiated, and so there was no integration. This structure, however, quite likely "embodied a type of ecological wisdom" and was "more in tune with natural wisdom, with the Earth and its many moods". Wilber is "in complete sympathy with that approach" but rejects "the attempt to turn back the clock and elevate this structure to a privileged status of integrative power that it simply did not possess" (Wilber, 1995/2000, pp. 170–171).

37 Especially critical realism (via its critique of the philosophical discourse of modernity, especially classical modernity: e.g Bhaskar (2002b); see also Bhaskar and Hartwig (2010, p. 198) on Western modernity as a specifically capitalist and European version of axial rationality) and complex thought (via its critique of the paradigm of simplicity's Cartesian reductionism and disjunction: see e.g. Morin (1991/2009, 2008)). Integral theory takes a more general, positive view of what it calls the rational or orange level of consciousness, manifested both in axial and modern rationality, without distinguishing

greatly between the two. Jean Gebser, however, whose work Wilber and integral theory integrate, with some reserves, distinguishes between the *efficient* (*menos*) and *deficient* (*ratio*) forms of the 'mental structure of consciousness', stressing that Western modernity manifested rationality and the mental structure in its more deficient form – coinciding more closely with Bhaskar's and Morin's critiques of modernity. See Gebser (1949 and 1953/1985), and also Feuerstein (1987); Combs (2002); Wilber (1995). See also Marshall (2016), for a more detailed discussion of the mental/rational structure of consciousness and its different expressions during the Axial Age (more balanced) and European modernity (less balanced).

38 See the section on spirituality for a discussion on the possibilities of cross-fertilisation between integral theory and metaReality via their different approaches to spirituality.

39 See e.g. Morin (1993/1999).

40 See Morin (1951/1974, 1994/2005).

41 See e.g. Wilber (1999; 2006); and Gebser (1949 and 1953/1985).

42 They focus on its coincidence with the rise of capitalism and industrialisation and the instrumental rationality and exploitation they promoted; its ethno-/Eurocentrism and consequent domination of other non-European, non-modern cultures; its anthropocentrism and resulting exploitation of nature; its 'paradigm of simplicity' that violates the complexity of reality; its abstract universality and consequent disrespect for singularity and pluralism; its atomistic, isolated ego possessed of rational autonomy and the splitting of humans from nature; its naïve epistemology. See e.g. Bhaskar (2002b); Morin (2005/2009).

43 Wilber talks of both the "dignity and disaster" of modernity. He especially critiques its instrumental rationality, and exclusive use of analytical thought/*Verstand*. He adds, for example, an emphasis on the repression of the biosphere (nature, body, sexuality) by the noosphere – as manifested in what Wilber calls the ego camp (e.g. Descartes, Kant, Fichte) and their opposing eco camp (e.g. the Romantics, Rousseau, Spinoza). He also critiques its reduction of the Great Chain of Being to its first rung (matter) and the colonisation by science (It/Its quadrants) of the other value spheres of art and morals (I and We quadrant, respectively). See e.g. Wilber (1995/2000, 1998/2000, 1999).

44 Wilber highlights its differentiation of the value spheres (art, morals, science), which allowed each sphere to develop freely, reason and evidence over arbitrary mythic authority, individual freedom, dignity and flourishing, democracy and universal rights, abolition of slavery. Bhaskar (Bhaskar with Hartwig, 2012, p. 213) calls the idea of the individual and individual flourishing the "golden nugget" of modernity – but stresses that the philosophical discourse of modernity, however, only espoused an abstract universality and ended up with just an atomistic egocentric individuality. Morin (2005/2009, ch. 2), embraces the benevolent, emancipatory and "fraternal face of [modernity's] humanism" (which found expression in the critical and self-critical rationality of Montaigne, Montesquieu and Voltaire; the declaration of the rights of man and citizens; Hugo's and Lamartine's synthesis of the spirit of Romanticism and the Enlightenment; a universalist aspiration towards greater equality and freedom and human flourishing that was expressed by the utopian socialists, anarchists and Marx), and rejects the 'dominant face' (which "puts man in the place of God, in fact the only subject of the universe, and gives him the mission of conquering the world", p. 41). This leads, he argues, to the complex, dialectical idea of a Europe that dominates and at the same time carries the emancipatory, humanistic ideas that facilitate liberation from this domination.

45 Critical realism provides a much more nuanced historical and philosophical analysis of modernity than integral theory, breaking it down into five phases and including postmodernity as just one of these phases, rather than as separate from modernity. See also Morin (2005/2009) for a historical overview and critique of modernity.

46 For example in Greece. See notes 37 and 48.

47 In Feuerstein's account, Roman civilisation, unlike classical Greece, "achieved … the heightened individualism that is associated with the mature mental consciousness" (Feuerstein, 1987, p. 100). This was reflected, comments Combs (2002), in the examination of individual

characters and personalities in art and literature, rather than the Greek concern with universal perfection. It was complemented by Plotinus and Neoplatonism, where self-reflective awareness reached a peak and also the interiority of St Paul and St Augustine (not only the latter's *Confessions* but also his stress on the certainty of one's immediate awareness or basic wakefulness – which was a precursor to Descartes' *cogito*). Christianity also contributed to the mental structure of consciousness first through its embrace of all humanity, and second by moving from the cyclical conception of time that represented the mythical structure of consciousness to a linear, forward-looking 'arrow' of time.

48 During the Renaissance there developed a capacity for objectivity and perspectival awareness, which was crucial to the development of modern philosophy and to its huge scientific advances. Mirrors appeared once again – after being popular in Rome but having disappeared during the dark ages – and personal diaries emerged, which "began to imply an internal subjective referent equatable to a personal self or ego. Objectivity began to take on a new meaning as the ego identified its location as a point separated and distanced from the rest of the world" (Combs, 2002, p. 98). Perspectival awareness can be seen in Descartes' creation of "the spatial mathematics of analytical geometry" (Combs, 2002, pp. 97–98) and in art after Leonardo's discovery of the laws of perspective. But for Gebser, this was not an advance over the first manifestation of the mental structure as seen in, for example, ancient Greek thought. The efficient form of the mental structure is *menos*, "balanced directional thought as seen, for instance, in the dialogues of Plato" (Combs, 2002, p. 98). But with the Renaissance and later, individualism and the "fixed location of the ego in objective perceptual space led … to rigidity and a self-centred inability to go beyond one's own narrow confines" (p. 99). This was the result of the deficient form of the mental structure, *ratio*, which for Gebser is characterised by division, calculation and atomisation and leads to isolation. Like Morin (and most critics of reductionist thought), Gebser points to Descartes' role in the consolidation of reductionist, divisive, atomistic thought. He also distinguishes, as do Kant and Hegel, between *Verstand* and *Vernunft*, arguing that the former unbalanced by the latter is unhealthy.

49 Martin Luther can be seen as the archetypal expression of the rational/mental/orange structure of consciousness (or Kegan's fourth order of consciousness/self-authoring stage): the individual asserting his own critical stand and criteria against established, conventional authority. See Laske (2006) for this observation.

50 At least in theory. Its abstract universality, however, ended up promoting an ethno-/ Eurocentrism that imposed its will on the rest of the world.

51 See Marshall (1991) for a discussion on Chomsky's approach to classical liberalism and the Enlightenment, especially his view of anarchism as a confluence of classical liberalism and socialism. With respect to Rousseau, Chomsky highlights his libertarian *Discourse on Inequality* rather than his more authoritarian *Social Contract*. The 'fraternal face of humanism' is taken from Morin (2005/2009) (see note 44), in contrast to the 'dominant face' that was bent on conquering nature and the world.

52 For example, Morin (1994/2005); Wilber (1995); Bhaskar (1993).

53 See e.g. Wilber (1998, 1999) and Bhaskar (2002a, 2002b) for integral theory and critical realist discussions of postmodernism.

54 See e.g. Wilber's *Integral Psychology* and *The Marriage of Sense and Soul*.

55 See e.g. Esbjörn-Hargens (2010); Marshall (2012a, 2012b); Hedlund-de Witt (2013); Wilber (2012, 2013). See also the next chapter by Nicholas Hedlund, which is an updated version of Hedlund-de Witt (2013).

56 Bhaskar (1993).

57 Bhaskar (1994, p. 185).

58 See Groff (2013, p. 7), who mentions the above writers and the "first book-length arguments for a powers-based ontology" being Harré and Madden's *Causal Powers* and Bhaskar's *A Realist Theory of Science* – both in 1975.

59 Groff (2013, p. 7) and Groff (2009, p. 275).

60 Both quotations from Bryant, Srnicek, and Harman (2011, p. 3).

61 Quoted in Combs (2002, p. 96).
62 Wilber (1999, p. 163). In full: "[A]ll Right-Hand exteriors, even if we superimpose conceptions upon them, nonetheless have various intrinsic features that are registered by the senses or their extensions, and in that general sense, all Right-Hand holons have some sort of objective reality." Wilber continues: "Even Wilfrid Sellars, generally regarded as the most persuasive opponent of 'the myth of the given' – the myth of direct realism and naïve empiricism, the myth that reality is simply given to us – maintains that, even though the manifest image of an object is in part a mental construction, it is *guided* in important ways by *intrinsic features* of sense experience, which is exactly why, as Thomas Kuhn said, science can make real progress. A diamond will cut a piece of glass no matter what words we use for 'diamond', 'cut' and 'glass', and no amount of cultural constructivism will change that simple fact" (pp. 163–164). As we can see, Wilber here is championing a weak social constructivism, which he tends to abandon for a much stronger form in phase five.
63 See Bhaskar (2012). See also Hedlund-de Witt (2013), for examples and an excellent discussion on this. Also, Marshall (2012a, 2012b).
64 See Wilber (2012) and Marshall (2012c).
65 Wilber (2013, p. 1–2). Wilber (2014) has also just published *The Fourth Turning*, a short ebook version of a longer book to be published shortly, which stresses ontology and ontological reality more, placing it on a more equal footing with epistemology (very different from the stance in *Integral Spirituality*). For example: "how one looks at a phenomenon helps co-determine the nature of the phenomenon seen, and the nature of the phenomenon seen helps co-determine what is seen" (2014, p. 100). This can be construed as a form of weak social constructionism, which both critical realism and complex thought, in their own ways, also endorse. Also: "These [interior] objects are absolutely real and ontologically there" and have a "real causal impact on the sensorimotor world" (2014, pp. 120, 122). With respect to the first part of this quotation, *Integral Spirituality* said much the same but left 'ontological' in scare quotes: "All the levels up to turquoise are now real, 'ontological', *actually existing structures* in the Kosmos" (2006, p. 247). (With respect to the second part, the stress on 'causal impact' and its relation to ontology is not seen in *Integral Spirituality*. And it happens to be the criterion that critical realism uses for the adjudication of reality, so perhaps this indicates an influence from critical realism). So all past actuals (or 'kosmic habits'), in all quadrants, are ontologically real and have causal impacts. Put all together, and now without the cultural need to deny, or reduce or be embarrassed by ontology – thanks to the demise of postmodernism's strong social constructionism, the acceptance in many quarters of a weak social constructionism that avoids the myth of the given and the rehabilitation of ontology and realism in both analytical and continental philosophy (a process in which critical realist depth ontology has played a significant role) – the gap between integral theory's previously (mid-phase five) strong social constructionism that wished to avoid ontology, and critical realism, especially, and also complex thought, is arguably more bridgeable.
66 Both integral theory and complex thought lack an explicit (depth) ontology, which leaves them vulnerable to sliding towards the dominant implicit 'flatland' ontology that underlies all current mainstream metatheories: empirical realism and ontological actualism (see next note). Their emphasis on emergence and stifled or unrealised potential, however, aligns them naturally with a critical realist depth ontology, an adoption of which would arguably strengthen them both in a number of ways (see main text). The essentially realist approach (in that they both presuppose the existence of a mind-independent reality) of both complex thought and integral theory up to and including phase four would facilitate such an adoption and grounding. As to integral theory's less realist postmetaphysical phase five, a number of problems from the perspective of critical realism have already been mentioned: it commits the epistemic fallacy, confusing the transitive and intransitive dimensions, and enters into a number of contradictions and inconsistencies (see Bhaskar, 2012, and Hedlund-de Witt, 2013). Furthermore, its view of metaphysics is limited – ruling out ontology by following

"Kant's critical philosophy" that "replace[s] ontological objects with structures of the subject" (Wilber, 2006, p. 231) – and its notion of enactment, which claims that "the meaning of a statement is the injunction of its enactment" (Wilber, 2006, p. 268), reflects the verificationist principle of logical positivism (according to Bhaskar, its "theory of enactment is an isomorph of the verificationist principle [of logical positivism]" – personal communication, 7 January 2014. (See also Hedlund-de Witt, 2013 for a good discussion on this point.) The logical positivists had insisted that only statements that were empirically verifiable (or formal statements) were meaningful (and thus really real) – which rules out much of traditional philosophy, and also of course a depth ontology that posits a deeper real domain of causal structures that lies beyond the actual and empirical domains (see Marshall, 2012b, for an account and critique of logical positivism). For his part, Wilber, driven by an understandable desire to accommodate spirituality within "modernity's demand for objective evidence and postmodernity's demand for intersubjective grounding" – especially given that when one makes "positive, ontological claims [about Spirit] the critics roar" (2006, pp. 234, 262) – devises his own version of positive verification. His solution is to place "spiritual realities … on the same footing as any other referents" (p. 262), insisting that "any ontic or assertic mode (+) must be able to specify the kosmic address of the referent of the signifiers, and this is true whether the referents are material, emotional, mental, spiritual, it doesn't matter. Spiritual realities are on exactly the same footing as electrons, Gaia, rocks, and the square root of a negative one" (p. 264). By means of this 'GigaGloss', all realities are subjected to the same criteria of verification, so that "[t]he problem of the proof of God's existence simply evaporates. The existence of Spirit is no harder to prove than the existence of rocks, electrons, negative ones, or Gaia. Simply look it up in the GigaGloss" (p. 266). What is now required when talking about any reality, according to this 'mega-phenomenological'/GigaGloss approach, is to specify the kosmic address of the perceived object and that of the perceiving subject, which implies also specifying "injunctions that bring forth or enact the particular worldspaces" (p. 266). Hence "the meaning of an assertion is the means of enactment" (p. 266); or "The meaning of an assertic or ontic statement is the means or injunctions of its enactment" p. (267); or, in short, "the meaning of a statement is the injunction of its enactment" (p. 268). While this approach highlights the fundamental role played by structures of consciousness (and methodology) in our knowledge of reality – an insight that would bolster both critical realism and complex thought – it is problematic for a number of reasons. First, any verificationist principle is wide open to immanent critique: how can it itself be verified? Second, and more importantly, it tends to reduce ontology to epistemology and methodology (enactment) – i.e. commits the epistemic fallacy. In order to make spiritual realities acceptable to modernity and postmodernity, integral theory's postmetaphysical phase has forfeited ontology (as expressed in *Integral Spirituality*. His latest writings, e.g. 2014, change this position – see previous note.) Third, there is arguably a more persuasive way to make spirituality acceptable to both modernity and postmodernity, and one which not only leaves ontology intact but also allows it to play a major role. By combining the different versions of spirituality of critical realism/ metaReality and integral theory, we can give spirituality a philosophical, ontological and contemplative phenomenological grounding. We can ground spirituality, as the philosophy of metaReality does, in a philosophical (not scientific) ontology that was initially established via transcendental argument from experimental activity and then expanded and deepened to include mind, intentional agency, social structures, non-being and nonduality. MetaRealism uses the same philosophical (or 'metaphysical' – see below) tool of transcendental argument – this time from everyday social activities – to establish, to 'assert', the existence of spiritual realities: of a cosmic envelope (secular version of transcendent Spirit), the ground-state of all being (secular version of immanent Spirit), an absolute realm of nonduality and identity that underpins and sustains the relative world of duality and difference – a nondual ground that is the ontological foundation of the cosmos. By combining this philosophical assertion of spiritual realities with the contemplative phenomenological evidence emphasised by integral theory, together with its notion of kosmic address and stress on enactment (in weaker versions that allow for ontology), we would arguably have a more compelling case for spirituality. And to that we could add preliminary scientific support for an immanent spirituality that envisions the cosmos as imbued with creativity and self-organisation via complex thought's notions of *physis* as active organisation and the tetragram, with the additional backing of Deacon's theory of emergent dynamics (see section on spirituality for further discussion on these points). Such a 'complex integral realist' spirituality would need to adopt a broader notion of metaphysics, one that is very different from traditional metaphysics (which both integral theory and critical realism critique), and one in which transcendental argument plays a significant role. Critical realism talks of 'metaphysics α' and 'metaphysics β', the former including transcendental argument and immanent critique, the latter including "the Leibnizian art of decoding and deciphering conceptual schemes" and concrete utopianism (Hartwig, 2007, p. 353). And transcendental argument is, in fact, argues Bhaskar (1986/2009, p. 11), related to science in that it is "a species of the wider genus of retroductive argument characteristic ... of scientific activity generally". This broader, updated vision of metaphysics, tied to the above philosophical, ontological, phenomenological and even (in a preliminary way) scientific grounding of spirituality, would mean that there is, in fact, another "avenue open to spiritual philosophy in the modern and postmodern world" apart from integral theory's "post-Kantian postmetaphysics" (Wilber, 2006, p. 248). A spiritual philosophy that includes a depth ontology that is clearly disambiguated from epistemology (which remain distinct and at the same time inseparable), transcendental argument, contemplative phenomenology and weaker versions of the kosmic address and enactment, and that drinks from the latest findings of the physical and biological sciences, is quite possible and potentially more robust. Such a possibility will be considered more thoroughly in Marshall (2016). And the recent moves and openness of integral theory towards critical realist ontology (starting with Esbjörn-Hargens, 2010, continued by Hedlund-de Witt, 2013, and including Wilber's latest writings – see main text and note 65), and of critical realism towards a number of insights of integral theory (Bhaskar, for example, openly recognises areas where integral theory can strengthen critical realism – see also Marshall 2012a, 2012b; Despain, 2013) bodes well for a deeper collaboration and cross-fertilisation in this area – as well as the other areas discussed in this chapter. As, of course, does the dialogue between integral theory and critical realism that is the focus of this whole book.

67 Empirical realism denies the existence of underlying 'real' mechanisms and structures that are not 'actual' (appear in experience) but that cause 'actual' events and phenomena; i.e. it equates what is real with what is 'actual'. It is the implicit ontology (ontological actualism) of empiricism – and also of Kantian, neo-Kantian, hermeneutic and social constructionist metatheories – all of which accept the Humean equating of causal laws with 'constant conjunction of events'. Empiricist epistemology is thus conjoined with an actualist ontology, involving the epistemic fallacy (ontology reduced to epistemology) and the denial of ontological stratification.

68 The quotation from Wilber above agrees, and Morin's weak social constructionism, with a similar emancipatory intent, even more so.

69 That is, especially the levels and lines components, but it also includes the other upper-left quadrant components (types, states, etc.), which, as discussed in the section on post-formal perspective, need to be considered dialectically in conjunction as a causally recursive transformational system.

70 See, especially, vols 3 and 4 of *La Méthode*. Among these sources, summarised in Morin (2001a), are mental errors (or perceptions, self-deception – our need for self-justification, egocentricity, tendency to project; conception – which is infiltrated by an 'independent psychic world' of fantasies, needs, desires, ideas, etc.); intellectual errors (our systems of

ideas that resist any information and argument that does not fit); errors of reason (an open, constructive and critical rationality protects against error and illusion but it can degenerate into rationalisation which is closed to dispute, fails to see the limits of formal logic, deduction and induction and rejects subjectivity, affectivity, contradictions as irrational); blinding paradigms (that prescribe and proscribe); and possession by ideas (which we need to dialogue with, not conflate with reality).

71 For example, Esbjörn-Hargens (2006); Hedlund (2010).
72 Without forgetting the subtle energies stressed by integral theory in this 'upper-right quadrant' aspect.
73 Individual-society-species; brain-mind-culture; reason-affectivity-impulse. Summarised in Morin (2001a).
74 See Bhaskar (1975).
75 Bhaskar (1979).
76 See Bhaskar (2010) and Bhaskar and Danemark (2006).
77 The expression 'taxonomy of epistemic structures' is borrowed from Hedlund-de Witt (2013).
78 See e.g. Bhaskar (2010); Morin (1999/2010); Stein (2007).
79 Bhaskar and Danemark (2006); Bhaskar (2010).
80 Bhaskar (2010) also talks of the need for, on the ontological side, *multidisciplinarity* (which adds together knowledge of generative mechanisms from different emergent levels of reality) and *intradisciplinarity* (that recognises changes in the actual generative mechanisms that result from the interdisciplinary synthesis); and, on the epistemological side, *crossdisciplinary* understanding (between teams composed of members from different disciplines).
81 Bhaskar (2010).
82 This Who × How × What formula is from Esbjörn-Hargens (2010a), an important article that constituted the first move within integral theory to a more ontology-friendly position.
83 See the section above on ontology and epistemology, especially note 66; Marshall (2012b) and Hedlund-de Witt (2013) for a discussion on integral theory's postmetaphysical phase's strong social constructionism.
84 Bhaskar (1994, p. 100).
85 On explanatory critique see Bhaskar (1979). For emancipatory axiology and critical realist ethics in general, see Bhaskar (1994, ch. 7); Hartwig (2007, pp. 157–164); Norrie (2010, ch. 5). As we saw in the section on post-formal perspective, integral theory's levels and critical realism's and complex thought's dialectical messiness can mutually enrich each other in their approach to directionality.
86 Bhaskar (2002c, p. xxiv). Later, p. 83, Bhaskar adds: "Indeed the central question today is that of the struggle between nonduality and demi-reality for the world of relative reality, that is the planet as it would be without instrumental reasoning and the totality of master–slave relations. For the first time in recorded history there is no alternative to the dominant system at the level of duality, so the real struggle is no longer between two opposing sets of oppressive systems or sets of master–slave relationships, but between demi-reality, in its monological globally hegemonic form, and its nondual basis and ground. This itself gives a reason for (relative) optimism that, especially in view of our extraordinary global interconnectedness, the nondual realm that entirely sustains this system, contains the seeds of a qualitatively different and potentially universal kind of social order."
87 It should be noted, however, that integral theory is being applied to many areas, some of which can have a potentially very significant social emancipatory effect. One such area is in organisations and businesses, and one exciting piece of recent research on integral organisations and their truly democratic and liberating potential is Frederic Laloux's *Reinventing Organisations* (2014). Marshall (2016) discusses Laloux's research in more detail.

88 Notions like (a) the *basic moral intuition* that aims "to protect and promote the greatest depth [level of development] for the greatest span [number of beings]"; (b) the *basic spiritual intuition* ('honour and actualize Spirit', which manifests in all four quadrants (Wilber, 1995/2000, pp. 640–641). And distinctions like (a) *ground value* (all beings/entities are equally a full expression of Spirit and thus demand regard); (b) *intrinsic value* [all holons, as *wholes*, have value in themselves, and the greater its depth/development (wholeness) the greater its intrinsic value – or its 'significance']; and (c) *extrinsic or instrumental value* (all holons, as *parts*, have instrumental value for others that depend on them, so that the greater number of wholes that depend on them – i.e. the lower they are in the holarchical sequence – the more *fundamental* they are and more extrinsic value they have) (Wilber, 1995/2000, pp. 544–545). Integral theory also talks of rights and responsibilities, where greater depth comes with greater responsibilities and rights (Wilber, 1995/2000, pp. 544–545). See also Wilber, Patten, Leonard, and Morelli (2008) for a discussion of integral ethics.
89 Morin (1993/1999, p. 141).
90 Morin (2005/2009, part 1, ch. 1).
91 Morin (2005/2009, p. 102).
92 Morin (2005/2009, p. 103).
93 For example, inner complexity, multiple personalities, blind spots, the mechanisms of self-justification and self-deception, the influence of emotion on reasoning, etc.
94 Morin (2005/2009, p. 106).
95 Morin (2005/2009, p. 110).
96 Including *homo ludens, homo imaginarius, homo consumans* and *homo poeticus* alongside the more emphasised *homo faber, homo empiricus, homo economicus* and *homo prosaicus*.
97 Morin (2005/2009, p. 55).
98 Morin with Tager (2008/2010, p. 168).
99 Morin (1977/2009, pp. 74–75).
100 Bhaskar with Hartwig (2012, p. 206).
101 For the dialogue between Bhaskar and Wilber on panpsychism, see Bhaskar (2012); Wilber (2012); Marshall (2012c). For the dialogue between Deacon and critical realism/metaReality see note 35 and Hartwig's (2013) review of Deacon's *Incomplete Nature* (2012), which includes a response by Deacon. For a conversation between Deacon and Terry Patten (representing integral theory), see http://beyondawakeningseries.com/blog/archive/.
102 See Wilber (2012).
103 See Bhaskar (2012). Hartwig (2013) says that panpsychism is an inappropriate term for metaReality and suggests instead 'panpsychism p' or panentheism to describe metaReality's position.
104 Hartwig (2013, p. 236). See also note 107 for a short comment on Wilber and Bhaskar's different positions on panpsychism.
105 Marshall (2016) discusses in some detail a 'new axial creation story' that integrates the positions of the three integrative metatheories and Deacon. This new 'creation story' also discusses at some length the notions of panpsychism, panentheism and nonduality, which form an integral part of it.
106 Morin (1993/1999, pp. 140–141).
107 See note 23.
108 See Marshall (2012c); Bhaskar (2012); Wilber (2012). Wilber's essential position is that "epistemology and ontology are inseparable aspects of the being/consciousness of every holon, and that goes all the way down. And that fundamentally changes the nature of what we consider real" (quoted in Marshall, 2012c, p. 36). Bhaskar retorts that "My 'panpsychism' is ontologically differentiated. It is not committed to any doctrine of the inseparability of being and knowledge of being (ontology and epistemology). Furthermore, it respects the distinct evolutionary processes of being and knowledge, and of beings of different types, in distinct evolutionary 'rhythmics' and trajectories and at different moments of them" (Bhaskar, 2012, p. 41). Bhaskar's ontologically differentiated

panpsychism is closer to Morin's and Deacon's more scientific accounts of evolution through the spheres, and would seem the most appropriate.

109 This argues that the four major states of gross, subtle, causal and nondual can be experienced by anyone at virtually any structure-stage, but that the individual's interpretation of that state will be determined by her structure-stage.

110 Bhaskar illustrates the way these three notions or mechanisms connect as follows: "[T]hink of two ground-states on the cosmic envelope; then when an embodied personality becomes one with their ground-state they will have an intimation of the co-presence of another ground-state within them, given where they are, on the cosmic envelope. Both ground-states will be on the cosmic envelope, and so co-present within each other.... And so reciprocity, me smiling back at you, is just a superficial form of co-presence, and transcendental identification is what happens when our two consciousnesses come together" (Bhaskar with Hartwig, 2012, p. 207).

111 See Gafni (2012). The True Self and Unique Self are Gafni's terms. Marc Gafni has developed, in close collaboration with Ken Wilber and integral theory, his particular synthesis of Western and Eastern Enlightenment.

112 See Bhaskar (1993; 1994); Wilber (1995); Morin (1991/2009), for example.

113 Marshall (2016); provides a detailed complex integral realist critique of the western tradition, as well as outlining a new axial vision for the 21st century that is based on a complex integral realism.

114 Edgar Morin was, together with Roy Bhaskar and Sean Esbjörn-Hargens representing integral theory, a keynote speaker at the 2013 Integral Theory Conference.

References

Basseches, M. (2005). The development of dialectical thinking as an approach to integration. *Integral Review*, 1, 47–63.

Bhaskar, R (1975/2008). *A realist theory of science*. London: Verso.

Bhaskar, R. (1979/1998). *The possibility of naturalism: A philosophical critique of contemporary human sciences*. London: Routledge.

Bhaskar, R (1986/2009). *Scientific realism and human emancipation*. London: Routledge.

Bhaskar, R. (1993/2008). *Dialectic: The pulse of freedom*. London: Routledge.

Bhaskar, R. (1994/2010). *Plato etc*. London: Routledge.

Bhaskar, R. (2002a). *From science to emancipation*. New Delhi: Sage.

Bhaskar, R. (2002b). *Reflections on metaReality*. New Delhi: Sage.

Bhaskar, R. (2002c). *MetaReality: The philosophy of metaReality, Vol. 1*. New Delhi: Sage.

Bhaskar, R. (2010). Contexts of interdisciplinarity: A research agenda to support action on global warming. In R. Bhaskar, C. Frank, K. G. Hoyer, P. Næss, & J. Parker (Eds.), *Interdisciplinarity and climate change*. London: Routledge.

Bhaskar, R. (2012). Considerations on 'Ken Wilber on critical realism'. *Journal of Integral Theory and Practice*, 7(4), 39–42.

Bhaskar, R., & Danemark, B. (2006). Metatheory, interdisciplinarity and disability research: A critical realist perspective. *Scandinavian Journal of Disability Research*, 8(4), 278–297.

Bhaskar, R., with Hartwig, M. (2010). *The formation of critical realism*. London: Routledge.

Bhaskar, R., with Hartwig, M. (2012). (Re)-contextualizing metaReality. In M. Hartwig & J. Morgan (Eds.), *Critical realism and spirituality* (pp. 206–217). London: Routledge.

Bryant, L., Srnicek, N., & Harman, G. (2011). Towards a speculative philosophy. In L. Bryant, N. Srnicek, and G. Harman (Eds.), *The speculative turn: Continental materialism and realism* (ch. 1, pp. 1–18). Melbourne: re.press.

Combs, A. (2002). *The radiance of being: Understanding the grand integral vision.* St. Paul, MN: Paragon House.

Commons, M. L., & Bresette, L. M (2006). Illuminating major creative scientific innovators with postformal stages. In C. Hoare (Ed.), *Handbook of adult development and learning* (pp. 255–280). New York: Oxford University Press.

Deacon, T. (2012/2013). *Incomplete nature: How mind emerged from matter.* London: W. W. Norton.

Deacon, T., & Cashman, T. (2012). 'Eliminativism, complexity and emergence'. In J. W. Haag, G. R. Peterson, & M. L. Spezio (Eds.), *The Routledge companion to science and religion* (pp. 193–205). London and New York: Routledge.

Despain, H. (2013). Integral theory: The salubrious chalice? *Journal of Critical Realism, 12*(4), 507–517.

Esbjörn-Hargens, S. (2006). Integral research: A multi-method approach to investigating phenomena. *Constructivism in the Human Sciences, 11*(1), 79–107.

Esbjörn-Hargens, S. (2010a.) Ontology and climate change. Integral pluralism and the enactment of multiple objects. *Journal of Integral Theory and Practice, 5*(1), 143–174.

Esbjörn-Hargens, S. (2010b.) An overview of integral theory. In S. Esbjörn-Hargens (Ed.), *Integral theory in action: Applied, theoretical and constructive perspectives on the AQAL model* (pp. 33–64). New York: SUNY Press.

Esbjörn-Hargens, S. (2013). The meta-praxis of defining and developing integral theory. Keynote presentation given at the Integral Theory Conference, July 2013. Downloaded from: https://foundation.metaintegral.org/ITC/Papers.

Feuerstein, G. (1987). *Structures of consciousness: The genius of Jean Gebser.* Lower Lake, CA: Integral Publishing.

Gafni, M. (2012). *Your unique self: The radical path to personal enlightenment.* Tucson, AZ: Integral Publishers.

Gebser, J. (1949 and 1953/1985). *The ever-present origin.* Athens, OH: Ohio University Press.

Groff, R. (2009). Introduction to the Special Issue. *Journal of Critical Realism, 8*(3), 267–276.

Groff, R. (2013). *Ontology revisited: Metaphysics in social and political philosophy.* London: Routledge.

Hartwig, M. (Ed.). (2007). *Dictionary of critical realism.* London: Routledge.

Hartwig, M. (2013). The power of absence: Dialectical critical realism, metaReality and Terrence W. Deacon's account of the emergence of ententionality. *Journal of Critical Realism, 12*(2), 210–243.

Hedlund, N. (2010). Integrally researching integral research: Enactive perspectives on the future of the field. *Journal of Integral Theory and Practice, 5*(2), 1–30.

Hedlund-de Witt, N. (2013). *Towards a critical realist integral theory: Ontological and epistemic considerations for integral philosophy.* Paper presented at the Integral Theory Conference, San Francisco, July 2013.

Laloux, F. (2014). *Reinventing organisations: A guide to creating organisations inspired by the next stage of human consciousness.* Brussels: Nelson Parker.

Laske, O (2006). *Measuring hidden dimensions: The art and science of fully engaging adults.* Melford, MA: Interdevelopmental Institute Press.

Laske, O. (2008). *Measuring hidden dimensions of human systems.* Melford, MA: Interdevelopmental Institute Press.

Laske, O. (2012). CDF: The end of developmental absolutism and reductionism? *IDM Hidden Insights Newsletter, 8*(3), 10–21. Downloaded from: http://interdevelopmentals. org/idm-newsletter-8-3/.

Marshall, P. (1991). Noam Chomsky's anarchism. *Our Generation, 22*(1–2), 1–15. Canada: Our Generation.

Marshall, P. (2012a). The meeting of two integrative metatheories. *Journal of Critical Realism*, 11(2), 188–214.

Marshall, P. (2012b). Toward an integral realism: Part 1: An overview of transcendental realist ontology. *Journal of Integral Theory and Practice*, 7(4), 1–34.

Marshall, P. (2012c). Ken Wilber on critical realism. *Journal of Integral Theory and Practice*, 7(4), 35–38.

Marshall, P. (2016). *Towards a new axial vision: A complex integral realist perspective*. London: Routledge.

Mingers, J. (2014). *Systems thinking, critical realism and philosophy*. London: Routledge.

Morin, E. (1951/1974). *El hombre y la muerte* (Man and death). Barcelona: Kairós.

Morin, E. (1977/2009). *El método 1: La naturaleza de la naturaleza* (The method 1: Nature of nature). Madrid: Ediciones Cátedra.

Morin, E. (1986/2009). *El método 3: El conocimiento del conocimiento* (The method 3: Knowledge of knowledge). Madrid: Ediciones Cátedra.

Morin, E. (1991/2009). *El método 4: Las ideas* (The method 4: Ideas) Madrid: Ediciones Cátedra.

Morin, E. (1993/1999). *Homeland Earth: A manifesto for the new millennium*. Cresskill, NJ: Hampton Press.

Morin, E. (1994/2005). *Mis demonios* (My demons). Barcelona: Kairós.

Morin, E. (1999/2010). *La mente bien ordenada* (A well-organised mind). Barcelona: Seix Barral.

Morin, E. (2001a). *Seven complex lessons in education for the future*. Paris: Unesco.

Morin, E. (2001b/2009). *El método 5: La humanidad de la humanidad* (The method 5: Humanity of humanity). Madrid: Ediciones Cátedra.

Morin, E. (2004/2009). *El método 6: Ética* (The method 6: Ethics). Madrid: Ediciones Cátedra.

Morin, E. (2005/2009). *Breve historia de la barbarie en Occidente* (A short history of barbarism in the West). Barcelona: Ediciones Paidós Ibérica.

Morin, E. (2008). *On complexity*. New Jersey: Hampton Press Inc.

Morin, E., with Tager, D. K. (2008/2010). *Mi camino: La vida y la obra del padre del pensamiento complejo* (My way: The life and work of the father of complex thought). Barcelona: Editorial Gedisa.

Norrie, A. (2010). *Dialectic and difference: Dialectical critical realism and the grounds of justice*. London: Routledge.

Stein, Z. (2007). Modeling the demands of interdisciplinarity: Toward a framework for evaluating interdisciplinary endeavors. *Integral Review*, 4, 91–107.

Wilber, K. (1995/2000). *Sex, ecology, spirituality*. London: Shambhala.

Wilber, K. (1998/2000). *The marriage of sense and soul*. In Collected Works of Ken Wilber, Vol. 8 (pp. 81–270). London: Shambhala.

Wilber, K. (1999). *Integral psychology*. London: Shambhala.

Wilber, K. (2006). *Integral spirituality: A startling new role for religion in the modern and postmodern world*. London: Integral Books.

Wilber, K. (2012). In defense of integral theory: A response to critical realism. *Journal of Integral Theory and Practice*, 7(4), 43–52.

Wilber, K. (2013). Response to critical realism in defense of integral theory. Addendum. Downloaded from: http://integrallife.com/integral-post/response-critical-realism-defense-integral-theory?page=0,4.

Wilber, K. (2014). *The fourth turning: Imagining the evolution of an integral Buddhism*. London: Shambhala.

Wilber, K., Patten, T., Leonard, A., & Morelli, M. (2008). *Integral life practice*. Boston, MA: Integral Books.

5

RETHINKING THE INTELLECTUAL RESOURCES FOR ADDRESSING COMPLEX TWENTY-FIRST-CENTURY CHALLENGES

Towards a critical realist integral theory

Nicholas Hedlund

> Today the spark of a renewal of metaphysics is rising from the ashes of negativism – whether this be a version of metaphysics asserting itself in the wake of Kant or one that is blatantly scrambling back behind Kant's transcendental dialectic.
>
> *(Habermas, 1992/1996, p. 28)*

Introduction[1]

As postmodernism's anti-realism continues to wane, and its inadequacies as an intellectual response to the complex global challenges of the twenty-first century become ever more glaring, there is an urgent need for more sophisticated and efficacious alternatives. But what will rise from the rubble – the fertile clearing – that postmodernism has bequeathed us?[2] What intimations of an alternative intellectual formation more apt for our planetary moment can be discerned? And what are (or will be) its key motifs and thematics?

To begin to address these questions one can start by noting some of the leading philosophies in the academy that are gaining credence as alternatives to postmodernism – namely, critical realism (CR),[3] integral theory (IT), and speculative realism.[4] These approaches are broadly united in an interest in the revindication of ontology[5] or some variant of *realism* in the face of the neo- and post-Kantian epistemological critiques undergirding postmodernism's myriad inflections of anti-realism.[6] Concomitantly, they diverge in important ways in terms of their particular approaches and histories related to surmounting these challenges to the status of ontology and their impact. In contrast to critical realism, for whom the revindication of ontology in philosophy has been a central and consistent goal explicitly developed since the 1970s, integral theory has approached the issue from a more interdisciplinary[7] metatheoretical perspective, has been less consistent in its position (e.g., its 'postmetaphysical' moments of opposition to ontology in phase 5, discussed below), and has only recently begun to address the issue, which remains somewhat peripheral, more explicitly (Esbjörn-Hargens, 2010a; Wilber, 2012a, 2012b).[8] Finally, speculative realism is itself a very new movement, emerging in 2007, which employs a number of divergent approaches to the revindication of ontology,[9] and has, to some extent, been influenced by critical realism (see, e.g., Bryant, 2011).[10]

Of the aforementioned approaches, I will focus on only two here: the respective positions articulated by the contemporary European-based philosophy of Critical Realism, founded by Roy Bhaskar, and the American-based metatheoretical approach of Integral Theory,[11] founded by Ken Wilber. While certain currents within the much more heterogeneous and loosely connected philosophical movement known as Speculative Realism are also worthy of consideration (see, e.g., Graham Harman's (2002) Object Oriented Philosophy and Levi Bryant's Onticology (2011)), for purposes of this short essay, I limit myself to addressing only IT and CR.

Thus, in this chapter, I want to suggest that both of these movements have substantial relevance for the iterative and reflexive process of envisaging and forging an integrative (or post-postmodern) metatheory that is apt for the twenty-first century and its complex global crises. Rather than a singular approach or particular theory (e.g., Ken Wilber's articulation of the AQAL model), I argue that integrative metatheory might be better understood as a broad and pluralistic sphere of thought (i.e., inclusive of multiple schools or streams) defined largely as an emergent structural formation arising in the wake of the philosophical discourse of both modernity and postmodernity[12] and characterized by the key motif of a resurgence of 'ontology,' or '*the new realism*,' regardless of the degree to which specific schools convincingly break with anti-realism.[13] In this way, I am suggesting that we may indeed be in the early phases of integrative metatheory's rise as a definitive alternative to postmodernism and its marked limitations – but of course, only time will tell. Yet if integrative metatheory is to constitute an authentically novel movement within the geo-historical trajectory of Western thought, rather than a mere recapitulation or variant of postmodernism (or regressive championing of [pre]modern approaches under the guise of the new[14]), then it must be more than an alternative – it must go *beyond* or transcend both modernism and postmodernism while simultaneously including their most important enduring contributions. That is, integrative metatheory, I want to suggest, should forge a higher-order *sublation (Aufhebung)* or transcendence and non-preservative synthesis of the philosophical discourse of both modernity and postmodernity. However, as we will see, this sublation necessarily is of a transformative-negational variety. Thus, rather than a mere recapitulation or re-iteration of the core tenets of modern or postmodern metatheory, I argue that a definitive signature of integrative metatheory is its fundamental *break* or asymmetry and transformative negation in relation to the ontological and epistemic foundations of its antecedent philosophical formations concomitant with the enfoldment of their enduring moments of virtue. It thereby must be an emergent, non-preservative dialectical sublation that negates, modifies and re-patterns aspects of their architechtonics, on the way to birthing an emergent holistic conceptual pattern or structure. In short, integrative metatheory, defined as such, should strive to enact a kind of *post*-postmodernism worthy of such a designation in a definitive structural sense, as opposed to the all too common rhetorical 'post-'holing that often seems to reflect trivial academic fence-building more than a substantive differentiation or break from antecedent approaches.[15]

Based on these proposed criteria or guiding principles for integrative metatheory (i.e., a post-postmodern intellectual formation sublative of the philosophical discourse of modernity and postmodernity; a mature or post-critical championing of ontology) I argue that CR and IT appear to be among the most comprehensive and sophisticated expressions of a still yet to be fully consolidated integrative, post-postmodern metatheory. Both CR and IT explicitly situate themselves not only as alternatives to postmodernism, but claim to go beyond both positivism and social constructivism while integrating key aspects of their respective philosophical discourses.[16] In the face of radicalized forms of post-Kantian skepticism and anti-realism characteristic of postmodernism, both approaches champion a higher-octave return to ontology – a return to some form of realism that substantially integrates the epistemic advances of both (post)positivism and social constructivism and thus is not a regression to a form of pre-critical, first philosophy (*prima philosophia*) or dogmatic metaphysics. Both CR and IT articulate unique justifications for such a return to an 'ontology' inclusive of the post-Kantian, postmodern principle of *epistemic relativity* in some form, to some degree (although, as we will see, while the same signifiers [e.g., 'ontology'] are used, there may be little referential overlap across these metatheoretical streams in their present form). They both seem to acknowledge that knowledge can no longer be formulated from what Thomas Nagel (1986) calls the 'view from nowhere,' which characterizes most metaphysical projects. Rather, they both self-reflexively argue that it should necessarily be *situated* in relation to various positionalities, such as geo-historical trajectories, cultural milieus, psychological structures, or otherwise. As such, they are both attempting to fashion the emergent contours of an integrative metatheoretical discourse through a epistemologically sophisticated return to 'ontology' or '(neo-) realism,' but have very different, partly incommensurable, yet potentially complementary understanding of what that means.

As I will contend, IT, as it has been expressed to date, maintains a post-Kantian position and develops a sophisticated, postmetaphysical theory of enactment, the strengths of which lie primarily in the epistemic domain.[17] In contrast, CR expounds a powerful critique of neo- and post-Kantianism, yet uses a Kantian-inspired method of transcendental argumentation to derive a 'depth ontology,' which is arguably its signature advance and principal strength. Thus, in this chapter I aim to explore the most salient strengths (moments of truth and coherence) and weaknesses (absences and contradictions) of both CR and IT[18] within the domains of ontology and epistemology, highlighting their striking complementarities, on the way to forging the outlines of a provisional non-preservative synthesis of these two approaches to being and knowing – that is, an integral realism[19] or *Critical Realist Integral Theory* (CRIT).[20] Crucially, the principle (knowledge-constitutive) interest motivating such a synthesis is the rethinking and advancement of the intellectual resources with which we can effectively address our complex, twenty-first-century challenges (such as climate change), with sufficient integrative span and emancipatory potency. As such, I am broadly attempting to begin to do with CR and IT what they each claim to do with the philosophical discourse of modernity and postmodernity – namely, to transcend and integrate them into an emergent intellectual formation. However, to be sure, my method here is dialectical in a *transformative-sublatory* sense (à la Bhaskar), as opposed to preservative-synthetic (à la Hegel) (Bhaskar, 1993/2008; Norrie, 2010).[21] By that I mean that I aim to engage each metatheory with an eye to identifying generative contradictions and absences (or other inconsistencies, anomalies, and aporias), while (hopefully) shedding some preliminary light on some of their potential causes. Such a method initiates a movement toward the rethinking of (aspects of) each metatheory's architectonics – beginning to chart a trajectory toward an expanded conceptual field (namely, a CRIT) that eschews and remedies absences and contradictions in each theory's pre-existing form. Importantly, this involves a negative transfiguration of elements within both theories. Thus, when I refer to 'synthesis' in the context of developing a CRIT, it should be understood in this explicitly non-preservative sense.[22]

First, I begin by providing a synoptic overview of IT in the domains of ontology and epistemology, followed by a comparable exposition of CR. I then critically analyze (delineating apparent absences and contradictions) IT in light of CR, before likewise exploring CR from the perspective of IT. Finally, I sketch some initial propositions with respect to how aspects of the two schools might begin to be transfigured and synthesized into a more comprehensive and robust (expression of) integrative metatheory – a CRIT – that could potentially unite the strengths of both while addressing and beginning to transform their respective liabilities (absences and contradictions). I conclude by reflecting on the social and ecological relevance of the deep and seemingly abstract ontological and epistemological questions underpinning this inquiry, suggesting that something like a CRIT may offer crucial intellectual resources for addressing the complex global challenges of the twenty-first century, such as climate change.

Integral theory's ontology and epistemology

Since a comprehensive overview of IT's ontology and epistemology is beyond the scope of this chapter, I will, rather, summarize certain key features relevant to my argument. To begin, IT, at least in a formal philosophical sense, lacks an explicit, fully articulated and justified (*a priori*) philosophical ontology; it thus remains largely implicit and therefore will be assessed in a reconstructive manner.[23] Having clarified this caveat, IT, as it has been expressed to date, builds on the German philosopher and social theorist Jürgen Habermas' (1992/1996, 2003) postmetaphysical thinking in articulating a post-Kantian theory of enactment, or integral postmetaphysics (also called phase 5 in the development of Wilber's approach). Integral postmetaphysics, as expounded by Wilber[24] (2001, 2003a, 2006) and Esbjörn-Hargens[25] (2010a) links ontology to epistemology and methodology such that (at least in some sense) it appears to assert the primacy of epistemology and methodology over ontology. That is, I argue that in practice it underscores the ways in which ontology is essentially derivative of, or contingent on, epistemology (and methodology), despite countervailing claims that they are synchronically emergent ("arise concurrently") and mutually interdependent ("co-enact concurrently").[26] Moreover, maintaining the primacy of epistemology (and methodology) over ontology is closely connected to IT's postmetaphysical attempt to jettison ontology or metaphysics in its pre-critical or dogmatic form. As Wilber (2006) articulates it:

> If metaphysics began with Aristotle, it ended with Kant. Or at any rate, took a turn that has defined the way sophisticated philosophers think about reality ever since. Kant's *critical philosophy* replaced ontological objects with structures of the subject. In essence, this means that we do not perceive empirical objects in a completely realistic, pregiven fashion; but rather, structures of the knowing subject impart various characteristics to the known object that then appear to belong to the object – but really don't; they are, rather, co-creations of the knowing subject. Various *a priori* categories of the knowing subject help to fashion or construct reality as we know it. Reality is not a perception, but a conception; at least in part. Ontology per se just does not exist.
>
> *(p. 231)*

Thus, Wilber's articulation of his postmetaphysical position appears to involve a relatively strong post-Kantian irrealist and constructivist stance,[27] including an alignment with Kant's basic notion that the *a priori* categories and structures do not have independent, real referents in the world (that is, *categorial irrealism*), but, in Wilber's terms, 'enact' the referent.[28] Wilber (2006) goes on to note that:

> [Ontological] objects come into being, or are enacted, only at various developmental levels of complexity and consciousness. Whether they exist in some other way CANNOT BE KNOWN in any event, and assuming that they do exist entirely independently of a knowing mind is nothing but the myth of the given and the representational paradigm – that is, is just another type of metaphysical thinking and thus not adequately grounded. At any event, postmetaphysical thinking does not rely on the existence of a pregiven world and the myth of that givenness.
>
> *(p. 252, capitals in original)*

This passage seems to reveal Wilber's correlation of ontology and epistemology: the ontological, mind-independent existence of objects "CANNOT BE KNOWN," and therefore, in a (characteristically postmodern) radicalization of Kant, if they can't be known, then sophisticated philosophy or metatheory, for Wilber, would make no claim to their existence: the ontological status of an object is contingent on its epistemological enactment vis-à-vis developmental structures and methods. Accordingly, Wilber seems to suggest that we cannot have knowledge of being (the ontic) *as such*, but only being as it is known by subjects (human and non-human), and therefore we can collapse Kant's transcendental dialectic and functionally equate being with *access* to being, being itself with the (inter)subjective interpretation or enactment of being: "there is no 'apart from' how a thing appears; there is simply how it appears" (Wilber, 2006, p. 252); thus "'enter consciousness' and 'exist' are essentially identical in the post/modern world" (Wilber, 2006, p. 250). Therefore, in the face of this Kantian *problem of access*, Wilber argues for what seems to be a subject-oriented position, albeit a(n) (arguably non-anthropocentric) panpsychic one,[29] that apparently sees no way for there to be realities that are fundamentally mind-independent – he sees no way to grant ontology an autonomy from epistemology[30] (and methodology) without regressing to dogmatic metaphysics, or some kind of pre-critical ontotheology that sidesteps the demands of modern *procedural rationality*[31] (Habermas, 1992/1996; Taylor, 1989). Thus, from the perspective of integral postmetaphysics, which is centrally committed to a procedural rationality, any claim to a truly mind-independent object-world is apparently a form of the 'myth of the given,' or pre-critical metaphysics.[32]

To be sure, Wilber's (2006, 2012a, 2012b) notion of "intrinsic features," and related distinction between "subsist" and "exist," adds complexity and nuance to his scheme, and *prima facie*, appears to undercut the assessment that "any claim to a truly mind-independent object-world is apparently a form of the 'myth of the given.'" However, Wilber (2006) goes on to point out that his 'intrinsic features' "are not intrinsically intrinsic features," but rather that "whatever is actually 'intrinsic' to the Kosmos changes with each new worldspace; and thus both what ex-ists and what sub-sists are con-structions of consciousness" (pp. 250–251). Moreover, he goes on to reiterate this position by claiming that "signifiers have real referents in the only place that referents of any sort exist anyway: in a state or structure of consciousness. All referents exist, if they exist at all, in a worldspace" (p. 266). Thus, while Wilber argues for the existence of 'real' objects, referents, and 'intrinsic features' that subsist, upon scrutiny, it seems that such notions are, for Wilber (2012b), an idealistically contingent function of mind/consciousness/interiority and its structures: "when we actually get down to explaining what this subsistence reality is – the 'real' – it changes with each new structure (red, amber, orange, green, etc.)" (p. 44). So for Wilber, it appears that there are realities that are not totally mind-dependent in the sense of what is brought forth synchronically in the human epistemic, subject-centered process of enactment (that is, "intrinsic features" that "subsist" relatively independent of a given human subject's perception of it), but those realities are themselves inexorably mind-dependent (at least in the Whiteheadian sense of prehension[33]).[34] So we might thereby conclude that, according to integral postmetaphysics, realities are not only constituted individually and synchronically, but also diachronically and relationally, and they are contingent on specific developmental structures. While this can certainly help to distinguish Wilber's enactivist position, for example, from solipsism and classical (e.g., Berkeleyian) forms of subjective idealism, to my mind, it does little to establish a foothold in the domain of a realism that honours the epistemic anteriority and independence of the world. Such a form of ontological realism, critical realism would argue, is a *sine qua non* of an authentic and substantive break from the radicalized forms of social constructivism and epistemic relativism. While Wilber has recently shifted his rhetorical emphasis with respect to ontology, moving from statements such as "ontology per se just does not exist" (Wilber, 2006, p. 231) to making explicit that "ontology is real" (quoted in P. Marshall, 2012a, p. 37), it seems relatively clear that for Wilber, and IT at large, ontology is enactively or *empirically contingent* (i.e., a product or "co-creation" of the knowing-consciousness or experience of sentient beings/holons), *developmentally stratified* (i.e., according to species and psychological levels of consciousness), and therefore *pluralistic* (i.e., there are multiple ontologies and many worlds that may or may not referentially overlap). In short, IT champions an irrealist *ontology of the phenomenal*, which, as we will see, is in marked contrast to that of CR (for which it wouldn't really be considered an ontology at all).[35]

Despite positing this inexorable post-Kantian coupling of epistemology (and methodology) and ontology, and the interrelated rejection of the possibility of generating a critical/post-Kantian, realist ontology (i.e., an ontology that is disambiguated from epistemology and thereby makes claims about being as such or objects that exist independent of mind and method), it is important to emphasize that Wilber attempts to differentiate his position from that of most strong forms of postmodern social constructivism[36] and untempered epistemic relativism in, for example, the following ways: (1) he argues for a weaker form of social constructivism by virtue of the fact that he claims to not deny *entirely* the existence of a real world 'out there' by reference to his "intrinsic features" and "ex-ist"/"subsist" distinction; (2) by emphasizing the highly structured (e.g., through developmental structures), interactively performative, and therefore non-arbitrary process of enactment on both epistemic and methodological levels (which could be said to resonate with aspects of structuralist anti-humanism[37]); and (3) through his underscoring of the principles of *epistemic reflexivity* and *positionality* implied in his articulation of the notion of 'kosmic address.'

Moreover, in the domain of epistemology, it should be noted that IT possesses a sophisticated epistemic taxonomy, including its matrix of (inter)subjective structures (e.g., levels, lines, states, types; see Figure 5.1[38]), as well as its methodological taxonomy known as Integral Methodological Pluralism (IMP; see Figure 5.2).[39] IT's taxonomy of such myriad (inter)subjective epistemic structures builds on the pioneering work of the Swiss psychologist and philosopher Jean Piaget (1896–1980). Piaget (1928, 1932, 1971a, 1971b, 1972, 1977, 2000/1969) employed empirical methods to observe and code the patterning of diverse capacities for thought and action, disclosed as human beings develop from infancy to various stages of adulthood. In this way, he rationally reconstructed the conditions for the possibility of various cognitive skills/events, and designated numerous (epistemic) structures that he saw as the fundamental causal mechanisms necessarily undergirding them. Over the course of his career, Piaget amassed a copious body of evidence for his developmental theory – known as *genetic epistemology* (referring to the genesis or origins of knowledge, *not* genes or biological genetics) – essentially birthing the field of developmental-structuralism and inspiring many researchers to further probe, test, and expand his model to delineate the higher reaches of adult development (i.e., beyond his 'formal operational' stage of linear rationality). As such, this neo-Piagetian stream of developmental-structuralism has subjected Piaget's general model to careful scrutiny within multiple research paradigms, and the essence of the model has generally stood the tests of time and demonstrated both its scientific validity and cross-cultural universality across the globe (Gardiner & Kosmitzki, 2004).[40] At the same time, the neo-Piagetians have introduced a number of important nuances and distinctions that do much to address a number of common objections and criticisms to developmental models, including their potential abuses when coupled with simple 'growth to goodness' normative assumptions, their purported uni-linear and uni-directional trajectory of 'progress,' and their alleged 'Eurocentricity,' to name a few.[41] Additionally, various researchers have used a broadly neo-Piagetian developmental-structural approach to delineate their own similarly forged (and generally more advanced) stage models in a number of domains or lines such as cognition (Basseches, 1984; Commons, Richards, & Armon, 1984; Dawson, 2001, 2002, 2004; Fisher, 1980; Fisher & Biddle, 2006; Rose & Fischer, 2009); reflective judgement (King & Kitchener, 1994); socio-emotional development (Kegan, 1982, 1994, 2001); ego-identity (Cook-Greuter, 1999, 2000, 2002; Loevinger, 1977, 1987); and morality (Armon, 1984; Kohlberg, 1984). IT, based on neo-Piagetian developmental-structural psychology, thus posits that empirical human knowing is situated within an invariant, though dialectical and non-unilinear, trajectory through hierarchically-structured stages – stages that function as key generative mechanisms in the enactment of what "ex-ists" out of the "subsist" level. Based on a meta-analysis of many of the best neo-Piagetian theories, IT articulates a synthetic metatheory that is arguably the most comprehensive taxonomy of these epistemic structures to date (Wilber, 2000, 2006).[42]

In addition to its matrix of (inter)subjective structures, IT also articulates a robust methodological taxonomy, IMP, that can be seen as an important aspect of its overall epistemic taxonomy (Esbjörn-Hargens & Wilber, 2006; Wilber, 2003b, 2006). IMP is a meta-methodological map of eight *event horizons* that situate eight corresponding methodological families to explore and disclose the dynamic interrelationships between (inter)subjective and (inter)objective aspects of reality. IMP also articulates the systematic interrelationships between each of the major methodological families, allowing the researcher to thereby combine, coordinate, and *systematically integrate* the multiplicity of methodologies and methods (both qualitative and quantitative) available for scientific inquiry. IMP has been operationalized as a practical framework, known as Integral Research (IR), which supports researchers to reflect on and self-reflexively situate the unique interpretive lens (and its strengths and weaknesses) that each researcher brings to their inquiry (Esbjörn-Hargens, 2006;

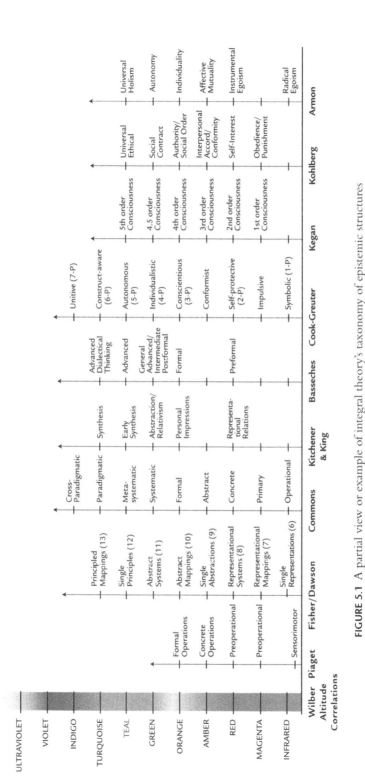

FIGURE 5.1 A partial view or example of integral theory's taxonomy of epistemic structures

Hedlund, 2008, 2010). In these ways, it offers a (broadly) scientific framework that goes beyond the unprincipled eclecticism that plagues many other integrative and multi-methodological approaches.

IT's overall epistemic taxonomy can thus be understood to represent an important scientific ontology that must be grappled with by any panoptic or comprehensive metatheory. In short, while IT lacks an explicit philosophical ontology, it nonetheless has an implicit comprehensive and sophisticated, systematically structured scientific ontology of the psychological, cultural, and methodological mechanisms that help to construct knowledge. Taken together IT's epistemic taxonomy constitutes a kind of robust metatheory, based largely on scientific findings, of the varied and often divergent ways that human beings experience and relate to aspects of the world – and is therefore among its primary contributions.

Critical realism's ontology and epistemology

In this section, I will provide a synoptic overview of CR's basic (transcendental realist and critical naturalist) ontology and epistemology (also see P. Marshall, 2012b, for a broad overview), while omitting CR's more complex dialectical and spiritual turns, since they deepen, but do not fundamentally shift or depart from, CR's basic ontology and epistemology.[43] In contrast to IT, CR has an explicit philosophical ontology, deploying a variation on a Kantian transcendental mode of argument[44] in relation to conceptualized human activities such as experimentation, both in science and more generally, to arrive at a definitively non-Kantian (object- rather than subject-oriented), transcendental realist position.[45] This position argues for a world composed of things possessing causal powers and generative mechanisms in virtue of their structure and existing and acting anterior to and *independently* of human interpretation, knowledge, enactment, or discourse.[46] As such, CR thoroughly de-couples and disambiguates ontology from epistemology, while making epistemology secondary to ontology (the former is 'constellationally contained' by the latter), since knowledge of the world (in some domain) depends evidently on the nature of the world (i.e., what the world is like in that domain).[47] This stands in stark contrast to IT's neo-Kantian position that leads with epistemology and developmental levels in expounding its notion of 'enacted objects.' Bhaskar (1975/2008) arrives at CR's basic ontology by asking an (inverted) Kantian-transcendental question: not, as Kant asked, "What must the mind be like for science to be possible?" but rather "What must the *world* be like for science to be possible?" As Bhaskar (1975/2008) highlights through rigorous transcendental or presuppositional analysis involving retroductive and deductive logic, as will be delineated below, it is the ontological reality and existence of a mind-independent object-world that must be presupposed on an *a priori* philosophical level, if *a posteriori* science is to be intelligible at all – it is a necessary condition for the possibility and intelligibility of experimental science. (This premise of human experimental practice is later generalized to include all forms of human practice.) More precisely, Bhaskar (1975/2008) claims that a necessary condition for the possibility of science is the existence of "intransitive objects," by which he does not mean simple gross-material entities (as in IT's upper-right quadrant), but rather real generative mechanisms, structures, and powers that exist autonomously of human minds and can be uncorrelated or "out of phase" with actual patterns of events or empirical observations (p. 13). Thus, according to CR, all socially produced scientific theories or interpretive knowledge-claims (the *transitive* dimension) are concerned with an absolutely (most natural mechanisms) or relatively (most social mechanisms) theory-independent object-world (the *intransitive* dimension),[48] whether they explicitly acknowledge it or not. Referring to this notion that "knowledge" has both a hermeneutical (transitive) as well as realist (intransitive) element, Bhaskar (1975/2008) writes:

> Any adequate philosophy of science must find a way of grappling with this central paradox of science: that men in their social activity produce knowledge which is a social product much like any other, which is no more independent of its production and the men who produce it than motor cars, armchairs or books, which has its own craftsmen, technicians, publicists, standards and skills and which is no less subject to change than any other commodity. This is one side of 'knowledge'. The other is that knowledge is '*of*' things which are not produced by men at all: the specific gravity of mercury, the process of electrolysis, the mechanism of light propagation. None of these 'objects of knowledge' depend on human activity. If men ceased to exist sound would continue to travel and heavy bodies fall to the earth in exactly the same way, though ex hypothesi there would be no-one to know it.
>
> *(p. 21, original emphasis)*

Thus, as Bhaskar suggests in this passage, CR holds that with the emergence of human (and other) forms of consciousness the world is characterized by a kind of duality in which (intransitive) objects (in a general categorical and dispositional/ tendential sense) have their own existence (and agency) outside of human knowledge and interpretation, but can only be known in their specific contents, rich textures, and nuances in and through (transitive) scientific inquiry and human interpretation/construal.

The proposition that intransitive objects can be (and often are) "out of phase" with actual patterns of events means that certain aspects of an object's generative powers may either act or lie dormant depending on various conditions and complex, dynamic interrelations with other objects. Thus, an intransitive object (generative mechanism) will not produce the same actual events in all contexts. Bhaskar (1975/2008) justifies his proposition that intransitive objects are the necessarily presupposed condition for science by transcendental analysis of the social practice of scientific experiment, stating that:

> [A]n experiment is necessary precisely to the extent that the pattern of events forthcoming under experimental conditions would not be forthcoming without it. Thus in an experiment we are a causal agent of the sequence of

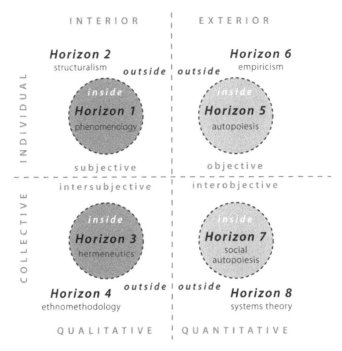

FIGURE 5.2 Integral theory's methodological taxonomy (Integral Methodological Pluralism) of eight horizons (zones) of scientific inquiry, eight corresponding methodological families, and their systematic interrelationships

events, but not of the causal law which the sequence of events, because it has been produced under experimental conditions, enables us to identify.

(p. 33)

Thus, as Bhaskar elucidates, the (closed systemic) experimental conditions draw out or disclose a particular pattern of events that would not otherwise have manifested (in an open systemic context), thus eliminating others while illuminating and identifying the real mechanisms producing the empirically observable pattern of events – the experiment brings the real and the actual temporarily into phase. In the extraordinary circumstance of an experimentally closed systemic context, objects tend to "obtain" or disclose unique sequences or patterns of events, or aspects of their potential event horizon. But in the extra-laboratory context of nearly ubiquitous open systems, objects/generative mechanisms can be either dormant or occluded by the complexity ("multi-mechanicity") of other causes within a network of mechanisms. Furthermore, the experience of particular patterns of events can also be "out of phase" with the events themselves. It is on this basis that CR posits that the world is structured or stratified in terms of three overlapping but distinct domains: the *real* (generative mechanisms, tendencies and powers plus events and experiences), the *actual* (events plus experiences), and the *empirical* (experiences)

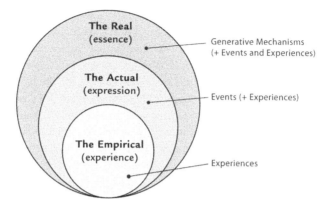

FIGURE 5.3 Three levels of depth in CR's ontology

Stratum in CR's Depth Ontology	Refers to:
The Real = Generative Mechanisms (+ Events and Experiences)	Underlying generative (causal) mechanisms or structures or fields that co-produce the flux of phenomena (events). These are themselves depth-stratified or layered (e.g., mechanisms of the inorganic world, the biosphere, and the sociosphere).
The Actual = Events (+ Experiences)	Events (whether observed or not) (e.g., Big Bang, the French Revolution, a human action)
The Empirical = Experiences	Experiences, empirical observations of events (e.g., what you see through microscopes or in historical documents)

(see Figure 5.3). Moreover, as the intelligibility of scientific change and development shows, the domain of the real is itself depth-stratified or ontologically deep such that the levels overlap in a nested manner: the real>the actual>the empirical, where '>' means co-includes or constellationally overreaches.

In noting the different expression of objects in open and closed systemic contexts (i.e., what Bhaskar refers to as their "transfactuality") and distinguishing between objects/generative mechanisms (level of the real), events/actualities (level of the actual), and the experiential and semiotic (level of the empirical), CR is, in effect, espousing a profoundly anti-reductionistic notion that one might call the *infinitude of potentiality*, in which the real is bursting forth to actualize its inexhaustible possibilities and potentials and unfold its creative fecundity on a level that eludes our dominion and control. That is, for CR, the being or essence of an object is always so much more vast, superabundant, and charged with potential than any patterns of events manifested and experienced on the level of the actual and empirical (or even the sum of those actual and empirical qualities).[49] For example, taking a human social actor, the being of that human is always deeper – seeded with incalculable possibilities – and in that sense beyond the particular ways it is manifesting and being experienced/enacted by other actors; it cannot be reduced to the pattern of its manifestation and/or interpretation in any context.[50] As such, CR lands a powerful blow on all forms of (post)positivism, empirical verificationism, and the like – even in their most expanded forms that are inclusive of interiority (e.g., James' "radical empiricism" and Wilber's "deep/broad empiricism"). In short, CR's ontology posits the existence of a real, differentiated, and depth-stratified world, independent of human knowledge and methodology, in which the domains of the real, actual, and empirical are categorically distinct. At the level of the real, objects have an undeniable, but often somewhat opaque and elusively vast, existence and potential. Working from the level of the actual and the empirical, aspects of the real can be disclosed through human inquiry, and rich knowledge of the nuances, contours, and textures of objects' contextual manifestations can be obtained, despite the inevitable fallibility and partiality of human knowledge production.

Thus, CR offers a compelling ontology that shares positivism's interest in the objective world and identifying causes, yet it diverges radically from it in claiming that the study of the empirical, in-and-of-itself, is too superficial, since it disregards the unobservable generative mechanisms that produce the actual events and empirical phenomena that positivists seek to measure and explain.[51] CR argues simultaneously for a weak constructivism and (critical) ontological realism – that is, an epistemological relativism that simultaneously acknowledges a universal, intransitive ontological dimension to reality. And just in virtue of ontological realism and epistemic relativity, it espouses a third (mediating) element in its "holy trinity": *judgmental rationality* – the possibility of arriving at non-arbitrary views about the world. CR is therefore a higher-order sublation (transcendence and inclusion) of naturalistic positivism and constructivist hermeneutics that articulates an ontology and epistemology honouring not only the creative agency of the human subject, but also the reality (and agency) of objects in the world (Alvesson & Sköldberg, 2009). CR thus argues persuasively against the reduction of ontology to epistemology (referred to as the "epistemic fallacy"), and against the reduction or conflation of the domain of the real to the domains of the actual/empirical (known as "actualism"[52]). That is, it argues for the irreducibility of the reality of causal structures and generative mechanisms to the manifest patterns of events that they produce (Alvesson & Sköldberg, 2009).

Having now provided a synoptic overview of IT's and CR's respective basic ontologies and epistemologies, I will now evaluate IT from the vantage point of CR.

Integral theory in the light of critical realism

From a critical realist standpoint, it could be argued that IT's postmetaphysical coupling of ontology and epistemology (and methodology) constitutes a form of neo-Kantian reductionism that CR refers to as the '*epistemic fallacy*,' a philosophical stance that harks back to ancient Greek philosophy (i.e., Parmenides, Protagoras, and Plato),[53] and has arguably been dominant in Western thought since the seventeenth century, which can be largely attributed to the work of Descartes, Hume, and Kant.[54] According to Bhaskar (1975/2008), the epistemic fallacy

consists in the view that statements about being can be reduced to or analysed in terms of statements about knowledge; i.e., that ontological questions
can always be transposed into epistemological terms. The idea that being can
always be analysed in terms of our knowledge of being, that it is sufficient for
philosophy to 'treat only of the network, and not what the network describes',
results in the systematic dissolution of the idea of a world (which I shall here
metaphorically characterize as an ontological realm) independent of but
investigated by science.

(pp. 36–37)

In short, the epistemic fallacy refers to the conflation of ontology and epistemology – the reduction of being as such to our knowledge of being. To be sure, IT's
postmetaphysical approach commits the epistemic fallacy in claiming that the being
of ontological objects is constituted through a subject's epistemic structures (e.g.,
developmental levels of consciousness) and methodological injunctions in the process of enactment.[55] It appears that IT therefore transposes or reduces questions of
the ontological status of being as such to epistemological questions of being as it
is brought forth and known in actual events and (broad) empirical experience. In
Wilber's (2006) words, the ontological status of objects in themselves "CANNOT
BE KNOWN," and thus IT posits that the object has no ontic status, or reality outside of the "con-structions of consciousness" (pp. 250–251).[56] While CR would
concede that *actual events* cannot be known outside of the epistemic translations
inevitably associated with substantive empirical inquiry, it would, of course, claim
that the ontological status of objects in their most essential and categorical features,
can be known through transcendental analysis and indeed must be presupposed.
Moreover, for CR, there is always a difference in principle between the transitive,
epistemic dimension of anything – an experience, event or mechanism – and its
intransitive ontic reality. So, for example, our knowledge (the transitive dimension)
of the French Revolution is not to be confused with the French Revolution as
such (the event, in the intransitive dimension). This is a key difference between CR
and IT: for CR ontological questions can in principle be clearly differentiated and
answered without being transposed into epistemological ones, whereas for IT, the
former is always fused to the latter.

In short, it appears that IT is essentially saying the following: the traditional
concept of knowing has now lost its cachet, since there is actually no given
thing or object to be known. Hence, knowing and being *implode* in the notion
of enactment – knowing is co-constitutive of being, ontology and epistemology
(and methodology) are mutually comprising. The claim here is that the ontological status or being of an object is brought forth through the consciousness
(epistemic structures) and behaviour (methodological injunctions) of the knowing subject – the being or agent engaged in the enactment. But what then, a critical realist might ask, is the ontological status of the one who enacts? This appears
to be overlooked by IT as it has been explicitly articulated to date, yet there
appears to be an implicit presupposition and thus concession of the ontological

existence or reality of at least one object – that is, the being engaged in the process of enactment – since in order for that being to enact anything at all, it must first exist as a real entity or object.[57] Thus, IT and its postmetaphysical theory of enactment seems to necessarily presuppose the ontological existence of at least one *intransitive object*. How can the being of an object be constituted through the process of enactment, if the process of enactment is inexorably driven by – and contingent on – a being that is *itself* an object? For example, when Wilber (2006) states that "[ontological] objects come into being, or are enacted, only at various developmental levels of complexity and consciousness," he is, at a minimum, logically presupposing at least one epistemic subject, with some level of development of consciousness, capable of employing methods to enact ontological objects (p. 252). But for that claim to be intelligible, that subject must itself have some ontological status. That is, the epistemic subject (or enactive agency) must itself be an ontologically real object.

Whether considering a human or an atom, the argument holds: IT's panpsychism (or paninteriorism) appears to be unable to help it escape the necessity of a realist position, and so must result in a *TINA formation*. To illustrate this point, I will offer an illustration. Again, having made the ontological status of the being of objects for humans contingent on *access* to them, IT then points out that different entities (e.g., quarks, atoms, molecules; cells, reptiles, mammals; humans at different stages in their psychological development) access or enact the world and its objects differently. For example, drawing on Maturana and Varela's (1980, 1987) biological phenomenology (zone 5 in the IMP map), IT claims that a frog's 'view from within' brings forth or cognizes a tree in a very different way than a human. As Wilber (2012b) states, "the frog enacts its own reality – its own epistemology and consciousness brings forth and co-creates its own ontology or world" (p. 45). Thus, within the frog's *Umwelt* (Von Uexküll, 1934/2010), the 'tree' is brought forth very differently, and may not even exist at all as a discrete qualitative pattern. And the same would be true for an atom's prehension of the 'tree.' Based on apparently Kantian presuppositions, this experiential divergence is an important basis for IT's rejection of CR's ontological realism. (Although CR's realism can of course take on board that frogs construe the world from unique perspectives and causally interact with their *Umwelt*.) As Wilber (2012b) states:

> [A]ccording to IT, the level of the 'real' described by CR doesn't exist as CR describes it. Rather in IT's view, in actuality it is either the product of both the prehensive-feeling-knowing plus holonic-being-isness of each of the holons at the particular level of the real (e.g., quarks, atoms, molecules, genetics) and their relations – all of which are tetra-enacted and tetra-evolved; and/or it is the result of the way the world emerges and is tetra-enacted at and from a particular level of consciousness-being.
>
> *(p. 45)*

Furthermore, Wilber adds:

[T]hese levels of being-consciousness (red, amber, orange, green, turquoise, etc.) are not different interpretations of a one, single, pregiven reality or world, but are themselves actually *different worlds* in deep structure (an infrared world, a red world, an amber world, an orange world, a green world, a turquoise world, etc., *each of which is composed of Nature's or Kosmic habits tetra-created by the sentient holons at those levels*, as are atomic, molecular, cellular, etc., worlds).

(*p. 45*)

In short, the being of objects has no existence or ontological status apart from the sentient holons enacting them at their own level of complexity and consciousness – and these different worldviews or *Umwelts* actually enact different worlds. But in all of these cases, the being of each of these holons, whether a frog, an atom, or a human, is presupposed to exist as an ontologically *real* entity or object. For the frog to enact the tree, the frog must first exist as a real ontological entity – and the same holds for the tree and the human in their enactment of their environment or objects in their worlds. In short, IT's panpsychic position still must presuppose an ontic reality independent of and anterior to the epistemic process of enactment. It thus does not escape the epistemic fallacy – it merely renders it non-anthropocentric, although for CR that would also be debatable.[58]

In this way, from the vantage point of CR, in order to begin the process of enacting or knowing anything, one must presuppose some kind of philosophical ontology – some kind of 'metaphysics' if you will. Furthermore, following Bhaskar's powerful transcendental arguments,[59] such an ontology or metaphysical proposition must presuppose the existence of an enactment-independent or intransitive world. Therefore, when Wilber claims that "postmetaphysical thinking does not rely on the existence of a pregiven world," he appears to be unaware of the *performative (self-) contradiction (performativer Widerspruch)* undergirding this so-called postmetaphysical position, as an implicitly pre-given or mind-independent world is *precisely* what it relies on.[60] And this problem is not unique to IT, but is the inevitable outcome of any philosophy or theory that commits the epistemic fallacy, which as we can see now is indeed a *fallacy* in the proper sense. Put differently, CR might say that IT's commitment of the epistemic fallacy condemns it to rely on an implicit ontology. As Bhaskar (1975/2008) elucidates:

> The metaphysical mistake the analysis of experimental episodes pinpoints, viz. the epistemic fallacy, involves the denial of the possibility of a philosoph-ical ontology. But if transcendental realism is correct, and ontology cannot in fact be reduced to epistemology, then denying the possibility of an ontology merely results in the generation of an *implicit ontology* and an *implicit realism*. In the empirical realist tradition the epistemic fallacy thus covers or disguises an ontology based on the category of experience, and a realism based on the presumed characteristics of the objects of experience, viz. atomistic events, and their relations, viz. constant conjunctions.

(*pp. 39–40*)

Thus, it is precisely IT's implicit philosophical ontology and implicit realism, because it has not been sufficiently justified and thereby sidesteps its own demands for methodological and epistemic transparency, that it cannot self-reflexively situate and coherently sustain itself – its postmetaphysical commitments are thus necessarily metaphysical commitments. Without an explicit and procedurally transparent (and hence, postmetaphysical) philosophical ontology, the internal logic of IT's own postmetaphysics inexorably eclipses itself, thereby unconsciously "scrambling back behind Kant's transcendental dialectic," to borrow a phrase from Habermas (1992/1996, p. 28), and to some extent succumbs to the very pre-critical position that it sought to depart from.[61] Put differently, IT's own internal commitments logically lead it towards the incorporation of a procedurally rational ontological foundation, like that of CR's transcendental realism.

Furthermore, as Bhaskar explicates in the above passage, the epistemic fallacy has its roots in the tradition of empirical realism, which is closely connected to logical positivism and its *verificationism*. Bhaskar (1975/2008) goes on to explain that:

> The logical positivists committed it [the epistemic fallacy] when arguing, in the spirit of Hume, that if a proposition was not empirically verifiable (or falsifiable) or a tautology, it was meaningless. Verificationism indeed may be regarded as a particular form of the epistemic fallacy, in which the meaning of a proposition about reality (which cannot be designated 'empirical') is confused with our grounds, which may or may not be empirical, for holding it.
>
> *(p. 37)*

This logical positivist verificationism bears a striking resemblance to IT's postmetaphysical dictum, "*the meaning of a statement is the injunction of its enactment.... No injunction, no enactment, no meaning,*"[62] which implies that without specification and disclosure of the methodological conditions of a statement about reality, it is considered to be meaningless (Wilber, 2006, p. 268). Thus, in the light of CR, IT's postmetaphysical approach can be seen, at least with respect to ontology, as a kind of empirical verificationism marred by the epistemic fallacy and unable to intelligibly sustain its own ontological and epistemological commitments. Furthermore, the epistemic fallacy is rooted in actualism – the reduction of underlying mechanisms to events or patterns of events. Thus, without adopting a critical realist stratified depth-ontology to avoid such a reduction of the real to the actual (i.e., actualism), postmetaphysical enactivism might therefore better be understood as a kind of metaphysical *(en)actualism*.

From a CR perspective, however, IT's interest in formulating a post-critical, post-postmodern metatheory need not inevitably lead to a neo-Kantian, subject-centered (strong) constructivism (and thus an entanglement in the epistemic fallacy and [en]actualism).[63] As Bhaskar's work highlights, the use of transcendental argumentation is a transparent *methodology* that arguably meets the demands of procedural rationality (a key criterion, or even *sine qua non*, of a postmetaphysical approach) and thus constitutes the key pathway to a post-critical revindication of an ontological realism that is not committed (implicitly or explicitly) to the epistemic fallacy and an actualist ontology. It is a methodologically sophisticated approach to forging a realist ontology that, in effect, sublates the essential epistemic advances of neo- and post-Kantian philosophy, without succumbing to performative contradiction or tautology. It may therefore, in practice, be more 'postmetaphysical' in relation to integral theory's implicit realist ontology on the one hand, and 'minimalist metaphysics' on the other, which remain procedurally opaque and lacking adequate justification vis-à-vis the mandates of its own post-metaphysical position. On these grounds one could convincingly refer to CR as a 'post-postmetaphysical' philosophy or metaphysics.[64] Moreover, as CR implicitly highlights, transcendental argumentation is a method of knowing that is *not* included in IT's meta-methodological map (IMP), which claims to account for all the major categories of human knowing. While one might speculate with respect to if and where transcendental argumentation might fit in the context of IMP's categories, as we can see by way of Bhaskar's theory, transcendental argumentation can be considered a foundational (*a priori*) method for garnering knowledge of the basic status and categorical structure of reality – and at present, it has no clear place in IT's meta-methodological map.[65] In short, from a CR vantage point, IT's attempt to jettison pre-critical metaphysics and arrive at an integral post-metaphysical position has not been entirely successful and appears to be entangled in a number of intractable philosophical problems and contradictions, including its reliance on an implicit realist ontology it cannot self-reflexively account for.

These problems and contradictions run deep, revealing penetrating ruptures in IT's ontological and epistemic architectonics that, I argue, cannot be resolved with surface-level theoretical patches[66] akin to the late Ptolemaic philosophers adding more sophisticated epicycles while avoiding any negative transfiguration at a root level. As such, without a serious rethinking of the ontological and epistemic foundations of IT's metatheoretical edifice, specifically the irrealism of its enactivism, it is at risk of collapse. I therefore argue that the absence of a transcendental realist ontology and epistemology leads IT to inexorable contradictions that may only be remedied by its adoption, which implies a deep transformation in which much needs to be shed.[67]

Critical realism in the light of integral theory

When examined in the light of IT, it could be argued that CR, given its lack of an adequate epistemic taxonomy, is not sufficiently nuanced and careful in its consideration of the epistemic categories that it uses to describe the world – and at a meta-level, of *reflexivity*, its own epistemic theorizing about it. While CR appears to have a solid ontological foundation and epistemology (in the sense of a formal philosophical theory with which to generally and categorically justify how humans acquire/produce knowledge), from the perspective of IT, CR has not paid sufficient attention to the variety of *epistemic* structures through which the world is known substantively, as well as the problem of epistemological self-consciousness in the sciences.[68] CR thus appears to be somewhat deficient in terms of providing a detailed account of the various distinct epistemic structures or categories that explain and shape (the transitive dimension of) knowledge production in our contemporary world – that is, it does not have an adequate explanatory taxonomy of the different specific structures or patterning undergirding the widespread phenomenon of inter-individual epistemic-hermeneutic variability (e.g., the interwoven ontological, epistemological, methodological, axiological, anthropological, and societal visionary orientations, or worldviews that individuals inhabit) (De Witt & Hedlund, 2015, in press; A. Hedlund-de Witt, 2012). While CR does have a model that accounts for certain abstract and transcendental aspects of inter-individual epistemic-hermeneutic variability, and analyses these as necessary for communication (Bhaskar, 1979/2015, pp. 152–158), to date it lacks a richly differentiated, substantive, and empirically grounded model of the structures and mechanisms that generate such variability.

In contrast, IT has this sort of rich and nuanced taxonomy of such myriad epistemic structures, which can be understood to represent an important *scientific ontology* of the categories of human knowing, which could strengthen CR's theory of the substantive psychological and cultural mechanisms that help to condition knowledge (the transitive dimension), and successfully be integrated with its compelling *philosophical ontology* (the intransitive dimension).[69] Moreover, given CR's commitment to *epistemic relativism* (that is, the principle that all knowledge is socially produced, and thus transient and fallible, and is conditioned by a geo-historically determined epistemic framework) and the concept of *developing integrative pluralism* (that is, incorporating the findings of valid empirical inquiry in the form of an evolving scientific ontology), CR's own internal commitments[70] logically lead it toward the incorporation of a broader taxonomy of epistemic categories like that of IT (Bhaskar, 1986/2009).[71]

Following Kant's (1791/1998) basic intuition regarding the *a priori* categories and structures of the mind, which contemporary scientific research (e.g., neo-Piagetian developmental structuralism) has arguably established, honed, and advanced, IT underscores the extent to which our psychological/subjective structures mediate and profoundly shape our knowledge of the world, not to mention the various neuro-biological, cultural, and social structures. As mentioned above, IT's epistemology is deeply informed by the work of Piaget and the neo-Piagetians, who have empirically illumined (or retroduced) the conditions for the possibility of various events disclosed in consciousness, designating numerous epistemic structures that they saw as the fundamental generative mechanisms necessarily undergirding them. Thus, as Piaget (1971b, 1972) suggested in his discussions of epistemology, the developmental structures of cognition he (and many others in his wake) identified are essentially a more nuanced and empirically grounded articulation of Kant's structures of the understanding or mind. Hence they can be conceptualized as neo-Kantian structures identified *a posteriori*.[72]

While CR concedes that knowledge is indeed transitive, situated within a geo-historical trajectory and social context, and thus fallible, when compared to IT, it seems to largely overlook such neo-Kantian/neo-Piagetian epistemic structures of consciousness that are so deeply implicated in the production of substantive knowledge. These structures, I argue, cannot be written off simply on the basis of a critique of (neo-)Kantian irrealism. The evidence presented in the neo-Piagetian literature makes abundantly clear that these structures are causally efficacious with respect to how humans construe the world, and therefore cannot be curtly cast aside as relics of a neo-Kantian epistemic fallacy. It is indeed possible, I propose, that such neo-Kantian/neo-Piagetian structures can be coherently rethought and construed in a transcendental realist manner. CR already acknowledges the existence of categories (e.g., space, time, and causality) and structures, situating them not as (transitive) epistemic impositions on the world by the subjective human mind (as Kant would have it), but as having real reference in the (intransitive) world. In Bhaskar's writings he stresses that the Kantian categories (and structures) are in the world (categorial realism). What I am suggesting in the context of a CRIT, however, is that the neo-Kantian/neo-Piagetian structures are both in the world and in the human mind. This proposition appears to be commensurable with CR's categorial realism as it in no way is implying that the neo-Kantian structures are mere subjective impositions, but rather that they mediate accurate renderings of intransitive objects. However, these categories and structures, part and parcel of an intransitive ontological world, when inhabited and employed in the context of inquiry are also transitive epistemic structures that fashion our construal of that intransitive world, as ontology necessarily precedes and constellationally contains or enfolds epistemology – and this means that knowing subjects and their epistemic structures are part of the world, part of ontology. Thus, CR rejects (neo-)Kantian '*categorial irrealism*' while embracing a categorial realism, allowing it, in principle, to include the Kantian categories and structures while jettisoning their status as unreal subjective impositions of the mind. However, the neo-Kantian structures (e.g., those disclosed by Piaget and his followers) do exist as (inter)subjective structures necessary for disclosing aspects of the world – they are structures in the transitive dimension that refer to real entities in the intransitive dimension. Concomitantly, since these neo-Kantian categories and structures are clearly causally efficacious generative mechanisms in the real domain of consciousness, they are themselves, by definition, constitutive objects of the (intransitive) world. Categories (and structures), "if valid, are constitutive of reality as such, irrespective of their categorization by observers or thought" (Bhaskar, 1997, pp. 140–141). In this way, for example, formal operations, in the (neo-)Piagetian scheme, refers to the structural capacity of a human subject to see or disclose linear causality, a reality which actually exists in the world. Similarly, meta-systematic operations (Commons *et al.*, 1984) refers to the capacity to disclose the *holistic causality* emerging from the interaction of multiple causal mechanisms across multiple nested systems, which again has an independent and anterior existence as a reality in the world. This meta-systematic structure discloses, meta-reflexively, the pluralism of interwoven epistemic structures that are themselves also part of the intransitive world – the world itself generates the structures through which facets of its own depth and complexity can be disclosed in consciousness. More of the complexity of reality is revealed in the later-stage epistemic structures, and thus with each higher-order structure there may be a tendential directionality toward a progressive de-centration or diminishing of what Bhaskar (2002, 2002/2012a) refers to as the "demi-real" elements, or that which is falsely premised but real, due to its causal efficacy. However, for CR there often appears to be an unreflected presupposition that individuals somehow naïvely, or almost voluntaristically choose to, disclose cognitively skills like the capacity to reflect on complex systems (e.g., the dynamics of a capitalist socio-sphere) or understand holistic causality – skills that are potentially critical conditions for the possibility of actualizing its emancipatory aims in practice.[73] To help remedy this and other absences, CR, therefore, could, after shedding its moments of irrealism, adopt aspects of IT's robust taxonomy of the cognitive capacities, or neo-Kantian epistemic structures rooted in neo-Piagetian developmental structural research, integrating them in transfigured form into its scientific ontology and epistemology in a coherent transcendental realist manner. Moreover, such a move seems particularly apt given the dialectical (and implicitly developmental) logic already present within CR.

Beyond its theoretical value, the realist transformation and integration of IT's epistemic taxonomy into CR's ontology and epistemology also would strengthen CR in the context of applied scientific research, potentially advancing it particularly in the context of social scientific research. While CR's critical naturalist approach to social science (see, e.g., Bhaskar, 1998) and "critical methodological pluralism" (Danermark, Ekström, Jakobsen, & Karlsson, 2002) has been lauded in the academy as a leading alternative to both (post)positivism and social constructivism alike, it has also been criticized for its insufficient engagement, in practice, on the level of the transitive, epistemological dimension, which appears to be due in part to its lack of a robust scientific ontology of epistemic structures (such as that of IT). From the vantage point of IT's intricate taxonomy of epistemic structures and its appreciation of the profound importance of the transitive-constructivist dimension of knowledge production, CR may run the risk of unknowingly hypostatizing various subjective and intersubjective phenomena, thus potentially transposing various epistemic elements into 'ontological' elements in an insufficiently critical manner. For example, Alvesson & Sköldberg (2009) state, in their discussion of critical realism as a leading alternative to (post)positivism and social constructionism, that while critical realist researchers

> are aware of the precarious nature of research (as inevitably problematic and arguable) … little space is granted to such discussions, apart from occasional confessions that come across as highly peripheral to what they otherwise consider themselves to be doing.… [T]he approach runs the risk of becoming rigid and lacking in terms of reflexivity, presenting subjective and arbitrary representations as self-evident and robust findings.
>
> (p. 49)

Thus, while CR acknowledges the constructivist element (or transitive dimension) in social scientific inquiry, devoid of a robust epistemic taxonomy, it may tend to pay too little attention to these transitive elements and their crucial role in the social process of knowledge production. CR social science might therefore be at risk of insufficiently accounting for the transitive dimension of inquiry and therefore insufficiently safeguarding against the potential import of hidden ideologies (see, e.g., Foucault, 1966/2002, who discusses such hidden ideologies in the context of the human sciences; 1972). It may thus run the risk of being written off or marginalized by those concerned with the hermeneutical and social constructivist complexities of inquiry, thus diminishing its emancipatory potential in the world. Concomitantly, CR social science may likewise run the risk of being co-opted by those with a positivist affinity who do not acknowledge the intricacies of knowledge construction in any substantive way. Those individuals who consider themselves to be under the broad umbrella of critical realism, yet (perhaps tellingly) propose to drop the 'critical' from 'critical realism', might indeed be suspected of such an implicitly positivistic disposition.

CR's insufficient account of the complexities of the transitive dimension, rooted in its lack of a model of inter-individual epistemic-hermeneutic variability, leads to a number of other problems in practice as researchers apply CR's DREIC schema (Bhaskar, 1998; Danermark *et al.*, 2002) to social scientific research. In the DREIC schema, researchers attempt to *describe* a particular pattern of events, *retroduce* an explanatory model, *eliminate* competing explanations, *identify* principal generative mechanisms, and *correct* the model in an iterative manner. Without an adequate epistemic model, such an approach may be somewhat problematic in practice. As Alvesson & Sköldberg (2009) argue:

> [D]ifferent researchers have different views regarding the 'necessary constitutive properties' and even if one had the good fortune to find researchers sharing the assumption about such properties, they would most likely come up with different ideas on the nature of such properties, and they would probably disagree over the events that the objects can be seen as capable of producing. Use of different perspectives would probably lead to different properties and different produced objects.
>
> *(p. 45)*

Thus, in order to effectively engage in explanatory social science, particularly with respect to the elimination of competing explanations, data and explanatory theories need to be situated within comprehensive methodological and epistemic taxonomies. Integral theory's emphasis on situating the positionality of the researcher in relation to its epistemic taxonomy (N. Hedlund, 2010) could help to mitigate problems of inter-individual hermeneutic-epistemic variability – critical realists need only re-contextualize this in terms of making transparent salient socially produced, fallible elements of our knowledge of objects. The epistemic and methodological positionality of the researcher is not constitutive of the ontological reality of an object, but it does profoundly shape not only the ways in which the researcher cognizes and interprets the object of inquiry, but also interfaces with – and impacts – the object of inquiry internally as it comes into a relational assemblage as a part of a complex totality or open system. This internal relationality thus potentially generates specifically structured forms of what social scientists call *reactivity* (e.g., 'the Hawthorne effect'), wherein individuals modify aspects of their behaviour or attitudes due to the effects of being studied, including a simple awareness of being observed (Heppner, Wampold, & Kivlighan, 2008, p. 331).

The heightened self-reflexivity that IT's epistemic taxonomy supports can help both to mitigate and situate specific reactivity effects, which in turn may help CR social scientists articulate more reliable and valid explanatory models. Thus, IT's methods for fostering such methodological and epistemic reflexivity by 'researching the researcher' (N. Hedlund, 2008, 2010) and locating one's scientific positionality vis-à-vis IT's taxonomy of structures (Integral Epistemological Pluralism) and meta-methodological map (IMP), may have much to offer CR in general, and its emancipatory social scientific approach in particular.

While CR claims to go beyond the myth of a God's-eye view or Nagel's 'view from nowhere' by self-reflexively locating its own theorizing within a geo-historical trajectory, it could substantially enhance its epistemological self-reflexivity by adopting IT's epistemic taxonomy (or at least some aspects of developmental-structuralism) as a tool for generating much more specificity in terms of its own positionality within a matrix of structures. Bhaskar (2002/2012b) refers to "reflexivity, or the capacity of a theory or discourse to coherently situate and sustain itself, is very important, indeed the supreme, criterion of philosophy" (p. 176). In short, IT holds the potential to complexify CR's scientific ontology and theory of the transitive dimension with its taxonomy of epistemic structures to complement its depth ontology.

Lacking such a robust scientific ontology of human knowing, CR generally seems to deal with divergence by leaning towards the philosophical ideal of *rational adjudication*, which IT would acknowledge is important under certain conditions, but is inadequate as an overall approach from IT's developmental-structural vantage. From an IT perspective, it is not always practical or ethical to try to rationally adjudicate disagreements that reflect deep structural differences in cognitive-epistemic capacity and worldview. This is not always a simple matter of rational adjudication, but requires an understanding of developmental differences, as well as an appropriate strategy for compassionately and effectively relating across worldview structures (De Witt & Hedlund, in press). While it is more obvious when one considers a case of child development, the same principle holds for adults and their (more subtle) disputes, as they continue to develop through the many structure-stages articulated by IT. IT might therefore lean towards an integrative-pluralistic concept of what could be called *rational-structural adjudication*, rather than the more monistic rational adjudication that a CR approach would tend toward. Conceptualized as such, rational adjudication, devoid of the kind of insight given by developmental-structuralism, seems to be a kind of 'flat' notion of rationality that is presumed to be available universally. Such rational-structural adjudication would attempt to mediate divergence in perspective not only on the basis of a singular rationally founded reality, but would attempt to do so also by acknow-ledging a multiplicity of transitive (inter)subjective structures and their corresponding 'demi-realities' imbued with varying degrees of falsehood and truth.

Overall, when viewed in light of IT, there are some important absences in the epistemic domain that CR arguably must come to terms with. These absences, which may also lead to contradictions in practice, can be addressed by rethinking aspects of its epistemic model in light of IT's epistemic taxonomy, or minimally some key findings in developmental psychology. Having critically assessed CR in light of IT, I now offer my concluding remarks.

Conclusion: towards a critical realist integral theory for planetary flourishing

In this chapter, I set out to explore the most salient strengths (moments of truth and coherence) and weaknesses (absences and contradictions) of both CR and IT within the domains of ontology and epistemology, attempting to reveal their key points of complementarity, and in doing so, moving towards the forging of a pro-visional metatheoretical synthesis: a *Critical Realist Integral Theory* (CRIT). A dia-lectical method was used, involving a transformative sublation driven by absences and contradictions in each metatheory. In the process I sought to begin to pre-liminarily illuminate aspects of their potential causes while starting to: rethink key elements of each metatheory's architectonics; negatively transfigure them; and chart a provisional course toward an expanded conceptual field (a CRIT) that brings them together in a non-preservative synthesis. Importantly, as I will elab-orate on in this section, my central underlying motivation for this project was the rethinking and development of the intellectual resources that can adequately address the complex and urgent global challenges of the twenty-first century (such as climate change).

I began by providing a synoptic overview of IT in the domains of ontology and epistemology, noting that IT's post-metaphysical approach asserts the primacy of epistemology (and methodology) over ontology, thus emphasizing the phenomenal pole of Kant's transcendental dialectic, and championing a kind of subject-oriented, enactivist ontology, rich with epistemic distinctions and categories. I then offered a comparable summary of CR, noting that its transcendental realism and critical nat-uralism use the method of transcendental argument to assert the primacy of ontol-ogy over epistemology (and methodology), thereby emphasizing the noumenal pole of Kant's transcendental dialectic and articulating an object-oriented, realist depth-ontology equipped with multiple distinct and stratified categories. I then crit-ically analysed IT in the light of CR, demonstrating the ways in which IT's enac-tivism and post-metaphysics is marred by performative contradiction rooted in its commitment to *inter alia* what CR calls the 'epistemic fallacy,' which reduces ontol-ogy to epistemology and necessarily presupposes an implicit philosophical ontology or pre-critical metaphysics. I then highlighted the consequent problematic of IT's inability to coherently account for and sustain itself on a meta-level (i.e., its lack of adequate *philosophical self-reflexivity*) and contrasted it with CR's transcendental realism, which offers a sophisticated, procedurally rational pathway to arriving at a philosophical ontology that IT would do well to consider, and, indeed, may be its only viable alternative. Finally, I evaluated CR in light of IT, illustrating the ways in which it lacks nuance and sophistication vis-à-vis the epistemic categories it uses to describe the world and its own substantive theorizing (i.e., its lack of adequate *scientific self-reflexivity*) and suggested that this deficiency also amounts to a blind spot in terms of CR's account of inter-individual epistemic-hermeneutic variability and may therefore undermine its commitment to seriousness and real-world emancipation. I then contrasted CR's model with IT's epistemic taxonomy, which offers a robust scientific ontology or meta-framework of the varied categories of human knowing and their processual unfoldment, and which might support both CR's scientific and emancipatory projects in decisive ways. To be sure, my critique of each metatheoretical stream reveals serious problem fields and contradictions in both. However, it also reveals a somewhat asymmetrical picture in which the contradictions in IT to relate its very foundations – its ontological and epistemic architectonics – which, I argued, cannot be resolved with superficial theoretical patches, but rather demand negative transfiguration at a root level. In essence, this would mean the shedding of its irrealist enactivism and (en)actualism and the adoption of a critical realist ontology. In contrast, the absences revealed in CR seem to relate to areas for further metatheoretical development, rather than foundational shedding and transformative negation. In my view, however, this does not mean that the problems noted with respect to CR are not critical or do not potentially have far-reaching implications both in theory and practice. Clearly, there are some important absences in the epistemic domain related to processes and generative structures that mediate or disclose accurate renderings of intransitive objects. IT, having scanned across the horizon of extant theories in development-structural psychology and developed a meta-level epistemic taxonomy, can be instructive here, either on the level of adoption of its framework or inspiring similar metatheoretical analyses in this field of developmental psychological research.

While this account of CR's and IT's respective ontological and epistemological foundations is notably limited by the synoptic method I have employed in this essay (as opposed, for example, to a more detailed comparative philosophical method), as well as by virtue of my own epistemic-hermeneutic positionality as a researcher and embodied personality,[74] I nonetheless have attempted to be as precise and even-handed as possible, striving to highlight salient absences and internal contradictions in each approach in an effort to incite reflection and foster the theoretical development of both. Moreover, aspects of my interpretations have been informed by the Critical Realism and Integral Theory symposia,[75] which could be seen here to constitute a kind of informal and loose peer-validation of a number of these perspectives, thereby arguably enhancing their validity. Whether one agrees with my substantive interpretations in full, I hope to at least have drawn attention to some problem fields that need to be considered and addressed in both communities of discourse in the coming years.

With respect to the project of sublation or non-preservative synthesis of the two schools, my analysis has, in addition to revealing absences and inconsistencies, arguably begun to demonstrate how the respective internal logoi of both CR and IT naturally flow in the direction of their transformation and integration into a more comprehensive and sophisticated metatheory (or meta-metatheory) that can unite the strengths of both while jettisoning their respective shortcomings. For IT I argued that this relates to its postmetaphysical commitments to a procedural rationality; while for CR, I suggested that it connects to its commitments to a developing integrative pluralism that ongoingly incorporates and coheres with valid scientific findings, as well as its commitment to seriousness, or the coherence of theory and practice, and reflexivity ('the supreme criterion'). In my view, CR and IT are in essence clearly born from the same dynamic patterning – cut from the same integrative, emancipatory cloth – as evidenced in their stunning conceptual resonance and similarity across many domains (e.g., CR's four-planar social being and IT's four quadrants;[76] CR's emergent levels and IT's developmental levels) (Marshall, 2012a). Yet, as I hope to have highlighted in this chapter, CR and IT are not mere recapitulations of one another, but rather through their differences (and points of incommensurability) each bring forth unique and complementary gifts that cannot be found in the other in their present form – the strengths of each remarkably seeming to coincide with the deficiencies, or areas in need of further theoretical reflection and development, in the other. This feature, which in fact seems to be catalysed by their architectonic dissonances and dialectical tensions, thus suggests a propitious, mutually enriching encounter between these approaches – and highlights the potential for forging a fruitful non-preservative synthesis. Such a synthesis would rethink and unite elements of the panoptic visions of both CR and IT into a more encompassing integrative approach that transcends them both – a CRIT. While the specific contours of such a CRIT will have to be the subject of future writings and indeed is intended to be developed at length in my PhD research (Hedlund, forthcoming), I have begun, in this chapter, to articulate a basis for such a synthesis.

In the domains of ontology and epistemology we can readily envision CR's philosophical depth ontology emboldened by IT's scientific ontology of epistemic categories. Such a basic sublation would potentially help move towards an integration of approaches along the two poles of the axis of Kant's transcendental dialectic, IT representing a sophisticated subjected-oriented, predominantly epistemological approach (emphasizing the primacy of the *phenomenal* pole), while CR's transcendental realism represents a compelling object-oriented approach that underscores ontology (emphasizing the primacy of the *noumenal* pole).[77] A CRIT might better honour and integrate these two key dialectically constellated approaches in ways that sublate the philosophical discourse of modernity and postmodernity and can revindicate ontology for our contemporary intellectual climate. CR's transcendental realist arguments offer a fundamental break from, and transcendence of, the irrealist philosophical discourse of (post)modernity, while IT's deep appreciation of the complexities of knowledge production ensure that a CRIT has sufficiently included its enduring epistemological insights. Furthermore, a CRIT could bring together the superior moments of self-reflexivity with regard to the philosophical and scientific aspects of metatheorizing within CR and IT, respectively.

Together, given their particular philosophical and scientific strong suits, along with their shared interdisciplinary, integrative, metatheoretical natures, a CRIT would likely be notably powerful as an approach to studying and addressing (hyper) complex twenty-first-century phenomena and global 'wicked problems,' such as climate change.

Amidst all this somewhat arid talk of ontology and epistemology, it is crucial to note that these debates have profound, far-reaching implications for real-world practice and social and ecological well-being. Debates about what is real and how we know ultimately invoke the normative and political aspects of social life. In some sense, ontological and epistemological questions are key determinates of a formative process that determines a view of who we are as human beings, our conception of nature, the divine, our ethical and aesthetic values, and our social imaginary. And the totality of those perspectives – our worldview at large – is deeply implicated in our contemporary practice and social order. Pulling back from our given method and practice to a deeper level of ontological and epistemological metatheory is very important, as we start to see the ways in which our manner of approaching our practice is profoundly shaped by our basic ontological and epistemic disposition. Take, for example, the ontological and epistemological position of the epistemic fallacy and its impact on how we see ourselves in relation to nature, building our practices and institutions on that vision. As the critical realist Andrew Collier (1994) put it:

> If there is a single philosophical idea which reflects more closely than any other this commercial (rather than technological) spirit, it is the epistemic fallacy, which reduces nature to our cognitive appropriation of it, just as this spirit reduces it to our economic appropriation of it. This epistemic fallacy has dominated philosophy for just the same period. In offering us the chance to break decisively with this fallacy, and the consequent anthropocentric worldview (Russell's 'three centuries of subjectivistic madness'), Bhaskar's realism makes possible … a much greater respect for the integrity of things independent of us.
>
> *(p. 149)*

As this passage suggests, our ontological and epistemic suppositions are fundamentally intertwined with our collective social formations and ecological well-being – and we can infer from this that our dominant philosophy in these domains desperately needs to transform. As the profound social and ecological crises of the twenty-first century indicate, we are being forced at a species level to move beyond anthropocentrism and the philosophy of the (inter)subject – to honour the integrity of things and beings independent of us, while also coming to a greater wisdom and humility with respect to our own epistemic and agential powers as a species and how they can be rightly used to support a just and thriving world for all. In light of the intractable global crises that we face, it does not seem at all far-fetched to suppose that the world itself may be telling us something – that the reality principle or natural necessity may be asserting itself – and thus we need an epistemically sophisticated (neo-)realism – an integral realism or CRIT – that can help us more keenly listen to the soul whispers of the field of nature, honour reality, and unfold the opportunities for collective spiritual maturation that these challenges seem to ultimately (re)present. Perhaps, I will be so audacious as to suggest, something like a CRIT could potentially offer precisely the kind of intellectual resources that are urgently needed on the planet right now. In their own right, I see both CR and IT (and other integrative metatheories) as harbingers, on a formal intellectual level, of an emergent cultural formation or (neo)integrative worldview, perhaps somehow responding to the whisperings of a higher-order reality or morphic attractor, to which they importantly shape and are recursively shaped by.[78] Yet perhaps it is possible that in their (self-)transformation and joining forces in their shared emancipatory commitments they can become something greater than their sum – a force that might thereby more powerfully address urgent global challenges of the twenty-first century and help to forge the foundations for the possibility of a sustainable, eudaimonistic planetary society in which all are free to flourish.

Acknowledgements

I am forever grateful to my dear friend and late mentor Roy Bhaskar for his unwavering encouragement of my vision, for the many lively intellectual exchanges that profoundly shaped my thinking on this piece (and beyond), and for his invaluable, precise comments on various drafts of this chapter. Sean Esbjörn-Hargens was also incredibly supportive throughout the entirety of the process, helping to inspire this chapter in its very inception and providing important comments as the piece evolved. I likewise want to acknowledge and thank Annick de Witt for her loving support in my writing process, her help in structuring my thoughts that informed the early drafts of this chapter, as well as her editorial feedback on a later draft. Bruce Alderman, Mervyn Hartwig, Paul Marshall, Petter Næss, John O'Regan, Michael Schwartz, Zak Stein, Paddy Walsh, and Roger Walsh all provided excellent feedback and encouragement in writing this piece, for which I am deeply thankful. I would also like to acknowledge and thank the participants of the Critical Realism and Integral Theory symposia series for informing and inspiring this chapter – this chapter has truly emerged out of a community dialogue. I would also like to thank Adam Robbert for reviewing my statements regarding speculative realism. Finally, I would like to thank professors Robert McDermott and Sean Kelly at the California Institute of Integral Studies Philosophy, Cosmology, and Consciousness Program, for their mentorship, friendship, and support for my philosophical endeavours.

Notes

1 An earlier version of this chapter is published as: N. Hedlund (in press). Towards a critical realist integral theory: Ontological and epistemic considerations for integral philosophy. In S. Esbjörn-Hargens & M. Schwartz (Eds.), *Dancing with Sophia: Integral philosophy on the verge*. Albany, NY: SUNY Press.

2 When referring to 'postmodernism' in the chapter, I am using it in a broad sense of the term, not beholden to any single theoretical perspective on it. I will assume it to be relatively unproblematic at this point to postulate that, while there is heterogeneity in perspective among scholars such as Jürgen Habermas, Charles Taylor, Roy Bhaskar, and Ken Wilber, there also appears to be substantial referential overlap and broad agreement among them with respect to postmodernism. While I highlight its limitations, it should be noted that postmodernism has pioneered many important theoretical advances of enduring value that any aspiring integrative, post-postmodern approach ought to deeply engage. For example, see Gary P. Hampson's (2007) important and insightful article for a rich discussion of such enduring advances and the need for integral studies to engage and include them more extensively. For a discussion of the problematics associated with postmodernism, including the myriad instantiations of its 'performative contradiction,' see, e.g., Karl-Otto Apel (1994); Jürgen Habermas (1987/2000, 1990); John Searle (1995); Thomas Nagel (1997); Charles Taylor (1989); Ken Wilber (1995); and Roy Bhaskar (2002/2012a).

3 See Bhaskar (2002/2012a, ch. 1). Also see Lopez & Potter (2001). It is important to note here that for Bhaskar, modernism and postmodernism are a kind of dialectically constellated assemblage, and thus postmodernism is *not* to be understood as a fundamentally novel or discrete intellectual and cultural formation vis-à-vis modernity. Rather, postmodernism is seen as merely one of five phases in the development of the philosophical discourse of modernity. These stages are as follows: (1) classical modernism; (2) high modernism; (3) modernization theory; (4) postmodernism; and (5) bourgeois triumphalism and endism/renascent fundamentalism. For an exposition of this conception of postmodernism as a sub-movement within the philosophical discourse of modernity, see Bhaskar (2002/2012a). For a more concise overview, see Hartwig (2011).

4 Other philosophies could be noted here, such as that of the contemporary French philosophers Edgar Morin and Alain Badiou, who also profess to be neither modern nor postmodern, but my intention here is not to be exhaustive. Jorge N. Ferrer's (2002, 2008) participatory approach could also be explored in this light. However, this will have to be taken up in possible future writings.

5 While much more could be said with respect to the similarities shared by these three approaches, my interest here is focused on the domains of ontology and epistemology.

6 Beyond the neo-and post-Kantian critiques of realism, which were radicalized by the postmodernists, (according to Bhaskar (2002/2012a), "the post-modernists are non-dialectical post-Kantians" (p. 30)), it is important to note, following numerous theorists, including Roy Bhaskar and Quentin Meillassoux (see, e.g., 2008), that most of Western philosophy, running all the way back to the ancient Greeks (e.g., Parmenides, Plato, and Protagoras) has somewhat of an 'irrealist' or 'correlationist' tendency, which privileges epistemology over ontology in some form.

7 Technically, integral theory situates itself as *postdisciplinary* or *metadisciplinary*, which it contrasts with transdisciplinary, crossdisciplinary, multidisciplinary, and interdisciplinary (see, e.g., Esbjörn-Hargens & Zimmerman, 2009). However, here I am using interdisciplinary as a general 'catch-all' phrase to signify scholarship that pursues some form of integration across disciplinary boundaries.

8 However, issues of ontology are becoming increasingly discussed amongst the integral community. For example, a major theme of the 2013 Integral Theory Conference (ITC) in San Francisco was the exploration of the relationship between integral theory and critical realism, inevitably raising key questions of ontology. Roy Bhaskar delivered a keynote address, and numerous paper presentations at the conference were devoted to exploring

points of contact between these two metatheories. For more on these developments, including the Critical Realism and Integral Theory symposia series, see the Introduction to this volume.

9 Speculative realism is a broad and heterogeneous family of emerging philosophical positions that are generally understood to be responses to the French philosopher Quentin Meillassoux's (2008) "correlationism" thesis. As Bryant (2011) states, speculative realism is "a loosely affiliated philosophical movement that arose out of a University of London, Goldsmith's College conference organized by Alberto Toscano in 2007. While the participants at this event – Ray Brassier, Iain Hamilton Grant, Graham Harman, and Quentin Meillassoux – share vastly different philosophical positions, they are all united in defending a variant of realism and in rejecting anti-realism or what they call 'correlationism'" (Bryant, 2011, p. 26). In this way, many speculative realists argue for various inflections of realist ontology that avoid the treatment of objects as mere constructions or correlates of the human subject/mind or culture/language, and in that sense seems to diverge from postmodernism (Bryant, 2011, p. 26). Finally, it is worth noting that Robert Jackson (2013) has provisionally outlined four main schools or strains within speculative realism, mapped along two axes: (1) "the primacy of epistemological fact/knowledge" vs. "the primacy of ontological existent"; and (2) "intensional" vs. "extentional." His blog-article provides a clarifying overview of the relationships among the various positions within the speculative realism movement.

10 With respect to critical realism's influence on speculative realism, the foundation of Bryant's "Onticology" is grounded in Bhaskar's transcendental realism, and therefore appears to be largely critical realist in terms of its fundamental ontological and epistemological positions, although he builds on it in novel ways. Bryant also seems to share a general resonance with critical realism's sublative disposition in relation to the philosophical discourse of modernity and postmodernity. As Bryant (2011) states, the aim of his book is to develop a "a post-humanist, realist theory of being capable of breaking with correlationism, that is nonetheless capable of integrating the most important and significant findings of the correlationists" (p. 42).

11 This chapter assumes readers to be basically familiar with both Integral Theory and Critical Realism. For an introductory overview of IT, see Esbjörn-Hargens (2010b) and Wilber (2006). For an introductory overview of CR, see Bhaskar (1998); N. Hedlund-de Witt (2012); Bhaskar & Hartwig (2010).

12 In this chapter, I am employing a generally dialectical, developmental view of consciousness, culture, and society. It is important to note that this position contrasts in important ways with the notion of development in its modernist connotations – that is, of a uni-linear, triumphalist developmental progression from 'primitive' levels of social evolution towards the 'civilized' status represented by the modern West. Such an approach has, in my eyes rightfully, been deconstructed by (notably postmodern) philosophers, anthropologists, and sociologists alike, mainly because of its Eurocentric, neocolonial, and derogatory implications, and its commitment to an oversimplified ontological parsimony that is out of step with the complexities and messiness of the empirical evidence (see, e.g., Ferguson, 2002; G. Marshall, 1998). Rather, I argue for a much more complex, dialectical, open-ended, and unpredictable process of change. In this understanding, development is de-coupled from the notion of 'progress' (i.e., one can also speak of negative developments), while some form of qualitative or structural change can nonetheless be observed. This means that not only do certain qualities increase or decrease according to specific criteria, but also that different criteria are appropriate for an adequate description of a new developmental stage. Thus, in a developmental movement two or more qualitatively different stages can always be systematically distinguished (Van Haaften, 1997). Moreover, new stages do not randomly arise, but they evolve out of, and are in some sense 'produced' by, the antecedent stage. In the words of Van Haaften, the later stages "depend on the earlier ones in the sense that the prior stages are necessary (but not sufficient) conditions for the coming about of the later ones. It is in this sense that several stages can be identified as causally and conceptually connected parts of a single

developmental sequence" (1997, p. 18). Thus, I invoke a notion of development as a structural change towards increasing complexity, differentiation, and integration, in line with the insights of the developmental-structuralists (or constructive developmentalists) in the field of psychology (see, e.g., Cook-Greuter, 1999; Kegan, 1982; Kohlberg, 1984; Piaget & Inhelder, 2000/1969) as well as with, for example, Inglehart and Welzel's (2005) notions of non-linear societal development, based on the empirical finding that over time the *direction* of change changes. This notion of development is thus complex and dialectical (rather than uni-linear and triumphalist), and describes a process without an *a priori* positable telos, endpoint, or formal trajectory. As Hartwig (2011), writes, "while rejecting any view of geo-history that sees it as an inexorable process of development towards a pre-ordained goal, viewing it rather as a radically contingent, uneven and multiform process punctuated by regression and foldback, critical realism does hold that there is a certain 'tendential rational directionality' in history" (p. 501). The view I am espousing here also implies that the later stages of development are not univocally "better" – morally or otherwise. Similarly, Habermas (1976) speaks of the *dialectics of progress*, observing that "evolutionarily important innovations mean not only a new level of learning but a new problem situation as well, that is, a new category of burdens that accompany the new social formation" (p. 164). Moreover, as Kegan (1982) argues, "A developmental perspective naturally equips one to see the present in the context both of its antecedents and potential future, so that every phenomenon gets looked at not only in terms of its limits but its strengths" (p. 30). Thus, despite what are in my eyes warranted (largely postmodern) critiques, part and parcel of our understanding of dialectical development is a critical distancing from the "growth to goodness" assumptions that have often plagued the discourse, and a concurrent differentiation between *descriptive* and *normative* dimensions of development (see, e.g., Stein, 2012).

13 In this way, integrative metatheory should be concerned with some form of ontological realism and going beyond anti- or irrealist philosophy, but may nevertheless fail to fully actualize this in a compelling and coherent manner. Moreover, as a very provisional suggestion, there are several other elements of integrative metatheory, or a metatheory for the twenty-first century, that we might want to delineate. As articulated in the Introduction to this volume, integrative metatheory, or metatheory 2.0, is grounded in the following principles or criteria: methodological transparency or judgemental rationalism, epistemic reflexivity and relativity, ontological realism and comprehensiveness, and integrative pluralism. Various other principles or criteria could be proposed (as we can see in several contributions to this volume), including a focus on the scholarship of integration (Boyer, 1990), a post-formal or dialectical mode of thought, and a break with the characteristically post/modern bias toward anthropism or anthroporealism, to name but a few.

14 This is not to say that interest in premodern or modern approaches is inherently regressive. Premodern and modern philosophy are clearly rich repositories of knowledge and wisdom – aspects of which can, and likely need to be, drawn on in forging viable contemporary integrative approaches. For example, Habermas' interest in contributing to the 'unfinished project of Enlightenment' seeks to redress some of the core problems in modern philosophy. Likewise, some speculative realists (e.g., Graham Harman) have highlighted the value of returning to Aristotle for inspiration in developing new ontologies. Neither of these projects seems particularly regressive to me. Furthermore, as I hope to clarify below, I do not see Western philosophy (or any other development, for that matter) to have a pre-given trajectory. In my view development or evolution (a descriptive evaluation) is de-coupled from notions of progress (mostly a normative judgment). Development is thus seen as a complex dialectical process that is radically contingent, multidimension, and non-unilinear – not a triumphalist, simple 'growth to goodness'.

15 That said, I do not generally prefer the term 'post-postmodern,' which necessarily must sustain itself in dialectical constellation with the post/modern. 'Integral' or 'integrative'

are better general terms in my view, but 'post-postmodern' can nevertheless be a useful term for certain rhetorical purposes, especially invoking a sense of geo-historicity and directionality.

16 It is also worth noting that both CR and IT not only claim this themselves, but also various secondary commentators have recognized them as such. This obviously doesn't mean they have necessarily achieved it, or are on equal ground here. Note also that positivism and social constructivism are invoked here as key (ontological and epistemological) moments within a constellation of modern and postmodern philosophies, respectively. They thereby are not to be conflated with the larger totalities of modernism and postmodernism.

17 Here I am generally using 'epistemic' in the sense of relating to informal knowledge or cognition, in contrast to 'epistemology,' which refers to formal *theories* of knowledge and how it is produced or acquired. However, these terms often overlap and can be used interchangeably in some contexts.

18 Also see Marshall (2012b) for an excellent overview of the points of connection and complementarity between Critical Realism and Integral Theory as integrative metatheories.

19 An earlier version of this chapter was originally titled "Towards an integral realism: Ontological and epistemic considerations for integrative philosophy." However, when Paul Marshall's (2012b) exceptional article with the same primary title, "Toward an integral realism. Part I: An overview of transcendental realist ontology," was published in the *Journal of Integral Theory and Practice* prior to this essay, I decided to change the title.

20 In many ways, this chapter was inspired by and born out of my participation in the first Critical Realism and Integral Theory symposium, held on September 15–18, 2011, at John F. Kennedy University, in the San Francisco Bay Area, and hosted by Integral Institute and the Integral Research Center. See the Introduction to this volume for more details on the symposia series.

21 In this way, my approach, inspired by dialectical critical realism, is ontologically polyvalent, rather than ontologically monovalent (the doctrine that being is purely positive and present), like that of Hegel's dialectic (Bhaskar, 1993/2008, 1994/2009).

22 Transcendence implies first a transformative negation (which is only partly preservative), whereas synthesis can imply a more purely positive and summative approach (Bhaskar, 1993/2008).

23 Wilber (2012a), in response to recent publications on the relationship between CR and IT, states that "virtually all of them say the same thing" in pointing out that Integral Theory can benefit from Critical Realism through "essentially, 'a grounding in ontology.'" He goes on to state that "in some ways this is unfair to Integral Theory. As several responding critics have pointed out, Integral Theory has an extensive ontology – from 'involutionary givens' to the 20 tenets, whose first tenet is: 'Reality is composed neither of things nor of processes, but of holons.' Holons, of course, are wholes that are parts of other wholes (as a whole atom is part of a whole molecule, a whole molecule is part of a whole cell, a whole cell is part of a whole organism, etc.). This is sometimes worded, 'Reality is composed of perspectives that are holons' (for reasons explained below). Since all of the items in the quadrants are holons, the Integral map is drenched in ontology" (p. 1). In some sense, I agree with Wilber's assessment here: integral theory does have an ontology. However, he goes on to indicate that, unlike in critical realism "this is an ontology inseparable from epistemology and methodology, all interwoven aspects of the Whole". But what seems to cause some confusion here is the failure to differentiate *philosophical* from *scientific* ontologies, which I see as a crucial distinction. To be sure, integral theory does indeed have a philosophical ontology (since, as we will see below, there is no alternative), but to my mind, it is essentially *implicit*. An exception to this is Wilber's (2006) admission that integral theory's post-metaphysical position actually relies on a "minimalist metaphysics," which includes his aforementioned "involutionary givens," such as *Eros*, *Agape*, and a *morphogenetic field of potentials* (see note 26 in Wilber's (2003a) "Excerpt A: An integral age at the leading edge"). This so-called minimalist metaphysics

indeed seems to be the closest proxy to an explicit philosophical ontology in integral theory, although in my view, if it is to cohere with its post-metaphysical position, it is in need of elaboration and justification vis-à-vis its methodological status. Until then, it is in contradiction with its postmetaphysical commitments. In many of Wilber's writings, despite claims that IT is post- or minimally metaphysical, it often appears to be the case that his metaphysics are explicit and not at all transcended or minimalist, but that IT relies to some extent on a neo-Hegelian metaphysics of Spirit-in-action. Wilber attempts to resolve the contradiction (between postmetaphysics and metaphysics) by dropping the 'metaphysics' of his early work based on the perennial philosophy and adopting a 'deep empiricism' in which various elements of his metaphysics of Spirit-in-action can be postmetaphysically justified. This is a potentially promising direction, in my view, but it is underdeveloped in his overall system, and his position, as he acknowledges in the above quote, remains metaphysical. Wilber largely claims that his metatheoretical narrative isn't metaphysical, while occasionally admitting that it is minimally so, but in reality it appears to be (non-minimally) metaphysical (methodologically opaque and unjustified) and in contradiction with his postmetaphysical stance. When it comes to the 20 tenets (see Wilber, 1995), my view is that they constitute an important aspect of integral theory's *scientific* ontology, although they are far from exhaustive of it. The 20 tenets, as I understand them, are essentially the result of Wilber's impressive coding of the meta-patterns or tendencies governing evolution in the purely physical domain of the universe or "physiosphere." They are derived from a deep study of the systems/complexity sciences, which have their basis largely in the physical sciences. Thus, unless otherwise argued for and justified, the 20 tenets should be regarded, in my view, as aspects of Integral Theory's scientific ontology. The situation gets more convoluted when Wilber moves from his (Wilber-4) statement that "reality is composed neither of things nor processes, but of holons" to his (Wilber-5) stronger constructivist statement that "reality is composed of perspectives." In doing so, it seems that Wilber has extrapolated from (the first tenet in) his scientific ontology a quasi-philosophical ontological proposition in which to attempt to ground his post-metaphysical position. However, the procedure or method by which he arrived at this claim has not been made transparent, and therefore it appears to be, by default, an essentially 'metaphysical' claim based on speculation. Interestingly, Wilber (2012b) augments his position by claiming in note 1 that "'Reality is composed of holons' is often stated 'Reality is composed of perspectives that are holons'," thus explicitly linking a key ontological proposition in Wilber-4 with that of Wilber-5 for the first time in a published work (p. 2). In my view, this appears to be an important (retrofit) move towards redressing problematic aspects of his (phase 5) post-metaphysical stance and grounding it clearly in his earlier (phase 4) work. On the other hand, Wilber's recent writings on CR tend to skirt the key issues, in my opinion, continuing to avoid a substantive engagement with Bhaskar's transcendental argument for the disambiguation or differentiation of ontology and epistemology. Such differentiation is clearly not the same as them 'being violently torn from each other.' Rather, differentiation, according to Wilber's own developmental logic, is the necessary condition for the possibility of authentic integration, in contradistinction to pre- or de-differentiated fusion. Bhaskar's argument implies that integral theory is *necessarily* beholden to ontological realism in the manner of TINA formation – *There Is No Alternative*. That is, IT is dependent on an implicit ontology that precedes, and therefore can be disambiguated or de-coupled from epistemology/methodology, and cannot intelligibly claim otherwise (i.e., at least not without simultaneously succumbing to a fundamental performative self-contradiction or self-referential paradox). This point will be returned to below. Furthermore, Wilber's position here depends in large part on his "genuine panpsychism," which, methodologically speaking, is in need of a justification to show its alignment and coherence with his phase 5 post-metaphysical emphasis on methodological reflexivity and transparency and demonstrate that it is not "just another type of metaphysical thinking and thus not adequately grounded" (Wilber, 2006, p. 252). Based on published articulations to date, Wilber's panpsychic position appears to be largely unjustified from a methodological perspective. I intuitively resonate with panpsychism/paninteriorism, but I do not think it can be coherently proclaimed (in an apparently metaphysical manner) as a crucial component of his "postmetaphysical" philosophy without a more elaborated justification.

24 However, it is important to note that integral post-metaphysics, which stereotypically "overcomes and rejects a metaphysical viewpoint and replaces it with an empirical, phenomenological, experiential, and evidential approach" (Wilber, 2001, p. 2) does not appear to be able to justify itself in accord with its own criteria. As Wilber (2006) admits, integral post-metaphysics cannot actually transcend metaphysics in practice, but rather relies on a "minimalist metaphysics," as mentioned above. Specifically, in order to cohere his philosophy, Wilber posits a number of "involutionary givens" such as *Eros*, *Agape*, and a *morphogenetic field of potentials*. These involutionary givens are apparently grounded only in substantive speculation and presupposed as ontological givens.

25 While Esbjörn-Hargens (2010a) refers to his extension of Wilber's (2001, 2003a, 2006) approach as "Integral Enactment Theory," I will, for the purposes of this chapter, include it under the umbrella of "Integral Post-Metaphysics" or simply "post-metaphysics," since its fundamental innovation is to thematize ontology and make explicit integral theory's previously implicit ontological pluralism.

26 In my view this assessment holds, despite some obfuscating statements arguing for the synchronically emergent and mutually interdependent nature of ontology and epistemology – e.g., Wilber's (2012a) claim that "epistemology (and methodology) and ontology are all integrally interwoven and mutually enactive, each contributing an irreducible aspect of the whole of reality, and none can be privileged (without resorting to first tier thinking).... This approach neither commits the epistemic fallacy (epistemology is privileged and ontology derived from it) nor the ontic fallacy (ontology is privileged and epistemology derived from it). Nor does it see ontology separated and consigned to its own realm, and epistemology separated and consigned to its own realm – but rather both arise concurrently (as part of a four-quadrant tetra-arising), co-evolve concurrently, and co-enact concurrently" (p. 1). As will be expounded, these claims seem to becloud the otherwise clear logic of integral post-metaphysics, which precisely depends on the transposing of ontology into epistemology such that the former is derived from the latter. Merely claiming (and not providing an argument) that they both co-arise and co-enact each other concurrently does nothing, in my view, to resolve the contradictions between such claims and other statements such as the following: "[ontological] objects come into being, or are enacted, only at various developmental levels of complexity and consciousness" (Wilber, 2006, p. 252), or "critical (Kantian) philosophy replaced metaphysics (or ontological objects) with epistemology (or structures in the subject), and this general move is unavoidable in the post/modern world" (Wilber, 2006, p. 271).

27 I argue that Wilber's position is indeed a strong (but not extreme) constructivism, despite his inclusion of various qualifiers and apparent caveats such as "we do not perceive empirical objects in a *completely* realistic, pregiven fashion" and "reality is not a perception, but a conception; *at least in part*" (italics added). This should clarify as my argument unfolds and I address Wilber's 'ex-ist'/'subsist' distinction in more depth.

28 As Kant stated, "hitherto it has been assumed that all our knowledge must conform to objects," but he then offers a new proposition: "that objects ... conform to our knowledge" (quoted in Braver, 2007, p. 35).

29 Wilber (2012b) also refers to his neo-Whiteheadian position as "pan-interiorist," wherein the Kosmos is composed of sentient holons with perspectives from humans all the way down to sub-atomic particles (who have "prehension"). For Wilber, his pan-interiorism constitutes a key point of demarcation between his position and that of Bhaskar: "CR maintains that there are ontological realities that are not dependent upon humans or human theories – including much of the level of the 'real' – including items such as atoms, molecules, cells, etc. – and IT agrees, with one important difference: IT is panpsychic (a term I'm not fond of, preferring 'pan-interiorist,' meaning all beings have interiors or proto-consciousness, à la Whitehead, Peirce, Leibnitz, etc.) – to wit, atoms do not depend upon being known by humans, but they do depend upon being

known by each other. The 'prehension' aspect of atoms (proto-knowing, proto-feeling, proto-consciousness) helps to co-enact the being or ontology aspect of the atoms for each other – their own epistemology and ontology are thus inseparable and co-creative. The atom's prehension is part of its very ontology (and vice versa), and as each atom prehends its predecessor, it is instrumental in bringing it forth or enacting it, just as its own being will depend in part on being prehended/known/included by its own successor" (p. 43). While the panpsychic qualification of Wilber's postmetaphysical/enactivist position does seem to distinguish it from the standard anthropocentric expressions of actualism and the epistemic fallacy, to my mind, it does little to refute the core critiques that CR levels against it. Wilber's panpsychic enactivism still necessarily must presuppose a mind- or prehension-independent world – an implicit ontology anterior to enactment. This is what CR refers to, as mentioned above, as a TINA formation. So while Habermas (1992/1996) argues that "there is no alternative to post-metaphysical thinking," we can be fairly certain that there is indeed a viable post-critical or post-postmetaphysical alternative to post-metaphysical thinking in critical realism, and its transcendental realism in particular (to which there appears to be no alternative). (Alternatively, transcendental realism could be considered to be highly post-metaphysical in certain respects, as will be explained.) I will discuss this critique of enactivism/post-metaphysics in the section "Integral theory in the light of critical realism" below.

30 For CR, however, ontology is relatively autonomous from epistemology, but not separate or discrete (see note 47).

31 According to Habermas (1992/1996) procedural rationality is a mode of knowledge production that came to prominence in the seventeenth century through the rise of the empirical methods of the natural sciences, while expanding its influence and reach in the eighteenth century via formalism in moral and legal theory as well as the institutions of the constitutional state (p. 33). Its emergence was importantly linked with a project of undermining a totalizing and dogmatic tendency toward the speculative assertion of *a priori* concepts such as 'the One' in premodern philosophy. Such a tendency was strongly associated with a kind of *substantive* (or theoretical) rationality whose claims were implicitly to be assessed in terms of a "rationality of contents" rather than a rationality of procedure or method concerned with "the validity of results" (p. 35). The former mode, which generates *anamnestic* knowledge, is associated with first philosophy or what Habermas calls 'metaphysical thinking,' while the later concerns itself with *discursive* knowledge and is associated with the epistemological and methodological transparency and rigour associated with modern science (p. 31). Procedural rationality, for Habermas, is closely connected, as a key criterion, to 'post-metaphysical thinking.'

32 For Wilber (2006), "there is no pregiven world, existing independently and apart from all perception of it. Nor are all things merely perceptions. Rather, there is a sum total of the mutually disclosing things and events that disclose themselves relative to each other (i.e., relative to each other's perspective)" (p. 255). Moreover, he states, "assuming there is something pre-existing in an ahistorical world and waiting to be seen is just metaphysics (and the myth of the given).... [T]here is no 'apart from' how a thing appears; there is simply how it appears, and it ALWAYS ALREADY appears as a perspective" (p. 252).

33 See Whitehead (1978).

34 Bruce Alderman (personal communication, September 26, 2014) informed me that he has offered some similar commentary in his post on the Integral Life website regarding the diachronic and synchronic dimensions of Wilber's framing of enactment and intrinsic features. See: www.integrallife.com/node/226886#comment-7995.

35 For CR, an 'ontology' generally signifies a realist ontology, which would crucially imply that the being of an object is not fundamentally contingent on any epistemic-hermeneutic functions of consciousness, it is existentially and causally intransitive.

36 The critical realist Andrew Collier (1994) makes the distinction between 'strong' and 'weak' forms of social constructivism, claiming that CR is a weak social constructivism, in contrast to strong, voluntaristic forms of social constructivism (e.g., post-structuralism).

While I occasionally deploy these terms in this chapter, it should be noted that Bhaskar (personal communication, June 16, 2013) prefers to refer to "the social construal of reality," or *social construalism* to describe CR's position, rather than a weak social constructivism. For Bhaskar, there is always a pre-given structural starting point for agential action and thus construction is not voluntaristic – hence his preference of the term 'construal' over 'construction.'

37 While I would not go so far as to claim that Wilber's enactivism should be called a form of 'structuralist anti-humanism,' I do see some notable resonance in aspects of it in the sense that it emphasizes that reality is not merely a construction of an individual human mind flowing from the personal agency of transcendental subjectivity, but rather is more of a product of impersonal or anonymous structures that are partly autonomous from any such agency (see, e.g., Bryant, 2011). To be sure, Wilber's staunch defence of the subject/agent and anti-reductionism (of individual subjectivity and agency to collective and impersonal intersubjective structures, as often championed by postmodern theorists) disavows him of such a designation (P. Marshall, personal communication, June 16, 2013).

38 While the epistemic structures in Figure 5.1 are depicted vertically, and therefore appear as unilinear sequences of levels, this is merely one possible visual metaphor or signifier that both reveals and conceals aspects of the more complex referents of these models. Thus, this depiction is more of an ideal typical metaphor, underscoring the hierarchical and linear aspects of the models. However, many of these models, and IT at large, acknowledge nonlinear elements (e.g., regressions), processual complexities (e.g., inhabiting multiple structures in a probabilistic manner), and use multiple metaphors (such as 'waves' and 'streams' for levels and lines, respectively) as well. To see these levels and lines depicted vertically, as in Figure 5.1, and conclude that they are merely unilinear structures 'stacked on top of each other', in my view, may imply a lack of in-depth understanding of the models in question as well as a lack of epistemic reflexivity or awareness of both the symbolic and limited nature of visual representations, as well as how those representations are being experienced and construed, perhaps idiosyncratically, in the observing subject. Ironically, engagement with those very models may help to avoid such reification on a semiotic and empirical level and serve to develop such (lacking) epistemic reflexivity. See note 12 for more on the complexities of developmental models.

39 See Esbjörn-Hargens and Wilber (2006) for an introductory discussion of IMP.

40 As Gardiner and Kosmitzki (2004, p. 123) state, "These stages have been studied from a cross-cultural perspective, and research evidence suggests that some aspects may be universal (the sequence of stages) while others (the stage of formal operations) may not." More specifically, most researchers in the field appear to agree that Piaget's stage-sequence and fundamental model is cross-culturally valid, yet this does not mean that all people in all cultures will reach the formal operational stage. Moreover, researchers in the neo-Piagetian tradition have found evidence for cognitive development beyond the level of formal (abstract, rational) operations – that is, various levels of *post-formal* (systemic, dialectical) thinking (Commons, Richards, & Armon, 1984; Kegan, 1994; Rose & Fischer, 2009).

41 See note 12 for a summary of these critiques and some rebuttals to them.

42 Wilber (2000) articulates a detailed metatheory of psychological development based on a review of over 100 developmental systems, delineating a sequence of "correlative basic structures" of cognition. Subsequently, Wilber (2006) augments his theory with reference to his system of "altitudes" or generalized "levels of consciousness" which, rather than referring to specific cognitive structures, are devoid of content and refer to the context (consciousness) in which particular contents arise. This is less a metatheory in the proper sense, but more a metatheoretical generalization. In both cases, Wilber's approach is (meta)theoretical, in contrast to the other developmental models in Figure 5.1, which are firmly grounded in empirical research.

43 The later two phases in the development of critical realism, dialectical critical realism and the philosophy of metaReality, respectively, both therefore bring greater depth,

complexity, and internal coherence to the ontology articulated in basic critical realism, but fundamentally do not alter the basic propositions of basic critical realism. Basic critical realism articulates an ontology in which being is *structured and differentiated* (in terms of the domains of real, the actual and the empirical; the intransitive and the transitive dimensions). Dialectical critical realism deepens the basic critical realist ontology by explicitly thematizing the primacy of *negativity* or ontological absence (and highlighting its essential role for an adequate theorization of process and change). It also highlights that objects are complex *totalities* with internal relatedness and holistic causality; and by thematizing *transformative agency and reflexivity* as inherent in being. MetaReality thematizes the *inwardness* or interiority and spirituality of being; being as *re-enchanted* and thus possessing intrinsic value and meaning; and being as incorporating identity over non-identity, or *nonduality*.

44 A transcendental mode of argument, or transcendental argument, is generally understood to be a philosophical argument that takes some manifest phenomenon or aspect of experience as given, and then deduces the necessary conditions for the possibility of that phenomenon – that which must be the case for it to be possible or intelligible.

45 One of Bhaskar's innovations is to propose a decoupling of transcendental modes of argumentation from their characteristically Kantian orientation toward subjective and intersubjective structures. As Bhaskar (1975/2008) writes, "If philosophy is to be possible (and I want to contend that it is in practice indispensable) then it must follow the Kantian road. But in doing so it must both avoid any commitment to the content of specific theories and recognize the conditional nature of all its results. Moreover, it must reject two presuppositions which were central to Kant's own philosophical project, viz that in any inquiry of the form 'what must be the case for Φ to be possible?' the conclusion, X, would be a fact about us and that Φ must invariably stand for some universal operation of the mind. That is to say, it must reject the idealist and individualist cast into which Kant pressed his own inquiries" (p. 5).

46 As we will see, human knowledge and interpretation is not separate from the world, but rather a (participatory) part of it.

47 However, it is important to note that such a disambiguation is understood by CR not in the sense that ontology and epistemology are fundamental split off from each other, but rather that ontology constellationally contains (or hollarchically embraces) epistemology, meaning that they are two differentiated (not dissociated) and asymmetrically related facets of a unity. Hartwig (2007) underscores this point, stating that "the two dimensions, whilst distinct, are not discrete; dialectically speaking, they … constitut[e] a constellational identity …" wherein "epistemology/the TD is seen as constellationally contained within ontology/the ID…. There is not a transitive dimension 'in here', and an intransitive one 'out there', though of course the causal laws of nature endure and operate independently of us. Everything – including the knowledge-seeker – is within being, of which epistemology/the TD is an emergent stratum" (p. 256).

48 By "intransitive" Bhaskar does not mean to suggest that objects/generative mechanisms are somehow static (they are more like dynamical morphic attractors), but rather that, they are either relatively or absolutely independent of human knowledge and practices in relation to them. Throughout the universe, including the social world, objects are existentially absolutely independent in the sense that, once constituted, nothing can then alter the reasons for this, while the fundamental generative structures of the natural world are causally absolutely independent and those of the social world relatively so.

49 It is worth noting some resonances between what I am calling CR's 'infinitude of potentiality' and the notion of 'withdrawal' in continental philosophy. 'Withdrawal' was originally coined by Martin Heidegger (1889–1976), but has been reinvoked and transformed by the speculative realists, particularly Harman and Bryant. See Harman (2002, ch. 1) for an analysis of the emergence of the term and his subsequent transformation of it. CR would emphasize, in contrast to the emphasis on the notion of withdrawal, that while the being of an object is deeper than ways in which it is being actualized and experienced

and is beyond our dominion and control, it is not completely elusive and unknowable. Rather, it is, in principle, knowable via various philosophical and scientific transcendental procedures. It is important to note, however, that from a CR perspective any employment of the notion of withdrawal would need to cut both ways, rather than as a one-sided, anthropocentric phenomenon. This means that humans and their experience would need to be understood as withdrawn from the object (whether human or non-human) we are encountering, too – from the perspective of objects in the world, knowing subjects and their experience are likewise withdrawn from objects in the world. It is also worth noting here that integral theory has it own implicit notion of inexhaustibility or withdrawal, as seen, for example, in Esbjörn-Hargens & Zimmerman's (2009) "there is no single tree" section of their impressive book, *Integral ecology: Uniting multiple perspectives on the natural world*. They claim that all the enactments of the tree (be they human or non-human) do not exhaust the tree.

50 Technically, for CR, a human being is "a concrete singularity – a unique product of a multiplicity of mechanisms (1M) in process (2E) subject to innumerable particular mediations (3L) issuing in a concretely singular result (4D). The result of this causal chain could always have been very different, and is wholly unlikely and immensely unpredictable" (M. Hartwig, personal communication, June 23, 2014).

51 See Alvesson and Sköldberg (2009).

52 Actualism can concisely be defined as the proposition that the domain of the real can be reduced to the domain of the actual (actually manifest events and patterns of events).

53 Bhaskar (1993/2008) insists that the roots of the epistemic fallacy were laid down by the Greeks – especially Parmenides (in his two ways of knowledge) and then more explicitly by Plato (in his theory of Forms). Bryant (2011) also ascribes Protagoras the status of a root-source philosopher asserting epistemology over ontology (i.e., correlationism). Also see Norrie (2010).

54 The Greek move towards crowning the primacy of epistemology was consummated by Descartes, who 'subjectivized and inwardized' the rational criteria for knowledge. Descartes also initiated what would later become known as the 'Cartesian-Lockean-Humean-Kantian paradigm,' which holds that we can only know reality from the immediate data of consciousness (P. Marshall, personal communication, June 16, 2013). See Descartes (1637/2006); Hume (1739/2000, 1748/1999); and Kant (1791/1998).

55 While Wilber (2012a, 2012b) claims that IT does not commit the epistemic fallacy, I hope to make a convincing case in this chapter to the contrary. Without a stratified ontology that distinguishes the real, the actual, and the empirical, as well as the intransitive and transitive dimensions, it is likely that it will continue to succumb to the epistemic fallacy – to be stuck in the 'correlationist circle', as the speculative realists would call it. Wilber (2012b) also argues that his distinction between 'ex-ist' and 'subsist' is: "similar to CR's transitive (ex-ist) and intransitive (subsist) with one major exception: as noted, IT is panpsychic – epistemology and ontology/consciousness and being cannot be torn asunder. What we call 'pre-human ontology' is actually a *pre-human sentient holon's epistemic-ontic Wholeness*, and not merely a disembodied, floating, 'view-from-nowhere' ontology. As molecule's prehension-knowing-proto-feeling is an inseparable part of its being-ontological makeup at the molecular level, and both are necessary to co-create each other. Ignoring prehension (and consciousness) just leaves ontology-being for the molecule, and epistemology-consciousness is just given to humans (or higher mammals), not to all sentient beings – they only get being, not knowing. But if a human consciousness-knowing is not involved in co-creating the ontology of atoms, molecules, or cells, *their own* consciousness-prehension is involved, all the way down (à la Peirce and Whitehead)" (Wilber, 2012b, p. 44). So while Wilber compares his ex-ist/subsist distinction to critical realism's transitive/intransitive distinction, respectively, I argue that they differ in a number of important ways (beyond just IT's panpsychism), most prominently that both Wilber's 'ex-ist' and 'subsist' refer to realities that are both fundamentally

constructions of consciousness. Subsistent realities can apparently be distinguished from ex-istent realities on a perspectival and temporal basis – they are constructions of consciousness that are perspectivally anterior to a given subject's process of enactment in the present moment, and may or may not exist for other subjects depending primarily on the developmental complexity of that subject's consciousness. To be sure, as Bruce Alderman (personal communication, September 26, 2014) reminded me, Wilber (2006) does acknowledge the groundlessness of his scheme (i.e., no non-perspectivally enacted being anywhere), and compares this vision to a dizzying hall of mirrors: "endless reflections of a Kosmos in a hall of mirrors" (p. 266). So, rather than accepting the reality of at least one being (the observer), Wilber seems to posit instead a slippery, infinite regress of perspective-taking with no perspective-independent beings anywhere (including the so-called perceiver). Graham Harman (2011), responding to Steven Shaviro (2011), criticizes a nearly identical orientation in Whitehead, claiming that Whitehead keeps passing off the 'hot potato' to the next entity, in infinite regress. Furthermore, on the issue of panpsychism, CR clearly does not reserve consciousness in the sense of prehension only for humans, but rather ascribes it to all entities in the form of various gradations of what Bhaskar calls 'enfolded consciousness.' So to be sure, Bhaskar's philosophy is not opposed to panpsychism.

56 To be sure, these "con-structions of consciousness" include its subsistence prior to the epistemic-hermeneutic process of enactment and ex-istence thereafter.

57 Bhaskar (1993/2008, ch. 4.3) makes essentially the same argument. Also see Bryant (2011) for a similar argument drawing on CR's transcendental realism.

58 Leading critical realist Mervyn Hartwig (personal communication, June 23, 2014) is not convinced that IT's panpsychism is indeed non-anthropocentric "given that the consciousness involved is 'proto' human. Also, to commit the epistemic fallacy is itself anthropic [i.e. anthropocentric/morphic]."

59 Principally, Bhaskar's transcendental arguments take the form of presuppositional reasoning and retroduction.

60 IT's post-metaphysics can be said to commit a performative (self-)contradiction in the sense that in the act of stating its central argument, the propositional content of the statement contradicts the implicit claims or presuppositions of its assertion (Habermas, 1990). Bhaskar makes a similar argument with respect to the central problematic of irrealist philosophies in *Dialectic: The pulse of freedom* (1993/2008, ch. 4.3), which he refers to as a 'self-referential paradox.'

61 While one could argue that much of Wilber's speculation and argumentation is in the form of a Habermasian 'reconstructive science,' which in principle bears some strong methodological resemblances to that of transcendental argument and could therefore be considered to possess a procedural rationality, in practice the necessary epistemic self-reflexivity and transparency necessary to substantiate such claim appears to be lacking, as theorists such as Edwards (2010) have pointed out.

62 In many ways, Wilber's (2006) articulation of Integral Post-Metaphysics seems to amount to a kind of expanded or 'broad' empirical verificationism in which the self-reflexive and transparent disclosure of the positionality of the researcher (i.e., the "means" of enactment) is theoretically paramount. Wilber calls this the positionality "Kosmic address," and states that at a minimum, it should include the specification of key epistemic structures and methodological injunctions employed by an author in making an ontic claim. According to Wilber, "metaphysics from an AQAL perspective means anything that does not (or cannot) generally specify the quadrant, level, line, state, and type of an occasion. If a writer does not specify those components – that is, if some version of a kosmic address is not specified – it is virtually always because that writer is unconsciously assuming that those components are pregiven and thus don't need to be specified.... So they present their maps of reality as if there is a pregiven reality and they have the correct representation of it. That is horrid metaphysics even according to the postmodern definition of metaphysics!" (p. 257). Wilber continues: "But I am going a step further and claiming that even the postmodernists who claim to overcome metaphysics are actually caught

in subtler versions of it, because metaphysics is anything that does not self-consciously disclose all of the AQAL components of any occasion. When a writer does not disclose those components it is almost always because he or she doesn't know they are there; and not knowing they are there, cannot stop those realities from unconsciously slipping into extensive versions of the myth of the given" (p. 257). However, Wilber's only reflexive disclosure of his positionality in *Integral spirituality* was (jokingly?) as follows: "say, in a cognitive 3rd-person stance by a male (let's be generous and say that I am) at an ultra-violet altitude in line/cognitive" (p. 266). So it seems that some integralists (in this case Wilber) "who claim to overcome metaphysics" by evoking the *rhetoric* of postmetaphysics, yet "do not self-consciously disclose all of the AQAL components of any occasion … are actually caught in subtler versions of it." But as I am attempting to show in this chapter, failure to disclose one's epistemic positionality is not the only subtler version of metaphysics that post-metaphysics can find itself caught in; far more consequential, in my view, is when post-metaphysics attempts to deny its dependence on a philosophical ontology, thereby implicitly committing itself to a form of pre-critical metaphysics.

63 Wilber (2006), however, sees the neo-Kantian approach as the only viable philosophical pathway in our contemporary context: "critical (Kantian) philosophy replaced metaphysics (or ontological objects) with epistemology (or structures in the subject), and this general move is *unavoidable* in the post/modern world" [emphasis added] (p. 271).

64 M. Hartwig, personal communication, June 23, 2014.

65 This raises the issue of what other important methods may be left out of the IMP map at present, along with the issue of the precise placement of various philosophical methods. Sean Esbjörn-Hargens has suggested (personal communication, March 16, 2013) that the philosophical method of transcendental argument may be a Zone-1 method in combination with a Zone-6 focus, following Wilber's claim that mathematics and logic are associated with the 'eye of mind' in his 'three eyes' scheme (the other two being the 'the eye of flesh' and 'the eye of spirit') and thus are fundamentally a facet of subjective mental experience, or introspection (i.e., Zone-1). However, I argue that since transcendental argumentation is a (relative and conditional) *a priori* philosophical method (that is, it refers to that which is *prior to* the subjective experience associated with Zone-1), such a valid placement in the IMP map seems questionable. In my view, IMP, as it has been expounded to date, is a map of the *a posteriori* scientific methodologies of human knowing. Such an understanding points to the possibility of developing *philosophical methodological pluralism* to complement its scientifically oriented methodological pluralism. Such a development might lead to a more comprehensive articulation of IMP. Thus, I am not necessarily trying to criticize IMP for omitting transcendental argument, but rather highlighting the potential for developing a more comprehensive taxonomy of methods that includes *a priori* philosophical methods such as transcendental argument.

66 See Nunez (2013) for the notion of 'patch' and 'patching' in relation to TINA compromise formations.

67 The orthodox practitioners of IT will tend to reject such a deep and non-preservative transformation, as it calls so much into question and in some ways may even contradict a desire to parsimoniously interpret the theoretical development of IT in a unilinear progression of preservative synthesis à la Hegel. On the other hand, the orthodox critical realists will tend to be uninterested in the meeting of CR and a transfigured IT, assuming perhaps that IT is 'a poisoned chalice' (Rutzou, 2012) that can't be salvaged and that the dialogue with IT does not reveal any important absences or contradictions which insights from IT might help absence or resolve. I, of course, would disagree with these views and argue that the revelation of deep problems in IT's architectonics do not preclude it revealing and absenting absences in CR on the way to a non-preservative synthesis in a CRIT. I would offer the path of non-preservative synthesis of the two metatheories seems to be reserved for the daring, heterodox practitioners willing to risk some degree of alienation from the orthodoxy of both metatheoretical streams. For me such a risk doesn't feel so much like a choice, but the natural result of a commitment to following

the golden thread of truth (however fallibly) and the quest for the intellectual resources that can truly be of transformative impact for a world in deep socio-ecological crisis.

68 While it has been suggested by some integral theorists that CR tends towards an *ontic fallacy* (e.g., Esbjörn-Hargens, personal communication, September 17, 2011) in the loose sense of an insufficient consideration of its epistemic categories, in a proper sense, the ontic fallacy can be said to refer to a reduction of epistemology to ontology wherein knowledge is conceptualized as a direct or unmediated representation of being by a disengaged subject in which the psychological, cultural, and social mechanisms through which knowledge is constructed vis-à-vis antecedent knowledge are either denied or ignored. It is important to note that, from a CR perspective, the ontic fallacy follows closely from the epistemic fallacy. As Hartwig (2007) puts it "the epistemic (together with its logicising variant) and ontic fallacies are dialectical counterparts or duals which, while apparent antagonists, in reality mutually presuppose and support each other" (p. 174). Thus, for CR to commit the ontic fallacy, according to its own definitions, it would also have to commit the epistemic fallacy, which it does not. Clearly, given CR's concept of the transitive dimension and fallibilist epistemology, which acknowledges that knowledge is always already situated within a geo-historical trajectory, CR does *not* commit an ontic fallacy in any proper sense. However, viewed from the vantage point of IT's robust taxonomy of epistemic structures and its appreciation of the profound importance of the transitive-constructivist dimension of knowledge production, CR, I argue, may run the risk of unknowingly hypostatizing various subjective and intersubjective phenomena, thus potentially transposing various epistemic elements into ontological elements in an insufficiently critical manner.

69 A philosophical ontology delineates the most abstract, general categorical features and form of the world, which science and other social activities presuppose. A scientific ontology discloses the *specific contents* of the world established by substantive scientific theory. It is one thing to have a theory generally positing that psychological, cultural, and social elements help to condition human knowing – it is quite another to have a detailed theory that actually specifies them as discrete, substantive mechanisms, grounded in far-reaching synthesis of scientific evidence.

70 As Bhaskar (2002/2012b) articulates, critical realism "remedies incompleteness' in *its* own discourse itself, that is in its previous phases: thus critical realism is a process of development in thought which builds ever more complete and rounded totalities, continually self-critical in a process of self-transcendence without any conceivable *a priori* positable end. This duplex dialectical process means that critical realism always consists in a double immanent critique – of the external manifold of received theory, and of its own dialectical past" (pp. 178–179).

71 Of course, it should be noted that IT does not have a monopoly on developmental psychology and the epistemic processes and structures it describes. For those critical realists who do not find the move toward a CRIT compelling, I would, at the least, hope that my discussion (in tandem with other contributions to this volume and its companion volume, particularly that of Zachary Stein) stimulates some interest in developmental-structural psychology and the ways in which it may help CR address some of its potential problems and/or develop into a more complete and serious emancipatory metatheory.

72 Paul Marshall (2012c) also makes a similar point in his excellent article "Toward an integral realism. Part 1: An overview of transcendental realist ontology" published in the *Journal of Integral Theory and Practice*.

73 Also see Zachary Stein's chapter "On realizing the possibilities of emancipatory metatheory: beyond the cognitive maturity fallacy, toward an education revolution" in the companion volume to this book. His important work, in resonance with and expanding on my critique, names this as the 'cognitive maturity fallacy.'

74 See N. Hedlund (2010, 2008) for detailed, albeit now somewhat outdated, accounts of my own positionality as a researcher, situated in relation to IT's epistemic taxonomy.

75 See the Introduction to this volume for a historical overview of the Critical Realism and Integral Theory symposia.

76 CR's four-planar social being, introduced in the late 1970s and published in Bhaskar (1986/2009), preceded that of IT's four quadrants, which were published in Wilber (1995).

77 In this way we might regard IT's ontology as a *subject-oriented ontology*, in contrast with CR's object-oriented approach to ontology.

78 The German philosopher Karl Jaspers (1968) was the first to propose the notion of the Axial Age, ranging from approximately 800 to 200 BCE. This period witnessed the essentially synchronic manifestation of many of the world's great wisdom traditions, including the first Greek philosophers (e.g., Thales, Pythagoras, Plato, and Aristotle), Siddhārtha Gautama Buddha, the Bhagavad Gita, Zoroastrianism, Confucianism, Taoism, and the Jewish prophets (from Isaiah to Ezekiel). See also Karen Armstrong's (2006) work for a more contemporary view on the Axial period. Much like the way in which many of the worlds great wisdom traditions of the Axial Age – from Platonism to Buddhism to Taoism – synchronically emerged across the globe (Jaspers, 1968) devoid of direct communication or physical mediation, one might speculate that the vanguards of the post-postmodern, integral age (e.g., CR and IT) seem to be being birthed together, each revealing and bringing forth unique facets of a larger emergent totality. Experimental evidence suggests that patterns of actual events and behaviours tend to resonate with and formatively influence other similar patterns of actual events, which apparently cannot be explained via material cause or direct physical mediation, but rather must be explained in terms of deeper generative mechanisms, or morphic attractors, that probabilistically influence the formation, patterning, and evolutionary trajectory of given phenomena on the level of the actual (Sheldrake, 1981/2009). This is one speculative hypothesis that might explain such non-locally co-emergent phenomena.

References

Alvesson, M., & Sköldberg, K. (2009). *Reflexive methodology: New vistas for qualitative research* (2nd ed.). London: Sage.

Apel, K. O. (1994). Transcendental semiotics and hypothetical metaphysics of evolution. In E. Mendieta (Ed.), *Karl-Otto Apel: Selected essays* (Vol. 1). Atlantic Highlands, NJ: Humanities Press.

Armon, C. (1984). Ideals of the good life and moral judgement: Ethical reasoning across the lifespan. In M. L. Commons, F. A. Richards, & C. Armon (Eds.), *Beyond formal operations: Late adolescent and adult cognitive development* (pp. 357–381). London: Praeger.

Armstrong, K. (2006). *The great transformation: The beginning of our religious traditions*. New York: Knopf.

Basseches, M. (1984). *Dialectical thinking and adult development*. Norwood, NJ: Ablex.

Bhaskar, R. (1975/2008). *A realist theory of science* (3rd ed.). London: Routledge.

Bhaskar, R. (1979/2015). *The possibility of naturalism: A philosophical critique of the contemporary human sciences*. London: Routledge.

Bhaskar, R. (1986/2009). *Scientific realism and human emancipation*. London: Routledge.

Bhaskar, R. (1993/2008). *Dialectic: The pulse of freedom*. London: Routledge.

Bhaskar, R. (1994/2009). *Plato etc.: The problems of philosophy and their resolution* London: Routledge.

Bhaskar, R. (1997). On the ontological status of ideas. *Journal for the Theory of Social Behavior*, 27(2/3), 136–147.

Bhaskar, R. (1998). General introduction. In R. Bhaskar, M. Archer, A. Collier, T. Lawson, & A. Norrie (Eds.), *Critical realism: Essential readings* (pp. ix–xxiv). London: Routledge.

Bhaskar, R. (2002). *From science to emancipation: Alienation and the actuality of enlightenment*. New Delhi: Sage.

Bhaskar, R. (2002/2012a). *The philosophy of metaReality: Creativity, love and freedom.* London: Routledge.

Bhaskar, R. (2002/2012b). *Reflections on metaReality: Transcendence, emancipation and everyday life.* London: Routledge.

Bhaskar, R. & Hartwig, M. (2010). *The formation of critical realism: A personal perspective.* London: Routledge.

Boyer, E. (1990). *Scholarship reconsidered: Priorities of the professoriate.* New York: Carnegie Foundation for the Advancement of Teaching.

Braver, L. (2007). *A thing of this world: A history of continental anti-realism.* Evanston, IL: Northwestern University Press.

Bryant, L. (2011). *The democracy of objects.* Ann Arbor, MI: Open Humanities Press.

Collier, A. (1994). *Critical realism: An introduction to Roy Bhaskar's philosophy.* London: Verso.

Commons, M. L., Richards, F. A., & Armon, C. (Eds.). (1984). *Beyond formal operations: Late adolescent and adult cognitive development.* New York: Praeger.

Cook-Greuter, S. R. (1999). *Postautonomous ego development: A study of its nature and measurement* (Unpublished doctoral thesis). Harvard University, Cambridge, MA.

Cook-Greuter, S. R. (2000). Mature ego development: A gateway to ego transcendence? *Journal of Adult Development, 7*(4), 227–240.

Cook-Greuter, S. R. (2002). A detailed description of the development of nine action logics in the leadership development framework: Adapted from ego development theory. Retrieved April 12, 2007, from www.Cook-Greuter.com.

Danermark, B., Ekström, M., Jakobsen, L., & Karlsson, J. (2002). *Explaining society: Critical realism in the social sciences.* London: Routledge.

Dawson, T. L. (2001). Layers of structure: A comparison of two approaches to developmental assessment. *Genetic Epistemologist, 29*(4), 1–10.

Dawson, T. L. (2002). A comparison of three developmental stage scoring systems. *Journal of Applied Measurement, 3*(2), 146–189.

Dawson, T. L. (2004). Assessing intellectual development: Three approaches, one sequence. *Journal of Adult Development, 11*(2), 71–85.

De Witt, A., & Hedlund, N. (in press). Reflexive communications for climate solutions: Towards an integral ecology of worldviews. In S. Mickey, S. M. Kelly, & A. Robbert (Eds.), *Integral ecologies: Culture, nature, knowledge, and our planetary future.* New York: SUNY Press.

Descartes, R. (1637/2006). *Discourse on method* (I. Maclean, Trans.). Oxford: Oxford University Press.

Edwards, M. G. (2010). *Organizational transformation for sustainability: An integral metatheory.* New York: Routledge.

Esbjörn-Hargens, S. (2006). Integral research: A multi-method approach to investigating phenomena. *Constructivism and the Human Sciences, 11*(1), 79–107.

Esbjörn-Hargens, S. (2010a). An ontology of climate change: Integral pluralism and the enactment of multiple objects. *Journal of Integral Theory and Practice, 5*(1), 143–174.

Esbjörn-Hargens, S. (2010b). An overview of integral theory. In S. Esbjörn-Hargens (Ed.), *Integral theory in action: Applied, theoretical and constructive perspectives on the AQAL model* (pp. 33–64). New York: SUNY.

Esbjörn-Hargens, S., & Wilber, K. (2006). Towards a comprehensive integration of science and religion: A post-metaphysical approach. In P. Clayton & Z. Simpson (Eds.), *The Oxford handbook of religion and science* (pp. 523–546). New York: Oxford University Press.

Esbjörn-Hargens, S., & Zimmerman, M. E. (2009). *Integral ecology: Uniting multiple perspectives on the natural world.* Boston, MA: Integral Books.

Ferguson, J. (2002). Development. In A. Barnard & J. Spencer (Eds.), *Encyclopedia of social and cultural anthropology.* London: Routledge.

Ferrer, J. N. (2002). *Revisioning transpersonal theory: A participatory vision of human spirituality.* Albany, NY: SUNY.

Ferrer, J. N., & Sherman, Jacob H. (2008). *The participatory turn: Spirituality, mysticism, religious studies.* Albany, NY: SUNY.

Fisher, K. W., & Biddle, T. (2006). Dynamic development of psychological structures in action and thought. In W. Damon & R. M. Lerner (Eds.), *Handbook of child psychology: Theoretical models of human development* (Vol. 1, pp. 1–62). New York: John Wiley & Sons.

Fisher, K. W. (1980). A theory of cognitive development: The control and construction of hierarchies of skills. *Psychological Review,* 87(6), 477–531.

Foucault, M. (1966/2002). *The order of things: An archaeology of the human sciences.* London: Routledge.

Foucault, M. (1972). *The archaeology of knowledge and the discourse on language* (A. S. Smith, Trans.). New York: Pantheon Books.

Gardiner, H. W., & Kosmitzki, C. (2004). *Lives across cultures: Cross-cultural human development* (3rd ed.). Boston, MA: Allyn & Bacon.

Habermas, J. (1976). *Communication and the evolution of society.* (Thomas McCarthy, Trans.). Boston, MA: Beacon Press.

Habermas, J. (1987/2000). *The philosophical discourse of modernity: Twelve lectures* (F. Lawrence, Trans.). Cambridge, MA: MIT Press.

Habermas, J. (1990). *Moral consciousness and communicative action* (C. Lenhardt & S. Nicholsen, Trans.). Cambridge, MA: MIT Press.

Habermas, J. (1992/1996). *Postmetaphysical thinking: Philosophical essays.* Cambridge, MA: MIT Press.

Habermas, J. (2003). *The future of human nature.* Cambridge, UK: Polity Press.

Hampson, G. (2007). Integral re-views postmodernism: The way out is through. *Integral Review,* 4, 108–173.

Harman, G. (2002). *Tool-being: Heidegger and the metaphysics of objects.* Peru, IL: Open Court.

Harman, G. (2011). Response to Shaviro. In L. Bryant, N. Srnicek, & G. Harman (Eds.), *The speculative turn: Continental materialism and realism* (pp. 291–303). Melbourne: re. press.

Hartwig, M. (Ed.). (2007). *Dictionary of critical realism.* London: Routledge.

Hartwig, M. (2011). Roy Bhaskar's critique of the philosophical discourse of modernity. *Journal of Critical Realism,* 10(4), 485–510.

Hedlund, N. (2010). Integrally researching Integral Research: Enactive perspectives on future of the field. *Journal of Integral Theory and Practice,* 5(2), 1–30.

Hedlund, N. (in press). Towards a critical realist integral theory: Ontological and epistemic considerations for integral philosophy. In S. Esbjörn-Hargens & M. Schwartz (Eds.), *Dancing with Sophia: Integral philosophy on the verge.* New York: SUNY Press.

Hedlund, N. H. (2008). Integrally researching the integral researcher: A first-person exploration of psychosophy's holding loving space practice. *Journal of Integral Theory and Practice,* 3(2), 1–57.

Hedlund-de Witt, A. (2012). Exploring worldviews and their relationships to sustainable lifestyles: Towards a new conceptual and methodological approach. *Ecological Economics,* 84, 74–83.

Hedlund-de Witt, N. H. (2012). Critical realism: A synoptic overview and resource guide for integral scholars. Retrieved December 12, 2012, from https://foundation.metaintegral. org/sites/default/files/Critical%20Realism_4-12-2013.pdf.

Heppner, P., Wampold, B., & Kivlighan, D. (2008). *Research design in counseling.* Belmont, CA: Thompson.

Hume, D. (1739/2000). *A treatise on human nature.* Oxford: Oxford University Press.

Hume, D. (1748/1999). *An enquiry concerning human understanding.* Oxford: Oxford University Press.

Inglehart, R. F., & Welzel, C. (2005). *Modernization, cultural change, and democracy: The human development sequence.* New York: Cambridge University Press.

Jackson, R. (2013). The fourfold of speculative realism: A work in progress. Retrieved April 5, 2013, from http://robertjackson.info/index/2013/04/the-fourfold-of-speculative-realism-a-work-in-progress/

Jaspers, K. (1968). *The origin and goal of history* (M. Bullock, Trans.). New Haven, CT: Yale University Press.

Kant, I. (1791/1998). *Critique of pure reason* (P. Guyer & A. W. Wood, Trans.). Cambridge: Cambridge University Press.

Kegan, R. (1982). *The evolving self: Problem and process in human development.* Cambridge, MA: Harvard University Press.

Kegan, R. (1994). *In over our heads: The mental demands of modern life.* Cambridge, MA: Harvard University Press.

Kegan, R. (2001). *How the way we talk can change the way we work: Seven languages for transformation.* San Francisco, CA: Jossey-Bass.

King, P. M., & Kitchener, K. S. (1994). *Developing reflective judgment.* San Francisco, CA: Jossey-Bass.

Kohlberg, L. (1984). *The psychology of moral development: The nature and validity of moral stages.* San Francisco, CA: Harper & Row.

Loevinger, J. (1977). *Ego development: Conceptions and theories.* San Francisco, CA: Jossey-Bass.

Loevinger, J. (1987). *Paradigms of personality.* New York: W. H. Freeman.

Lopez, J., & Potter, G. (2001). *After postmodernism: An introduction to critical realism.* London: Athlone Press.

Marshall, G. (1998). *The Oxford dictionary of sociology.* Oxford: Oxford University Press.

Marshall, P. (2012a). Ken Wilber on critical realism. *Journal of Integral Theory and Practice,* 7(4), 35–38.

Marshall, P. (2012b). The meeting of two integrative metatheories. *Journal of Critical Realism,* 11(2), 188–214.

Marshall, P. (2012c). Toward an integral realism. Part 1: An overview of transcendental realist ontology. *Journal of Integral Theory and Practice,* 7(4), 1–34.

Maturana, H. R., & Varela, F. J. (1980). *Autopoiesis and cognition: The realization of the living.* Boston, MA: D. Reidel.

Maturana, H. R., & Varela, F. J. (1987). *The tree of knowledge: The biological roots of human understanding.* Boston, MA: Shambhala.

Meillassoux, Q. (2008). *After finitude: An essay on the necessity of contingency.* New York: Continuum.

Nagel, T. (1986). *The view from nowhere.* Oxford: Oxford University Press.

Nagel, T. (1997). *The last word.* Oxford: Oxford University Press.

Norrie, A. (2010). *Dialectic and difference: Dialectical critical realism and the grounds of justice.* London: Routledge.

Nunez, I. (2013). Transcending the dualisms of activity theory. *Journal of Critical Realism,* 12(2), 141–165.

Piaget, J. (1928). *Judgement and reasoning in the child.* London: Littlefield and Adams.

Piaget, J. (1932). *The moral judgment of the child.* Chicago: University of Chicago Press.

Piaget, J. (1971a). *Biology and knowledge.* Chicago: University of Chicago Press.

Piaget, J. (1971b). *The insights and illusions of philosophy.* New York: The World Publishing Company.

Piaget, J. (1972). *The principles of genetic epistemology* (W. Mays, Trans.). London: Routledge.

Piaget, J. (1977). *The essential Piaget: An interpretive reference guide.* New York Basic Books.

Piaget, J., & Inhelder, B. (2000/1969). *The psychology of the child.* New York: Basic Books.

Rose, L. T., & Fischer, K. W. (2009). Dynamic development: A neo-Piagetian approach. In U. Muller, J. Carpendale, & L. Smith (Eds.), *The Cambridge companion to Piaget* (pp. 400–421). Cambridge: Cambridge University Press.

Rutzou, T. (2012). Integral theory: A poisoned chalice? *Journal of Critical Realism,* 11(2), 215–224.

Searle, J. (1995). *The construction of social reality.* New York: The Free Press.

Shaviro, S. (2011). The actual volcano: Whitehead, Harman, and the problem of relations. In L. Bryant, N. Srnicek, & G. Harman (Eds.), *The speculative turn: Continental materialism and realism.* Melbourne: re.press.

Sheldrake, R. (1981/2009). *Morphic resonance: The nature of formative causation.* Rochester, VT: Park Street Press.

Stein, Z. (2012). *On the use of the term integral: Vision-logic, meta-theory, and the growth-to-goodness assumptions.* Paper presented at the 2nd Biennial Integral Theory Conference, Pleasant Hill, California.

Taylor, C. (1989). *Sources of the self: The making of the modern identity.* Cambridge, MA: Harvard University Press.

Van Haaften, W. (1997). The concept of development. In W. Van Haaften, M. Korthals, & T. Wren (Eds.), *Philosophy of development: Reconstructing the foundations of human development and education* (pp. 13–29). Dordrecht: Kluwer Academic.

Von Uexküll, J. (1934/2010). *A foray into the worlds of animals and humans.* Minneapolis: University of Minnesota Press.

Whitehead, A. N. (1978). *Process and reality.* New York: Free Press.

Wilber, K. (1995). *Sex, ecology, spirituality: The spirit of evolution.* Boston, MA: Shambhala.

Wilber, K. (2000). *Integral psychology: Consciousness, spirit, psychology, therapy.* Boston, MA: Shambhala.

Wilber, K. (2001). On the nature of a post-metaphysical spirituality: Response to Habermas and Weis. http://wilber.shambhala.com/html/misc/habermas/index.cfm/.

Wilber, K. (2003a). Excerpts A, B, C, D, G from the Kosmos trilogy, Vol. 2. www.kenwilber. com/professional/writings/index.html.

Wilber, K. (2003b). Foreword. In F. Visser (Ed.), *Ken Wilber: Thought as passion* (pp. xi–xv). New York: SUNY Press.

Wilber, K. (2006). *Integral spirituality: A startling new role for religion in the modern and postmodern world.* Boston, MA: Integral Books.

Wilber, K. (2012a). Critical realism revisited (pp. 1–3): MetaIntegral Foundation. Retrieved December 5, 2012 from: https://foundation.metaintegral.org/sites/default/files/Critical%20Realism_Revisited-1.pdf.

Wilber, K. (2012b). In defense of integral theory: A response to critical realism. *Journal of Integral Theory and Practice,* 7(4), 43–52.

6

AFTER INTEGRAL GETS REAL

On meta-critical *chiasma* of CR and IT

Michael Schwartz

Power₁ and non-exclusion

The dialogue between Critical Realism (CR) and Integral Theory (IT) is maturing. A conversation best conducted, then, not as what CR calls a power₂ master–slave interaction of defending a prior position against perceived threats, but rather as a mature power₁ encounter of mutual enhancement and celebration, each metatheory inviting the other – as well as itself – to discern absences, pathologies, theory/practice tensions, partialness, and respective strengths and weaknesses, therein sparking creative emergence, empowering the other and itself into greater wholeness and emancipatory potency. Respectful of the boundaries of both approaches, while at the same time open to incipient lines of co-creative emergence, this ethos also takes to heart the IT regulative principle of non-exclusion, summarized in pith as no position is 100 percent in error; in effect a dissolving of allergies to otherness enabling more nuanced critical learning processes. Three interwoven trajectories thereby emerge: (1) CR learns from its encounter with IT and adjusts its bearings *qua* CR; (2) IT learns from its encounter with CR and adjusts its bearings *qua* IT; (3) insights spark forth no longer principally contained in either metatheory (a) in degree and (b) in kind. By orienting within the dialogue field in this manner, we disarm background *Vorurteilen* (pre-judgments within the hermeneutical circle of understanding) that otherwise animate, behind our backs, power₂ forms of speaking and listening as well as categorical-allergic reactivity to unfamiliar positions and claims.

We begin our comparative inquiry with a topic that emerged early in the brief history of the metatheory exchange: *the question whether IT commits what CR calls the epistemic fallacy*. This leads immediately into the theme of being and knowing, itself inseparable from both approaches' stance on nonduality and its importance for individual and collective emancipation. Our exploration of these themes will result in concrete suggestions: (1) how CR can adjust its ways, (2) how IT can adjust its ways, and (3) one way co-creative metatheorizing can begin to move beyond the predominant gravitational pull of either approach.

This chapter underlabors for the dialogic encounter between CR and IT, all the while conducting a conversation between the two metatheories within the discursive space opened by this underlaboring.

Being and knowing

Beginning with the Fall 2011 symposium, there have been various claims, of differing force and from various argumentation angles, that IT commits the *epistemic fallacy*: the post/modern irrealist error of overweighing the knowing subject or, as with Heidegger, the human clearing (*Lichtung*) of beings; such that epistemology or disclosiveness overdetermines and delimits the scope of what is said to be. In counter-measure to such irrealist views, CR distinguishes three levels of ontological depth: experiences, events, and generative mechanisms. The domain of the real is inclusive of all three, the domain of the actual only of the first two. By focusing on and looking for regularities in experiences and events, as conditioned and centered in the human subject's finite capacities, irrealist ontologies become defined by epistemology or human disclosiveness, such that generative-causality is wrongly sought exclusively within and amongst experience and events, floundering on what CR calls the error of *actualism*.

CR demonstrates instead that the natural sciences set up experiments to generate closed systems such that regularities of events show forth, the scientist now able to discern the real generative mechanisms causative of that regularity. These intransitive mechanisms are non-identical to events and experience; purchase on causative structures leads to the capacity to predict actualities in the context of an artificially closed system. In contrast, the social sciences cannot set up experiments that generate closed systems; they must learn about generative mechanisms without access to the experimental establishment of regularities of events. Explanation of causality is possible, but there can be no decisive predictive tests for theories.

In this light, does IT commit the epistemic fallacy?

In the recent "exchange" between Bhaskar and Wilber, the latter denies the charge that IT commits this fallacy (Bhaskar, 2012a; Marshall, 2012; Wilber, 2012a, 2012b). Is this a mere denial? Or might it be more – perhaps marking an absence, a symptom of a yet to be thematized comparative line of inquiry? Taking the latter course, I want to suggest that both parties, unintentionally and in part, are in this case talking past one another. Taking up CR terms, Bhaskar tends to be focusing on the *non-anthropic generative mechanisms of the real*; while Wilber is stressing the *non-pregivenness of actuals* – a view which, in its unsaid, entails that *specific actuals are a necessary condition of formally knowing certain kinds of generative mechanisms*. When Wilber speaks of (actuals) sub-sisting and ex-isting, he is pointing to a reserve of non-being, the actuals of which come forward *only* within a given tetra-arising worldspace, the latter inclusive of specific waves of cognitive development. Specific actuals are not pre-given; determinate subjects and objects only coming forward in specific worldspaces – in the example offered in Wilber's paper, atoms do not come forward and ex-ist as specifiable actuals prior to the modern scientific worldspace (even though they sub-sist independently of human observation), nor does formal operational thinking, a capacity requisite for engaging atoms in a scientific manner that accounts for their generative capacities. For IT both objects of causal knowledge and competent knowing subjects are non-pregivens. If for CR the transitive activity of scientists sets up experimental conditions of closed systems as a restrictive re-configuring of the coming forth of actuals, hence as a kind of Heideggerian clearing (minus the at times fusing of ontology and epistemics proper to Heidegger's view of disclosure) enabling the testing for generative mechanisms that are non-identical to the ontological strata of experience and events, for IT the clearing of actuals is not only that of the experimental scientist, but always already tetra-arising – with experimental science a special or second-order instance.

According to IT the coordinates for the coming forth of actuals *qua* actuals (ex-istence) are the four quadrants and eight primordial hori-zones (each zone associated with a set of perspective-chains; see Fuhs, 2010). One of these is the UL with its zone 2 disclosures of neo-Kantian schemas and capacities of knowing – *as this zone locates the site not only of actual subjects but also generative mechanisms proper to knowing itself*. For example, the subjective conditions of being able to differentiate real depth strata, proper to CR, requires a certain minimum level of non-pregiven cognitive development (Wilber cites turquoise somewhat metaphorically to signify "very high development"). Furthermore, for IT such high cognitive waves of conceptual cognition are not the end of the story, as it posits so-called third-tier waves of gnosis (which have points of contact with metaReality's views of the intuitive intellect and supramental consciousness) – opening up questions, yet to be investigated in a sustained communal and philosophical manner, of just what such modes of knowing are and how they revise our understanding of prior distinctions, such as that of the actual and real domains. For example, do the subtle and causal "sheaths" have respective depth dimensions that are in some sense *generative*?

Given these preliminary distinctions and clarifications, let us say then that when the IT model is enacted with a secreted foundation in the UL quadrant of human beings, *as it most often has been*, it comes to appear as both necessarily and fatally committed to the epistemic fallacy. In part this appearance is due to a theory–practice contradiction endemic to IT.

In presenting the AQAL model, IT states that all four quadrants are equiprimordial, that none is prior to, nor one-sidedly determinative of, another. In practice, however, there is a hyper-stressing of the UL and zone 2, such that in a secreted foundational manner, objects (and subjects) are said to tetra-arise – but in fact are presented as overdetermined by the subjective conditions of cognitive developmental waves. Theoretically committed to the equiprimordial co-arising of all four quadrants of an individual holon, the enactment of the model typically diverges from this theoretical premise.

The UL, however, need not be the quadrant through which the other three are seen and sensed; any quadrant can serve in that way, such that the epistemic knowing subject itself (UL) can be disclosed in light of other quadrant-perspectives. For example, Marxian theories descending from Lukács (1971), centered in the LR, can shed light on the textures of the subject's lived experience, as with Debord's notion of spectacle (Debord, 1994; Schwartz, 2011), about which psychological methods of the UL have nothing direct to say. CR, in its turn, has offered re-readings of Hegel's account of the unfolding of self-consciousness, taking up and surpassing Marx's own critique of that dialectic, demonstrating how identity formation warps due to capitalistic systemics and exchanges, calling for us to redress the disaster of reification by developing a self-understanding of ourselves as integrated-agential *embodied personalities*. None of this, to be clear, is to dismiss zone 2 developmentalism, but only to de-center its deeply embedded habit as secreted foundation when enacting the AQAL model.

Further, calling the early modern capitalist formation "orange" – as IT has – is to look *through* zone 2 developmental value waves of the UL quadrant proper *at* LR techno-economic systems. This can yield insights. And yet in a formal-theoretical sense it violates the IT restriction of validity claims and their specific methodologies to their own quadrant domain or hori-zone; that methods proper to one quadrant or hori-zone cannot be legitimately brought to bear on the matters of other quadrants or hori-zones (raising the question, with regard to the Lukácsian tradition just cited, to what extent if at all IT forges an inter-quadrant approach with its own distinctive methodologies). Calling capitalism "orange" then, while useful as a metaphor in generating insights (and having echoes of, while not precisely enacting, what IT calls a *judgment*, which moves between and amongst quadrants; see Wilber and Fuhs, 2010), can readily have the effect of imposing results from a psychological method onto an ontologically different quadrant domain, in this example suppressing the specific systems contours of techno-economic regimes, overriding proper analysis of them – which is all too common in the IT community, given its neglect of social holons (see below). In light of this theory–practice contradiction, IT can benefit by turning toward a post-foundational *integral kaleidoscopics*, where any one of the quadrants can be the center of gravity and fulcrum through which the other three quadrants are sensed and seen to disclose insights (Schwartz, 2012 and in press); remaining mindful of the limits of this approach with regard to formal methodologies and their validity claims as domain/quadrant specific.

In the end, by decentering the human UL and zone 2 as secreted foundation, while incorporating the CR ontological depth distinction between actuals and generative mechanisms (and thereby letting go of any strong claims for the circularity of epistemology and ontology), IT updates itself, moves past any hints of the epistemic fallacy, and "gets real" – able to leave in place the quadrant matrix and the notion of perspectives, now schematizing taxonomies of actuals *and* of generative mechanisms.

CR would do well, in turn, to heed three closely interrelated insights from this exchange with IT.

First, the actuals that ex-ist condition what generative mechanisms can be investigated. This point can be unpacked. The first half of the sixth of IT's Twenty Tenets says that "the lower sets the possibilities of the higher." This has some bearing on the CR depth strata of the real. Generative mechanisms are intransitive and may exist independently of human existence. In one sense events exist independently of human existence as well, in another sense this claim is misleading. We can surmise that all kinds of events are ongoing about which human beings do not and may never know; let's call these unspecified events. For any event to be specifiable there must be either direct or indirect experience of the event or some facet or effect of the event. In this sense, experience is the condition of possibility of specifying events as certain kinds of events, this distinction assuring that there is no slippage into an "abstract universalism" of events-in-general that would have the effect of flattening the import of experience. (For only once specified, do we rightly understand that those kinds of events are ongoing independent of direct experience of them.) The ranges of experience, as coordinated through the kinds of worldspaces that arise, delimit in this *decisive* manner the range of specifiable events and in turn the forms of possible knowledge. This is not trivial. It points to how the matrix of any individual holon is a kind of mega-phenomenology that strongly bears upon the transitive activities of researchers, hence on what kinds of causal knowledge is possible.

Second, and extending from this first point, while CR honors the dynamic and emergent character of being, at stake is the degree to which, and the domains within, such a view of non-givenness is fleshed out and enacted. CR can benefit from a much deeper appreciation and methodological specification of the variations in the contours of experience and actuality amongst individuals per their concrete singularity, inclusive of (while neither reducible to nor necessarily centered in) developmental waves, wholeheartedly acknowledging that zone 2 neo-Kantian developmentalisms are an important part of the picture – pointing to non-physicalist but real generative mechanisms of the human ability to know actuals and generative mechanisms themselves. When properly and metatheoretically contextualized, and de-centered from a theoretical function of grounding or underwriting all other modes of inquiry, developmentalisms become an important part of a meta-critical approach (able to complement CR's discernment of the various modes of contemporary alienation and their various moral-ideologies), able to sidestep the pitfalls of the epistemic fallacy, and profoundly clarify aspects of the stratification of concrete embodied personalities within the folds of four-planar social being.

Third, if more nuanced, and in part coming out of the first two points, CR can foreground stronger core valuation of actuality, and of experience itself, as strata of the real. There is in the early phases of CR – which is to be sure outshone in metaRealism (where the primacy of transcendental critique is supplemented by an enhanced phenomenology of experience) – a tendency of not giving much attention to the contours, specificities, and importance of actuals like that of direct lived experience. Not a categorical denigration, to be sure, and orientated by proper focus on the topics at hand (that of rectifying irrealist philosophies of the natural and social sciences), but a kind of neglect or minimization nonetheless (for example, the "concept of the actual as an instance of the necessary, possible, or universal, divorced from actualism, is unobjectionable," Bhaskar, 1993, p. 235 – a rare positive statement on actuality itself, if indirect in its affirmation). There are various symptoms of this non-focus: (1) The term used in early CR to speak of mistaken theories of scientific theory is "actualism" – without regular, strong, and robust accompanying statements on the importance and value of actualities. (2) In the singular *Dialectics* volume (Bhaskar, 1993), followed by *Plato Etc.* (Bhaskar, 1994), there are powerful critiques of ontological monovalence coupled with arguments for the priority of the negative – the negative as the not yet actual, dialectics as the critical and practical bringing forward of absences. This has the tacit valuation, again by no means direct or categorical, of prioritizing what sub-sists over what ex-ists. (3) Aesthetics, as inquiry into the significance of the sensible, has no major place in CR's brilliance. While there are important placeholders for aesthetics, prior to the metaRealism phase, as in passages noting the need for an aesthetics of existence (cf. Bhaskar, 1993, p. 15); aesthetics as such is never "fleshed out" until metaRealism activates notions like enchantment. (4) Art, as concerned with actualities in a most intimate way, has no fundamental place in CR's founding studies, while approaches like of that of Jameson (1979) on the political unconscious of artworks can nourish CR's emancipatory dialectics and concern for concrete utopias. To be clear, CR's profound emancipatory impulse, there from the start, is not the contemplation of generative mechanisms for their own sake, but oriented towards reducing suffering and enhancing freedom – where suffering and freedom are of our *actual* lives. The methodological expansion in metaRealism towards greater inclusion of a phenomenology of experience might then be unleashed even more into engagement with the everydayness of experience and events; aligning with, complementing, and fleshing out even further the critique of modern abstract universalism proper to the dialectical phase of CR and its forwarding of concrete universalism = concrete singularity.

To approach this from another angle, we may turn to the theme of post-metaphysics. In IT the sense of post-metaphysics has some affinities with Habermas' *Postmetaphysical Thinking* (Habermas, 1994; cf. Wilber, 2006, Appendix II) and its de-ontologizing inclinations, an orientation about which CR, in its championing of ontology and its critique of the overemphasis in modern thought of the epistemic, would be dubious. However, another and distinct major strain of post-metaphysical inquiry is founded in a lineage of major philosophers that includes Heidegger, Derrida, and Sallis. This critical strain notes two recurrent interwoven components of the Western metaphysical tradition: (1) a metaphysics of presence, and (2) a metaphysics of the sensible–intelligible binary – where with the latter, the sensible (or some correlative term) is denigrated, bypassed, or devalued in light of its transparency or its negligible conditioning impact upon the intelligible/knowledge of the intelligible. CR's notion of the non-identity of the stratified real, in its critique of ontological monovalence, brilliantly and productively moves past the first metaphysical knot. But what about the second? While CR posits a three-strata view of the real, its evaluation of current philosophical and theoretical practices speaks regularly in binary terms of the actual/real, or more precisely, of the actual/generative mechanism distinction. As noted already, the "neglect" of the actual *qua* actual in early CR shifts in DCR with the theme of concrete singularity, which in principle opens up the space for fuller engagement with actuality (and the empirical); while in the metaReality phase the increased deployment of phenomenological insight opens towards an enhanced intimacy with empiricities. Yet, stemming from the initial distinctions developed in and proper to the transcendental realistic critique of prior philosophies of science, there has been a lingering tendency in CR throughout towards sustaining a metaphysics of the sensible–intelligible binary that downplays the former term, bypassing sustained explication of what an event is (Mingers, 2014, p. 33) and even more so short-changing exploration of the domain of the empirical itself; inclining to override attention towards and the valuing of the actual in lieu of causal mechanisms and structures as the stratum of explanatory intelligibility. Contrarily, post-Husserlian phenomenologies (e.g., Levinas, Sallis) and related streams of post-phenomenology (e.g., Deleuze) have mounted important and irreducible insights into sensation, sensibility, elementals, vibrations, the senses of sense, and more that are not merely or simply reducible to perception, but open into a rich field of descriptive (and more-than-descriptive) inquiry that contours what might be called the field of aesthetics. Leaving little room for the fullness and richness of the actual, this lingering metaphysic knot underwrites in part CR's thin approach to deep self-transformation and the correlative underappreciation of the import of the multidimensional trajectories of self-transformation for our nuanced and singular ways of concrete lived existence.

In the end, there is in CR a theory–practice imbalance between (1) brilliant and innovative theorizing of the stratified embodied personality as concrete universal↔concrete singularity and (2a) the absence of an adequate mapping of the complex and profound spectra of those stratifications, coupled with (2b) the absence of extensive injunctional pathways for developing such capacities (as with the high cognitive development required for enacting dialectical thought, which is a non-pregiven power still rare amongst the population; see Laske, 2008). While the metaReality teachings begin to redress 2a and 2b, CR would do well to greatly expand and dimensionalize its mapping and exercising of the various stratifications of the embodied personality cum transcendental-spiritual Self.

Negativity and nothingness

Negativity is important in both metatheories. In the dialectical phases of CR, the critique of ontological monovalence offers profound philosophical engagements with themes of negativity, absence, non-being, and social change, putting forward a seminal version of dialectics (confirmed, in the main, by cognitive research; Laske, 2008) consisting of the four moments of non-identity, negativity, open totality, and transformative praxis. IT has a neo-Whiteheadian thesis of micro-genesis (creativity as processual change) that remains on the level of actuals, the notions of sub-sist and ex-ist pointing to determinate or quasi-determinate non-being, as does the thesis of involution/evolution, where the most general patterns and broad orientations of evolution are said to be set out ahead of time. What both metaviews might foreground more than they perhaps already do are Heideggerian insights, recently reworked in Sallis' post-deconstructive phenomenology (2000 and 2012) and in a different direction in Harman's object-oriented ontology (Harman, 2011) of the concrete withdrawal of being/s, such that actuals already in ex-istence hold in reserve yet to be disclosed aspects and potencies.

Going further, negativity is to be distinguished from nothingness. The former involves determinate or quasi-determinate non-beings, the latter as radical counterpoint/complement to being in general. Schelling asked the question (*pace* Hegel of the *Logic*): why is there something rather than nothing? As Tyler Tritten (2012) argues, this question is not in the first instance cosmological but existential, an inquiry into the depth significance of manifestation and its bearing upon human existence. Heidegger's various meditations on this question, including his later articulations of ontological difference and *Ereignis*, led him to conclude that human being is the shepherd or placeholder of being – an anthropic conclusion if there ever was one. IT in its turn has approached this question not as did Heidegger – who attempted a twisting free from the metaphysical tradition so as to inaugurate another beginning that clears attunement to being – but as a mega-phenomenology of experience and actuality coupled with methodologically gleaned generalizing orientations about manifestation's tendency to evolve. Spirit, as Conscious Nothingness, births manifestation as Its own kosmic Play and through this Play strives for Self-recognition. Having from the start gotten lost in the game and forgotten its own Supreme Identity, Spirit evolves into forms of manifestation that have requisite capacity to serve as the site of Self-recollection, humans being one of these sites. It is not clear to me how CR might take up and respond to Schelling's question; how it would value a given answer – or whether CR would even sanction the question itself (cf. "Leave aside the [Schellingian and] Heideggerian question of why there is something rather than nothing," Bhaskar, 1993, p. 46; also p. 239).

Co-creative emergence

Having considered CR and IT on matters of being, knowing, negativity, and nothingness, we are better placed to consider and discern that each puts forward what I call *schemes*. Such schemes are the explicit or implicit diagrammatic expressions of taxonomies inseparable from positions on themes like ontology, epistemology, ontics, epistemics, methodology, enactment, and so forth (cf. Schwartz 2014) – hence are more than taxonomic. Both approaches offer schemes that are in part constituted through horizontal (depth) and vertical (nest) ontological axes. CR is especially strong in its view of a *stratified ontology of horizontal depth* of the real as the site of generativity amidst the non-identity of the three ontological strata (and where from the frame of metaRealism all these strata are immanent within the domain of metaReality). IT is especially strong in its view of a *stratified ontology of vertical height* of development and evolution (where from the frame of the one True Self all these vertical strata are immanently nondual).

These specific strengths are complementary, the intersection of axes is able to be mapped in any number of ways. Using in this instance the IT framework as point of departure (which is how "horizontal" and "vertical" have been deployed in this instance), horizontal strata of depth are inclusive of the actual and its real generative mechanisms intersecting with vertical strata of height, inclusive of (if not exhausted by) the upwards nesting of the physio-, bio-, noo-, and theospheres proper to individual holons. The quadrants and hori-zones show the sites of and relationships among actuals, real absences, and generative mechanisms. For example, zone 2 (via developmental psychology) marks the site of non-physicalist generative mechanisms of cognition, while zone 5 (via cognitive science) marks the site of physicalist generative mechanisms of cognition – calling for a meta-method to inquire into how these two generative mechanisms coordinate in their generativity (Edwards, 2009).

Each of these axial strengths also has its own internal limits or lacunae. The CR ontology of real *depth* has a complex and by means straight forward tendency, as already discussed above (and most proper to its earlier phases), to valorize depth over surface, as with the philosophical attention upon generative mechanisms over comparable focus on the immediacy of lived experience. The IT ontology of evolving *height* has a complex and by no means straightforward tendency to valorize upwardness over what lies below, ascent over descent, prioritizing the kosmic drive of masculine Eros over feminine agape – Eros as the drive that brings forth novel capacities in achieving new heights, agape as the embracing drive, reaching down to integrate the new growth with prior structures and processes. But in the wake of insights stemming from Sri Aurobindo (2006) to A. H. Almaas (2004) and Michael Washburn (2003), the IT sense of agapic descent seems truncated and undervalued. The Higher can enter so deeply into the Lower that the union of High and Low brings forth novel actualities and capacities distinct from those of transforming ascent. I call this creative intensity of agapic descent *transfiguration*, such that sufficient upward transformation comes to be a condition of possibility of an effective downward transfigurement (see also Hedlund, 2008). To go further, CR has important insights as regards vertical nests within the real; while IT has important insights as regards ontological depths – with regard to the latter, there is an entire discussion to be had on IT's view of the interplay of the four kosmic drives as explanatory (non-predictive) of tendencies proper to manifestation *in general*; the four drives are neither available in direct experience nor mere patterns of events but intransitive. CR in contrast focuses on *domain-specific* generative mechanisms, such that the causative structures of physics are not those of human economies. Holding both these accounts, mindful of and honoring the different methodological approaches proper to each, contours a space of inquiry that expands consideration of generativity.

In this instance, I have been initiating the various sketched trajectories of co-creative emergence from a starting point within the quadrant model. As Sean Esbjörn-Hargens (2012) has however noted, there is an important family resemblance between IT's four quadrants and CR's four-planar social being: the four quadrants of an individual holon being its interior, exterior, cultural, and social-system dimensions; four-planar social being as the matrix of material transactions with nature, inter/intra-subjective personal relations, social relations, and agencial subjectivity of the embodied personality. While having much overlap, the precise make-up and relation amongst the respective categorical distinctions in the two schemes are incommensurable, terms like "social" signifying differently.

Beyond the appeal of its diagrammatic symmetry, the logic of the four quadrants makes sense given arguments proper to holonic theory and as well as to the precise perspectives-chains of integral math. It is to be sure a map of an *individual* holon. The CR scheme, in contrast, is explicitly of the *social*. While IT possesses the notion of a social holon, it has undervalued, undertheorized, and rarely deployed this concept in any ramified way, resulting in integral analyses of social-cultural phenomena most often being enacted through the quadrant matrix, amounting to what I have elsewhere argued is a wayward form of methodological individualism (Schwartz, 2013). Since IT forwards in theory the co-arising of individual and social holons – the lower two quadrants of an individual holon being the loci of the where and the how of an individual's membership in a given social holon – there is a theory–practice contradiction that parallels the one (discussed above) that hyper-stresses the UL quadrant. If from the IT logic of individual holons and its perspective-chains the CR model looks like it is committing category mistakes in how it differentiates and aligns its four planes of social being, IT has yet to embrace the view of individual *and* social holons as the within and without of one another in the perspectival Flesh of the world, let alone deploy this bi-focal model to explicate complex socio-cultural phenomena via detailed methodological enactments. CR, on the other hand has proven itself one of the most important and praxis-oriented social theories available, establishing entire research fields across the disciplinary domains.

The status of the individual body-mind in the two approaches is instructive. From the view of the quadrant model, the relation of body and mind is seen as the co-arising and correlation of interior and exterior occasions, honoring the principle of non-exclusion while going a long way towards redressing the so-called mind-body identity problem. Yet the analytic separation, keyed by the figure of the quadrant diagram, between the UL and UR (and underwritten by a view that interiors and exteriors are distinct ontological dimensions current throughout manifestation as a whole), has tended to invite in the back-door, throughout the integral community, a dissociation of these dimensions of being – the imbalanced focus on the UL quadrant and psychology the case in point – not then the deepest intent and hope of the metatheory itself in its advocating of centauric and post-centauric modes of selfhood. CR's notion of a stratified embodied personality (as underwritten by the view that mind is an evolutionary emergent from the body and the material universe), as one of the four planes, avoids this rift, grounded in a profound re-reading of Hegel's phenomenology of self-consciousness, in light of social-cultural conditions, where the various dissociations of mind and body are diagnosed as a dis-ease of modernity and postmodernity that thwarts intentional-embodied praxis for social change. Both views of the individual body-mind have merit – IT on the non-exclusion and complementarity of both physicalist and non-physicalist research paradigms; CR on the integration and integrity of the embodied personality as condition for emancipatory praxis. What must, then, be noted is missing from this very brief comparative study is how the scheme of four-planar social being might be deployed as an alternative means of initiating co-creative metatheoretical emergence. And, too, it is important to keep in mind that in constellating new schemes by drawing on the two metatheories, the diagrammatic figures reference, *but often without the needed signification*, various kinds of (1) perspective switching (CR) and (2) perspective chains (IT).

Let me give an example of how diagrams cannot be brought together outside of such considerations. Integral has regularly overburdened the quadrant model as if it was sufficient in all cases to map a social holon. Squeezing techno-economic stage-structures into the LR quadrant is misleading, as an individual holon, as grounded in a first-person perspective, would entail most directly that the LL and LR quadrants locate the ways an individual participates and is located in various social holons – for example, a facet of the LR quadrant not as an evolutionary string of techno-economic modes, but instead the site where the individual is a member of a given techno-economic regime. In turn, a social holon is composed of members, where the various dimensions of the LL and LR quadrants organize their interrelationships, breaking from the quadrant diagram when pointing to the distribution patterns of members as they are dynamically woven and rewoven as a social holon. In this way individual holons and social holons are "the within and without of one another" – they flip or reverse, in Merleau-Ponty's sense of chiasm, from one into the other as proper to *the perspectival Flesh of the world* (Schwartz, 2013). Whereas the individual quadrant model is framed as first-person, a given social holon diagram, if yet to be fleshed out in its own right, is framed in the first instance as third-person. Moving between the two holonic schemes is to switch between an embracing-framing first- and third-person perspective. When we turn to four-planar social being, its diagram has as its framing perspective the third-person, such that the embodied personality is seen for the most part from the "outside" (to echo a conversation I have had with Otto Laske on this topic), interiority only coming forward as a principal dimension or moment of being in the post-dialectical phases of CR and the positing of 5A in the unfolding of the MELDARA presentation. As such, the quadrant diagram and that of four-planar social being do not map onto one another readily, as their respective framing-embracing perspective orientations differ. Furthermore, a given diagram of a social holon well might not correlate with that of four-planar social being, despite both being third-person in their framing-embracing perspective, in that the categories of the two views are not in all cases the same. The upshot is that we do well to be cautious and careful in generating novel schemes that draw on diagrams from both metatheories.

Nonduality

In bringing this comparative exploration to a close it must be noted how rare it is among academic philosophies to boldly foreground a nondual view as both CR and IT do – CR in its notion of metaReality and IT in recasting the Buddhist terms of absolute and relative. For both metatheories, individual and collective emancipation is unlikely without our humanity awakening to or at the least tasting nondual Love. This is not New Age, but Old Age – wisdom for All Ages.

IT has claimed that all is "absolutely relative" (Wilber, 2006, appendix II). CR-inspired views have tended to interpret this assertion as an instance of the epistemic fallacy, that all is relative to the knowing subject. I suggest instead that this phrase is most compacted and complex, animated by senses of Sat-Chit-Ananda, Lila, and the primordiality of perspectives (the latter a yet to be unpacked notion in IT having a philosophical ancestry that includes Leibniz). Some of the resonant senses of this phrase include: (1) actuals cannot escape their relativity or relationality as co-dependent arising, as they always already interdependently coexist, echoing Buddhist philosophical views; (2) perspectives are elemental of actualities, the one True Self sees through each and every sentient being with which it is nondual, the display of the Kosmos relative to a given monadic perspective; only God sees, but God has no God's-eye view, instead possessing infinite perspectives on Herself; (3) all three holonic values – ground, intrinsic, extrinsic (Wilber, 2000, pp. 543–547) – are always already in play, such that all is equally an expression of ground value as seamlessly divine and sacred ("absolute"); while at the same time there are senses of better and worse ("relative"). The phrase "absolutely relative" is not then an expression of a strong or fatal commitment to the epistemic fallacy, but is a compacted speculative view of the Kosmos – God seeing Herself immanently from countless angles in an endless dance of evolving creative play.

The metaReality phase of CR shifts philosophical focus from the nonidentity of the domain of the real to the identity/unity of the metaReal that embraces and permeates the real and its depth strata. Actuality is inseparable from this identity/unification, equally enchanted and sacred; the strata distinctions remaining operative. MetaReality saturates the real with a Love that when realized by human beings radically changes the sense of what is and what can be, inspiring praxis towards the bringing forth of what CR calls the eudaimonistic society (complementary to IT's call for the liberation of all sentient beings).

An interesting distinction between CR and IT is the "cut" on nonduality as humanly recollected. For CR, each human being has a ground-state defined as non-dual, where the various individuated ground-states are united in the *cosmic envelope*. For IT, there is "at bottom" the witness or True Self, the one without another, where the human monad can become non-dual with the ever-present witness. In addition, the human monad can evolve into a boundless Unique Self "nondual" with the True Self (Gafni, 2012). Ground-state in CR and Unique Self in IT are non-identical, as are the senses of cosmic envelope and witness, despite the substantial overlap in the two views. In both metaviews, to awaken to or at least taste the nondual Love that always already is, empowers our effortless efforts to bring forth the individual emancipation of each and the eudaimonistic society for all – a claim unable to be assessed through a primacy or one-sidedness of conceptualization and theorization. To do so is to commit the *rationalistic fallacy* – the confounding of encompassing modes of gnosis and experience with the ways and means of concepts and language as proper to rational waves of cognition as if those are the only or highest waves possible for human beings (therein a fallacy aligned in part with what CR calls the linguistic fallacy, which knowingly or tacitly brackets strong referentiality, and also aligned in part with what IT calls the pre/trans fallacy, the confounding of pre-rational and post-rational waves of cognition as centered in the norm of discursive rationality). What seems not to be happening in large sectors of the CR community is what IT calls the taking up and enacting of the three strands of knowing (knowing in the sense of disclosing domains of actuality). These are: (1) taking up an injunction, "do this," e.g., meditate; (2) gleaning direct evidence over time, e.g., all arises as the texture of love-bliss, coming over time to outshine afflictive emotions; and (3) checking collective knowledge and expertise proper to this injunction domain, e.g., the world's sundry contemplative traditions repeatedly speak to this transformational result. This route enables "nondual Love" to have its real referent as the needed complement to and rewiring of linguistic signification.

Conclusion

Returning to the opening of this chapter, and the various trajectory outcomes, we can now summarize our results.

(1) CR can enhance itself by rectifying a theory–practice imbalance with regard to the stratified embodied personality of concrete singular individuals, specifying in much greater detail the ways and tendencies of human development-potencies and how one can bring online (as well as coordinate and knit) these intra-active capacities via sustained transformative practice; where this imbalance has had the consequence of underestimating the flexible constitution of human experience as a constellated field that decisively conditions and delimits (i) the specifiability of events and therein (ii) the causal mechanisms that can be brought to light. And where this much greater specification of trainable capacities becomes a metacritical complement to the CR analyses of the primary modes of contemporary alienation, for example, an individual living (and suffering from) a slave moral ideology of personalism might also be locked into a low wave of faith development (UL), growth frozen by the pervasive cultural pre-understanding of faith (LL) that confounds a fundamentalist level of faith capacity with the entire line of development, a modern pathology that IT calls the line/level fallacy (Wilber, 2006) – these various factors (moral personalism, pre-rational faith development, line/level fallacy as background *Vorurteil*) constellating an existential field of real suffering and constraining ills. (2) IT can enhance itself by taking to heart the view of a depth-stratified ontology of the real, relaxing any tendencies towards anthropism; while addressing and

correcting two theory-practice contradictions: (i) the over-weighting of the UL quadrant with regard to an individual holon and (ii) the balancing out and integrating of individual holonic and social holonic analytics proper to the perspectival Flesh of the world. (3) One tactic of seeding co-creative metatheoretical emergence is to combine aspects of the diagrammatic schemes from each metatheory, birthing new integrative configurations which are to include clear indications of perspective switches and perspectival chains.

It is my surmise that at this still quite early stage of discussion, the holding open of these various regulative trajectories within the dialogic field yields the best possible theory–practice outcomes in service to the emancipation of each and all.

References

Almaas, A. H. (2004). *Inner journey home: The soul's realization of the unity of reality*. Boston, MA: Shambhala.

Aurobindo, S. (2006). *The life divine* (7th ed.). Pondicherry: Sri Aurobindo Ashram.

Bhaskar, R. (1993). *Dialectic: The pulse of freedom*. New York: Routledge.

Bhaskar, R. (1994). *Plato etc.: The problems of philosophy and their resolution*. London and New York: Verso.

Bhaskar, R. (2008). *A realist theory of science* (3rd ed.) London and New York: Verso.

Bhaskar, R. (2012a). Considerations on "Ken Wilber on critical realism". *Journal of Integral Theory and Practice*, 7(4), 39–42.

Bhaskar, R. (2012b). *The philosophy of metaReality* (3rd ed.). London and New York: Routledge.

Debord, G. (1994). *The society of the spectacle*. New York: Zone Books.

Edwards, M. (2009). *Organizational transformation for sustainability: An integral metatheory*. New York and London: Routledge.

Esbjörn-Hargens, S. (2012). *Tetra-dynamics: quadrants in action*. Sebastopol, CA: MetaIntegral Foundation.

Esbjörn-Hargens, S., and Zimmerman, M. E. (2009). *Integral ecology: Uniting multiple perspectives on the natural world*. Boston, MA and London: Integral Books.

Fuhs, C. (2010). An integral map of perspective-taking. In S. Esbjörn-Hargens (Ed.), *Integral theory in action: Applied, theoretical and constructive perspectives on the AQAL model* (pp. 273–302). Albany, NY: SUNY Press.

Gafni, M. (2012). *Your unique self: The radical path to personal enlightenment*. Tucson, AZ: Integral Publishers.

Habermas, J. (1994). *Postmetaphysical thinking: Philosophical essays*. Cambridge, MA and London: MIT Press.

Harman, G. (2011). *The quadruple object*. Alresford, Hants: Zero Books.

Hedlund, N. H. (2008). Integrally researching the integral researcher: A first-person exploration of psychosophy's holding loving space practice. *Journal of Integral Theory and Practice*, 3(2), 1–57.

Jameson, F. (1979). Reification and utopia in mass culture. *Social Text*, 1, 130–148.

Laske, O. E. (2008). *Measuring hidden dimensions of human systems: Foundations of requisite organization*. Medford, MA: Interdevelopment Institute Press.

Lukács, G. (1971). *History and class consciousness: Studies in Marxist dialectics*. Cambridge, MA: MIT Press.

Marshall, Paul. (2012). Ken Wilber on critical realism. *Journal of Integral Theory and Practice,* 7(4), 35–38.

Mingers, J. (2014). *Systems thinking, critical realism and philosophy: A confluence of ideas.* London and New York: Routledge.

Sallis, J. (2000). *Force of the imagination: The sense of the elemental.* Bloomington and Indianapolis: Indiana University Press.

Sallis, J. (2012). *Logic of the imagination: The expanse of the elemental.* Bloomington and Indianapolis: Indiana University Press.

Schwartz, M. (2011). Beyond the spectacle of postmodern sheen. *Integral life art galleries.* Retrieved November 20, 2013, from http://integrallife.com/art-galleries/virtually-so.

Schwartz, M. (2012). *The call of integral virtues.* What Next Integral Conference. Denver, CO, December 28, 2012–January 1, 2013.

Schwartz, M. (2013). On social holons, ideologies of integral, and the kosmopolitan call of politics: Beyond methodological individualism in integral theory and praxis. *Journal of Integral Theory and Practice,* 8(3–4), 163–164.

Schwartz, M. (2014). Diagrammatic art – and the art of philosophy. *Integral life art galleries.* Retrieved May 25, 2014, from http://integrallife.com/art-galleries/transformative-interface.

Schwartz, M. (in press). Tetra call of the good. In: M. Schwartz and S. Esbjörn-Hargens (Eds.), *Dancing with Sophia: Integral philosophy on the verge.* Albany, NY: SUNY.

Tritten, T. (2012). *Beyond presence: The late F. W. J. Schelling's criticism of metaphysics.* Boston, MA and Berlin: De Gruyter.

Washburn, M. (2003). Transpersonal dialogue: A new direction. *Journal of Transpersonal Psychology,* 35(1), 1–19.

Wilber, Ken (2000). *Sex, ecology, spirituality: The spirit of evolution* (rev. ed.). Boston, MA and London: Shambhala.

Wilber, K. (2004). *The simple feeling of being: Embracing your true nature.* Boston, MA and London: Shambhala.

Wilber, K. (2006). *Integral spirituality: A startling new role for religion in the modern and postmodern world.* Boston, MA: Integral Books.

Wilber, K. (2012a). In defense of integral theory: A response to critical realism. *Journal of Integral Theory and Practice,* 7(4), 43–52.

Wilber, K. (2012b). Critical realism revisited (pp. 1–3): MetaIntegral Foundation. Retrieved August 28, 2015 from https://foundation.metaintegral.org/sites/default/files/Critical%20Realism_Revisited-1.pdf.

Wilber, K., and Fuhs, C. (2010). Core integral. *Essential integral: Lesson two,* electronic interactive course. Retrieved August 28, 2015 from www.coreintegral.com/programs/courses.

7

WHY I'M A CRITICAL REALIST[1]

Mervyn Hartwig

> We two – how long we were fool'd!
> Now transmuted, we swiftly escape, as Nature escapes;
> We are Nature, long have we been absent, but now we return;
> …
> We have circled and circled till we have arrived home again – we two have;
> We have voided all but freedom and all but our own joy.
>
> Walt Whitman, 'We two – how long we were
fool'd' (1860, 1881), Leaves of Grass

At the level of personal history there are of course a thousand and one reasons why I'm a critical realist. You could say that I began taking critical realism in with my mother's care. My mother was a simple country woman with little formal education and terribly oppressed, but she was very much in her ground-state and had a profound implicit understanding of the fundamental importance of love, trust and solidarity for human well-being. Like many critical realists, she understood that love and trust have priority over reciprocity and exchange and that spirituality, as the deep yearning to transcend alienation and realize unity, is pervasive, though hidden, in everyday life in the demi-real. When I was about ten, rounding up the cows early one morning on our tenant farm in southern Queensland, Australia, I came upon a troupe of brolga dancing a courtship ritual in the mist on the banks of the Moocooboola River. Visitors from another world, it seemed to me, which is in this one,[2] these elegant large birds had migrated many times miles and more from their habitat in the north to take advantage of the (then) record floods we were experiencing. I watched in awe, and understood that the world as such is always already enchanted. Such experiences, relived many times over a lifetime, are the practical basis of my spirituality. I took them as intimations of a domain of real creative fecundity far transcending (exceeding) the actual world we inhabit. Later I shed the religious faith I was brought up in, but I have always understood the universe and all beings within it to be interconnected at a fundamental level, as quantum mechanics[3] and metaRealism indicate and many great artists and thinkers divine.

That's about as far as I'll try to follow my story on this occasion, though. Personal world-lines or lifelines or rhythmics[4] are always highly contingent and unique. They criss-cross each other and those of other beings in countless ways, connecting, branching, rupturing, jumping, blocking and switching; and they run their courses on the surface of an inexhaustible sea of potentiality that could have resulted in very different outcomes. The chances of me being me (or you you) are googolplexically improbable. Besides, readers will doubtless be interested less in how I came to be a critical realist than in why I think critical realism articulates the most adequate metatheory we have for understanding and changing the world.[5]

So let me start from where I am, we are – in the sociosphere within the bio-sphere of that 'star among stars',[6] planet Earth – the magnificent mother of us all, as Indigenous people have understood from time immemorial. By 'sociosphere' I mean that emergent level of the physio-bio-sphere, distinct but not discrete, com-prised of humans and their material, social and cultural structures and infrastruc-tures.[7] Right now the sociosphere is in a terrible mess of our own making, and getting worse by the minute. This is attested by a large and rapidly growing number of scientists across a wide array of approaches to understanding the world.[8] Critical realism diagnoses a planetary polycrisis[9] manifesting at all four planes of social being, corresponding to the moments of the self-structuration of being as such: our rela-tions with nature (4D), each other (3L), our social structures (2E) and our selves (who we are and who we think we are) (1M).

The direst of these crises is undoubtedly the first – that of our relations with our natural environment, which I refer to as the (socio-)*ecological crisis*. For the first time in recorded history it is no longer possible for anyone undeluded by the demi-real to die feeling confident that the human species will even survive, let alone thrive, for very long after their departure. The ecological crisis is the expression of a straightforward contradiction: a *finite*, unique and delicately equilibrated planet-ary system, relatively closed as natural systems go, spaceship Earth and its biosphere, coming into conflict with a dominant globalized human mode of production, capitalism, that needs to grow *in-finitely* at an average of about 2.5 per cent per annum just to stay in business – and even so necessarily leaves a massive trail of human destitution and injustice in its wake.[10] It should thus be thought of as a crisis of a (socio)*ecosystem*: capitalism-*in*-nature, not capitalism *and* nature.[11] That is, capitalism-in-nature comprises a *duality* or dialectical unity with real internal distinctions and contradictions and not a (non-illusory) *dualism* or split-off of dis-crete entities.[12] The dualist view is, of course, widespread, but it is an illusion or demi-reality that fools us, as Walt Whitman saw so clearly: nature itself recoils from it and makes its escape when we transform ourselves.[13] The elements of this (partial) totality (within totality) are in significant respects internally related. Thus capitalist crisis (the 'financial' crisis, the great recession, etc.) directly affects our relations with non-human nature by, for example, keeping jobs and growth at the forefront of our consciousness to the occlusion of anthropogenic climate change; and conversely, depletion of resources (soil depletion, peak oil, water shortages, etc.) occasioned by short-sighted focus on growth directly exacerbating capitalist crisis. This makes the ecological crisis particularly explosive, with possibly dire implications for the biosphere as a whole – not just in terms of the ongoing increase in the 'background' rate of extinction of species and the consequent loss of biodiversity, but with the potential to cause another sudden mass extinction event. Think what would happen if the sun went out, for example, as a result of nuclear catastrophe on Earth in the context of escalating wars over resources. Blotted out, it would still be shining, but its life-enabling free energy would no longer reach the planet.

Myrmecologists tell us that ant colonies sometimes develop into supercolonies stretching 6,000 kilometres or so underground. A human supercolony[14] now bestraddles the entire planet, pleonexically battening on it and exploiting its resources in a highly entropic way,[15] not just under and on the ground but on, under and through all the seas and oceans and all the atmosphere and beyond, constrained and enabled by an invisible layered meshwork of cultural and social structures. As Earth-system scientists like to say, something has to give, and it won't be the laws of physics. Or as Goethe put it in 1824, commenting on the disastrous floods in St Petersburg of that year: 'Nature goes her own way, and all that seems to us an exception is really according to order.'[16] This nicely expresses what critical realists call the *ecological asymmetry*.[17] Whereas nature is existentially and in its fundamental modes of operating causally *independent* of humans, as natural beings constituted by and emergent from nature we are utterly *dependent* on it.[18] When they clash, it is the species, not the environment or nature as such, that goes under. 'When nature expresses abhorrence, she does so out loud', Goethe warns, '… the creature that lives falsely is destroyed early.'[19] We clearly have to move on to a post-capitalist way of doing things if the species is to avoid the fate of myriad species in the course of biological evolution that failed to correlate reliably with their environment. Climate-change deniers themselves understand this very well, as they demonstrate every time they try to discredit the ecology movement as 'anti-capitalist' – as though that in itself is an argument. The social status quo needs to be justified every bit as much as departure from it. Critical realism's fundamental message here is that we have to stop behaving as though we are masters (*sic*) of the universe and get back in tune with nature; and that explanatory-critical science can assist importantly in this by showing, for a start, that the notion that you can have infinite economic growth within a finite biosphere is false, and identifying and recommending removal of the sources in the capitalist political economy of this perilous false view.[20] Critical realism thus inverts the slogan, 'There Is No Alternative to capitalism' (TINA) to read 'Capitalism Is No Alternative to a sustainable sociosphere' (CINA).[21]

What is necessary, then, is an *epochal transition* to a new form of social life.[22] Perhaps it has already begun. Epochal transitions involve the transformation, rather than reproduction, of the deep structures of a dominant form of life.[23] They should be distinguished from developmental transitions within a form of life, such as the transitions within capitalism to its various phases. If you look at past epochal transitions, starting with the one that took us from feudalism to capitalism (or, if you prefer, from premodernity to modernity, or pre-industrialized to industrialized society), two things stand out in the present context. First, the *epochal crisis*[24] during the 'long' fourteenth century (*c.* 1300–1450) that presaged the transition to capitalism resembled our own polycrisis in at least several important respects. It was a crisis of a socio-ecosystem, centrally involving soil exhaustion, famine, disease and demographic collapse as well as proliferating peasant revolts and the escalation of warfare. Then again feudalism, like capitalism, was a system of power-over, exploitation and exclusion: a master–slave-type mode of production geared around the extraction of a surplus from the direct producers (the peasantry) by a dominant class (the militarized aristocracy), resulting in neglect of agricultural sustainability – a neglect that capitalism, which is based on the lies that wage-labour is not forced and not exploited, has globalized.[25] Second, the transition to the modern ecosystem involved fundamental transformation across the board in the sociosphere, a thoroughgoing shift in worldview and associated practices: social, cultural, economic and political, scientific, religious and philosophical. You cannot have such a shift without a far-reaching shift in philosophy and social theory along with everything else.[26] This is the main reason why we need integrative metatheories such as critical realism and integral theory aspire to be.[27] For me critical realism is above all the philosophy and social theory of transition to a post-capitalist sociosphere. It grounds philosophically and builds on Marx's understanding of the moral aletheia or objective of the human species as 'the free development of each as a condition for the free development of all', which Marx called communism and critical realists call universal free flourishing or eudaimonia – a dialectically universalized and universalizing version of the Golden Rule, which is coming to be understood as the Platinum Rule.[28] And it sketches an emancipatory dialectic at a high level of engagement showing how explanatory-critical social science and concrete utopianism articulated with social movements might help us get there. That is, critical realism or a philosophy very like it, is a part of what is necessary to move beyond capitalism to a better way of life; to attain eudaimonia it is necessary, as Bhaskar put it in the late 1980s, to 'win the intellectual high ground' for it.[29] But it is only one part of what is necessary: the struggle goes on at every level, each of which is essential.

What *are* the indispensable things that critical realism does in relation to this transition? Two things above all. It demonstrates that the intellectual underpinnings of modernity are false, misleading or inadequate. And it shows that people as such for their part are fundamentally free (1M), creative (2E), loving (3L), right-acting (4D), spiritual (5A), enchanted (6R) and nondual (7A/Z) beings and, although they are everywhere in chains, have the resources and capacities to build a sustainable planetary sociosphere of free flourishing.[30]

The philosophical underpinnings of modernity have been furnished above all by Hume, Kant and Hegel. Critical realism runs fundamental critiques of all three – provisionally definitive world-historical critiques that take on board their positive contributions but demolish key tenets of their problematics. It finishes off positivism,[31] and in my view Kantianism too, as a fount of empirical realism and actualism,[32] and demonstrates contra Hegel that the ideal is not autonomous but embedded in a socio-material context.[33] Against Hume, it demonstrates that natural necessity is real, and that far from being applicable to the social world, empiricism and positivism do not even work for the natural world; and it shows that 'value must exist in the world, whether human beings do or not'[34] and that we can make transitions from facts to values and fallibly establish moral truths. This critique is of vital importance because the Humean outlook has dominated the entire philosophical discourse of modernity from the outset, in the form of a worldview structured around the couple of (1) an atomistic ego (whether a person, group, class, gender, nation or some mix of these) set over against (2) the world described in abstractly universal terms, 'which is the object of the ego's action (manipulation and exploitation)'; and in strong resonance with capitalism's logic of commodification and the reification, alienation and McDonaldization it generates.[35] This couple is at the heart of *irrealism*, understood as a combination of anthroporealism or 'the reduction of being to a superficialized knowledge' and its necessary compensating complement, the transcendent realism of a Disneyfied fantasy world 'as the imaginary reward for real drudgery'.[36] Against Kant, critical realism shows that objective reality is not immanent to experience, as empirical realism has it, rather the world is relatively or absolutely independent of experience – the categories are in the world, not just in our heads, and it is possible to fallibly know something of things-in-themselves.[37] Contra the related 'linguistic turn', while inadequate or false categorizations of the world are real and powerful, we are not prisoners of discourse. Far from alienating us irremediably, the entry into language makes it possible, in the new conditions of self-consciousness and referential detachment, to stay in touch with the world: that's what language is for![38] Against Hegel, critical realism vindicates and justifies philosophically Marx's critique. It shows that Hegel cannot sustain concepts of intransitivity, transfactuality, ontological polyvalence and transformative praxis; that there is far more to the world than concepts and discourse; and that social contradictions have to be resolved in practice, not just in theory.[39]

In arguing that people already have the resources to build eudaimonia, critical realism is fundamentally at odds with approaches such as Lacanianism and the currently fashionable Lacano-Hegelianism of Slavoj Žižek and others. This reproduces a version of the people/nature split in Hegel. The human being's true original nature for Hegel is alienation of themselves as Spirit from natural being. Similarly, in an atheistic version of original sin that bears the unmistakable imprint of capital's Faustian pleonexia, the Žižekian story has it that the 'ground-state' of the subject is inconsistency and self-division, i.e. our fate is endless self-alienation and striving to create consistency and coherence. It is not the case that we are inconsistent and divided because we are thwarted by social constraints, we are thwarted by constraints because we are aboriginally self-divided.[40] Alienation is foundational and irremediable. The entry into language leaves a permanent gash in our being. If we fail in our emancipatory projects, the point is to fail better next time and to split ourselves off even further from nature – the further the better.[41] Critical realism maintains, far more plausibly, that the first act of referential detachment in the dawn of human geo-history carried with it, not alienation as such, but the potential for it, which was later contingently actualized.[42] It argues, moreover, that there are real limits to alienation at all four planes of social being: at 1M the transcendentally real self or ground-state, including freedom of the will;[43] at 2E the transcendental principles of universal solidarity and axial rationality that underpin our social practices; at 3L the transcendental identity consciousness that is an irreducible feature of social interaction with others; and at 4D the fact that we are natural beings and, no matter how much we evolve or transform ourselves, can never get away from that.[44] What links and grounds these limits is a fundamental human need and desire for non-alienation, i.e. unity, union, identity-in-difference.

Rousseau famously noted that people as such are free yet everywhere in chains. This is the antinomy of (essential) freedom and (actual) slavery.[45] As an emancipatory philosophy,[46] critical realism's fundamental drive is to resolve this antinomy, a drive that takes it all the way from basic critical realism to metaRealism. Basic critical realism does I think successfully resolve many of the key antinomies of Western modernity (naturalism/anti-naturalism, structure/agency, individualism/collectivism, body/mind, causes/reasons, facts/values) but full resolution (in theory) of the antinomy of freedom and slavery had to await the metaRealist understanding that the difference prioritized over unity in Western philosophy, including critical realism, presupposes underlying unity or identity-in-difference.[47] There are a number of milestones along the way to this result. First, the basic structure of emancipatory critique and the theories of the TINA formation and the demi-real[48] that it entrains is already given in the argument of transcendental realism for the inexorability of ontology: not only is ontology necessary, but if your ontology is inadequate you will necessarily presuppose in your practice a more or less adequate one.[49] Second, this already presupposes ontological and alethic truth – that truth is fundamentally a real feature of the world. Third, implicit within the notion of alethic truth is a concept of truth or reality as absolute.[50] Fourth, implicit within that in a context of depth-stratification is the notion of an ultimate or metaReal stratum of identity-in-difference, already mooted in *Dialectic* (Bhaskar 1993), ingredient in and sustaining everything else, analogously to the ingredience of fundamental particles in emergent levels of being – the absolute as such, otherwise known in metaRealism as the ground-state and cosmic envelope. Fifth – and this is crucial – the experience of union or identity in the moment of absolute transcendence in any process of learning or discovery can be rendered fully intelligible only on the basis that it involves 'the union between something already enfolded within the discovering agent, brought up to consciousness by a moment of Platonic anamnesis or recall, with the alethic self-revelation of the being known, existing outside him';[51] that is, it involves the union of two beings at the level of the implicit, supramental consciousness of their ground-states, entailing the theory of generalized co-presence or interconnectedness – that at the level of fundamental possibility everything is implicitly contained within everything else. From there it is but a short step to link 'the latent immanent teleology of praxis'[52] (the pulse of freedom of *Dialectic*) to the immanent teleology of the ground-state and cosmic envelope, and to view everything in the universe as enchanted and as 'in the process of becoming one with its ground-state'.[53] And so you arrive at metaReality, a zone of nonduality, unity and identity, a level at which everything is fundamentally interconnected, in virtue of which the world is always already enchanted and the ultimate source of human powers of creativity, love, right action and so on.

This move constitutes an immanent critique of Marx's theory, which 'does successfully capture a deep, perhaps the deepest dual level, in our social structure',[54] but

> one which presupposes, and depends on the efficacy of a deeper, untheorized level, that of the ground-state qualities of unrecognized (non-commodified) creativity and unconditional love and other ground-state qualities that Marx did not theorize, just as his vision of a communist society actually depends on the process of self-realization or enlightenment and its universalization that the individual process ['the free development of each'] both implies and presupposes for its completion.[55]

It is also an immanent critique of critical realism which, although it provides 'the best account of what we have to get rid of',[56] no more than Marx can satisfactorily resolve the paradox or antinomy of the co-presence of realism and irrealism, freedom and slavery, potential plenty and dire scarcity.[57]

> If realism is true ... why is it that irrealism is so dominant? Well irrealism is so dominant because it reflects the irrealist, reified, heteronomous, oppressive structures of the societies in which we exist. Realism can only be conceived to be true if it reflects a deeper, more basic level which most of us have not fully developed or have so overlaid with structures that are irrealist in character that we find it difficult either to see why most people are irrealist, reified or unfree or to believe that realism, freedom, spontaneity, creativity, love, can actually be alethically true.[58]

The antinomy is resolved, then, by the thesis, first articulated in *From East to West* and the seminar presentations leading up to it, and thereafter given a more secular cast, that

> man is essentially godlike, subsisting and acting in a world of relativity and duality. A difference springs up only as a product of illusion. And it is the essential nature of man to come to see through this illusion and to realize their self-consciousness as free and/or godlike.[59]

What Bhaskar is beginning to articulate here is a naturalism that completely recasts the naturalism espoused by the positivistic, and tacitly endorsed by the Kantian tradition.[60] The great aporia of the former is its inability to sustain an account of intentional causality, and the great mirroring aporia of the latter is the unknowability of the self that confers intelligibility on the world.[61] The partial critical realist resolution of both aporias is carried through in metaRealism. Both self and world are knowable and human consciousness and intentional agency are emergent powers of the fundamental structure of possibility of the universe. This immediately entrains a critique of those religious traditions that emphasize God's ontological transcendence at the expense of God's immanence, as well as of the doctrine of original sin or fallenness and of emancipation or salvation as coming from without rather than, necessarily, from within: a transcendent god entails an immanent god, that people have the potential within them to conform to God's will.[62]

How did essentially free beings come to be enslaved? Basically we forgot who we are – creatures who emerged from nature and so are part of its overall unity and creativity.[63] So we became alienated or split off from nature, each other, our social structures and our real selves. Initially only some of us forgot, those who became the oppressors or alienators and imposed their will on the rest of us. For tens of thousands of years we had had social mechanisms in place that successfully guarded against the alienator,[64] but these contingently broke down with the emergence of master–slave-type societies and irrealist categorial structures. Insofar as they act falsely in regard to what people essentially are, master-classes necessarily develop irrealist categories that occlude alethic truth. However, alethic truth (natural necessity insofar as it has been encountered by humanity) is inexorable and cannot be wholly disregarded in practice. So you get endemic theory–practice contradiction: denial in theory by the false of the truth on which it depends, acknowledgement of it in practice. This is the fundamental basis of ideology or what critical realism calls TINA compromise formations and demi-reality: we keep patching[65] our theories to try to hide the contradictions and end up prisoners of a vast meshwork of false or inadequate (irrealist) theories and social practices of our own making that act as constraints on our capacities for free flourishing. Hence our polycrisis is among other things a profound crisis of rationality.[66]

What we above all have to do to effect a transition to sustainable free flourishing is to shed demi-reality and consistently act in and from our ground-states. The greatest resource we have for building eudaimonia is people and their fundamental capacities. Human agency is relatively autonomous of social structures; it is not the case that we are through and through constituted and determined by social structures and/or discourse.[67] True, the transformational model of social activity suggests that in explanations of geo-historical events the social context will as a rule be primary. But creativity comes from agents, from people, from 'below', and in a major crisis the context cracks, the flaws in the old way of doing things become more evident and it starts to lose its hold. A powerful case can be made in anthropology, not just philosophy, that the most basic mode of human being is, not exchange, reciprocity and recognition, as the liberal metanarrative has it, but trust, care, love and solidarity, and that there is a real striving and yearning for freedom deep down in all humans (the pulse of freedom).[68] Critical realist and other scholarly depth-strugglers can assist with explanatory critiques that tell us what needs to be changed and why, exercises in concrete utopias, theories of transition and dialectics of freedom and solidarity organically linked with social movements.

We are Nature, long have we been absent, but now we return.

Notes

1　This chapter started out as a talk to Roy Bhaskar's postgraduate seminar at the International Centre for Critical Realism, Institute of Education, London, October 2013. Roy asked me to make some general introductory remarks about critical realism and I decided that a good way to do this was to try and say why I'm a critical realist. I am grateful to Roy and Nick Hedlund for encouraging me to develop my remarks, and to Sean Esbjörn-Hargens for his thoughtful editing. My comments in these notes on integral theory as propounded by Ken Wilber in particular have been added in an effort to meet Sean's and Nick's request for greater reflexivity; I have confined them to notes to minimize disruption to the flow of the original essay. Where '>' means 'constellationally contains', 'critical realism' refers throughout to metaRealism > dialectical critical realism > original critical realism, except where the context indicates otherwise.

2　'There is another world/But it is in this one'. Paul Éluard, cited in White 1966/1969, epigraph. These lines are White's rendition of part of a sentence that appears in Paul Éluard, *Oeuvres complètes* (Paris: Gallimard, 1968), vol. 1, p. 986: 'Il y a assurément un autre monde, mais il est dans celui-ci' (cited by Wark 2014). A Nobel-prize-winning Australian novelist, White had a profound understanding of nonduality and enchantment. The characters in his novels, though ensnared in the mundacity of the demi-real, from time to time catch glimpses with their 'blind blue eyes' of the other world that is in this one. 'Blind' speaks of the blockism of the demi-real (cf. Hans Despain's chapter in the companion volume to this, *Metatheory for the Anthropocene*), 'blue' of its transcendence. I am indebted to my wife, Rachel Sharp, for teaching me how to read White.

3　This is not to say that quantum mechanics 'proves' or 'grounds' spirituality or to hitch philosophy's star to current physics, just that it indicates that reality is interconnected at the level of underlying fields of potentiality (entanglement, non-locality); Mark Edwards (this volume) makes a similar point under the rubric of science's 'pointing-out' capacities in relation to the nondual. Ken Wilber is in my view untrue to his own integrative insights in holding that no support for integral spirituality can be drawn from quantum physics. This view, which conforms to the modern dogma of NOMA (the notion that science and religion have non-overlapping jurisdictions or magisteria), endorsed by mainstream science and theology alike (see e.g. Shkliarevsky 2011), ultimately derives from the Kantian and Hegelian dualism of phenomena and noumena, nature and spirit, critiqued by critical realism as premised on an untenable Humean ontology of empirical realism in regard to the natural world and enshrined in fundamental Wilberian concepts such as cosmic evolution and geo-history as the evolution of Spirit; the four quadrants and eight zones (interior/ exterior, depth/surface, interpretation/observation); and the Kosmos as comprised of separate domains of sensibilia, intelligibilia and transcendelia uniquely knowable by empirical, rational and transcendental inquiry (contemplation, meditation, intuition), respectively. In classic hermeneutical fashion (cf. e.g. Habermas, a key philosophical mentor), the whole of the right-hand (RH) half of the four quadrants and of the 'exteriors' of the eight zones is ceded to positivistically conceived science by Wilber – a move that pre-empts the possibility of a non-positivist naturalism or unification of the social and natural sciences. Wilber, for whom causality entails 'strict determinism' (Wilber 2013) and who prides himself on including all major forms of knowledge acquisition, lacks a realist theory of science (natural or social) and a depth-stratified ontology of things possessing transfactually efficacious causal powers in virtue of their intrinsic structure – ontology is subsumed within epistemology, and structures are viewed as collectivities (groups) of individual agents plus their interactions ('stable patterns of events', Wilber 2000, 13) rather than, as in critical realism, the intrinsic (interior!) qualities of anything in virtue of which it possesses causal powers. The dualism of subject (LH) and object (RH) along the vertical axis of AQAL is thus mirrored in the split between individual (Upper) and collective (Lower) along its horizontal axis – missing here is any notion of social, including epistemological, activity as the reproduction and/or transformation of structures. (The profound social atomism of the integral tradition is epitomized in Sean Esbjörn-Hargens' alignment of the epistemological process with 'the Who?' – the individual subject with a 'perspective'.) The notion that the deployment of AQAL in research ensures that 'no major part of any solution is left out or neglected' (Esbjörn-Hargens 2010, 35) is thus deeply problematic. It is important to note that the LH/RH distinction does not align with the distinction between the transitive and intransitive dimensions in critical realism, because for critical realism all LH ('subjective' and 'intersubjective') as well as RH ('objective' and 'interobjective') realities have an existentially intransitive dimension. For critical realism, philosophy and science investigate the same world, which is either absolutely or relatively intransitive to their activities, and because 'what is synthetic *a priori* is also (contingently) knowable a posteriori' (Bhaskar 1979/2015, 6), the findings of philosophy must in the long run be consistent with those of science; for Wilber, physics has no jurisdiction in the domain of Spirit except qua 'petrified' – it deals with only one of six levels of being, a level that is the least significant and ultimately illusory. There is thus a fundamental split in Wilber between theology and philosophy, on the one hand, and science on the other, and their respective objects – a split that is of course disavowed by Wilber but only at the heavy cost of correlationism (see note 37, below) and 'full-spectrum empiricism' (see note 47, below, and Wilber 1983/2011, 'Preface to the third edition, revised [2000]' and ch. 2), underpinned by an actualist meta-ontology of the cosmos 'tetra-arising' as the evolution of Spirit (note 5, below). On the quantum issue, see e.g. Wilber with Niehaus, 1984/2001 and Wilber, 2006, Appendix III. Actually, Wilber is not consistent on this issue, as on many others, for his own synthetic method presupposes the 'valid and tested' results of the sciences (as well as of philosophy and 'the wisdom tradition') and he himself is sometimes not averse to citing quantum mechanics in support of his con-fusion of epistemology and ontology, consciousness and being (Wilber 2013).

4   Rose 1997. For the concepts of world-line and rhythmic see Bhaskar 1993/2009 and Hartwig 2007c, 2007d.

5   This is in no way to imply that critical realism cannot learn from dialogue with other philosophies and metatheories, only that I think it articulates the most adequate metatheory currently available for understanding the relative world we inhabit. Clearly, it can become more adequate and will in due course be superseded: the claim is geo-historically relative, not uniquist or absolutist; unlike integral theory, critical realism makes no claim to provide a 'neutral framework' (Wilber 2006, 31). The work of systematically appraising the relative strengths and weaknesses of critical realism and integral theory is being pursued apace in a number of quarters, including this book and its successor volume and the pages of *Journal of Critical Realism*. Although I do not think integral theory 'a poisoned chalice', I find myself in agreement with the substance of Timothy Rutzou's (2012, 2014) fundamental philosophical critique of it. Wilber's bold project, very much against the grain of the zeitgeist at first, to articulate a spirituality for our times (which however excludes atheists and agnostics) and an integrative metatheory is I think important, indeed urgent, but there are fundamental problems with the way he goes about this, as I hope these notes will indicate. The key source of critical realism's relative strength in my view is its principled method of philosophical argument, transcendental critique (transcendental argumentation plus immanent critique of rival theories); see Hartwig 2015b and the works by Bhaskar referenced therein on this topic. This imparts to Bhaskar's work a developmental consistency lacking in that of Wilber, whose synthetic method, which amounts to little more than 'traditional scholarship methods of essentially reading a broad, but idiosyncratic, selection of writings and research and then making of it what they will according

to their own assumptions and predilections' (Edwards 2013, 183), functions to paper over contradictions, absences and differences by taking 'largely agreed upon orienting generalizations from the various branches of knowledge (from physics to biology to psychology to theology) and … *string[ing] these orienting generalizations together*' to 'arrive at … a broad orienting map of the place of men and women in the Universe, Life and Spirit' (Wilber 1995/2000, 5, my emphasis). However, in my view the work of comparative appraisal is not comparing like with like, though for the most part it is conducted as if it is (e.g. by Sean Esbjörn-Hargens and Paul Marshall in this volume). Critical realism is most fundamentally a *post-postmetaphysical philosophy* or metaphysics that proceeds by transcendental critique, a metaphysics that aspires to 'sustain … the development of a general metatheory for the social sciences' (and indeed science more generally) (Bhaskar 1993/2008, 2). Integral theory, by contrast, purports to be a *postmetaphysical metatheory*, not a metaphysics, based on the method of synthesizing the 'best' results of the various sciences, social theories and philosophies (cf. Edwards 2013, 180–1; Stein this volume). As a metaphysics, critical realism thus proceeds at a more abstract level than integral theory (insofar as the latter really is postmetaphysical), is not in competition with it and indeed can underlabour for it and other metatheories (and within that social theories), including those articulated under its own auspices. That said, Wilber's 'postmetaphysical' correlationism, which conflates epistemology and ontology (see note 37, below), is in reality expressly premised on an (actualist) Hegelian-Whiteheadian meta-ontology or *metaphysics* of the cosmos as the evolution of Spirit from a groundless Ground or Emptiness (nonduality) in which subject and object are ultimately identical (cf. Rutzou 2012, 2014) – a dimension that Edwards (2013) ignores in locating integral theory exclusively within a tradition of *scientific* big-picture building. The combination of correlationism and this ontological process of Spirit's inexorably ascending drive to self-realize – to negate and preserve, transcend (Eros) and include (Agape) – may aptly be designated a (foundationalist, cf. Schwartz this volume) *onto-theology* or sequence of ontotheologies in the Heideggerian and Derridean sense (see e.g. Thomson 2000 and 2011, ch. 1; Skempton 2010). There is little in common, it should moreover be noted, between integral theory's synthetic method and transcendental realist argumentation (a species of the retroductive-analogical procedure that is central to science). In contrast to critical realism's 'naturalized transcendentalism' (McWherter 2015), Wilber (1995/2000, 824 n. 228) identifies the transcendental with what is transcendent to the cosmos and transcendental inquiry with meditation and direct intuition/experience. Were Hans Despain's (2013) question to Rutzou as to why he favours engagement with integral theory, in spite of his fundamental critique of it, addressed to myself, my main response would be that metatheories and metaphysics *matter* and critique is the lifeblood of both.

6   Paul Klee, cited in Moholy-Nagy 1970, 6–11, 9; the phrase is borrowed from J. G. Herder's *Ideas on a Philosophy of the History of Mankind*, 1784–91. Like Bhaskar and (in a different way) Wilber, Klee encouraged his students to approach their work anthropocosmically – from the perspective of the cosmos – and to interpret the visual as tokens of fundamental structural order as well as of flux and becoming.

7   Alternative concepts to sociosphere currently in use include anthrosphere, technosphere and noosphere. However, the first two seem to downplay (non-material) culture and social structure, and the focus of the latter, favoured by Wilber, is too exclusively on human consciousness, more generally culture. An unfortunate consequence of this orientation in Wilber, reflecting ontological idealism and actualistic acceptance of Hegel's bias towards linear negation (see Bhaskar 1993/2008, 5–8, 24–8), is the inversion of the real relation between the noosphere and the biosphere (and between the biosphere and the physiosphere) and an account of the world of Form (relative reality in metaRealism) as composed of the evolution of neatly nested hierarchies or stages of unfolding of Spirit (the Great Holarchy or Chain or Nest of Being) that is at odds with its demonstrable unevenness and complexity. See e.g. Wilber 1995/2000, ch. 3 ('the biosphere is a part of the noosphere, and not vice versa' (p. 97)); *pace* Mark Edwards (this volume), Bhaskar's

account of the relationship between demi-reality, relative reality and absolute reality does not involve 'a nested holarchical relationship' in the Wilberian sense. In the counterpart of Hegel's monovalent reinstatement of positivity, negativity is undone in Wilber in an account of the world of Form as becoming 'Fuller and Fuller and Fuller' or more plenitudinous as it 'tetra-arises', culminating for humans in the Integral Age (Wilber 2006, 236f.). There are of course many passages in Wilber that in effect acknowledge that negation is by no means always radically preservative or linear – e.g. 'half' of the findings of the modern systems sciences are discarded by his own metanarrative (1995/2000, 41) – but these can only serve to reveal his radical inconsistency and to unravel the Great (linear) Holarchy itself ('There is nothing that isn't a holon (upwardly and downwardly forever))' (1995/2000, 41), i.e. *nothing* that is not a *whole* that is simultaneously part of other wholes. This unravelling is hardly surprising given that Wilber's Great Chain of Being merely superimposes an evolutionary story of increasing cosmic self-understanding onto the traditional metaphysical conception.

8   See e.g. Hilary 2013; Potter 2010; Foster 2013; and Kunkel 2014.

9   As we suggest in the Introduction to this volume, an even more adequate term than 'polycrisis' might be 'metacrisis'. Bhaskar's equally appropriate term for this is 'crisis system' (Bhaskar 2016, forthcoming).

10   Of course, if capitalism does not exist as a real social kind but is just a convenient fiction on the part of investigators, as social theorists commonly suggest (e.g. Little 2010), or if social structures are merely collectivities (groups) of people, as in integral theory, there would seem to be less to be concerned about. For an argument that social structures, understood as internally related social practices such as those between capitalists and wage-earners, are real and causally efficacious on whatever scale and geo-historical range empirically based research reveals, see Hartwig 2015b.

11   It would be more accurate, but too cumbersome, to say 'the capitalism-dominated sociosphere-in-nature'. For the concept of 'capitalism-in-nature' see Moore 2011, who however collapses nature to its 'production' in capitalism, i.e. the processes and practices whereby humans come to know nature, thereby committing the epistemic fallacy.

12   For the difference between 'dualism' and 'duality' see e.g. Hartwig 2007a.

13   A demi-reality is illusory but real in terms of its causal efficacy, which like that of a mirage in the desert is dependent on the truth it occludes – a real illusion. See Bhaskar 2000, 3–4, 24, 32–8. Its fundamental cause is human error and forgetting, which is a prominent theme also in Wilber.

14   Cf. Nadeau 2013, 26. Nadeau likens the human supercolony to a superorganism.

15   See especially Geogescu-Roegen 1971/1999 and Biel 2011.

16   Goethe 1998, 75 (December 9, 1824).

17   Already in the late 1970s Bhaskar warned that what is now at stake is not just civilized survival, but 'survival, non-extinction' as such, given that humanity is in the grip of 'the infantile fantasy' that, contrary to what the ecological asymmetry shows, the world was made for us to manipulate and control rather than that we were made for it; 'we survive as a species only insofar as second nature respects the overriding constraints imposed upon it by first nature'. The effective deployment of explanatory critical science comprises 'perhaps the only chance' of survival for the human species. Bhaskar 1986/2009, 221–2. Although published in 1986, *Scientific Realism* was written for the most part in the late 1970s and completed in 1983. For the concept of the ecological asymmetry see *ibid.*, 139–41. Cf. Wilber 1995/2000, ch. 1; however, Wilber lacks a concept of social science as explanatory critique.

18   Bhaskar 2012, 11.

19   Goethe 1794–5/2011, 446.

20   See e.g. Næss 2006. Explanatory critique presupposes that, contrary to 'Hume's law', a logical transition from facts to values, theory to practice, is possible. Bhaskar's arguments for this have been sharply criticized within critical realism, but in my view carry the day; see e.g. Hartwig 2015b. For a powerful and more detailed elaboration and defence of explanatory critique see Craig Reeves, forthcoming. Note that when the conditions

of possibility of human life as such are threatened, natural scientists, unlike many philosophers and social theorists, see no problem in transiting from facts to values; see the science of global warming.

21 Despain 2013 and his chapter in our companion volume, *Metatheory for the Anthropocene*.

22 Cf. Gallopin and Raskin 2002.

23 The criterion for significant geo-historical events I am using here is generated by critical realism's transformational model of social activity (TMSA).

24 Moore 2011; Foster 2013.

25 Moore 2002.

26 This point is of course emphasized also in integral theory.

27 For Wilber (see 1995/2000, 12f., and *passim*), the ecological crisis is largely the outcome of the 'fractured worldview' of modernity and its remedy accordingly is the worldview proffered by integral theory. From a critical realist perspective this emphasis on consciousness, while important, downplays the role of human material transactions with nature and of social structure understood not as collectivities (as in integral theory), but as spatio-temporally distanciated ensembles of interrelated but asymmetrically weighted social practices.

28 Interpreted not as an abstract universal, but as 'presupposing dialectical universality and concrete singularity': do unto others, not as you would do unto yourself, but as you would do unto them if you were they, not you. Bhaskar 2002b/2012, 344–5. I am grateful to Stephen Shashoua of the Three Faiths Forum, London, for calling my attention to the fact that this rule is known in interfaith and other circles as the Platinum Rule.

29 Bhaskar 1989/2011, 1.

30 People also have capacities to do great evil, of course, but critical realism argues that these are secondary to and dependent on their ground-state capacities, and moreover systematically promoted by capitalist modernity with its supreme values of money and power-over, having and controlling. Integral theory also emphasizes the richness of human potentials and possibilities, but lacks a thoroughgoing critique of irrealism (of which it is itself a form) and the demi-real and an adequate theory of master–slavery ('dominator hierarchies', according to Wilber's metanarrative, came to an end in modernity!). As Hans Despain has noted (2013, 512 and his chapter in our companion volume *Metatheory for the Anthropocene*), Wilber's theory of the Atman project, or rather of what blocks it, does have significant affinities with the theory of the demi-real. Mark Edwards' (2013 and this volume) 'integral meta-studies' acknowledges the demi-real.

31 Vandenberghe 2014, 4.

32 Cf. Ferraris 2004/2013.

33 Cf. Bhaskar 1979/2015, 72.

34 Bhaskar 2012, 14.

35 See especially Bhaskar 2002c/2012, chs 1 and 3 (p. 168 for the quotation) and Hartwig 2011. Nicholas Hedlund (this volume) picks up on this point.

36 Bhaskar 2012, 18–19.

37 See especially McWherter 2013. The anthropic conflation of ontology and epistemology (a form of the epistemic fallacy), though pervasive in the discourse of Western post/modernity, is nowhere more thoroughly manifest than in the work of Wilber, for whom 'both what ex-ists and what sub-sists [in the Kosmos] are con-structions of consciousness' (Wilber 2006, 251n.), and many times over at that. For '*consciousness … goes all the way down*', i.e. consciousness that is 'proto' to, or an early form of, the consciousness of humans, so that even atoms have an epistemology and know each other, co-creating or 'enacting' their world (Wilber 2013, original emphasis) – a very different conception from the non-anthropic implicit consciousness that pervades the cosmos according to metaRealism. This co-creation is then repeated indefinitely in the great unfolding of being-consciousness as the world of atoms is transcended and included in a higher, genuinely different epistemic-ontic Whole co-produced or enacted by consciousness at that level. Moreover, it is *doubled* whenever human epistemology enacts a level of being-consciousness, so that the world of atoms (in our

example) is enacted first by atoms themselves (at which stage it sub-sists) and then by humans (whereupon it ex-ists). This com-prehensive con-fusion finds its pithiest expression in Wilber's statement that 'the world of Form is AQAL' (2006, 288n.). It is usefully critiqued by speculative realism as 'correlationism': the view that the real exists solely in and through the co-constitutive activity of subjectivity. See e.g. Assiter 2013. One consequence of Wilber's correlationism is that, *pace* Paul Marshall (2012, 191f.; cf. Esbjörn-Hargens this volume), there is no 'general correspondence' between the four quadrants and Bhaskar's four-planar social being, more generally the MELD schema – for Wilber quadrants are not only dimensions of being-becoming, as 1M–4D are in MELD, whose moments correspond to the concrete universal, but '*first and foremost* perspectives' of a subject – 'all things are perspectives before they are anything else' (Wilber 2006, 252–3, my emphasis). The first moment of the concrete universal (corresponding to 1M), universality understood as natural necessity or the intrinsic natures of things in virtue of which they possess causal powers, is completely absented in Wilber in many formulations, along with intransitivity (which Wilber conflates with critical realism's domain of the real), as in postmodernism more generally: '[*t*]here … *is no such thing as "the dog"* … to which our conceptions give varying representations, but rather *different dogs* that come into being or are enacted with our evolving concepts and consciousness' (260, original emphasis). For critical realism, while the universal is indeed only ever instantiated in historically specific concrete singulars, it is a real dimension or category of being; a dog is *inter alia* an instance of a natural kind in virtue of its genetic constitution. But here again Wilber is arguably not consistent, for on his own showing Spirit is universal to all beings and is correlated with 'depth' and 'interiors', so he should at least accept with Alain Badiou that the Idea of the dog (the Idea of the horse in Badiou's example) is universal (Badiou 2006/2009, 16–20), for while 'the dog' does not indeed exist (except in discourse), in Wilber's world, Spirit in its doggy Form must. Sean Esbjörn-Hargens' ingenious attempt (this volume) to map integral theory's correlationism onto a critical realist depth-ontology, although attempting a step in the right direction, does not in my view succeed for the simple reason that they are fundamentally incompatible. When our theories change (transitive dimension) the fundamental laws of nature (intransitive dimension) do not change with them. Although we might understand, say, gravity, better and how to counteract it in particular contexts, it continues to operate as before. It cannot be enacted, co-produced or 'brought forth' by humans. It is existentially and causally *absolutely* intransitive in relation to human activity. It is true – and this is fully acknowledged in critical realism – that in the sociosphere (and to a lesser extent the biosphere) there is causal interdependence. People reproduce and/or change their social contexts. But many social phenomena exhibit a *relative* intransitivity that the (voluntarist) mantra of enactment fails to acknowledge. Is it really the case that every time we go to a shop its entire physio-bio-sociospherical context and supply-system 'co-arise', i.e. are 'co-nascent – literally', with our intentional act (Esbjörn-Hargens 2010, 37, 39)? Think of the difficulty of reversing the effects of anthropogenic global warming, e.g. the thawing tundra (which would persist for some time, despite our best efforts, in accordance with laws of nature that we are helpless to change), or of fundamentally changing the structure of the capitalist system. Of course, if a social structure is understood as a group or collective of individuals rather than as a spatio-temporalized stretch-spread of interrelated positioned-practices asymmetrically related in terms of power$_2$, the task will seem much easier! Wilber's 'full-spectrum empiricism' (see note 47, below) remains intact in the 'complex integral realism' of Esbjörn-Hargens, whose next step in the right direction would be to revise correlationism and take intransitivity fully on board, entailing the abandonment of mix-and-match synthesis as a cardinal method – a method that he mistakenly attributes to critical realism and that is wholly unfit for his grand purpose of (more or less) preservatively sublating existing metatheories in a meta-metatheory. It is not at all clear that the method recommended for the same purpose by Mark Edwards (2010, 2013), a key influence on Esbjörn-Hargens, is not a continuation at a more abstract level of the very synthetic method that he (Edwards) so tellingly criticizes in Wilber; Edwards wants to do 'big picture science', but neglects the heavy reliance of science on transcendental procedure. Zachary Stein's reconstructive metanarrative approach (this volume), which could explicitly be combined with transcendental critique, offers I think a more promising way forward, providing a way of articulating important commonalities while respecting key differences; as does Nicholas Hedlund's canvassing of the possibility of transcendental critique leading eventually to the sublation of existing metatheories in a higher order conceptual formation. Bhaskar's own philosophical ontology may be thought of as a 'rational reconstruction' of the discourse of science, including social science, articulating the formal conditions of possibility of its practice (Bhaskar 1975/2009, 176).

38 I owe this way of putting the matter to Roy Bhaskar (personal communication).

39 See Bhaskar 1993/2009; Hartwig 2007b; Norrie 2010.

40 Roberts 2013, 88. There is a similar tale of primordial self-division in the work of Wilber, who argues that the human neonate, being unconscious of its union with Ground, is already in 'the pits of alienation … unconscious Hell', from which it proceeds to the 'conscious Hell' of 'the Fall into self-consciousness'. Wilber 1980/1996, 7 (Foreword to the second edition), 17. In *Up from Eden*, ch. 17, 'Original sin', Wilber (1981/1983), in accordance with a certain reading of Hegel, splits alienation itself into 'theological' and 'scientific' alienation: the former is contemporaneous with Creation, marking the beginning of the illusory separation of all beings from God (Nature as self-alienated Spirit in Hegel); the latter is completed in the second millennium BCE, when 'evolution produced the first fully self-conscious beings [*sic*]' (312) (in Wilber's Hegel, Spirit awakening in humans as the Unhappy Consciousness of self-consciousness). However, unlike Žižek, Badiou and others, Wilber remains true to the Hegelian notion that these splits can be healed. While nature is 'asleep in sin' (self-alienated or involuted Spirit), evolution is a story of climbing back to union with Spirit. Adrian Johnston's 'transcendental materialism', which likewise posits a primal split between mind and matter, acknowledges a Hegelian-Marxian pedigree but parts company with that tradition on the issue of whether it can be overcome. Johnston 2014, esp. 180. Derrida also proclaims an originary insurmountable or 'inalienable alienation', but deconstruction in its Heideggerian and Derridean form can be read as 'itself a development of the critique of reification and alienation. The target of deconstruction, the ontotheological metaphysics of presence, is itself the alienated condition of givenness and positivity. The unalienated condition, in its generative determinability, is itself *différance*, *différance* freed from the presence that is its own effacement' (Skempton 2010, 198).

41 'New Age bullshitters are telling us we have lost contact with nature. I say: no we haven't lost *enough* contact with nature…. [W]e should not only denaturalize nature but ourselves' (Slavoj Žižek, cited in Jeffries 2011, original emphasis).

42 Alienation is thus a geo-historically relative concept. Most fundamentally estrangement from our essential selves (absence of totality), the split is not between a fixed inner real self and one's actual self, but between what one has become (essentially is and is tending to become) and what one socially is obliged to be or thwarted from becoming. Its possibility is situated by the TMSA, in which people and society are understood as, though interdependent, 'radically different kinds of thing' (Bhaskar 1979/2015, 33).

43 Critical realism understands freedom of the will, with Rousseau, as part of what a human being essentially is. To eliminate it you would have to eliminate human being. On Rousseau, see MacLean 2013.

44 Contrary to what a literal reading of the title of Stein's 'Beyond nature and humanity' (this volume) suggests. See Bhaskar 2012, 22–3.

45 Cf. Bhaskar 2002a/2012, 128f., 156, 171f.

46 Note that emphasis on emancipation does not mean that we necessarily preface our search for truth with our politics; on the contrary, as the theory of explanatory critique shows (note 20, above), our politics can flow from the search for truth.

47 Though five years younger, Wilber arrived at this insight more than a decade earlier than Bhaskar. See his 1979/2001. However, Wilber makes the mistake throughout his oeuvre of arguing for nonduality from its experience alone, a strategy that can cut no ice with those who have not had the relevant experience (whom Wilber merely dismisses as not 'qualified to make the judgement' (2006, 268)). In *Eye to Eye* Wilber (1983/2011; cf. Wilber 2000, 8) explicitly views this as an extension of empiricism into the higher realms of Spirit, which he dubs 'full-spectrum empiricism' (xxiii–xxiv); it is thus by no means wholly correct to say with Marshall (2012, 192) that integral theory has been engaged in 'exhuming' (i.e. ex-Hume-ing) the interior of the subject from the outset. In this Wilber is faithful to Hegel's case for God, which depends upon identification with the divine of human experience of the possibility of freedom as rational self-determination; for a useful account see Wallace 2014. Bhaskar's justification for metaRealism includes experiential (phenomenological and practical) components, but only as ancillary to complex transcendental realist argumentation that nonduality is a necessary condition of human social life – a strategy that is unavailable to Wilber while ever he disavows all forms of metaphysics in favour of 'postmetaphysics' and postmodernism, viewed as Spirit's latest stage of AQAL manifestation ('Spirit's postmodern turn') or the latest 'kosmic habit' (i.e. ontotheology). Instead of accusing Bhaskar of 'cheating' by 'adding' a spiritual dimension to his system, Wilber (2013) would be better advised to engage with the arguments for metaReality. At their broadest, postmetaphysics for Wilber is integral theory, and metaphysics is any non-integral-theoretic view, i.e. any view that does not or cannot specify for its referents a kosmic address or AQAL location together with the injunctions necessary to enact them (which can be looked up in the integral 'GigaGlossaries' that can be read off from the parameters of AQAL); if it cannot do so, its claims are mere 'assertions without evidence', hence meaningless 'metaphysical gibberish'; if it can, the referents are real, and problems of proof – e.g. of God's existence – simply don't arise. Integral 'mega-phenomenology' is thus a '*mega-positivism*' in this one specific sense, Wilber notes with approval, for when positivists 'concluded that "the meaning of a statement is the means of its verification" they were at least hitting on the fact that part of any reality is the means of its enactment' (Wilber 2006, 257–8, 267–9, 273, my emphasis). As Wilber here acknowledges and Bhaskar has pointed out, Wilber's 'theory of enactment is an isomorph of the verificationist principle [of logical positivism]' (cited by Marshall this volume; cf. Hedlund this volume). It is unsurprising, therefore, that Wilber's account of the relation between the advance of reason and the retreat of mythology ('ideology') exactly mirrors that of the positivist tradition (Wilber 1995/2000, 456–7 and *passim*). In Bhaskar 1993/2009 Hegel is critiqued as 'the supreme "*logical positivist*", *avant la lettre*' (90–1, original emphasis), in four main respects, all of which in my view find their counterpart in Wilber: dialectic as a logical process of reason (Wilber's transcend and include or Spirit-in-action); ontological monovalence (Wilber's view of relative reality as increasingly plenitudinous and positive); Hegel's presupposing the findings of the science of his day (or those he agrees with) (Wilber's synthetic method) and tacit endorsement of empiricism (Wilber's explicit full-spectrum empiricism); and Hegel's endism or 'eternalization of the status quo' (Wilber's triumphalist liberal worldview and attempt to accommodate integral theory to postmetaphysics and post/modernity in pretty well every respect).

48 The fundamental structure of a TINA compromise formation, a concatenation of which constitutes the demi-real or web of *maya* (illusion), is identical with the structure apprehended, tacitly or otherwise, in emancipatory thought: 'the suppression by the false of the truth on which it depends and which sustains it' (Bhaskar 2002a/2012, 219).

49 Bhaskar 2002a/2012, 172, 217.

50 Bhaskar 2002a/2012, 187. Cf.: '[O]ne's account of the real grounds or reasons for something is fallible, but the grounds themselves are not.... Ontological "infallibilism" is necessary for epistemic fallibilism.' Bhaskar with Hartwig 2010, 131–2.

51   Bhaskar 2002a/2012, xii. This does *not* mean, Bhaskar subsequently explains (*ibid.*, 244), that knowledge is, as for Plato, 'basically recollection'; rather that the potential to see it, which is always already enfolded within us, is awakened.

52   Bhaskar 1994/2010, 154.

53   Bhaskar 2002a/2012, 277.

54   Bhaskar 2002c/2012, 356.

55   Bhaskar 2002c/2012, 356, n. 10. On Enrique Dussel's persuasive reading, Marx does actually theorize the non-commodified creativity of 'living labour', which by contrast to labour-power stands outside capital as 'not-capital' and is the ultimate source of value, though of course he cannot ground this at the level of the absolute. See Dussel 1988/2001 and Arthur 2002.

56   Bhaskar, Bhaskar 2002a/2012, 266.

57   Bhaskar 2002a/2012, 128f, 156, 171f.

58   Bhaskar 2002a/2012, 171.

59   Bhaskar 2002a/2012, 129. Cf. the great realist scientist, Albert Einstein (1954): 'A human being is part of a whole, called by us the universe, a part limited in time and space. He experiences himself, his thoughts and feelings, as something separated from the rest, a kind of optical delusion of his consciousness. This delusion is a kind of prison for us, restricting us to our personal desires and to affection for a few persons nearest us. Our task must be to free ourselves from this prison by widening our circles of compassion to embrace all living creatures and the whole of nature in its beauty. The true value of a human being is determined by the measure and the sense in which they have obtained liberation from the self. We shall require a substantially new manner of thinking if humanity is to survive.' The self here is of course, in Bhaskarian terms, the atomistic egocentric self, not the transcendentally real self. There are a number of slightly varying versions of this quotation, dating from 1954, in circulation. It puts metaRealism in a nutshell *avant la lettre*. It is cited in part by Wilber 1981/1983, 6.

60   Cf.: '[N]ature without humanity contains almost all the categories of the dialectic', with the exception of categorial error (Bhaskar 2002a/2012, 77), and the rational kernel of Hegelian dialectic, involving transcendence and emergence, though not for Bhaskar in a process of linear radical negation, applies 'by slight extension of the argument' to the non-human world (57). The charge of 'anti-naturalism' has been brought against Bhaskar's *The Possibility of Naturalism* (Benton 1981), but in my view Bhaskar rescues naturalism by thoroughly revising our understanding of nature. '[H]ow strange the truth about physical reality must be', writes Galen Strawson, professed Spinozan (a)theist and 'new Humean', 'given that consciousness is itself a wholly physical phenomenon' (Strawson 2011, 26). But of course there is a sense in which it is not so strange, it is natural, and we are natural beings. It is we who are estranged from an adequate understanding of our relation to nature (cf. Dickens 2011). According to metaRealism, the potential for consciousness as we know it is implicitly enfolded in 'physical reality' from the outset – the universe is an implicitly conscious developing material system – but (in contrast to Wilber, in whose work one gets the sense of humans having pre-eminent significance in nature) it is highly contingent that human consciousness has emerged and whence it will evolve.

61   Bhaskar 2002a/2012, 11.

62   Bhaskar 2002a/2012, 358. See also Bhaskar with Hartwig 2011. *Pace* Jolyon Agar, Bhaskar espouses transcendence-within-immanence, not immanence-within-transcendence. See Agar's interesting *Post-Secularism, Realism and Utopia* (2014). For Wilber, by contrast, God (Spirit, hence the human real Self), is completely transcendent (outside and prior to) as well as ('paradoxically') completely immanent to (within) nature. Bhaskar is agnostic as to what lies beyond the cosmos; the cosmic envelope is immanent to the cosmos but transcendent with respect to the ground-states of concretely singular beings. It has another 'side' but this cannot be 'seen' by philosophy and science.

63   Cf. Wilber 1983/2011, 'Preface to the third edition, revised [2000]'. For Bhaskar's view of the real self, see especially his 2002b/2012, ch. 2, 'Who am I?'.

64   For Wilber, by contrast, 'in the relatively "equalitarian" societies of the past (such as early horticultural and some foraging), the "equality" was kept in place, not by legal and moral (or noospheric) determinants, but by luck' (Wilber 1995/2000, 396, original scare quotes). Wilber's account of human societies prior to the rise of master–slave-type society is immensely patronizing and crude, as Neil Hockey suggests in his chapter in our companion volume *Metatheory for the Anthropocene*. They are portrayed as not having differentiated the noosphere (where 'right makes might') from the biosphere (where 'might makes right', hence as dominated by their biology (530–1). This is the view from the capitalist demi-real (cf. Rutzou 2014, esp. 81, n. 19).

65   I am indebted to Iskra Nunez (2014) for her apt gloss on the TINA formation as 'patched': patching merely postpones eventual disintegration as the reality principle (alethic truth) asserts itself. Nunez's work is *inter alia* a useful reminder that the cardinal philosophical mistake on which the interpretivist tradition to which Wilber belongs is premised is uncritical acceptance of Humean empiricism in relation to the natural world. Bhaskar's theory of the demi-real is explored by Mark Edwards in this volume.

66   Bhaskar 2007, 200. The answer to Rainer Maria Rilke's question: 'Who has turned us round like this, so that,/whatever we do, we always have the aspect/of one who leaves?' is thus: 'We have' (Rilke 1912, 1922/ 2001, eighth elegy – '*Wer hat uns also umgedreht, daß wir,/was wir auch tun, in jener Haltung sind/von einem, welcher fortgeht?*'). Cf. current fantasies about migrating to the stars.

67   See especially Archer 2000 and Smith 2010, 2015.

68   Graeber 2011; Hartwig 2015a. In the work of Wilber, by contrast, recognition, respect and reciprocity have priority over trust, solidarity and sharing, and the few exceptional '*individuals*' who have trodden the path to Atman ... were, and are, the great Heroes of mankind' (1981/1983, 68, original emphasis). This elitist and vanguardist ('leading edge of history') orientation is evident throughout Wilber's oeuvre, resonating with a pervasive violence of expression in relation to aspects of worldviews that he doesn't agree with, most recently evident in his comments on critical realism (Wilber 2013). 'Short of that emergence [of Hegelian/Habermasian mutual recognition as the end of history]', writes Wilber, citing Francis Fukuyama in support, 'history is a brutalization of one self or group of selves trying to triumph over, dominate, or subjugate others' (Wilber 1995/2000, 321). This is *inter alia* an anthro-ethno-ego-present-centric (Bhaskar 1993, 91; cf. Hostettler 2013) travesty of our Indigenous past, revealing Wilber's 'honouring' of earlier forms of life as bogus: 'the [foraging] tribal structure has this family or kinship lineage, and different tribes, with different kinship lineages, have very, shall we say, testy relations with each other. You are on the fucking side or you are on the killing side' (Wilber 1996, 46). It is a travesty, moreover, that functions to valorize the plutocracies we inhabit today as 'pluralistic democracies, forged by a passion for tolerance' (Wilber 1995/2000, 391). That Wilber goes on to suggest in characteristic fashion that this end of history is not really the end of history does nothing to diminish the pervasive denigration of past 'stages' of human cultural development, the earlier of which, along with most institutional religion, pertain, as in any nineteenth-century unilinear evolutionary schema, to the 'childhood' of humanity, and the later of which are spearheaded by the West – a view critiqued by critical realism as Eurocentrism, modernization theory and bourgeois triumphalism; as Rutzou has suggested, notwithstanding Wilber's (belated) postmodern turn, in the final analysis the combination of AQAL and a meta-ontology of 'the actualist evolutionary development of self-realizing Spirit ... reinstates modernity against postmodernity' (Rutzou 2012, 222). This metanarrative of cultural evolution is arrived at by a highly eristic transposition of the stages of developmental psychology into the domain of culture. For Wilber, in keeping with full-spectrum empiricism, the pulse of freedom did not even exist prior to the emergence of modern 'pluralistic rationality' (1995/2000, 397), and the atomistic ego that dominates modernity and its philosophical discourse according to critical realism is largely conjured away – retrojected to the 'archaic' or 'egocentric' stage of cultural evolution – in favour of the postconventional worldcentric rational

stage on its irresistible way to Kosmocentric forms of life with Integral selves, and beyond (1996, ch. 5f.). In this triumphalist spiritualized Western liberal worldview less 'developed' levels of being-consciousness, though emanating from the same Ground, are less real and have less value ('intrinsic' as well as 'extrinsic') than more developed ones (1995/2000, 544–5); in 'the great developmental unfolding … to worldcentric and higher', 70 per cent of the world's current population has not yet made it beyond 'the ethnocentric or lower levels of development', which puts them in the same league as 'Nazis' and indicates that they are 'less intelligent' than the intelligent people who dismiss metaphysics (Wilber 2006, 179, 274); and it is a problem of the first order (that 'really drove us nuts') 'how individuals at even some of the lower stages of development … could still have profound religious, spiritual, and meditative state experiences' (Wilber 2006, 91). Thus I cannot agree with Marshall (2012, 204) that the story told by Wilber of 'Spirit-in-action' is fundamentally similar to the thesis of the rational directionality of geo-history (the pulse of freedom) in critical realism and metaRealism. Above all, while Wilber does acknowledge countervailing forces, the upshot at the level of the actual is the inexorable unfolding of the neatly nested Great Holarchy of being-consciousness toward 'the pinnacle of cosmic self-comprehension' (Rutzou 2014, 79) and the idealist inversion of the relations between the noosphere, the biosphere and the physiosphere (the noosphere transcends and *includes* the biosphere and the biosphere the physiosphere). In critical realism, only the general tendency at the level of the real is inexorable, i.e. operates with the force of natural (not logical) necessity – what happens at the level of the actual is messy and highly contingent (including the very existence of humans); and it is a tendency universal to the human species, earthed in human embodied agency as such, a pulse that knows no West nor East nor South nor North, and no red nor orange nor teal nor indigo, etc. either. Of course, as Zachary Stein suggests (this volume), there is nothing to prevent integral theory from taking on board the critical realist analysis and critique of master–slave-type social forms and their de-agentification of human agency, but this would entail very substantial revision of Wilber's correlationism and the 'provocative' metanarrative that underpins it. As Stein also suggests, integral theory's strength in developmental and transpersonal psychology can undoubtedly contribute powerfully to *re*-agentification (cf. Despain 2013). However, Stein's critique of Bhaskar in our companion volume *Metatheory for the Anthropocene* on the basis that Bhaskar does not elaborate a substantive developmental psychology, is not immanent but transcendent because it has been no part of Bhaskar's aim to elaborate such a psychology. Rather, his philosophy aims to articulate the possibility of a relatively autonomous science of psychology and an orienting metatheory that can underlabour for psychology and other sciences. It is perfectly possible to elaborate a developmental psychology under the auspices of that metatheory, and indeed Margaret Archer's (2000) theory of personal emergent powers has taken important steps along that road. Integral theory does not have a monopoly on developmental psychology!

References

Agar, J. 2014. *Post-Secularism, Realism and Utopia: Transcendence and Immanence from Hegel to Bloch*. London: Routledge.

Archer, M. 2000. *Being Human: The Problem of Agency*. Cambridge: Cambridge University Press.

Arthur, C. J. 2002. *The New Dialectic and Marx's 'Capital'*. Leiden: Brill.

Assiter, A. 2013. 'Speculative and critical realism'. *Journal of Critical Realism* 12(3): 283–300.

Badiou, A. 2006/2009. *Logics of Worlds: Being and Event, 2*. London: Continuum.

Benton, T. 1981. 'Realism in social science: some comments on Roy Bhaskar's *The Possibility of Naturalism*'. *Radical Philosophy* 27: 13–21.

Bhaskar, R. 1975/2008. *A Realist Theory of Science*. London: Routledge.

Bhaskar, R. 1979/2015. *The Possibility of Naturalism: A Philosophical Critique of Contemporary Human Sciences*. London: Routledge.

Bhaskar, R. 1986/2009. *Scientific Realism and Human Emancipation*. London: Routledge.

Bhaskar, R. 1989/2011. *Reclaiming Reality*. London: Routledge.

Bhaskar, R. 1993/2009. *Dialectic: The Pulse of Freedom*. London: Routledge.

Bhaskar, R. 1994/2010. *Plato Etc.: The Problems of Philosophy and their Resolution*. London: Routledge.

Bhaskar, R. 2000. *From East to West: Odyssey of a Soul*. London: Routledge.

Bhaskar, R. 2002a/2012. *From Science to Emancipation: Alienation and the Actuality of Enlightenment*. London: Routledge.

Bhaskar, R. 2002b/2012. *Reflections on MetaReality: Transcendence, Emancipation and Everyday Life*. London: Routledge.

Bhaskar, R. 2002c/2012. *The Philosophy of MetaReality: Creativity, Love and Freedom* London: Routledge.

Bhaskar, R. 2007. 'Theorizing ontology'. In *Contributions to Social Ontology*, ed. C. Lawson, J. Latsis and N. Martens, 192–202. London: Routledge.

Bhaskar, R. 2012. 'Critical realism in resonance with Nordic ecophilosophy'. In *Ecophilosophy in a World of Crisis: Critical Realism and the Nordic Contributions*, ed. R. Bhaskar, K. G. Høyer and P. Næss, 9–24. London: Routledge.

Bhaskar, R. 2016, forthcoming. *Critical Realism in a Nutshell*. London: Routledge.

Bhaskar, R. with Hartwig, Mervyn 2010. *The Formation of Critical Realism: A Personal Perspective*. London: Routledge.

Bhaskar, R. with Hartwig, Mervyn 2011. 'Beyond East and West'. In *Critical Realism and Spirituality*, ed. Jamie Morgan and Mervyn Hartwig, 187–202. London: Routledge.

Biel, R. 2011. *The Entropy of Capitalism*. Leiden: Brill.

Despain, H. G. 2013. '"It's the system stupid": structural crises and the need for alternatives to capitalism'. *Monthly Review* 65(6): 39–44.

Dickens, P. 2011. 'Society, subjectivity and the cosmos'. *Journal of Critical Realism* 10(1): 5–35.

Dussel, H. 1988/2001. *Towards an Unknown Marx: A Commentary on the Manuscripts of 1861–3*, trans. Yolanda Angulo, ed. Fred Moseley. London: Routledge.

Edwards, M. G. 2013. 'Towards an integral meta-studies: describing and transcending boundaries in the development of big picture science'. *Integral Review* 9(2): 173–188.

Einstein, A. 1954. [Excerpt from untitled letter]. www.workingwithoneness.org/about.

Esbjörn-Hargens, S. 2010. 'An overview of integral theory: an all-inclusive framework for the twenty-first century'. In *Integral Theory in Action: Applied, Theoretical, and Constructive Perspectives*, ed. S. Esbjörn-Hargens, 33–64. Albany, NY: SUNY Press.

Ferraris, M. 2004/2013. *Goodbye Kant! What Still Stands of 'The Critique of Pure Reason'*, trans. Richard Davies. Albany, NY: SUNY Press.

Foster, J. B. 2013. 'Epochal crisis'. *Monthly Review* 65(5): 1–12.

Gallopin, R. C. and Raskin, P. D. 2002. *Global Sustainability: Bending the Curve*. London: Routledge.

Geogescu-Roegen, N. 1971/1999. *The Entropy Law and the Economic Process*. Cambridge, MA: Harvard University Press.

Goethe, J.W. von. 1794–5/2011. *Wilhelm Meister's Apprenticeship*. In J. W. von Goethe, *Wilhelm Meister*, trans. H. M. Waidson, 3–465. London: Alma Classics.

Goethe, J.W. von. 1998. *Conversations of Goethe with Johan Peter Eckermann*, trans. John Oxenford. Cambridge, MA: Da Capo Press.

Graeber, D. 2011. *Debt: The First 5,000 Years*. New York: Melville House.

Hartwig, M. 2007a. 'Duality and dualism'. In *Dictionary of Critical Realism*, ed. M. Hartwig, 149–50. London: Routledge.

Hartwig, M. 2007b. 'Hegel–Marx critique'. In *Dictionary of Critical Realism*, ed. M. Hartwig, 225–29. London: Routledge.

Hartwig, M. 2007c. 'Process'. In *Dictionary of Critical Realism*, ed. M. Hartwig, 387–8. London: Routledge.

Hartwig, M. 2007d. 'World-line'. In *Dictionary of Critical Realism*, ed. M. Hartwig, 502. London: Routledge.

Hartwig, M. 2011. 'Bhaskar's critique of the philosophical discourse of modernity'. *Journal of Critical Realism* 10(4): 485–510.

Hartwig, M. 2015a. 'All you need is love'. *Journal of Critical Realism* 14(2): 205–24.

Hartwig, M. 2015b. 'Introduction' to Roy Bhaskar, *The Possibility of Naturalism: A Philosophical Critique of the Contemporary Human Sciences*, vii–xxxvii. London: Routledge, orig. pub. 1979.

Hilary, J. 2013. *The Poverty of Capitalism: Economic Meltdown and the Struggle for What Comes Next*. London: Pluto Press.

Hostettler, N. 2013. *Eurocentrism: A Marxist Critical Realist Critique*. London: Routledge.

Jeffries, S. 2011. 'A life in writing: Slavoj Žižek'. *Guardian*, London, 15 July.

Johnston, A. 2014. *Prolegomena to any Future Materialism, Volume 1: The Outcome of Contemporary French Philosophy*. Evanston, IL: Northwestern University Press.

Kunkel, B. 2014. *Utopia or Bust: A Guide to the Present Crisis*. London: Verso.

Little, D. 2010. *New Contributions to the Philosophy of History*. Dordrecht: Springer.

MacLean, L. 2013. *The Free Animal: Rousseau on Free Will and Human Nature*. Toronto: University of Toronto Press.

McWherter, D. 2013. *The Problem of Critical Ontology: Bhaskar contra Kant*. London: Palgrave Macmillan.

McWherter, D. 2015. 'Metaphilosophical naturalism and naturalized transcendentalism: some objections to Kaidesoja's critique of transcendental arguments in critical realism'. *Journal of Critical Realism* 14(1): 54–79.

Marshall, P. 2012. 'The meeting of two integral metatheories'. *Journal of Critical Realism* 11(2): 188–214. Moholy-Nagy, Sibyl 1970. 'Introduction' to Paul Klee, *Pedagogical Sketchbook*. New York: Praeger, orig. pub. 1925.

Moore, J. W. 2002. 'The crisis of feudalism: an environmental history'. *Organization and Environment* 15(3): 301–322.

Moore, J. W. 2011. 'Transcending the metabolic rift: a theory of crises in the capitalist world-ecology'. *Journal of Peasant Studies* 38(1): 1–46.

Nadeau, R. L. 2013. *Rebirth of the Sacred: Science, Religion and the New Environmental Ethos*. Oxford: Oxford University Press.

Næss, P. 2006. 'Unsustainable growth, unsustainable capitalism'. *Journal of Critical Realism* 5(2): 192–227.

Norrie, A. 2010. *Dialectic and Difference: Dialectical Critical Realism and the Grounds of Justice*. London: Routledge.

Nunez, I. 2014. *Critical Realist Activity Theory: An Engagement with Critical Realism and Cultural-Historical Activity Theory*. London: Routledge.

Potter, G. 2010. *Dystopia: What Is to Be Done?* Waterloo, Canada: CreateSpace.

Reeves, Craig forthcoming. *The Idea of Critique*. London: Routledge.

Rilke, R. M. 1912, 1922/2001. *Duino Elegies*, trans. A. S. Kline. www.poetryintranslation.com/.

Roberts, J. 2013. 'Dialectic and post-Hegelian dialectic (again): Žižek, Bhaskar, Badiou'. *Journal of Critical Realism* 12(1): 72–98.

Rose, S. 1997. *Lifelines: Biology beyond Determinism*. Oxford: Oxford University Press.

Rutzou, T. 2012. 'Integral theory: a poisoned chalice?' *Journal of Critical Realism* 11(2): 215–24.

Rutzou, T. 2014. 'Integral theory and the search for the Holy Grail: on the possibility of a metatheory'. *Journal of Critical Realism* 13(1): 77–83.

Shkliarevsky, G. 2011. 'The God debate and the limits of reason'. *Cosmos and History: The Journal of Natural and Social Philosophy* 7(2): 70–93.

Skempton, S. 2010. *Alienation after Derrida*. London: Continuum.

Smith, C. 2010. *What Is a Person? Rethinking Humanity, Social Life, and the Moral Good from the Person Up*. Chicago: University of Chicago Press.

Smith, C. 2015. *To Flourish or Destruct: A Personalist Theory of Human Goods, Motivations, Failure, and Evil*. Chicago: University of Chicago Press.

Strawson, G. 2011. 'Religion is a sin'. *London Review of Books* 33(11): 26–28.

Thomson, I. D. 2000. 'Ontotheology? Understanding Heidegger's *Destruktion* of metaphysics'. *International Journal of Philosophical Studies* 8(3): 297–327.

Thomson, I. D. 2011. *Heidegger, Art, and Postmodernity*. Cambridge: Cambridge University Press.

Vandenberghe, F. 2014. *What's Critical about Critical Realism? Essays in Reconstructive Social Theory*. London: Routledge.

Wallace, R. M. 2014. 'Hegel's God: how we know it, and why it deserves to be called "God"'. http://robertmwallace.blogspot.co.uk/2014/04/hegels-god-how-we-know-it-and-why-it.html.

Wark, M. 2014. 'There is another world, and it is in this one'. www.publicseminar.org/2014/01/there-is-another-world-and-it-is-this-one/#comments.

White, P. 1966/1969. *The Solid Mandala*. Harmondsworth: Penguin.

Wilber, K. 1979/2001. *No Boundary: Eastern and Western Approaches to Personal Growth*. Boston, MA: Shambhala.

Wilber, K. 1980/1996. *The Atman Project: A Transpersonal View of Human Development*. Wheaton, IL: Quest Books.

Wilber, K. 1981/1983. *Up from Eden: A Transpersonal View of Human Evolution*. Boulder, CO: Shambhala.

Wilber, K. 1983/2011. *Eye to Eye: The Quest for the New Paradigm*. Boston, MA: Shambhala.

Wilber, K. 1995/2000. *Sex, Ecology and Spirituality: The Spirit of Evolution*. Boston, MA: Shambhala.

Wilber, K. 1996. *A Brief History of Everything*. Dublin: New Leaf.

Wilber, K. 2000. *Integral Psychology: Consciousness, Spirit, Psychology, Therapy*. Boston, MA: Shambhala.

Wilber, K. 2006. *Integral Spirituality: A Startling New Role for Religion in the Modern and Postmodern World*. Boston, MA and London: Integral Books.

Wilber, K. 2013. 'Response to critical realism in defence of integral theory'. http://integral-life.com/integral-post/response-critical-realism-defense-integral-theory?page= 0,0.

Wilber, K. with Ann Niehaus, eds, 1984/2001. *Quantum Questions: Mystical Writings of the World's Great Physicists*. Boston, MA: Shambhala.

8

CONTRIBUTIONS OF EMBODIED REALISM TO ONTOLOGICAL QUESTIONS IN CRITICAL REALISM AND INTEGRAL THEORY

Tom Murray

Introduction: everybody is right, everything is real

One could sum up the motivating orientations behind integral theory and critical realism by pointing to Ken Wilber's "*everybody is right*" and Roy Bhaskar's "*everything is real*."[1] Both philosophers narrate our historical moment in terms of the failings of modernity and post-modernity and offer integrated and inclusive visions of what is possible to come. Critical realism (CR) and integral theory (IT) both encompass hard science, social science, ethics, and spirituality in their spacious metatheoretical purview. Both were conceived to defend a humble yet rigorous rational empiricism in a postmodern milieu in which truth, realness, and valid knowledge were dismissed. "Everybody is right" and "everything is real," properly understood, convey a pragmatic hopefulness, even an exuberant blessing, which is medicine for the existential ailments and grave challenges of our time.

Bhaskar (like Habermas) sees a primary role of philosophy as, not so much to discover its own exalted truths, but in a humbler role as *underlaborer* for other disciplines. Bhaskar and Wilber see the role of philosophy as fundamentally ethical and *emancipatory*. Philosophy can underlabor other disciplines in the hope of furthering human happiness, flourishing, freedom, and/or evolution. Emancipation is very much about reducing what Bhaskar calls the demi-real – beliefs and conceptions that do not correspond well with reality. Andrew Collier notes that a philosophy takes on the function of critique (as in "critical theory" and "critical realism") "when it exposes internal contradictions in the beliefs implicit in the practice" of some theory or ideology (1994, p. 18). Critical theories are usually thought of as critiquing social norms, especially dominant narratives and ideologies, but can also be used self-reflectively to critique a theorist's, group's, or discipline's *own* stance. Critical self-reflection upon one's own demi-reality is thus *self-emancipatory* (and part of what Bhaskar would call the "pulse of freedom" within all persons). CR and IT are mature post-post-modern theories whose members already engage in self-critical processes, and my offerings here are merely to contribute to this process with some additional tools and concepts.

It is not enough to point out the demi-reality or the systematic biases in reason. *Ameliorating* demi-reality involves identifying its *sources*, i.e. the causal and structural mechanisms that produce it (doing what CR would call an explanatory critique using retroduction). In this chapter I draw on trends in cognitive-science-based *embodied philosophy* that reveal some of the structural sources of the demi-real. I draw primarily from Lakoff and Johnson's embodied realism (ER), and provide some extensions to it related to "epistemic drives". As Bhaskar and Wilber well note, all ideas, models, and theories are fallible. Demi-reality is not just about false ideas but also about the fuzzy edges and limitations inherent in ideas – i.e. their indeterminacy. The demi-real involves not just erroneous ideas, but an erroneous *certainty* in ideas.

Much of the quotidian appeal of CR is in its invitation to "get real" in the face of theories that, in Bhaskar's terms, "lack seriousness" and allow idealism and abstraction to outstretch pragmatic intuitions and concrete facts (this is an aspect of the "reality principle"). In alignment with this concern, my approach in this chapter is aligned with Habermas' concept of postmetaphysics, which critiques the "strong concept of theory, its grasp of the totality, and its claim to a privileged access to truth" (1992, p. 6) that was endemic to positivist philosophies. Though CR and IT critique positivist philosophy, post-metaphysical principles must perennially be re-applied to theories that are as far reaching and compelling as CR and IT.[2]

Embodied realism and metaphorical pluralism

Between ontology and epistemology

The play of philosophical themes between IT and CR concerns ontology and epistemology, and their interrelationship. That is, questions about what can be considered real; how to best conceptualize the layers, elements, or properties of reality; and the bounds of what can be understood about reality. At stake is what can be considered *real* (vs. epiphenomenal, derivative, illusory, or "merely" subjective), and what is considered real or to exist is often at the core of disagreements about the *truth* of claims – giving ontological considerations significant importance in dialogue that may not on the surface seem to contain ontological themes.[3]

Contemporary metatheoretical and post-metaphysical approaches such as CR an IT share the goal of skillfully combining the gifts of classical and positivistic philosophies with the caveats and unsettling disclosures that emerged in postmodern and deconstructivist philosophies. A conundrum being worked out by such approaches is: how to make strong claims while remaining appropriately humble and acknowledging of a fallibilism that is compatible with postmodern/constructivist critiques of knowing.

One can distinguish three coordinated gestures that many contemporary approaches have in common, and that parallel CR's "holy trinity" of base principles

(Marshall, 2012a, p. 14). The first gesture is aligned with CR's "ontological intransitivity" – the realist claim that a reality exists outside of our knowing or perceiving of it (even if any particular claim about that reality is fallible). This is the weakest form of realism.[4] Wilber includes this step within IT in his discussion of subsistence. This first gesture is often supported with transcendental arguments or rational reconstruction, to the effect that we always already make this assumption, or that this assumption is a necessary condition for the possibility of further (serious) philosophical deliberation (or is necessary for any reasoned action or communication). That is, to deny that there is a reality is to engage in performative contradiction or absurdity ("non seriousness" in Bhaskar's terminology).[5] These arguments give one permission to make claims about a reality independent of human thought. (In CR alethic truth is truth of things distinct from propositions and interpretation.)

The second gesture is a constructivist move that is acknowledged by both integral theory and critical realism. That is to acknowledge that there are epistemic limitations and fallibilities to *all* human knowledge and propositions, as in CR's "epistemic relativity." This is implied in Wilber's adages "the map is not the territory," "everyone is at least partially right" and in his Three Strands description of scientific inquiry.

The third gesture is meant to coordinate and extend the first two, and offers a middle path between ontology and epistemology: to claim that *validity is graded* such that some claims are stronger than others, and that some claims more closely correspond with reality (what Habermas calls "the unforced force of the better argument" (1999). This corresponds to CR's "judgmental rationality" and with Wilber's "we can accept the valid truth claims … insofar as they make statements about the existence of their own enacted and disclosed phenomena" (Wilber, 2003b).

These three gestures are much more accepted in current scholarly circles than they were in the mid-twentieth century when Wilber and Bhaskar (and others including Habermas) were working out their original contributions, in full battle gear against the excesses of postmodernism and positivism that were endemic to academia and culture at the time. As an example of the wider contemporary agreement, in *Philosophy in the Flesh* (*PITF*) Lakoff and Johnson describe traditional "disembodied objective scientific realism" as containing three claims or assumptions (p. 90): (1) There is a world independent of our understanding of it; (2) We can have stable [practical, trustable] knowledge of it; and (3) Our concepts and forms of reason are *not* constrained by physicality, allowing science to discover absolute truths. They take the first two as true, paralleling the three gestures above, and see the last as highly problematic.

Following these three gestures, the problem of exactly *how* to argue for strong validity or confidence in specific truth claims is more problematic. IT and CR diverge here, with some within CR accusing IT of the "epistemic fallacy" of leaning too far toward epistemic relativity in its quest for a judgmental rationality that resolves the conundrum.[6] Following the three gestures integral theory often moves quickly on to "so let us find and use the best model we possibly can" (i.e. AQAL; and see discussion of Kosmic Address later), and proceeds with a relatively positivistic style.[7] And though CR is more cautious on this front, I do not believe that its theoretical force produces an escape velocity that allows the distance from epistemology that it presumes in its claim that ontology underpins epistemology (more on this later).

Lakoff and Johnson's Embodied Realism, one focus of this chapter, speaks directly to this quandary. Their claims, though radical in the context of metatheories such as CR and IT, must be reckoned with. Embodied Realism reveals unavoidable sources of the demi-real that, if not exposed and integrated, threaten to weaken the portability of these metatheories as they spread into wider circles of culture and academia.

Lakoff and Johnson make the radical claim that "the question of what we take truth to be is therefore a matter for cognitive science because it depends on the nature of human understanding…. Truth is, for this reason, not something subject to definition by an a-priori philosophy" (*PITF*, p. 108). They go on to claim that "more than two millennia of a priori philosophical speculation about [certain] aspects of reason are over," and that because "findings from the science of the mind are inconsistent with central parts of Western philosophy … philosophy can never be the same again" (p. 3). These claims come from a deeply epistemological orientation, and may chafe uneasily at critical realism's focus on ontology. In addition they challenge the performative conviction within integral theory's categorical models and grand "orienting generalizations."

Coping with the symbolic impulse: toward softer categories

Embodied Realism draws on empirical cognitive science to show how the structural nature of categories and concepts influence how we reason. According to empirical research on prototype theory (Mervis & Rosch, 1981) the concepts and categories we use (in thought and language) admit to fuzzy boundaries and other types of indeterminacies (including "family resemblance" structures). The mind, or, we could say, the symbolic nature of language, has a tendency to perceive or interpret phenomena in mutually exclusive black-and-white terms. As Gregory Bateson says: "[the] world begins by making splits, then drawing boundaries, then solidifying these boundaries. Then we fool ourselves into believing what we have made ourselves see" (1979). When we employ the knife of the conceptual category (as all terms do, at least nominally), we risk two types of error. First, that we ignore or misclassify phenomena that fall within the fuzzy *overlap* at the conceptual split (i.e. at the gray area between democrat vs. republican, state vs. stage, or transitive vs. intransitive). Second, we ignore or misclassify phenomena that fall *outside* the conceptual scheme (if we are focused on classifying things within fruits, then vegetables may go unnoticed). I call the tendency to interpret or enact categories as having definitive boundaries the "symbolic impulse."[8]

The shock (or irritation, or plague) of indeterminacy is more significant the more *abstract* the concepts being discussed, and philosophical concepts (truth, reality, freedom, causality, object, being, knowledge, etc.) are among the most abstract of all. Of interest here is how philosophical arguments, and reason in general, might be reframed when categorical boundaries are *softened* (actually when they are treated as softened, since studies show that they always *are* fuzzy).[9]

Lakoff and Johnson point out that since *propositions* are composed of concepts one must cope with the graded nature of abstract propositions as well. Concepts are explicitly described by definitions but implicitly, or cognitively, determined by (enacted through) complex abstractions over *exemplars* that are impossible to definitively describe or enumerate. Disagreements are often the result of interlocutors tacitly assuming different spaces of exemplars for their concepts, and thereby talking past each other. This has implications for what we might call post-rational discourse.[10] Rather than claiming that a statement is categorically wrong, one can ask "in what sense is it true and in what sense is it false?" Or: "what assumptions would I have to make about the definitions of its terms and the nature of reality for the claim to seem true?" (and similarly for a counter-claim). This relates to the type of dialectic that Bhaskar proposes (in *DPF*), which, rather than being constrained to the Hegelian and Wilberian transcend-and-include dialectic, can also accommodate a dialectic that deconstructs on its way toward more real(istic) (non-categorical, including rhizome-like) understandings.[11]

Metaphorical pluralism

In their "Primary Theory of Metaphor" Lakoff and Johnson argue that thought and reason are *primarily* and *fundamentally* metaphorical, and that the metaphors we employ are grounded in our embodiment – that abstract thought is composed of conceptual building blocks at the sensorimotor level. The key implication is that if it can't be built up from basic sensorimotor primitives, we can't think it.[12] Example metaphors include: knowing or understanding as seeing or grasping; similarity as closeness; organization as physical structure; change or transformation as motion; relationships as enclosures (*PITF*, pp. 50–54). Importantly, "metaphor is not the result of … interpretation [it is] a matter of immediate conceptual mapping via neural connections" (*PITF*, p. 57). The metaphorical grab-bag that one has access to in thinking about abstract ideas is fully constrained by one's embodiment (and, of course, is influenced by other factors, such as one's cognitive development and culture).

Lakoff and Johnson go on to show that many abstract concepts are understood in terms of a "metaphorical patchwork, sometimes conceptualized by one metaphor, and at other times by another." For example, our concept of time is based on a patchwork conglomerate of more fundamental experiences and schema, mostly involving space and motion (from *PITF*, ch. 10). The future is in *front* of us and the past *behind* us. We *face* the future. Time *passes* by or the time has *arrived*. Time durations can be *large* or *small*. Research has "found that we cannot think (much less talk) about time without those metaphors" (*PITF*, p. 166). These metaphors are not just *an aspect* of our understanding of time, together they *comprise* our understanding of time.

Lakoff and Johnson go on to "consider the classical ontological question: *Does time exist independent of minds*, and if so, what are its properties?… [We] *reject the question*. It is a loaded question" (*PITF*, p. 167). Pragmatically, answers to such questions are meaningless or not useful. "Yet the biological and cognitive construction of time does not make it subjective or arbitrary or merely cultural … the metaphors are not arbitrary; they are deeply motivated [by physical reality]. They permit the measurement of time, our very notion of history, the science of physics [and modern technology], and much more" (*PITF*, p. 168). The metaphors are "apt" and extremely useful, but "being metaphors, can get us into silliness if we take them literally" (*ibid.*).

Research has shown that we unreflectively jump from one metaphorical basis to another and that these metaphors can be incompatible or contradictory. *Causation*, for example, is understood in terms of a loose collection of features and exemplars having a fuzzy "family resemblance" or "multivalent radial structure" but have no precise definition, specific nature or essence beyond human thought. Though having diverse facets, these concepts have an *experiential sense* of undeniable unity. The various senses of "causality" have enough overlap of use and understanding that the mishmash holds together as a single gestalt. Lakoff and Johnson's analysis shows that "over the course of history, philosophers have formulated a wide variety of theories of causation, each substantively different from the others and therefore each with its own distinct logic" (*PITF*, p. 173). Are they talking about the same thing? "Philosophers may disagree as to what is the *right* theory of causation, but the philosophical community [erroneously] recognizes all of them as theories of the same thing" (*ibid.*).

In *PITF* Lakoff and Johnson describe at length the metaphorical pluralisms and other indeterminacies of concepts. "Our most fundamental concepts – time, events, causation, the mind, the self, morality [truth, reality, object, being, and freedom] – are multiply metaphorical" (or metaphorically pluralistic, p. 128). These are, of course, key concepts within CR and IT. For ER such constructs "have no precise definition, specific nature or essence beyond human thought" (*ibid.*). This presents a serious challenge to CR's strong orientation to ontology, and bolsters IT's leanings toward epistemology and its claim that epistemology and ontology are symmetrically co-determinate.

We can note the word "precise" in the last *PITF* quotation about "no precise definition." Definitions and definitive claims are important and unavoidable and we must do our best to bring clarity and precision to claims and definitions. Embodied Realism simply points out the inherent limits in doing so. ER makes some philosophical claims, but its use for emancipatory critique is not so much in its refutation of any particular proposition, but rather it challenges the *force* of arguments, exposing fallibilities at a level below propositions, i.e. the level of *concepts* – the building blocks from which propositions are made. It challenges certainty and partially explains the hermeneutic challenges of multiple and perspectival interpretation.

Applications to CR and IT

There are numerous implications of ER for CR, IT, and the current attempts to compare or integrate them.[13] ER can add "seriousness" (in Bhaskar's sense) to philosophical controversies by challenging the performative seriousness (or certainty) of the debates. Indeterminacies might be safely ignored within "the choir" of a particular community or worldview, but become problematized as a philosophical framework (1) critiques others or responds to critique, and (2) attempts to disseminate its ideas to a wider community. I call this the "idea portability principle": that understanding and dealing with the indeterminacy of ideas is more important the greater the distance between the worldviews or beliefs of interlocutors. I note some applications of these ideas below.

(1) Marshall (2012b, p. 195) says "IT's ontology has only been implicit, never fully elaborated by Wilber, and in its post-metaphysical phase moved to a fairly strong social constructionist position … which subordinates ontology to epistemology, methodology and enactment." In a series of articles Wilber and Bhaskar debate these issues.[14] Does IT commit the epistemic fallacy? This is a current area of contention. "The Epistemic Fallacy" (EF) is a concept that must (like all concepts) admit to graded boundaries. This may seem obvious but could it be that the clamor would dissipate if this indeterminacy principle were taken more deeply? Posing questions categorically invites an inflammation of the symptoms of indeterminacy. The more nuanced questions are "in what *sense* does IT commit the EF, and what sense does it *not* commit the EF?" or "to what degree (or where) does IT lean too far toward epistemology and what problems does that create?" (and similarly for CR and ontology). Indeed most scholars working at the intersection of CR and IT are approaching the question with this type of nuance. Embodied Realism shows why it is not only prudent and generous, but necessary to do so.

Does ontology subsume epistemology? Bhaskar claims that "Everything is contained (constellationally) within ontology (including epistemology and ethics) – or rather its referent, being (including knowledge and values)" (OSI, p. 142). Yet Norrie notes that CR sees a complex, co-embedded, constellational relationship between ontology and epistemology, "not a clear analytical distinction" (2010, p. 17).[15] ER shows us why concrete metaphors are problematic for ideas, concepts, and theories (and other transitives). Ideas and concepts can have paradoxical, recursive, or intractably complex topological relationships. One theory can contain, contextualize, completely describe, or take a privileged perspective on another; while the second theory can also contain, contextualize, completely describe, or take a privileged perspective on the first (see Roy, 2006). Figure/ground relationships can become flipped or muddled in the transitive realm. Transitives (e.g. ideas) are in no way constrained to follow the laws of the physical world, yet we are constrained (in a sense) to conceptualize them in terms of concrete sensorimotor metaphors – a perennially unsatisfying phenomenon. Esbjörn-Hargens' (2010) description of ontology and epistemology as co-(or tetra-)arising and interpenetrating seems more in line with the principles of CR, IT, *and* ER.

Strong claims are challenged in light of ER's critique of foundationalism. Consider Wilber's "all objects are first and foremost perspectives. NOT 'are seen from perspectives,' but ARE perspectives ... there is no 'apart from' how a thing appears [... things] do not exist in a pregiven world" (2006, p. 252). Wilber also states that "objects come into being, or are enacted, only at various developmental levels of complexity and consciousness". Whether they exist in some other way CANNOT BE KNOWN in any event, and assuming that they do exist entirely independently of a knowing mind is nothing but the myth of the given" (Wilber 2006, p. 252).[16] This contrasts strikingly with Bhaskar's "categories are not to be viewed as something which the subjective observer imposes on reality; rather categories such as causality, substance, process, persons, etc. – if valid – are constitutive of reality as such, irrespective of their categorization by observers or thought" (OSI, p. 140).

Yet even within this strong ontological claim Bhaskar tips his hat to epistemology. The addition of the qualification "if valid" is telling. The only test or argument for such validity is through discursive, i.e. epistemological, means (as empathized by Habermas).[17] Wilber also says "this does not mean 'to be is to be perceived' ... nor is this to say that perception creates being ... rather to say that being and knowing are the same event" (2003c, p. 142). One can find moments within Wilber's and Bhaskar's work that support both ontological and epistemological positions.

It can be rhetorically and strategically productive for theorists to posit claims with definiteness. The heat behind categorical statements that seem to presume direct access to knowledge of the structure of reality can ignite conviction and loyalty, yet, in the face of alternative perspectives, can generate a searing flame and a wincing smoke that impedes generative outcomes. One can appreciate and make good use of both "sides" of an argument without committing categorically to one or the other, and one can intuit a larger truth that holds them both, though this larger perspective may be more difficult to articulate definitively. *Within* any framework, one might make arguments about foundations or essences, but in the *metatheoretical* work of comparing and integrating theories, the more inclusive stance is pragmatically preferred, especially given that reason alone cannot adjudicate deep philosophical problems (one must go developmentally "up" a level in both positivistic abstraction/generality *and* in negative capability and openness). The ping-pong ball bounding between epistemology and ontology can't be subdued into a stillness on either side through rational argumentation, including transcendental argumentation. Our only hope for quiescence is in a post-rational post-paradoxical holding of the opposites in dynamic interplay (also called vision-logic).

(2) In other papers (Murray 2010, 2013, in press) I explore how Embodied Realism impacts IT claims based on AQAL categories including subject/object, singular/plural, state/stage, levels, types, and lines. Strong categorization can precipitate overreaching claims that ignore territories in between or outside of the category's definition. What gets ignored when one assumes that phenomena must be subjective or objective, but not both or neither? What gets marginalized when one attempts to classify a human capacity in terms of the canonical set of developmental lines usually listed by Wilber? In categorical systems such as AQAL, the symbolic

impulse is what tempts one to shoehorn phenomena into neat packages when the situation calls for a more nuanced analysis. Paul Marshall speaks to this in describing the "pathology of the paradigm of simplicity [of] Cartesian clear and distinct ideas, analytical reductionism of whole into parts, and isolation of objects from their environmental contexts" (2012a, p. 21).

Wilber and others in IT readily acknowledge the indeterminacies of these categories, and IT speaks to the interaction, co-definition, and co-(tetra)emergence within categorical dualities; and it references higher-level constructs that transcend and include dualities. Still, IT is sometimes weak on the negative capability of being explicit about the limitations of the constructs themselves, and in specifying exemplars that exist in the liminal areas between or outside of a polarity or category system. Also, because of the exceptional and seductive explanatory power of the framework, IT scholars and practitioners tend toward misplaced concreteness (reification – see below) in (1) assuming that the categories exist in and constrain the (intransitive) real, and (2) treating the conceptual boundaries as mutually exclusive.

(3) CR does not rely as heavily on categorical models at IT, but is of course not immune to considerations introduced by ER. CR makes a considerable contribution to philosophical thought in arguing that ideas, mechanisms, absences, and nonduality are each real. But these concepts are massively indeterminate, and in particular the concept of the real. To its skeptics CR must answer the question, "Is negation (or nonduality, etc.) *really real*?" ER suggests that the question is unanswerable in any definitive way that would satisfy most critics. It is better to, as Bhaskar does, explain the *sense* in which each of these things is real, and what that implies more broadly.

Perspectivally engaging different facets of a metaphorical pluralism may only be an intermediate step from which disagreement might proceed at a more nuanced level of discourse. Interlocutors might still disagree with the explanation of how "X is in a sense Y, and in another sense not Y." The goal is not agreement or finality, but a process of increasing clarity, mutual understanding, flexibility, and generativity. This is a basic assumption in procedural rationality (see Habermas, Rawls) but is taken ever deeper as the indeterminacies of propositions revealed by ER are acknowledged.[18]

(4) Another application of ER is in the controversy of whether IT's panpsychist (or pan-interiorist) theory amounts to an epistemic overreach. Wilber, following Whitehead, claims that sentience, prehension, and consciousness are extended all the way down to subatomic particles. Some make the (misplaced concreteness) mistake of creating a metaphysics of this principle. Consciousness is mistakenly seen as a substance that permeates atoms – as something that infuses humans in abundance and is sprinkled into rocks and subatomic particles. What Wilber and Whitehead have accomplished is to show how the ideas of consciousness, prehension, and sentience can, quasi-metaphorically, be stretched usefully, even to an extreme, such that plants, asteroids, and even sub-atomic particles can be said to have these attributes (*proto*-consciousness, proto-sentience, etc.).

This stretching at first challenges our understanding of "consciousness" and then it enriches our understanding of the referents (e.g. people and rocks). We see them in a new way. No new properties, observations, substances, or even hidden causal mechanisms need to be added. Particles and rocks still do what we understand them to do. But seeing their behavior, nature, and interactions in terms of prehension opens up new avenues of understanding and creative exploration – not only for particles but also for humans and other objects imbued with our "old" meaning of prehension. In this way metaphors not only link things "metaphorically," but extend meaning from its foundation.[19]

(5) I will give two final short applications, without getting into the details of the controversies. First is the controversy within the IT/CR confluence on whether objects and processes in reality are "enacted." I believe that much of the difficulty within this conversation, as with other topics noted above, stems from metaphorical pluralism, and the fact that our descriptions and understanding are fundamentally limited by sensorimotor metaphors. It seems possible to articulate the senses in which reality, under certain senses of the word, is enacted, while noting senses in which reality is not enacted, without needing a single ruling on the question (which is impossible from an ER perspective). We can increase nuance and create important differentiations through a continuous movement between exemplars and abstractions, to generate a space of mutual understanding (see Lakatos, 1976, on how a concept's meaning is co-determined within the two spaces of abstract definitions and concrete exemplars).

Second is the question of whether one can "gain access to" a mind-independent reality, as CR claims is possible. On the surface, epistemologically oriented ER gives a definitive "no." But we can, as an immanent critique, apply ER's principles of fallibility to its own conclusions to nuance the dilemma. "Access" is a graded concept and a metaphorical pluralism, so we can ask, under what senses of access is CR's claim valid, and under what senses is it not? It is best to do so using exemplars (again, see Lakatos on this generative epistemic dynamic).[20]

Pragmatism and metaphysics

Pragmatism revisited

Embodied Realism has a strong resonance with pragmatism. The philosophy of Pragmatism is summed up by Louis Menand, perhaps the leading contemporary expert on the subject, who says that Pragmatism is an idea about ideas: "The idea is that ideas – theories, beliefs, convictions, principles, concepts, hypotheses – are essentially means of adaptation.... Ideas are not 'out there' waiting to be discovered, but are tools that people devise" (2001, pp. 1, 8). This is a strong statement of epistemic relativity (the "second gesture" from above).

CR's critique of Pragmatism (see *PIF*) does not take the Pragmatist's full scope and import, as articulated by Menand, into account. Bhaskar's critique of Pragmatism focuses on the neo-pragmatist Richard Rorty, who, though aligning himself with the early pragmatists, takes the radically non-pragmatic (and deconstructivist) route of de-valuing all reference to reality and valid knowledge. This contrasts with the core sensibilities of the early Pragmatists (James, Peirce, Dewey, etc.), who are sympathetic with the so-called Reality Principle (from Freud) – the call to ground ideation in experience so as to avoid the overreaching of an intellect attempting a "view from nowhere."

I find the essence of Pragmatism to have much alignment with CR and the "seriousness" of "getting real" that CR implies (and see Bhaskar's invocation of the reality principle in *DPF*, p. 55).[21] CR's "holy trinity" arguably implies a deeply pragmatic philosophy, one that argues for the usefulness and reasonableness of ideas in the service of deeper knowledge-building dialogue and more effective ethical action; and one that is ever open to both empirical and rational modes of critique and development. However, Menand notes that Pragmatism "does not solve the problem of objectivity…it just ignores it" (2001, p. 11).[22] This might explain CR's distancing from Pragmatists, despite the compatibilities.

Metaphysics, transcendental argument, and strata of reality

The ontological status of abstractions/generalities such as foundations, essences, totalities, and universals is problematic, as noted above. Such referents occupy an uncomfortable position between interiorities (ideas) and concrete exteriorities. Like Platonic forms/ideals, they seem to "exist" in a realm that is not fully real and not fully idea(l); they do not exist in space and time and yet are claimed to have an objective existence independent of mind. This is the realm of metaphysical postulation which many, including Habermas in his post-metaphysics, try to avoid. In his description of post-metaphysics, Wilber associates metaphysical thinking with "the myth of the given" and "postulating fixed, eternal, [ahistorical,] independently existing archetypes" (2006, p. 247). The call to post-metaphysical argumentation is not a call to abandon metaphysical notions as much as a call for transparency about the limits, tradeoffs, and risks of making metaphysical claims, and a nuancing that anticipates the indeterminacies involved. It is difficult, and some would say meaningless, to categorically argue for or against the ontological status or "reality" of such objects, as metaphysical thinking might have us attempt. So more nuanced approaches are needed.

ER shows, from a cognitive science perspective, that even the concepts of "real," "exist," and "object" are metaphorical pluralisms and graded concepts, admitting to significant indeterminacy. Thus ER gives us permission (or requires us) to move beyond categorical treatments and investigate the *degree or sense* in which something is real. ER thus supports Bhaskar's claims that "the relevant question is not whether ideas are real, but what kind of reality they have, and whether ideas of different type (e.g. kind, epistemological or ethical status) have different kinds of reality" (OSI, p. 142). In contrast, many philosophies less developmentally sophisticated than IT and CR resort to rebukes, using terms like "illusory" or "epiphenomenal", because they constrain themselves to a strict categorical understanding of "reality."[23]

I will mention three approaches to nuancing types or senses of "reality": one from IT and another from CR; but first I will make a more general observation. Linguists and philosophers have explored how each of these things are real in different ways: concrete individual objects (the dog); classes and abstractions over concrete objects (e.g. dogs, mammals); properties such as red or bigness; processes and gerunds (e.g. reproduction, running); so-called social constructs such as money and gender (see Searle, 1995); and natural laws and causal mechanisms such as gravitation and evolution (see *RTS*; Elster, 1999). Some scholars still hold to the notion that "reality" can point to a single totalizing referent. From ER we can say that to ask *whether* of each of these things is real is uninteresting, but articulating *in what sense* each is real, or should be treated as real, is useful.[24]

What I have yet to see worked out is an analysis of the specific types of indeterminacies, categorical errors, or fallacies that each of these facets of reality is susceptible to. Such an analysis would allow us to move away from charging others with "committing" the X fallacy, and work from a common understanding of the vulnerabilities inherent in making different types of ontological commitments.

IT's approach to expanding the construct of reality is the integral pluralism and integral postmetaphysics of Wilber and Esbjörn-Hargens, which involves reframing the question of *whether* something exists to ask *how* it exists *for whom*. IT says that what is perceived to exist depends on the methodology used to inquire and the developmentally determined capacity of the observer/inquirer to perceive (Wilber 2006, in process; Esbjörn-Hargens, 2010). It proposes frameworks for classifying methodologies (using eight "primordial perspectives" or "methodological zones") and developmental capacity (Wilber's Levels of Consciousness stage model). (I have given a very brief summary of Integral Pluralism here and discuss it more in Murray, PME, in press).

CR's approach uses transcendental argumentation for the reality of a strata of hidden (non-concrete) causal entities such as mechanisms, structures, laws, and tendencies within nature.[25] CR is "neither empiricist nor positivist" and presupposes the existence of transcendental entities "assessable by implication" that are "neither empirical nor actual" (Price, 2013, p. 5), and "beyond observation and logic" (Marshall, 2012a, p. 4). CR differentiates the nested domains of the empirical (experienced events), the actual (which includes non-experienced physical events), and the real (which includes processes and *mechanisms* that underlie events) (*RTS*, p. 13). In Critical Realism deep, non-observable ("generative") structures, mechanisms, and tendencies have an equal ontological status to concrete objects and events (because they are "causally efficacious").[26] Thus we can claim a type of reality (and thus a type of validity) for constructs like language, freedom, values, and survival, which exists at particular levels or strata of reality.

All three of the above approaches to nuancing "what is real" are post-metaphysical in nature. According to Cooke (summarizing Habermas, 1992) post-metaphysical approaches include a movement from substantive to procedural grounding for claims – i.e. a claim is valid if the method for arriving at it is valid. *Transcendental* arguments posit what must be the case for empirical facts or observations to be possible. They often take the forms of "X is a necessary condition for the possibility of Y." There are two variations of these arguments: a weak epistemological and a strong ontological one. The epistemological version is what Habermas calls "rational reconstruction."[27] "Reconstructive" sciences and reconstructive modes of inquiry make arguments about the (usually implicit or intuitive) preconditions, pre-understanding, or know-how that underly basic human competencies. They posit assumptions that are necessarily, or always and already, made when thinking, speaking or acting. For example the "first gesture" mentioned above argues that, at least implicitly and unconsciously, people speak and act with the assumption that a reality exists independent of human thought and activity.

Bhaskar uses transcendental argumentation in its strong ontological form for many of his claims. For example, in his model of a stratified structure of reality, he argues for the reality of invisible mechanisms as being necessary for the possibility of the scientific process, and more generally necessary for the intelligibility of experience. But it is not clear how Bhaskar moves from the weaker claim about the nature of the (human) processes of experimental scientific inquiry to make claims about reality qua reality, independent of any knowing subject.[28] Bhaskar showed that science (and other types of reason) make unexamined ontological presuppositions – unreflectively yet inescapably acting as if these were true. But is there any practical difference between an ontological claim that something must exist (alethically) and making the more epistemological claim that human reason always already must make such-and-such an assumption about reality; i.e. that the relationship between the structure of reality and the structure of human cognition is such that humans are constrained to have such-and-such an assumption? I would argue not, based on the already mentioned fallibilities explored in ER.

CR's transcendental realism is framed as curative to problems with Kant's transcendental idealism (Marshall, 2012a). Kant proposed that categories such as space, time, and causality were the result of structures of consciousness and that, as Marshall puts it, "any attempt to venture beyond the bounds of actual and possible experience into the world for things in themselves will result in empty metaphysics" (p. 4). Marshall implicates this idealist attitude in a number of social and philosophical pathologies which CR means to correct, noting that this idealism inadvertently "moves humans to the center rather than the periphery," leading to the much maligned problems of post-modernity that "ended up separating the knowing subject from objective reality" (p. 5). CR's solution is the transcendental realist move of placing time, space, causality, structure, and mechanism back out into the world but within a strata of reality that contain that intransitives.[29]

This "revindication of ontology" provides strong footholds for integrative metatheories that attempt to include the strengths and jettison the weaknesses of modernist and postmodern philosophies, as CR and IT attempt to do. However, ER offers an alternative solution that does not require strong ontological moves. The notion, shared today by most embodied approaches to cognition, argued scientifically, and unavailable in Kant's time, is that the structure of human cognition is determined by evolutionary forces and is deeply motivated by the structure and properties of physical reality. Animal survival depends on perception and reason producing a good-enough representation and interpretation of reality to promote survival and reproduction. The structures and laws of *reality* have molded cognition in both species/evolutionary ways in individual/psycho-historical/developmental ways. We do not need to assume that time, space, causation, etc. subsist in reality with any fidelity to our perceptions, understanding, or theories of them – so long as the distortions, filters, and biases introduced by our wet-ware do not create levels of demi-reality that threatened the survival of our predecessors.[30] From *PITF*: "Embodiment keeps [truth from having to be] purely subjective. Because we all have pretty much the same embodied basic-level and spatial-relationship concepts, there will be an enormous range of shared 'truths' … [in addition] social truths are based on an enormously wide [shared] understandings and experiences" (p. 107).

Mysticism, spirituality, and epistemic drives

As noted in Marshall (2012a, p. 2) CR and IT "both embrace spirituality, thus confronting a taboo that is deeply entrenched within the academy … and endorse a directionality in evolution toward the realization of Spirit (or the ground-state)." Along the further reaches of the spiritual or psychological path to radical stages of freedom from conditioning one encounters certain types of well-documented experiences. These include profound states of emptiness, bliss, boundlessness, expansiveness, one-pointedness, oneness, and/or compassion. Bhaskar and Wilber, like many philosophers and spiritualists throughout time, incorporate insights and pointing-out injunctions sparked from deep encounters within this territory. Along the way IT and CR track deeply into metaphysical territory – despite that fact that both theories include sophisticated post-metaphysical arguments and attitudes.[31] For example, Wilber makes claims about Spirit, Nondual reality, the Absolute, Eros, and Involution; while Bhaskar speaks of the nondual ground-state, universal solidarity, and ultimate or alethic truth. In speaking persuasively to questions of "ultimate concern" it is difficult to avoid claims about universals, totalities, essences, and foundations, i.e. metaphysics – but it is done at a price. ER can shed some light on this conundrum as well, providing additional tools for the post-metaphysical framing of spiritual insights and concepts. In particular we can suggest that, in philosophy's role as a humble underlaborer, it is prudent to err on the side of speaking from phenomenology over metaphysics.

Mystical vs. metaphysical claims

In *Mysticism and Logic* Bertrand Russell describes *metaphysics* as "the attempt to conceive the world as a whole by means of thought" (1917, p. 6). In philosophy this is usually done through the application of *rational* arguments, including transcendental arguments. *Mystical* claims, on the other hand, purport a direct access to universal knowledge of reality based on *experience*. The spiritual claims within IT and CR have both mystical and metaphysical elements.

The mystic "knows" and must struggle to articulate the intuitions gained through a privileged access to a deeper reality.[32] The first problem in mystical knowledge is whether experience or knowledge can in fact include "direct access to reality" and to truths that are not subject to empirical or discursive validation. If this implies an ideal objective "view from nowhere," we can categorically reject the possibility (from the second "gesture" above). However, if what is implied is knowledge of a *deeper* reality, or more *valid* knowledge of reality, then we can and should allow for the possibility (from the third gesture). Then with mystical knowledge the primary problem becomes how one bridges from intuitive or pre-symbolic knowledge to language that articulates an insight. We are left then with the plurality of problems with language, mentioned by many a mystic, some of which are explored from a cognitive science perspective in ER. (We also face developmental issues of *adequatio*, i.e. whether the listener has built up (or taken down) structures that allow her to understand what is being referred to.)

Metaphysical clams have different (though overlapping) challenges vs. mystical claims. Many of these challenges have been summarized above. Foundations, essences, and universals such as consciousness, life, Spirit, Eros, Ground of Being are abstractions subject to significant indeterminacy, which implicate the certainty or precision with which they are professed. Metaphysical entities/processes are more than mere ideas that are rational abstractions or generalizations over observed phenomena – they are inferred from observation through reason, yet are said to exist in some realm of reality (not ideation). Actual objects in concrete reality are "replete" and cannot be completely described with a finite number of properties (they are also said to "withdraw" from being captured by ideas or language). The structures and mechanism mentioned in CR are not "actual" concrete entities and are more like abstractions in this sense. We are not justified in attributing properties to these objects beyond what observation and logic imply. However, metaphysical objects such as Gaia, Spirit, and Eros are usually treated as existing within the actual world. But if so they must be replete with properties beyond our initial conceptualization of them. And in the narratives surrounding such entities many additional properties are assigned *ad hoc*, such as intentionality, and omnipresence.

Metaphysical/mystical spiritual concepts have important meaning-generative potential. They provide linguistic footholds for those experiencing certain truths to deepen and share their understanding of this territory, and they are targets and boosts for those aspiring to new depths of wisdom. But, as is widely known, ideas containing flavors of totalization, fundamentalism, or essentialism can be "dangerous in the wrong hands" and are susceptible to distorted interpretation. Even in "the right hands" they have a seductive pull on the ego.

It is good to map out and present the possible limitations of metaphysical ideas. Totalizing or "re-enchanting" types of claims may be inevitable in certain types of inquiry, and IT and CR go to great lengths to frame propositions and acknowledge fallibilities. They contain explicit critiques of reductionism, fundamentalism, and absolutism.[33] Yet as metatheories they are still vulnerable. One example is the "evolution (and involution) as Spirit in action" theme in IT. In importing teleological and intentional agencies into evolution one opens the door to a stream of mystical and magical thought.

As another example of the risks of leaning too far toward metaphysics, consider Bhaskar's concept of metaReality, which might take on too much. In Bhaskar's explanation, metaReality begins in ideas about radical (and everyday) transcendence-through-negation and expands to become an explanatory model of universal solidarity and transcendental love, and a basis for envisioning the eudaimonian (ideal) society. The results spill from description and explanation into prescription. Doing so is valid given that fact and value interplay, but it seems problematic to build explanations of complex human phenomena from such elementary foundations. The significant "epistemic distance" from hard facts to an essence like nonduality allows for questionable conclusions such as Bhaskar's "principle of universal solidarity" which specifies that "in principle, any human being can empathize with and come to understand any other human being" (Bhaskar, 2010b, p. 18). An embodied perspective would say that, as animals sharing the same emotional pallet, affective empathy is potentially universal among humans, but cognitive empathy, and the ability for any to understand the *ideas* of any other, is not universal, and is in fact sometimes practically impossible.

Spirituality is a controversial theme for contemporary philosophers for many reasons, in part because of the prevalence of metaphysical (or quasi-metaphysical) entities often introduced. To further explore why metaphysical (and mystical) ideas are both powerful and troublesome, I will introduce the notion of epistemic drives.

Epistemic drives

The symbolic impulse, as mentioned above, biases one to be blind to the prototype-structure, graded boundaries, and metaphorical pluralisms revealed in ER. Sophisticated modern thinkers *intellectually* know that things do not exist according to black and white categories, and one's language often tries to compensate for the distortions introduced by this symbolic impulse with, for example, qualifiers and glosses. However, the symbolic impulse and its consequences go deeper than most imagine and have an insidious influence on all thought.[34] The symbolic impulse is one type of "epistemic drive," an umbrella term I use for tendencies of thought that influence what is believed to be real or true (in everyday conversation and in philosophical arguments).

In PME (table 2) I list over a dozen epistemic drives including drives toward purity, perfection, simplicity, generality, universals, abstraction, permanence, and fundamental/essential causes or roots. I propose that for each such drive there exists a balancing drive (for example, the drives to concreteness, specificity, change, multiplicity, partiality, novelty, and imperfection). How one balances these drives in any moment is a function of personal style, context, culture, and many other things. It would seem that those drawn to metatheories (often unreflectively) privilege the first set of drives listed over the other balancing drives (and this seems true of Western thought in general).

I use the term "drive" to make the analogy to biologically innate "emotional" drives such as the reproductive drive, fight/flight/freeze responses, territoriality, social dominance/submission, etc., though epistemic drives presumably involve higher brain centers. Like other drives, we experience a large number of epistemic drives (hard-wired urges or tendencies) that may or may not exhibit prominently at any given time, and often operate in competition with each other (in CR terms they are potentially dormant powers). Similar to other types of drives, one can experience and observe their phenomenology. For example there is a sense of ease, certainty, and mastery when one can ignore details and differences and trust a sturdy generality. There is a sense of elegance and wholeness when one can embrace many things into a circle of unity. There is a certain satisfaction in ordering things or collecting them into tidy groups, or in discovering the root cause, source, or foundation of things. One can observe the feelings of disorientation when things don't fit together, or when things that once fit together start to unravel. Like other drives, epistemic drives are largely unconscious processes that, on the one hand, can have unseen control over us, and on the other hand, can be observed, managed, and controlled to some degree through learned metacognitive (and meta-affect) skills.

Misplaced concreteness (mentioned above and coined by Whitehead) is another epistemic drive. It is related to what CR calls the ontic fallacy, and what IT refers to as the myth of the given or the map–territory confusion[35] – the tendency to imbue abstract concepts with the properties of concrete objects such as definitive boundaries. Misplaced concreteness is further explained by ER. ER illustrates cognitive mechanisms and biological/evolutionary origins of misplaced concreteness. Misplaced concreteness is further elaborated through the notion of epistemic drives, which helps explain the prevalence of cognitive biases in particular contexts (i.e. why misplaced concreteness might prevail despite its unmasking). (Collier (1994, p. 47) frames misplaced concreteness, using CR terms, as treating something from the level of mechanisms and structures as if it were from the strata of the actual.)

Epistemic drives seem to play a large part in the creation and dissemination of spiritual and metaphysical ideas. Such drives toward generality, abstraction, purity, wholeness, certainty, etc. can contribute to reliable understanding of reality but they can also over-function or function pathologically to generate demi-reality and the folly (or violence) which, in the extreme, leads to grandiosity, hegemony, elitism, absolutism, and proto-fascism. In less extreme ways the subtle (and not so subtle) influence of epistemic drives pervades the creation, consumption, and promotion of theories, models, and belief systems. The general need for meaning and certainty (and the avoidance of dissonance-incurring uncertainty, doubt, or unknowing) is an epistemic drive. (As mentioned above the demi-real includes not only the content of ideas, but the certainty with which they are held.)

Though philosophers and intellectuals may not be prone to its more primitive manifestations, they are not immune to the influence of epistemic drives, which manifest differently at different levels of abstraction and development (see PME, p. 108). Though it may seem unusual to ask scholars to reflect on how epistemic drives influence their ideas, the more mundane analogy to emotional drives is clear: in both social and scholarly communication one expects a more developed individual to reflect upon or have in-the-moment awareness of how emotions such as anger or jealousy influence how they act, what they say, and what they believe, and to make balancing adjustments accordingly. We can extend this from psychosocial drives to epistemic drives.

In considering epistemic drives we shift our treatment of embodied philosophy into phenomenology, including what it *feels like* to generate ideas and take on beliefs.[36] Recall that the arguments I present in this chapter are oriented to self-emancipation. That is, ideas and modes of critique are offered as tools for practitioners in IT, CR, and any knowledge-building community, to lessen the demi-reality of their models and to ease the process of reaching from one theory or community towards another. Self-emancipatory work necessarily mixes first-, second-, and third-person perspectives. Self-inquiry includes moments of sensing into what it *feels like* to do philosophy, and observing the relationship between one's ideas and one's actions (this is yet another aspect of "embodied" philosophy). How does one's relationship to these drives influence self-understanding and the collective knowledge-building process?[37] This is a worthwhile meditation.

IT and CR are explicitly normative projects and both allow for a nuanced treatment of the fact/value is vs. ought distinction. IT and CR allow that value-judgments play a role in discovering and communicating factual truths; and that values (and morality) are motivated by and grounded in considerations of reality. These notions can be applied self-reflexively (toward self-emancipation) to ask how epistemic drives impact the models, claims, and modes of illocution enacted within the IT and CR communities. This is not a purely intellectual exercise, but a phenomenological process of feeling into the movement of such drives as sensations within the body, as they arise in the moments of thought and discourse and then bringing this self-inquiry into a dialogic space of we-inquiry.

The feeling of truth about reality

Foundational and universal claims, including spiritual or quasi-metaphysical claims about the nature of reality, reach far into fields of indeterminacy, yet they are sometimes posited with a performative definitiveness. In Murray (2013, in press) I examine Wilber's claims that perspectives are primordial, his narrative around the evolutionary impulse, and quasi-metaphysical statements such as "ultimate realization of the ever-present, spaceless and therefore infinite, timeless and therefore eternal, formless and therefore omnipresent, Condition of all conditions and Nature of all natures and radically groundless Ground of all grounds."[38] The aim is not to discredit these constructs and claims, since they have strong meaning-generative potential. As mystical claims they can be said to be pointing to insights stemming from profound experience (states), and from a stable realization of developmentally advanced territory (stages). But as totalizing metaphysical claims about the nature of reality they are still problematic, especially in terms of the styles of justification and confidence that are performed as idea memes flow into and through knowledge-building communities and out into cultures at large.

As noted, mystical experiences, including those gained through contemplative practices, include felt senses of vast spaciousness, emptiness, boundarylessness, oneness, and single-pointedness. What could support the move from phenomenological experience into claims about ultimate reality?[39] From an embodied perspective, the mind can neither experience nor properly conceive of (actual) infinities (including complete emptiness). Esoteric traditions are rife with adepts claiming to have discovered an even *more* infinite, essential, or totalizing reality than the *ultimate* truth that was previously described by another adept. If something *feels* infinite, omnipresent, empty, or universal, *is* it? Our answer must be "no" in a post-metaphysical milieu.[40] There is still room for mystical and metaphysical claims, however. We could say that Wilber is trying his best, despite the limitations of language, to point to something that is more metaphorically than literally infinite. One who newly gains the experience and insight that Wilber points to might say that their usual and prior understanding of the word "infinite" does not apply literally, but that infinite is still the closest metaphor available that captures the experience. The challenge is that, for those of us trying make sense of the insights articulated by mystic-scholars like Bhaskar and Wilber, as Lakoff and Johnson put it: when we take our metaphors too seriously we risk stepping into "silliness," or worse.

Russell, in *Mysticism and Logic*, compares scientific/logical with mystical modalities and says that those great thinkers who skillfully blend the two represent "the highest eminence … that it is possible to achieve in the world of thought." Yet he also discusses at length the characteristics and risks of mystical claims. He notes the tendency for the passion of the mystic to conflate "the good with the truly real"; and that those who "are capable of absorption in an inward passion" can experience "the loss of contact with daily things [and] common objects." He says that "logic used in the defense of mysticism seems to be faulty as logic" and "[renders such] philosophers incapable of giving any account of the world of science and daily life" (1917, p. 15). He concludes with "while fully developed mysticism seems to me [a mistaken outcome of the *emotions*], I yet believe that by sufficient restraint, there is an element of wisdom to be learned by the mystical way of *feeling*, which does not seem to be attainable in any other manner [and which is] to be commended as an attitude toward life, not as a creed about the world" (p. 12; emphasis mine; see Murray (2010) for more on Russell and mysticism). Again, the invitation is to ground such themes in phenomenology more than metaphysics.

Toward construct-aware metatheories

Our embodied and post-metaphysical treatment of CR and IT has travelled through philosophical, psychological and phenomenological territory, and now enters into developmental concerns. That is, what human capacities should be assumed or supported in the course of comparing, improving, using, or disseminating these metatheories; and what capacities are needed to enact the embodied and post-metaphysical approach to metatheory espoused herein? It is generally agreed that one area in which IT can contribute significantly to CR is IT's articulation of interior development (strongest for individual development, but also substantial for cultural development).[41] Though one might question the specific categories of stages and lines enumerated in IT's AQAL model, the fact that human skill acquisition follows developmental trajectories has been rigorously empirically demonstrated.[42] Development has at least three implications for metatheories motivated by emancipation and social change: first, in strategies for *applying* them, second, in strategies for *promulgating* them; and third, in self-reflexive modes of *creating* them.

As emancipatory projects motivated by visions of social change, IT and CR envision (four-quadrant and four-planar being) changes in socio-politico-economic systems and in the beliefs and capacities of individuals and collectives. It is critical that we understand and anticipate what individuals and groups are capable of in terms of idea and skill transformation, the speed at which it can be expected to happen, and the types of motivations and methods that are expected to support it. For most of the envisioned social change efforts referencing CR or IT it is not essential that the stakeholders and beneficiaries understand or use the principles and models in IT and CR – these models are used by change agents as means to an end.

However, these emancipatory metatheories also have goals to promulgate specific ideas, skills, and worldviews – i.e. IT and CR principles and models *per se*. In disseminating (meta-)theories it is generally understood that communicating to different audiences requires different levels of depth and nuance, but developmental theory offers specific principles in this regard. (Also, since education and learning are essential elements of social change, cognitive science is an essential tool in emancipatory strategies.) From a developmental perspective we can say that many of CR's and IT's constructs require post-rational, vision-logic or construct-aware stages of development to be correctly understood (Wilber, 2006; Cook-Greuter, 2005; or metasystematic/paradigmatic in Commons & Richards, 1984). Below we note several capacities associated with these later levels of development how the accurate dissemination of metatheoretical ideas may be constrained to particular audiences. These capacities include negative capability, construct awareness, causal or nondual modes of experience, complex epistemic forms, deep self-reflection/self-understanding, and empathy.

One capacity of post-formal thought is the "negative capability" of flexible conceptualization that helps one understand or experience language and thought in the ways ER describes them. In this chapter we have grappled with ontological and epistemological nuances in metatheoretical concepts including: enactment, panpsychism, negativity/absence, "direct access" to reality, primordial perspectives, categories (as constituent of reality), and nonduality. The inescapable gradedness and metaphorical pluralism of these language constructs means that we will perpetually be confronted with paradox and indeterminacy. The invitation is for a more fully construct-aware (post-formal or post-rational) holding of these concepts. Formal-operational thought will, in a positivistic mode, forever search for the best explanation using ever more refined differentiations, precision, and ever broader perspectives incorporated systematically. Construct-aware thought includes more "negative capability" and sees the house of mirrors that positivistic logic can construct. It can make informed tradeoffs between pushing ahead and letting go. Cook-Greuter says of construct-aware thought:

> [One becomes] cognizant of the pitfalls of the language habit [and starts] to realize the absurdity [or] limits of human map making. [The] linguistic process of splitting into polar opposites and the attending value judgments can become conscious ... variables are now seen as interdependent, causality experienced as cyclical and boundaries of objects as open and flexible... [one remains] aware of the pseudo-reality created by words ... [and becomes] aware of the profound splits and paradoxes inherent in rational thought.... Good and evil, life and death, beauty and ugliness may now appear as two sides of the same coin, as mutually necessitating and defining each other.
>
> *(Cook-Greuter, 2000, pp. 21, 30)*[43]

In working with the metatheoretical concepts in CR and IT one encounters graded categories and claims that suggest that we should ask "To what extent" or "In what sense is [X] true (or real)? And in what sense not true (or real)?" – and resist the compulsion to find a proposition (at that same level) that integrates the answers. One encounters apparent paradoxes, such as: "Is nonduality empty or full?" One encounters metaphorical pluralisms that confound attempts to square one theoretical system with another. One encounters fractal-like conceptual structures, and relationships among abstract or transitive objects that will not conform to sensorimotor metaphors (for example, theoretical frameworks that can each claim to fully contain the other). Is mind within matter or matter within mind? Is ontology within epistemology or is it the other way around? Is nondual realization above and transcending regular consciousness or below and underpinning it? A theoretical framework may have a definitive answer to these questions. But the deeper truth is that reality goes sort of both ways – a fact that can be acceptable to those capable of gracefully holding paradox.

ER implies that paradox is an experience more than a fact of reality, and is a by-product of embodied cognition and the symbolic impulse. When all one has to work with are metaphorically based concepts such as full and empty, or wave and particle, then any reality that is not well described by the available concepts will appear paradoxical or otherwise confusing (or invisible).[44] One might (in a formal-operational mode) pursue the question until one identifies more appropriate language, but using construct-aware thought also allows for the play of language and its limitations.

A second capacity of post-formal thought is a deep phenomenological contact with so-called causal modes of experience. CR constructs such as absence, negation, totality, and nonduality have developmental implications pointing to causal states. These concepts can be understood as empty formal referents, but to fully understand them, they must be established within experience and intuition. CR grounds nonduality and mystical sensitivity in ubiquitous ordinary experience, e.g. Marshall speaks of the "nondual states of everyday transcendence" (2012b, p. 202).[45] This orientation provides a needed complement to IT's focus on "rarefied" states and stages. But, as Terri O'Fallon (2013) is finding in her research extending Cook-Greuter's work, turning the subjective experiences of emptiness, formlessness, non-being, Kosmic connectedness, or nonduality into stable objects of awareness and dialogue (causal objects, in her terminology) requires a high developmental capacity.[46] The nondual may be ordinary, but it might require non-ordinary capacities to understand this, limiting the audience for this message.

A third post-rational capacity (actually one that begins to form in the prior stages) is an ability to comprehend relationships and structures in complex and interpenetrative ways. The understanding of models, theories, and principles can be framed in terms of "epistemic forms" that are grounded in concrete metaphors (abstract schema for structuring knowledge and know-how, see Collins & Ferguson, 1993). Linear or categorical (black and white) structures are simpler than graded/spectral, network, or branching/manifold structures; which are in turn simpler than co-referential interpenetrating, paradoxical, fractal/recursive, constellations/meshworks; meta-systematic, autopoietic or cybernetic, or massively interdependent/ecosystemic structures. For example, above we noted how "figure/ground relationships can become flipped or muddled."[47]

Thus there is a developmental trajectory of the complexity with which one can understand the relationships, structures, systems, and co-dependent origination of things. Clearly both Wilber and Bhaskar make use of complex epistemic forms in sections of their writing, introducing different levels of challenge for the reader. (Wilber, as a more populist writer, skillfully includes a range of epistemic forms, allowing access points for different developmental levels.)

A fourth post-rational capacity is a deeper witnessing capacity in self-understanding and reflexive capacity. Cook-Greuter's description of construct-aware thought includes: "the ego becomes transparent to itself; [one] looks at all experience fully in terms of change and evolution [and one becomes] aware of the ego's clever and vigilant machinations at self-preservation" (2000). The understanding of interiors includes increasingly deep understanding of the nature of language, thought, emotion, self/ego, and the influences of group/cultural identification and immersion on the self. The development of ego (also called "wisdom skill") includes a deeper awareness of both interiors and exteriors and their interrelationship; leading to deepening integration of theory/ideation and practice. Empathy, compassion, and self-compassion also have developmental trajectories. Development includes transformations of value-systems and motivations that make it more likely (and easier) to let go of overly simple structures, open to new possibilities, tolerate dissonance and uncertainty, and actively seek critique. One is increasingly motivated to align one's being with one's capacity for complexity and depth, because the differences (absences) are felt more acutely.

Consistently in this chapter, the invitation has been to understand and *experience* concepts (and the claims that incorporate them) with softer boundaries, perspectival pluralism, and indeterminacy. The dance between boring headlong into finer distinctions and grander generalizations vs. letting go and opening up to (actual) unknowing requires skill that each theorist develops with her own style. The invitation is not to the acclaimed originators of our metatheories, but to members of the knowledge-building communities surrounding them. As individuals many of us have the "second-tier" skills required to interpret complex and nuanced philosophical ideas skillfully, but we, and the species as a whole, have barely scratched the surface of what it might be like for entire communities to embody these capacities. Esbjörn-Hargens echoes this sentiment in noting in a an ITC 2015 presentation that "even theories can do shadow work." For example, it is not yet clear what reflection on the *embodied* nature of ideas and theories as described by ER might look like if noted regularly within a collective inquiry or discipline. Thus we don't have much experience navigating the tradeoffs in avoiding the paralysis of recursive reflection as we strive to be generative and self-emancipatory.

Conclusions

Lakoff and Johnson, argue that "reason is not 'universal' in the transcendent sense; that is, it is not part of the structure of the universe … it is [however] a structure shared universally by all human beings" (*PITF*, pp. 4–8). They continue with the more radical claim that, "What we take truth to be is … a matter for cognitive science because it depends on the nature of human understanding" (p. 108).

Though CR and IT are correct in pointing out the dangers and fallacies possible in epistemological and constructivist orientations to reason and reality, a realist approach to philosophy must incorporate the hard facts about the embodied nature of cognition. The bio-psycho-evolutionary perspective on reason and cognitive biases was unavailable to the classical and post-structuralist philosophies that CR and IT are designed to rectify. Studies of "bounded rationality" were just emerging as Wilber and Bhaskar developed their theories. This chapter offers some small steps toward integrating the emerging embodied perspective into metatheoretical work.

The implications are important beyond academic philosophy, because as Lakoff and Johnson say, "radical change in our understanding of reason [leads to] a radical change in our understanding of ourselves" (*PITF*, p. 3). Embodied approaches open up avenues for personal and community-wide self-emancipation, and a more stable link between experiential truths revealed through mystical encounters with reality and metaphysical ideas developed through the dance of rational deliberation.

In *The Art of Waiting*, Martin Keogh says: "When myriad possibilities appear in each moment, the opportunities for self-criticism [diminish and] the pathway you end up taking is simply what you are contributing to the dance…. How do we increase our capacity to live in the unresolved? … [L]et the animal brain and body have a stronger voice … letting the river flow [and as James Hillman suggests] 'learn to accept a self that remains ambiguous no matter how closely it is scrutinized'" (2010, p. 15).

Notes

1 Bhaskar: "Ideas … are part of everything and everything is real" (OSI, p. 139); "Everything is real [including] absences" (*RMR*, p. 37). Wilber: "I have one major rule: everybody is right. More specifically, everybody … has some important pieces of the truth"; from Wilber's "non-exclusion principle" (1993, p. 6).
2 Note that CR distances itself from Habermas and postmetaphysics and sees itself as post-postmetaphysical, while in this chapter I focus on the similarities between them.
3 Bhaskar says "'Is' and 'real' discharge the burden of ontology" (*DPF*, p. 46).
4 Collier notes that "Heidegger … argues forcefully that non-realism is a non-starter, as it presupposes a worldless subject, and we are essentially Being-in-the-world" (Collier, 1994, p. 30).
5 Antecedent to this first step, and supported by similar arguments, is the assumption (epistemologically speaking) or claim (ontologically speaking) that reality has stable forms of structure, regularity, and pattern (which, for example, allow experiences of external reality that are more stable than dreams or imaginations, and from Bhaskar's work, underpin the scientific method). As Lakoff and Johnson put it, though all knowledge is fallible "we are not likely to discover that there are no such things as cells or that NDA does not have a double-helix structure" (*PITF*, p. 89).
6 Bhaskar defines the epistemic fallacy as "the view that statements about being can be reduced to or analyzed in terms of statements about knowledge; i.e., that ontological questions can always be transposed into epistemological terms" (OSI, p. 36).
7 Positivistic as in "positive capability" vs. "negative capability" (Murray, 2011). Positivistic approaches provide models, insights, and distinctions enabling more reasoning power, more meaning generation, and increased clarity and confidence. Negative capability includes high tolerance of and skill with the cognitive dissonance, fallibility, ignorance, mystery, and paradox (also discussed within CR's 2E edge of negation), which can reveal or accompany ever deeper unsettling territories of unknowing and fallibility.
8 The symbolic impulse creates what Bhaskar calls the world of (or perception of) duality, while nonduality includes both reality and perception of reality that is not mediated by the symbolic impulse.
9 Bruno Latour echoes this sentiment in his critique of the academic "business" of critique, which sets up dichotomous positions that seem to be at odds with each other when the reality of individual circumstances is more nuanced. "Do you see now why it feels so good to be a critical mind? [no matter which position you take] you're always right!" (2004, pp. 238–239).
10 John Stuart Mill famously said "in all intellectual debates, both sides tend to be correct in what they affirm, and wrong in what they deny." Knowledge might more efficiently progress through perspective-taking moves than through traditional antagonistic argumentation.
11 In Murray (2010) I suggest that scholarly communities package their theories and frameworks with an "indeterminacy analysis" of key concepts to make the ideas more portable outside the community.
12 Ideas and concepts build hierarchically upon each other (Fischer 1980; Commons & Richards 1984), so ideas need not be expressed directly in concrete metaphors, but each component concept is, if one drills down a few levels, grounded in sensorimotor concepts.
13 I am careful not to claim that Wilber or Bhaskar is unaware of the types of indeterminacies and tradeoffs that I speak of; nor do I judge that they are in any way trying to mislead their readers or followers. Rather, to the extent that my arguments critique their

claims or performative style, I prefer to assume that they have made informed strategic decisions based on their goals and assessments of their audience.

14 Unfortunately, the debate had not reached a level of "dialog" when Bhaskar passed away; and, looking at the three or four short documents produced, Wilber and Bhaskar did not engage deeply enough with each other's material to avoid oversimplification. The deeper and more nuanced dialogue between IT and CR has been taken up by others in these communities, notably the authors in this volume.

15 Marshall notes that "Bhaskar discusses the problem of incommensurability in a number of places," mentioning how meanings change and evolve within communities of practice (2012a, p. 15).

16 As pointed out by Hedlund-de Witt (2013), to claim that all reality is mind-dependent begs the question of whether minds are mind-dependent, suggesting a performative contradiction.

17 For example, though CR claims that "categories exist in nature," ER says even the concept of "category" admits to graded boundaries and metaphorical pluralism, such that those drawing opposing conclusions are very likely grounding in different metaphors.

18 Note that for each conversational context one must make the pragmatic call of how deep to push the challenge of indeterminacy, while taking certain concepts as unproblematic, in order to avoid "analysis paralysis."

19 A similar case can be made for the extension of the concepts of "agency" and "actor" to inanimate objects as suggested by both Latour and Bhaskar.

20 Imagine someone who does not have physical access to trees wanting to learn about and experience a tree; and that person wears thick gloves on their hands. They are allowed to enter a botanical garden to satisfy their desires. They have thus *gained direct access* to the tree – an actual object. However, as with the numerous limitations to all human sense experience, intuition, and reason, we will say that the gloves cannot be removed, and in this sense the person can not have *full* unadulterated access to the reality of the tree. Additionally, "direct" (or any other word one could use in its place) is a graded metaphorical pluralism, adding to the overall indeterminacy of the issue.

21 Pragmatism and the Reality Principle are also echoed in the 1M movement in MELD, which proclaims the priority of existence over essence (in *DPF*).

22 And this is largely true of Habermas, who, to my reading, rather than "committing" the epistemic fallacy, simply chooses not to play that particular game because his philosophical interests lie elsewhere, and the omission does not impede his project.

23 Those who misappropriate quantum physics to explain consciousness fall into a similar trap in having no way to explain entities that are both real and non-physical. Those struggling to "solve the mind-body problem" have similarly painted themselves into a corner in treating mind and matter as discrete categories (a misplaced concreteness) that exist *a priori* in nature.

24 For example, science struggles with the admission that, if probed deeply, it does not really know what a force is, or whether forces really exist. It also invents quasi-metaphysical objects such as "dark energy" to account for observed anomalies.

25 In addition, both IT and CR give subjective (transitive) processes equal ontological status vs. concrete reality, and both make claims about the reality of a radically empty nondual source underlying manifest reality. CR's ontological justification for these claims is more rigorous, and builds on CR's arguments about the reality of negation and absence.

26 CR posits that within the domain of the real there are strata of emergence such as material (physics), living (biology), and rational (culture) (others, including Koestler (1967) and Wilson (1998), have proposed similar models of emergence; and see Corning, (2002)). CR proposes that structures, mechanisms and tendencies exist in "layers of nature, and are ordered.... [The] more basic layer will have more explanatory power [yet] we are [not] able to predict a higher level mechanism from our knowledge of a more basic one" (Collier, on Bhaskar's work, 1994, pp. 46, 110). (Similarly, Wilber (2000) notes that lower layers set the *possibilities* for higher ones, while higher layers set the *probabilities* for lower ones.)

27 Habermas (widely acknowledged for his work on post-metaphysics) says that the main task of philosophy is not in establishing infallible truths, but in "rationally reconstructing the intuitive pre-theoretical knowledge of competently speaking, acting and judging subjects" (Habermas, 1992, p. 38). Cooke (1994) summarizes Habermas' notion of post-metaphysical philosophical trends as having "replaced foundationalism with fallibilism" with regard to valid knowledge and how it may be achieved.

28 The strengths and weaknesses of transcendental arguments are described in Taylor 1995, ch. 1.

29 This category does not seem to be given a name by itself, but when combined with the actual and empirical strata which sublate it, is called "the real".

30 Theoretical physics is constantly illustrating ways in which the mundane understanding of basic structures as time, location, distance, order, dimensionality, etc. could be misleading or limiting (e.g. see Kuhlmann, 2013).

31 CR seems to distance itself from Habermas, despite many areas of overlap, and may not associate itself with the term post-metaphysical. However, overall CR does fall under Habermas' definition of post-metaphysical as I understand it (Murray, 2011).

32 The same issues arise in describing a mundane experience such as the taste of chocolate or what it is like to be a female to one who has never had the experience. Esoteric spiritual experiences are different in that they are rarer, and require non-normative practices to attain – but all experience is, in one sense, equally ineffable.

33 Note Bhaskar's "side polemic against monism, reductionism, and fundamentalism, including the ideas of unique beginnings, rock bottoms and fixed foundations, all of which smack of anthropic cognitive triumphalism" (*DPF*, p. 45).

34 In addition, the symbolic impulse to view phenomena in terms of simplistic categories is exacerbated under conditions of strong emotion or ego/identity attachment.

35 And similar concepts including reification, hypostatization, concretism, and delusions of reference.

36 This is in line with IT's methodological pluralism (Esbjörn-Hargens, 2010), which recommends (or requires) approaching inquiry from multiple methodological perspectives.

37 The notion of epistemic drives can be mis-used in shoot-from-the-hip psychoanalysis of scholars or communities. For example, is IT motivated by an unexamined need for a reassuring purposeful role for humans in an otherwise lonely universe? Is CR driven by an unexamined need for the security of a knowable and stable reality amidst its apparent chaos and indeterminacy? It is more fruitful to apply the concepts from ER in *self*-reflection as tools for greater nuance and flexibility; rather than as petty weapons wielded in an *ad hominem* critique of the theories of others.

38 From Wilber's Excerpt A of the in-progress vol. 2 of the Kosmos Trilogy.

39 Contemporary scholars of Buddhist scholastic and scriptural texts are usually cautious to describe advanced states in terms of phenomenology rather than truths about reality (e.g. the vijñānas or janas of the Satipatthana Sutta).

40 Certainty and understanding are not only products of reason; they are *feeling* states that arise independently of rational validity. This is evidenced when one feels completely certain and yet turns out to be wrong, or when one leaves a lecture feeling that it was fully understood, soon to realize that one can't explain the ideas to another.

41 Critical realists have been aware of developmental factors. For example, Bhaskar describes "levels of rationality" (*PIF*, p. 157); and Price speaks of how the logical positivist perspective "simply cannot 'see' the non-empirical structures and mechanisms that help to construct our existence" (2013, p. 7). But IT's developmental theories add significantly to this.

42 Surprisingly, Lakoff and Johnson do not reference developmental modes in *PITF*. The inclusion of developmental considerations, like the addition of epistemic drives, extends the philosophy of ER.

43 Studies indicate that an awareness of cultural embeddedness within belief systems and worldviews comes at the pluralist stage, which precedes the construct-aware stage. This

awareness begins with seeing how *others'* beliefs are culturally determined, and later includes an awareness of how one's own beliefs are culturally determined. Cook-Greuter notes that "At the Construct-aware stage not just cultural conditioning is seen through, but the predicament of living in language" (2000, p. 29).

44 Marshall notes that "Bhaskar discusses the problem of incommensurability in a number of places," mentioning how meanings change and evolve within communities of practice (2012a, p. 15).

45 ER also provides an alternative approach to the reality of nonduality. The apperception of duality, in terms of categorical thinking, can be seen as a specious outcome of the symbolic impulse. Most or all dualities do not exist in reality, which, for the most part, has a more complex and seamless structure than simple categories can capture. Thus nonduality need not be an esoteric state of consciousness or being but a natural state of affairs. To experience reality in this way *feels* esoteric and spiritual; as, for most of us, it is only in (often blissful-feeling) non-ordinary states that the symbolic impulse is bypassed or disabled.

46 From advanced developmental stages "reality is now understood as the undifferentiated phenomenological continuum or chaos, the creative ground … [in] this awareness of an underlying unity [they] experience themselves and others as part of ongoing human-ity, embedded in the creative ground, [feeling] embedded in nature – birth, growth and death, joy and pain are seen as natural occurrences, patterns of change in the flux of time" (Cook-Greuter, 2005, p. 32).

47 In *DPF* Bhaskar says "presences and absences may be recursively embedded and system-atically intermingled in all sorts of fascinating ways [with] all sorts of topologies … loops, hierarchies, holes, blocks, intersecting … intertwined, punctured" (p. 48).

References

RTS: Bhaskar, R. (1975/2008). *A realist theory of science.* New York: Routledge.

DPF: Bhaskar, R. (1993/2008). *Dialectic: The pulse of freedom.* New York: Routledge.

PIF: Bhaskar, R. (1991). *Philosophy and the idea of freedom.* Oxford & Cambridge, MA: Blackwell.

OSI: Bhaskar. R. (1997). On the ontological status of ideas. *Journal for the Theory of Social Behaviour,* 27(2/3), 135–147.

RMR: Bhaskar, R. (2002/2012). *Reflections on metaReality: Transcendence, emancipation and everyday life* (2nd ed.). New York: Routledge.

PITF: Lakoff, G., & Johnson, M. (1999). *Philosophy in the flesh: The embodied mind and its chal-lenge to Western thought.* New York: Basic Books/Perseus Books Group.

PME: Murray, T. (2011). Toward post-metaphysical enactments: On epistemic drives, negative capability, and indeterminacy analysis. *Integral Review,* 7(2), 92–125.

Bateson, G. (1979). *Mind and nature: A necessary unity* (Advances in Systems Theory, Complexity, and the Human Sciences). New York: Hampton Press.

Bhaskar, R. (2010a). *AQAL 2210: A tentative cartology of the future; or how do we get from AQAL to A-perspectival?* Presented at the Integral Theory Conference, July, 2010.

Bhaskar, R. (Ed.). (2010b). *Interdisciplinarity and climate change: Transforming knowledge and prac-tice for our global future.* London: Taylor & Francis.

Collier, A. (1994). *Critical realism: An introduction to Roy Bhaskar's philosophy.* New York: Verso.

Collins, A., & Ferguson, W. (1993). Epistemic forms and epistemic games: Structures and strategies to guide inquiry. *Educational Psychologist,* 28(1), 25–42.

Commons, M. L., & Richards, F. A. (1984). A general model of stage theory. In M. L. Commons, F. A. Richards, & C. Armon (Eds.), *Beyond formal operations: Late adolescent and adult cognitive development* (pp. 120–141). New York: Praeger.

Cooke, Maeve. (1994). *Language and reason: A study of Habermas's pragmatics.* Cambridge, MA: MIT Press.

Cook-Greuter, S. R. (2000). Mature ego development: A gateway to ego transcendence. *Journal of Adult Development*, 7(4), 227–240.

Cook-Greuter, S. R. (2005). Ego development: Nine levels of increasing embrace. Available at www.cook-greuter.com.

Corning, P. A. (2012). The re-emergence of emergence, and the causal role of synergy in emergent evolution. *Synthese*, 185(2), 295–317.

Elster, J. (1999). *Alchemies of the mind: Rationality and the emotions*. Cambridge: Cambridge University Press.

Esbjörn-Hargens, S. (2010). An ontology of climate change: Integral pluralism and the enactment of multiple objects. *Journal of Integral Theory and Practice*, 5(1), 143–174.

Fischer, K. (1980). A theory of cognitive development: The control and construction of hierarchies of skills. *Psychological Review*, 87(6), 477–531.

Habermas, J. (1992). *Postmetaphysical thinking: Philosophical essays*. Cambridge, MA: MIT Press.

Habermas, J. (1999). *Moral consciousness and communicative Action*. Cambridge, MA: MIT Press.

Hedlund-de Witt, N. (2013). *Towards a critical realist integral theory: Ontological and epistemic considerations for integral philosophy*. Presented at the Integral Theory Conference, July, 2013.

Keogh, M. (2010). *The art of waiting: Essays on contact improvisation*. Self-published and available from the author at martinkeo@aol.com.

Koestler, A. (1967). *The ghost in the machine*. New York: Macmillan.

Kuhlmann, M. (2013). What is real? *Scientific American*, 309(2), 40–47.

Lakatos, I. (1976). *Proofs and refutations: The logic of mathematical discovery* (J. Worrall & E. Zahar, Eds.). Cambridge, MA: Cambridge University Press.

Latour, B. (2004). Why has critique run out of steam? From matters of fact to matters of concern. *Critical Inquiry*, 30(2), 225–248.

Latour, B. (2005). *Reassembling the social: An introduction to actor-network-theory*. Oxford: Oxford University Press.

Marshall, P. (2012a). Toward an integral realism. *Journal of Integral Theory and Practice*, 7(4), 1–34.

Marshall, P. (2012b). The meeting of two integrative metatheories. *Journal of Critical Realism*, 11(2), 188–214.

Menand, L. (2001). *The metaphysical club: A story of ideas in America*. New York: Farrar, Straus, & Giroux.

Mervis, B., & Rosch, E. (1981). Categories of natural objects. *Annual Review of Psychology*, 32, 89–115.

Murray, T. (2010). Exploring epistemic wisdom: Ethical and practical implications of integral theory and methodological pluralism for collaboration and knowledge-building. In S. Esbjörn-Hargens (Ed.), *Integral theory in action: Applied, theoretical, and constructive perspectives on the AQAL model* (pp. 345–368). Albany. NY: SUNY Press.

Murray, T. (2011). Toward post-metaphysical enactments: On epistemic drives, negative capability, and indeterminacy analysis. *Integral Review*, 7(2), 92–125.

Murray, T. (2013). *Mystical claims and embodied knowledge in a post-metaphysical age*. Presented at the Integral Theory Conference, July, 2013.

Murray, T. (in press). Embodied realisms and integral ontologies: Toward self-critical theories. In S. Esbjörn-Hargens & M. Schwartz(Eds.), *Dancing with Sophia: Integral philosophy on the verge*. Albany, NY: SUNY.

Norrie, A. (2010). *Dialectic and difference: Dialectical critical realism and the grounds of justice*. London: Routledge.

O'Fallon, T. (2013). *The senses: Demystifying awakening*. Presented at the Integral Theory Conference, July, 2013.

Price, L. (2013). *Re-enchanting research: Transdisciplinarity as practical mysticism*. Presented at the Integral Theory Conference, July, 2013.

Roy, B. (2006). A process model of integral theory. *Integral Review,* 3, 118–152.

Roy, B. (2015). Born in the middle: The soteriological streams of integral theory and meta-Reality. *Integral Review,* 10(1), 187–201.

Russell, B. (1917). *Mysticism and logic, and other essays.* London: Allen & Unwin.

Searle, J. (1995). *The construction of social reality,* New York: Free Press.

Taylor, C. (1995). *Philosophical arguments.* Cambridge, MA: Harvard University Press.

Wilber, K. (1983). *A sociable God: A brief introduction to a transcendental sociology.* New York: New Press.

Wilber, K. (1993). *The spectrum of consciousness.* Boston, MA: Shambhala.

Wilber, K. (2000). *Sex, ecology, spirituality* (Collected Works of Ken Wilber, Vol. 6). Boston, MA: Shambhala.

Wilber, K. (2003a). Excerpt A: An integral age at the leading edge, Part I. Available at www.kenwilber.com/Writings/.

Wilber, K. (2003b). Excerpt B: The many ways we touch: Three principles helpful for an integrative approach. Available at www.kenwilber.com/Writings/.

Wilber, K. (2003c). Excerpt C: The ways we are in this together: Intersubjectivity and interobjectivity in the holonic Kosmos. Available at www.kenwilber.com/Writings/.

Wilber, K. (2006). *Integral spirituality.* Boston, MA: Shambhala.

Wilber, K. (in process). *Integral semiotics.* Available at www.kenwilber.com/Writings/.

Wilson, E. O. (1998). *Consilience: The unity of knowledge.* New York: Random House.

AFTERWORD

Markus Molz

Being invited by the editors to contribute the Afterword to this unprecedented volume on metatheory for the twenty-first century is closing a loop, and possibly starting new loops, as I will outline at the end. The loop that is going to be closed started five years ago when I invited all of the editors of the present volume, among dozens of other metatheory aficionados, to participate in the symposium "Research across Boundaries."[1] The symposium was organized at the University of Luxembourg, with Mark Edwards, Jonathan Reams, and Helmut Reich joining me in the scientific committee. The papers are compiled in a two-part special issue of *Integral Review* (Molz & Edwards, 2013, in press a).

Against this background, I am particularly grateful for the opportunity to contribute this Afterword. I will make use of this opportunity to expose a loosely coupled past-present-future sequence in order to surface a number of critical issues that I see in integrative emancipatory metatheorizing. As for the past, I will spot a significant thread in my subjective biographical experience that might sound negative but that ultimately, through a constructive transformation, led to the Luxembourg symposium. As for the present, I will briefly assess the achievements of the encounters of critical realism with integral theory that led to this volume, among other outcomes, while exploring some ingredients of this success story. As for the future, I will point out several challenges that I believe need to be addressed or more strongly focused on in order to further the emerging arena of constructive cross-stream metatheory dialogues.

The prehistory: a personal account

I am living my life under late modern conditions that favor short-term patchwork over long-term purpose. Boundary-crossing emancipatory metatheories belong to the sense-making tapestry that I need, among other ingredients, to develop and cohere transformative work. My work, and my life, would otherwise fall apart in disconnected bits and pieces of little to no significance. These metatheories also help me prevent cynicism and nihilism as they nourish the hope that "another world is possible" – far from guaranteed, but at least possible. Among complementary pursuits, I have therefore been studying an ever-growing range of metatheories for more than a quarter of a century.

I have been reading and meeting lead authors and discussing with followers and practitioners of various metatheoretical streams that are animated by an integrative and emancipatory impulse. I am sympathetic with all the meta-streams I came across, finding loads of nuggets (lenses) in all of them (among cryptic stuff I do not understand, and shadows that lead to unnecessary internal inconsistencies and external tensions). For a fairly long time, I observed a predominance of self-contentment within many meta-streams, with little overall willingness to even notice other streams, let alone become acquainted with at least some others in commensurable depth. I did not notice many attempts of active engagement in generative dialogues across streams. Rather, often an attitude of *a priori* superiority of the stream somebody was already identified with was displayed, an *a priori* limitation of streams considered worth noticing was set, or a biased agenda on the basis of the assumptions, standards, and arenas of one side that were structurally devaluing the other before a dialogue could even start.

I also came across a significant number of representatives of various metatheoretical streams that enacted fractures between key principles of their espoused metatheory and their actual life practice. I would therefore dare to say that alongside great contributions there is a pattern of misuse of integrative metatheories. This pattern led me to believe that it is crucial to spell out and cultivate an ethics of metatheorizing before, during, and after developing and making use of metatheories. The very same metatheory can be put to good emancipatory uses as it can also be employed as a self-inflating weapon for immunizing oneself against criticism or for labeling if not dismissing others. Let me reiterate that the above is a purely subjective personal account and that it is hopefully in no way representative. However, I know from many conversations that I am not the only one who has had ample opportunity to make such observations.

The situation where leading proponents of integrative metatheoretical streams that I cherish did not, or only monologically and in a cursory manner, engage with the works of living fellow pioneers from other streams was highly unsatisfactory for me. I experienced this as a violation of their (basically shared) dialogical, emancipatory, and planetary principles and aspirations. For many years, I did not quite know what to do with the nagging discontent resulting from the striking isolation of contemporary boundary-crossing metatheories from each other. But I could not bypass metatheories and pass on to other things because of their promise "as humanity's vocabulary of self-transformation" (Stein, this volume).

An unavoidable side effect of parallel study of various metatheories is that the *de facto* pluralism of such endeavors remains always evident. Every new metatheory I discovered sharpened the sense that each stream and voice features specific foci, strengths, and weaknesses, that a huge, un- or under-exploited potential for mutual criticism and enrichment is lying untouched in front of us, and that it is not too difficult to scratch the surface and dig up elements of untold metatheoretical genealogies (Molz, 2010b; Molz & Hampson, 2010; Stein, this volume). On this basis, I kept hoping

> that the different strands of progressive integral efforts, which are still in competition with each other, may evolve towards a stage of consolidation and mutual communication [and] be accepted and critically advanced in close dialogue with differing cultural and academic traditions.
>
> *(Benedikter & Molz, 2011, p. 66)*

In the context of my painful experience of the ongoing double bind of finding promising emancipatory metatheories in performative self-contradiction in their relation to each other, the idea of a dialogical symposium matured in me, as an intuition first, and as a design concept second. I envisioned a specifically conceived and facilitated dialogue space in which trans-, post- and meta-disciplinary researchers with metatheoretical interests and frameworks that come from different backgrounds and that had never met before could personally engage with each other. The deeply felt need was there, as was the basic concept of how to configure such a gathering. But I did not have a budget to realize this idea.

I was astonished to see what this intention eventually ended up attracting. This is how it happened: The university in which I was working at that time was in its early phase of development and the recipient of heavy public investments. It so happened that there was a pot of unspent money at the end of an administrative year. It had either to be spent quickly or returned. Leaping at this opportunity, I wrote up the concept for the "Research across Boundaries" symposium, applied successfully for the funds, and found myself unexpectedly in the fortunate position to realize my dream. All of a sudden, the means to fly in more than 30 metatheory pioneers from all over the world were at my disposal. Not very serendipitously, the window of opportunity to make this symposium happen coincided with the period reserved for the writing up of my PhD dissertation. It was completely unreasonable to attempt to do both at the same time, but how could I let go of the emerging opportunity to organize the symposium I dreamed of? I absolutely wanted to see what happens when some of the brightest contemporary metatheorists came together, and so I ventured into one of the craziest times of life. As a big surprise, and confirmation, 90 percent of the invitees actually joined the event, including the editors of these twin volumes and a few of the chapter contributors.

Appreciation of the achievements

It is rare in the scattered field of metatheorizing to see serious discussions of a metatheory that are not bound to a single academic discipline. Even more rare, if not quite exceptional, is the encounter of two or three boundary-crossing metatheories.

The intense engagement of the critical realism and integral theory communities with each other at and since the Luxembourg symposium is therefore nothing less than awe-inspiring. It is the most intensive and long-lasting interaction between two meta-streams resulting in the strongest and fastest metatheoretical creativity and evolution of all those that could be sparked by the Luxembourg symposium. The dynamics that unfolded greatly exceeded my expectations, even though they have unfortunately been overshadowed by Roy Bhaskar's passing away. The sustained mutual engagement shows that generative dialogues between metatheoretical streams is perfectly possible. It shows that they can be a fruitful endeavor imbued with critical and sometimes hard-hitting reflective mirroring, but also that this can be done joyfully and respectfully.

What every reader can find in this volume goes light years beyond the mutual default ignorance, defensive reflexes, and superficial arguments that can be found elsewhere – beyond predictable results from short-lived events with immediate return to business as usual, beyond simple compilation of individual contributions in an edited volume. This volume is the result of a much deeper and longer mutual engagement than usual. There is more in it than assimilation of "useful stuff" to patch one's own preferred metatheory without changing anything in its architectonics. This volume reflects metatheorizing as a living process in a way I have not seen before. What exactly happened? What are the ingredients for this generative outburst in what was a desert with hardly any vegetation and barely an oasis? What can we learn from this exemplary sustained engagement for facilitating other generative dialogues?

Thinking about these questions, let me try to give a few tentative answers as hypotheses to be further explored. First of all, I believe that the possibility to meet in person is an initial condition that can hardly be replaced by anything else. I think that Adam Oxford was right in his catchphrase that "there is no substitute for the creativity of warm bodies in a room." Second, there is certainly something about interpersonal chemistry that cannot be brought about in a targeted way, in this case the friendship that developed between Sean Esbjörn-Hargens and Roy Bhaskar (among others). This friendship freed enthusiasm and energy in others also and was certainly one of the drivers for organizing further gatherings across the Atlantic. Third, the encounter was about lifetime oeuvres, of Wilber and Bhaskar (and Morin) that each matured over several phases, over decades, in parallel. There was something substantial to show to each other, there was much thinking and former criticism baked already into each component of each of these metatheories. Fourth, the arrangement was not about two lead authors meeting each other, which could have caused a spiral of criticism–defense–counter-criticism, but about communities with their respective internal diversity in terms of the personalities, cultures, and generations that were present, including a third group of people acquainted with the metatheories under discussion without being proponents of either– in my view a key move for enabling and sustaining a fruitful dialogical dynamic. Fifth, in relation to the previous point, the places in which the gatherings took place were alternated, starting from a third place (the Luxembourg symposium) and then including mutual visits, so to speak, in California and England.

These and possibly other ingredients unleashed enough energy to let a beautiful relational history unfold, from a first short but sparkling encounter to a honeymoon phase and from there to serious engagement in which identities and differences resurfaced while being processed in a climate of respect. On this basis, offspring were created in terms of new metatheories composed of memetic material from the "parents." In my observation, two main strategies have been employed in this relation:

- the flipsides of defense of one's stream and criticism of the other (Hartwig in this volume, Wilber in his comments on critical realism elsewhere);
- variants of integration of metatheories from different streams into new syntheses (Esbjörn-Hargens, Hedlund, Marshall in this volume).

It was predictable, despite the undeniable creativity displayed in this book, that these strategies would be deployed in the encounters. The reason is simple: they always are. Historical research shows that millennia ago it was no different:

> Evidence from the fourth century BCE reveals not one but a broad range of exegetical attitudes, all of which would reappear in some guise in later periods of textual growth: exegetes heatedly defending or attacking the integrity of single traditions or "schools"; high-level syncretists ... fusing traditions with abandon; and, at the opposite extreme, anti-text radicals, reacting to the "clamour of the schools."
>
> *(Farmer, Henderson, & Witzel, 2000, pp. 69–70)*

The "anti-metatheorists" have not been included as authors in this volume for the understandable reason that they do not produce metatheory, but seek to undermine all metatheory (apart from the implicit metatheory underling their general disbelief in metatheories). But "anti-metatheorists" not only exist, they often represent the dominant forces in contemporary research institutions in which specialized empirical research is considered the only legitimate, or at least the privileged form of research.

Besides the two main strategies mentioned above, another two strategies came to be used:

- expansion of the discourse space by adding more perspectives or entire metatheories to the picture (Murray, Stein in this volume, and myself in the remainder of this Afterword);
- detailed analytical comparison of how selected lenses are used in two or several metatheories (Edwards, Schwartz in this volume).

This also is not astonishing, given that it has been established a long time ago through meta-studies that unification or synthesis, with its promise of increased understanding through increased economy of thought, is a member of a triplet of themata, one of its antithetical aspects being multiplicity (or complexity, variety), the other being … resolution rather than synthesis. Each of these three members of the triplet has its uses.

(Holton, 1975, p. 332)

As in the past, we can expect this universal set of strategies to be reproduced over and over again in the future. It structures the field in which metatheories (and many other things) develop. The different strategies either enhance or question each other. Both functions are important to advance metatheorizing. Consequently, the deployment of all these strategies needs to be supported in balanced and interactive ways. This requires conscious care to avoid the usual shift of each strategy splitting off in its own community, in its own discursive space, in its own methodology, becoming blind to how much it depends on coexisting with the other strategies. One of the greater merits of this volume is not only to invite the expression of various strategies within the same space but also to have brought forth reflection on this variety.

Possible future pathways

Besides nurturing the encounter of a healthy mix of strategies, what else might be good advice for maintaining and enhancing generativity in the emerging field of "dialogical and co-creative emancipatory metatheorizing"? Let me go through the W questions to highlight challenges and to bring to light a few possible pathways or orientations that could help cope with them.

Why?

Integrative emancipatory metatheorizing has several purposes, as mentioned and exemplified in different contributions to these twin volumes. On the one hand, an integrative impulse is present in critical realism, integral theory, and other metatheories, as they are constructed by collecting, situating, and connecting many sense-making devices (lenses). When metatheories meet that went separately through this construction process of developing sets of lenses, the integrative impulse clicks in on the next meta-level, and some (see strategies, above) seek to combine the richness of two or more such sets of lenses. If the integrative impulse plays out as an isolated orientation it can become voracious, though. There is no end to integrating ever more lenses or perspectives. The integrative drive has an in-built tendency to build a tower of Babel. In other words, metatheories can also grow too fat, so to speak, and thus become impractical. The ideology that as many perspectives as possible need to be integrated within one and the same metatheory is doing exactly the same to us as the idea of endless economic growth. It works for a while, but ultimately it is an impossible agenda. As much as there are ecological limits to economic growth, there are cognitive limits to metatheory growth. And in practice, there are time and resource constraints to seriously exploit more than a limited set of lenses in a piece of research, in conveying them through teaching, or in including them impactfully in transformative practice.

When we take the human condition into account, the more we follow the voracious integrative impulse the less emancipatory a metatheory might turn out to be in practice. It is therefore worth noticing that the integrative function of metatheory and the emancipatory function of metatheory can be in tension and that they can even grow apart from each other. Pursuing the integrative impulse ever further, from a certain point onwards it might well no longer increase the emancipatory power of a metatheory but rather diminish it. This is because the emancipatory power of a metatheory is not a linear function of the number of perspectives that have been integrated. There are other factors that play a role, such as the cognitive processing capacity, the level of prior education necessary to understand a metatheory, and the number of people taking a metatheory up, explicitly or implicitly. In general, simpler metatheories spread more easily and hence become more influential than more sophisticated ones, even though the former are less comprehensive than the latter.

Coming back to the purpose of metatheory dialogues, a prominent purpose is to serve humanity in its contemporary Great Transformation, by means of stimulating, empowering, orienting, supporting, and legitimizing ethical and catalytic transformative practices. Relating metatheories to each other as thoroughly as undertaken in the encounters presented in this volume undeniably takes substantial amounts of time, resources, and attention. Why shall we pursue this? Why is this relevant? And how could it become even more relevant? The guiding question in this regard might be how we can expand Kurt Lewin's famous adage from "there is nothing so practical as a good theory" to "there is nothing so practical as a good metatheory." There is a topos that appears over and over again in the context of emancipatory approaches, which is that they have value when they remain tied to practice:

> For an ecology of knowledges, knowledges-as-intervention-in-reality is the measure of realism, not knowledge-as-a-representation-of-reality. The credibility of cognitive construction is measured by the type of intervention in the world that it affords or prevents.
>
> *(Sousa Santos, 2007, p. 70)*

> Good thinking, then, enhances our ability to live well, to do what it is good to do.
>
> *(Carp, 2001, p. 72)*

> We urgently need to bring about a revolution in universities so that the basic intellectual aim becomes, not knowledge merely, but rather wisdom – wisdom being the capacity to realize what is of value in life, for oneself and others.
>
> *(Maxwell, 2013, p. 77)*

> The action paradox – that we learn more about our reality when our primary intent is to change it rather than inquire into it – affirms practical primacy.
>
> *(Heron, 1996, p. 40)*

The "primacy of the practical," as Heron calls it, leads us to ask ourselves what difference metatheoretical differences make in practice. What practical differences in which real life contexts are evidenced that can be traced back to specific differences between metatheoretical positions? It is easier to analyze conceptual differences between metatheories and we can indeed explicate them in more and more depth, detail, and sophistication. But how do we know which metatheoretical differences make any notable difference in practical fields? My contention is that we know as yet very little about this. The "primacy of the practical" calls us to sharpen our awareness in this respect and to find answers to these questions.[2]

It is relatively easy to point to marked differences between practices and their outcomes and consequences that flow from metatheories underlying and stabilizing the current mainstream systems in contrast to those that flow from almost any sound emancipatory metatheory. This type of contrast is therefore generally preferred by emancipatory metatheorists to show the merits, or the superiority, of their preferred metatheory over its conventional counterparts. However, a comparison of practical differences resulting from the (often subtle) metatheoretical differences between different emancipatory metatheories is much more difficult and (therefore?) rarely undertaken.

How can extended conversations among proponents of different emancipatory metatheories be tuned to make tangible contributions that stimulate the development of more powerful transformative practices than each emancipatory metatheory has already inspired on its own, and this within a reasonable timeframe? How can we develop a sense of which of the basically limitless options of metatheoretical criticism, comparison, and integration are well worth the effort because they bring forth substantial systemic leverage in the current societal transition dynamics? On which shall we concentrate our limited time, attention, and resources in an era of transformational urgency?

These questions pertain to what could be called a metatheory pragmatism. Metatheory pragmatism pushes us to make new distinctions and to find out which conditions influence the degree to which the following two opposite scenarios apply in particular instances:

1   Practitioners in the same field inspired by different emancipatory metatheories (each composed of a complex set of lenses) but by similar values employ tools, methods, and practices that have similar practical effects (a point some practitioners make themselves to say that it does not matter too much which emancipatory metatheory you are inspired by).

2   A single new subtle conceptual differentiation within a single metatheoretical lens opens up entire new seams of insights and fields of transformative practice (a point Edwards makes in this volume).

In the first case, time and resources would be better invested directly in the practical pursuits than in further metatheoretical sophistication. In the second case, this particularly significant finding arising from metatheory dialogues would need to be communicated to communities of practitioners in ways that they can process.

Who?

Who is invited to cross-stream emancipatory metatheory dialogues? Who actually makes it to join in? In the current situation the problem implied by these questions is as much present in this volume as in many other contexts: mostly or exclusively white male contributors located mostly or exclusively in the North Atlantic belt mostly or exclusively sharing similar presuppositions come together. How can this situation evolve towards substantially more gender-, culture-, and paradigm-balanced, i.e. truly planetary dialogues about our deep assumptions enshrined in each other's favorite metatheories?

Why are there are so few women participating in the metatheory dialogues? Besides the persistence of the well-known stereotypical gender imbalances in different occupations, what is it that women might tend to find unappealing in metatheorizing, even if they were totally unconstrained in choosing their engagements? And what would make it more appealing? Two hypotheses that I discuss in more detail in the "How?" section, below, might play a role in finding answers to these questions: palpable connection to practice and co-creation. Further possible reasons for the observable imbalance need to be explored more systematically and strategies developed to overcome it.

Another structural imbalance concerns the cognitive injustice between the global North and the global South, which are no longer geographical notions but positions in the globalized political economy of the contemporary world system after five centuries of dominance of the global North. We must understand that cognitive injustice is the outcome of the present geopolitical structuration of power and its reflection in research, education, and publishing, among other sectors, in particular the economy. We must understand that contributing to bringing about global cognitive justice requires sustained countervailing efforts that get traction by outsmarting the almost automatic, institutionally supported reproduction of the imbalanced status quo. We must further understand that cognitive injustice is an often overlooked root cause for a broad range of other ills and evils that emancipatory metatheories seek to address and help overcome.

> Global social injustice is … intimately linked to global cognitive injustice. The struggle for global social justice must, therefore, be a struggle for global cognitive justice as well. In order to succeed, this struggle requires a new kind of thinking.
>
> *(Sousa Santos, 2007, p. 52)*

We cannot therefore afford to have emancipatory metatheory dialogues reinstating rather than reducing cognitive injustice. Is there any field better suited than emancipatory metatheory dialogues to come to grips with rampant cognitive injustice? What can be learned from fields in which issues of cognitive justice/injustice are already clearly problematized, such as in intercultural philosophy (Dussel, 2012), cultural epistemology (Sousa Santos, 2014), or the emerging contours of world anthropologies (Restrepo & Escobar, 2005)? It is of course true that integrative metatheorists naturally seek to include many sources from many disciplines, cultures, and eras when building their metatheories. But integration is always selective, however far it is reaching out and embracing diversity of perspectives. What sources from across the world are taken into account and how the integration task is approached depend strongly on positionality. It is a different matter to attempt this from a central positionality in the world system than to do it from a peripheral positionality, or from the epistemologically privileged in between positionality, arising from experiences in both the center and the periphery and thus allowing for metatheoretically creative "border thinking" (Samman, 2002). There are many interesting metatheoretical proposals arising from border thinking, such as Ananta Giri's (India/world) weak integration (Giri, 2013; Molz, 2013), Enrique Dussel's (Argentina/Mexico) philosophy of liberation (Dussel, 2006), or Roberto Unger's (Brazil/USA) twenty-first-century upgrade of pragmatism undergirding an "experimentalist cooperation" that is culturally contextualized (Unger, 2007), among many others.

Even though social systems/structures/institutions are of course theorized by both critical realism and integral theory, they are much more concretely dealt with in border-thinking work such as Dussel's and Unger's. The point is that there is no neutral positionality. One's own positionality is always located somewhere in the geopolitics of knowledge in which structural and symbolic power is exercised all the time, in which socioeconomic and legal conditions and institutions enable or hinder participation along what de Sousa Santos (2007) calls "abyssal lines," in which there are dominant languages, entailing a host of issues related to existing/non-existing, possible/impossible translations and accessibility/non-accessibility of sources. Metatheoretical streams arising from peripheral positionalities are hidden from the perspective of central positionalities as long as they do not manage to appear in a dominant language, or rather the dominant language (English), and in publishing channels of the global North. There is generally much more awareness in the global South of what is going on in the global North than the other way round, which creates a bad situation for metatheorizing on both sides, for opposite reasons, not to mention the fact that South–South cooperation is also underdeveloped because there is little supporting infrastructure for this in a world system dominated by the global North.

Let me give just two striking examples of the dramatic effects positionality can have on metatheorizing. First, the notion of development is core in practically all contemporary Western metatheories, both conventional and emancipatory, whereas it is problematized if not abandoned in contemporary metatheories arising from the global South as a consequence of devastating effects experienced by many in these regions as effects of technosocial developmentalism promoted for instance by modernization theory, a developmentalism based on a linear, universalist understanding of progress. Second, the notion of transmodernity arising from Dussel's philosophy of liberation (Dussel, 2006) encapsulates a vision for what comes next after modernity (or would be desirable to come next). Transmodernity is neither like postmodernity nor integralism as postulated in the global North. It does not sit clearly in the neat scheme of levels of consciousness or unfolding eras of cultural evolution that is a central pillar of integral theory, for instance.

Metatheoretical work arising from different positionalities in the world system, rooted in different cultural contexts and expressed in different languages, also usually comes in a different style. The best translation cannot iron out a certain strangeness in the perception of people used to another style. There are many styles not corresponding to the Anglo-Saxon habits of reasoning, arguing, and conveying information (which have become the *de facto* international standard). A mistake that is often made is to consider work expressed in a different style from the dominant one as insufficiently well conceived or argued. On this basis, the question needs to be raised how metatheories become eligible in the first place to be invited to metatheory dialogues. The fact that metatheories come in different styles makes *a priori* setting of criteria about which metatheories to include and which to exclude from integration or dialogue problematic, because they are the criteria of only one side. How then can we set criteria together, which give voices and streams a chance to be heard and contribute on an equal footing that do not necessarily comply with the so-called international (aka Anglo-Saxon) standards? And whose enforced compliance with these standards would precisely hamper or destroy the originality of their contribution.

Another relevant target group that has not so far been invited to the "emancipatory metatheory party" are metatheorists whose presupposition is that integration is not possible and should therefore not be attempted. It is by no means certain that they would come to the party, but if they are not invited it is certain that they cannot even make up their mind whether there is an interest for them to join or not. As far as I can see, there are mutual dislikes. The non-integrative presupposition seems to be counterintuitive for metatheorists who are starting from the opposite presupposition that strong integration is *a priori* always the best strategy. This presupposition is in-built into integral theory and leads to the illusionary claim of "all-inclusiveness" (Edwards & Molz, in press). It cannot be warranted, though, that integration is always possible nor that it is always good to attempt integration. Both presuppositions, integrative and non-integrative, are just that: presuppositions. Critical realism, with its notion of absence and its principle of epistemological relativism, defends a more flexible intermediate position. This position leaves space for epistemic diversity while refuting both the purported possibility of strong integration in terms of all-inclusiveness and the purported impossibility of integration in terms of multiple incommensurable worlds or ontologies.

The opposite extreme positions can be refuted as self-contradicting, but various positions in between can be defended with equal plausibility. If it is not a simple matter of taste which position to choose on the sliding scale between strongly and weakly integrative presuppositions, what is it that creates strong identifications with a particular presupposition? I think it is one of the mistakes of integral theory to relegate non-integrative or weak integrative thinking to a "postmodern-pluralist" level of consciousness alone. There is sufficient evidence that there is also a reconstructive postmodernism, not only a deconstructive one. Furthermore, it is possible to find integrative (monist) and disintegrative (pluralist) positions on all higher levels of consciousness. For instance, Banerji (2012, p. 89) distinguishes Aurobindo's supermind

> from the inclusivistic structures either of a transcendental monism or a totalistic developmental systems theory.... To think an integral consciousness, one must think radical monism and radical pluralism at the same time preserving pluralism in its fullness.

John Law (2004) is a good example of a scholar artfully and consistently arguing for a "baroque" research orientation "looking downward" straight into what he does not hesitate to call "the mess," rather than the "romantic" orientation that is "looking upward" to an orderly sky of neat categorical abstractions. Looking downward is a perspective that seeks to capture concrete examples of local disordered singularities in their everyday non-coherence that escape larger schemes while revealing the necessary and unavoidable heterogeneity of knowledge about a multiplicity of realities that are considered as only partially related to each other, at best. Law presents an emancipatory metatheoretical programmatic, just like any author in this volume, with the difference that it is not an integrative one. As an earlier example of such an orientation, Magoroh Maruyama's (1977) heterogenistics might be mentioned, which is starting from the observation that we are living in an *increasingly* heterogenizing universe. Heterogenistics draws conclusions from this insight for epistemology. A still earlier example is William James' pluralistic world hypothesis with which he confronted the dominant monism of his times:

> Things are "with" one another in many ways, but nothing includes everything, or dominates over everything. The word "and" trails along after every sentence. Something always escapes. "Ever not quite" has to be said of the best attempts made anywhere in the universe at attaining all-inclusiveness. The pluralistic world is thus more like a federal republic than like an empire or a kingdom. However much may be collected, however much may report itself as present at any effective centre of consciousness or action, something else is self-governed and absent and unreduced to unity.
>
> *(James, 1977/1909, p. 148)*

My contention is that non-integrative metatheoretical positions, or mixed (partly integrative and partly non-integrative) positions can be generated by the same level of consciousness and cognitive complexity as integrative ones, can be as emancipatory in their intent, can bring forth programs of research and practice that are as productive, insightful, and transformative as is the case for integrative positions. Consequently, there is little reason not to invite representatives of non- or only partially integrative positions to the table of metatheory dialogues, even though their positions are more or less strongly adverse to integrative metatheories. The character of non-integrative metatheories is also different. They do not build up big conceptual architectures. This would be at odds with their presupposition. They can operate on the basis of just a few flexible guiding principles. Certain adjustments in Esbjörn-Hargens' ten criteria (in this volume) would therefore be necessary to recognize them as equals.

We cannot expect that an integrative metatheorist will ever convince a non-integrative metatheorist to change their respective presupposition, or vice versa. What we can expect is a new and more fundamental tension that does not exist among metatheories sharing similar presuppositions whose tensions are more about details. The role of these additional participants in metatheory dialogues could consist of providing examples that cannot be integrated in the integrative metatheories, that evidence cracks and omissions in the neat conceptual constructions, and thus provoke revisions. Integrative metatheorists tend to believe that they can always patch their metatheories and integrate whatever is not yet integrated. This is precisely the reflection of their presupposition, which also makes them prone to over-assimilation (Edwards & Molz, in press). Metatheorists espousing a baroque orientation for their part believe that their counter-examples are capable of giving integrative metatheories a deathblow. This idea results from their presupposition. But it is well known that theories and metatheories generally are not given up because of a few counter-examples. The art of hosting a dialogue among metatheorists starting from opposite presuppositions would need to consist in consciously cultivating the fundamental opposition as a productive tension. As it is a big tension it has the potential to instigate bigger shifts and greater developments than among metatheories sharing key presuppositions, but it will evidently also be more challenging to uphold the generativity of the dialogue.

In the next sections I will address future perspectives of the "What?" and the "How?" of metatheory dialogues. Who is invited in the first place and who is eventually *de facto* in the position to participate in such dialogues evidently has a great influence on what is discussed and how. I believe that consciousness-raising and additional organizational efforts are in order to engage more equitably with women, colleagues from the global South, and proponents of paradigms starting from opposite presuppositions, among others.

What?

After what has been said on the purpose of and the participants in emancipatory metatheory dialogues, let us focus on what they could do to further the flourishing of metatheoretical creativity and transformative impact. Without any pretension to be prescriptive or exhaustive, the following threads could be among the promising avenues to be developed in the future.

1   The power of in-depth conversations across two to three metatheories has been demonstrated in this volume. Contrasting a small set of metatheories is one of the proven approaches for uncovering and creating awareness for metatheoretical lenses, for different degrees of differentiation within the same lens, and for the unique set of lenses constitutive of each metatheory. Such conversations are a proven way of finding out about the strengths and weaknesses of particular metatheories, of how they can complement each other, and what the incommensurable specifics are that resist integration in a fusion of metatheories. It is difficult to imagine that more than a small set of metatheories can be included in such in-depth conversations at a time without losing the specific quality of the conversations and their outcomes. This limitation requires approaches complementary to this kind of metatheory dialogues.

2   Another approach would consist of progressively establishing an internationally shared "lens repertoire" that allows for participatory criticism, improvement, and expansion. Such a repertoire is not itself a metatheory, because it does not connect lenses with each other in specific configurations and does not load them with specific semantics. But it would collect, describe, and categorize (or flexibly tag) the building bricks of theories and metatheories across disciplines and cultures. There are precursors of this kind of work. Gerald Holton (1975) extracted over 50 lenses (which he calls themata) underlying the work of prominent researchers in physics. Unfortunately, they are not accessible in one place but dispersed across Holton's life work. Archie Bahm (1970) described the variants of polar lenses in philosophy, which is a specific subset of lenses. Andrew Abbott (2001) retraced lenses used in the social sciences since their inception and shows how they are fractally reproduced over time, across and within different paradigms. More recently Edwards (2010) and I (Molz, 2010) unearthed a number of metatheoretical lenses that seem to be pervasively used in the social sciences, categorizing them according to lens shapes (like polarity, path, or holarchy). Holton and Abbott concur, by the way, that very few new lenses have appeared in the history of modern science over the past century. It can therefore be hypothesized that there are a limited number of fundamental lenses from which (meta)theorists choose and combine a selection in idiosyncratic ways. The pervasively used lens shapes can be traced back to kinesthetic image schemata that all humans share rather than to the affordances of specific fields of study; an observation that aligns with embodied cognition research in which such shapes are described and how they are used and reproduced in metaphorical sense-making (Kimmel, 2013; see also Murray, this volume). They seem to be part of the universal cognitive equipment of humans that evolved over long periods of time as embodied beings in this world. No attempt has yet been made to my knowledge to create a systematic lens repertoire and to use it as a toolbox for metatheory construction. Much as the introduction of

the periodic table boosted advances in chemistry and the creation of pattern languages in design disciplines and software engineering, the creation of a lens repertoire could have the potential to boost metatheorizing.

3   In light of the "primacy of the practical" mentioned above and in face of socio-cognitive and economic constraints, metatheory dialogues could be oriented towards the creation of intentionally bounded metatheories designed for specific purposes, especially when the possibility has been created to draw from a universal lens repertoire. As we know, the map is not the territory. The map you need does not only depend on the territory but also on the purpose with which you are crossing it, your mode of transportation, your general experience with navigation, your level of acquaintance with the area, etc. A certain convergence is required between the purpose the mapmaker had in mind and the situation of the user, for instance in relation to the resolution of the map. The digital maps we can use today for geographical navigation allow zooming in and out seamlessly. The conceptual maps we use are still far from this possibility. Therefore, we need maps of different resolution. Furthermore, there are instances in which a reliable, orthodox map exists. In this case, a single map does the job. There are other instances, e.g. when new territory is being explored, in which there are different maps with some helpful and some unhelpful indications in each. In such a situation, you better make use of all available maps without trusting any of them entirely.

   Maps that are fit for a purpose are an alternative to the self-defeating agenda of building purportedly unbounded, "all-inclusive" metatheories (Edwards & Molz, in press). It is true that certain boundaries, especially inherited boundaries of social and knowledge organization, need to be questioned and changed, if necessary. But boundaries can also be intentionally set to devise metatheories that are tailored for specific purposes, contexts, or target groups. This strategy could enhance the potential of metatheory to inspire the creation of actual transformative impact, such as through a metatheory of "high transformation teams" (rather than "high performance teams"), meta-methodologies that help in generating entrepreneurial or educational system innovations, new stories that inspire cross-sector partnerships to collaborate on systemic institutional transformation, or frameworks for assessing the quality of trans-, post-, and metadisciplinary research. The list could go on, evidently. There are many fields relevant for catalyzing the contemporary Great Transformation in which metatheories of good quality and practical import are lacking.

4   Still another thread of metatheorizing concerns cultural-historical, genea-logical, and biographical reconstructions of metatheories and metatheoretical streams. When we are metatheorizing we are standing on the shoulders of historical giants. We are simply often not aware of it. How many times has a metatheoretical wheel been reinvented because of lack of historical awareness? Genealogies are also problematic. As far as my observation goes, metatheoreti-cal streams tend to make up a genealogical story that makes them look good by claiming certain ancestors. These genealogical stories neither coincide with

actual genealogies, i.e. traditions directly transmitted from generation to generation (which is rarely ever the case), nor with much more complex genealogical networks. For instance, there are important integral traditions that integral theory leaves out of its genealogical account, such as socialist/anarchist integral, Catholic integral, and Slavonic integral, even though these streams were among the earliest operating with the notion of integral (Molz, 2010b, Molz & Hampson, 2010). In another context, Roland Benedikter and I have written that:

> [T]he comparative historical study of attempts at integrative worldviews becomes essential for enabling us to develop new forms of such attempts. In studying the history of integrative thought and practice in the twentieth and twenty-first centuries, a mind-set can be cultivated that allows us to anticipate, to outline and practically to establish a new integrative worldview.
>
> *(Benedikter & Molz, 2011, p. 67)*

Within each genealogy that can be uncovered through thorough research, interesting diversity tends to appear, including opposite positions under the same heading and similar positions under different headings. Abundant diversity within the same stream can be annoying and threatening to its identity, but it can also facilitate bridge-building across streams.

Interesting insights could also be gained by retracing the geographical and professional patterns of uptake, application, and falling back into oblivion of particular metatheories. I got the impression, for instance, that critical realism is more widespread and better accepted in academia than integral theory, which is no wonder as critical realism started as a philosophy of science and integral theory after Wilber deliberately left academia. In contrast, it might well be the case that more practitioners in various fields pick up integral theory than critical realism, as integral theory comes along more nicely packaged for the taste of busy practitioners. Another example is that Edgar Morin's complex thought seems to be widely received in Southern Europe and Latin America – more, if not much more, than critical realism or integral theory – even leading to first cases of institutionalization (institutes and a university), whereas much of Morin's prolific stream of publications is not even translated into English, which limits international uptake elsewhere. To my knowledge, there are no systematic studies yet on how such distributions of influence evolve. But fortunately over time overlaps between "spheres of influence" have developed, making the metatheory dialogue presented in this volume possible. It can be assumed, though, that other metatheoretical streams have not yet overlapped.

Finally, biographical research on metatheorists is a further complement that can bring up interesting insights. For instance, if we accept that metatheories consist of sets of lenses, what in the life of the metatheorist co-determines which lenses are included to which degree of differentiation (Molz, 2010)? Holton's research program revealed that fundamental themata are set early in the life of a researcher and played out consistently and unquestionably over long periods, if not the whole life.

> The thematic commitment of a scientist typically is remarkably long-lived.... To a much larger degree than either paradigms or world views, thematic decisions seem to come more from the individual than from the social surrounding.
>
> *(Holton, 1975 p. 334)*

As for the followers, the question is different: what factors co-determine with which metatheory somebody identifies? How is it that some identify strongly with one specific metatheory and others do not? There is generally little awareness of what goes into making such choices. They remain largely unconscious and hence they cannot be criticized, softened, and actively developed.

How?

I have already applauded the achievement of bringing two to three important metatheoretical streams to interact in constructive ways, as reflected in this volume. It seems difficult, however, to imagine how more than two to three streams at a time can engage with each other in the required depth and continuity. As already discussed, this brings up the question of how the two to three streams moved into a joint reflexive space are selected from the many candidate metatheories that exist. Sean Esbjörn-Hargens (this volume), having scanned a range of such candidates, lists ten good arguments why he selected the three metatheories that he included in his brave meta-integration attempt at a level that he calls "order 4." This cannot prevent, however, other metatheorists drawing up their own list of criteria and selecting two or three other candidates from a different pool of candidate metatheories and possibly processing them on the basis of another of the above-mentioned strategies (see, for instance, the examples of Gidley, 2007; Martin & Martin, 2014; and Molz, 2010).

If this possibility exists, and the examples show that it does, however much we wanted to see dialogues of integrative metatheories taking place, these very attempts can also paradoxically bring about a new fragmentation (or rather reproduce unintendedly the fragmentation that exists on lower levels that integrative metatheorizing originally set out to overcome). If order 3 integration called for order 4, order 4 integration calls for order 5, given that there are several order 4 attempts and there will be more in the future. Where do we stop? The visual joke in Figure A.1 perhaps better reveals in a few lines the structural issue at stake than any philosophical treatise.

An important aspect of how to metatheorize in the future seems therefore to consciously calibrate the appropriate level of reflexivity in the context of an

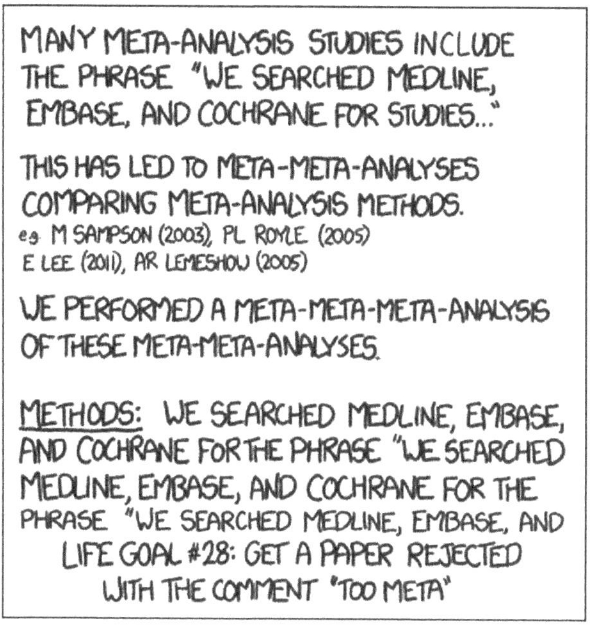

MANY META-ANALYSIS STUDIES INCLUDE THE PHRASE "WE SEARCHED MEDLINE, EMBASE, AND COCHRANE FOR STUDIES..."

THIS HAS LED TO META-META-ANALYSES COMPARING META-ANALYSIS METHODS.
eg M SAMPSON (2003), PL ROYLE (2005) E LEE (2011), AR LEMESHOW (2005)

WE PERFORMED A META-META-META-ANALYSIS OF THESE META-META-ANALYSES.

METHODS: WE SEARCHED MEDLINE, EMBASE, AND COCHRANE FOR THE PHRASE "WE SEARCHED MEDLINE, EMBASE, AND COCHRANE FOR THE PHRASE "WE SEARCHED MEDLINE, EMBASE, AND LIFE GOAL #28: GET A PAPER REJECTED WITH THE COMMENT "TOO META"

FIGURE A.1 Too meta (from http://blogs.worldbank.org/impactevaluations/node/1233)

"action/reflection ratio." The point here is that not only is there a lack of reflexivity in the world that needs to be overcome – the default situation in many contexts that explicit metatheories and more so metatheory dialogues help address (but generally for a very small number of persons only); but it is also possible to overdo it with reflexivity by piling up meta-levels on each other that are more and more remote from transformative action in the social and material world. Metatheorizing by default delays action by investment of individual and collective effort in increasing reflexivity rather than in immediate action. This is justified inasmuch as the increased reflexivity facilitates and accelerates ensuing transformative action while multiplying its leveraging power.

But we should not forget that metatheorizing takes place in the world. Metatheoretical reflexivity needs therefore to include its own social, economic, and environmental preconditions and consequences. The hope that the consequences will be positive in the long run and cover up the more immediate negative consequences is an unwarranted assumption. It can happen, but must not be assumed to happen. What we have here is structurally the same situation as the case of researchers, activists, or politicians flying to international conferences to promote measures against climate change, while causing themselves an extra load of carbon emissions. These long-distance flights could be justified only if the results of the deliberations offset or prevented future release of substantially more carbon than was released into the atmosphere in order to attend such meetings.

When we cannot be sure that advances in transformative action and its impact occur within reasonable timeframes, we might have done too much of the same, we might have gone "too meta." Anyone who has read R. D. Laing's *Knots* (1970) understands where excesses of reflexivity in relationships can end: in convolutions of negative spirals based on unwarranted assumptions driving the participants apart from each other and into frustrating isolation from which there seems to be no way out, every further move adding an iteration to the same blockage.

> In sum, some balance between the extremes of unreflexive, "flat" description, which presents a supposedly "objective" picture of the phenomenon, and convoluted, meta-reflexive textual presentations, which move too far away from the phenomenon in question, is recommended.
>
> *(Gough, 2003, p. 32)*

So, how do we strike the right balance? It is certainly true that there are many more people in the world acting with little reflection than there are metatheorists reflecting with little ensuing action. The benefit of the doubt is on the side of the metatheorists: what they are doing is potentially necessary. Nevertheless, as they are the world champions of reflexivity, they also have more responsibility than any-body else to calibrate reflection and action appropriately. The following orienta-tions might help in making progress on this issue:

- Metatheory communities shall make themselves accountable for how their investment of individual and collective effort in metatheorizing geared to transform cognitive/narrative realities relates to investments of effort in pursuits of transformational work in institutional/material realities.
- Metatheoretical reflexivity as practiced in this volume among metatheoreticians shall be extended in ways that enhance reflexivity in non-metatheoreticians, making their activities more emancipatory.
- Metatheory dialogues shall become directly embedded in transformative pro-jects and programs that have the goal of catalyzing system transformations.

Another "how" question concerns the mode through which metatheorizing occurs. In the past, the typical mode was monological. A single bright brain absorbed loads of materials, ordered them, and wrote the result up as the metatheory of X (a field, or in some cases "everything"), authored by Y (a single person). Which metatheory of the past is not single-authored? The present metatheory dialogues introduce a dialogical mode across metatheory communities. This is new and stirs metatheoreti-cal creativity. But ultimately, after the dialogue has taken place, the mode reverts typically to single-authored texts. A trialogical mode in which co-creation is kept going across all phases of the research, conversation, and publishing cycle and that results in collectively authored texts has yet to be fully conquered by metatheorists. But as this is practiced in other fields already, there is no reason why it could not also be practiced by metatheorists in the future.

Where?

It is well known that the location in which an encounter between different parties takes place has an influence on how it unfolds, whether people like to stay, and whether they feel invited to come back. The metatheory dialogues documented in this volume unfolded in an interspace between universities to which individual members of the metatheory communities were affiliated and NGOs created by groups of metatheorists, such as the International Centre for Critical Realism, the Institute for Integral Studies, and the Integral Research Center/MetaIntegral Foundation. It is certainly a good idea to develop metatheory dialogues in such an interspace. This diminishes the risk of falling prey to institutional agendas that are not helpful for developing emancipatory metatheory further. So far, however, this interspace has been feeble, has not had a continuous existence, has had to be created and recreated again and again.

How could it become stronger and bigger, able to host more metatheory dialogues, involving more streams, and this continuously? The answer is evident: academia needs to become more hospitable (again) to metatheorizing and dedicated NGOs need to be better funded based on their own agenda, not on the funders' agenda. However, trans-, post-, and metadisciplinary metatheorizing does not have a strong foothold in academia, if at all. It does not fit into institutional structures and incentives that are strongly attuned to foster disciplinary and interdisciplinary empirical science, which are still by far the predominant forms of inquiry in universities (Molz & Edwards, in press b). As emancipatory metatheories are about transformation, including institutional transformation, the dialectical question is in order: how can they help (themselves and others) advance institutionalization of spaces in which metatheorizing is a legitimate core activity?

Institutionalization is necessary if metatheory dialogues are not to depend mostly on rare, happy circumstances that tend to dissolve again in a short time. Institutionalization is also one of the missing links between metatheory and practice. Institutionalization can happen by two means: transformation of existing institutions inside out and creation of new institutions based from the outset on a different design. The most powerful transformation strategy can likely be realized when individuals, teams, and communities involved in both kinds of endeavors start to imagine and co-create institutional transformation together, and to advance their work, precisely, in interspaces between established and emerging institutions.

It is far from clear as yet, however, what emancipatory metatheory communities contribute to targeted institutional transformation or institution-building in terms of integrative universities (Awbrey & Scott, 1997), for instance. There have been several attempts in the past by single streams that failed. There are some newly emerging attempts which, however, are only partially, indirectly, or not at all related to emancipatory metatheory communities. My contention is that linking emancipatory metatheory to transformative practice works best by contributing actively to institutionalization. I suppose that metatheorists would generally be in favor of more inviting and stable contexts for their work. Stein (this volume) volunteers by saying: "I support the institutionalization of metatheoretically guided knowledge production." Many others are certainly as willing. But what could they do concretely? How to bring this basic willingness together into concrete endeavors of institution-building that are not dominated by a single stream, and thus avoided by people who feel at home in other streams (or in none of the streams)?

There is no lack of brilliant junior and senior metatheory aficionados. But they are not only dispersed across institutions. They are also often isolated within their respective institution. In mainstream institutions a boundary-crossing metatheoretical orientation tends to be perceived as strange and alien. There are no identifiable institutional hubs yet in which the international metatheoretical vanguard across streams would be able to gather for sustained joint work. Besides small-scale experiments, often inspired either by only one metatheory or none in particular, where are broader, targeted, participatory, co-creative efforts guided by several emancipatory metatheory communities and tuned to become hosts of sustained metatheory dialogues and at the same time hubs of transformative practice? Without an institutionalized critical mass, it will be most difficult to channel the invaluable contributions of emancipatory metatheories in the twenty-first century into a transformative force large and powerful enough to offset the self-destructive trends pervading our civilization. Therefore:

> [T]he first priority is the establishment of a decent continuity in facilitating integrative paradigm building on an academic and scientific level, and to build a modern foundation of historically informed erudition, memory and comparative research about the integrative movements. This is important for laying the foundations for the first joint identity of integral worldviews of our time in the broadest sense, and for enabling them to build sustainable bridges between themselves. This first joint identity may not be a common cultural identity, but might rather consist in a shareable basis of common sense that respects differences and diversity within federation building.
>
> *(Benedikter & Molz, 2011, p. 66)*

The second priority is to concentrate efforts across streams in the most promising endeavors of institution-building that are designed in such a way that multiple emancipatory streams feel invited to dwell in the emerging new (inter)spaces.

Conclusion

In this Afterword I first looked back at my personal biographical relation to integrative emancipatory metatheories, in particular the performative contradictions (which made me feel that "everything was imperfect"). On this basis, my surprise could not be greater at how forcefully and positively generative metatheory dialogues between critical realism and integral theory (and other metatheories) started to unfold, as reflected in this volume ("everything is perfect"). After this appreciation

I laid out a few possibilities in regard of how metatheory dialogues can be further enhanced in the future ("everything can be perfected"). It is not too much to predict that the encounters and developments that have been started in *Metatheory for the Twenty-First Century* have a promising future, that there is great potential for further expansion, and that this movement is direly needed to help redirect the contemporary Great Transformation in ways that enable a dignified life for present and future generations of all sentient beings.

Notes

1 http://dica-lab.org/rab.
2 The organizers of the Integral Theory Conference 2015 are animated by a similar reflection. The conference will be devoted to exploring "Integral impacts: Using integral metatheories to catalyze effective change."

References

Abbott, A. D. (2001). *Chaos of disciplines*. Chicago: University of Chicago Press.

Awbrey, S. M., & Scott, D. K. (1997). *Creating integrative universities for the twenty-first century*. Paper presented at the 19th EAIR Forum, University of Warwick. Retrieved from www.umass.edu/pastchancellors/scott/papers/creatingU.html.

Bahm, Archie J. (1970). *Polarity, dialectic and organicity*. Albuquerque, NM: World Books.

Banerji, D. (2012). Structure and process: Integral philosophy and triple transformation. *Integral Review*, 8(1), 85–95.

Benedikter, R., & Molz, M. (2011). The rise of neo-integrative worldviews. In M. Hartwig & J. Morgan (Eds.), *Critical realism and spirituality* (pp. 29–74). London: Routledge.

Carp, R. M. (2001). Integrative praxes: Learning from multiple knowledge formations. *Issues in Integrative Studies*, 19, 71–121.

Dussel, E. (2006). Transmodernity and interculturality: An interpretation from the perspective of philosophy of liberation. *Poligrafi*, 41–42(2), 5–40.

Dussel, E. (2012). A new age in the history of philosophy: The world dialogue between philosophical traditions. *Journal of Philosophical Research*, 37(Special Supplement), 151–166.

Edwards, M. G. (2010). *Organizational transformation for sustainability: An integral metatheory*. New York: Routledge.

Edwards, M. G., & Molz, M. (in press). On the fallacy of integration without boundaries. In S. Esbjörn-Hargens (Ed.), *True but partial*. Albany, NY: SUNY Press.

Farmer, S., Henderson, J. B., & Witzel, M. (2000). Neurobiology, layered texts, and correlative cosmologies: A cross-cultural framework for premodern history. *Bulletin of the Museum of Far Eastern Antiquities*, 72, 48–90.

Gidley, J. M. (2007). The evolution of consciousness as a planetary imperative: An integration of integral views. *Integral Review*, 5, 4–226.

Giri, A. K. (2013). Towards a new art of integration. *Integral Review*, 9(2), 113–122.

Gough, B. (2003). Deconstructing reflexivity. In L. Finlay & B. Gough (Eds.), *Reflexivity: A practical guide for researchers in health and social sciences* (pp. 21–35). Oxford: Blackwell.

Heron, J. (1996). Quality as primacy of the practical. *Qualitative Inquiry*, 2(1), 41–56.

Holton, G. (1975). On the role of themata in scientific thought. *Science*, 188(4186), 328–334.

James, W. (1977/1909). *A pluralistic universe*. Cambridge, MA: Harvard University Press.

Kimmel, M. (2013). The arc from the body to culture: How affect, proprioception, kines-thesia, and perceptual imagery shape cultural knowledge (and vice versa). *Integral Review, 9*(2), 300–348.

Laing, R. D. (1970). *Knots.* London: Penguin.

Law, J. (2004). And if the global were small and non-coherent? Method, complexity and the baroque. *Society and Space, 22,* 13–26.

Martin, H., & Martin, A. K. (2014). *Ken Wilber, Joseph Campbell, and the meaning of life* (Vols. 1 & 2). Sebastopol, CA: AK Publishing.

Maruyama, M. (1977). Heterogenistics: An epistemological restructuring of biological and social sciences. *Acta Biotheoretica, 26*(2), 120–136.

Maxwell, N. (2013). From knowledge to wisdom: Assessment and prospects after three dec-ades. *Integral Review, 9*(2), 76–112.

Molz, M. (2010a). *Toward an integral pluralism in sociocultural research* (Unpublished doctoral dissertation). University of Luxembourg.

Molz, M. (2010b). *The many faces of integral: Towards a reflexive genealogy of streams and a dia-logical ecology of voices.* Presentation at the Integral Theory Conference, JFK University, Pleasant Hill, CA, August 1.

Molz, M. (2013). Weak integration: Reflection of a neo-integrative worldview. *Sociological Bulletin, 62*(1), 111–115.

Molz, M., & Edwards, M. G. (Eds.). (2013). Research across boundaries: First part of the spe-cial issue. *Integral Review, 9*(2).

Molz, M. & Edwards, M. G. (Eds.). (in press a). Research across boundaries: Second part of the special issue. *Integral Review.*

Molz, M., & Edwards, M. G. (in press b). Crossing boundaries, stimulating creativity: The horizon of integral meta-studies. In A. K. Giri (Ed.), *Pathways of creative research: Towards a festival of dialogues.* Delhi: Primus Books.

Molz, M., & Hampson, G. P. (2010). Elements of the underacknowledged history of integral education. In S. Esbjörn-Hargens, J. Reams, & O. Gunnlaugson (Eds.), *Integral education. New directions for higher learning* (pp. 35–46). Albany, NY: SUNY Press.

Restrepo, E., & Escobar, A. (2005). Other anthropologies and anthropology otherwise. Steps to a world anthropologies framework. *Critique of Anthropology, 25*(2), 99–129.

Samman, K. S. (2002). The convergence of world-historical social science: "Border think-ing" as an alternative to the classical comparative method. In R. Grosfoguel & A. M. Cervantes-Rodríguez (Eds.), *The modern/colonial/capitalist world-system in the twentieth cen-tury. Global processes, antisystemic movements, and the geopolitics of knowledge* (pp. 267–285). Westport, CT: Greenwood.

Sousa Santos, B. de. (2007). Beyond abyssal thinking: From global lines to ecologies of know-ledge. *Review, 30*(1), 45–89.

Sousa Santos, B. de (2014). *Epistemologies of the South: Justice against epistemicide.* Boulder, CO: Paradigm Publishers.

Unger, R. M. (2007). *The self awakened: Pragmatism unbound.* Cambridge, MA: Harvard University Press.

INDEX